DICTIONARY

For Shelagh Boyd

from

Mario Reading

February 2002

Written & Compiled by Mario Reading
With images courtesy of The Kobal Collection

DICTIONARY OF

CINEMA

HOUSE OF
STRATUS

This edition published in 2001 by House of Stratus, an imprint of
House of Stratus Ltd, Thirsk Industrial Park, York Road, Thirsk, North Yorkshire, YO7 3BX, UK.
Also at: House of Stratus Inc., 2 Neptune Road, Poughkeepsie, NY 12601, USA.

www.houseofstratus.com

Typeset, printed and bound by House of Stratus.

A catalogue record for this book is available from the British Library and the Library of Congress.

ISBN 0-7551-1347-0

For my wife, Claudia, and my son, Lawrence, boon companions
in cinema's enchanted forests of the mind

Acknowledgements

I owe a large debt of gratitude to Phill Walkley, co-ordinator of the Purbeck Film Festival, who kindly agreed to read through the manuscript and point out any glaring errors – it was he who tactfully brought to my attention an entry in which I had inadvertently given Jean Renoir, instead of Marcel Carné, credit for directing *Les Enfants Du Paradis* (45); of such things nightmares are made. Also to Dougie Mayhew, for the DFA machine story; Ned Halley, for an inimitable contribution to Worst Films and for having the nous to suggest the whole idea to me in the first place; Ole Rummel, for his science fiction expertise (particularly with *Star Trek*); William Windham, for his help on the technical minutiae of camera and servo-control mechanisms; Phil Moad, of The Kobal Collection, and Amanda Russell, for their enthusiasm and sensitivity in steering me towards the right photographs; and Jason Cox, for the book's outstanding design. In addition, a very special thank you is due to my editor, Jenny Rayner, for her tireless work, endless enthusiasm and excellent (occasionally painfully excellent) advice. Finally, my deepest love and thanks to my wife, Claudia, for her patience, grace and forbearance in times of Phocensian despair.

ntroduction

My first visceral memory of film, and one that I have never quite succeeded in shaking off, is of fear. Fear of the unseen. The image came in David Lean's *Oliver Twist* (48), and I'm still not one hundred per cent certain that I remember it correctly, for I've never, for obvious reasons, chosen to watch the film again. As I recall it now (and I last saw the film around 1958, when I was five years old), Robert Newton's Bill Sykes, in an ungovernable fit of temper, kills the innocent Nancy, played by Kay Walsh, but Lean, being the consummate and inventive filmmaker that he is (and possibly swayed by censorship considerations), chooses to show the murder only in shadow – the shadow of the rise and fall of Sykes's club, accompanied by Nancy's terrified and increasingly feeble screams. The recollection of this appalling scene has haunted me for years (and continues to do so), and provides an awesome example of the simple power of the moving image to imbrue reality.

Later images from my childhood viewing are less unsettling but equally forceful, and comprise the shooting of the dog in Robert Stevenson's *Old Yeller* (57), a memory which has forever barred me from discovering the ending to Lewis Milestone's *Of Mice And Men* (39), (for even to this day I can never get past the scene where the old man's dog is taken out of the bunkhouse to be shot, without bursting into tears and asking someone to switch off the television set), and curious flashbacks to a film in which a murderer finds himself sealed up in an entirely electrified room – heaven alone knows what the film was called, but I, for sure, never wish to find out.

No happy memories, you ask? Hundreds, but they are usually non-specific, as though one tends to remember simply the feeling of happiness rather than any particular scene to that effect. No, the visceral memories are reserved for psychological horror (analysts, please don't call me – I'll call you), and are unnervingly specific. Oh dear. Another one has just sprung to mind concerning a torture sequence (probably very mild) in a Second World War-based spy movie. It was the screams of course, and my imagining of what was happening, that were so very much more telling than the brutal, and probably not very descriptive reality.

These films certainly distressed me, but they probably also prepared me, much as Grimm's *Fairy Tales*, Heinrich Hoffmann's *Der Struwwelpeter* (*Shock-headed Peter*), and Wilhelm Busch's *Max and Moritz* had done before, for the understanding that life was not necessarily always going to be sweetness and light. To that extent it was right of my parents to let me watch the films, and I don't at all regret the uneasiness some of the scenes may have engendered. Later, movies became a source of comfort rather than unease, and to this day I get an excited and fluttery feeling in my stomach when I am finding my seat in a cinema before the showing of a film I particularly want to see, and which I suspect will have 'heart'.

Now to the *Dictionary*. I wrote it because I love film. It is also a sly effort to justify a misspent youth, teenager-hood, young adulthood, early middle age and middle age spent watching extraordinary numbers of the things, often when I should have been otherwise occupied. This way I can console myself that all those tens of thousands of hours glued to the screen or to the television set were simply research for the *magnum opus* I always knew I would perpetrate on an unsuspecting world. During all those solitary (but never lonely) hours, I developed opinions which inevitably find themselves reflected here – not in the technical entries, of course, which I have endeavoured to make succinct and non-technical (in so far as that is possible), so much as in the individual ones, which I hope you will find stimulating, occasionally enervating, but always, I trust, honest. If I tell you that I have had to leave out seventy single-spaced pages chock-full with potential entrants, you will realise that space, and a desire to give full value to the people who do appear, has inevitably engendered casualties – I also admit that there are a number of individuals whom one might expect to see but whom I have refused to include because, in my opinion, they simply don't merit the space.

The layout, I hope, is self-evident. Everything is in pure alphabetical order, with cross-references to guide you to related snippets throughout the book. Under each non-technical entry there is a list entitled Other Key Films – this is my entirely subjective choice, from the often extensive filmographies available to me, of movies that I think best reflect that individual's skills. In the case of still-living, still-working personalities, I have added nearly all their most recent films simply to reflect the state of that particular person's career as it is, rather than as they would have it be. Also, on occasion, I have added, under the title Key Line(s), a *bon mot*, quip or quote by somebody else that I trust may add a little extra enjoyment to my summation. As far as foreign titles go, I have tended to leave them in the original, except where they are better known to English-speaking audiences in their English versions – in that case I give both (unless they are exceedingly well-known) with the original title first, followed by the English title. Film release dates present further difficulties, because they vary, according to the practice of the country, depending on whether the film is an American, a British, a Continental, or an International film, so that what may initially appear as an anomaly is simply the release date in a different country.

Now to birth dates and death dates. I don't give them. In my opinion they get in the way. A quick glance at the dates in the filmographies together with an even cursory reading of the text will give a passable idea of what age a person was when they did what film. Neither do I show courtesy titles – as far as I am concerned 'Lord This', 'Dame That', or 'Sir Somebody Other', usually didn't start out that way, and it's their *career* I'm writing about, not the end result of it – it wasn't Lord Olivier, for example, who starred as Heathcliff in William Wyler's *Wuthering Heights* (39); it was plain, simple, common-or-garden Laurence Olivier.

Within the main body of the text, I invariably attach the director's name to films they are known to have directed; however, I don't carry this over to the Key Films section for reasons of space, except when the Key Films refer to the career of a non-actor or a non-director (cinematographers, screenwriters, composers, etc.) in which case I do include them for ease of reference. Now is the moment I'd better come clean. Modern media conglomerates bore me – I've done my best, and the entries are as up to date and as entertaining as I can make them, but I find the subject rather turgid, and most of the moguls who run these monoliths rather grey. Another blind spot is producers – the great ones are all here, warts and all, but I draw the line at the not-so-greats, unless they have some particular idiosyncrasy that marks them out as interesting.

In addition to the main body of the text, I have included a few highlighted sections that I hope will amuse, entertain and engender discussion. These include my personal choice of films in the following classes: Adventure Films, All-time Best Films, Animated Films, Big-budget Action Films, Children's Films, Comedy Films, Crime Films, Cult Films, Detective Films, Documentary Films, Dramas, Epics, *Film Noirs*, Gangster Films, Ghost Films, Horror Films, Love Films, Monster Films, Musical Films, Political/Satirical Films, Psychological Dramas, Science Fiction Films, Sentimental Films, Silent Films, Spy Films, Swashbucklers, Thrillers, War Films, Weepies, and Western Films. These lists, culled from more than 25,000 movies, are not intended to be definitive (such an ambition would be palpably absurd), but are simply designed as a quick guide to readers who may be setting out on – rather than on their way back from – a lifetime's voyage of cinematic discovery. Finally, I've added a small section of Worst Films (limiting myself to the last ten years or so), Erotic Moments, and a separate section entitled Heartstopping Moments, which consists of a small series of subjective, but, one hopes, perspicaciously chosen peak moments in cinema.

Books such as the *Dictionary of Cinema* are usually written by committees, with all the disadvantages in terms of consistency and wit, and the advantages in terms of shared responsibility and multi-tasking. The shared responsibility for this book is entirely mine. The opinions are also mine, for better or worse, as is the choice of entries. I admit that the book is idiosyncratic. So am I. But it was a labour of love, for film has been both my comfort and my educator – a prop in times of sickness, a joy in times of health, and a boon at moments (rare, these) of intellectual growth.

Well, there you have it. I've made my excuses, explained what I'm doing here, and now all that's left is to wish you the same enjoyment reading the *Dictionary of Cinema* that I've had writing and researching it. '*Salud, y forza al canuto.*'

– Mario Reading, 2001

Aardman Animations

Home to Plasticine superheroes Wallace and Gromit and the entire *Chicken Run* (00) research team, Aardman is one of the most successful of all the independent animation studios. Founded by Peter Lord and David Sproxton in 1972, Aardman now has the blessing – and the mountains of cash that go with it – of **Steven Spielberg's DreamWorks SKG**. Based in Bristol, Aardman was originally responsible for Morph, of BBC TV's *Take Hart* fame, after which it branched out into music videos and advertising. Nick Park joined as co-director in 1985, bringing Wallace and Gromit with him, and the rest is history. Park now has three **Oscars** under his belt, and an untold multitude of other awards, and remains as committed to Plasticine, rather than to computer animation, as ever. <u>Author's Note</u>: Has anyone noticed that Nick Park's real-life grin is the exact image of Wallace's?

OTHER KEY FILMS: *A Grand Day Out* (89); *Creature Comforts* (91); *The Wrong Trousers* (93); *A Close Shave* (95)

KEY LINE:

'Poultry in motion.'

Abbott and Costello

A hit-and-miss comedy duo that never really matched the heights achieved by their famous antecedents, **Laurel and Hardy**. Arthur Lubin's *Buck Privates* (41) began their rise, Charles Riesner's *Lost In A Harem* (44) consolidated it, Charles Barton's *Abbott And Costello Meet Frankenstein* (48) steadied them on their way down, while the same director's *Dance With Me Henry* (56) saw them finally hit rock bottom.

OTHER KEY FILMS: *Hold That Ghost* (41); *The Naughty Nineties* (45)

Abby Singer, The

The last-but-one shot of the movie shooting day, named after a production manager who was in the habit of optimistically calling out 'Last Shot!', only to find the director insisting on just one more, this time absolutely final, take.

Above The Line

Euphemism for the cost of a film before shooting begins.

Abrahams, Jim

Co-director, with **David** and **Jerry Zucker**, of the comic hit *Airplane!* (80), Abrahams is also partly responsible for the extremely popular *Naked Gun* series (88-94) and the two 'Hot Shots' movies, *Hot Shots!* (91) and *Hot Shots! Part Deux* (93). Best of all, he was co-executive producer on **John Waters's** sublime *Cry-Baby* (90), which is far funnier and more inventive than all this dynamic trio's most recent output put together.

OTHER KEY FILMS: *The Kentucky Fried Movie* (77); *Top Secret!* (84); *Ruthless People* (86); *Big Business* (88); *Jane Austen's Mafia!* (99)

Abril, Victoria

Best known for being one of director **Pedro Almodóvar's** favourite stars, Abril is considerably more famous in her native Spain than internationally despite twin art-house successes in Almodóvar's sexually explicit *Tie Me Up! Tie Me Down!* [*Átame!*] (89) and Josiane Balasko's sexually and emotionally convoluted *French Twist* [*Gazon Maudit*] (95). In *French Twist*, Abril, fed up to the back teeth with her macho and serially unfaithful husband, takes up with a lesbian drifter who is then impregnated by the despondent husband (in a particularly weird *ménage à trois*), after which the two women bring up the child as their own while the husband is outed for the closet gay he has always been by a rich bisexual playboy whose drinking toast of choice is 'Salud, y forza al canuto.' [Cheers, and more power to the p★★★★] Wow!

OTHER KEY FILMS: *Robin And Marian* (76); *Law Of Desire* (uncredited) (87); *High Heels* (91); *Kika* (93); *Jimmy Hollywood* (94); *Libertarias* (96); *Entre Las Piernas* (99); *101 Reykjavík* (00); *Mari Del Sud* (01)

KEY LINE:
'She moves like a panther prowling to a flamenco beat…' [Robert J Pardi on Abril's feline appeal]

Abstract Film

A film which communicates solely through the expedient of visual or abstract design, and which bears no relation whatsoever to work that we normally consider as exemplifying 'narrative reality'. Man Ray and Henri Chomette were the most famous abstract filmmakers during the 1920s (the era of the genre's inception) while Ralph Steiner, Norman McLaren, Francis Thompson and John Whitney have since followed in their footsteps.

Academy Leader

See **Standard Leader**

Academy Of Motion Picture Arts And Sciences

The US bellwether organisation for all aspects of film and filmic endeavour was founded in 1927. Distinguished 'players' from every branch of the film world are, from time to time, invited to become members of the Academy, and to vote, once a year, for their choice of recipient for an Academy Award, or **Oscar**.

Accelerated Montage

The increasingly rapid juxtaposition of shots at the climax of a scene (e.g. a car chase) to instil excitement in the viewer.

Victoria Abril demonstrating her feline credentials as Marina, in Pedro Almodóvar's heady Átame! (89)

Accelerated Motion

The trick of speeding up certain parts of a scene (e.g. a gunfighter's draw) to create the appearance of heightened skill or pace. A classy example of this occurs in **Howard Hughes's** *The Outlaw* (43), when Jack Beutel's Billy The Kid outdraws Thomas Mitchell's Pat Garrett at such an accelerated speed that it is impossible to catch sight of his guns during the process.

Acetate

The base for most modern film stock, and the successor to the highly inflammable **nitrate** base, which was used until the late 1940s. See **Safety Film**

Acteurs De Composition

A category of French actor who, unlike the **monstres sacrés** of **Jean Gabin**, **Jules Berry**, **Michel Simon**, **Fernandel**, **Arletty** and their ilk, could readily assume any number of different personae, allowing themselves more flexibility, if less obvious acclaim, in the choice of their parts. These include Pierre Fresnay, **Charles Vanel**, **Madeleine Renaud** and **Jean-Louis Barrault**.

Action

Film director's cue for the cameras to begin rolling. Also any and every move in front of the camera.

Action Still

A still photograph taken directly from a developed frame of film and blown up to normal photographic proportions. See **Still**

Actor's Studio

Home of 'The **Method**' school of acting, this New York workshop was founded in 1947 by Robert Lewis, Cheryl Crawford and **Elia Kazan**, with Lee Strasberg as its artistic director. Method acolytes have included **Montgomery Clift**, **James Dean**, **Marlon Brando**, **Rod Steiger**, **Paul Newman**, and, very briefly, **Marilyn Monroe**, whose performance as Cherie in Joshua Logan's *Bus Stop* (56) undoubtedly benefitted from Strasberg's influence.
KEY LINE:
'My first reaction would be to say it set me back about ten years. But that's facetious, because I did learn a lot about subtext. I learned that very often the best writing is the line that says the opposite of what the person means.' [Screenwriter Arnold Schulman, who scripted Robert Mulligan's *Love With The Proper Stranger* (63) amongst others, on **The Method**]

Actual Sound

The sound heard on a movie soundtrack that stems from a visually traceable source on screen.

Acutance

The measurement by microdensitometer of the sharpness of any given image or frame on a film.

Adam, Ken

Influential and multi-talented production designer (a.k.a. **Art Director**) responsible for the overall look of some of the most successful of the **James Bond** films, including **Guy Hamilton's** *Goldfinger* (64), Terence Young's *Dr No* (63) and *Thunderball* (65), and **Lewis Gilbert's** *The Spy Who Loved Me* (77). Other highlights of this extraordinary career include the multitude of inventive set pieces on Michael Anderson's *Around The World In 80 Days* (56), the brilliantly conceived war room in **Stanley Kubrick's** *Dr Strangelove* (63), and the gorgeous look of the whole of Kubrick's *Barry Lyndon* (75).
OTHER KEY FILMS: **Thorold Dickinson's** *The Queen Of Spades* (49); **Robert Siodmak's** *The Crimson Pirate* (52); Sydney J Furie's *The Ipcress File* (65); Herbert Ross's *Pennies From Heaven* (81); Barry Sonnenfeld's *Addams Family Values* (91); Nicholas Hytner's *The Madness Of King George* (94); Frank Oz's *In & Out* (97); István Szabó's *Taking Sides* (01)

Addinsell, Richard

English romantic composer whose many screen credits include the wildly popular Warsaw Concerto for piano and orchestra, heard for the first time in Brian Hurst's *Dangerous Moonlight* (41), which featured a Paderewski-like and elegantly dashing **Anton Walbrook** playing the piece in a bombed-out house.
OTHER KEY FILMS: Sam Wood's *Goodbye Mr Chips* (39); **Thorold Dickinson's** *Gaslight* (40); **David Lean's** *Blithe Spirit* (45); **Alfred Hitchcock's** *Under Capricorn* (49); **Laurence Olivier's** *The Prince And The Showgirl* (57); Ted Kotcheff's *Life At The Top* (65)

Addison, John

Successful composer of an impressive number of the key British films of the 1960s (many of which just happen to have been directed by **Tony Richardson**) and which include *The Entertainer* (60), and *Tom Jones* (63), Addison is best seen in the context of his predecessor and compatriot, **Richard Addinsell**, with both men proving to be so totally professional and self-effacing that no one, apart from the occasional keen-eyed film buff, has ever heard of them.

OTHER KEY FILMS: Tony Richardson's *Look Back In Anger* (59), *A Taste Of Honey* (61), *The Loneliness Of The Long Distance Runner* (62), *The Loved One* (65) and *The Charge Of The Light Brigade* (68); Guy Green's *Luther* (73); Herbert Ross's *The Seven Per Cent Solution* (76)

Additional Camera

A second cameraman brought in to cover or complement the main camera operator during a particularly tricky or complex shot.

Adjani, Isabelle

Glacially beautiful and politically uncompromising star of **François Truffaut's** *The Story Of Adèle H* (75), Adjani also shone in **Werner Herzog's** *Nosferatu The Vampyre* (79), **Luc Besson's** *Subway* (85) and Bruno Nuytten's *Camille Claudel* (89). She made something of a comeback in Patrice Chereau's *La Reine Margot* (94), but, despite her cult status, she still remains (voluntarily, one suspects) on the periphery of her profession.
OTHER KEY FILMS: *Possession* (80); *Quartet* (81); *One Deadly Summer* (83); *Diabolique* (96); *Paparazzi* (98)

Adlon, Percy

Adlon's greatest mainstream hit came with the quirky *Bagdad Café* (88) in which an indubitably chubby Marianne Sägebrecht (whom Adlon has regularly used in his films) made an appealing and unlikely heroine, and which, coincidentally, relaunched **Jack Palance's** then rather moribund career. Adlon's later movies, such as *Salmonberries* (91) with k d lang, have tended to appeal more to alternatively inclined film festival audiences, but *Sugarbaby* (85), possibly Adlon's best film, though undoubtedly avant-garde in appearance, is nevertheless cosily populist in intent.
OTHER KEY FILMS: *Celeste* (81); *Rosalie Goes Shopping* (89); *Younger And Younger* (93); *Hotel Adlon* (96); *Die Strausskiste* (99); *DogShit* (00)

Advance

The marginal differential on a piece of film between the soundtrack and its corresponding image. Also money paid up front, in good faith, following a verbal or written agreement.

Isabelle Adjani in characteristically glacial form as Anna/Hélène, in Andrzej Zulawski's visionary Possession *(80)*

Best Adventure Films

Henri-Georges Clouzot's *Le Salaire De La Peur* [*The Wages Of Fear*] (53); Jacques Feyder's *Knight Without Armour* (37); **John Ford's** *The Hurricane* (1937); **Henry Hathaway's** *The Lives Of A Bengal Lancer* (35); **Howard Hawks's** *To Have And Have Not* (45); **Werner Herzog's** *Aguirre, Wrath Of God* (72) and *Fitzcarraldo* (82); **Alfred Hitchcock's** *The 39 Steps* (35); **John Huston's** *The African Queen* (51) and *The Man Who Would Be King* (75); **Zoltan Korda's** *The Four Feathers* (39); **Akira Kurosawa's** *Throne Of Blood* (61); **Ernest B Schoedsack** and Ernest Pichel's *The Most Dangerous Game* (32); **Ridley Scott's** *The Duellists* (77); **Steven Spielberg's** *Jaws* (75) and *Raiders Of The Lost Ark* (81); **John Sturges's** *The Great Escape* (63); J Lee Thompson's *North West Frontier* (59)

Affleck, Ben

One of the most talented of the up-and-coming stars of the new Hollywood generation, Affleck has a surprisingly extensive filmography already under his belt, including a joint **Oscar**-winning scriptwriting credit on **Gus Van Sant's** excellent *Good Will Hunting* (97), which he shares with his childhood friend (they were both born in Cambridge, MA) **Matt Damon**. Genuinely talented, and with a powerful screen presence, if Affleck chooses his mature parts well and proves that he can carry a movie on his shoulders rather than simply as part of a larger group, he will almost certainly become a force to be reckoned with in Hollywood.

OTHER KEY FILMS: *School Ties* (92); *Dazed And Confused* (93); *Mallrats* (95); *Chasing Amy* (97); *Going All The Way* (97); *Armageddon* (98); *Forces Of Nature* (99); *Boiler Room* (00); *Deception* (00); *The Third Wheel* (01); *Pearl Harbor* (01)

Agee, James

Influential and often acerbic film critic for *Time* and *The Nation* magazines, Agee scripted **John Huston's** *The African Queen* (51) and **Charles Laughton's** *Night Of The Hunter* (55), proving that, unlike most film critics, he was also able to produce the creative goods when called upon. His film reviews have recently been republished, and go a long way towards confirming his critical prescience in a world fogged by the effects of the Second World War and its aftermath – one can, in the circumstances, just about forgive him for his curious blindness to the merits of *film noir*. He received a posthumous Pulitzer Prize for his novel, *A Death In The Family*, crowning his all too brief forty-five-year lifespan of achievement.

Agent

An agent acts on behalf of his or her client, finding them work, drawing up contracts and clarifying working conditions. A customary fee of between ten per cent and fifteen per cent is then levied on any and all income the client obtains through the agency's efforts.

AIP

Masters of both schlock horror and teen drive-in movies, American International Pictures combined both genres in Gene Fowler Jr's *I Was A Teenage Werewolf* (57) during the showing of which countless now comfortably middle-aged Americans were probably conceived. Other highlights include the Beach Party series with Frankie Avalon, and **Roger Corman's** *The Masque Of The Red Death* (64), in which **Vincent Price** scared the pants off a further generation of US teenage mothers and their eager swains.

Albers, Hans

One of Germany's greatest screen actors, Albers had an unusually wide range, acting in comedy, in tragedy, and as a romantic lead. Towards the end of his life, age and decrepitude consigned him to character roles, but he remained much loved, and his wartime incarnation as Baron Münchhausen proved immensely popular on both sides of the conflict.

OTHER KEY FILMS: *Zigeunerblut* (11); *Lola Montez* (19); *Grand Hotel Babylon* (19); *Der Prinz Und Die Tänzerin* (26); *The Blue Angel* (30); *Münchhausen* (43); *Blue-Beard* (51); *Der Letzte Mann* (55)

Alda, Alan

Popular character actor (born Alphonso D'Abruzzo) who made his mark in the smash hit television series *M*A*S*H*, Alda has successfully run parallel careers on stage, screen, and as a writer and director with *The Four Seasons* (81), *Sweet Liberty* (86) and *A New Life* (88). He was outstanding as a self-obsessed film director in **Woody Allen's** *Crimes And Misdemeanours* (89), but many consider his best screen performance to have been in Jerry Schatzberg's *The Seduction Of Joe Tynan* (79), which he also scripted.

OTHER KEY FILMS: *The Extraordinary Seaman* (69); *To Kill A Clown* (72); *California Suite* (78); *Betsy's Wedding* (90); *Manhattan Murder Mystery* (93); *Everyone Says I Love You* (96); *Mad City* (97); *The Object Of My Affection* (98); *What Women Want* (00)

Aldrich, Robert

Cult filmmaker who alternately hit and missed the spot with a succession of fascinating and often shocking films. Pick of the bunch must be *Kiss Me Deadly* (55) in which Aldrich came closer than anyone has ever done to transferring no-holds-barred hard-boiled **pulp fiction** onto the screen. He resuscitated the careers of **Bette Davis, Joan Crawford** and **Olivia de Havilland** with the melodramatic *Whatever Happened To Baby Jane?* (62) and its follow-up, *Hush…Hush Sweet Charlotte* (64), and set the seal on his own success as a commercial director with the evergreen *The Dirty Dozen* (67).

OTHER KEY FILMS: *Vera Cruz* (54); *Apache* (54); *The Big Knife* (56); *The Killing Of Sister George* (68); *Too Late The Hero* (70); *Ulzana's Raid* (72); *The Choirboys* (77); *The Angry Hills* (81)

Allefex Machine

A machine used in silent movie theatres to mimic certain sound effects – a slap, a shot, thunder and lightning, etc.

5

Allégret, Marc

A favourite of André Gide, Allégret made his reputation with *Fanny* (32), which, with the two other films in the trilogy, **Alexander Korda's** *Marius* (31) and author Marcel Pagnol's own *César* (36), represented, perhaps, the first tentative emergence onto the screen of the since rather dumbed-down 'soap opera' genre. Allégret went on to specialise in romantic melodrama, a style typified by the fervid *Blanche Fury* (48), in which the illegitimate but passionately cold **Stewart Granger** tries to claim his dubious inheritance by murdering his legitimate brother and uncle in a Gothic atmosphere that sometimes borders on the fey.

OTHER KEY FILMS: *Les Amants Terribles* (36); *Heart Of Paris* (37); *L'Arlésienne* (42); *Lunegarde* (46); *Blackmailed* (51); *Les Démons De Minuit* (61); *Les Parisiennes* (62)

Allen, Woody

A critically acclaimed director whose turbulent private life has of recent years regrettably come to overshadow his talent as a filmmaker, Allen began his career as a stand-up comedian, progressed to screenwriting with Clive Donner's *What's New Pussycat?* (65), then proceeded to direct himself in the film version of his Broadway hit *Play It Again, Sam* (72). More popular in France than in his native New York, Allen is renowned for using the women in his life as the main female protagonists in his films – **Diane Keaton** graced both *Annie Hall* (77) and *Manhattan* (79), while **Mia Farrow** (with whom he later had an injurious bust-up) appeared in, amongst other films, *Hannah And Her Sisters* (86) and *Husbands And Wives* (92). A rarity among American filmmakers, Allen always retains full creative control over his own material.

OTHER KEY FILMS: *Zelig* (82); *The Purple Rose Of Cairo* (85); *Radio Days* (88); *Crimes And Misdemeanors* (89); *Manhattan Murder Mystery* (93); *Bullets Over Broadway* (94); *Mighty Aphrodite* (95); *Deconstructing Harry* (97); *Celebrity* (98); *Sweet And Lowdown* (00); *Small Time Crooks* (00); *The Curse Of The Jade Scorpion* (01)

KEY LINES:

'When I die I want to come back as **Warren Beatty's** little finger.' [Allen on sex]

'Los Angeles is not good for me – it's carcinogenic.' [Allen on the Big Orange]

'Hey, don't knock masturbation. It's sex with someone I love.' [Allen on onanism]

'I don't tan, I stroke.' [Allen on sunbathing]

Allied Artists

Taken over by Lorimar in 1980 after it had filed for bankruptcy, Allied Artists was originally a subsidiary of **Monogram**, but they reversed names in 1953, and backed into each other. Before its takeover, AA had specialised in the importation and distribution of foreign films following the liquidation of its in-house production studio in 1967. Core interests now include music, soundtracks and television.

All-time *Best* Films

Ingmar Bergman's *The Seventh Seal* (57) and *Wild Strawberries* (57); **Robert Bresson's** *Le Journal D'Un Curé De Campagne* (51); **Marcel Carné's** *Les Enfants Du Paradis* (43-4); **Jean Cocteau's** *La Belle Et La Bête* (45); **Michael Curtiz's** *Casablanca* (42); **Jean Eustache's** *La Maman Et La Putain* (73); **Federico Fellini's** *8½* (63); **Victor Fleming's** *Gone With The Wind* (39); John Ford's *The Searchers* (56); **Akira Kurosawa's** *The Seven Samurai* (54); **Yasujiro Ozu's** *Tokyo Story* (53); **Roman Polanski's** *Chinatown* (74); **Satyajit Ray's** *The Music Room* (63); **Carol Reed's** *The Third Man* (49); **Jean Renoir's** *La Règle Du Jeu* (39) and *Une Partie De Campagne* (36); **Vittorio de Sica's** *Bicycle Thieves* (48); **Andrei Tarkovsky's** *Andreï Rublev* (66-7); **Jean Vigo's** *L'Atalante* (33-4); **Orson Welles's** *Citizen Kane* (41); **Billy Wilder's** *Some Like It Hot* (59)

Allyson, June

With her torch singer's voice and impishly sweet smile, Allyson was a dead cert to play girl-next-door roles and good, unthreatening female chums, and wholesome old **MGM** made certain that those were the parts that she got. Following nearly a decade in musicals, Allyson moved into drama, probably at the instigation of her husband, **Dick Powell**, but the studio only once let her stretch her wings and play completely against type, as the shrewish wife in **José Ferrer's** *The Shrike* (55). They then proceeded to scupper the whole shebang by tacking on a ridiculously upbeat ending.

OTHER KEY FILMS: *Thousands Cheer* (43); *The Sailor Takes A Wife* (46); *Secret Heart* (46); *Words And Music* (48); *Little Women* (49); *The Glenn Miller Story* (54); *Executive Suite* (54); *Woman's World* (54); *Stranger In My Arms* (59)

Almendros, Néstor

Influential **cinematographer** who first made his mark in **Barbet Schroeder's** sun-drenched drug-culture curiosity *More* (69), which he soon followed with **Eric Rohmer's** exquisitely carnal *My Night At Maud's* (69) and *Claire's Knee* (71). Almendros worked frequently with **François Truffaut**, most notably on *The Story Of Adèle H* (75) and *The Last Metro* (80), but his global reputation rests strongly on his miraculous camerawork for **Terrence Malick's** *Days Of Heaven* (78) and on the superlative job he did for **Alan J Pakula** on *Sophie's Choice* (82).

OTHER KEY FILMS: Eric Rohmer's *La Collectionneuse* (71) and *Pauline at the Beach* (83); **Barbet Schroeder's** *Maîtresse* (76); **Robert Benton's** *Kramer Vs Kramer* (79), *Places In The Heart* (84) and *Billy Bathgate* (91)

Almodóvar, Pedro

Scabrous and anarchic, Almodóvar has been obsessed, ever since his earliest underground films, with the delirious convolutions of gay and female sexual desire. A stylist of the first order (and the coincidental discoverer of **Antonio Banderas**), Almodóvar found a large international audience with *Women On The Verge Of A Nervous Breakdown* (88), closely followed by *Tie Me Up! Tie Me Down!* (89), *High Heels* (91), and *Kika* (94), which the United States misguidedly banned as a result of feminist pressure. His latest films, including *The Flower Of My Secret* (95), *Live Flesh* (97) and *All About My Mother* [*Todo Sobre Mi Madre*] (99), have proved immensely popular with European-oriented and iconoclastically inclined audiences.

OTHER KEY FILMS: *Pepi, Luci, Bom* (80); *Matador* (86); *Law Of Desire* (87); *Mutante Action* (93)

Altman, Robert

After his extraordinary breakthrough with *M★A★S★H* in 1970, Altman took his improvisatory techniques to new heights in *Nashville* (75), which cemented his reputation as an actor's director. Over the ensuing twenty-five years he has followed his own star on the outer edge of the Hollywood system, alternating flops and triumphs with a commendably independent nonchalance. Highlights of his career include *The Long Goodbye* (73), a radical reworking of **Raymond Chandler** that somehow contrives to remain true to the original, and *The Player* (92), which boasts the longest and most successful first travelling shot since **Orson Welles's** scintillating *Touch Of Evil* (58) set the standard in these matters.

OTHER KEY FILMS: *McCabe And Mrs Miller* (71); *Thieves Like Us* (74); *A Wedding* (78); *Come Back To The Five And Dime, Jimmy Dean, Jimmy Dean* (82); *Streamers* (83); *Short Cuts* (93); *Prêt-A-Porter* [*Ready To Wear*] (94); *Kansas City* (96); *Wild Card* (97); *The Gingerbread Man* (98); *Cookie's Fortune* (99); *Dr T And The Women* (00); *Gosford Park* (01)

A-movies

Big-budget feature films designed for screening as part of a double bill alongside a smaller-budgeted secondary feature.

Alwyn, William

A fine screen composer as well as a prolific and successful mainstream conductor and musician, Alwyn's name appears on the score of a remarkable number of prestigious 1940s and 1950s British films, including Sidney Gilliat's *The Rake's Progress* [a.k.a. *Notorious Gentleman*] (45), **Carol Reed's** *Odd Man Out* (47) and Anthony Pelissier's *The Rocking Horse Winner* (49). His most popular and affecting score was for Reed's brilliant psychological study of childhood, *The Fallen Idol* (48).

OTHER KEY FILMS: Anthony Asquith's *The Winslow Boy* (48); **Jean Negulesco's** *The Mudlark* (50); **David Lean's** *Madeleine* (50); **Robert Siodmak's** *The Crimson Pirate* (52); Ken Annakin's *Swiss Family Robinson* (60)

American Film Institute

Founded in 1967, the AFI is the American equivalent of the former **British Film Academy** (which amalgamated with the Society Of Film And Television Arts in 1959) with its main aim being to advance the cause of film in whatever form it deems necessary throughout the American mainland.

American International Pictures

See **AIP**

Anamorphic Lens

The lens that puts the squeeze into images on a normal-frame 35mm film, removing the squeeze in projection to produce a wide-screen effect. First used in 1953 **CinemaScope**, and now most often seen in **Panavision**.

Anderson, Lindsay

Politically committed and awesomely well-informed about cinema (he wrote the best-ever book about **John Ford**) this theatre director and occasional documentarist shattered British middle- and lower middle-class illusions about the working classes in *This Sporting Life* (63), and went on to attack the middle classes themselves in *If...* (68), a masterpiece of poeto-anarchic fabulism (oops!), in which the inmates of an English public school turn

the tables on their masters and massacre them with machine-guns, rifles, and hand grenades from the very edifices they are being trained to protect. The film went on, quite rightly, to win the Palme D'Or at the **Cannes Film Festival**. See **Free Cinema**
OTHER KEY FILMS: *O Lucky Man!* (73); *Britannia Hospital* (82); *The Whales Of August* (87); *Glory! Glory!* (89); *Is That All There Is?* (92)

Andersson, Bibi
Along with **Liv Ullmann**, Andersson is the best-known actress to emerge from director **Ingmar Bergman's** extraordinary body of work. Catching sight of her on stage at Malmö during a theatrical production, Bergman immediately cast her in his gentle comedy of manners, *Smiles Of A Summer Night* (55) – just three years later she followed up her success with a significant triumph at the **Cannes Film Festival** with Bergman's *Brink Of Life* (58). Although she later moved into the commercial mainstream, it is as the complex heroine of such powerful and uncompromising emotional dramas as Bergman's *Persona* (66) and *The Touch* (71) that she will always be remembered.
OTHER KEY FILMS: *The Seventh Seal* (56); *Wild Strawberries* (57); *The Magician* (58); *The Devil's Eye* (60); *The Pleasure Garden* (61); *All These Women* (64); *The Rape* (67); *The Passion Of Anna* (69); *Scenes From A Marriage* (73); *Babette's Feast* (87); *Dreamplay* (94); *Shit Happens* (00)

Andress, Ursula
No great shakes as an actress, Andress was, nevertheless, something of an event in cinematic history, bursting onto the screen in what, in retrospect no doubt, seemed a rather sturdy white bikini, in Terence Young's *Dr No* (62). (For the next few years her poster image, complete with Freudian knife at belt, graced the walls and the minds of an untold number of spotty teenagers.) Trading on her new-found fame she went on to appear in a succession of blatantly commercial British films which culminated in her public cuckolding of her husband John Derek (of *Tarzan The Ape Man* (81) and Bo Derek fame), with actor **Jean-Paul Belmondo**, in a primitive version of what has now become the much-loved modern paparazzi-fest tradition. And that's about it.
OTHER KEY FILMS: *She* (65); *What's New Pussycat?* (65); *The Blue Max* (66); *Clash Of The Titans* (81); *Liberté, Égalité, Choucroute* (85); *Cremaster 5* (97)
KEY LINE:
'I can assure you my intentions are strictly honourable.' [Connery to Andress in *Dr No*]

Andrews, Dana
Curiously unquantifiable (he wasn't *really* handsome) but invariably interesting lead actor who shone as the obsessed detective in **Otto Preminger's** fascinating whodunit *Laura* (44), and much later as the unbelieving psychic investigator in **Jacques Tourneur's** cult horror masterpiece *Curse Of The Demon* (57). *Film noir* aficionados will cherish the often-underrated Andrews's performance in Preminger's little-known (and **Ben Hecht**-scripted) *Where The Sidewalk Ends* (50), in which he plays a cop gone seriously to the bad, with the gorgeous **Gene Tierney**, who also played the elusive Laura, featuring once again as his love interest.
OTHER KEY FILMS: *Ball Of Fire* (41); *Swamp Water* (41); *Boomerang!* (47); *Beyond A Reasonable Doubt* (56); *While The City Sleeps* (56); *Battle Of The Bulge* (65)

Andrews, Harry
A fine and in many ways scandalously underrated actor (one presumes on account of his typecast, square-jawed, military look) Andrews always appeared comfortable in front of the cameras, and exuded that rare thing – spontaneous integrity. He moved from the stage to a thirty-year career in films, and finally to television, where he also excelled, producing some of his best work in that medium, most notably in Michael Wilcox's 1985 BBC TV drama, *Lent*. On film he was particularly good as the gruff but tender sergeant Tom Pugh in J Lee Thompson's *Ice Cold In Alex* (58), and also as **Trevor Howard's** argumentative elder brother, Lord Raglan, in **Tony Richardson's** *The Charge Of The Light Brigade* (68).
OTHER KEY FILMS: *The Red Beret* (52); *The Black Knight* (54); *Saint Joan* (57); *Barabbas* (62); *55 Days At Peking* (63); *The Hill* (65); *The Sea Gull* (68); *Entertaining Mr Sloane* (70); *The Ruling Class* (72); *The Mackintosh Man* (73)

Andrews, Julie
Always eager to belie the squeaky-clean, perpetual virgin image which the studios foisted upon her in such perennial family fare as Robert Stevenson's *Mary Poppins* (64) and **Robert Wise's** *The Sound Of Music* (65), Andrews has also chosen to act in more 'adult' material, such as husband **Blake Edwards's** *S.O.B.* (81) in which she famously bared her breasts at the not-so-advanced age of forty-six. Many of her die-hard fans felt that by doing so she had rather missed the point.
OTHER KEY FILMS: *Torn Curtain* (66); *Star!* (68); *Victor/Victoria* (81); *Duet For One* (86); *Relative Values* (00)

KEY LINE:
'Working with her is like being hit over the head with a Valentine's card.' [Attributed to **Christopher Plummer,** her co-star in *The Sound Of Music*]

Anger, Kenneth

Famous in film buff circles for his schlock exposé of Hollywood's most grotesque secret lives in his books *Hollywood Babylon* (1958) and *Hollywood Babylon 2* (1984) (must reading for all aficionados of camp), Anger is also a very talented **avant-garde** filmmaker (and occasional actor), obsessed with mysticism and the occult, whose work includes the notorious and orgiastic *Inauguration Of The Pleasure Dome* (54–66). **OTHER KEY FILMS:** *Fireworks* (47); *The Story Of O* (59-61); *Scorpio Rising* (64); *Lucifer Rising* (73);

Best Animated Films

Tex Avery's *The Cat That Hated People* (48) and *Little Rural Ridinghood* (49); Frédéric Back's *L'Homme Qui Plantait Des Arbres* (87); **Tim Burton's** *The Nightmare Before Christmas* (94); **Walt Disney's** *Snow White And The Seven Dwarfs* (37), *Pinocchio* (40), *Fantasia* (40) and *The Jungle Book* (67); Paul Grimault's *Le Roi Et L'Oiseau* (79); **Hanna/Barbera's** *The Cat's Concerto* (Tom & Jerry) (47); John Lasseter's *Toy Story* (95); Nick Park's (see **Aardman**) *Wallace & Gromit Tetralogy* (89-95); **Robert Zemeckis's** *Who Framed Roger Rabbit* (88)

Animatics

The equivalent of an animated form of picture-board which is used to pre-plan or block out shots and sequences for later use in a feature film, advertisement or music video.

Animation

The art of imitating motion by illusion – most often by a series of hand- or computer-generated frames.

Animation Camera

A specially mounted camera specifically designed for animation photography, which utilises a sensitive stop-motion mechanism so that individual frames may be filmed for later animation.

Animation Stand

A composite term for the illuminated table, the stop-motion animation camera, and the specially constructed camera stand that are used in the creation of animated features.

Animator

The key artist in any animation sequence who pens in the final positions of the animated object.

Animatronics

The art of moving puppets by the use of internal mechanisms that can be computer-, cable- or radio-controlled.

Anime

A peculiarly Japanese form of animation technique (pronounced animé), which stemmed from the popular comic books endemically available all over Japan. Now sometimes pejoratively used to imply a particular form of pornographic or fantasy cartoon.

Annaud, Jean-Jacques

Annaud's career runs parallel, in many ways, to his near contemporary **Ridley Scott**. Both started out in advertising, moved smoothly through their own domestic markets, and have since ended up making large, internationally promoted middlebrow films. *Quest For Fire* (81) was Annaud's first big success in this sphere, notable for the fact that its dialogue consisted of an entirely made-up language (by novelist Anthony Burgess) with **subtitles**, ensuring the film the widest possible commercial airing. Annaud pulled off a similar trick with *The Bear* (88) (the dialogue this time consisting of grunts and screams), which followed his very successful foray into Umberto Eco territory with *The Name Of The Rose* (86). Very popular in France, where he is seen as living proof that French sensibility can indeed attract a mass international following, Annaud is also notable for the very few projects he takes up. **OTHER KEY FILMS:** *Black And White In Colour* (76); *Hothead* (79); *The Lover* (92); *Wings Of Courage* (95); *Seven Years In Tibet* (97); *Enemy At The Gates* (01)

Answer Print

Sometimes known as a 'trial' or 'approval' print, an answer print is the first sound-inclusive print to be sent to the producer for approval. Everything about the print is then meticulously checked and the print is sent back (often on a number of occasions) for fine-tuning. The final answer print is then used as the standard by which all subsequent **release prints** are compared.

Antonioni, Michelangelo

One of the undoubted masters of the Italian cinema, Antonioni's uncanny visual sense was evident from his very first directing job, the

black-and-white documentary *The People Of The Po Valley* (47). Everything counts in an Antonioni film, from the colour of a fur coat to the positioning of two alienated people on a bridge. In his famous trilogy comprising *L'Avventura* (59), *La Notte* (60) and *L'Eclisse* (62), Antonioni uses the marvellous faces of Monica Vitti and **Jeanne Moreau** to mirror the breakdown of a series of intense interrelationships. With *Blow-Up* (66), Antonioni turned his attention to swinging London, and in *Zabriskie Point* (70) to irony-free California, which he proceeded (paradoxically really, given the title of his previous film) to blow up, in one of the longest and most graphic explosion shots in film history. **Jack Nicholson** gave one of his best-ever screen performances in Antonioni's *The Passenger* (75), which explored, at times painfully, the sometimes tenuous fragmentation of personal identity, a subject of which this director has proved himself a master.
OTHER KEY FILMS: *Story Of A Love Affair* (50); *Red Desert* (64); *The Three Faces Of A Woman* (65); *Identification Of A Woman* (82); *Beyond The Clouds* (95); *Destination Verna* (00)

Aperture
The opening in a camera, through which light enters.

APO
An acronym for 'action print only', to imply a film print without the soundtrack added.

Apple Box
Awesomely complicated device (in the cunning shape of a simple box) that is used to lift vertically challenged male actors over their often-taller female co-stars. Disdaining the use of the box, five-foot six-inch **Alan Ladd** asked his technicians to dig a slit trench for his leading ladies to walk in instead.

Apted, Michael
Director Michael Apted's debut feature, *Triple Echo* (72), was a curious, rather underrated piece of work, in which a Second World War deserter disguises himself as the sister of his mistress (by cross-dressing) in order to avoid capture, only to find himself the object of a Military Police sergeant's lewd advances (a gloriously gloating **Oliver Reed**). A hell of a plot, when you come to think of it, and considerably before its time in its investigation of sexual identity. Apted went on to international success with *Coal Miner's Daughter* (80), *Gorky Park* (83), *Gorillas*

In The Mist (88) and *Nell* (94) – as well as trying his hand, very effectively, at a **James Bond** movie, in *The World Is Not Enough* (99) – but none have had quite the same mystery or sense of place as *Triple Echo*. *Extreme Measures* (96), starring **Gene Hackman** and **Hugh Grant**, was an outstanding thriller, however, and Apted remains a director to watch.
OTHER KEY FILMS: *Stardust* (74); *Critical Condition* (87); *The Long Way Home* (89); *Class Action* (90); *Thunderheart* (92); *Moving The Mountain* (95); *Inspiration* (97); *Always Outnumbered* (98); *Enigma* (01)

Aquarium
Hollywood jargon for the booth in which sound is mixed and edited.

Arau, Alfonso
Mexican director of *Like Water For Chocolate* (92), which was written by his ex-wife Laura Esquivel, and the even more 'chocolaty' *A Walk In The Clouds* (95), Arau began life as an actor on such movies as **Sam Peckinpah's** *The Wild Bunch* (69), and **Robert Zemeckis's** *Romancing The Stone* (84). His own films vary from out-and-out thrillers to social commentaries, and he now runs his own LA production company, specialising in films for a predominantly Latin American audience.
OTHER KEY FILMS: *The Barefoot Eagle* (67); *Calzonzin Inspector* (74); *Wetback Power* (80); *Chido Guan* (84); *Picking Up The Pieces* (00)

Arbuckle, Fatty
'Poor' Fatty tasted both the fruits of heady success and the bitter aloes of public contumely. The former 'king of comedy' (who was earning $5,000 a week in 1917) saw his career plummet when he was accused of rape and murder after inadvertently causing the death of gaiety girl Virginia Rappe by rupturing her bladder *in flagrante delicto* at an orgy. Though finally acquitted on all charges (for lack of evidence – most of the other revellers were drunk at the time and the chief witness was dead), Fatty was banned from acting and his $3,000,000 contract with **Paramount** torn up. The disgraced former plumber eventually ended up drunk and dead himself, aged only forty-six, in a New York apartment. **James Ivory** later made a film inspired by the Arbuckle affair, starring James Coco, called *The Wild Party* (75).
OTHER KEY FILMS: *The Rounders* (14); *A Cream Puff Romance* (16); *Rough House* (17); *The Cook* (18); *The Garage* (19); *The Dollar-A-Year Man* (21); *Brewster's Millions* (25)

Arc Lamp

The one-time major source of studio lighting, consisting of a vivid white light produced by either a carbon or a mercury and xenon electrode.

Ardant, Fanny

A favourite actress of avant-garde director **Alain Resnais** (and the widow of film director **François Truffaut**) the Monte Carlo-born Ardant has been notably successful on both stage and screen, as much on account of her offbeat, bluestocking looks, as for her undoubted talent. Her filmography is astonishing, the more so as she is virtually unknown outside France except in enlightened film buff circles. Her recent performance in **Patrice Leconte's** majestically comic *Ridicule* (96) has, of course, done absolutely nothing to change this unreasonable state of affairs.

OTHER KEY FILMS: *Les Chiens* (79); *The Woman Next Door* (81); *Vivement Dimanche!* (83); *Un Amour De Swann* (84); *Next Summer* (85); *Mélo* (86); *Afraid Of The Dark* (92); *The Deserter's Wife* (92); *Colonel Chabert* (94); *Beyond The Clouds* (96); *Pédale Douce* (97); *Elizabeth* (98); *La Cena* (98); *La Débandade* (99); *Le Fils Du Français* (99); *Le Libertin* (00); *Callas Forever* (01)

Arkin, Alan

A much-garlanded character actor, Arkin is best known for his portrayal of the deaf-mute in Robert Ellis Miller's *The Heart Is A Lonely Hunter* (68) and for his bravura performance as Yossarian in **Mike Nichols's** otherwise disappointing *Catch 22* (70). He was absolutely outstanding in James Foley's film version of **David Mamet's** stage play, *Glengarry Glen Ross* (92) and recent turns in **Tim Burton's** *Edward Scissorhands* (90), Joe Johnston's *The Rocketeer* (91) and Andrew Niccol's *Gattaca* (97) prove that his career is still in gear.

OTHER KEY FILMS: *The Russians Are Coming! The Russians Are Coming!* (66); *Wait Until Dark* (67); *Inspector Clouseau* (68); *Freebie And The Bean* (74); *Hearts Of The West* (75); *Simon* (80); *Big Trouble* (85); *Grosse Pointe Blank* (97); *Jakob The Liar* (99); *Arigo* (00) (also dir.)

Arlen, Harold

Son of a New York cantor, the multi-talented Arlen composed the music for **Victor Fleming's** *The Wizard Of Oz* (39) and **Vincente Minnelli's** all-black *Cabin In The Sky* (43), which united such jazz luminaries as Lena Horne, **Louis Armstrong**, Duke Ellington and Ethel Waters. The best song in the movie, and one of the best ever written, is Arlen's 'Happiness Is Just A Thing Called Joe'.

OTHER KEY FILMS: Anatole Litvak's *Blues In The Night* (41); George Seaton's *The Country Girl* (54); **George Cukor's** *A Star Is Born* (54)

Arletty

Quintessential French actress who steadfastly refused all offers to go to Hollywood, Arletty later found herself accused of collaboration with the Germans after her war-time affair with a high-ranking Nazi officer came to light. Her name has since become synonymous with that of director **Marcel Carné**, for whom she acted in four absolutely outstanding films – *Hôtel Du Nord* (38), *Le Jour Se Lève* (39), *Les Visiteurs Du Soir* (43), and *Les Enfants Du Paradis* (44), the last of which, thanks in part to her outstanding performance as Garance, is generally recognised as one of the greatest films of all time.

OTHER KEY FILMS: *Un Chien Qui Rapporte* (30); *Pension Mimosas* (35); *Faisons Un Rêve* (36); *Les Perles De La Couronne* (37); *Désiré* (38); *Fric-Frac* (39); *Madame Sans-Gêne* (41)

Armendariz, Pedro

He was Mexico's very own version of **Rudolph Valentino**, and his following remains strong to this day in a country still emotionally wedded to its past and to the cult of poetic and sentimental machismo which he personified. Armendariz killed himself at the age of fifty-one on learning that he had cancer, after starring in a succession of great films from the golden age of Mexican cinema, including **Emilio Fernandez's** *Maria Candelaria* (43) and *The Pearl* (45). He had a flourishing career, too, across the border with the US, with notable parts in **John Ford's** *Three Godfathers* (49) and a wonderful last fling as **James Bond's** lasciviously daredevil Turkish friend, Kerim Bey, in Terence Young's *From Russia With Love* (63).

OTHER KEY FILMS: *Maria Elena* (35); *La Reina Del Rio* (39); *Simon Bolivar* (41); *Flor Sylvestre* (44); *Enamorada* (46); *The Fugitive* (47); *Fort Apache* (48); *We Were Strangers* (49); *La Malquerida* (49); *The Big Boodle* (57); *La Cucaracha* (58)

Armstrong, Gillian

Armstrong's career began strongly with *My Brilliant Career* (79), to the extent that she seemed on the verge of a heady international breakthrough, but her subsequent choice of resolutely low-profile material seems to have worked against her (while saying much for her integrity). *Mrs Soffel* (84) may have been a touch worthy, but *High Tide* (87), with the excellent **Judy Davis**, was a magnificent return

11

to form, and Armstrong's version of *Little Women* (94) is the best since the 1933 **George Cukor/ Katharine Hepburn** movie.

OTHER KEY FILMS: *The Singer And The Dancer* (76); *Starstruck* (82); *Fires Within* (91); *The Last Days Of Chez Nous* (92); *Not Fourteen Again* [doc.] (96); *Oscar And Lucinda* (97); *Charlotte Gray* (01)

Armstrong, Louis

Hardly a film actor (not a lot of people know that…) so much as a walking, singing, trumpet-playing legend, who starred in a number of films simply to please his fans and to boost box office takings – mind you, he had a neat line in repartee and he lit up the screen whenever he appeared, which must put him somewhere near the top rank of the acting profession. He partnered **Bing Crosby** in Norman McLeod's *Pennies From Heaven* (36), and then again, twenty-one years later, in **Charles Walters's** *High Society* (56), but if you *really* want to see Satchmo swing, check out Bert Stern's *Jazz On A Summer's Day* (59) documentary, and in particular his duet with trombonist Jack Teagarden on the evergreen 'Lazy River'. Sublime!

OTHER KEY FILMS: *Artists And Models* (37); *Dr Rhythm* (38); *Cabin In The Sky* (43); *Hollywood Canteen* (44); *A Song Is Born* (48); *The Glenn Miller Story* (54); *The Five Pennies* (59); *Paris Blues* (61); *Hello Dolly!* (69)

Arnold, Malcolm

Distinguished composer and coincidental scorer of film soundtracks, Arnold is best known in cinema circles for his work on **David Lean's** *The Sound Barrier* (52), *Hobson's Choice* (54), and *The Bridge On The River Kwai* (57), but he also scored Ronald Neame's *Tunes Of Glory* (60) and Delbert Mann's rather disappointing – when compared with the 1935 **George Cukor** version – *David Copperfield* (70).

OTHER KEY FILMS: Anthony Kimmins's *The Captain's Paradise* (53); Henry Cornelius's *I Am A Camera* (55); **Carol Reed's** *Trapeze* (56); Stuart Heisler's *Island In The Sun* (57); Ronald Neame's *The Chalk Garden* (64); **Anthony Mann's** *The Heroes Of Telemark* (66)

Arquette, Patricia

Very sexy, rather offbeat American actress who has brought considerable depth to her roles, particularly in **Sean Penn's** *The Indian Runner* (91), John Madden's *Ethan Frome* (93), and Tony Scott's *True Romance* (93), Arquette was a natural

choice for a **David Lynch** 'heroine' in *Lost Highway* (97), and her rather fey mixture of sensuality and street wisdom certainly marks her out from the usual Hollywood herd.

OTHER KEY FILMS: *Time Out* (87); *Far North* (88); *Trouble Bound* (93); *Ed Wood* (94); *Beyond Rangoon* (95); *The Secret Agent* (96); *The Hi-Lo Country* (98); *Stigmata* (99); *Bringing Out The Dead* (99); *Little Nicky* (00)

Arquette, Rosanna

Very different from her sister, Patricia, but equally versatile, Arquette had her first big critical success with Susan Seidelman's *Desperately Seeking Susan* (83), followed by **Lawrence Kasdan's** *Silverado* (85), and the **Luc Besson** cult hit *The Big Blue* [*Le Grand Bleu*] (88). In 1997 she starred in **David Cronenberg's** controversial and erotic *Crash* (97), which allowed her undoubted talent full rein, even if the film itself was something of an unsatisfactory hybrid.

OTHER KEY FILMS: *After Hours* (85); *Nobody's Fool* (86); *New York Stories* (89); *Black Rainbow* (91); *Nowhere To Run* (93); *Pulp Fiction* (94); *Search And Destroy* (95); *Gone Fishin'* (96); *Buffalo '66* (98); *Pigeon Holed* (99); *The Whole Nine Years* (00); *Things Behind The Sun* (01)

Arranger

The musician or composer who adapts and arranges existing music for a film score, e.g. yet another version of 'Greensleeves', for a Henry VIII movie, or of 'La Marseillaise' for anything involving the French.

Arriflex

The camera behind many of the shaky hand-held shots we see in French **New Wave** films of the late 1950s and early 1960s, this 16mm or 35mm reflex camera has since been largely superseded by the **Steadicam**, but its influence on **avant-garde** filmmakers and on **cinéma vérité** documentarists can hardly be over-emphasised.

Art Department

The studio production team in charge of set building and design.

Art Director

Chief of the **Art Department** and ultimately responsible for the total architectural and aesthetic look of a film. Alternatively known as the production designer. See **Alfred Junge** and **Van Nest Polglase**

Art-House Cinema

A cinema that shows classic, independent, cult and director's season films as a point of faith. The world centre for such cinemas is in **Paris**, but most major cities have a number of these 'havens from everyday life' tucked away down back streets. They are often, but not always, run by **cinéphiles**. The term art-house cinema can also be applied as a catch-all for the types of film customarily shown at such venues.

Arthur, Jean

Arthur only really shone when **Frank Capra** directed her, but then this husky-voiced tomboy of an actress – who always gave the impression that she was game for anything – made movie magic, as in *Mr Deeds Goes To Town* (36), *You Can't Take It With You* (38) and *Mr Smith Goes To Washington* (39). Her career ended on a sour note thanks to a contractual dispute with **Columbia Studios**, but she lit the screen up one last time as embattled homesteader **Van Heflin's** wife, quietly and decorously in love with gunfighter **Alan Ladd** in **George Stevens's** magnificent **Western** *Shane* (53).
OTHER KEY FILMS: *The Whole Town's Talking* (35); *The Plainsman* (37); *Arizona* (40); *The Devil And Miss Jones* (41); *The Talk Of The Town* (42)
KEY LINE:
'I'm hard to get, Geoff. All you have to do is ask me.' [Arthur to Cary Grant in **Howard Hawks's** *Only Angels Have Wings* (39)]

Artifact

Unfortunate visual defects or blurs appearing on a film due to misuse or malfunctioning of the image-bearing equipment. See also **Cinch Marks**

Artificial Light

Any and every light on a film set that is produced by anything other than natural conditions.

Arzner, Dorothy

Along with **Ida Lupino**, who was infinitely her superior in instinct, if not in technique, Arzner was one of the few female film directors to work commercially in the era of the great studios. A superb editor, and a more than competent scriptwriter, Arzner's first directing job was **Paramount's** *Fashions For Women* (27). Among her later films, both *Nana* (34) and *Dance Girl Dance* (40), with its slight feminist twist, are particularly worthy of mention.
OTHER KEY FILMS: *Manhattan Cocktail* (28); *The Wild Party* (29); *Merrily We Go To Hell* (32); *Christopher Strong* (33); *First Comes Courage* (43)

ASA

The American Standards Association rating for film emulsion speed that is to be found on nearly all undeveloped film and which indicates the extent of a film stock's light sensitivity.

ASC

Acronym for The American Society of Cinematographers, founded in 1919. See also **BSC**

Ashby, Hal

Oscar-winning editor-turned-director Ashby struck a public chord with *Harold And Maude* (71), in which twenty-year-old Bud Cort falls in love with seventy-something Ruth Gordon. *The Last Detail* (73) followed, with **Jack Nicholson**, as Buddusky SM1, on the top of his form, and bringing Ashby a welcome measure of critical success, while *Being There* (79), Ashby's paean to simplicity about a foundling gardener turned presidential adviser, brought **Peter Sellers** his very own late-career **Oscar** nomination. Despite these promising beginnings, and such mid-career successes as *Coming Home* (78), Ashby never seemed able to take advantage of his status, and he died in 1988 after a sudden, drug-related falling-off of quality, and with relatively few films to his credit.
OTHER KEY FILMS: *The Landlord* (70); *Shampoo* (75); *Bound For Glory* (76); *8 Million Ways To Die* (86)

Ashcroft, Peggy

A great stage actress who gave only a few screen performances, Ashcroft had the rare ability to subsume herself totally inside any part that she was playing. As the downtrodden crofter's wife in **Alfred Hitchcock's** *The Thirty-Nine Steps* (35), her intense five minutes on film unaccountably linger in the mind long afterwards, and it was only just that she received a belated best supporting actress **Oscar** for her role of Mrs Moore, in **David Lean's** *A Passage To India*.
OTHER KEY FILMS: *The Wandering Jew* (33); *Rhodes* (36); *The Nun's Story* (59); *Secret Ceremony* (68); *Sunday Bloody Sunday* (71); *She's Been Away* (89)

Aspect Ratio

The simple measurement of the width-to-height ratio of a feature film image when projected against a screen. Until the 1950s the customary aspect ratio of most movies was 1.33:1, but this changed, with the appearance of wide-screen cinema, to anything up to 2.55:1. The aspect ratio is a key element of a film's visual composition, something often ruined by ill-considered and visually truncated TV presentations.

13

Asquith, Anthony

Known as 'Puffin' to chums such as **John Mills**, Asquith was actually the son of a British Prime Minister, and the director of several of the most prestigious films in the history of British Cinema. His longest-lasting collaboration was with playwright Terence Rattigan, from whose scripts he directed the haunting *The Way To The Stars* (45) [a.k.a. *Johnny In The Clouds*], *The Winslow Boy* (50) and *The Browning Version* (51). Asquith was a real master at portraying the stultifying inhibitions of the upper and middle classes, and his films were often subtly anarchic, reflecting his deeply held and egalitarian political views.

OTHER KEY FILMS: *Pygmalion* (38); *French Without Tears* (39); *Fanny By Gaslight* (44); *The Importance Of Being Earnest* (52); *Carrington VC* (54); *The Yellow Rolls-Royce* (64)

Assembly

A primary editing stage in which, for the first time, a move towards a first **rough cut** of the film is attempted by the tentative splicing together of pre-edited footage.

Assistant Cameraman

The camera technician in charge of focus pulling, loading and unloading film, keeping logs and general maintenance of the camera apparatus.

Assistant Director

A fertile training area for budding young directors, the AD is responsible for rehearsals, schedules, crowd organisation and confirming that all the film crew are on hand during **call**.

Assistant Editor

The editor's dogsbody, responsible for keeping records, labelling, maintaining order, and general rather than creative cutting and splicing.

Assistant Producer

The producer's right hand, responsible for carrying out generalised supervision and coordination duties and representing the studio's interests whenever the producer is not on the set.

Associated British Picture Corporation

An early British production company, created in 1932 by John Maxwell through the merger of his British International Pictures (which owned **Elstree Studios**) with Associated British Cinemas, owners of the ABC circuit of cinemas. ABPC, together with **Rank**, held a virtual stranglehold over British production, distribution and exhibition, until they were taken over in 1969 by the EMI conglomerate.

Associate Producer

Not to be confused with the assistant producer, the AP is directly involved in creative decision-making on and off the set, and functions as the producer's second in command.

Astaire, Fred

The most elegant of all screen dancers, Astaire encapsulated the magic and glamour of Hollywood better than anyone else, whether dancing alone – one has only to think of his 'put her to sleep, sandman' tap-dance in front of Edward Everett Horton in Mark Sandrich's *Top Hat* (35) – or in partnership with **Ginger Rogers** (check out their magical pairing in **George Stevens's** *Swing Time* (36)), **Rita Hayworth** or Cyd Charisse, who all did their best work with him. Like every great dancer, he made his partners look beautiful, and his light, apparently untrained tenor voice was perfect for those subtle **Cole Porter** numbers which are so very much harder to master than they first appear when one foolishly attempts to sing along to them in the shower. Later, when his dancing days were over, Astaire proved himself a sensitive and modest actor, most notably as Julian Osborn in Stanley Kramer's *On The Beach* (59). A true master.

OTHER KEY FILMS: *Flying Down To Rio* (33); *The Gay Divorcee* (34); *Follow The Fleet* (36); *Shall*

*Fred Astaire and ten-time partner **Ginger Rogers**, in a typically elegant scene from William A Seiter's* Roberta *(35)*

We Dance (37); Carefree (38); Holiday Inn (42); The Sky's The Limit (43); Blue Skies (46); Easter Parade (48); Let's Dance (50); The Band Wagon (53); Silk Stockings (57); Funny Face (57); The Towering Inferno (74); That's Entertainment (compilation) (74)

KEY LINE:
'Can't act. Can't sing. Slightly bald. Can dance a little.' [Verdict on Astaire's first screen test in 1932]

Asther, Nils

If Asther were only ever remembered for one part, that part would be the eponymous effete Chinese warlord in **Frank Capra's** The Bitter Tea Of General Yen (33). Using all the well-honed techniques he learnt during his salad days as a star of silent cinema, Asther somehow transcended the absurdity inherent in a tall, finely chiselled Swede playing a Chinaman, to produce an odd and heady effect that is infinitely seductive, and, by the end of the film, almost unbearably poignant – we are certainly not surprised that gorgeous **Barbara Stanwyck**, as Megan Davis, threw caution (and her boring missionary husband) to the winds on his account. The final scene on board the boat, with Stanwyck and Walter Connolly reminiscing about Yen, never fails to bring a tear to the eye, (at least to this writer's).

OTHER KEY FILMS: The Cossacks (28); Adrian Lecouvreur (28); Wild Orchids (29); The Sea Bat (30); Letty Lynton (32); Madame Spy (34); The Crime Doctor (34); Night Monster (42); That Man From Tangier (53); When Darkness Falls (60)

Astigmatism

Named after the human optical defect, camera astigmatism is a focusing imperfection that causes blurring or deformation at the outer edges of the frame.

Astor, Mary

Astor is most fondly remembered for her unwanted part in the 'Mary Astor sex diaries scandal', in which she detailed her exotic shenanigans with four-times-a-night curtain-raiser, playwright George S Kaufman. The diaries unaccountably fell into the hands of Astor's then husband, who blatantly used them against her in the ensuing child custody proceedings. Astor's movies could hardly fail after that, and eager fans breathlessly scrutinised (with entirely new eyes, one supposes) her ice-cool performance as Brigid O'Shaughnessy opposite **Humphrey Bogart's** Sam Spade in **John Huston's** The Maltese Falcon (41), and her glittering comic turn as sexy serial divorcée Princess Centimillia in **Preston Sturges's**

The Palm Beach Story (42) [French title, Madame Et Ses Flirts!], which also happens to be one of the funniest films ever made.

OTHER KEY FILMS: Beau Brummell (24); Red Dust (32); Dodsworth (36); The Hurricane (37); The Prisoner Of Zenda (37); The Great Lie (41); Across The Pacific (42); Meet Me In St Louis (44)

KEY LINE:
'Ah, desert night – with George's body plunging into mine, naked under the stars…' [A brief excerpt from Astor's diary, unfortunately subsequently burnt by order of the judge.]

Mary Astor proving that all those 'desert night' stories weren't apocryphal

Asynchronism

When the sound track and the image are out of synch on the screen – not to be confused with 'dubbing', when the sound track and the image are *always* out of synch (that's a joke, by the way!).

Asynchronous Sound

See Synchronous Sound

Attenborough, Richard

Attenborough made his first real mark as the tormented, razor-toting Pinkie in **John Boulting's** *Brighton Rock* (47), and followed this up with a seemingly countless number of stiff upper lip and gor blimey jobs in worthy Second World War films. Talent will always out, however, and he soon matured into more nuanced performances, culminating in his chilling portrayal of serial killer John Reginald Christie in Richard Fleischer's *10 Rillington Place* (71). By this time Attenborough had transmogrified into a gifted director with his screen version of Joan Littlewood's stage production of Charles Chilton's play, *Oh! What A Lovely War* (69), which he followed up with the equally successful *Young Winston* (72), the first of a number of sometimes rather worthy biopics that took him through the 1980s and 1990s. Now a Lord, and something of a power behind the scenes in British Cinema, he has recently delighted his loyal audience by a tremendous return to form as a director with the touching and still underrated *Shadowlands* (93).

OTHER KEY FILMS: *In Which We Serve* (42); *The Gift Horse* (52); *The Angry Silence* (60); *The Great Escape* (63); *Gandhi* (82); *Cry Freedom* (87); *Chaplin* (92); *In Love And War* (96); *Grey Owl* (99)

Atwill, Lionel

A fine character actor (and renowned lecher and orgiast) who, like his successor **Vincent Price**, developed a lucrative secondary career in horror movies, Atwill's booming English stage voice and lean, tormented features enlivened many a dreary murder scene. The performance for which he is best remembered came as the doomed protagonist in Sidney Lanfield's classic *The Hound Of The Baskervilles* (39), but he also did sterling supporting work as diplomats, aristocrats, colonial governors and stern fathers in some of the greatest films of Hollywood's golden age.

OTHER KEY FILMS: *Indiscretion* (21); *The Mystery Of The Wax Museum* (33); *Stamboul Quest* (34); *The Devil Is A Woman* (35); *Captain Blood* (35); *The Lives Of A Bengal Lancer* (35); *The Last Train From Madrid* (37); *The Great Waltz* (38); *The Three Musketeers* (39); *Johnny Apollo* (40); *Boom Town* (40); *To Be Or Not To Be* (42)

KEY LINE:

'All women love the men they fear. Their preference is…for a Master!' [Atwill on himself]

Audiovisual

Normally used in the context of an 'audiovisual aid' to describe demonstration techniques which benefit from both visual and sound back-ups.

Audition

A test performance for a future or mooted film production, usually held in the presence of the director, the talent scout and the producer.

Audran, Stéphane

A former wife of director **Claude Chabrol** and the star of many of his films, Audran perfectly encapsulated the brittle, sophisticated and sensual French ideal of beauty that **Luis Buñuel** so perfectly satirised in *The Discreet Charm Of The Bourgeoisie* (72). A highly intelligent actress and markedly careful with her choice of roles, Audran showed a vast international audience just how good she was with the performance of a lifetime in Gabriel Axel's now perennial *Babette's Feast* (87), although her most famous role is that of Hélène, **Jean Yanne's** potential victim in Chabrol's *Le Boucher* [*The Butcher*] (70). If any American actress had produced the same body of work in the US that Audran has done in France, she would be a national treasure.

OTHER KEY FILMS: *Les Cousins* (59); *Le Tigre Aime La Chair Fraiche* (64); *Les Biches* (68); *Just Before Nightfall* (71); *Violette Nozière* (78); *Eagle's Wing* (79); *Coup De Torchon* [*Clean Slate*] (81); *Le Choc* (82); *Quiet Days In Clichy* (90); *Betty* (92); *Maximum Risk* (96); *Arlette* (97); *Belle Maman* (99); *Le Pique-Nique De Lulu Kreutz* (00)

August, Bille

Denmark's most prestigious filmmaker, August soon made his national mark with *Twist And Shout* (86), and his international one with *Pelle The Conqueror* (87), with which he won a Palme D'Or at the **Cannes Film Festival**. His more recent films, such as *The House Of The Spirits* (93) and *Smilla's Sense Of Snow* (97) have disappointed some of his fans, and, despite his undoubted talent, he has yet to establish himself firmly as a major international player.

OTHER KEY FILMS: *Zappa* (83); *The Best Intentions* (92); *Jerusalem* (96); *Les Misérables* (98); *A Song For Martin* (00)

August, Joseph H

One of the great unsung cinematographers of the American cinema, August was a master of light and shade, which he used to fine effect in **John Ford's** *The Informer* (35) and *They Were Expendable* (45), and particularly in his final film, **William Dieterle's** haunting *Portrait Of Jennie* (48). The highlight of August's career (for aficionados only, of course) was the scene in Henry Otto's *Dante's Inferno* (24) where August photographed the interior of Hell in a now notorious ten-minute sequence in which greased up musclemen (complete with helmets and togas) thoroughly enjoy themselves thrashing (for the victim's own good, no doubt) an eclectic assortment of naked and chained starlets.

OTHER KEY FILMS: Lambert Hillyer's *The Narrow Trail* (17); John Ford's *Up The River* (30); **Howard Hawks's** *Twentieth Century* (34); **George Cukor's** *Sylvia Scarlett* (35); **George Stevens's** *A Damsel In Distress* (37)

Aurenche, Jean

One of the greatest and most consistent of all French screenwriters, Aurenche is responsible for such brilliantly disparate films as **Marcel Carné's** *Hôtel Du Nord* (38) and, together with his collaborator, Pierre Bost, **Claude Autant-Lara's** *Le Diable Au Corps* [*Devil In The Flesh*] (46), and **René Clément's** *Jeux Interdits* [*Forbidden Games*] (52). Criticised by some **New Wavers** for his adherence to the 'tradition de qualité' which they felt had cramped French films for a generation, Aurenche finally won through, despite nearly a decade in the doldrums, with **Bertrand Tavernier's** *Coup De Torchon* [*Clean Slate*] (81) and Pierre Granier-Deferre's *L'Étoile Du Nord* (82), which perfectly illustrate the need for both cinematic traditions.

OTHER KEY FILMS: Jean Delannoy's *La Symphonie Pastorale* (46); **Claude Autant-Lara's** *L'Auberge Rouge* [*The Red Inn*] (51), *Le Rouge Et Le Noir* [*The Red And The Black*] (54) and *En Cas De Malheur* [*Love Is My Profession*] (57)

Autant-Lara, Claude

That paradoxical figure, an anti-establishment right-winger, Autant-Lara made the notorious *Le Diable Au Corps* [*Devil In The Flesh*] (46) in which a schoolboy conducts a passionate affair with an absent soldier's wife. A stylish, commercially successful filmmaker, Autant-Lara found himself increasingly marginalised during the late 1950s and early 1960s by the arrival of the French **New Wave**, which criticised him for his slick virtuosity and concentration on technique. He made something of a belated riposte, however, with *En Cas De Malheur* [*Love Is My Profession*] (57), which starred a conspicuously rosy-cheeked Brigitte Bardot.

OTHER KEY FILMS: *Ciboulette* (33); *Le Rouge Et Le Noir* (54); *A Pig Across Paris* (56); *Le Journal D'Une Femme En Blanc* (65); *Gloria* (77)

Auteuil, Daniel

Now internationally known thanks to his performances in **Claude Berri's** *Jean De Florette* (86) and *Manon Des Sources* (86), Auteuil descends from a family of itinerant opera singers, and the comic brio he brings to some of his roles, together with a wry, occasionally awkward self-deprecation, reflect this, marking him out as a natural screen presence. Superb as the tormented Protestant king, Henri de Navarre, in **Patrice Chereau's** *La Reine Margot* [*Queen Margot*] (94), he is equally at home in such contemporary dramas as **André Téchiné's** *Ma Saison Préférée* [*My Favourite Season*] (93) and **Claude Sautet's** *Un Coeur En Hiver* [*A Heart In Winter*] (93). One can always infer more from Auteuil's sensitive, perpetually tormented face than his skilful use of screen dialogue would suggest, putting him in friendly contention with such great French cinema actors of the past as **Louis Jouvet** and **Jean Gabin**.

OTHER KEY FILMS: *L'Amour En Douce* (85); *Romuald Et Juliette* (89); *Lacenaire* (90); *The Separation* (94); *Les Voleurs* (96); *Lucie Aubrac* (97); *Le Bossu* (97); *La Fille Sur Le Pont* (99); *Mauvais Passe* (99); *La Veuve De Saint-Pierre* (00); *Sade* (00); *L'Adversaire* (01)

Auteur Theory

A concept, first put forward in 1954 by **François Truffaut** in **Cahiers du Cinéma** magazine, equating film with high art, insofar as each film might be considered as the exclusive and identifiable work of the director, rather than as a more conventional collaboration between many.

Authenticator

The person who ensures that fatal anachronisms do not mistakenly creep into movies — the wristwatch worn by one of the slaves in **Stanley Kubrick's** *Spartacus* (52) springs inexorably to mind, as does the eminently pickable lock on the *inside* of the Sarah Connor/**Linda Hamilton** character's isolation cell in **James Cameron's** *Terminator 2: Judgment Day* (91).

Automatic Dialogue Replacement

The addition of dialogue after actual filming is completed, comprising either dubbed foreign dialogue, the replacement of faulty or badly recorded dialogue, or the insertion of additional dialogue when the characters concerned are either off-camera, or their backs are turned. See also **Looping**

Autry, Gene

Singing cowboy star who, with his horse, Champion, almost single-handedly kept **Republic Studios** from going under during the late 1930s and early 1940s, and who became massively wealthy as a result. Writer of more than 200 songs, Autry's films were long on action and short on romance, something that obviously appealed to the youthful pre-war audiences that were his staple.

KEY FILMS: *Tumblin' Tumbleweeds* (35); *Melody Ranch* (40); *Heart Of The Rio Grande* (42); *Rim Of The Canyon* (49)

Avant-garde

Used from the early part of this century as a catch-all phrase for non-mainstream, independent and experimental work that is ahead of its time; it literally means 'in the vanguard'.

Avery, Tex

A far greater cult figure in France than he is in the USA, Avery was the supreme fantasist of cartoon animation, with many of his 1930s and 1940s shorts reaching almost surreal levels of macabre and ironical humour. A classic example is his placard-carrying '*Eat At Joe's*' bear — it is only belatedly that we realise that the bear *is* Joe, and that he lures hungry victims into a fake diner to provide for his own meals. Falsely described as a screwball stylist, Avery actually understood the attraction and cathartic effect of horror just as well as Bruno Bettelheim or the brothers Grimm, and his vital, sexy cartoons stand up, to this day, as well as ever.

OTHER KEY FILMS: *Uncle Tom's Bungalow* (37); *The Blitz Wolf* (42); *Red Hot Riding Hood* (43); *The Shooting Of Dan Magoo* (45); *Uncle Tom's Cabana* (47); *Señor Droopy* (49) ...let's face it, watch anything by Avery you can.

Avid

A modern, non-linear computer editing system, named after the company that invented it, Avid Technology, Inc.

Aykroyd, Dan

Famous for appearing in the cult John Landis movie *The Blues Brothers* (80), Aykroyd has nevertheless failed to attain true star status — he's unlikely to be complaining, however, since making a mint out of co-writing and co-starring in the mega Ivan Reitman hit *Ghostbusters*, in 1984. Since then he's given a number of amusing performances, most notably in Tom Mankiewicz's otherwise run-of-the-mill *Dragnet* (87), but he has failed to find the public's pulse to any real extent in any of his ensuing comedy vehicles.

OTHER KEY FILMS: *Trading Places* (83); *Into The Night* (84); *Driving Miss Daisy* (89); *Sneakers* (92); *Grosse Pointe Blank* (97); *Diamonds* (99); *Stardom* (00); *The Curse Of The Jade Scorpion* (01); *Hitting The Wall* (01); *Pearl Harbor* (01)

Ayres, Lew

Ayres's finest moment came as young German army recruit Paul Baumer, killed while reaching for a butterfly, in Lewis Milestone's great anti-war film *All Quiet On The Western Front* (30), after which he spent long, and no doubt profitable years, dangling his stethoscope as Dr Kildare. A gentle, kindly man, he took both of those parts with him to the Second World War, in which, as a conscientious objector, he agreed only to serve as a medical orderly (albeit under fire). When he was eventually allowed back into the Hollywood fold, he made one or two effective *film noirs,* with **John Sturges's** downbeat *The Capture* (50) a real standout.

OTHER KEY FILMS: *Night World* (32); *The Last Train From Madrid* (37); *The Unfaithful* (47); *Johnny Belinda* (48); *Donovan's Brain* (53); *Advise And Consent* (62)

Azéma, Sabine

Along with **Fanny Ardant**, Azéma is a favourite actress of director **Alain Resnais** — he used her in his Alan Ayckbourn-inspired curiosity *Smoking/No Smoking* (93) — and she is a fine stage performer as well. She invariably gives committed performances, and the highlights of her screen career include **Bertrand Tavernier's** *Un Dimanche À La Campagne* [*A Sunday In The Country*] (84), Resnais's *Mélo* (86), and the provision of consummate and touching support for **Philippe Noiret** in Tavernier's majestic *La Vie Et Rien D'Autre* (89).

OTHER KEY FILMS: *La Dentellière* [*The Lacemaker*] (77); *Cinq Jours En Juin* (89); *Trois Années* (90); *On Connaît La Chanson* (97); *Le Schpountz* (99); *La Bûche* (99); *Tanguy, 28 Ans, Habite Encore Chez Ses Parents* (01); *La Chambre Des Officiers* (01)

Aznavour, Charles

One of the great French torch singers of the 1950s and 1960s (although he was, in fact, of Armenian extraction), Aznavour was also a surprisingly good actor, a fact first recognised by **François Truffaut** in *Tirez Sur Le Pianiste* [*Shoot The Piano Player*] (60), in which Aznavour plays Charlie Kohler/Edouard Saroyan, the unwitting and elusive piano-playing brother of a minor crook who subsequently re-enters his life and inveigles him into mayhem. He carried Claude Bernard-Aubert's very funny *Le Facteur S'En Va-T-En Guerre* [*The Postman Goes To War*] (66) on his own, and he was about the best thing in Claude Lelouch's otherwise rather turgid *Edith Et Marcel* (83), which told of the brief love affair between *chanteuse* Edith Piaf and boxer Marcel Cerdan. His most celebrated international hit, which he sang in magnificently broken English, was 'She', an American cover version of which appeared on the soundtrack of Garry Marshall's *Pretty Woman* (90), sung by another artist (how dumb can you get?). Try to catch Aznavour's original French version if you can.

OTHER KEY FILMS: *Le Testament D'Orphée* (60); *Taxi For Tobruk* (61); *The Adventurers* (73); *The Blockhouse* (73); *The Tin Drum* (79); *Viva La Vie* (84); *Les Années Campagne* (91); *Le Comédien* (97)

B-movies

Low-budget feature films designed for screening as part of a double-bill alongside a big-budget main feature.

KEY LINE:

'All characters in B-movies are too smart.' [Ex-**Paramount** producer, Joe Sistrom]

Babenco, Hector

Argentinian-born Babenco is the prime example of a film director lauded in his own country for the controversial yet committed nature of his early work, who then tries, and fails, to achieve the same trick in the United States under the triple burden of stars, money and his own political expectations. *Pixote* (81), with its uncomfortable use of real street children whom the audience voyeuristically know stand little chance of eventual survival after the filmmakers no longer need them, finds itself in marked counterpoint to the smooth, equally committed, yet undeniably theatrical *Kiss Of The Spider Woman* (85) and *Ironweed* (87), in both of which the audience can be perfectly sure that the stars will return to their lives of luxury and plenty as soon as their low-life make-up is taken off. A paradox? Of course. That is the nature of cinema.

OTHER KEY FILMS: *King Of The Night* (75); *At Play In The Fields Of The Lord* (91); *Foolish Heart* (98)

Baby Spot

A miniature spotlight mainly used to illuminate a star's face in extreme close-ups.

Baby Tripod

A squat, low-level camera tripod for acute, almost ground-level camera angles.

Bacall, Lauren

Her first film was **Howard Hawks's** *To Have And Have Not* (44), she was nineteen, and the wiggle she gave future real-life husband **Humphrey Bogart** in the last scene of the film is one of the sexiest moments in all cinema – full of invitation and promise and devil-may-care youth. She followed this up with a sizzling performance as Vivien Sternwood in Hawks's *The Big Sleep* (47) and then, apart from a fine, more mature appearance in **John Huston's** *Key Largo* (48), she virtually disappeared from the scene as a major Hollywood player, although she was to appear successfully on the stage and in a further mixed bag of twenty-five movies – some reasonably memorable, as in **Jean Negulesco's** *How To Marry A Millionaire* (53), and others decidedly less so. She did, on the other hand, become something of an icon as the former Mrs Bogart, and this part (despite many protestations) she has always played very well indeed.

OTHER KEY FILMS: *Dark Passage* (47); *Young Man With A Horn* (50); *Blood Alley* (55); *Written On The Wind* (57); *North West Frontier* (59); *Harper* (66); *Murder On The Orient Express* (74); *The Shootist* (76); *Mr North* (88); *Misery* (90); *The Mirror Has Two Faces* (96); *Day And Night* (97); *The Venice Project* (99); *Presence Of Mind* (99)

KEY LINES:
'Maybe just whistle. You know how to whistle, don't you, Steve? You just put your lips together and blow.' [*To Have And Have Not*]

'I know. I know. You don't give a hoot what I do. But when I do it you get sore.' [*To Have And Have Not*]

Bacharach, Burt

One of the greatest of the 1960s generation of composer/songwriters, Bacharach's name is on literally dozens of film scores, sometimes for a single song, as in **John Ford's** *The Man Who Shot Liberty Valance* (62), and sometimes for the whole score, as in his **Oscar**-winning efforts for George Roy Hill's *Butch Cassidy And The Sundance Kid* (69), in which he won an additional Oscar for the title song alone, 'Raindrops Keep Falling On My Head'. Scorning simple melodies, Bacharach's hallmark has always been the complexity of his rhythms, which, while making his songs seem eminently hummable when sung by professionals, nevertheless presents significant difficulties to your average shower singer.
OTHER KEY FILMS: Clive Donner's *What's New Pussycat?* (65); **Lewis Gilbert's** *Alfie* (66); Charles Jarrott's *Lost Horizon* (73); Steve Gordon's *Arthur* (81); Bud Yorkin's *Love Hurts* (91); **The Coen Brothers'** *Fargo* (96); P J Hogan's *My Best Friend's Wedding* (97); Andrew Bergman's *Isn't She Great* (00)

Background

Everything that goes on behind the main action, and, in consequence, possibly the single most important contributor to a film's atmosphere. In **Josef von Sternberg's** *Shanghai Express* (32), for instance, we find ourselves as fascinated by the exotically moving and heaving throng behind **Marlene Dietrich** and Clive Brook when they indulge in their final, heady kiss at Shanghai Station, as we are by the stars themselves.

Background Noise

This is the added-value noise to be heard behind the **dialogue**, and which, as with the visual **background**, adds immeasurably to the atmosphere of a scene. Certain filmmakers, such as **Orson Welles** and **Josef von Sternberg**, made a particular virtue of dense, multi-layered background tracks and it is arguable that, since the virtual demise of the silent film, background noise is the single most important addition to the complex art of filmmaking. Paradoxically, the sudden lack of background noise (see **Jean Renoir's** *La Grande*

Illusion (37) in **Heartstopping Moments**) can be equally effective, creating a sudden vacuum which may then be filled with a different, unexpected emotional content.

Backing

Used extensively in **Alfred Hitchcock's** *Rear Window* (54), 'backing' is topography painted on a screen and used to mimic a geographical location that exists beyond the confines of the interior of a set – a moonlit night outside a window, a block of flats across the way, the interior of a hall, etc.

Back Lighting

Marlene Dietrich was regularly backlit in the films she made with her mentor and erstwhile lover, **Josef von Sternberg**. His preferred lighting arrangement for the star consisted of a number of spotlights, hidden directly behind her, which threw carefully constructed shadows over her face while at the same time creating an other-worldly aura around her hair. The best known backlit shot of her occurs in von Sternberg's *Shanghai Express* (32) (see cover illustration), when Dietrich stands alone in a railway carriage silently smoking a cigarette, looking up, for all the world like Dante Gabriel Rossetti's Beata Beatrix, while the camera and the audience make equally silent love to her image.

Back Lot

An area inside the confines of a studio lot but outside the studio buildings which is used for mimicking expensive exterior locations without the necessity of moving and relocating the entire cast and crew.

Back Projection

Film projected onto a screen behind the actors to suggest a non-studio location, and to enable distant objects to appear in focus.

Back-up Schedule

An alternative shooting schedule that can be used in the event of foul weather or administrative mix-ups, thus ensuring that the day is not a total loss.

Bacon, Kevin

A talented character actor who seems most at ease as part of a group rather than carrying a film on his own, Bacon had a big hit with Herbert Ross's dance drama *Footloose* (84), but has since tended to play the role of a friend, or subsidiary to the hero, in such movies as John Hughes's *Planes, Trains & Automobiles* (87) and Rob Reiner's *A Few Good*

Men (92). Bacon made an excellent directing debut with *Losing Chase* (96), which starred Helen Mirren and Bacon's wife, Kyra Sedgwick.

OTHER KEY FILMS: *Starting Over* (79); *Diner* (82); *Flatliners* (90); *JFK* (91); *The River Wild* (94); *Apollo 13* (95); *Sleepers* (96); *The Hollow Man* (00); *Novocaine* (01)

Bacon, Lloyd

Bacon was a typical Hollywood studio director who turned out dozens of mostly nondescript feature films, with, however, one or two real gems hidden away amongst them. He cut his teeth directing **Mack Sennett** shorts, and later worked extensively for **Warners**, where he appeared to shine most directing musicals, of which the brilliant *42nd Street* (33), great-uncle of all backstage musicals, has best stood the test of time.

OTHER KEY FILMS: *The Singing Fool* (28); *Footlight Parade* (33); *Wonder Bar* (34); *Gold Diggers Of 1937* (36); *Marked Woman* (37); *The Oklahoma Kid* (39); *Brother Orchid* (40); *Action In The North Atlantic* (43)

Baffle

Anything that reflects or muffles either sound or light.

BAFTA

Britain's answer to the US-run **Academy Of Motion Picture Arts And Sciences** (which hands out the **Oscars** at its annual awards ceremony), the British Academy Of Film And Television Arts feels itself, quite rightly, to be something of a country cousin to its more prestigious and lucrative transatlantic rival. Its annual BAFTA awards, however, are treasured by their recipients despite, or perhaps because of, the sometimes rather perverse (dare one say arbitrary?) nature of their assignments. Stephen Fry's brilliantly ironical speech at the 2001 BAFTAs, from its glorious first line beginning 'Ladies, Gentlemen, and Americans', may be taken as a welcome model for the enlightened and highly literate mock-amateurishness which differentiates the British from their more focused transoceanic cousins.

Baker, Joe Don

Good supporting actor, best known for dependable, somewhat violent, good buddy roles, Baker was the only man ex-con **Robert Duvall** could count on in John Flynn's excellent gangster drama *The Outfit* (74). The somewhat portly, usually reliable, and always swift-thinking Joe Don

could also play a mean CIA man, and an even meaner villain, as his Brad Whitaker, in John Glen's **James Bond** outing, *The Living Daylights* (87), so consummately proves.

OTHER KEY FILMS: *Cool Hand Luke* (67); *Junior Bonner* (72); *Charley Varrick* (73); *The Natural* (84); *Fletch* (85); *Cape Fear* (91); *Goldeneye* (96); *Tomorrow Never Dies* (97); *Vegas, City Of Dreams* (01)

Baker, Rick

One of the great special effects make-up men, Baker is particularly good at recreating apes, which he has done for John Guillermin in **King Kong** (76) (acting as the great Kong himself), for Hugh Hudson in *Greystoke* (84) and for **Michael Apted** in *Gorillas In The Mist* (88), amongst others. His miraculous transformation of **Eddie Murphy** into a grossly overweight, lovelorn professor in Tom Shadyac's *The Nutty Professor* (96) and Peter Segal's *Nutty Professor II: The Klumps* (00) is particularly inspired.

OTHER KEY FILMS: **William Friedkin's** *The Exorcist* (73); **George Lucas's** *Star Wars* (77); **Brian De Palma's** *The Fury* (78); John Landis's *An American Werewolf In London* (81); **David Cronenberg's** *Videodrome* (83); Joel Schumacher's *Batman Forever* (95); Barry Sonnenfeld's *Men In Black* (97); **Ron Howard's** *How the Grinch Stole Christmas* (00); **Tim Burton's** *Planet Of The Apes* (01)

Baker, Stanley

Tough-guy actor who cut his teeth on the new breed of 'realist' British crime films of the 1950s, Baker's brooding, apparently innate talent was quickly recognised by **Joseph Losey**, who used him to good effect in *The Concrete Jungle* (60), the frustratingly perverse *Eva* (61), and later in the far more successful (though still perverse) *Accident* (67). He could play an embittered, angry man better than anyone else in cinema, but he also shone in more complex roles, such as that of Lt Chard in Cy Endfield's *Zulu* (63). He later branched out into film production, and latterly, before his early death at the age of forty-nine, in 1976, he seemed to be losing just a little of his earlier edge.

OTHER KEY FILMS: *Eye Witness* (50); *The Cruel Sea* (53); *Hell Drivers* (57); *Campbell's Kingdom* (58); *Violent Playground* (58); *Hard Drivers* (60); *Hell Is A City* (60); *Robbery* (67); *The Games* (70); *The Last Grenade* (70)

Balance

Sergei Eisenstein was obsessed, almost to the point of mania, by the pictorial balance in each shot that appeared in his films, and he became renowned for his use of the five, six or seven figure framework in which actors and actresses were filmed in long shot or from the waist up, with some in the foreground, others in the background, to produce an effect of striking visual felicity and harmonious design. Eisenstein's most notable move in this direction came with the uncompleted *Que Viva Mexico!* (32), in which filming was aborted just before the final part was due to be shot, thanks largely to his sponsor, novelist Upton Sinclair, getting cold feet over time and expense.

Balancing Stripe

A thin strip of material taped to the back of the magnetic strip on a reel of film stock to counterbalance its general thickness and to ensure a smooth and unjerky projection.

Balcon, Michael

Founder of Gainsborough Films, and later chief of production at **Ealing Studios**, Balcon was one of the mainstays of pre- and post-war British cinema, responsible for successes such as **Alfred Hitchcock's** *The Thirty-Nine Steps* (35), **Sam Wood's** *Goodbye Mr Chips* (39), and the multi-directed *Dead Of Night* (45), possibly the single best ghost film of all time. After the war he produced many of the **Ealing comedies**, including **Robert Hamer's** *Kind Hearts And Coronets* (49) and **Alexander Mackendrick's** *Whisky Galore* (49) and *The Man In The White Suit* (51).

OTHER KEY FILMS: **Robert Flaherty's** *Man Of Aran* (34); **Alfred Hitchcock's** *The Man Who Knew Too Much* (34), *Sabotage* (36) and *The Secret Agent* (36); **Alberto Cavalcanti's** *Nicholas Nickleby* (47); Henry Cornelius's *Passport To Pimlico* (49); **Basil Dearden's** *The Blue Lamp* (50); Charles Crichton's *The Lavender Hill Mob* (51); Charles Frend's *The Cruel Sea* (53); **Alexander Mackendrick's** *The Ladykillers* (55)

Baldwin, Alec

Elegant leading man and gifted screen actor who considers his stage work to be every bit as important as his film parts, Baldwin appeared to hit the big time as Jack Ryan in John McTiernan's *The Hunt For Red October* (90), but blew his chance for a follow up in Phillip Noyce's *Clear And Present Danger* (94) after a contract dispute, and has since seemed satisfied to aim at critical rather than commercial success. He was outstanding in James Foley's *Glengarry Glen Ross* (92), adequate in Roger Donaldson's *The Getaway* (94), and realistically edgy in Lee Tamahori's aptly named *The Edge* (97).

OTHER KEY FILMS: *Beetlejuice* (88); *Working Girl* (88); *Malice* (93); *The Juror* (96); *Mercury Rising* (98); *The Confession* (99); *Thomas And The Magic Railroad* (00); *Pearl Harbor* (01)

Ball, Lucille

You either loved her or you hated her (and America loved her) in the 'I Love Lucy' TV series, but no one can deny that Ball had supreme comic timing, a talent to which her TV filmography amply testifies. One of the most successful producers in Hollywood history with her Desilu production company, Ball started off on the screen as a **Ginger Rogers** clone but soon graduated to her very own brand of slapstick humour in **Lloyd Bacon's** *The Fuller Brush Girl* (50), followed by a series of **Bob Hope** vehicles, of which the best was undoubtedly George Marshall's *Fancy Pants* (50). Jamestown, in New York State, where she was born, has become something of a shrine to her memory, and Lucy-Desi Days are held there every year to celebrate her life and achievements.

OTHER KEY FILMS: *Roman Scandals* (33); *Top Hat* (35); *The Big Street* (42); *Du Barry Was A Lady* (43); *Ziegfeld Follies* (46); *Forever Darling* (56)

Ballard, Lucien

Ballard was one of the greatest of the black-and-white cinematographers, something recognised by that doyen of the **monochrome**, **Josef von Sternberg**, who used him on *Morocco* (30), *The Devil Is A Woman* (35) and *Crime And Punishment* (35). Ballard's greatest achievement came with **Stanley Kubrick's** *The Killing* (56), in which he managed to suggest a seemingly washed-out but actually deeply contrasted suburban and rural America, an effect that was later imitated but never bettered by such leading directorial lights as **Martin Ritt, Peter Bogdanovich,** and **Terrence Malick.** Ballard's final films were mostly **Westerns**, and include **Sam Peckinpah's** elegiac *Ride The High Country* (62), the same director's seminal *The Wild Bunch* (69) and nostalgic *Junior Bonner* (72), not to mention **Henry Hathaway's** sensationally good (and sensationally well-shot) **John Wayne** oater, *True Grit* (69). Part Cherokee, Ballard was once married to **Merle Oberon**.

OTHER KEY FILMS: John Brahm's *The Lodger* (44); **Jacques Tourneur's** *Berlin Express* (48); Henry Hathaway's *Nevada Smith* (66); **John Sturges's** *Hour Of The Gun* (67); Tom Gries's *Will Penny* (68); Sam Peckinpah's *The Ballad Of Cable Hogue* (70)

23

Ballhaus, Michael

One of the most innovative of recent **cinematographers**, Ballhaus made his reputation working for **Rainer Werner Fassbinder** on films as disparate as *Chinese Roulette* (76) and *The Marriage Of Maria Braun* (78). In recent years his edgy, constantly moving style has won over the likes of **Martin Scorsese** with *GoodFellas* (90) and *The Age Of Innocence* (93), and **Robert Redford**, with *Quiz Show* (94), to his Hollywood camp.

OTHER KEY FILMS: Rainer Werner Fassbinder's *The Bitter Tears Of Petra Von Kant* (72) and *The Stationmaster's Wife* (77); **Martin Scorsese's** *The Color Of Money* (86) and *The Last Temptation Of Christ* (88); Steve Kloves's *The Fabulous Baker Boys* (89); **Wolfgang Petersen's** *Outbreak* (95); **Barry Levinson's** *Sleepers* (96); **Mike Nichols's** *Primary Colors* (98); Barry Sonnenfeld's *Wild Wild West* (99); Robert Redford's *The Legend Of Bagger Vance* (00); Martin Scorsese's *Gangs Of New York* (01)

Balsam, Martin

Fine character actor best known for his heady descent down the stairs at the point of **Anthony Perkins's** knife (sorry, I've given the secret away) in **Alfred Hitchcock's** *Psycho* (60), Balsam's laconic face and his ability to look hunted, marginally devious and yet still somehow decent stood him in good stead in more than sixty very often distinguished films – he was one of Hollywood's greatest second rankers.

OTHER KEY FILMS: *On The Waterfront* (64); *12 Angry Men* (57); *Breakfast At Tiffany's* (61); *Seven Days In May* (64); *Hombre* (67); *Little Big Man* (70); *The Stone Killer* (73); *Cape Fear* (91); *Soldato Ignoto* (95); *Legend Of The Spirit Dog* (97)

Bancroft, Anne

Bancroft is the one and only Mrs Robinson (despite **Kathleen Turner's** and Jerry Hall's recent performances on stage in London's West End) and she brings the same acute intelligence and commitment to all her parts. Before her iconic status as Mrs R in **Mike Nichols's** *The Graduate* (67), Bancroft triumphed in **Arthur Penn's** *The Miracle Worker* (62) and in Jack Clayton's *The Pumpkin Eater* (64) and looked set for a major movie career, but her inclinations were otherwise, and she has since contented herself with the occasional juicy role in such quality vehicles as David Jones's *84 Charing Cross Road* (87). She is married to comedian and film director **Mel Brooks**.

OTHER KEY FILMS: *The Raid* (54); *Seven Women* (66); *Young Winston* (72); *The Elephant Man* (80); *To Be Or Not To Be* (83); *Mr Jones* (93); *How To Make An American Quilt* (95); *G. I. Jane* (97); *Great Expectations* (98); *Up At The Villa* (00); *Keeping The Faith* (00); *Heartbreakers* (01)

Banderas, Antonio

Following his initial success in a number of **Pedro Almodóvar's** films, most notably *Law Of Desire* [*La Ley Del Deseo*] (87) and *Women On The Verge Of A Nervous Breakdown* (88), Hollywood picked up this good-looking and athletic Spaniard and imaginatively cast him as a Cuban in Arne Glimcher's *The Mambo Kings* (92). **Alan Parker's** *Evita* (96) followed (this time Banderas was Argentinian), and Martin Campbell's rather good *The Mask Of Zorro* (98), but it is unlikely, on present showing, that Banderas will ever have the range of his illustrious predecessor in the Zorro part, **Tyrone Power**. Note for Film Buffs: It was Banderas who introduced Catherine Zeta-Jones to **Michael Douglas**. Isn't that interesting?

OTHER KEY FILMS: *Labyrinth Of Passion* (82); *Matador* (86); *Tie Me Up! Tie Me Down!* (90); *Philadelphia* (93); *Interview With A Vampire* (94); *Assassins* (95); *The 13th Warrior* (99); *Play It To The Bone* (99); *The Body* (01); *Spy Kids* (01); *Original Sin* (01)

Bank

As in a 'bank of lights', meaning a collection of incandescent lamps set into a simple reflector and used for general illumination.

Bankhead, Tallulah

A renowned high liver, gaiety girl and wit (and the seductress of numerous young Etonians) Bankhead was always a stage actress at heart and rarely turned her hand, or anything else for that matter, to film. However when she did she was great fun (if rather creakingly theatrical), and her best-known role was as millionairess Connie Porter cast adrift in **Alfred Hitchcock's** *Lifeboat* (44) with Walter Slezak, **William Bendix** and her mink coat for company. She'd have made a great dinner companion, though.

OTHER KEY FILMS: *The Trap* (19); *Tarnished Lady* (31); *Devil And The Deep* (32); *Main Street To Broadway* (53)

KEY LINES:

'Cocaine habit-forming? Of course not. I should know. I've been using it for years.' [Bankhead on substance abuse]

'I'm as pure as the driven slush.' [Bankhead on virtue]

Banky, Vilma

Banky deserves a place in this book if only for her name, which many people instantly recognise without ever having seen any of her films. She was actually one of the top three or four stars of her day, acting silently alongside the young **Ronald Colman** and the even younger **Gary Cooper**, and simply giving up her career when sound came along. Her most famous part was in George Fitzmaurice's *The Son Of The Sheik* (26), in which she partnered **Rudolph Valentino** in what was arguably his best film.

OTHER KEY FILMS: *The Lady From Paris* (24); *The Dark Angel* (26); *The Winning Of Barbara Worth* (26); *The Night Of Love* (27); *Two Lovers* (28); *This Is Heaven* (29)

Bannen, Ian

An intense character actor who specialised in men under pressure, Bannen acted in dozens of high-quality British films and one or two US ones, although he never really looked comfortable on the far side of the Atlantic. He came close to winning an **Oscar** for his supporting role of Crow, in **Robert Aldrich's** *The Flight Of The Phoenix* (65), but his best performance was as the putative child molester, Kenneth Baxter, tormented by **Sean Connery's** Detective Sergeant Johnson, in **Sidney Lumet's** *The Offence* (73). He died tragically, in a car accident near Loch Ness in Scotland, in November 1999.

OTHER KEY FILMS: *A Tale Of Two Cities* (58); *The Hill* (65); *Jane Eyre* (71); *The Mackintosh Man* (73); *Eye Of The Needle* (81); *Ghandi* (82); *Gorky Park* (83); *Defence Of The Realm* (86); *Hope And Glory* (87); *The Cherry Orchard* (91); *Damage* (92); *Braveheart* (95); *Waking Ned* (98); *To Walk With Lions* (98); *Best* (00)

Bara, Theda

Her name is an anagram of 'Arab Death', and she was **Fox's** answer to the anodyne **Mary Pickford**. Famous overnight as the '**vamp**' following her appearance in *A Fool There Was* (15) (which was based on Rudyard Kipling's poem 'The Vampire'), Bara made a film a month for Fox in the following three years, incarnating such vampish heroines as Cleopatra, Camille, Du Barry and Cigarette – but the public slowly tired of her, and she ended up parodying her own image during the 1920s in a vain attempt to keep their interest in her alive.

OTHER KEY FILMS: *Carmen* (16); *Serpent Of The Nile* (16); *The She-Devil* (18)
KEY LINE:
'Kiss me, my fool.' [*A Fool There Was*]

Barbera, Joseph

With his partner William Hanna, and their producer Fred Quimby, Barbera was the mastermind behind the **Tom & Jerry** cartoons for **MGM**. The Hanna–Barbera team then went freelance to produce a seemingly endless series of top-rated cartoons, largely for American daytime TV. 'Top Cat' and 'The Flintstones' were theirs, as well as 'Yogi Bear', 'Huckleberry Hound' and 'Quick Draw McGraw'.

OTHER KEY FILMS: *Yankee Doodle Mouse* (43); *The Cat Concerto* (46); *The Two Mouseketeers* (51); *Life With Loopy* (60); *Just A Wolf At Heart* (62)

Bardem, Juan Antonio

One of Spain's most prestigious filmmakers, Bardem became the visual historian and invisible conscience of all those persecuted during the Franco era through the medium of such films as *Muerte De Un Ciclista* (55) and *Calle Mayor* (56). Following the success of his early films with international critics, Bardem became the focus of sustained governmental interference, and it is only since the death of Franco that he has been able to continue systematically mapping the tormented post-war history of the Spanish people.

OTHER KEY FILMS: *Welcome Mr Marshall* (52); *Felices Pascuas* (54); *La Venganza* (58); *El Ultimo Dia De La Guerra* (69); *Behind The Shutters* (73); *El Poder Del Deseo* (76); *Lorca, La Muerte De Un Poeta* (87); *Resultado Final* (98)

Bardot, Brigitte

Known as 'the sex kitten' and also as the 'girl with the best bottom in the business' – which she unabashedly showed in numerous steamy films, most notably in front of her defence lawyer, **Jean Gabin**, in **Claude Autant-Lara's** *En Cas De Malheur* [*Love Is My Profession*] (57) – Bardot encapsulated the modern, sexually uninhibited woman well before such a state was widespread. Married to, amongst others, film director **Roger Vadim** and multi-millionaire playboy Gunther Sachs, Bardot retired from the screen (with no apparent regrets) at the early age of forty, to devote the remainder of her life to animal welfare.

OTHER KEY FILMS: *Doctor At Sea* (55); *Et Dieu Créa La Femme* [*And Woman Was Created*] (56);

25

Une Parisienne (57); *Babette S'En Va-T-En Guerre* (59); *La Vérité* [*The Truth*] (60); *Le Mépris* [*Contempt*] (63); *Viva Maria* (65); *Masculin-Féminin* (66); *Les Femmes* (69); *Don Juan 1973* (73)

KEY LINE:
'Garbo's visage had a kind of emptiness into which anything could be projected – nothing can be read into Bardot's face.' [Simone de Beauvoir on Bardot]

Barker, Lex

He was a good Tarzan in some very bad films, and later the unforgettable Winnetou and Old Shatterhand in a series of German **Westerns** (based on the best-selling books of Karl May) that were hardly ever seen outside Europe. Barker's most competent straight performance came in **Federico Fellini's** *La Dolce Vita* (60), but he was perhaps best known for his five (mostly rather brief) marriages to a variety of actresses, including **Lana Turner**, of whom another famous husband, bandleader Artie Shaw, once said, 'Lana was an airhead – she was a beautiful ornament.' (I don't know what this has to do with anything, but there it is.)
OTHER KEY FILMS: *Crossfire* (47); *Mr Blandings Builds His Dream House* (48); *Tarzan's Peril* (51); *The Deerslayer* (57); *Winnetou* (63, 64 & 65); *Old Shatterhand* (64)

Barkin, Ellen

An excellent actress with an offbeat, sexy face (her beauty somewhat along the lines of a **Frances McDormand**), Barkin had a real hit with Jim McBride's excellent *The Big Easy* (86), followed by Harold Becker's equally excellent *Sea Of Love* (89). Then what? A good but small part in Mike Newell's *Into The West* (93) and some fun with Walter Hill's *Wild Bill* (95), but nothing in there to match her obvious talent and screen presence.
OTHER KEY FILMS: *Diner* (82); *Tender Mercies* (82); *Down By Law* (86); *Siesta* (87); *This Boy's Life* (93); *The Fan* (96); *Fear And Loathing In Las Vegas* (98); *Drop Dead Gorgeous* (99); *Money* (00); *Crime And Punishment In Suburbia* (00); *Someone Like You* (01)

Barn Doors

The adjustable flaps around the opening of a spotlight to allow for directional beaming.

Barnes, George

Barnes plied his camera for virtually all the great names of the Hollywood golden age, and was perhaps the most consummately professional and consistent cinematographer of his day. He worked on George Fitzmaurice's *The Son Of The Sheik* (26) and *Raffles* (30), and he was co-photographer on **Henry King's** gorgeously **Technicolor**-ed *Jesse James* (39); but his best work came later for **Alfred Hitchcock** on *Rebecca* (40) and *Spellbound* (45), and Robert Stevenson's *Jane Eyre* (43), notable for its wildly atmospheric lighting.
OTHER KEY FILMS: Ray Enright's *Dames* (34); **Lloyd Bacon's** *Marked Woman* (37); Mitchell

Brigitte Bardot in pouting 'sex kitten' mode

Leisen's *Frenchman's Creek* (44); Richard Wallace's *Sinbad The Sailor* (47); Abraham Polonsky's *Force Of Evil* (48)

Barney

A cover designed to protect the camera from temperature upheavals and extraneous sound.

Barrault, Jean-Louis

Politically committed theatrical impresario inevitably paired in the French public's eye with his wife, **Madeleine Renaud**, Barrault will be remembered by devoted filmgoers for his majestic performance as the mime, Baptiste Debureau, in **Marcel Carné's** masterpiece *Les Enfants Du Paradis* (45). He made a belated appearance in Ettore Scola's *La Nuit De Varennes* (82), but Barrault's heart was always in the theatre, and particularly with the Comédie Française and the Théâtre de France, from whose ranks he was unceremoniously jettisoned after supporting the students during the May 1968 riots.

OTHER KEY FILMS: *Les Beaux Jours* (35); *Drôle De Drame* (37); *Orage* (38); *D'Homme À Hommes* (48); *La Ronde* (50); *Le Dialogue Des Carmélites* (60)

Barry, John

Near-ubiquitous during the 1960s, Barry scored just about every big British movie of the decade, and a quick glance at his extended filmography suggests that he must have had precious little time left over from work to taste the swinging side of 1960s London. His first major commission came with Bryan Forbes's *The L-Shaped Room* (62), but Barry really began to be noticed with his catchy theme and variations for Terence Young's *From Russia With Love* (63), which one has only to think of momentarily to instantly start humming the tune. The James Hill-directed *Born Free* (66) theme was his too, together with the beautifully scored Anthony Harvey film, *The Lion In Winter* (68). His most memorable scoring, however, involves a toss-up between **John Schlesinger's** *Midnight Cowboy* (69) and **Sydney Pollack's** *Out Of Africa* (85), with *Out of Africa* winning by a short head. Mind you, his score for **Lawrence Kasdan's** *Body Heat* (81) was also outstanding.

OTHER KEY FILMS: **Guy Hamilton's** *Goldfinger* (64); James Clavell's *The Last Valley* (70); **Nicolas Roeg's** *Walkabout* (71); Graeme Clifford's *Frances* (82); **Francis Ford Coppola's** *The Cotton Club* (84); Richard Marquand's *Jagged Edge* (85); **Kevin Costner's** *Dances With Wolves* (90); Adrian Lyne's

Indecent Proposal (93); Roland Joffé's *The Scarlet Letter* (95); Beeban Kidron's *Swept From The Sea* (97); Harold Becker's *Mercury Rising* (98); **Michael Apted's** *Enigma* (01)

Barrymores, The

Scions of a famous theatrical family, Ethel, John and Lionel Barrymore succeeded in films almost despite their nineteenth-century selves. Ethel never took films seriously, even when she received a best-supporting **Oscar** for Clifford Odets's *None But The Lonely Heart* (44), but her brother John, on the other hand, was a natural show-off to whom films offered untold dramatic opportunities, and whose career would have been even more astonishing but for his heavy drinking and womanising, which he parodied so beautifully in Edmund Goulding's *Grand Hotel* (32). Lionel out-hammed even his brother, particularly in **King Vidor's** *Duel In The Sun* (46), but he somehow contrived to restrain himself during the filming of **John Huston's** *Key Largo* (48) to turn in a dignified and powerful performance as the paraplegic James Temple. Together, all three notched up a mind-boggling number of film performances, somehow contriving to stifle virtually all critical faculties on the part of their ever-faithful public.

OTHER KEY FILMS: Ethel: *Rasputin And The Empress* (33); *The Spiral Staircase* (46); *The Paradine Case* (48); *Portrait Of Jenny* (49); *Deadline USA* (52); **John**: *Dr Jekyll And Mr Hyde* (20); *Moby Dick* (30); *Dinner At Eight* (33); *The Great Profile* (40); **Lionel**: *The Temptress* (27); *David Copperfield* (35); *Camille* (37); *Captains Courageous* (37); *It's A Wonderful Life* (46)

KEY LINE:
'For an actress to be a success, she must have the face of a Venus, the brains of a Minerva, the grace of a Terpsichore, the memory of a Macaulay, the figure of Juno, and the hide of a rhinoceros.' [Ethel on acting]

Basher

A studio spotlight that can either be fixed or hand-held to highlight a given area or person.

Basinger, Kim

A curiously on/off actress who has made more than one comeback and more than one mistake, not least by refusing to appear in Jennifer Chambers Lynch's *Boxing Helena* (93), for which she was sued by the makers and forced to pay multimillion dollar damages. If looks alone could make a star, Basinger would be it, but

27

her acting ability has always been just a little doubtful, despite good critical reception for her recent role as a **Veronica Lake** look-alike in Curtis Hanson's excellent *LA Confidential* (97).
OTHER KEY FILMS: *Never Say Never Again* (83); *The Natural* (84); *Fool For Love* (85); *Blind Date* (87); *Batman* (89); *The Getaway* (94); *I Dreamed Of Africa* (00); *Bless The Child* (00)

Bass, Saul

Bass changed the way movie titles and credit sequences are designed, turning them from the often turgid succession of filmed names an audience is eager to get through, to something which reflects the movie they are about to watch, and acts as a sort of foreword, or *amuse-gueule*, preparing punters for whatever treat is in store. Notable examples of his work occur in **Billy Wilder's** *The Seven Year Itch* (55), **Alfred Hitchcock's** *Vertigo* (58), **Otto Preminger's** *Anatomy Of A Murder* (59) and **Martin Scorsese's** *GoodFellas* (90).
OTHER KEY FILMS: Otto Preminger's *The Man With The Golden Arm* (56); **Stanley Kubrick's** *Spartacus* (60); **John Frankenheimer's** *Grand Prix* (66)

Batch Number

A number attached to a can of film to prove that the emulsion used was created heterogeneously – the number is significant because different emulsions have different qualities and it wouldn't do to mix two different batches during the shooting of an important piece of film.

Bates, Alan

Important British stage actor who has appeared in a number of seminal films, including **John Schlesinger's** *A Kind Of Loving* (62) and **Ken Russell's** *Women In Love* (69), in which he indulged in the infamous naked wrestling scene with **Oliver Reed** – illiterate critics of Russell have often missed the point of this scene, however, for it is completely Lawrentian and totally in keeping with the tone of the book. Bates, for his part, has always chosen his roles with extreme care, and his filmography is an impressive one, with remarkable few clinkers. His best performances have come in Clive Donner's *Nothing But The Best* (64) and in Schlesinger's *Far From The Madding Crowd* (67), as the faithful but somewhat ill-starred Gabriel Oak.
OTHER KEY FILMS: *The Entertainer* (60); *Whistle Down The Wind* (61); *Zorba The Greek* (64); *Georgy*

Girl (66); *King Of Hearts* (66); *The Fixer* (68); *The Go-Between* (70); *A Day In The Death Of Joe Egg* (71); *The Shout* (78); *Quartet* (81); *Return Of The Soldier* (82); *Britannia Hospital* (82); *Secret Friends* (91); *Silent Tongue* (93); *The Grotesque* (95); *Varya* (99)

Bates, Kathy

A fine, understated actress, who finally found the international recognition she deserved in Rob Reiner's *Misery* (90), in which she famously smashed **James Caan's** ankles with a sledgehammer. Jon Avnet's *Fried Green Tomatoes* (91) followed, but her best role to date has undoubtedly been as the eponymous title character in Taylor Hackford's *Dolores Claiborne* (95), in which Bates showed just what subtlety and stillness she can bring to difficult and at times unsympathetic parts.
OTHER KEY FILMS: *Taking Off* (71); *Come Back To The Five And Dime, Jimmy Dean, Jimmy Dean* (82); *Dick Tracy* (90); *Shadows And Fog* (92); *Used People* (92); *North* (94); *Angus* (95); *Diabolique* (96); *Titanic* (97); *Primary Colors* (98); *Bruno* (00); *Unconditional Love* (01)

Bath

A receptacle used during film processing. Also the chemical solution used inside that receptacle.

Batteries

Batteries are needed to power both cameras and technical recording equipment at outdoor locations. There are three principal battery types – wet cell, dry cell and nickel-cadmium.

Bazooka

Slang term for the piece of equipment used to steady and secure spotlights on a catwalk.

BCU

Acronym for a Big Close Up of an actor or actress's face.

Béart, Emmanuelle

The gorgeous, St Tropez-born daughter of French pop star Guy Béart, Emmanuelle first came to general notice playing the part of the vengeful Manon in **Claude Berri's** *Manon Des Sources* (86), and then proved that she could act as well as look beautiful in Claude Sautet's *Un Coeur En Hiver* (93), in which she co-starred with her real-life lover **Daniel Auteuil**, who had the Herculean task of convincing the audience that his screen persona was frigidly capable of rejecting her.

*Emmanuelle Béart
as the mysterious
Claire, in Brian de
Palma's* Mission:
Impossible *(96)*

OTHER KEY FILMS: *L'Amour En Douce* (85); *Ruptures* (93); *Belle Epoque* (94); *L'Enfer* (94); *Mission: Impossible* (96); *Don Juan* (98); *Voleur Du Vie* (98); *Le Temps Retrouvé* (99); *Elephant Juice* (99); *La Bûche* (99); *Les Destinées Sentimentales* (00); *Voyance Et Manigance* (01)

Beatles, The

Hardly renowned for their film careers when considered in relation to their musical achievements, their performance as a group in Richard Lester's *A Hard Day's Night* (64) is nevertheless worthy of mention, if only on account of the film's energy and their iconic presence in it when seen against the miracle of the 1960s and the effect they had on popular culture during that decade. Of the quartet, drummer Ringo Starr has paradoxically enjoyed the most 'successful' acting career, but his performances are, for the most part, simply adequate, and have never indicated either the need or even the possibility of a radical mid-term vocational change on his part. George Harrison, on the other hand, through his production company Handmade Films, has been either the co- or the executive producer on a number of fine British films, including **Terry Gilliam's** *Time Bandits* (81), **Neil Jordan's** *Mona Lisa* (86) and **Bruce Robinson's** *Withnail & I* (87).
OTHER KEY FILMS: *Help!* (65); *Yellow Submarine* (68) [in animated form]; *Let It Be* (70)

Beatty, Warren

Beatty is good-looking, charismatic and politically impeccable (in recent Hollywood terms), but the jury must surely still be out on his acting ability. He has the typical mannerisms of a major star, but these get in the way of any real performance, although, no doubt, they please his many fans. He hasn't acted in that many films compared to, say, his exact contemporary **Jack Nicholson**, but of the films in which he has appeared, particular plaudits must go to **Elia Kazan's** *Splendor In The Grass* (61), **Alan J Pakula's** *The Parallax View* (74), and also to *Reds* (81), which Beatty himself directed.
OTHER KEY FILMS: *The Roman Spring Of Mrs Stone* (61); *Lilith* (64); *Bonnie And Clyde* (67); *McCabe And Mrs Miller* (71); *Shampoo* (75); *Heaven Can Wait* (78); *Dick Tracy* (90); *Bugsy* (91); *Bulworth* (98); *Town And Country* (01)

Beineix, Jean-Jacques

Beineix had a well-justified international smash hit with *Diva* (81), which he followed up with the turgid and mannered *La Lune Dans Le Caniveau* [*The Moon In The Gutter*] (83). *Betty Blue* (86) reset the score in his favour (for a while) but Beineix has never really followed up on all the hype that was associated with his name in the early 1980s, and his recent films have been radically disappointing, if the quality of his initial promise is taken into account.
OTHER KEY FILMS: *Roselyne Et Les Lions* (89); *IP 5: The Island Of Pachyderms* (92); *Otaku* (94); *Mortel Transfert* (00)

Belafonte, Harry

Belafonte has recently come back into his own again thanks to the role of hoodlum Seldom Seen, in **Robert Altman's** *Kansas City* (96), after many years spent concentrating on his concert career to the exclusion of films. Despite the fact that he will always be best known for his gorgeous singing of hits like 'Jamaica Farewell', he has turned in some outstanding screen performances, most notably in **Robert Wise's** *Odds Against Tomorrow* (59), as Johnny Ingram, the butt of fellow crook **Robert Ryan's** inveterate racism.
OTHER KEY FILMS: *Carmen Jones* (55); *Island In The Sun* (57); *The World The Flesh And The Devil* (59); *Buck And The Preacher* (72); *Ready To Wear* (94); *White Man's Burden* (95)

Belmondo, Jean-Paul

Quintessential French actor (son of the sculptor, Paul Belmondo) who has never managed to secure a true international audience, Belmondo came closest

29

with his Bogart-influenced young man on the run, Michel Poiccard, in **Jean-Luc Godard's** *À Bout De Souffle* [*Breathless*] (60). With his wide-boy, ex-boxer's face, and his eyes perpetually screwed up against a cloud of Gitanes smoke, Belmondo personified the free-spirited soul of the 1960s, moving successfully into action roles in the 1970s and 1980s, and then into straight drama in the 1990s, a move which culminated, unfortunately, in Claude Lelouch's disastrously pretentious *Les Misérables* (95). His best films came early, and include Philippe de Broca's *That Man From Rio* (64), Godard's excellent *Pierrot Le Fou* (65), and Jacques Deray's influential *Borsalino* (70). Of Belmondo's extremely successful action-man period, Henri Verneuil's *Night Caller* (75) stands out as almost perfect of its type.

OTHER KEY FILMS: *Les Tricheurs* (58); *Web Of Passion* (59); *Moderato Cantabile* (60); *Cartouche* (61); *Le Doulos* (63); *Le Voleur* (67); *Stavisky* (74); *L'Alpageur* (76); *L'As Des As* (82); *Le Marginal* (83); *Itinéraire D'Un Enfant Gâté* (88); *Désiré* (96); *Une Chance Sur Deux* (98); *Peut-Être* (99); *Les Acteurs* (00); *Amazone* (00)

Benchley, Robert

A successful and sophisticated American humorist with a dry, acerbic, *New Yorker*-style wit, Benchley was an extremely popular character actor during the 1930s and 1940s, appearing in numerous shorts and feature films, often in the guise of an irascible, fast-talking fly-in-the-ointment of the US bourgeois lifestyle.

KEY FILMS: *How To Sleep* [short] (35); *China Seas* (35); *A Night At The Movies* [short] (37); *The Trouble With Husbands* [short] (40); *Bedtime Story* (41); *I Married A Witch* (42); *Practically Yours* (44); *The Bride Wore Boots* (46)

KEY LINE:

'Let's get out of these wet clothes and into a dry Martini.' [Benchley on sex, booze and the 1930s Manhattan lifestyle]

Bendix, William

Bendix was instantly recognisable, with his sloppy, crumpled face and his renowned capacity for playing mentally challenged losers, but his acting was a good deal more intelligent than the good buddy/bad buddy parts he was normally given, and he was particularly memorable as the injured and bewildered ex-GI murderer in George Marshall's **Raymond Chandler**-scripted *The Blue Dahlia* (46), and, again with **Alan Ladd**, as the ex-flyer's possibly slightly more than platonic crony, in **John Farrow's** *Calcutta* (47).

OTHER KEY FILMS: *China* (43); *Lifeboat* (44); *The Dark Corner* (46); *Two Years Before The Mast* (46); *Streets Of Laredo* (49); *The Big Steal* (49); *Macao* (52)

Benigni, Roberto

Sometime flavour-of-the-month since his athletic **Oscar** triumph (he jumped across the seats to reach his award) for the self-directed *Life Is Beautiful* (97), the Benigni-cult has been a long time a-coming, and will most probably peter out just as quickly. He was, however, very good indeed as the comic Italian prisoner in **Jim Jarmusch's** *Down By Law* (86), and his stock in his home market of Italy (he was born, paradoxically for a comedian, in a place called Misericordia) has always been extremely high – and will doubtless continue that way – despite the possibility that his mixture of sentimentality twinned with coy self-awareness may pall very quickly for international audiences.

OTHER KEY FILMS: *Wild Beds* (79); *Tuttobenigni* (85); *La Voce Della Luna* (90); *Johnny Stecchino* (91); *Night On Earth* (91); *Astérix Et Obélix Contre César* (99)

Bening, Annette

Now married to the much-used **Warren Beatty**, Bening is a far better actress than her more famous husband, as she has recently shown in her **Oscar**-winning turn in Sam Mendes's *American Beauty* (99). This followed a number of other outstanding performances, notably in **Milos Forman's** disastrously underrated *Valmont* (89), and in **Stephen Frears's** superb **film noir,** *The Grifters* (90). An actress to watch, and almost certainly a stayer, Bening's is the face and figure we see on the recently revamped **Columbia** film logo.

OTHER KEY FILMS: *Postcards From The Edge* (90); *Bugsy* (91); *Guilty By Suspicion* (91); *Regarding Henry* (91); *Love Affair* (94); *The American President* (95); *Richard III* (95); *Mars Attacks!* (96); *The Siege* (98); *In Dreams* (98); *What Planet Are You From?* (00)

Bennett, Charles

Screenwriter of seven early **Alfred Hitchcock** films, including *The Thirty-Nine Steps* (35) and the much-underrated *Young And Innocent* (37), the exuberant, polo-playing Bennett eventually moved to Hollywood to script or co-script such wonderfully quirky oddities as **John Farrow's** *Where Danger Lives* (50), and **Jacques Tourneur's** *Curse Of The Demon* (58). His later scripts, under the Irwin Allen aegis, were a little pedestrian, and Bennett was known to opine, in later years, that he bitterly regretted ever having gone to Hollywood.

OTHER KEY FILMS: Maurice Elvey's *The Clairvoyant* (34); Herbert Smith's *Night Mail* (35); Robert Stevenson's *King Solomon's Mines* (37)

Benny, Jack

Achingly funny American comedian with an impeccable sense of timing, Benny could make even his silences hilarious, as in his famous 'your money or your life' sketch, in which Benny, threatened by a highwayman, cannot make up his mind which course he ought to take. He was sublime in **Ernst Lubitsch's** *To Be Or Not To Be* (42), and widely reckoned to be one of the nicest men in Hollywood. What more can you want?

OTHER KEY FILMS: *The Medicine Man* (30); *It's In The Air* (35); *Artists And Models* (37); *Man About Town* (39); *Charley's Aunt* (41); *George Washington Slept Here* (42); *A Guide For The Married Man* (67)

KEY LINE:

'I don't deserve this, but I have arthritis, and I don't deserve that either.' [Benny, on receiving an award]

Berenger, Tom

Berenger has often flirted with the big-time, but never quite seems to have made it. He suggested what he was capable of in **Richard Brooks's** *Looking For Mr Goodbar* (77), impressed again in **Lawrence Kasdan's** *The Big Chill* (83), and finally appeared to have hit his box-office stride with **Oliver Stone's** *Platoon* (86), in which he played the devil-driven and booze-addicted bad angel, Sgt Barnes, to **Willem Dafoe's** hash-powered quasi-saint, Sgt Elias. **Ridley Scott**, too, used him to good effect as the smitten cop letting down his blue-collar wife in *Someone To Watch Over Me* (87), but since then he seems to have had an on/off love affair with the public (and, quite possibly, himself). He was excellent in **Wolfgang Petersen's** *Shattered* (91), and one cannot help wishing for yet another belated career resurrection for this exceptional screen actor.

OTHER KEY FILMS: *Flesh And Blood* (TVM 79); *Beyond Obsession* (85); *Love At Large* (90); *The Field* (90); *At Play In The Fields Of The Lord* (91); *Sniper* (93); *Last Of The Dogmen* (95); *The Substitute* (96); *The Gingerbread Man* (98); *Shadow Of Doubt* (98); *Takedown* (99); *Fear Of Flying* (00); *Eye See You* (01)

Beresford, Bruce

Don's Party (76), *The Getting Of Wisdom* (77) and *Breaker Morant* (79) signalled the arrival of a major directing talent, but Hollywood has never quite known how to use this idiosyncratic Australian. His *Tender Mercies* (83), with the excellent, always understated **Robert Duvall**, was superb, and with an **Oscar** under his belt for *Driving Miss Daisy* (89) Beresford's star seemed to have risen for good; but his recent eclectic choice of material (good for him!) and his staunch refusal to be typed have tended to dilute his box-office appeal.

OTHER KEY FILMS: *King David* (85); *Crimes Of The Heart* (85); *Mr Johnson* (91); *A Good Man In Africa* (94); *Silent Fall* (94); *Last Dance* (96); *Paradise Road* (97); *Double Jeopardy* (99); *Ataturk* (00); *Bride Of The Wind* (01)

Berger, Helmut

Odd, off-beat star of Continental films, the good-looking Berger first made an impression in **Luchino Visconti's** *The Damned* (69), and his best later parts always echoed that same theme of decadence. He was excellent, again, as Alberto, in **Vittorio De Sica's** gorgeous *The Garden Of The Finzi-Continis* (71), believably wayward as Visconti's *Ludwig* (73), and seriously disturbing as a bisexual cross-dresser in Tinto Brass's weird and perverse *Salon Kitty* (76).

OTHER KEY FILMS: *Dorian Gray* (70); *Ash Wednesday* (73); *The Romantic Englishwoman* (75); *The Godfather Part III* (90); *Stille Wasser* (96); *Die 120 Tage Von Bottrop* (97); *Unter Den Palmen* (99)

Bergman, Ingmar

Indisputably one of the greatest film directors of all time, Bergman managed to correlate his personal development as a human being with his artistic development as a filmmaker to produce one of the most astonishingly consistent bodies of work on record. It is impossible to over-emphasise the excitement with which his new films were received in intellectual and artistic circles during the 1950s, 1960s and 1970s, and his success must be seen as an object lesson to young filmmaking aspirants that integrity and excellence must always count for more than merely commercial success in the sum total of human endeavour. *Smiles Of A Summer Night* (55), *The Seventh Seal* (57), *Wild Strawberries* (57), *The Virgin Spring* (60), and *Through A Glass Darkly* (62) are all masterpieces of the highest order, and even in his lesser films (of which there are few), his commitment to a personal vision is so intense that most forms of criticism seem, in many respects, redundant.

OTHER KEY FILMS: *Summer Interlude* (51); *Summer With Monika* (53); *The Magician* (58); *The Devil's Eye* (60); *Winter Light* (63); *The Silence* (63); *Persona* (66); *Hour Of The Wolf* (68); *The Shame* (68); *The Touch* (71); *Cries And Whispers* (72); *Scenes*

From A Marriage (73); *The Magic Flute* (74); *The Serpent's Egg* (77); *Autumn Sonata* (78); *Fanny And Alexander* (83); (Script) **Liv Ullmann's** *Faithless* (00)
KEY LINE:
'After years of playing with images of life and death, life has made me shy.' [Bergman on filmmaking]

Bergman, Ingrid

Like the fiery arc of a short-lived meteor, this serenely beautiful but fatally masochistic actress fell foul of a Hollywood system that reckoned it owned her and which knew how to thrust home its dagger, Cassius-like, when she eventually rejected its blandishments. After Gregory Ratoff's 1939 remake of her Swedish success *Intermezzo*, it seemed that Bergman could do no wrong; first with **Michael Curtiz's** *Casablanca* (42), then with **Sam Wood's** *For Whom The Bell Tolls* (43), followed by **George Cukor's** *Gaslight* (44) and **Alfred Hitchcock's** *Spellbound* (45) and *Notorious* (46) – successes every one, with a possessive producer (**David O Selznick**) only too ready to start calling the shots. Crisis-stricken, and feeling that her career was largely out of her own hands, Bergman ran away to Italy at the age of thirty-five, leaving her husband and daughter behind her. She conceived a son with director **Roberto Rossellini** during the filming of

Stromboli (50), followed by twin girls, and it took Hollywood all of six long years to forgive her, her punishment being the very mediocrity of nearly all of her future parts within the studio system.
OTHER KEY FILMS: *Dr Jekyll And Mr Hyde* (41); *The Bells Of St Mary's* (45); *Arch Of Triumph* (48); *Under Capricorn* (49); *Voyage To Italy* (53); *Eléna Et Les Hommes* (56); *Indiscreet* (58); *Aimez-Vous Brahms?* [*Goodbye Again*] (61); *Autumn Sonata* (78)

Berkeley, Busby

Sex was Berkeley's stock-in-trade, and no individual in the history of film purveyed it better. Turning gorgeous chorus girls into gigantic sexual kaleidoscopes through the use of soaring fixed lenses, Berkeley revelled in the camera's voyeuristic ability, until all of us, the audience, the filmmaker, the technicians and the actors, become voyeurs with him in a giant, musically accompanied orgy of lubricity. Even **Eddie Cantor** became infected by this merry bacchanal, and the scene in Leo McCarey's *The Kid From Spain* (32) where Cantor emerges from under the bedclothes in a Vassar-style girls' dormitory which then magically transforms itself into a gigantic swimming pool seems somehow to sum up all the glories of devil-may-care Hollywood's depression era chutzpah.

Ingrid Bergman as Alicia Huberman, winning over **Cary Grant's** *initially frigid Devlin, in* Notorious *(46)*

OTHER KEY FILMS: *Whoopee!* (30); *42nd Street* (33); *Footlight Parade* (33); *Gold Diggers Of 1933* (33); *Roman Scandals* (33); *Dames* (34); *Fashions Of 1934* (34); *Twenty Million Sweethearts* (34); *Stars Over Broadway* (35); *Babes In Arms* (39)

Berlin Film Festival

One of the largest cinema talent showcases in the world and a perennial threat to **Cannes**, the Berlin festival was founded in 1951, with its chief and most prestigious award being the Golden Bear for Best Film.

Berlin, Irving

A sublimely talented songwriter who could hardly play a note on the piano unless it was tuned to the correct key, Berlin was responsible for such perennial hits as 'Alexander's Ragtime Band', 'Cheek To Cheek' and 'White Christmas', which was so memorably and lucratively (it went on to become the best-selling song of all time) sung by **Bing Crosby** in Mark Sandrich's *Holiday Inn* (42). Recipient of a Medal of Merit, a Congressional Gold Medal, a French Légion D'Honneur and the Medal of Liberty, Berlin survived to the ripe old age of 101, and may, with some justification, be considered the most successful songwriter who has ever lived.

OTHER KEY FILMS: Alan Crosland's *The Jazz Singer* (27); Roy Del Ruth's *Kid Millions* (34); Mark Sandrich's *Top Hat* (35); **Charles Walters's** *Easter Parade* (48); George Sidney's *Annie Get Your Gun* (50); **Michael Curtiz's** *White Christmas* (54)

Berri, Claude

High-profile French director whose career has seen him through more ups and downs than most filmmakers – he began his career with an **Oscar** for his film short, *The Chicken* (63), then proceeded to blow his chances of an international career with a string of only occasionally successful comedies – Berri is now best known for his **Marcel Pagnol** duet, *Jean De Florette* (86) and *Manon Des Sources* (86), and for his more recent true-life resistance thriller, *Lucie Aubrac* (97) (featuring a luminous performance by Carole Bouquet), which followed a long period in which he concentrated on production rather than direction.

OTHER KEY FILMS: *Marry Me! Marry Me!* (69); *Le Cinéma De Papa* (70); *Le Sex Shop* (72); *Le Male Du Siècle* (75); *Le Maître D'Ecole* (82); *Tchao Pantin* (83); *Uranus* (91); *Germinal* (93); *La Débondade* (99)

Berry, Jules

One of the **monstres sacrés** of the 1930s golden era of French cinema, the sinister-voiced Berry worked for every director of note at the time, and had screenwriters of the quality of **Jacques Prévert** clamouring to write for him, on account of his extraordinary mastery of the spoken French language. His most characteristic performances occur in **Jean Renoir's** early masterpiece *Le Crime De Monsieur Lange* (36), as the abominable, but nonetheless sympathetic Paul Batala, and in **Marcel Carné's** *Le Jour Se Lève* (39) and *Les Visiteurs Du Soir* (42).

OTHER KEY FILMS: *Rigolboche* (36); *Arsène Lupin Détective* (37); *Carrefour* (37); *La Symphonie Fantastique* (42); *Le Voyageur De La Toussaint* (43); *Portrait D'Un Assassin* (49); *Les Maîtres Nageurs* (50)

Bertolucci, Bernardo

A co-writer on **Sergio Leone's** *Once Upon A Time In The West* (68), Bertolucci announced himself to the world with *The Spider's Stratagem* (70), closely followed by his first masterpiece, *The Conformist* (70), in which he established the complex visual patterns (with the help of his magnificent cinematographer **Vittorio Storaro**) which were to mark the films of his later maturity. *Last Tango In Paris* (72), for instance, deserved every accolade it was given, if only for daring to challenge the mainstream cinematic parameters of human sexuality, and although Bertolucci may have disappointed his admirers in recent years with his emphasis on surface textures to the detriment of his former emotional honesty, even his relative failures, like *The Sheltering Sky* (90), retain their ability to seduce both the eye and the mind.

OTHER KEY FILMS: *1900* (77); *La Luna* (79); *The Last Emperor* (87); *Stealing Beauty* (96); *Besieged* (98); *Paradiso E Inferno* (99)

Besson, Luc

French cult filmmaker who has successfully negotiated the crossover to commercial cinema without the total loss of integrity normally associated with such a move, Besson seduced the film buffs with *Le Dernier Combat* (84), the quasi-philosophers with *Subway* (85), and the sea-and-nihilism freaks with *The Big Blue* (88). He then went on to seduce the feminists with *La Femme Nikita* (91), and the sci-fi action loons with *The Fifth Element* (97) – not a bad run for this still relatively young (he was born in 1959) Parisian.

OTHER KEY FILMS: *Atlantis* (91); *The Professional* (94); *The Messenger: The Story Of Joan Of Arc* (99)

33

Best Boy/Girl

The principal assistant of the **gaffer** (a.k.a. the chief electrician) on the film set.

Best Titles

A particularly subjective one, this, but here are a few randomly chosen titles that might entertain, surprise and generally gladden the heart of film aficionados everywhere – they include the poetic, the inspired, and the downright schlocky, and some are so descriptive one hardly needs to see the film in order to deduce the plot:

D W **Griffith's** *The Musketeers Of Pig Alley* (12); De Grasse's *Hell Morgan's Girl* (17); Roy Del Ruth's *Love And Doughnuts* (21); Muhsin Ertuğrul's *The Shirt Of Fire* (23); **Robert Z Leonard's** *Adam And Evil* (27) and *Let Us Be Gay* (30); **Kenji Mizoguchi's** *Osen Of The Paper Cranes* (34); **Edgar G Ulmer's** *Tomorrow We Live* (42); William A Seiter's *Four Jills In A Jeep* (44); V Shantaram's *The Immortal Story Of Dr Kotnis* (46); Norman Foster's *Kiss The Blood Off My Hands* (48); **Jean Negulesco's** *Johnny Belinda* (48); Henry Levin's *The Mating Of Millie* (48); **Preston Sturges's** *The Beautiful Blonde From Bashful Bend* (49); **Howard Hawks's** *I Was A Male War Bride* (49); John Hubley's *Fuddy Duddy Buddy* (52); **Vittorio De Sica's** *Indiscretion Of An American Wife* (53); **Allan Dwan's** *Slightly Scarlet* (56); Serge Bourguignon's *Sundays And Cybele* (62); Christopher Morahan's *All Neat In Black Stockings* (69); Alexander Kluge's *Artists At The Top Of The Big Top: Disorientated* (68); Stan Brakhage's *Anticipation Of The Night* (58), *Window Water Baby Moving* (59) and *The Act Of Seeing With One's Own Eyes* (71); **George Cukor's** *Heller In Pink Tights* (60); Zhang Junli's *A Withered Tree Meets Spring* (62); Dong Kena's *A Blade Of Glass On The Kunlun Mountains* (62); Don Owen's *Nobody Waved Goodbye* (64); Aleksandar Petrovic's *I Even Met Happy Gipsies* (67); Joyce Wieland's *Rat Life And Diet In North America* (68); Halit Refiğ's *I Lost My Heart To A Turk* (69); Malcolm Le Grice's *Blackbird Descending* (77); Tsui Hark's *All The Wrong Clues (For The Right Solution)* (81); Katja von Garnier's *Abgeschminkt!* (93); Zhang Yuan's *Beijing Bastards* (93); Dwight Yoakam's *South Of Heaven, West Of Hell* (00)

See also **All-time Best Films, Erotic Moments, Heartstopping Moments, Worst Films**

Betty Boop

Max Fleischer's sexy cartoon heroine of the late 1920s and 1930s, who was based on the flapper concept behind Helen Kane's famous song rendition (later parodied by **Marilyn Monroe**) of 'I Want To Be Loved By You'. Come to think of it, Monroe's screen persona, particularly in **Billy Wilder's** *Some Like It Hot* (59), and in her upskirt scene in the same director's *The Seven Year Itch* (55), seems to owe a lot more than has ever been previously acknowledged to gorgeous Betty's antics – and Marilyn would have been between the ages of five and thirteen at the height of Betty's fame, and no doubt highly impressionable. Hmm. How about a PhD thesis on this, until now it seems, largely unexplored possibility? See **flash frame** for the full Betty Boop upskirt story.

BFFS

The British Federation of Film Societies, responsible for co-ordinating film societies, on a regional basis, all around the United Kingdom.

BFI

Founded in 1933, the British Film Institute, as well as promoting British cinema in any way possible, also runs the National Film and Television Archive and the network of RFTs through which archived films are subsequently distributed. In addition the BFI operates the National Film Theatre (home to the annual **London Film Festival**) on whose three screens over 2,000 immaculately preserved films are shown each year.

Best Big-budget Action Films

Luc Besson's *Léon* (94); **John Boorman's** *Excalibur* (81); **James Cameron's** *The Terminator* (84) and *Terminator 2 – Judgement Day* (91); Richard Fleischer's *The Vikings* (57); Brian G Hutton's *Where Eagles Dare* (69); Ted Kotcheff's *First Blood* (82); **George Lucas's** *Star Wars* (77); John Milius's *Conan The Barbarian* (82); **George Miller's** *Mad Max 2* (a.k.a. *The Road Warrior*) (81); J Lee Thompson's *The Guns Of Navarone* (61)

Billing

The publicity that stars receive on movie posters and film credits, and which to some extent determines their eventual status regarding payment and perks, billing is often the subject of many an acrimonious dispute as to who comes first, and whose name should be larger, blacker, in brighter lights, etc.

Bin

The padded container used for storing unwound film during the editing process.

Binoche, Juliette

French actress who has the ability to transcend the normal parameters of her all-too-obvious surface sex appeal to produce beautiful, touching performances that leave the spectator with an insight into femininity that few modern actresses ever have the capacity, far less the instinct, to attempt. She was the best thing in Philip Kaufman's otherwise unsatisfactory *The Unbearable Lightness Of Being* (88), as well as in **Louis Malle's** sadly underrated *Damage* (92), but her true possibilities were only belatedly and triumphantly captured by the great **Krzysztof Kieslowski** in the *Blue* (94) part of his colours trilogy. Her performance as Hana in **Anthony Minghella's** *The English Patient* (96) simply reinforced the fact that she is one of the best film actresses working anywhere today. Since then, she has produced marvellously nuanced performances in virtually all her films, most notably as the emotionally damaged Alice, in **André Téchiné's** *Alice Et Martin* (98), finding renewed strength through coping with her younger lover's breakdown, and as Vianne Rocher in Lasse Hallström's delightful fairy-tale, *Chocolat* (00).

OTHER KEY FILMS: *Les Nanas* (84); *La Vie De Famille* (84); *Mauvais Sang* (86); *Les Amants Du Pont Neuf* (91); *Wuthering Heights* (92); *The Horseman On The Roof* (96); *Les Enfants Du Siècle* (99); *La Veuve De Saint-Pierre* (00); *Code Inconnu* (00)

Biograph

One of the first ever film production companies, founded in New York in 1896, and responsible for many of the early **D W Griffith** shorts.

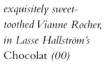

Juliette Binoche as the exquisitely sweet-toothed Vianne Rocher, in Lasse Hallström's Chocolat *(00)*

Biopic

The so-called biography of a famous person committed to celluloid and which sometimes, but not always, deserves the subtitle of hagiography. Famous biopics include **Michael Curtiz's** life of **Cole Porter**, *Night And Day* (46), and Alfred E Green and **Joseph H Lewis's** *The Jolson Story* (46), which purports, but fails, to trace the real life of **Al Jolson**, star of Alan Crosland's *The Jazz Singer* (27), the first ever talking picture.

Birkin, Jane

Willowy, absurdly English, yet somehow quintessentially European scion of the 1960s, Birkin seemed famous for only two things during much of her career – for being Serge Gainsbourg's mistress, and for her breathy orgasm on the soundtrack of his song 'Je t'aime...et moi non plus'. She is better than that of course, as the French have always known, and as the rest of us have only belatedly discovered in her exquisite performance opposite **Dirk Bogarde** in **Bertrand Tavernier's** *Daddy Nostalgie* (a.k.a. *These Foolish Things*) (90).

OTHER KEY FILMS: *Blow-Up* (66); *La Piscine* (69); *Don Juan* (73); *Dark Places* (73); *Le Diable Au Coeur* (76); *Death On The Nile* (78); *Evil Under The Sun* (82); *La Belle Noiseuse* (91); *Noir Comme Le Souvenir* (95); *On Connaît La Chanson* (97); *A Soldier's Daughter Never Cries* (98); *The Last September* (99); *Reines D'Un Jour* (01)

Bisset, Jacqueline

Stunningly attractive actress whose acting ability has never quite seemed to live up to the promise of her beauty, Bisset came closest as Yvonne Firmin in **John Huston's** *Under The Volcano* (84), and she was more than good in **Peter Yates's** otherwise turgid *The Deep* (77). With a bit of luck, and with just a little more skill, she could have been England's answer to **Catherine Deneuve**.

OTHER KEY FILMS: *Cul De Sac* (66); *Two For The Road* (67); *The Mephisto Waltz* (70); *Day For Night* (74); *The Spiral Staircase* (75); *St Ives* (76); *The Greek Tycoon* (78); *Rich And Famous* (81); *Class* (83); *High Season* (87); *Scenes From The Class Struggle In Beverly Hills* (89); *Wild Orchid* (90); *The Maid* (91); *La Cérémonie* (95); *Let The Devil Wear Black* (99); *New Year's Day* (00); *The Sleepy Time Gal* (01)

Bit Part

The minor role a minor role player plays.

Bit Player

What virtually every actor and actress starts out as – a minor role player.

Bitzer, Billy

Bitzer was the man who put director **D W Griffith's** vision up onto the screen in a series of the most famous films ever made. A former silversmith, Bitzer graduated towards the camera only slowly, finally beginning his most famous collaboration at the relatively advanced age of thirty-six. It was Bitzer's genius that captured the very spirit of silent film in Griffith's *The Birth Of A Nation* (15), *Intolerance* (16) and *Broken Blossoms* (19), and it was Bitzer, too, who developed and perfected the numerous technical innovations that Griffith has largely, and no doubt rightly, taken much of the credit for, and which include **back lighting** and the **iris**.

OTHER KEY FILMS: *In Old Kentucky* (09); *The Fugitive* (10); *The Lonedale Operator* (11); *Madame Rex* (11); *A Tale Of The Wilderness* (12); *The New York Hat* (12); *Hearts Of The World* (18); *Way Down East* (co-camera) (20); *Orphans Of The Storm* (co-camera) (22)

Black-and-White Film

It was only in the mid 1950s that colour began to outstrip the traditional black-and-white (monochrome) medium as the preferred choice of most Hollywood directors. Purists, however, still feel that black-and-white is far better able to capture the emotion, nuances, and sheer otherness of filmmaking, than the more blatant colour process. A recent trend towards the 'colorization' of such classics as **Michael Curtiz's** *Casablanca* (42) has rightly angered all those who cherish original intent over faddishness.

Black, Karen

A superb character actress who lit up the screen in **Bob Rafelson's** *Five Easy Pieces* (70) as Rayette Dipesto, **Jack Nicholson's** dumb yet sensitive blue-collar girlfriend, Black also made her mark in John Flynn's *The Outfit* (73), **John Schlesinger's** *The Day Of The Locust* (75) and **Robert Altman's** *Nashville* (75). For some incomprehensible reason her star began to wane during the 1980s and 1990s, leaving us to chew over the indelible images of her 1970s heyday and ponder what might have been – the scene in *Five Easy Pieces* where Black (with her scrupulously painted toenails perched coquettishly on the car dashboard) sings a country-and-western ballad to the over-educated but

under-motivated Nicholson, is one of the most heartrending reflections of almost-love in the history of cinema. Didn't they *know* what she had?
OTHER KEY FILMS: *Easy Rider* (69); *Drive He Said* (71); *Portnoy's Complaint* (72); *The Great Gatsby* (75); *Family Plot* (76); *Come Back To The Five And Dime, Jimmy Dean, Jimmy Dean* (82); *Children Of The Night* (92); *The Player* (92); *Cries Of Silence* (93); *New York Crossing* (96); *The Donor* (00); *House Of 1000 Corpses* (01)
KEY LINE:
'I'll go out with you, or I'll stay in with you, or I'll do anything that you like for me to do, if you tell me that you love me.' [Black to Nicholson's Robert Eroica Dupea, in *Five Easy Pieces*]

Blanc, Mel
The greatest of all voice-over artists, Blanc provided the voices for the characters in the **Looney Tunes** and **Merrie Melodies** series of animated cartoons.
KEY LINE:
'What's up Doc?' [*Bugs Bunny cartoons*]

Blaxploitation Movies
A series of 1970s films which glorified the black experience while at the same time endeavouring to gather in the largest possible paying audience to view the results. First and best of the genre was Gordon Parks's *Shaft* (71) (remade in 2000 by John Singleton with **Samuel L Jackson** in the title role of John Shaft), closely followed by the even more influential *Superfly* (72), which was directed by Parks's son, Gordon Parks Jr, who was killed in a plane crash seven years later. **Quentin Tarantino** paid homage to the genre by using a famous blaxploitation actress, Pam Grier, in his excellent *Pulp Fiction* (94) follow-up, *Jackie Brown* (97).

Blier, Bernard
Always the most unlikely-looking of screen stars, with his chamber pot belly and his bald head, Blier confounded the Gods of Appearance by constructing a distinguished and lengthy career in French cinema. He appeared in well over 100 films during his more than fifty-year film career, including **Marcel Carné's** *Hôtel Du Nord* (38) and *Le Jour Se Lève* (39), and **Henri-Georges Clouzot's** *Quai Des Orfèvres* (47). Made a Chevalier De La Légion D'Honneur by the French Government for his contribution to cinema history, Blier, who died in 1989, is the father of film director Bertrand Blier, of *Les Valseuses* (74) and *Trop Belle Pour Toi* (89) fame.

OTHER KEY FILMS: *L'Enfer Des Anges* (39); *La Symphonie Fantastique* (42); *Seul Dans La Nuit* (45); *Monseigneur* (49); *La Souricière* (50); *Avant Le Déluge* (54); *Le Dossier Noir* (55); *Crime Et Châtiment* (56); *L'Homme À L'Imperméable* (57); *Retour De Manivelle* (57); *Les Misérables* (58); *La Chatte* (58); *Germinal* (62); *Casanova* (70): *Le Corps De Mon Ennemi* (76); *Buffet Froid* (80); *I Picari* (87)

Blimp
The noise-dampening housing that surrounds a camera and which prevents the sound of the mechanism from registering on the soundtrack – most modern cameras are now self-blimped, meaning that they are designed to operate with little or no residual noise.

Block-booking
An iniquitous trick once used by the major studios to force distributors to buy and project second-rate films, if, and only if, they also wanted the right to run the most desirable commercial features. The practice was outlawed in 1948.

Blockbuster
A film that is either expected to be, or has been in the past, a massive box-office success – recent candidates include **Ridley Scott's** *Gladiator* (00) and **John Woo's** *Mission: Impossible 2* (00). Past candidates include **Victor Fleming's** *Gone With The Wind* (39) and **Steven Spielberg's** *Raiders Of The Lost Ark* (81).

Blocking
The total mapping out of a film scene before shooting commences to include camera, furniture and acting positions, often through the use of stand-ins.

Bloom
A special coating on a glass lens or surface, designed to offset reflected light.

Bloop
The click occasionally heard on a film soundtrack that is caused by faulty splicing. Also applies to the triangular first aid patch used to cover the offending splice.

Blooper
A large receptacle filled with water that is used for re-creating pneumatically produced underwater explosions.

37

Blow

Hollywood movie jargon for an actor or actress's verbal slip-up.

Blow-up

A blown up or expanded copy of a print or image from, say, 8 or 16 mm to 35. Can also be applied to the enlargement of a single frame to highlight one desirable feature at the expense of another.

Blue Movies

Referring to the mythical blue colour of the censor's pencil, the term is now used exclusively for pornographic films that are not available on general release. The most famous blue movie of them all was *Deep Throat* (71), starring the multi-talented Linda Lovelace.

Blue Pages

The coloured pages of additional material appended to a script during shooting to differentiate them from the original script.

Blue Screen Process

The process by which a number of different shots can be combined to produce the effect of a single, composite image, otherwise known as a **travelling matte**. Filming of the actors takes place in front of a blue screen, and the resulting image is then re-photographed through varying degrees of filter, following which the whole shot (with the additionally filmed material) is then reassembled using an **optical printer**. The process was successfully used in **Victor Fleming's** *Gone With The Wind* (39) to suggest the passing of **Clark Gable's** Rhett Butler and **Vivien Leigh's** Scarlett O'Hara in a buggy through the collapsing, fiery remains of Atlanta.

Body Double

A stand-in used specifically for sex scenes, in which the principal actor or actress, for reasons of vanity, squeamishness or uxorial *force majeure*, does not wish to participate.

Body Frame

The harness an operator uses to support a hand-held camera during non-static filming.

Body Make-up Artist

The person who, by convention in the UK, and by union regulation in the US, can apply make-up to all areas of the body not including the head, shoulders, hands and lower arms, which are the sole province of the general make-up artist.

Boetticher, Budd

One of the best-kept secrets of visually and emotionally literate American cinema, Boetticher was never allowed outside the **B-movie** format, but that suited both him and his style just fine. He made a series of **Westerns** with **Randolph Scott** in the final years of the 1950s, the best of which, *The Tall T* (57), *Buchanan Rides Alone* (58) and *Ride Lonesome* (59), must rank among the finest in a genre already overbrimming with talent in the likes of **John Ford**, **Howard Hawks**, **Sam Peckinpah** and **Anthony Mann**. Boetticher understood men and what motivates them, and as if in subconscious echo, he threw up his own burgeoning career to pursue a story in Mexico about an ill-fated matador, Carlos Arruza, that wrecked his health, destroyed his marriage and bankrupted both his future and his bank balance. One likes to imagine him, like Randolph Scott's Buchanan, shrugging off such absurd vicissitudes with a cracked smile and an airy laugh, geeing up his horse, and quietly continuing on his way.

OTHER KEY FILMS: *The Bullfighter And The Lady* (51); *The Magnificent Matador* (56); *Seven Men From Now* (56); *Decision At Sundown* (57); *Westbound* (59); *Comanche Station* (60); *The Rise And Fall Of Legs Diamond* (60); *Arruza* (71)

Bogarde, Dirk

For fifteen years, between 1948 and 1963, Bogarde winced his way through more than thirty mostly forgettable films (with the possible exception of **Basil Dearden's** *The Blue Lamp* (50) and *Victim* (61), and **Michael Powell** and **Emeric Pressburger's** *Ill Met By Moonlight* (57)) as a matinee idol who was forced to sew the flies of his trousers together to defend himself from over-eager female fans. Then **Joseph Losey** cast him as manservant Hugo Barrett in *The Servant* (63), and the second part of Bogarde's career began, ushering in a golden period in which he took on a series of increasingly challenging roles in a succession of English and European art-house films, which included Losey's *Accident* (68), **Luchino Visconti's** *The Damned* (69) and *Death In Venice* (71), and Liliana Cavani's controversial exercise in sadomasochism, *The Night Porter* (73). The third part of Bogarde's professional life was taken up with writing, but he gave a final, touching performance opposite **Jane Birkin** in **Bertrand Tavernier's** *Daddy Nostalgie* (90) (a.k.a. *These Foolish Things*), which neatly and elegantly brought this now eminent actor's filmic career to an end.

OTHER KEY FILMS: *Doctor In The House* (54); *The Sleeping Tiger* (54); *The Spanish Gardener* (56); *Campbell's Kingdom* (57); *A Tale Of Two Cities* (58); *King And Country* (64); *Darling* (66); *Le Serpent* (73); *Permission To Kill* (75); *Providence* (77); *A Bridge Too Far* (77); *Despair* (79); *The Vision* (87)

Bogart, Humphrey

Rediscovered and taken to its collective heart by the French **New Wave** of the 1950s and 1960s, Bogart, while remaining quintessentially a man of his own time, also managed, in terms of his image, to transcend it. Born a New York WASP, Bogart shone when playing cynical and worldly men, brought, often despite their own better instincts, to heroism. In this way he differed from **Jean Gabin**, to whom, in many ways, he can be compared. Gabin, though often beaten down, was never cynical – it needed Bogart's genius, particularly as Rick Blaine in **Michael Curtiz's** *Casablanca* (42), to exemplify the world-weary spleen of a knight in only-so-very-slightly-tarnished armour. In Bogie's final film, Mark Robson's *The Harder They Fall* (56), **Philip Yordan** (possibly with the help of a friend or two) wrote a cracking script about the boxing industry, and Bogart, as always, played it straight down the line, from heel to hero. A few weeks after the film came out he was diagnosed with the cancer that was eventually to kill him, a little under a year later, just nine days before his fifty-eighth birthday. Note for Film Buffs: Bogie's favourite movie was **William Wellman's** *A Star Is Born* (37). He used to run a 16-mm print of it every Christmas Eve and cry all the way through it. When asked why, he answered, 'I don't know. It just makes me cry.'

Humphrey Bogart as Dix Steele, and Gloria Grahame as Laurel Gray, in Nicholas Ray's smashing film noir, In A Lonely Place *(49)*

OTHER KEY FILMS: *The Petrified Forest* (36); *They Drive By Night* (40); *High Sierra* (41); *The Maltese Falcon* (41); *To Have And Have Not* (44); *The Big Sleep* (46); *Key Largo* (48); *The Treasure Of The Sierra Madre* (48); *In A Lonely Place* (50); *The African Queen* (51); *The Barefoot Contessa* (54); *The Caine Mutiny* (54); *The Harder They Fall* (56)

KEY LINES:

'Life, every now and then, behaves as though it had seen too many bad movies…' [Joseph L Mankiewicz's *The Barefoot Contessa* (54)]

'I used to play chess with Humphrey Bogart, but I couldn't afford it.' [Curt Siodmak, progenitor of *Curucu, Beast Of The Amazon* (56), and its follow-up, *Love Slaves Of The Amazon* (57), on the price of friendship]

Bogdanovich, Peter

Almost more important in film criticism and conservation than he is in creative cinema (which is a backhanded compliment to just that creativity), Bogdanovich has savoured the highs and lows more than most directors of his generation, and probably acknowledges his own shortcomings and failures as well as anybody. His successes are impressive, and include *Targets* (68), *The Last Picture Show* (71), *Saint Jack* (79) and *Mask* (85). His failures can usually be set down to either misplaced ambitions or vainglory – and who would dare to cast the first stone in that direction?

OTHER KEY FILMS: *What's Up Doc?* (72); *Paper Moon* (73); *Daisy Miller* (74); *Nickelodeon* (76); *Texasville* (90); *The Thing Called Love* (93); *The Substance Of Fire* (96)

Bohringer, Richard

Perennially Gitanes-smoking, hoarse-voiced French character actor, Bohringer made his mark with international audiences in **Jean-Jacques Beineix's** *Diva* (81), in which he played the quirky Gorodish, the one who explains the perfect way to butter a baguette and who peels onions wearing a snorkel. He remains, however, very much a local French actor, despite his second successful foray into international waters with **Peter Greenaway's** *The Cook, The Thief, His Wife And Her Lover* (89). Film fans who want to sample Bohringer's peculiarly eccentric style of acting should seek out a copy of Michel Deville's *Péril En La Demeure* [*Death In A French Garden*] (85), or **Patrice Leconte's** ironically misogynistic *Tango* (93), secure in the knowledge that they won't be let down.

OTHER KEY FILMS: *Le Dernier Métro* [*The Last Metro*] (80); *L'Addition* (84); *Subway* (85); *Le Paltoquet* (86); *Kamikaze* (86); *Après La Guerre* (89); *Dames Galantes* (90); *Le Parfum D'Yvonne* (94); *Les Caprices D'Un Fleuve* (96); *Tykho Moon* (96); *La Vérité Si Je Mens* (97); *Comme Une Bête* (98); *Cinq Minutes De Détente* (99); *La Soutane Écarlate* (00); *Ma Folle De Soeur* (01)

Bollywood

An amalgamation of the words Bombay and Hollywood, Bollywood is a term that has, in recent years, come to imply the whole of Indian cinema, but which should, strictly speaking, only be seen to apply to those films made and filmed near or around Bombay.

Bolt, Robert

An eminent playwright and the screenwriter on such films as **David Lean's** *Lawrence Of Arabia* (62), *Dr Zhivago* (65) and *Ryan's Daughter* (70), Bolt's finest hour came with the filming of his stage play about the tormented and finally doomed relationship between Henry VIII and Sir Thomas More in **Fred Zinnemann's** *A Man For All Seasons* (66). Bolt, who had been married to actress Sarah Miles, died in 1995, after a long and exhausting battle with illness.

OTHER KEY FILMS: Roger Donaldson's *The Bounty* (84); Roland Joffé's *The Mission* (86)

Bond, James

The brainchild of Ian Lancaster Fleming (and originally blond – of hair colour, not of name) Bond made his literary debut in *Casino Royale* in 1953, and his film debut in Terence Young's *Dr No* (62). Discounting the turgid, multi-directed and ostensibly comic 1967 version of *Casino Royale* (in which there were any number of Bonds, some even female), the nominally English super-spy has since been played by five different actors on the big screen, in the following, occasionally leap-frogging order: Scots-born **Sean Connery**, English-born **Roger Moore**, Australian-born George Lazenby, Welsh-born Timothy Dalton and Irish-born **Pierce Brosnan.** (The Americans did get a look in, way back in 1954, when Bond was played in a one-hour TV special by Barry Nelson.) The best Bond, by popular acclaim, appears to be Connery, but both Dalton and Brosnan are excellent, and Moore brought a cheerful wryness to the part that was as entertaining, in its way, as Connery's laconic intelligence was menacing. In recent years the

Bond brand name has moved from marketing tool to marketing miracle, swept along by the remarkable success of the 'Goldeneye' video game, which set a new standard in computer-game graphics. The Bond trademark has proved the most resilient and long-lasting of all the great movie brands, a fact testified to by the hundreds of Bond sites listed on the Internet.

OTHER KEY FILMS: Terence Young's *From Russia With Love* (63); **Guy Hamilton's** *Goldfinger* (64); **Lewis Gilbert's** *You Only Live Twice* (67); Guy Hamilton's *Live And Let Die* (73); John Glen's *The Living Daylights* (87); Martin Campbell's *Goldeneye* (95); Roger Spottiswoode's *Tomorrow Never Dies* (97); **Michael Apted's** *The World Is Not Enough* (99)

KEY LINE:
Bond: 'Do you expect me to talk?' Goldfinger: 'No, Mr Bond, I expect you to die.' [*Goldfinger*]

Bond, Ward

One of **John Wayne's** greatest chums, and a fine, though limited character actor in his own right, Bond specialised in playing hardened men who won't take any nonsense, despite, or even because of, their own semi-comical natures. His best part came as Captain The Reverend Samuel Clayton in **John Ford's** *The Searchers* (56) where he showed a level of incipient humanity that was lacking in many of his other characterisations.

OTHER KEY FILMS: *Dodge City* (39); *Young Mr Lincoln* (39); *Drums Along The Mohawk* (39); *The Long Voyage Home* (40); *They Were Expendable* (45); *My Darling Clementine* (46); *The Fugitive* (47); *Fort Apache* (48); *Three Godfathers* (48); *Wagonmaster* (50); *The Quiet Man* (52); *Johnny Guitar* (54); *Rio Bravo* (59)

Bonham Carter, Helena

Fearful of being forever typecast as an upper-middle-class English Rose, Bonham Carter has striven, sometimes unsuccessfully, to portray herself as a foul-mouthed, working-class American instead. The logic of this may seem inescapable to some, but the simple fact remains that what she does best is British costume drama, where inhibitions, cruet and corsets reign supreme. She was excellent in **James Ivory's** *Howards End* (92), and also in Mort Ransen's marginally more contemporary *Margaret's Museum* (95), and she will almost certainly go on trying to extend her range, which is a great deal more than can be said of most of the actors and actresses who have acquired for themselves such a cosy and potentially lucrative niche.

OTHER KEY FILMS: *A Room with A View* (86); *Maurice* (87); *Getting It Right* (89); *Hamlet* (90); *Where Angels Fear To Tread* (91); *Mary Shelley's Frankenstein* (94); *Mighty Aphrodite* (95); *Twelfth Night* (96); *Keep The Aspidistra Flying* (97); *Fight Club* (99); *Carnivale* (99); *Novocaine* (01); *Planet Of The Apes* (01)

Booking

A deal made between a film distributor and a cinema owner that specifies exactly when, where and for how long a movie may be shown.

Boom

An extendible arm to carry the microphone or the camera invisibly (one hopes) above the players on a film set.

Boom Man

The man who operates and manipulates the aforementioned **boom**.

Boom Shot

This is an extended, moving shot, using a variety of different camera angles and focuses, which is only made possible through the skilful and invisible use of a **boom** microphone.

Boorman, John

A well-informed and fanatical propagandist for film, Boorman is one of Britain's finest directors, and his career is something of a miracle given the shabby way filmmakers of talent are often treated by the London-based institutions and governing bodies that should be helping and encouraging them. Many of Boorman's best films have consequently been shot with US and other foreign funding, producing such gems as *Point Blank* (67), *Hell In The Pacific* (68) and *Deliverance* (72). *Excalibur* (81) is a visually and aurally stunning evocation of the Arthurian legends, and Boorman's *Hope And Glory* (87) showed just what British filmmaking had been missing over the years of its director's enforced creative exile. His recent John Le Carré outing, *The Tailor Of Panama* (01), miraculously transformed **Pierce Brosnan** from hunk to successful light comedian, by virtue of a literate script (by Andrew Davies), stunning photography (by Philippe Rousselot), and Boorman's steady and emotionally literate hand on the tiller.

OTHER KEY FILMS: *Leo The Last* (70); *Zardoz* (74); *The Emerald Forest* (85); *Beyond Rangoon* (95); *The General* (98)

Booster

A dynamo used for boosting the wattage of an existing light source on a studio set.

Booster Light

Powerful lamp used to heighten and intensify the natural effect of daylight.

Borgnine, Ernest

A natural 'heavy' as personified by his sadistic military policeman, Sgt 'Fatso' Judson, in **Fred Zinnemann's** *From Here To Eternity* (53), and as **Robert Ryan's** evil henchman, Coley Trimble, in **John Sturges's** *Bad Day At Black Rock* (54), Borgnine surprised everyone when he received an **Oscar** for his portrayal of the amorously ill-favoured Bronx butcher in **Delbert Mann's** *Marty* (55). (This was one of a new breed of filmed teleplays that revolutionised Hollywood's approach to screen dialogue in the mid-1950s.) His career has varied wildly since then, leaving the impression that, apart from the one blip, Borgnine has never been more than a talented, single-tracked team player.

OTHER KEY FILMS: *Johnny Guitar* (54); *Run For Cover* (55); *Violent Saturday* (55); *Jubal* (56); *The Vikings* (58); *Barabbas* (62); *The Flight Of The Phoenix* (65); *The Wild Bunch* (69); *Hustle* (75); *Escape From New York* (81); *Cane Arrabiatto* (85); *Skeleton Coast* (87); *Tides Of War* (90); *Gattaca* (97); *Abilene* (99); *Castle Rock* (00)

Borzage, Frank

A scandalously under-appreciated filmmaker whose particular brand of heady romanticism was eaten up and then spat out by the cheerful, rackety, patriotic hoo-ha that followed the United States' belated entry into the Second World War, Borzage could show the poetical side of a love story almost as well as the French, and he had a particular insight into the vulnerabilities and weaknesses of judgement such a love engenders. His best films, which include *Seventh Heaven* (27), *Bad Girl* (31), *History Is Made At Night* (37), *Three Comrades* (38) and *The Mortal Storm* (40), have heart (a rare thing in Hollywood), and as such deserve to be remembered and shown far more than they are. Borzage cared about love and friendship and the painful losses the one can cause to the other, and with films such as *A Farewell To Arms* (32) he paved the way for such later poets of the human condition as **Nicholas Ray** and **Charles Laughton**.

OTHER KEY FILMS: *Lazybones* (25); *Street Angel* (28); *The River* (29); *Man's Castle* (33); *No Greater Glory* (34); *Desire* (36); *Moonrise* (48)

Bost, Pierre

See **Jean Aurenche**

Boulting, John and Roy

A set of twins who either shared or alternated the producing, writing and directing work on a high-quality sequence of British features and documentaries of the 1940s and 1950s, including *Thunder Rock* (43), a seriously weird paean to commitment, and *The Guinea Pig* (a.k.a. *The Outsider*) (49), in which the working-class recipient of a scholarship, **Richard Attenborough**, struggles to make his way in an upmarket and initially unwelcoming private school. (In our newly enlightened and radically chic age, of course, the private schoolboys would now be struggling against each other, and not Attenborough, in order to take his discarded place at the substandard state school his academic brilliance so unwisely caused him to leave!) The Boultings' best joint projects were the **Graham Greene** and Terence Rattigan-scripted *Brighton Rock* (50), and a little-seen thriller, *Seven Days To Noon* (50), in which an atomic scientist threatens London in a rather misguided protest in favour of nuclear disarmament. When the brothers turned to comedy in the late 1950s, something of their magic unfortunately gave way in the process.

OTHER KEY FILMS: *Desert Victory* (44) (doc.); *Tunisian Victory* (45) (doc.); *Burma Victory* (47) (doc.); *The Magic Box* (51); *Single-handed* (54); *Private's Progress* (56); *Run For The Sun* (57); *Brothers In Law* (57); *I'm All Right Jack* (59); *Lucky Jim* (63); *Twisted Nerve* (68); *There's A Girl In My Soup* (73)

Bourvil

A much-loved comedian who changed his name from André Raimbourg to that of the town, Bourville, in which he had been brought up (in a delightful and typically French tribute to his rural roots), Bourvil had become something of a national treasure by the time of his death at the age of fifty-three in 1970. He was that rare thing, a comedian who could handle both the tragic and the slapstick elements inherent in all great comedy. His greatest success came in Gérard Oury's *La Grande Vadrouille* (66), in which he, Terry-Thomas and the great **Louis de Funès** play British pilots (!) escaping from the predictably demented Boches. Bourvil's best performance, however, came in another Gérard Oury story, this time directed by André Cayette, the considerably more downbeat *Le Miroir A Deux Faces* (58), which was later lamentably remade by a narcissistic **Barbra Streisand**, who had most emphatically not learned the lessons of the original.

OTHER KEY FILMS: *La Ferme Du Pendu* (45); *Les Trois Mousquetaires* (53); *Les Misérables* (58); *Un Drôle De Dimanche* (58); *Le Bossu* (59); *Le Corniaud* (65); *Les Grandes Gueules* (65); *L'Étalon* (70)

Bow, Clara

A rather tragic figure in retrospect, Bow, at the height of her brief fame, was known as Elinor Glyn's 'It' girl, and seemed to have the world at her feet, but fame, and the gradual loss of it after the advent of sound had cramped her style and highlighted her brassy accent, served to undermine her already fragile (and possibly inherited) mental state, and she spent a large part of her later life confined to various institutions. A direct precursor of such tragic goddesses of the screen as **Jean Harlow** and **Marilyn Monroe**, the best of Bow's films span the period 1927-9 (the run-up to the Great Depression, in other words) and parallel, by an awful sort of morphology, Bow's later descent into her own depressive cycle.

KEY FILMS: *It* (27); *Children Of Divorce* (27); *Wings* (27); *Red Hair* (28); *The Wild Party* (29); *The Saturday Night Kid* (29)

Box Office

Euphemism for a star's potential to return on outlay – he or she is either good or bad 'box office', in other words. The expression refers to the booth at the entrance to a cinema where the money is taken.

Box Office Receipts

The total gross amount taken from punters at all participating cinema box offices during the screen life of a film.

Boyer, Charles

Smoothly romantic star and heart-throb for nearly three separate generations of women, Boyer's magnetic powers of attraction may seem a little hard to understand now – but given a small amount of insight and an even smaller capacity for retrospective empathy, it becomes clear that Boyer represented the apparently opposing paradoxes of passion and security for his female audience, and that this otherwise quite unrealistic (and therefore quintessentially filmic) equation was something that the philosophically inclined Boyer instinctively understood and chose to make his own. Following a career permeated with lightness, professionalism and charm, Boyer died tragically, by his own hand, just two days after the death of his beloved wife, Pat, and thirteen years following the death by suicide of their only son, Michael.

KEY FILMS: *Le Capitaine Fracasse* (27); *L'Epervier* (33); *Liliom* (33); *Shanghai* (35); *Mayerling* (36); *The Garden Of Allah* (36); *Conquest* (37); *Orage* (37); *Algiers* (38); *All This And Heaven Too* (40); *Back Street* (41); *The Constant Nymph* (43); *Gaslight* (44); *Madame De…* (53); *Nana* (55); *La Parisienne* (57); *Stavisky* (74)

Brackett, Charles

Renowned for his inspired collaboration with **Billy Wilder** on *The Major And The Minor* (42), *Five Graves To Cairo* (43), *The Lost Weekend* (45), *The Emperor Waltz* (48) and *Sunset Boulevard* (50), the near-miraculous Brackett also collaborated on the scripts, or provided the storylines for, **Ernst Lubitsch's** *Ninotchka* (39), **Howard Hawks's** *Ball Of Fire* (42) and **Henry Hathaway's** *Niagara* (53). Hot diggety-dog! How many of the more-lauded, super-cosseted and better-paid directors who traditionally steal a screenwriter's thunder can match that sort of career tally? And look at the following – not a clinker amongst them.

OTHER KEY FILMS: Robert Z Leonard's *Piccadilly Jim* (37); Ernst Lubitsch's *Bluebeard's Eighth Wife* (38); Theodore Reed's *What A Life* (39); Mitchell Leisen's *To Each His Own* (46); **Jean Negulesco's** *Titanic* (53)

Branagh, Kenneth

Something of a multi-talented wunderkind who was raised so high after his initial successes on the stage, on the road, on television, and with his first motion picture – *Henry V* (89) – that it was almost inevitable that a *Frankenstein* (94), or something very much like it, would come along to melt or pare his wings. The fact remains that Branagh is a cultured bringer-together, a leader and galvaniser of men and women, and that this particular talent is in such short supply at the moment that to carp at his occasional excesses is tantamount to wishing that the literate part of the British film industry commit *seppuku* with a rusty dagger. Long may he continue striving on his, and our, behalf.

OTHER KEY FILMS: *Dead Again* (91); *Peter's Friends* (92); *Much Ado About Nothing* (93); *A Midwinter's Tale* (95); *Hamlet* (96); *Love's Labour's Lost* (00)

Brandauer, Klaus Maria

A consummate actor and manipulator of the screen, Brandauer is capable of the tricky feat of making us disapprove of the character he is playing while still liking the man who is playing him, thus providing the audience with a pretty moral conundrum indeed. Most notable along these lines was Brandauer's Baron Blor Blixen-Finecke in **Sidney Pollack's** *Out Of Africa* (85), who, despite giving **Meryl Streep** syphilis, ruining her and then running out on her – not necessarily in that order – remained so much more sympathetic and believable than the two main protagonists in the film that one found oneself cheering him on

during each separate perfidy. Brandauer had previously managed a similar trick, as the baddie, Largo, in Irvin Kershner's **James Bond** outing *Never Say Never Again* (83), and one is left with the feeling that were Brandauer ever to put himself forward as a benevolent dictator, in, say, his native Austria, he might have a darned good chance of snatching the job from under the noses of any notionally democratic opposition.

OTHER KEY FILMS: *Mephisto* (81); *Colonel Redl* (86); *Streets Of Gold* (86); *Hanussen* (88); *The French Revolution* (89); *The Russia House* (90); *White Fang* (91); *Mario And The Magician* (94); *Rembrandt* (99); *Dykaren* (00); *Vercingétorix* (01); *Jedermanns Fest* (01)

Brando, Marlon

A master of **Method Acting**, Brando cemented his screen career with three films in three years directed by **Elia Kazan** – *A Streetcar Named Desire* (51), *Viva Zapata* (52) and *On The Waterfront* (54). In 1953 he took a brief break from Kazan and starred as Mark Antony in **Joseph L Mankiewicz's** critically acclaimed *Julius Caesar*. Brando directed his own extraordinary first feature, *One-Eyed Jacks*, in 1961, but from then onwards his career has varied enormously. Later highlights include **Gillo Pontecorvo's** *Burn!* (70), **Francis Ford Coppola's** *The Godfather* (72) and *Apocalypse Now* (79), and a phenomenal performance as Paul, in **Bernardo Bertolucci's** *Last Tango in Paris* (72), in which he single-handedly extended the possibilities of screen acting.

OTHER KEY FILMS: *The Men* (50); *The Wild One* (54); *Guys And Dolls* (55); *Teahouse Of The August Moon* (56); *The Young Lions* (58); *The Fugitive Kind* (60); *Mutiny On The Bounty* (62); *The Chase* (66); *Reflections In A Golden Eye* (67); *The Missouri Breaks* (73); *A Dry White Season* (89); *Don Juan DeMarco* (95); *The Island Of Dr Moreau* (96); *The Brave* (97); *Free Money* (98); *The Score* (01)

KEY LINES:

'You don't understand. I could've had class. I could've been a contender. I could've been somebody…instead of a bum, which is what I am.' [*On The Waterfront*]

'An actor's a guy who, if you ain't talking about him, ain't listening.' [Brando on actors]

'The horror! The horror!' [*Apocalypse Now*]

'He has enormous regard for people who do useful things in the world. He thinks in some part of his soul that acting is silly. He has a kind of contempt for it. He considers it game-playing and trickery.' [Stewart Stern, who scripted George H Englund's *The Ugly American* (63), on Brando]

Marlon Brando as the brutish Stanley Kowalski, in Elia Kazan's A Streetcar Named Desire *(51). See further image at Edward Dmytryk.*

Brasseur, Pierre

Brasseur was a vastly impressive all-rounder, combining a forty-five-year film career with some exalted stage performances, the writing of numerous plays and the reputation of being a more than passable poet – the sort of civilised Renaissance man, in other words, the cinema so rarely throws up nowadays, except, perhaps, in the person of a **John Sayles** or a **Peter Bogdanovich**. Brasseur made his mark playing the vicious and cowardly little hood in **Marcel Carné's** quasi-nihilistic *Quai Des Brumes* (38) who ends the film by gunning down hero/anti-hero **Jean Gabin** from a passing car. The quality of many of the films Brasseur appeared in was astonishing, and he never let down either his directors or the screenwriters (particularly **Jacques Prévert**) who so adored writing for his elusive, ironical voice. His greatest screen performance came, not surprisingly, as Frédérick Lemâitre in Carné's miraculous *Les Enfants Du Paradis* (45).

OTHER KEY FILMS: *Les Deux Timides* (25); *La Fille De L'Eau* (25); *Quick* (32); *Pattes De Mouche* (36); *Les Portes De La Nuit* (46); *Les Amants De Vérone* (48); *Les Mains Sales* (51); *Barbe-Bleue* (51); *La Tour De Nèsle* (54); *Oasis* (54); *La Tête Contre Les Murs* (58); *La Loi* (58); *Vive L'Amour* (61); *King Of Hearts* (66)

Breakaway Prop

Purposely weak piece of prop furniture designed to shatter when fallen on or hit, preferably without injuring the actors – thus 'breakaway' glass, or a 'breakaway' bar stool.

Breakdown Script

The essential tool which allows a director to schedule shooting effectively and economically, and which consists of a total breakdown (by the assistant director) of any and every effect, prop, location, part-time actor, etc., into a sensible sequence, and which takes into account convenience and availability rather than any spurious notion of real-time filming.

Breathing

What happens when a piece of film buckles or gets caught up in the projector's gate, causing a blurring or fluttering effect on the screen.

Brennan, Walter

Winner of no less than three supporting actor **Oscars**, for **William Wyler's** *Come And Get It!* (36), David Butler's *Kentucky* (38), and Wyler's *The Westerner* (40), Brennan is the most famous character actor of them all, and his magnificent string of

performances in **Howard Hawks's** *To Have And Have Not* (45), where he played **Humphrey Bogart's** gimpy drunk companion Eddie, in **John Ford's** *My Darling Clementine* (46), as the evil Clanton paterfamilias, and in his supreme comic turn as **John Wayne's** crusty sidekick, Stumpy, in Hawks's sublime and still stubbornly underrated *Rio Bravo* (59), is surely more than enough to ensure Brennan's eternal seat in the great movie house in the sky.

OTHER KEY FILMS: *Bride Of Frankenstein* (35); *Barbary Coast* (35); *The Three Godfathers* (36); *Fury* (36); *The Adventures Of Tom Sawyer* (38); *Sergeant York* (41); *Swamp Water* (41); *Hangmen Also Die* (43); *Driftwood* (47); *Best Of The Badmen* (51); *Bad Day At Black Rock* (55); *The Proud Ones* (56)

KEY LINES:

'Say? Was you ever bit by a dead bee?' [Brennan to **Lauren Bacall** in *To Have And Have Not*]

'Drinking don't bother my memory. If it did, I wouldn't drink. I couldn't. I'd forget how good it was. Then where'd I be? Start drinking water again.' [*To Have And Have Not*]

Bresson, Robert

Watching any film by Robert Bresson is an experience so distinct from watching a film by any other director that one is forced to review one's expectations of the cinema accordingly. Bresson is a filmmaker of such awesome seriousness and integrity that one sometimes feels as if invited into the garden of a monastery, there to contemplate the human soul in an environment devoted to the noumenal and scrupulously detached from material things. Disdaining 'acting' per se, he uses faces, sounds, images and music, to highlight his search for some elusive truth to which he alone appears to hold the key – there are moments in his films that are so sublimely honest that one stands aghast at the triviality of much of one's normal filmic diet of pap, expediency, and *folie de grandeur*. Yes, there is a place for entertainment and joy and silliness, but there must also be one for art, and Bresson, **Jean Renoir**, **Ingmar Bergman**, and a bare few others remind us of our responsibilities and our humanity, and warn us that we trivialise the transformative power of faith and of exalted emotions at our peril.

See **Heartstopping Moments**

KEY FILMS: *Les Anges Du Péché* (43); *Les Dames Du Bois De Boulogne* (45); *Le Journal D'Un Curé De Campagne* (50); *Un Condamné À Mort S'Est Échappé* (56); *Pickpocket* (59); *Le Procès De Jeanne D'Arc* (62); *Au Hasard, Balthazar* (66); *Mouchette* (67); *Une Femme Douce* (69); *Quatre Nuits D'Un Rêveur* (71); *Lancelot Du Lac* (74); *Le Diable Probablement* (77); *L'Argent* (83)

Bridge

An incidental piece of music used to elide scenes in a movie.

Bridges, Jeff

Bridges was one of the best young actors of the 1970s and 1980s, appearing in one great movie after another, and then, for some reason, he went mainstream on us and the power of his performances tailed off, along with his youth, until he became merely a good working actor, and not the edgy and slightly dangerous presence he had been in his early prime. Still, his prime was enough (and more than many lesser talents ever had), and he gave outstanding performances as the lost young Texan, Duane Jackson, in **Peter Bogdanovich's** *The Last Picture Show* (71); as the young but fatally untalented boxing hopeful, Ernie Munger, in **John Huston's** magnificent film about losers, *Fat City* (72); as Lightfoot, the crazy boy **Clint Eastwood** takes under his wing only to see him die like a moth in a candle flame, in **Michael Cimino's** superb comedy thriller *Thunderbolt And Lightfoot* (74); and as Richard Bone in **Ivan Passer's** *Cutter's Way* (81), a man with no ambitions and no convictions who nonetheless ends up by rising to the quality of his friendships. These are great films and great performances by any standards, and there are more. In fact, Bridges remains the unsung hero of post-1960s melancholia, and his place in any discriminating viewer's movie pantheon is assured.

OTHER KEY FILMS: *Bad Company* (72); *The Last American Hero* (73); *Hearts Of The West* (75); *Stay Hungry* (76); *Winter Kills* (79); *Against All Odds* (84); *Starman* (84); *Jagged Edge* (85); *Tucker: The Man And His Dream* (88); *The Fabulous Baker Boys* (89); *The Vanishing* (93); *Wild Bill* (95); *White Squall* (96); *The Mirror Has Two Faces* (96); *The Big Lebowski* (98); *Arlington Road* (99); *The Muse* (99); *Simpatico* (99); *The Contender* (00)

Bridging Shot

A **montage** or similar sequence which suggests time passing, and which is used to connect one scene to another, e.g. the spinning hands of a clock, dated newspaper cover pages, the burgeoning and gentle fall of leaves.

British Film Academy

The British equivalent of the **American Film Institute**, the BFA was founded in 1946 for the declared purpose of advancing the cause of film in any and every way possible. It amalgamated in 1959 with the Society of Film And Television Arts.

British Film Institute

See **BFI**

British Lion

British Lion Film Corporation was founded in 1927, but was taken over in 1946 by **Alexander Korda**, who coveted British Lion's Shepperton Studio lot. Most of the great British moviemakers passed through its 'virtual' portals at one time or another.

Broadside

Large-bodied floodlight giving generalised light on a closed set.

Bronson, Charles

Bronson had one of the finest natural physiques ever seen on an actor, a gift (if that is the right word) from his years working down the Lithuanian coalmines. How such a man, from such a place, should ever have managed to reach the heady heights of Hollywood stardom is a story that almost makes one believe that the streets of the United States are indeed paved with gold. Bronson's greatest success, however, has always been in Europe, with European audiences, and his late flowering (he was almost fifty when he really hit the big time) is a tribute to his guts and staying power. His epiphany – when, briefly, he attained a quasi-mythological status in Italy and France – came with **Sergio Leone's** *Once Upon A Time In The West* (68), where his craggy, lived-in features seemed to suggest, in purely visual terms, of course (something which Leone, of all people, understood), the neutral, desiccated, almost sterile air of the great deserts of the American West.

OTHER KEY FILMS: *The Magnificent Seven* (60); *The Great Escape* (63); *The Dirty Dozen* (67); *Soleil Rouge* (71); *The Valachi Papers* (72); *Chato's Land* (72); *The Stone Killer* (73); *Death Wish* (74); *The White Buffalo* (77); *The Indian Runner* (91); *Death Wish V: The Face Of Death* (94)

Brooks, Louise

Brooks's star shone briefly in **G W Pabst's** *Pandora's Box* (29) and *Diary Of A Lost Girl* (29), and then again in the late 1950s and early 1960s when she was 'rediscovered' by film curator James Card, her pageboy bob and kohl-encircled eyes looming from a multitude of fresh posters and stills. But her star faded just as abruptly second time around, leaving the remainder of her life to be spent chasing the furtive image of that rekindled moment, or trying, in vain, to recreate a magic that

Louise Brooks –
pageboy bob, phallic
sets, elusive gaze and all

Young Frankenstein (74) amused by virtue of its skilful rehashing of music-hall and silent film conventions (but the fans were still having to stretch to keep their boy in contention). But that first brief spurt of originality seemed to have hamstrung its director, and with each post-1974 film he sank lower and lower down the scale, until his most recent films resemble a series of strung-together gags distilled from a how-to book for TV, rather than motion picture entities with some residual purpose beyond the simple fact that they might make money. It's a tragedy, really, and one returns to *The Producers* time and again as if to the work of some long-lost comic genius too modest and self-effacing to have ever thought of travestying himself.

OTHER KEY FILMS: *Silent Movie* (76); *High Anxiety* (77); *History Of The World Part One* (81); *To Be Or Not To Be* (83); *Spaceballs* (87); *Life Stinks* (91); *Robin Hood: Men In Tights* (93); *Dracula: Dead And Loving It* (95)

KEY LINE:
'Will the dancing Hitlers please wait in the wings! We are only seeing singing Hitlers.' [*The Producers*]

47

Brooks, Richard

A screenwriter turned director (akin, one supposes, to a poacher turned gamekeeper), Brooks made an impressive sequence of literate, high-quality films during the late 1950s and 1960s, including *Cat On A Hot Tin Roof* (58), *Elmer Gantry* (60), *Lord Jim* (65) and *In Cold Blood* (67). Each one was an adaptation of an existing work, and each one retained just the faintest trace of a Classics Illustrated approach, as if Brooks never expected the readers of the original works to bother turning up at the cinema. This is not to say that he wasn't a good director – for he was far more skilful, and brought far better material to the screen than most of his contemporaries – but merely that his work seemed to lack the spark of greatness which great adaptations need. His treatment of Truman Capote's bestselling novel *In Cold Blood* came closest, but one wonders how much of its effect relied on Conrad Hall's exquisite photography, which included the famous shot of droplets of rain streaming down a cell window and reflecting off killer Perry Smith's gut-stricken face as if they were tears.

OTHER KEY FILMS: *Deadline USA* (52); *The Blackboard Jungle* (55); *The Last Hunt* (56); *The Brothers Karamazov* (58); *Sweet Bird Of Youth* (62); *The Professionals* (66); *Looking For Mr Goodbar* (77); *Wrong Is Right* (82); *Fever Pitch* (85)

was as elusive as she, in the end, turned out to be. In the final analysis it was what Pabst made of her that counted, as if she were a canvas hewn from human skin for him to paint on, and it was this sad and bitter paradox that so swiftly, and so completely, brought her down.

OTHER KEY FILMS: *A Girl In Every Port* (28); *Beggars Of Life* (28); *Prix De Beauté* (30)

Brooks, Mel

Brooks made one of the funniest films in cinema history with *The Producers* (68) – inventive, acute, flamboyant and anarchic, his seemed a genuinely original voice at a time when cinema comedy had hit the post-TV doldrums. *Blazing Saddles* (74) was brasher and more obvious but still more or less on target (his fans said charitably) and the splendid

KEY LINES:

'The images come first, and with images, like music, the primary reaction is emotional…the effect has to be orchestral.' [Brooks on film]

'As long as it has that element in it that you can recognise in yourself, as long as it has a pinch of the truth in it – terrific!' [Brooks, on watching **Gary Cooper** movies in the Cambodian jungle, during the filming of *Lord Jim* (65)]

'There's only one real word of advice I have to give you. If you ever do make this into a movie, make a movie, don't make a book.' [Author Sinclair Lewis to writer/director Richard Brooks before the making of *Elmer Gantry* (60)]

Brosnan, Pierce

Better-looking and better-preserved than any man his age (he was born in 1953) has any right to be, Brosnan made a suave and believable James Bond in Martin Campbell's *Goldeneye* (95), Roger Spottiswoode's *Tomorrow Never Dies* (97) and **Michael Apted's** *The World Is Not Enough* (99), and a convincingly heroic figure in Roger Donaldson's *Dante's Peak* (96) and John McTiernan's *The Thomas Crown Affair* (99). His career has had a gentle lift-off, and his best part, before Bond rocketed him (briefly?) into the stratosphere, was as the cold-blooded Russian operative in John Mackenzie's *The Fourth Protocol* (87), an impressively tight, old-fashioned little thriller, and none the worse for that. Come to think of it, Brosnan is a rather old-fashioned sort of a star, and it's a fair bet that he will show considerably more staying power, in consequence, than many of the brasher, rasher, younger generation of rivals snapping at his heels, as his recent 'outing' as a closet light comedian, in **John Boorman's** *The Tailor Of Panama* (01), so persuasively suggests.
OTHER KEY FILMS: *The Long Good Friday* (80); *Mister Johnson* (90); *The Lawnmower Man* (92); *Mrs Doubtfire* (93); *Love Affair* (94); *The Mirror Has Two Faces* (96); *Grey Owl* (99); *Blood And Champagne* (01)

Brown, Joe E

Brown doesn't really merit a place here, but he's getting one because he was utterly brilliant in **Billy Wilder's** *Some Like It Hot* (59), where he played spoiled but soft-hearted multi-millionaire Osgood E. Fielding III, to **Jack Lemmon's** Jerry/Josephine. Osgood is the sort of man that everyone would like to have as a favourite uncle, and it takes genius, of a certain sort, to create such an enduring and much-beloved archetype.
OTHER KEY FILMS: *Song Of The West* (30); *The Tenderfoot* (32); *A Midsummer Night's Dream* (35); *Chatterbox* (43); *The Tender Years* (47); *Show Boat* (51); *Around The World In Eighty Days* (56); *It's A Mad Mad Mad Mad World* (63)
KEY LINE:
Jerry: 'We can't get married at all. I'm a man.' Osgood: 'Well. Nobody's perfect.' [*Some Like It Hot*]

Browning, Tod

The one work for which Browning is really known outside the quasi-Masonic and rarefied world of the film critic and theorist is his 1932 production *Freaks*. The principal reason for its fame may well lie in the fact that it was banned, and banning inevitably creates interest – but the true reason for its success is far subtler than that, and relies as much on Browning's early experiences as a circus entertainer as it does on the instinctive insights the film contains on the consequences of judging a thing or a person simply by their appearance. No film has ever brought this subject home with greater force, and *Freaks*, which would be virtually unfilmable today because of its non-politically correct subject matter, remains, to all intents and purposes, unique.
OTHER KEY FILMS: *The Unholy Three* (25); *The Unknown* (27); *The Thirteenth Chair* (29); **Dracula** (31); *The Iron Man* (32); *Mark Of The Vampire* (35); *The Devil Doll* (36)

Brute

The king of studio lamps, blasting out 10,000 watts of raw white light through a four-foot-wide lens.

Brynner, Yul

It's a little hard to fathom the extent of Brynner's screen success, inasmuch as the polished old chestnut (whoops) of women finding bald men irresistible because of their enhanced testosterone count could not possibly have applied to him, as Brynner shaved, rather than lost, his hair. Something of a one-track actor, Brynner could glower with the best of them, and his rugged and deeply masculine Siberian/Russian voice (at least one presumes it was Siberian/Russian, for Brynner was extremely vague about his antecedents) had a certain rough charm. But the real rub comes when one compares roles and actors. Take Brynner's Chris, the boss in **John Sturges's** *The Magnificent Seven* (60), then match it against Takashi Shimura's Kambei (exactly the same role) in **Akira Kurosawa's** *The Seven Samurai* (54). Well? Shimura suggested the veteran soldier's tiredness, his feeling for duty, his sense of fun and his noble soul – Brynner simply suggested Chris's eagerness to be at the enemy, and a certain simpering complicity in the various neuroses of his companions.

OTHER KEY FILMS: *The King And I* (56); *The Buccaneer* (58); *The Sound And The Fury* (59); *Le Testament D'Orphée* (60); *Taras Bulba* (62); *Villa Rides* (68); *The Madwoman Of Chaillot* (69); *Westworld* (73)

BSC

The letters **BSC** are the acronym for the British Society of Cinematographers.

Bugs Bunny

The most famous cartoon character *not* to come out of the **Disney** studios, the Brooklyn-accented, carrot-chomping rabbit first appeared in *Porky's Hare Hunt* (38), in the temporary guise of, you've guessed it, a hare!

OTHER KEY FILMS: *Who Framed Roger Rabbit* (88)

Bullet Hit

Small explosive device used to mimic the sound of a bullet striking flesh.

Bullock, Sandra

What to say? Daughter of a German opera singer, Bullock's best part to date has come in Randa Haines's *Wrestling Ernest Hemingway* (93) which thankfully predated her instant but undeserved leap to fame in Jan De Bont's *Speed* (94), allowing us to consider, for a moment, the perfectly acceptable actress she might have become had not celebrity and Hollywood hoopla clouded the issue.

OTHER KEY FILMS: *Demolition Man* (93); *The Net* (95); *A Time To Kill* (96); *In Love And War* (96); *Practical Magic* (98); *Forces Of Nature* (99); *28 Days* (00); *Gun Shy* (00); *Miss Congeniality* (00); *Exactly 3:30* (01)

Buñuel, Luis

It would be naïve to call Buñuel predominantly a surrealist, just as it would be false to call his early collaborator, Salvador Dalí, principally a painter – both were concerned with appearances, how little they matter, and how much fun they are to suborn. A comedian of anarchy, Buñuel turned any project he was given (or chose to take) into yet another facet of an all-consuming vision in which the Church, the middle classes, the worthy and the dull became fodder for his explosive visions. He despised the cinema of 'effect', and

chose to tell his stories and illustrate his themes in as uncomplicated a way as possible – but the depth of thought behind each image always comes through, and at his best, in *Los Olvidados* (50), *The Adventures Of Robinson Crusoe* (52), *Viridiana* (61), *The Exterminating Angel* (62), *Tristana* (70) and *The Discreet Charm Of The Bourgeoisie* (72), Buñuel reached a sort of paradoxical, because atheistic, sanctity.

OTHER KEY FILMS: *Un Chien Andalou* (28); *L'Age D'Or* (30); *Mexican Bus Ride* (51); *Wuthering Heights* (53); *The River And Death* (54); *The Criminal Life Of Archibaldo De La Cruz* (55); *Nazarin* (59); *Le Journal D'Une Femme De Chambre* (64); *Simon Of The Desert* (65); *Belle De Jour* (67); *That Obscure Object Of Desire* (77)

KEY LINE:
'Thanks to God, I am still an atheist.' [Buñuel on faith]

Burnett, W R

Either co-screenwriter, original novelist or story consultant on **Mervyn LeRoy's** *Little Caesar* (30), **Raoul Walsh's** *High Sierra* (41) and **John Huston's** *The Asphalt Jungle* (50), Burnett, though a gentle, non-violent man himself, understood the gangster mind wonderfully well, and has heavily influenced just about everybody (including **Quentin Tarantino** and **Martin Scorsese**) who has attempted the genre since. An inveterate gambler who succeeded in virtually bankrupting himself on more than one occasion, Burnett was effectively forgotten by the time of his death in 1982, having, himself, become the 'outsider' character he always depicted so well.

OTHER KEY FILMS: **Howard Hawks's** *Scarface: Shame Of A Nation* (32); Stuart Heisler's *I Died A Thousand Times* (56); **John Sturges's** *The Great Escape* (63)

KEY LINE:
'You're born, you're gonna have trouble, and you're gonna die. That you know. There's not much else you know.' [Burnett on life, living, and the pursuit of sapience]

Burnt Up

An overexposed piece of film that unwittingly suggests a burnt effect.

Burton, Richard

Together with **Robert Donat**, Burton was the screen actor with the finest speaking voice in the business, as is amply demonstrated in his definitive recordings of the poetry of Dylan Thomas. At his

Richard Burton, with attitude, on the set of Bob McNaught's Sea Wife *(57), in which he played the role of Biscuit*

best (and when he wasn't coasting along in blandly commercial film vehicles) Burton could electrify the screen more effectively even than **Marlon Brando**. He gave a magisterially self-referential performance as the drunken, railing, despairing unfrocked priest, the Reverend T Lawrence Shannon, in **John Huston's** *The Night Of The Iguana* (64), for unfortunately alcohol, and a fine, but ultimately underused intellect, were Burton's twin crosses in life. His readings in Donald Brittain and John Kramer's magnificent *Volcano: An Inquiry Into The Life And Death Of Malcolm Lowry* (76) showed what was lost when he didn't get to play the once-in-a-lifetime role of Lowry's alter ego, Geoffrey Firmin, in Huston's *Under The Volcano* (84).

OTHER KEY FILMS: *My Cousin Rachel* (52); *Bitter Victory* (57); *Look Back In Anger* (58); *Becket* (64); *The Spy Who Came In From The Cold* (65); *Who's Afraid Of Virginia Woolf* (66); *Where Eagles Dare* (69); *Villain* (71); *Under Milk Wood* (73); *1984* (84)

Burton, Tim

Burton has becoming something of a one-man cult, and deservedly so, for he brought a new, albeit Gothically inclined look to a 1980s commercial cinema in need of something (anything!) to redeem it from creeping mediocrity. *Batman* (89) was as good as it should have been thanks to Burton's genuine comic-book vision of a subject that lingers in the souls of most grown-up male children – call it the subliminal wish to be a hero if you like – and it is Burton's particular strength that he understands the child inherent in the man and caters to it, while bringing a demonstrably adult understanding and skill to the construction of his creations. *Edward Scissorhands* (90) was enormous fun, and *The Nightmare Before Christmas* (93) was a genuinely original slant on an overused, and for the most part under-imaginative, genre.

OTHER KEY FILMS: *Pee-Wee's Big Adventure* (85); *Beetlejuice* (88); *Batman Returns* (92); *Ed Wood* (94); *Mars Attacks!* (96); *The Legend Of Sleepy Hollow* (99); *Planet Of The Apes* (01)

Buscemi, Steve

Marvellously offbeat character actor whose scene-stealing turns in **Quentin Tarantino's** *Reservoir Dogs* (91) and **Joel** and **Ethan Coen's** *Fargo* (96) were enough to guarantee him cult status with those viewers who weren't aware of the cult status he already enjoyed thanks to his theatrical forays and appearances in independent, non-mainstream films. He benefits from a curiously memorable face which he uses as if it were a glove puppet, galvanising its features and eyes until the viewer either laughs, gives in, or in the case of his inept crook, Carl Showalter, in *Fargo*, runs.

OTHER KEY FILMS: *Parting Glances* (86); *Coffee And Cigarettes Part Two* (88); *Mystery Train* (89); *New York Stories* (89); *Miller's Crossing* (90); *Zandalee* (91); *The Hudsucker Proxy* (94); *Things To Do In Denver When You're Dead* (95); *Kansas City* (96); *Trees Lounge* [also dir.] (96); *Con Air* (97); *The Big Lebowski* (98); *28 Days* (00); *The Animal Factory* [also dir.] (00); *Double Whammy* (01)

Busch, Niven

Busch either co-scripted, wrote the original novel or provided the story for **Henry King's** *In Old Chicago* (38), **William Wyler's** *The Westerner* (40), Tay Garnett's *The Postman Always Rings Twice* (46), **King Vidor's** *Duel In The Sun* (47) and Raoul Walsh's *Pursued* (47), which adds up to a pretty good career, even if, unlike that of most directors and actors, it is far more difficult to pin down. An inveterate field sportsman and rancher, Busch really understood his subject, and this knowledge comes through in both his novels and the screenplays he was so often called upon to make of them.

OTHER KEY FILMS: Anthony Mann's *The Furies* (50); **John Sturges's** *The Capture* (50); Raoul Walsh's *Distant Drums* (51)

Business

Euphemism for any trick, tic, movement or expression an actor or actress uses to enhance their playing of a role.

Bust Shot

Close-up shot of an actor's torso and face, so that the view of what Fats Waller called the 'pedal extremities' is blocked.

Butterfly Scrim

Invisible screen in the shape of a butterfly which is used to dilute the effect of light on an actor or other stationary object on the set.

Buyer

The filmic equivalent of a prisoner-of-war camp scrounger, responsible for the provision of anything and everything needed on a film set in the way of props and costumes.

Buzz Track

Pre-recorded background noise that is only mixed into the action in the editing room.

Byrne, Gabriel

A dark, cerebral actor, whose features often suggest more than one might infer simply from his capacities as an actor, Byrne's career got off to a relatively late start (he was thirty-one) in **John Boorman's** *Excalibur* (81), in which he played a quick-tempered and utterly self-destructive Uther Pendragon. The image he often portrays on screen is a curious one, as full of apparent lethargy as a lion before the sudden, flashing movement that means death (in other words he hasn't ever been used as effectively as he might have been) and one looks to nuances in **Joel and Ethan Coen's** *Miller's Crossing* (90), Mike Newell's *Into The West* (93) and Bryan Singer's *The Usual Suspects* (95) to suggest a new and possibly more fruitful direction for this rather oddball actor to take.

OTHER KEY FILMS: *Defence Of The Realm* (86); *Gothic* (86); *A Soldier's Tale* (88); *The End Of Violence* (97); *Smilla's Feeling For Snow* (97); *This Is The Sea* (98); *The Man In The Iron Mask* (98); *Enemy Of The State* (98); *Stigmata* (99); *End Of Days* (99); *Canone Inverso – Making Love* (00)

CAA

Acronym for the Creative Artists Agency, a major Hollywood talent agency that specialises in the promotion and marketing of creative and commercial talent in both cinema and television. See **ICM**

Caan, James

Caan is a throwback to the great character actors of the 1930s and 1940s, and his screen career has been marked more by opportunities missed than by openings taken. He has never really been able to carry a movie on his own, being by nature more of a team player, although, paradoxically, many of his best performances have been as loners. He was the youth in the funny cowboy hat in **Howard Hawks's** *El Dorado* (67) (an excellent remake of Hawks's own *Rio Bravo* (59)), and then the vivacious, extreme-living Sonny in **Francis Ford Coppola's** *The Godfather* (72). Weightier parts came and went, most notably with Michael Mann's *Thief* (81), but it seemed that Caan had been sidelined forever. He spent five years away from the screen between 1982 and 1987, but returned, impressively, in Coppola's *Gardens Of Stone* (87), triumphantly in Rob Reiner's *Misery* (90), sinisterly in Steve Kloves's excellent but ultimately flawed *Flesh And Bone* (93). Now Caan hovers (contentedly, one supposes) just outside the normal lanes of the Hollywood mainstream, like an injured rogue shark waiting for the occasional picking from rich passing ships.

OTHER KEY FILMS: *The Rain People* (69); *Rabbit, Run* (70); *Freebie And The Bean* (74); *The Gambler* (74); *The Killer Elite* (75); *Rollerball* (75); *Comes A Horseman* (78); *Alien Nation* (88); *Dick Tracy* (90); *Things To Do In Denver When You're Dead* (95); *Mickey Blue Eyes* (99); *The Way Of The Gun* (00); *Viva Las Nowhere* (00)

KEY LINE:
'I play in order to lose. That's what gets my juices going.' [**Karel Reisz's** *The Gambler*]

Cableman

Member of the film crew in charge of all forms of cable handling, both for sound machinery, fixed and mobile cameras.

Cage, Nicolas

Cage is one of the most interesting of the current crop of Hollywood leading men, largely because he cut his teeth on independent and off-beat movies before graduating to the blockbusters he now appears in with such deadening regularity. A nephew of **Francis Ford Coppola** (a status which doubtless helped him in the early stages of his career but which has since been transcended by his talent), Cage's best roles came before his multi-million-dollar leap to superstardom, and include **Alan Parker's** *Birdy* (84) as bewildered Vietnam vet Al Columbato, **Joel and Ethan Coen's** *Raising Arizona* (87) in which he played soft-hearted ex-hoodlum H I McDonough, **David Lynch's** *Wild At Heart* (90) in which his Sailor Ripley ran the gamut of emotions from dementia back to dementia again, and, best of all, Mike Figgis's *Leaving Las Vegas* (95), in which Cage was miraculously good as the demon-possessed Ben Sanderson who drinks himself to death, eyes open, in one final, nihilistic binge.

OTHER KEY FILMS: *Rumble Fish* (83); *Peggy Sue Got Married* (86); *Moonstruck* (87); *Honeymoon In Vegas* (92); *Red Rock West* (93); *The Rock* (96); *Con Air* (97); *Face/Off* (97); *Snake Eyes* (98); *Gone In Sixty Seconds* (00); *Family Man* (00); *Captain Corelli's Mandolin* (01)

Cagney, James

Cagney was the best at what he did, and what he did was unique and virtually unintelligible to those who had never seen him on screen. He was mannered, small, ugly and obstreperous, and he was also elegant, witty, quick-witted and often beautiful in movement and design. How to explain him? Only through his films, which failed, thank God, to harness the energy of this half-Norwegian, half-Irish walking, darting – even singing and dancing, in **Michael Curtiz's** *Yankee Doodle Dandy* (42) – idiosyncrasy. Only Hollywood could have produced him, and only **Warners** really knew how to use him, in such timeless movies as **William Wellman's** *The Public Enemy* (31), Curtiz's *Angels With Dirty Faces* (38), William Keighley's *Each Dawn I Die* (39) and **Raoul Walsh's** *The Roaring Twenties* (39). Perhaps his greatest mature role came in Walsh's *White Heat* (49), but he was as brilliant in comedy as he was in drama, and **Billy Wilder's** *One Two Three* (61) provided a suitable valedictory to his magnificent career. Note for Film Buffs: Catch Cagney, if you can, in his later and scandously underrated **Westerns**, such as **Nicholas Ray's** *Run For Cover* (55) and **Robert Wise's** *Tribute To A Bad Man* (56), and see for yourselves how Cagney brought humanity to a since often dehumanised genre.

OTHER KEY FILMS: *Blonde Crazy* (31); *Winner Take All* (32); *Hard To Handle* (33); *Footlight Parade* (33); *Jimmy The Gent* (34); *A Midsummer Night's Dream* (35); *Ceiling Zero* (36); *Blood In The Sun* (46); *Love Me Or Leave Me* (55); *Mister Roberts* (55); *Man Of A Thousand Faces* (57); *Shake Hands With The Devil* (59); *Ragtime* (81)

KEY LINE:
'Anyway, Ma, I made it… Top of the world!' [*White Heat*]

Cahiers Du Cinéma

André Bazin's critical film journal, founded in 1951, which paved the way for French **New Wave** directors **François Truffaut, Eric Rohmer,** Jacques Rivette, **Claude Chabrol** and **Jean-Luc Godard,** and which began France's long flirtation with the **Auteur Theory,** leading to a re-evaluation of such otherwise marginalised Hollywood directors as **John Ford, Nicholas Ray, Samuel Fuller** and **Edgar G Ulmer.**

Cain, James M

Pulp fiction writer and guru of *film noir*, Cain was also an amateur of music, and music and musical forms abound in his crime novels, his screenplays, and in the myriad authorised and unauthorised adaptations made from his stories. The best of the unauthorised borrowings was **Luchino Visconti's** *Ossessione* (42), which was based, more than merely closely, on Cain's novel *The Postman Always Rings Twice,* but which brought with it a particularly Italianate sense of doomed and earthy passion. Cain also co-scripted John Cromwell's headily romantic *Algiers* (38), and the sum of his novels that have been made into first-rate feature films is quite simply awe-inspiring – and this despite Cain's oft-repeated reservations about cinema's artistic potential.

OTHER KEY FILMS: John M Stahl's *When Tomorrow Comes* (39); **Billy Wilder's** *Double Indemnity* (44); **Michael Curtiz's** *Mildred Pierce* (45); Tay Garnett's *The Postman Always Rings Twice* (46); **Anthony Mann's** *Serenade* (56)
KEY LINE:
'Most pictures aren't worth seeing. Let's face it, the moving picture never did lick reality. Pictures don't go deep. If a girl has a pretty face, that's as far as the camera can look.' [Cain on the movies]

Caine, Michael

The newly knighted Caine is a cosy establishment figure now, which is hardly surprising since he started out as a conservatively inclined (though vaguely anarchic) working-class boy made good. He always seemed to know he would make it, and that serene confidence has been his best friend during his successful mainstream career. He was utterly convincing both as **Lewis Gilbert's** *Alfie* (66) and as Harry Palmer in Sidney J Furie's *The Ipcress File* (65), and despite **Oscar**-winning performances in **Woody Allen's** *Hannah And Her Sisters* (86) and Lasse Hallström's *The Cider House Rules* (99), some of Caine's best performances have come in lesser films, such as James Clavell's *The Last Valley* (71), or films where he has played second lead, as in **Bob Rafelson's** under-appreciated *Blood And Wine* (96). Caine was always good at comedy but better at coldness, and his most memorable roles have reflected this aspect of his persona, as the eponymous Jack Carter in Mike Hodges's *Get Carter* (71), and as Kurt Steiner, the disillusioned German Wehrmacht war hero in **John Sturges's** *The Eagle Has Landed* (77).

OTHER KEY FILMS: *Zulu* (64); *The Italian Job* (69); *Too Late The Hero* (70); *Sleuth* (72); *The Man Who Would Be King* (75); *California Suite* (78); *Dressed To Kill* (80); *Educating Rita* (83); *The Holcroft Covenant* (85); *Mona Lisa* (86); *The Fourth Protocol* (87); *Noises Off* (92); *Little Voice* (98); *Quills* (00); *Miss Congeniality* (00); *Last Orders* (00)

KEY LINE:
'Not a lot of people know that.' [Catchphrase attributed to Caine, but vehemently denied by the man himself]

Calibration

The markings used to indicate the changes of focus an **assistant cameraman** (focus puller) must make during a long camera shot, while his chief is left free to concentrate on the shot itself. Also the markings used in **animation** to indicate how far a figure or background must move during each frame.

Caligarisme

A French term that describes German **Expressionist** style as exemplified by **Robert Wiene's** *The Cabinet Of Dr Caligari* (19).

Call

The direct responsibility of the **assistant director**, call represents the crucial summoning of all film technicians and staff to be on set and prepared for work at a specific, pre-ordained time.

Cameo Role

A walk-on celebrity bit part in a film, usually credited, but occasionally conducted in an anonymous spirit of fun by a famous guest or friend of the director. Some directors enjoy making cameo appearances in their own films, often as the result of superstition or audience expectation – **Alfred Hitchcock**, for instance, popped up in over thirty of his films, and was eventually forced to time his manifestations for the earliest possible moment so that the audience could return their concentration to the plot. He had become, if you like, his very own **McGuffin**.

Cameo Shot

A shot designed to highlight the star and not the background.

Camera Angle

The extent to which the camera is tilted to suggest height, smallness, emotional perspective, neutrality, etc.

Camera, Hand-held

See **Hand-held Camera**

Camera Jam

What happens when the perforations on **film stock** either get out of **synch** or disengage, leading to a piling up, or jam of film, inside the camera.

Cameraman

The person in charge of operating a motion picture camera, usually under the direct supervision of the **cinematographer**, and for ensuring that the pre-ordained camera moves are carried out correctly.

Camera, Motion Picture

See **Motion Picture Camera**

Camera Movement

Static cameras were pretty much the name of the game until **F W Murnau's** *The Last Laugh* (24) showed American directors and **cinematographers** just what they'd been missing. Murnau freed the camera to move up and down stairs (even to follow and mimic the jerky peregrinations of a drunken man), and his influence, and that of his post-war German contemporaries, opened the floodgates to the sea of innovation during the 1930s and 1940s, which culminated in **Orson Welles's** famous two-minute opening shot in *Touch Of Evil* (58).

Camera Operator

Another name for a **cameraman**.

Camera Rehearsal

A camera dress rehearsal for a particular shot or scene, usually using **stand-ins** in place of the real stars or protagonists of the scene.

Camera Report

A report handed in at the end of the day by the **assistant cameraman** detailing that day's shoot. It usually includes the number of feet shot, the number of takes, and the **cinematographer's** recommendations as to which takes seemed the most successful from the floor.

Camera Right/Left

Instructions detailing which part of the frame is under discussion or which direction the camera must pan, always bearing in mind the fact that the camera sees a picture the way the audience sees it, and not as the actors see it. The expression is derived from the analogous theatrical term, stage right/left, the most famous example of which must be William Shakespeare's 'exit pursued by a bear' from *The Winter's Tale* – the direction is left to the director's discretion.

Camera Speed

Normal camera speed averages out at about 24 frames per second, dropping to 18 fps for the now rarely used Super 8 film; video cameras function at a slightly faster 25 fps. On certain cameras it is possible to adjust the speed while filming, giving slow-, or accelerated-motion effects. <u>Note for Film Buffs</u>: Cinema films run faster on TV (25 as opposed to 24 fps), giving a marginally shorter running time.

Caméra-Stylo

Alexandre Astruc invented this phrase in his 1948 piece 'Le Caméra Stylo', using it to equate the camera with a pen that the director then uses to write with his or her own unique signature, much as a painter will use a brush, or a sculptor a chisel. This concept then formed the basis for the later French **New Wave** idea of the director as autonomous **auteur**.

Camera Trap

Trench dug to conceal a secondary camera from the sight line of the principal camera during filming.

Cameron, James

One of Tinseltown's most successful commercial directors following a lucrative string of hits which include *The Terminator* (84), *Aliens* (86), *The Abyss* (89), *Terminator 2: Judgment Day* (91) and *Titanic* (97), Cameron is a fastidious filmmaker who prepares his movies with an intricacy that may go a long way towards explaining their remarkable box-office record. His **blockbusters** often contain something more than mere surface characterisation, and this comes as a most welcome innovation in that most inhuman of vehicles, the mega-budgeted, studio-dominated Hollywood hit. A little creative imagination might not go amiss on his film titles, though.
OTHER KEY FILMS: *Xenogenesis* [short] (78); *Piranha II: The Spawning* (81); *Rambo: First Blood Part II* [co-script] (85); *True Lies* (94); *Strange Days* [screenplays and story only] (95)

Campion, Jane

New Zealander Campion began her career making shorts, and her success at Cannes with the ultra-short *Peel* (82) edged her steadily towards her debut feature, *Sweetie* (89), which first brought to the public's notice her predilection for plots involving awkward or marginal young women who have been badly let down by their families. She continued this theme with *An Angel At My Table* (90), the story of author Janet Frame's struggle for acceptance, and she finally found mainstream recognition with *The Piano* (93), an intensely irritating and mannered film that some people, it is only fair to say, loved. Her *Portrait Of A Lady* (96) was little better, and Campion seems to have fallen uncomfortably between two stools in recent years, not being able to decide whether she should concentrate on art-house cinema or on the commercial.
OTHER KEY FILMS: *Holy Smoke* (98); *In The Cut* (01)

Can

The metal container in which film stock is stored – the term 'in the can' implies the completion of a particular piece or section of film. The word 'can' may also be used to refer to a soundman's headphones or to a basic studio light.

Candela

Before 1936 candlepower was used to measure light – after 1936 the candela (abbreviation cd) superseded it.

Candid Camera

Now synonymous with the internationally famous TV shows in which innocent and unwary people are shown being duped into foolish acts, the term strictly means the filming of people without either their consent or their knowledge, a technique commonly used in **cinéma vérité** and **documentary**.

Candlepower

See **Candela**

Cannes Film Festival

Home of the coveted Palme D'Or and situated at the famous luxury resort on the French Riviera (think Hotel Du Cap, Eden Roc, The Carlton, etc.), the Cannes festival began in 1946 and has continued, May in, May out, amidst sometimes fervid but always entertaining controversy, ever since. Highlights have included an attack on **Jean-Luc Godard** by a custard-pie stalker, and the celebrated **paparazzi** snap of **Robert Mitchum** with a busty starlet.

55

Cantinflas

Mexico's most famous comedian and something of a household name in the US after his appearance as Passepartout in Michael Anderson's *Around The World In Eighty Days* (56). Cantinflas never managed to parlay his brief international success into the longer term, but that can hardly have bothered him since his reputation throughout the Spanish-speaking world began high, with Alejandro Galindo's *Ni Sangre Ni Arena* (41), and was sustained throughout the rest of his life, ensuring that he remained in demand even after his premature retirement.

OTHER KEY FILMS: *El Gandarme Desconcido* (41); *El Circo* (42); *Los Tres Mosqueteros* (43); *El Mago* (49); *Pepe* (60); *El Extra* (62); *El Padrecito* (64); *El Patrullero 777* (78)

Cantor, Eddie

Cantor was a genuinely funny man, and his demented brand of humour relied on the premise of a cowardly man levering himself out of sticky places through his gift of the gab – Cantor's patter certainly succeeded in levering him back into the fortune he had made on Broadway and lost to the Wall Street Crash of 1929. His films are sometimes hard to watch nowadays, with the gradual changes that have occurred in our perception of humour and its timing, but Leo McCarey's *The Kid From Spain* (32) remains tremendous and sexy fun (with its bevy of **Busby Berkeley** college girls) and Frank Tuttle's *Roman Scandals* (33) has a lot to recommend it too – Cantor had a surprisingly mellifluous singing voice which he could use to great effect, and his plots have a marked penchant for involving scantily clad dancing girls in their various shenanigans (which can't be a bad thing!).

OTHER KEY FILMS: *Kid Boots* (26); *Whoopee!* (30); *Palmy Days* (31); *Kid Millions* (34); *Strike Me Pink* (36); *Ali Baba Goes To Town* (37); *Thank Your Lucky Stars* (43); *If You Knew Susie* (48)

Canutt, Yakima

Most renowned of all Hollywood stuntmen, Canutt doubled for, amongst others, **John Wayne**, **Clark Gable** and **Roy Rogers**, and was largely responsible for the sensational chariot race in **William Wyler's** *Ben-Hur* (59), in which **Charlton Heston** gave Stephen Boyd his grisly comeuppance. When Heston queried some new trick Canutt was hatching, Canutt responded with: 'Chuck, just make sure you stay in the chariot. I guarantee you're going to win the goddamned race.' Canutt also designed and executed the famous 'man under the galloping horses' stunt in **John Ford's** *Stagecoach* (39), in which, doubling as an ignoble savage, Canutt jumps from his pinto onto the back of a team of four recklessly galloping horses, clambers to the cross bar, is shot by Big John Wayne (a.k.a. The Ringo Kid), falls between the galloping horses, hangs on to the cross bar for a moment while the stage drags him along the ground, then lets go, disappearing beneath the hooves of the horses and the wheels of the stage, eventually emerging, more or less intact, on the desert floor, where he proceeds, against all the odds, to play dead.

Caper Movies

See **Heist Movies**

Capra, Frank

Capra certainly started his career from the bottom, as a film splicer and general handyman around various minor studios, ending up as a gagman for **Hal Roach**. This meant that when **Harry Cohn** offered him the hitherto unheard-of opportunity to direct a series of films to counter the prevailing miseries of the Depression, Capra was the man for the job. Ever ambitious, Capra rode the Depression-era camera tracks to awesome effect, and his masterpiece of the period must be *It Happened One Night* (34), although *Platinum Blonde* (31) and *The Bitter Tea Of General Yen* (32), his magnificent story of a doomed cross-cultural passion in war-torn China between **Barbara Stanwyck's** soon-to-be missionary's wife and **Nils Asther's** blissfully decadent warlord, have considerably more heart to them, and strike one as less cold-bloodedly commercial. A number of Capra's later films, including *Mr Deeds Goes To Town* (36) and *It's A Wonderful Life* (46), have entered American folklore, and it would be invidious to criticise them with the public's response to their message verging on the irrational, but his earlier *Lost Horizon* (37) is a genuinely uplifting film, benefiting from a script by Capra's long-term collaborator **Robert Riskin**, brilliantly gleaned from James Hilton's worldwide bestseller about the utopian never-never-land of Shangri-la. Once cinema's greatest master of populism, Capra was shamefully neglected by the Hollywood hierarchy after 1950. See **Erotic Moments**

OTHER KEY FILMS: *The Strong Man* (26); *American Madness* (32); *Mr Smith Goes To Washington* (39); *Meet John Doe* (41); *Arsenic And Old Lace* (44); *Pocketful Of Miracles* (61)

KEY LINE:
'Capra would take the sneak previews to many different places...he had tape recorders set up all over the theatre, so he could find out where the laughs were and how long they were, and if they were too long and over-cutting another line, we'd leave room for them.' [Arnold Schulman, who scripted Capra's *A Hole In The Head* (59)]

Caption
Information appearing on the screen which tells the audience when, where or why a scene is occurring.

Carbon-arc Lamps
Electric light generated between carbon electrodes and used to power studio lamps and film projectors.

Cardiff, Jack
Cardiff (a lifetime achievement award winner at the 2001 Oscar ceremony, and the first ever technician to receive such an honour) understood the camera as few men before or since have understood it, and his black-and-white films, such as **René Clair's** *The Ghost Goes West* (35) and Jacques Feyder's wondrously romantic *Knight Without Armour* (37), together with his later rich **Technicolor** work on **Michael Powell's** *A Matter Of Life And Death* (46) and *Black Narcissus* (47), and on **Albert Lewin's** magical *Pandora And The Flying Dutchman* (51), attest to something more consistent than a mere

cameraman's (his own definition of himself) input – call it a cinematographer's eye, if you will. His later films, including those he directed himself (excepting *Sons And Lovers* (60) and *Young Cassidy* (65), which he co-directed with **John Ford**) were pedestrian in the extreme, and one remains astonished at how Cardiff could show so much critical acuity for so long behind the camera, only to blow it so consummately at the end of his career when he found himself in front of the lens.
OTHER KEY FILMS: Zoltan Korda's *The Four Feathers* (39); Gabriel Pascal's *Caesar And Cleopatra* (45); Michael Powell's *The Red Shoes* (48); **Alfred Hitchcock's** *Under Capricorn* (49); **John Huston's** *The African Queen* (51); **Joseph L. Mankiewicz's** *The Barefoot Contessa* (54); **King Vidor's** *War And Peace* (56); Lewis Teague's *Cat's Eye* (85); Jamie Payne's *The Dance Of Shiva* (98)
KEY LINE:
'Watch me very carefully when I have my periods.' [**Ava Gardner** to Jack Cardiff, while filming *The Barefoot Contessa*]

Cardinale, Claudia
She wasn't really an actress but more of an image, which is why **Sergio Leone** used her alongside **Charles Bronson** in *Once Upon A Time In The West* (68), and why **Federico Fellini** used her alongside **Marcello Mastroianni** in *8½* (63), and why **Luchino Visconti** used her opposite **Alain Delon**

Claudia Cardinale (as Toni Alfredo) in a curious state of undress, during the filming of Henry Hathaway's Circus World *(64)*

in *The Leopard* (63) – think of the actors, and the parts she played, and the reasons for her choice become clear. Her very voluptuousness was almost deadening, and one sometimes came away from her films feeling strangely tarnished, as if one's voyeurism were being cast back at one for being too obvious and for making the object of it too acute and empty an end. When she spoke, Cardinale sounded like a Neapolitan courtesan, and it was this paradox which saved her from the mediocrity that so much beauty would normally confer – one didn't watch a Cardinale performance so much as marvel at the vessel containing it, and Leone's undermining of her carefully nurtured image in *Once Upon A Time In The West* can now be seen, in retrospect, as a masterstroke of Italian fabulism.

OTHER KEY FILMS: *La Prima Notte* (59); *Rocco And His Brothers* (60); *Cartouche* (61); *La Viaccia* (61); *The Pink Panther* (63); *Gli Indifferenti* (64); *The Adventures Of Gerard* (70); *The Red Tent* (71); *La Pelle* (81); *Fitzcarraldo* (82); *La Storia* (85); *Briganti* (99)

Carné, Marcel

Carné's later career doesn't matter – all that matters is that in an astonishingly rich period of eight years he distilled the dreams, the ironical spirit of resignation, and the doomed romanticism of France, an ancient nation sold on the existential virtues of living and loving for the moment, rather than of storing up goods for a notional and anti-instinctual future. Carné presented the French to themselves as they wanted to be seen, and the French to us as we wanted to see them, and this was his true gift. With *Quai Des Brumes* (38), *Hôtel Du Nord* (38), *Le Jour Se Lève* (39), *Les Visiteurs Du Soir* (42) and *Les Enfants Du Paradis* (45), he guaranteed a sort of immortality to a state of mind the direct opposite of the commercial Armageddon we live in today. Carné's characters live briefly, love wildly, and die with their disillusions intact.

OTHER KEY FILMS: *Jenny* (37); *Les Portes De La Nuit* (46); *Juliette Ou La Clé Des Songes* (51); *Thérèse Raquin* (53); *L'Air De Paris* (54); *Terrain Vague* (60)

Carpenter, John

Carpenter has always drawn much of the inspiration for his films from the **B-Movies** of the 1950s, beginning with *Dark Star* (74), his cult sci-fi classic, continuing with the edgy *Assault On Precinct 13* (76) – a tribute to **Howard Hawks's** *Rio Bravo* (59) – and culminating in *Halloween* (78), which catapulted him into big-time horror and **slasher movie** territory. His *Escape From New York* (81) was a male adolescent's dream movie (hero Kurt Russell, as

Snake Plissken, even sported an eye-patch) and Carpenter has continued referentially entertaining us ever since, with such films as *The Thing* (82), *Christine* (83) and *Starman* (84). His tongue may have, on occasion, been fixed firmly in his cheek, but his films have always been honestly imbued with a real love of cinema and of the thrills and spills and Jills associated with the best of it.

OTHER KEY FILMS: *The Fog* (80); *Big Trouble In Little China* (86); *Memoirs Of An Invisible Man* (92); *Village Of The Damned* (95); *Escape From L.A.* (96); *Vampires* (98); *Ghosts Of Mars* (01)

Carrey, Jim

One of the most bankable of all recent box-office stars, Carrey can be genuinely funny, a talent which is rarer than gold dust in Hollywoodland. The self-directed *Ace Ventura, Pet Detective* (94) began Carrey's rise to superstardom, followed by Charles Russell's *The Mask* (94) and the sensationally sick Farrelly Brothers slapstick masterpiece, *Dumb & Dumber* (94), which took good taste to a new, triumphant low. After a scene-stealing performance as the Riddler in Joel Schumacher's *Batman Forever* (95) Carrey briefly suffered from a hefty dose of the worthies, but he has now re-emerged, humour triumphantly intact, in yet another Farrelly sickcom, *Me, Myself And Irene* (00).

OTHER KEY FILMS: *Ace Ventura: When Nature Calls* (95); *The Cable Guy* (96); *Liar Liar* (97); *The Truman Show* (98); *Man On The Moon* (99); *How The Grinch Stole Christmas* (00)

***

Irony Warning!! Irony Warning!!
Tests have proved that without the aforementioned irony warning, even highly literate readers will take the following tongue-in-cheek and affectionate paean to the *Carry On* version of essential English humour literally. So please read on, bearing in mind that I don't mean what I seem to be saying. Capisco?

Carry On Films

Appalling series of unfunny, would-be comic British films (58-92) that even otherwise sane people pretend to like. Gathering together a precociously awful armada of British comic has-beens, audiences have cheered such profoundly unedifying spectacles as Kenneth Williams's travestying of Julius Caesar at the point of his death, crying, 'Infamy! Infamy! They've all got it in for me!' Now is that funny, I ask you? Seriously, though…

KEY FILMS: Gerald Thomas's *Carry On Teacher* (59), *Carry On Nurse* (59), *Carry On Constable* (60), *Carry On Cleo* (64), *Carry On Cowboy* (65), *Carry On Up The Khyber* (68), *Carry On Camping* (69), *Carry On Henry* (71), *Carry On Matron* (72), *Carry On Behind* (75), *Carry On Emmanuelle* (78), *Carry On Columbus* (92)

Casablanca

Considered by some to be the single most romantic film of all time, **Michael Curtiz's** *Casablanca* (42) brought together the talents of **Humphrey Bogart**, **Ingrid Bergman**, Paul Henreid, **Sidney Greenstreet**, **Claude Rains**, **Peter Lorre** and **Conrad Veidt**, not to mention a veritable menagerie of screenwriters, three of whom (**Julius J Epstein**, Philip G. Epstein, and Howard Koch) eventually got their name on the credits (and an **Oscar** apiece). Dooley Wilson sang 'As Time Goes By', but didn't, incidentally, play the piano. Curtiz and his screenwriters stole from just about every genre there was to steal from, creating a heady concoction that had little, if nothing, to do with the Second World War, and a very great deal to do with an inspired escapism from it. Bogart based his character, Richard 'Rick' Blaine, on a mixture of **Jean Gabin**, in **Marcel Carné's** *Quai Des Brumes* (38), and **Gary Cooper**, in **Josef von Sternberg's** *Morocco* (30), with the ineffable homespun Bogart cynicism to leaven the dose. Bergman took the idea for her famous mackintosh from Michèle Morgan in *Quai Des Brumes* too, but the look and the sound of Ilsa Lund were triumphantly her own. The film, unlike many of the other commercial vehicles of the time, improves with every viewing.

KEY LINES:

'Play it, Sam, play "As Time Goes By".' [Bergman to Wilson]

'Major Strasser has been shot. Round up the usual suspects.' [Rains]

'Of all the gin joints in all the towns in all the world, she walks into mine.' [Bogart]

'Here's looking at you, kid.' [Bogart to Bergman]

'If she can stand it, I can. Play it!' [Bogart to Wilson]

'How extravagant you are, throwing away women like that. Someday they may be scarce.' [Rains to Bogart]

'I remember every detail. The Germans wore grey. You wore blue.' [Bogart to Bergman]

Cassette

The plastic casing inside which video film is stored. Alternatively a sealed container used for loading fresh, unexposed film in broad daylight without spoiling it.

Cast

The list of those actors who do actually appear in the finished article. Alternatively the act of deciding who is to appear in a film.

Casting Couch

The couch on which the casting director would, allegedly (only in the dim, bad old days of Hollywood, of course), take out payment in kind for favours given from callow young actresses, and occasionally, one supposes, from callow young actors too.

Casting Director

Person in charge of selecting suitable actors and actresses for subsidiary and bit part roles in a film.

Catchlight

The gleam in the eye of an actor caused by the reflection of light sources from the set. Alternatively the light used specifically to produce this effect.

Cattle Call

A general, catch-all audition for any bit parts left over in a film after the main actors and actresses have been selected.

Catwalk

A scaffolding walkway high above the stage set which allows electricians and other technicians easy access to lighting and sound set-ups.

Cell/Cel

Name for the single sheet of transparent cellulose acetate on which an animator draws an image that can then be superimposed onto an existing, pre-drawn background.

Celluloid

The actual use of celluloid for film stock is virtually obsolete, but the word is still used to denote every form of cinema film (barring, of course, the **digital** variety).

Cement

The glue used to splice two pieces of film together in an editing room.

Censorship

Government and State interference, on our behalves, in what can and cannot be shown on the screen. The first film censorship board in the US was established in Pennsylvania in 1911, specifying the need for a formal review (in front of the largely upper-class board) before any motion picture could be shown within the State's borders. Taboos covered anything to do with white slavery, abortion, drug use and venereal disease.

Central Casting Corporation

The Alliance of Motion Picture Producers set up Central Casting in 1926 to act as a repository and to keep book on all the actors and actresses legally available for film work, famously classifying them as blond, brunette, gawky, elegant, fat, thin, dumb, smart, etc. The Company became privatised in 1976.

Century Stand

A tripod on which light sources may be secured before diffusion.

CGI

Acronym for Computer Generated Imagery, CGIs are scenes directly fabricated on a computer and then added, often to live-action scenes, in order (paradoxically) to provide verisimilitude. First tentatively used in **Barry Levinson's** *Young Sherlock Holmes* (85), CGI has now overtaken conventional animation in the visual realism stakes to such an extent that in **DreamWorks's** recent *Shrek* (01), Princess Fiona (voiced by Cameron Diaz) became so convincing a dybbuk that one could even make out the corners of her mouth unsticking before she uttered a word. Joking aside, computed-generated imagery, advanced as it already appears, is only at the beginning of its journey, and the **Academy of Motion Pictures Arts and Sciences** is acknowledging this fact by introducing, in 2002, their first **Oscar** dedicated to animated feature films.

KEY FILMS: Disney's *Toy Story* (95); DreamWorks's *Antz* (98); Disney's *A Bug's Life* (98), *Dinosaur* (00), *Monsters, Inc.* (01); **Columbia's** *Final Fantasy* (01)

Chabrol, Claude

A sensationally variable director who, at his best, as in *Que La Bête Meure* [*This Man Must Die*] (69) and *Le Boucher* (70), could turn out some of the finest and most perspicacious (in terms of human motivation) thrillers ever, and at his worst, as in *Madame Bovary* (91), could astonish even die-hard fans with the sterility and matter-of-factness of his direction. From his very first film, *Le Beau Serge* (58), it was obvious that in Chabrol French cinema had something special – a director who could both fascinate and entertain – and in his second film, *Les Cousins* (59), he extended this range,

suggesting rather than explaining, much as a good novelist might do in similar circumstances. Eschewing tricks, Chabrol filmed straight down the line, something which failed to endear him to the **New Wave**, and his mid-period *Les Biches* (68), which concerns the uneasy affair between two lesbians and the architect who loves them both, is his finest film in this mode; for Chabrol, when he cares to be, is both the reluctant champion and the ultimate castigator of the French petit bourgeoisie, while **Eric Rohmer**, his elder in years, but near-contemporary in terms of film, remains its fondest observer.

OTHER KEY FILMS: *A Double Tour* (59); *The Tiger Likes Fresh Blood* (64); *Le Scandale* (67); *La Femme Infidèle* (69); *La Rupture* (70); *Juste Avant La Nuit* (71); *Les Innocents Aux Mains Sales* (76); *Les Magiciens* (75); *Violette Nozière* (78); *L'Enfer* (94); *The Ceremony* (96); *Au Coeur Du Mensonge* (99); *Merci Pour Le Chocolat* (00)

Chandler, Raymond

A magnificent though frustrated screenwriter (and a real lover of the film medium) as well as being the novelist/creator of the much-filmed private eye **Philip Marlowe**, Chandler scripted, amongst others, **Billy Wilder's** *Double Indemnity* (42), George Marshall's *The Blue Dahlia* (46) and **Alfred Hitchcock's** *Strangers On A Train* (51). A master of simile and metaphor, and a literate, erudite man, Chandler later succumbed to drink and melancholia following the death of his beloved wife, Cissy.

OTHER KEY FILMS: Irving Pichel's *And Now Tomorrow* (44); Lewis Allen's *The Unseen* (45)

KEY LINES:

'Everything written with vitality expresses that vitality; there are no dull subjects, only dull minds.' [Chandler on the art of writing]

Chaney, Lon

The son of deaf-mute parents, Chaney became, of necessity, a consummate mime. The original 'Man of a Thousand Faces', he died just as the advent of sound was about to change forever the way people viewed the silent cinematic image. In almost 150 films Chaney nearly always portrayed the tormented, the deformed and the marginal, giving his characters a nobility that speech would almost certainly have diluted. His was the greatest-ever Quasimodo in Wallace Worsley's *The Hunchback Of Notre Dame* (23), and no actor has ever understood the Phantom's reluctant donning of the cloak as well as Chaney did in Rupert Julian's *Phantom Of The Opera* (25). Great actors

such as **Charles Laughton** learned much of their craft from watching him, particularly in his capacity for stillness, and his ability to express extreme languor and sudden, violent resolution.
OTHER KEY FILMS: *Hell Morgan's Girl* (17); *The Miracle Man* (19); *Oliver Twist* (22); *The Unholy Three* (25); *The Blackbird* (26); *The Unknown* (27); *London After Midnight* (27); *Where East Is East* (29)

Changeover
The deft and (mostly) unnoticeable switching between reels and projectors in a cinema projection room, the frequency of which is dictated by the length (ergo number of reels) of the film being shown.

Changeover Cue
The mark projectionists look for on the top right-hand side of a frame to warn them to change projectors — usually ten seconds and two seconds before the end of a reel.

Changing Bag
A sealed, opaque bag used for changing film or investigating the causes of a **camera jam** even in direct sunlight.

Chaplin, Charlie
Sit any child in front of a Chaplin film and a strange change will occur — where before it had sought speed and constant stimulation, the child is now seen to relax, and its expectations simplify. The child will at first chortle, perhaps self-consciously, and then, slowly, it will give itself up to the magic that Chaplin so uniquely possessed. For Chaplin was the great communicator, and he communicates now beyond the grave to all those with the inclination, and the capacity, to see and hear him. When Chaplin touches us we remain touched, and images from his films remain with us as the stuff and dressing of our unconscious. It's easy to pull him down as a man, for he had more than his fair share of faults, but there must surely be a place for genius beyond stricture, for illumination beyond the conjecture of fools, and Chaplin holds firm, despite, or perhaps because of, these very shortcomings.
KEY FILMS: *The Tramp* (15); *Shanghaied* (15); *The Vagabond* (16); *The Rink* (16); *The Immigrant* (17); *A Dog's Life* (18); *Shoulder Arms* (18); *The Kid* (21); *A Woman Of Paris* (23); *The Gold Rush* (25); *The Circus* (28); *City Lights* (31); *Modern Times* (36); *The Great Dictator* (40); *Monsieur Verdoux* (47); *Limelight* (52)

KEY LINE:
'All I need to make a comedy is a park, a policeman and a pretty girl.' [Chaplin on comedy]

Character Actor
The familiar faces one catches sight of in supporting roles, often over many years, and of whom one can never remember the name. Doctors might reasonably define this condition as the 'Elisha Cook Jr syndrome', after the character actor of the same name who graced an untold number of **Humphrey Bogart** movies, usually as a gunsel, a bell-hop or a corpse, and of whom people regularly asked, 'Say, what's the name of that guy? You know. The one in the Bogart film who drinks the poison?' To give Elisha his due, he was given one of the main parts in **Stanley Kubrick's** *The Killing* (56), and delivered an electrifying performance as the hen-pecked but still decent minor thief, George Peatty. He ended up dead, of course.

Character Role
A subsidiary role in a film whose success depends more on archetype, eccentricity and the ability to be noticeable, than on any particular talent. The quality of the character actors is an essential addition to the success of any movie, and famous character actor archetypes from Hollywood's golden age include Eric Blore (the cynical, put-upon valet), **Thelma Ritter** (the feisty, working-class home help), and S Z Sakall (the cheerful, German-accented family waiter).

Chase Film
The most comprehensive of all genres, comprising **Westerns**, thrillers, **science-fiction** movies and demented love stories, the chase film involves both itself and the audience in an extended, often over-the-top chase, hopefully leaving everyone happy and exhausted by the final credits. Top of the bunch must be **Alfred Hitchcock's** *The Thirty-Nine Steps* (35) in which **Robert Donat** finds himself chased, not only by the baddies, but also by the police and an irate, gorgeously be-stockinged Madeleine Carroll in handcuffs.

Cheat Shot
Any shot that purports to show something that does not in fact happen; for instance the shot of **Tom Cruise**, in **John Woo's** *Mission Impossible II* (00), leaping from one bare piece of rock to another with two thousand feet of nothing looming beneath him. In reality the star simply does his stunt, drops onto a convenient hidden platform, then strolls off for his tea (hot or iced, as the case may be).

Chen Kaige

Forced to give up school to work on the land during Mao Zedong's Cultural Revolution, Chen Kaige used this hard-won knowledge in his first film, *Yellow Earth* (84), which was about the misunderstandings inherent between town and country, worker and peasant. With **Zhang Yimou** as his cinematographer, he went on to make *The Big Parade* (85) which showed how individuals must learn to relate to the institutions they are forced to join in a communal society, and which fell just as inevitably foul of the communist authorities. *Farewell My Concubine* (93) was Kaige's first major international success, sharing the Palme D'Or at **Cannes**, and he has recently completed the most expensive Asian film ever made, *The Emperor And The Assassin* (99), which is safely set in 221 BC, and deals with the reunification of the seven kingdoms by Emperor Ying Zheng, and the love and skulduggery that went hand in hand with it – in the film, Zheng's concubine, the exquisite **Gong Li**, falls in love with the assassin who is meant to fake an attempt on Zheng's life, which just goes to prove that the basic *film noir* plot was comfortably in existence over two thousand years ago.
OTHER KEY FILMS: *King Of Children* (87); *Life On A String* (91); *Temptress Moon* (97)

Chevalier, Maurice

In his French films Chevalier was tough, caustic, sexy and streetwise, and in his American films he was winsome, charming, coy and rather camp. Could it be the language? Perhaps French encourages candour and English encourages euphemism? Who knows. But the French films (apart from the US ones made by the European-orientated **Ernst Lubitsch**) are generally better, and the French Chevalier, with his brilliant vocal skills – he could scat, sing songs and wordplay ballads just as well as **Jean Gabin** and Berthe Sylva, which is really saying something – more accurately reflected his music-hall background. He ended his long career (despite a blip after the war when he was accused, then cleared, of collaboration) as the avuncular roué every woman would like to pretend she'd had a love affair with in her prime, shrugging and winking and charming his way through such delightful candyfloss as **Vincente Minnelli's** *Gigi* (58) and Walter Lang's *Can-Can* (60).
OTHER KEY FILMS: *The Love Parade* (29); *Playboy Of Paris* (30); *The Merry Widow* (34); *Folies Bergère* (35); *Avec Le Sourire* (37); *Le Silence Est D'Or* (47); *A Royal Affair* (50); *My Seven Little Sins* (54); *Love In The Afternoon* (57); *Can-Can* (60)

Best Children's Films

Ludwig Berger, Tim Whelan and **Michael Powell's** *The Thief Of Bagdad* (40); Josef von Baky's *Münchhausen* (43); Desmond Davis's *Clash Of The Titans* (80); **Walt Disney's** *One Hundred And One Dalmatians* (61); Richard Fleischer's *Twenty Thousand Leagues Under The Sea* (54); **Victor Fleming's** *The Wizard Of Oz* (39); **Terry Gilliam's** *Time Bandits* (81); David Hand and **Walt Disney's** *Bambi* (42); Nathan Juran's *The Seventh Voyage Of Sinbad* (58); Albert Lamorisse's *The White Stallion* [a.k.a. *White Mane*] (53); **Fritz Lang's** *Moonfleet* (55); Mike Newell's *Into The West* (91); **Satyajit Ray's** *The Golden Fortress* (74); Henry Safran's *Storm Boy* (76); **John Sayles's** *The Secret Of Roan Inish* (96); **Steven Spielberg's** *E.T. The Extra-Terrestrial* (82)

Child Stars

The little brats every actor and actress dreads being upstaged by. See **Macaulay Culkin**, **Judy Garland**, **Mickey Rooney**, **Shirley Temple**, etc.

Chinagraph Pencil

A cutting room tool used by editors to mark the work print with reminders of where to cut, fade, **dissolve**, synchronise, **splice**, reshape, refine, redesign or **wipe**.

Chinese Dolly

Non-euphemistic cinema term referring to the slanted camera tracks needed for a combined **travelling** and **pan** shot.

Choker

Filmmaker's argot for a tight close-up on an actor's or actress's face.

Choreographer

Fight scenes, gun battles, fiestas, and weddings all need to be choreographed, just as much as ballets, dance numbers and, very often, car chases. This is the main job of the choreographer, one of the forgotten heroes of the average film set.

Christie, Julie

Christie seemed unbelievably natural and carefree at a time when her contemporaries were busy tending their beehive hairdos and sanding their five lacquered layers of nail varnish. To see her strolling along a dull northern street, swinging her handbag and looking happy to be alive and young and with the future still ahead of her in **John Schlesinger's** *Billy Liar* (63), was suddenly to understand, through one moving image, what the 1960s should have been about. She gradually lost that unselfconsciousness (which is hardly surprising given the attention, the pressure, and the quantity of adulation she subsequently received) but in her best films, which include Schlesinger's *Far From The Madding Crowd* (67), **Nicolas Roeg's** *Don't Look Now* (73) and **James Ivory's** *Heat And Dust* (83), she reclaims it, delighting us with her spontaneity, and reminding us of who we might have been had not work, ambition and mediocrity got in the way. OTHER KEY FILMS: *Darling* (65); *Doctor Zhivago* (65); *Fahrenheit 451* (66); *The Go-Between* (70); *McCabe And Mrs Miller* (71); *Shampoo* (75); *Demon Seed* (77); *Memoirs Of A Survivor* (81); *The Return Of The Soldier* (83); *Dragonheart* (96); *Hamlet* (96); *Afterglow* (97); *Belphégor* (00)

Chromatic Aberration
This is what happens when a faulty lens causes the surrounds of an image to flare, or reflect unwanted colours.

Chronotography
The precursor to cinematography, chronotography consists of the recording of a large succession of individual but sequential photographic images which, when played fast, mimic natural motion.

Cimino, Michael
Cimino was a potentially good director who blew it, thanks, no doubt, to the usual character defaults, but also to a far greater than normal vainglory. *Thunderbolt And Lightfoot* (74) was a first-rate little thriller, which combined comedy, action and pathos to excellent effect, and *The Deer Hunter* (78) was a flawed but fascinating example of high movie hokum. *Heaven's Gate* (80), with its disastrously unrealistic production costs, became the symbol for all that was wrong with post-*Easy Rider* Hollywood, until it seemed that Cimino had hoist himself with his own petard. He has only really ever partially redeemed himself with the not bad (but not really very good either) *Year Of The Dragon* (85). OTHER KEY FILMS: *The Sicilian* (87); *Desperate Hours* (90); *The Sunchaser* (96); *The Dreaming Place* (99); *Brazil 1500* (00)

Cinch Marks
Marks which appear on a projected film and which are generally caused by abrasion or the faulty rewinding of a previous projection.

Cinéaste
Originally used by the French to mean an amateur of film (a film buff), the term is now in general usage and refers to anyone creatively involved in the making of motion pictures.

Cinecittà
One of the world's largest film production centres, started in 1936 and completed in 1937 (at the height of the Italian Fascist era) and situated only half a dozen miles from the centre of Rome, Cinecittà was home to **Mervyn LeRoy's** *Quo Vadis* (51), **William Wyler's** *Ben-Hur* (59), **Federico Fellini's** *La Dolce Vita* (60) and *8½* (63), and many, many more of the great US and Italian films of the 1950s and 1960s.

Cine-Fi Sound
A technique once used at US drive-in cinemas and which involved the soundtrack being broadcast on an AM radio wavelength, allowing clients to tune in their car or transistor radios to listen to the movie being shown in front of them.

Cinema Nôvo
A form of politically committed fantasy cinema, prevalent in Brazil during the 1960s, and which equates to the magical realism of certain Latin American novelists. Leader of the movement was Glauber Rocha, who used allegory, euphemism and bizarre symbolic juxtapositions to highlight what he and his followers felt were the wrongs of the Brazilian political machine.

Cinema
First used in 1910, 'cinema' is an abbreviation of the word **Cinématographe**, coined from the Greek word Kinēma, meaning movement, by the **Lumière** brothers in 1895, to describe their newly patented camera/projector machine.

CinemaScope
The first commercially applied wide-screen process, foisted on an astonished industry by **20th Century-Fox** in 1953 as a counterattack to television, until the far more effective **Panavision** came along and superseded it. An anamorphic lens magnified the compressed image produced inside the camera by another anamorphic lens, throwing an enormous, rectangular image, roughly two-and-a-half-times the length of its own height, onto cinema screens. The word CinemaScope has since become the everyday word for the wide-screen process, even though the last commercially exploited CinemaScope film was Richard Fleischer's *Fantastic Voyage* (66).

63

Cinematheque

An art-house cinema, which specialises in the showing of predominantly non-mainstream films.

Cinémathèque Française

The largest film library in the world, comprising more than 100,000 films and over a million stills.

Cinematic

Anything relating to film, or to the making, financing, producing and distributing of films. Can also apply to the particular filmic qualities of a location, scene or person, or to the potential that a story or idea has to be filmed.

Cinématographe

The original camera/projector used by the **Lumière** brothers and patented on 13 February 1895.

Cinematographer

Arguably the most important person on the set after the director, the cinematographer is responsible for both the lighting and the photography of a film. In the case of such great exponents of the art as **Gregg Toland**, **Sven Nykvist**, **Néstor Almendros**, **Gabriel Figueroa** or William H Daniels, it may be assumed that any director who used their services would rely on them almost completely for the final look of the film.

KEY LINE: 'The director describes the shot and the general camera placement, then the cinematographer goes to work creating the atmosphere, through lighting, in which the story will develop.' [Figueroa on the cinematographer's art]

Cinéma Vérité

A quasi-realistic documentary style first used in France in the 1960s. Using hand-held cameras, filmmakers would follow their subjects around until sheer force of habit made their presence tolerably acceptable. The ensuing footage would then be edited in as cursory a way as possible to retain the gritty, apparently authentic feel of the material.

Cinemicrography

Sometimes known as microcinematography, this is the technique by which microscopic particles are filmed through a microscope, and then later enlarged for detailed study.

Cinemiracle

A short-lived wide-screen process that aimed to do away with the unsightly joins that bedevilled its chief opponent, the tri-projector **Cinerama** process.

Cinemobile

A large, articulated vehicle used for moving motion picture-making equipment between locations and also for accommodating film crews. It superseded the fleet of lorries or trucks that were needed before its invention, circa 1965, by Fouad Said.

Cineorama

A pioneering multiscreen system designed by Raoul Gromoin-Sanson in the early 1890s, which used ten simultaneous projection units to throw ten images onto a vast circular screen. It was first used in 1900 at the Grande Exposition in Paris, but police interference on the grounds of crowd control rendered the system unworkable.

Cinéphile

A lover, or enlightened amateur of film – someone, in fact, who goes beyond a mere cursory knowledge of the stars, and interests themselves in the more tangential aspects of films and filmmaking.

Cinerama

Something of a fad in the 1950s and 1960s, Cinerama relied on three synchronised projectors working simultaneously to produce a large-screen effect which gave audiences the impression that they formed part of the film itself, particularly when faced with toboggan runs, big dippers, and log jams rushing towards roaring rivers, and so forth. The parallel and cheaper **CinemaScope** and **Panavision** processes (which relied on 70mm magnified film) soon superseded the system, which anyway proved to be prohibitively expensive. The multi-directed (**John Ford**, **Henry Hathaway** and George Marshall) *How The West Was Won* (62), one of the few films shot using the technique, was actually rather good.

Cinex Strip

A test strip of film showing the possible light gradations that may be used in the eventual processing of the completed film.

Circuit

The conglomeration of a number of cinemas under one company umbrella for the purpose of market-share-led economies of scale. International examples might include the Gaumont, Odeon, UGC, UCI, Virgin, Warner-Village and United Artists cinema chains.

Citizen Kane

It is hard to say anything about **Orson Welles's** *Citizen Kane* (41) that hasn't been said and resaid many times already. Suffice it to say that Welles was given *carte blanche*, under a virtually unprecedented contract from **RKO**, to make whatever film he wanted to. Following on from an idea he had sketched out with his co-writer, Herman J Mankiewicz, Welles began filming the story of William Randolph Hearst, newspaper tycoon and media monster, complete with insalubrious details of Hearst's private life with his mistress, Marion Davies (the name Rosebud, which figures so prominently in the film, was rumoured to be Hearst's nickname for Miss Davies's clitoris). Understandably incensed, Hearst did everything he could to get the film banned, and his vituperation continued long after his death, and possibly had something to do with Welles's later cold-shouldering by key elements of the Hollywood hierarchy. What really mattered, though, was the film, and it is for its extraordinary originality that *Kane* is justly renowned, and for which it regularly gets voted the best film of all time. Using virtually every technique the cinema had hitherto thrown up, Welles (already wise enough, aged twenty-five, to employ only the best of collaborators) also added some of his own, gleaned from his experiences in the theatre and in radio – **Gregg Toland's** deep focus photography, Mankiewicz's literate writing skills, **Bernard Hermann's** music and **Van Nest Polglase's** and Perry Ferguson's art direction all contributed to this masterpiece, but it is indisputable that Welles was the captain of his ship, and as such, while being the first to take credit, he should also be allowed the dubious, but only just privilege, of being last man off.

KEY LINE:
'As it must to all men, death came to Charles Foster Kane.' [Newsreel announcement of Kane's death]

City Symphonies

Filmed documentaries designed to conjure up the spirit of a great city like London, Berlin, Paris or New York. To be differentiated from feature films, like **Woody Allen's** *Manhattan* (79), which strive for the same effect using overtly fictional storylines.

Clair, René

Clair was a consummate filmmaker who started out by undermining, moved on to delighting, and ended up by challenging his audiences. Some of his silent films showed marked avant-garde tendencies, but Clair fortunately overcame this handicap to produce some of the most innocently happy films of the 1930s, including *Sous Les Toits De Paris* (30), *Le Million* (31) and *The Ghost Goes West* (35), with **Robert Donat** as both the ill-starred scion of a beleaguered Scottish dynasty, and his ghost, who find themselves vicariously removed to Florida by a rich American. *I Married A Witch* (42) is another gem, which contains **Veronica Lake's** best comedic work (and she *was* a good comedienne) and concerns a notorious family of New England witches who are burnt at the stake but return to haunt (in a delightfully irritating way) the unwitting ancestor of their nemesis, **Frederic March**. *It Happened Tomorrow* (44) was another US winner, and Clair returned to France after the war, his reputation enhanced, to direct a number of challenging and emotionally mature dramas, including *Les Belles De Nuit* (52) and *Les Grandes Manoeuvres* (55), films which harked back to that earlier period in France, before the war, in which he had made his reputation.

OTHER KEY FILMS: *Paris Qui Dort* (23); *The Italian Straw Hat* (27); *Le Dernier Milliardaire* (34); *The Flame Of New Orleans* (41); *And Then There Were None* (45); *La Beauté Du Diable* (50); *Porte Des Lilas* (57); *Les Fêtes Galantes* (65)

KEY LINE:
'René Clair was amazing. He had the only black pinstripe suit that I had ever seen that had crimson stripes. He was elegant, elegant. He looked like a ballroom dancer, like a Valentino. Very petite, intense, wonderful.' [Screenwriter Stewart Stern on being directed in a play, *The French Touch*, by Clair]

Clapper Board

Old-fashioned hinged clapping device for indicating, both on the set and on the soundtrack of a strip of film, that a new scene is beginning. An electronic device is now mostly used instead.

Clapsticks

Another word for a **Clapper Board**.

Claw

The pointed sprocket inside cameras and projectors which catches hold of the perforations at the edge of a strip of film and forces the film forward frame by frame.

Clean Entrance

A smooth entrance into frame by an actor or actress during the filming of a scene.

65

Clean Exit

You've guessed this, haven't you? Check out the previous entry and reverse it, making sure that you are not sidetracked by a process of spontaneous morphology.

Cleese, John

Cleese is perhaps not the comic genius some would suggest, but his manic style and his capacity for exalted anarchy, particularly in his television work with the Monty Python team, and also with his co-writer/one-time wife Connie Booth's sublime *Fawlty Towers* series, bring him perilously close on occasion. His film work has been variable, almost as if such an extended medium did not really interest him, but notable for a few particular highlights outside the Monty Python caucus — Christopher Morahan's *Clockwise* (86), for instance, was genuinely amusing and grows even better with repeated viewings, and it was in Charles Crichton's *A Fish Called Wanda* (88) that Cleese came closest to achieving the crossover of his talent from small screen to large.

OTHER KEY FILMS: *And Now For Something Completely Different* (72); *Monty Python And The Holy Grail* (75); *Monty Python's Life Of Brian* (79); *Monty Python's The Meaning Of Life* (83); *Silverado* (85); *Fierce Creatures* (97); *The World Is Not Enough* (99); *Isn't She Great* (00); *Harry Potter And The Sorcerer's Stone* (01)

Clément, René

Clément cemented his early reputation with *La Bataille Du Rail* (46), a heart-rending reconstruction of the often fatal Resistance activities of French railway workers during the Second World War; but his greatest war film came later, with *Jeux Interdits* (52), in which Clément and his scriptwriters, **Jean Aurenche** and **Pierre Bost**, discovered that by filming the war from the point of view of two natural and instinctive children who have no alternative but to create their own realities in the face of its absurdity, he could bring home its message and effect to a wider, still war-weary audience. Clément never quite matched that stroke of genius again, but his antiheroic *Knave Of Hearts* (54) became something of a cult on both sides of the Channel, and *Plein Soleil* (59), with **Alain Delon** at his coldest and most manipulative, provided **Anthony Minghella** with at least some of the cinematic wherewithal to attempt his *Talented Mr Ripley* (99), based on the same Patricia Highsmith story.

OTHER KEY FILMS: *Les Maudits* (47); *The Walls Of Malapaga* (49); *Gervaise* (56); *Le Jour Et L'Heure* (63); *Les Félins* (64); *Is Paris Burning?* (66); *The Deadly Trap* (71)

Cliffhanger

A now outmoded system for maintaining an audience's interest, based on the silent serial movie premise that if one left the hero or heroine hanging by their fingernails off the edge of a cliff, punters would return and pay to find out what happened the next week. Modern audiences are a good deal less amenable in their expectations, and want it all now.

Clift, Montgomery

Elizabeth Taylor noticed Clift's extraordinary intensity during the shooting of **George Stevens's** *A Place In The Sun* (51), where she was disturbed to find that this **Method** actor would often come off the set literally shaking with unresolved emotion. The highpoint of Clift's career came two years later, however, with his Robert E Lee Prewitt in **Fred Zinnemann's** *From Here To Eternity* (53), although he had previously given another convincing performance as Matthew Garth, in **Howard Hawks's** *Red River* (48). Appallingly disfigured in a car accident during the making of **Edward Dmytryk's** *Raintree County* (57), Clift's face was surgically reconstructed to afford at least a semblance of his former beauty, and he used this new (and real) vulnerability to good effect in **John Huston's** *The Misfits* (61) and *Freud* (62). Hounded throughout his career because of his homosexuality, and tragically prone to remorse and self-loathing on the same account, Clift died, four years later, aged just forty-five, of a heart attack.

OTHER KEY FILMS: *The Search* (48); *The Heiress* (49); *The Big Lift* (50); *I Confess* (53); *The Young Lions* (58); *Suddenly Last Summer* (59); *Wild River* (60); *Judgment At Nuremberg* (61); *The Defector* (66)

Clip

An extract from a film removed for advertising or critical purposes. Alternatively a length of film removed during the editing process.

Clooney, George

Clooney made his name as Dr Doug Ross in the television series 'ER', and that might have been the end of it, had not this nephew of singer Rosemary Clooney — together with one or two Hollywood studios desperate for a new romantic male action star to replace their ageing crop — decided it was time for him to take his chance on the big screen. The strange

George Clooney as bank robber Jack Foley (musing on happy endings?), in Steven Soderbergh's Out Of Sight *(98)*

thing is that Clooney apparently blew it, with Joel Schumacher's *Batman And Robin* (97) and Mimi Leder's *The Peacemaker* (97), but it was so obvious to everyone that he had what it takes that the studios persisted, the star barely resisted, and the rest will probably be history. His recent standout performance in the **Coen Brothers'** *O Brother, Where Art Thou?* (00) proves that he is the nearest thing to a reincarnated Clark Gable that Hollywood possesses.

OTHER KEY FILMS: *Return Of The Killer Tomatoes!* (88); *Unbecoming Age* (92); *From Dusk Till Dawn* (96); *One Fine Day* (96); *Out Of Sight* (98); *The Thin Red Line* (98); *Three Kings* (99); *The Perfect Storm* (00); *Spy Kids* (01); *Ocean's 11* (01)

KEY LINE:
'I don't believe in happy endings... it's a mean thing, life.' [Clooney on life]

Close, Glenn

Close is not predominantly a movie actress but a theatrical one, and it is conceivable that when the sum of her career is finally taken, film will only have a walk-on part. She was excellent, however, in a thankless role, that of Alex Forrest in Adrian Lyne's *Fatal Attraction* (87), but her Marquise De Merteuil in **Stephen Frears's** *Dangerous Liaisons* (88) was inferior to **Annette Bening's** Marquise in **Milos Forman's** *Valmont* (89). Her best screen role came as the ill-fated Sunny von Bulow in **Barbet Schroeder's** *Reversal Of Fortune* (90).

OTHER KEY FILMS: *The Big Chill* (83); *The Natural* (84); *Jagged Edge* (85); *Hamlet* (90); *Paradise Road* (97); *Cookie's Fortune* (99); *Things You Can Tell Just By Looking At Her* (00); *102 Dalmatians* (00)

Close Shot

Not as extreme as a close-up, a close shot will tend to highlight the top or bottom half of an actor, or to focus, in direct ratio to the size of the object being filmed, on one individual facet of a scene.

Close-up

Usually consisting of a full or partial face shot, close-ups are designed to reflect or highlight a given emotion. They are used more rarely for action purposes (in order not to gross out the audience, one supposes) but **Luis Buñuel** and Salvador Dalí had no such reservations, and in their surrealist masterpiece *Un Chien Andalou* (29), they showed a close-up shot of a woman's eyeball being sliced open by a razor. It was later found that a dead pig's eye had been craftily juxtaposed with the (fortunate) woman's face.

67

Cloud Wheel

An additional gizmo used to heighten the effect of an artificial skyscape during an indoor shoot, and which consists of light being filtered and refracted through a revolving disk onto a backdrop.

Clouzot, Henri-Georges

Clouzot was France's master of suspense and sadism, seeking his subjects behind twitching curtains or in crowded rooms. His second film was *Le Corbeau* (43), a magnificently dark thriller about a poison-pen letterist who turns an otherwise happy town against itself. Seen by many as a brave criticism of French collaboration with the Nazis, it paradoxically got Clouzot into trouble after the war for showing the French as too black and for laying itself open to use in German propaganda! The very sexy *Quai Des Orfèvres* (47) reinstated him (see **Erotic Moments**), and was followed, six years later, by the finest of all nail-biters, *Le Salaire De La Peur* [*The Wages Of Fear*] (53). Clouzot then went on to match *Le Corbeau* with its bourgeois counterpart, *Les Diaboliques* (55), a truly devious whodunit that leaves one guessing until the very last moment. His *Le Mystère Picasso* (56) was a brilliant and innovative documentary which had the happy idea of asking Picasso to paint on glass panels through which Clouzot's camera could film him – the feature-length result came perilously close to revealing the very magic that Picasso himself believed in so intensely.
OTHER KEY FILMS: *L'Assassin Habite Au 21* (42); *Manon* (49); *Les Espions* (57); *La Vérité* (60); *L'Enfer* (64); *La Prisonnière* (68)

Coburn, James

Thin, rangy, laconic – a man of odd movements and languid mien – Coburn was a loner hero in all his best films, and although he was surprisingly good at comedy, one remembers him most fondly for his knife-throwing Britt in **John Sturges's** *The Magnificent Seven* (60), for his bomb-loving ex-IRA gunslinger, Sean Mallory, in **Sergio Leone's** underrated *A Fistful Of Dynamite* [a.k.a. *Duck, you Sucker/Once Upon A Time There Was A Revolution*] (71), and for his disillusioned Sergeant Steiner in **Sam Peckinpah's** sensational *Cross Of Iron* (77).
OTHER KEY FILMS: *Ride Lonesome* (59); *Hell Is For Heroes* (62); *The Great Escape* (63); *Major Dundee* (65); *A High Wind In Jamaica* (65); *Our Man Flint* (66); *Pat Garrett And Billy The Kid* (73); *Death Of A Soldier* (86); *Maverick* (94); *Eraser* (96); *Keys To Tulsa* (97); *Intrepid* (00); *Proximity* (01)

Cobweb Spinner

Much used in such films as **Alexander Korda's** multi-directed production of *The Thief Of Bagdad* (40), **Steven Spielberg's** *Raiders Of The Lost Ark* (84) and in countless **Hammer Horror** movies, a cobweb spinner consists of a large fan used to imitate the cobweb-making actions of a spider by blowing skeins of rubber cement onto any surface that is deemed cobweb-worthy by ghoulish directors.

Cocteau, Jean

Cocteau was a phenomenon more than a man, and his talents read like the sort of list Narcissus would have drawn up for himself had he ever bothered to put stylus to wax tablet. Cocteau thought of himself predominantly as a poet, however, and this view permeated his films and allowed him the freedom to invent. *La Belle Et La Bête* (46) is the most successful of these dream fantasies, closely followed by *Orphée* (50), a film which cannot fail to move viewers when seen for the first time and at a young enough age, and provide them with some understanding of the imaginative possibilities of the cinema. Many further films were made from Cocteau's scripts and stories, and possibly the most successful of these is **Jean-Pierre Melville's** *Les Enfants Terribles* (50), in which we are drawn in, almost against our will, to the claustrophobic yet strangely liberating world of the semi-insane.
OTHER KEY FILMS: *Le Sang D'Un Poète* (30); *L'Aigle À Deux Têtes* (48); *Les Parents Terribles* (48); *Le Testament D'Orphée* (60)

Code Numbers

Figures marked on a working print and its matching soundtrack at one-foot intervals in order to indicate to an editor where synchronisation should occur.

Coen Brothers, The

Love them or hate them (and they are desperately popular with the more pretentious critics) Joel and Ethan Coen very definitely have talent, and for every turkey like *Barton Fink* (91) (and what a hell of a turkey that was: see **Worst Films**) they come up with three or four successes, including their debut *Blood Simple* (84), the hilarious *Raising Arizona* (87), the gloriously pulpy *Miller's Crossing* (90), and their near-masterpiece *Fargo* (96), a movie which improves with every viewing. Quirky, individualistic, and just a touch self-conscious, the Coens epitomise the brasher form of artist, not content to step back and let things be, but always aiming for effects that may not come off but certainly seem worth striving for at the

time. Their recent *The Big Lebowski* (98) featured an on-form **Jeff Bridges** playing the sort of man he might have become had he not taken up acting, aged eight, in his father's 'Sea Hunt' TV series, and *O Brother, Where Art Thou?* (00) is a paean to blues, road movies, jail films, and the magnetic talent of **George Clooney**.
OTHER KEY FILMS: *The Hudsucker Proxy* (94)

Co-feature

The intended partner for a main feature **A-movie** during the period (up to about the middle of the 1960s) when cinema chains regularly incorporated two films into their programme, as part of the expected double bill.

Coffee, Lenore

Yet another unsung screenwriter (except to the cognoscenti), Coffee's forty-year career, from silent to sound, included innumerable adaptations, scenarios, and script and dialogue credits, the best of which include Clarence Brown's *Possessed* (31), **Cecil B DeMille's** *The Squaw Man* (31) and David Miller's *Sudden Fear* (52). Like so many of her profession, Coffee ended up penniless and forgotten in a film industry-funded rest-home, while television audiences were still thrilling to **Bette Davis's** performance in **Edmund Goulding's** Coffee-scripted *The Great Lie* (41).
OTHER KEY FILMS: William Nigh's *Desert Nights* (29); **Michael Curtiz's** *Four Daughters* (38); Irving Pichel's *Tomorrow Is Forever* (46); **Edward Dmytryk's** *The End Of The Affair* (55)
KEY LINE:
'I like Graham Greene very much. He's a convert to Catholicism, too. He said something once that I will always remember, "I wouldn't want a God I could understand." ' [Coffee on her collaboration with Greene on *The End Of The Affair* (55)]

Cohn, Harry

Cohn was the man Hollywood loved to hate, and over the years he came to epitomise everything that was bad and grasping about the studio system. Founder of **Columbia Pictures** with his later-to-be-ousted brother Jack, Cohn used his new-found power to tyrannise his writers, directors and stars into performing his will, earning himself the nickname 'White Fang' from **Ben Hecht** in the process.
KEY LINE:
'On your first day there you were invited to lunch with Harry Cohn in the executive dining room.

You sat down. At which point he pressed a button, and the chair under you collapsed. And everybody laughed, laughed, laughed.' [**Charles Bennett** on his introduction to Columbia Pictures]

Cokuloris

See **Cookie**

Colbert, Claudette

Colbert wouldn't even have found a job on TV these days thanks to her currently unfashionable form of beauty, but that would have been television's, and our, loss. She was a witty, sparkling little thing, unquestionably strong (before feminine strength became an unpleasant buzzword with supremacist connotations). She had a light, pleasantly ironical touch in comedy, which was best brought out by a man's man, like **Clark Gable**, in *It Happened One Night* (34). She was brilliant at deflation, too, and one remembers her breezy magnificence in **Preston Sturges's** *The Palm Beach Story* (42), where she dealt, in turn, with the Weenie King, a heroically ineffectual **Joel McCrea**, the entire Ale & Quail club, **Mary Astor's** sexually voracious Princess Centimillia, and, best of all, Rudy Vallee's sublime J D Hackensacker III. All of which goes to prove, in the proverbial nutshell, that she was a consummate screen actress.
OTHER KEY FILMS: *The Sign Of The Cross* (32); *Imitation Of Life* (34); *Under Two Flags* (36); *Tovarich* (37); *Bluebeard's Eighth Wife* (38); *Zaza* (39); *Drums Along The Mohawk* (39); *It's A Wonderful World* (40); *Boom Town* (40); *Since You Went Away* (44); *Guest Wife* (45); *The Egg And I* (47); *Sleep, My Love* (48)
KEY LINES:
'I proved, once and for all, that the limb is mightier than the thumb.' [*It Happened One Night*]

'I just had the unpleasant sensation of hearing you referred to as my husband.' [*It Happened One Night*]

Colman, Ronald

One of the few actors to retain, and indeed increase, his audience appeal after the move from silent to sound film, Colman was still capable of fluttering female hearts at the relatively advanced age of fifty-seven, when he won an **Oscar** for his portrayal of a schizophrenic actor in **George Cukor's** *A Double Life* (47). His best parts came earlier, however, in **John Ford's** *Arrowsmith* (31), **Jack Conway's** *A Tale Of Two Cities* (35), John Cromwell's *The Prisoner Of Zenda* (37), and **Frank Capra's** recently restored *Lost Horizon* (37), where Colman's elegant and comforting voice perfectly matched the other-worldly atmosphere of Shangri-la.

69

OTHER KEY FILMS: *The White Sister* (23); *Beau Geste* (26); *Bulldog Drummond* (29); *Raffles* (30); *The Unholy Garden* (31); *Under Two Flags* (36); *Random Harvest* (42)

KEY LINE:
'I may not believe in myself, but I expect others to believe in me.' [*A Double Life*]

Colorization

The absolutely perfidious technique whereby black-and-white films are artificially coloured to please mindless grockles who wouldn't recognise a film classic if it came up and bit them in the face.

Colour

Hand-painted colour scenes were commonplace in films such as **Georges Méliès's** *A Trip To The Moon* (1902), and frame by frame tinting was used heavily throughout the 1910s and 1920s. Rouben Mamoulian's *Becky Sharp* (35) was the first major feature film to use the three-colour register strip **Technicolor** process (the scarlet uniforms of the British officers at the ball before the battle of Waterloo gave particular pleasure), and later **Michael Curtiz's** *The Adventures Of Robin Hood* (38), **Victor Fleming's *Gone With The Wind*** (39) and *The Wizard Of Oz* (39), together with **Henry King's** *Jesse James* (39), all made brilliant use of the system. Until the mid-1950s **black-and-white** film was still the medium of choice for many serious directors, but by the mid-1960s most had surrendered to the **Technicolor** revolution. <u>Note for Film Buffs</u>: Many of the cheaper 1950s and 1960s colour variants (particularly DeLuxe) are seriously beginning to fade.

Colour Chart/Grey Scale

The twin charts used side by side in order to estimate how colour film will convert to **black-and-white** should such a transformation be deemed necessary. For a simple home test all that is necessary is to gradually tone down the colour during the showing of any particularly luridly shot movie – the result may quite often be an improvement on the original.

Colour Cinematography

The colour process involves something in the region of double the expense of using **black-and-white** stock, and entails additional costs due to the increasing importance the qualities of weather and light will take on during location shooting. The matching of shots is also harder using the colour process, but all this pales into insignificance (when it comes to a choice between both processes) in the face of the majority of filmgoers who now resolutely refuse to shell out to watch first-rate black-and-white films, feeling that they are somehow being cheated. Ignorance, as the saying doesn't go, is in the eye of the wallet holder.

Colour Consultant

Due to the effectiveness of modern colour processes, the job of colour consultant is now virtually obsolete. The notorious Natalie Kalmus, first wife of joint **Technicolor** inventor Dr Herbert T Kalmus, maintained a near stranglehold on directors during the 1930s and 1940s by arrogating the role of colour consultant (and the accompanying screen credit on every single Technicolor film) to herself.

Colour Correction

The reworking of existing colours by means of filters to produce an original or desired effect, for example the washed-out **Western** tones **Vilmos Zsigmond** used in **Robert Altman's** *McCabe And Mrs Miller* (71), or in **John Huston's** now-notorious colour experiments (the photography was done by Aldo Tonti) in *Reflections In A Golden Eye* (67).

Colour Film

Film stock that contains colour sensitive emulsion.

Colour Filter

A filter of a particular colour used to strain out all other colours but its own.

Colour Sensitivity

The amount of sensitivity film stock has to visible spectrum colours.

Colour Sequence

A specific part of a film that is coloured differently from the main bulk of the work. **Sergei Eisenstein** used this concept to good effect in *Ivan The Terrible, Part Two* (46), and **Erich von Stroheim** tinted a military parade in honour of Emperor Franz Josef in his *The Wedding March* (28). Other classic examples are the colour differentiation between heaven and earth (earth is coloured) in **Michael Powell** and **Emeric Pressburger's** *A Matter Of Life And Death* (46), and the sudden interposition of cost-cutting black-and-white sequences in **Lindsay Anderson's** *If* (68).

Colour Temperature

The colour value of a light source as measured by a Kelvin calibrated three-colour-meter.

Columbia Pictures

Columbia's big break came nearly fifteen years after its founding by **Harry Cohn** and his brother Jack, when **Frank Capra** directed **Clark Gable** and **Claudette Colbert** in the massively successful **road movie**, *It Happened One Night* (34). Thirty years later it would throw itself behind **David Lean's** *Lawrence Of Arabia* (63), and twenty years after that throw off **Steven Spielberg's** *ET* (82), a move that cost it untold millions of dollars in lost receipts. Bought by Coca-Cola in 1982, the company was sold at a massive profit to Sony of Japan (who also own TriStar) seven years later.

Combined Print

See **Composite Print**

Comeback

What happens when an actor or actress is all but forgotten, and then returns triumphantly and unexpectedly to public awareness – the dream of many, of course, but a privilege accorded to few. **John Travolta** recently achieved it in **Quentin Tarantino's** *Pulp Fiction* (94), and **Gloria Swanson** certainly lived up to her name (and the pun it so nearly is) in **Billy Wilder's** *Sunset Boulevard* (50), in which her performance as Norma Desmond (herself as she might have been?) was nothing short of astonishing.

Best Comedy Films

Woody Allen's *Radio Days* (87); **Robert Altman's** *M*A*S*H* (70); Richard Benjamin's *My Favourite Year* (82); John G Blystone's *Blockheads* (38); **Mel Brooks's** *The Producers* (68); **Frank Capra's** *Arsenic And Old Lace* (44); **René Clair's** *I Married A Witch* (42); **George Cukor's** *The Philadelphia Story* (40); Bill Forsyth's *Local Hero* (83); **Terry Gilliam** and Terry Jones's *Monty Python And The Holy Grail* (74); **Robert Hamer's** *Kind Hearts And Coronets* (49); **Howard Hawks's** *Bringing Up Baby* (38), *Ball Of Fire* (41) and *I Was A Male War Bride* (49); James W Horne's *Way Out West* (37); **Buster Keaton's** *The Navigator* (24); **Stanley Kubrick's** *Dr Strangelove Or: How I Learned To Stop Worrying And Love the Bomb* (64); **Patrice Leconte's** *Tango* (92); **Ernst Lubitsch's** *Ninotchka* (39) and *To Be Or Not To Be* (42); Leo McCarey's *Duck Soup* (33) and *The Awful Truth* (37); **Alexander Mackendrick's** *The Ladykillers* (55) and *Whisky Galore* (48); Norman Z McLeod's *It's A Gift* (34); **Preston Sturges's** *Sullivan's Travels* (41) and *The Palm Beach Story* (42)

Commissary

The eating area in a film studio.

Compilation Film

A film compiled exclusively from existing footage, usually, but not always, taking the form of a **documentary**.

Composite Dupe Negative

A double of an existing negative that also contains synchronized sound.

Composite Master

The existing print from which a **composite dupe negative** is made.

Composite Photography

Otherwise known as **matte** or **blue screen** shots, composite photography is the art of splicing together two or more pieces of separately shot film to give the impression that the scene we are watching actually occurred more or less as we see it on the screen. Famous matte shots include the burning of Atlanta sequence in **Victor Fleming's** *Gone With The Wind* (39), which was actually shot three years earlier on the **MGM** backlot and resulted in the destruction of a number of unwanted sets and considerable local hysteria. This 1936 footage was then spliced into a 1939 sequence with two stuntmen driving a seemingly out of control carriage through the flames, creating the spectacular effect we see in the movie.

Composite Print

A film print in which sound and image are married together.

Compositing

The elision of two or more disparate images, separately shot, into one apparently seamless scene, by the use of **blue screen** or **digital** techniques. When Forrest Gump, in the person of **Tom Hanks**, shakes President Nixon's hand, the art of compositing enables us to be quite sure that Tricky Dicky didn't emerge from the grave either to appear in the scene or to receive his belated royalty cheque.

Computer Animation

The total opposite of what **Aardman** do, computer animation consists of the scanning of images into a digitally controllable form, which can then be manipulated as and how the animator wishes, by means of a computer

71

program. Both versions of **Disney's** *Toy Story* (95 and 00) were computer-animated, in total opposition to the **stop frame** processes so laboriously but effectively used by Aardman's *Chicken Run* (00).

Computer-Generated Imagery
See **CGI**

Cone Lights
A series of differently powered and sized but similarly formulated studio lights, used for the blanket illumination of large areas.

Connery, Sean
Recently voted the sexiest male of the century and the man who improves most as he gets older, by a significant cross-section of American womanhood, ex-bodybuilder Connery started his international career by pipping the likes of **Trevor Howard**, **Peter Finch**, **James Mason** and **Richard Burton** to the role of Ian Fleming's **James Bond** (probably because he came cheap). His increasing box-office success in the Bond part allowed Connery to branch out into more 'worthy' fare, and he made the curiously

underrated *Marnie* (64) for **Alfred Hitchcock**, followed by **Sidney Lumet's** unremittingly brutal *The Hill* (65). In recent years virtually everything the newly knighted Connery has done has turned to box-office gold, but despite this he remains, when he cares to be – as Daniel Dravot, for instance in **John Huston's** magnificent *The Man Who Would Be King* (75) and as Barley Blair, in **Fred Schepisi's** *The Russia House* (91) – an excellent actor and a consummate screen professional.

OTHER KEY FILMS: *Hell Drivers* (58); *Dr No* (62); *From Russia With Love* (63); *Woman Of Straw* (64); *The Molly Maguires* (70); *The Anderson Tapes* (72); *The Offence* (73); *The Wind And The Lion* (75); *Outland* (81); *Five Days One Summer* (83); *The Untouchables* (87); *The Rock* (96); *Entrapment* (99); *Finding Forrester* (00)

Console
The main panel in a sound studio or recording booth which is used for controlling all the different aspects of sound work including recording, mixing, looping, dubbing and re-recording.

Contact Printing
A basic and cheap form of printing that consists of the twin emulsions of the positive and negative film coming into contact while passing an exposing aperture.

Continuity
The illusion that the film we are watching was shot in exact sequence, due to the efforts of the **continuity girl** or **boy** to ensure that scenes actually shot out of sequence (the majority) match each other in any and every respect.

Continuity Girl (Boy)
The person on a film set responsible for making sure that the physical aspects of a scene remain consistent, even if the scene is shot and completed at wildly differing times. This nightmarish role extends to monitoring haircuts (rotten luck if an actor loses his hair between extended shots), drink measures, clothing and dress items such as earrings (**Yul Brynner** varied markedly in this respect during Walter Lang's *The King And I* (56), appearing first with one earring and then two within the same scene), and the placing of furniture. Notable boo-boos include the repetition of two exactly similar shots of Max von Sydow getting out his cross and holy water, but twenty minutes apart unfortunately, in **William Friedkin's** *The Exorcist* (73), the gradual change in **Elvis**

The evergreen Sean Connery as legendary thief Robert 'Mac' MacDougal, in Jon Amiel's Entrapment *(99)*

Presley's prison number in Richard Thorpe's *Jailhouse Rock* (57), and Celia Johnson's magically quick-drying raincoat in **David Lean's** *Brief Encounter* (45). A more recent clanger (all right, more an editing clanger than a continuity one, but what the hell) came in Roland Emmerich's *Universal Soldier* (92), when we see a shot of the motel owner's mother still reading her magazine *five minutes* after Dolph Lundgren and his cyborgs have opened fire with four zillion rounds of ammunition on **Jean-Claude Van Damme's** motel room (and the two rooms adjacent to his for good measure) just ten yards down the road from her office. Perhaps she was deaf? Yes, that must be it.

Continuity Sheets

The notes kept by the **continuity girl** or **boy** (or clerk, if we want to be politically correct, which we don't) and which relate to the physical and verbal aspects of each scene shot. They will be compared and married to further shots of the same scene conducted later, ensuring that no slip-ups or anachronisms belatedly come to light.

Continuity Title

Near-ubiquitous in silent film, the sort of continuity title which customarily took up the whole screen, explaining the plot, historical background, or simply giving dialogue, is now rarely deemed necessary except in mannered, re-creative or artificial settings. However the grand old tradition still continues, for some reason, in submarine films, where the continuity title is usually provided by mock computer printouts, together with assorted computer-like noises, to explain contexts like the Cold War and the reasons for nuclear deterrence to otherwise ignorant audiences.

Continuous Action

An extended take that is not interrupted by editing. Most famous of all was **Orson Welles's** spectacular two-minute opening sequence in *Touch Of Evil* (58), in which he follows the progress of a car and its doomed passengers through the streets of a Mexican border town. The sequence had to be re-shot a number of times because the border guard, overawed by the massed ranks of actors, technicians and hardware bearing down on him, consistently fluffed his lines.

Contract Player

Rather outmoded now, the contract player was a staple of 1930s and 1940s Hollywood, and was often chained to one particular studio (and the whims of the studio boss) by the intricate details of a long-term contract, which could frequently stretch to as much as seven years (and on occasion, even more). **Olivia de Havilland** and **Bette Davis** were among the first big stars successfully to fight the studios for the right to run their own artistic lives.

Contrast

Providing the effective gap between the brightest and most sombre areas of a shot, contrast is an essential tool, particularly in black-and-white productions of the *film noir* or **expressionistic** variety, in which tonal variations provide much of the visual effect of any particular scene.

Contrast Glass

The tool used by many cinematographers to resolve their lighting problems, consisting of a glass eyepiece through which lighting contrast, and the balance between key and **fill lights**, may be ascertained.

Conway, Jack

Conway learned the directing art under **D W Griffith**, and went on to make some of the best films of Hollywood's golden age, including the definitive *A Tale Of Two Cities* (35) with **Ronald Colman**. He also directed the one and only **Jean Harlow** in *Red-Headed Woman* (32), and in her final film, *Saratoga* (37), and was responsible for the sexiest Tarzan movie ever, *Tarzan And His Mate* (34), in which the smooth-buttocked **Maureen O'Sullivan** wore the famous cut-away loin cloth that has delighted and titillated discerning moviegoers for nigh on seventy years.
OTHER KEY FILMS: *Arsène Lupin* (32); *Libeled Lady* (36); *Too Hot To Handle* (38)

Cookie

Also known as a cuke or cokuloris, this is a solid sheet of material through which holes are cut to allow light to penetrate in order to raise contrast, heighten and disperse shadows, and reduce glare.

Cooper, Chris

One of the finest screen actors currently at work in Hollywood, Cooper is also one of the most self-effacing, and one cries out for him to be used more often while suspecting that he is very cannily managing his own career, thank you very much, and doesn't need any advice from outside parties. His best performance among many has come in **John Sayles's** cross-cultural American masterpiece *Lone Star* (97), in which Cooper plays Sheriff Sam Deeds, struggling to emerge

73

from beneath the shadow of his hero-worshipped (except by his son) dead father. This is indisputably one of the great films of the last thirty years, and deserves to be paired with the best of **John Ford**, but Cooper's performance is as utterly unlike **John Wayne's**, in, say, Ford's *The Searchers* (56), as it is possible to be. Deeds is an ordinary man in extraordinary circumstances, and he triumphs (if that is the word) specifically on account of that very, dogged, ordinariness. It takes a master to achieve such a trick.

OTHER KEY FILMS: *Bad Timing* (80); *Matewan* (87); *City Of Hope* (91); *Guilty By Suspicion* (91); *This Boy's Life* (93); *Money Train* (95); *A Time To Kill* (96); *Great Expectations* (98); *The Horse Whisperer* (98); *American Beauty* (99); *Me, Myself And Irene* (00); *The Patriot* (00)

Cooper, Gary

Awesomely good-looking even in later life and an inveterate womaniser (his mistresses included **Clara Bow**, **Marlene Dietrich**, **Carole Lombard**, **Ingrid Bergman**, Patricia Neal, **Grace Kelly**, Anita Ekberg and Lupe Velez), Cooper epitomised the laconic, slow-speaking (but hardly slow-witted) **Western** heroes the movie public have always yearned for. The son of British immigrants to the US, Cooper was pretty much top of the Hollywood heap for twenty of the thirty-five years of his acting career. Rated by contemporaries as the greatest film star of them all, he was both a fine comedian in films such as **Frank Capra's** *Mr Deeds Goes To Town* (36) and **Howard Hawks's** *Ball Of Fire* (41), and a superb dramatic lead in **Fred Zinnemann's** *High Noon* (52) and **Anthony Mann's** underrated *Man Of The West* (58), where he combined both these talents to almost mythic effect.

OTHER KEY FILMS: *Shopworn Angel* (28); *Morocco* (30); *Farewell To Arms* (32); *The Lives Of A Bengal Lancer* (35); *Desire* (36); *The Plainsman* (36); *The Westerner* (40); *Sergeant York* (41); *For Whom The Bell Tolls* (43); *The Fountainhead* (49); *Vera Cruz* (54); *Love In The Afternoon* (57)

KEY LINES:

'For me it's the first chapter. For what has my life been up to now? A preface? An empty foreword.' [Cooper's over-erudite linguistic expert, Bertram Potts, to **Barbara Stanwyck's** over-sexed gangster's moll, Sugarpuss O'Shea, in *Ball Of Fire*]

'He's hung like a horse and he can go all night.' [Clara Bow, musing on Cooper's jewellery collection]

'Gary Cooper was a very interesting, a very complex man. He was not a simple person at all. I think he was one of the best actors film has ever had.' [Wendell Mayes, who co-scripted Cooper's last **Western**, Delmer Daves's *The Hanging Tree* (59)]

'Everything Cooper does is original. He thinks about it. You have to watch it to realise what makes Gary Cooper on film. You don't just stand him up there; it's things that he does.' [**Henry Hathaway** on Cooper, whom he directed in *The Lives Of A Bengal Lancer* (35)]

Cooper, Merian C

Always an adventurer (he joined an expedition against Pancho Villa and was shot down a couple of times during the First World War), Cooper only really made movies as a means of raising money to fund his real love, flying. With his partner, Ernest B Schoedsack, he filmed a number of highly regarded documentaries, including the fictionalised *Chang* (27) about an embattled Siamese hill-tribe family, and the public's response to these eventually led him to try his hand at feature films. With the

Gary Cooper looking beautiful, in a classic 1930s Hollywood studio shot. See also image at Barbara Stanwyck

success of his first effort, *The Four Feathers* (29), he, Schoedsack and **RKO** decided to take a punt on a wild idea involving giant apes and New York skyscrapers, and the result was *King Kong* (33), the greatest and most original adventure story of all time. The film was so successful that Cooper was shunted upstairs to the executive lounge, and he continued on in film only as a producer – but it is to him, coincidentally, that we owe many of director **John Ford's** greatest early movies.

Coppola, Francis Ford

Coppola is an enigma – a man of extraordinary energy and varied passions whose generous encouragement of others, twinned with his magnificent work on the *Godfather* trilogy (72-90) and *Apocalypse Now* (79), should be enough to put him on a par with a **John Ford**, a **Nicholas Ray**, or a **Frank Capra**. The fact that he doesn't quite match his progenitors is not so much a criticism as a warning – recent American film lacks the soul and the poetry of its greatest antecedents, and Coppola, too, falls into this trap – it's as if by being given an enormous, magical box of tricks, directors like Coppola have forgotten that it is people, and not effects that count. Effects, however, can best be left to nature – what a movie audience wants to see is how people respond to extremes, and how these extremes bring out a communal and incipient humanity. John Ford understood this in *The Hurricane* (37) which was never intended to be simply about the storm, but rather about the people whose lives it changed; Nicholas Ray understood it in *They Live By Night* (49), which was not about crime but about youth; and Frank Capra understood it in *The Bitter Tea Of General Yen* (32), which wasn't so much about revolution, as about the lives and loves of the people caught up in it. *Apocalypse Now* is magnificent, and bears repeated viewings, but one finally comes to the conclusion, after being bowled over, yet again, by its brilliance – so what? It is impossible to imagine Martin Sheen's Capt. Willard as changed by the end of it. Or even wiser. He and the viewer have simply undergone an extraordinary experience together, and are content to part on those terms. But one never forgets Terangi and Marama, Bowie and Keechie, Megan Davis and General Yen.

OTHER KEY FILMS: *The Rain People* (69); *The Conversation* (74); *One From The Heart* (82); *The Outsiders* (83); *Rumble Fish* (83); *The Cotton Club* (84); *Peggy Sue Got Married* (86); *Gardens Of Stone* (87); *Tucker: The Man And His Dream* (88); *Bram Stoker's Dracula* (92); *Jack* (96); *The Rainmaker* (97)

Co-production

A production funded by two or more nations to take advantage of financial incentives and to increase audience sizes by sometimes filming scenes in a number of languages, thereby obviating the necessity for post-production dubbing.

Copter Mount

Also known as a Tyler Mount, the copter mount prevents the camera juddering during aerial filming in a helicopter.

Copy

Any print made from an already developed original.

Copyright

The exclusive right to reproduce or perform one's own work, and to authorise others to do the same. European copyright now lasts for life plus seventy years, as opposed to US and worldwide copyright, which lasts for life plus fifty.

Corman, Roger

Corman may be most renowned for his colourful horror films, but he was always more than simply a master of the macabre, and his innate sense of design and continual encouragement of other directors make him an important player in 1950s and 1960s cinema (he is the producer of more than 300 films). As a director his best films were undoubtedly those starring **Vincent Price**, and in particular the **Nicolas Roeg**-photographed *The Masque Of The Red Death* (64) and the **Robert Towne**-scripted *The Tomb Of Ligeia* (64), in both of which Price thankfully plays it straight. Both films had a heady visual style to them, and were essentially accurate portrayals of Edgar Allan Poe's interior world. Corman's championing of such 'difficult' European directors as **Ingmar Bergman** and **Federico Fellini** also redounds to his credit, and it is interesting to note that in recent years Corman has moved beyond his cult status to the status of grand old man of low-budget cinema.

OTHER KEY FILMS: *Machine Gun Kelly* (58); *The House Of Usher* (60); *The Pit And The Pendulum* (61); *X – The Man With X-Ray Eyes* (63); *The St Valentine's Day Massacre* (67); *Bloody Mama* (70); *Frankenstein Unbound* (90)

KEY LINE:
'He was only interested in saving money, so his intellect ground down to almost nothing... Roger's stuff was 99 per cent garbage and 1 per cent is of interest.' [Screenwriter Charles B Griffith on his many collaborations with Corman]

Costa-Gavras, Constantin

Costa-Gavras is a political director, and his films invariably reflect his background as the son of a Greek communist and former Second World War resistance fighter. *Z* (69), with **Yves Montand**, was the first film to signal his particular talents as a truth-seeker and propagandist against tyranny, and he followed this up with *The Confession* (70), *State Of Siege* (72) and *Special Section* (72), which concentrated on Czechoslovakia, Uruguay, and Vichy war-time France respectively. He succeeded in making even the CIA uncomfortable with *Missing* (73), but his most successful film, in both human and political terms, is the little seen *Betrayed* (88), which works surprisingly well with its portrayal of an FBI agent, **Debra Winger**, torn apart by her love for a man, **Tom Berenger**, whom at the same time she must inevitably betray for the rabid, though paradoxically attractive Ku Klux Klan activist that he is. Costa-Gavras deals brilliantly with such paradoxes throughout the body of his work, and his strength lies in never forgetting the human in favour of the epic.

OTHER KEY FILMS: *The Sleeping-Car Murders* (65); *Shock Troops* (67); *Clair De Femme* (79); *Hanna K.* (83); *Family Business* (86); *Music Box* (90); *La Petite Apocalypse* (93); *The Dreyfuss Affair* (94); *Rasputin* (95); *Mad City* (97)

Costner, Kevin

Now struggling for his commercial life after a sequence of own-goal turkeys, Costner is a genuine talent with an uncanny capacity to miss his own market. After a run of well-chosen hits with **Brian De Palma's** *The Untouchables* (87), Roger Donaldson's *No Way Out* (87) and his own well-directed *Dances With Wolves* (90), not to mention a first-rate performance in **Oliver Stone's** *JFK* (91), his star position seemed more or less unassailable. Kevin Reynolds's *Robin Hood: Prince Of Thieves* (91) followed, together with an excellent turn as a convict with a heart of gold in **Clint Eastwood's** *A Perfect World* (93), and then…yes, Reynolds's *Waterworld* (95) and Costner's own *The Postman* (97), both disasters on an epic scale. Why? **Sam Raimi's** *For Love Of The Game* (00) has done nothing to stop the slide, and despite good reviews for Roger Donaldson's *Thirteen Days* (00), Costner remains a man who is struggling. Is a **John Travolta**-like comeback on the cards? Only time, and the next edition of this book, will tell.

OTHER KEY FILMS: *Silverado* (85); *Bull Durham* (88); *Field Of Dreams* (89); *The Bodyguard* (92); *Wyatt Earp* (94); *Tin Cup* (96); *3000 Miles To Graceland* (01)

KEY LINE:
'It's a great cultural achievement, now, fame, and it doesn't stand for anything.' [Costner on himself]

Costume Designer

The most famous of them all was Edith Head, whose name appeared on the final credits of a seemingly untold number of films during the 1930s and 1940s. The recipient of eight **Oscars**, Head tops the list of Oscar receivers for individual creative achievement, and was also responsible for designing the single most expensive dress ever seen on film – Ginger Rogers's $35,000 mink and sequin dance costume, worn in Mitchell Leisen's *Lady In The Dark* (44).

Costume Drama

Sometimes disparagingly known as 'costumers', costume dramas deal with literary, social or historical subjects which require period dress. A particularly convenient trope wherever censorship prevails, **Sergei Eisenstein's** *Ivan The Terrible* (44-46), for instance, was made at the behest of Stalin (who thought, wrongly, that costumers were intrinsically safe) and who then condemned Part Two of the epic when it became clear that the director was using his portrait of Ivan's secret 'oprichniki' police in order to criticise Stalin's own repressive policies.

Costumer

A costumer's duty is to procure and provide all the clothes worn in a film production either from the studio itself, from rental agencies, or from theatrical costumiers, antique and thrift shops, and then to aid in the dressing and fitting of the stars and the secondary players before shooting begins.

Cotten, Joseph

Now seen as something of an **Orson Welles** protégé, Cotten never appeared to take his acting very seriously, and it seems almost by default that he turned in good performances. Apart from the ubiquitous *Citizen Kane* (41), Cotten's best roles were in Welles's sadly truncated *The Magnificent Ambersons* (42) and *Journey Into Fear* (42), and, most notably, **Alfred Hitchcock's** *Shadow Of A Doubt* (43), in which he played Uncle Charlie, a charmingly ingratiating killer. Once again, in **Carol Reed's** *The Third Man* (49), he pulled out all the stops alongside his friend Welles, in his incarnation of Holly Martins to Welles's Harry Line, but, woefully, Cotten's later work was pedestrian in the extreme.

OTHER KEY FILMS: *Gaslight* (44); *Duel In The Sun* (46); *Portrait Of Jenny* (48); *Under Capricorn* (49); *Niagara* (53); *Touch Of Evil* (58)

Counter Key

Also known as a modelling light, this is a spotlight designed to emphasise contour and texture rather than simply providing generalised illumination.

Counterpoint

A term taken from music which implies no strict correlation between image and sound, but rather a counterpointing, or symbolic differentiation, between the two mediums, the image telling of one thing, the music of another. See **Parallelism**

Coverage

Most directors aim for maximum coverage during the shooting of a scene, meaning that shots are taken from every possible angle to simplify and expedite the eventual editing process and to provide back-up if one or more takes are spoiled.

Cover Shot

Extra insurance in the form of additional shots taken of a scene in case the original footage falls short of the director's expectations.

Coward, Noël

Coward constructed his own image of himself and resolutely lived by it throughout his extraordinarily successful life. When his plays began losing popularity he moved to films, and when the film work began to dry up he began a new career as an entertainer, chanteur and occasional actor, and when he tired of this he took to writing, yet again about himself, or rather about who he wanted to be. All this is perfectly normal in an actor, and Coward made a virtue of it. The plays serve as his memorial, for it was generally others who made the best films of his stories, most notably director **David Lean** with *Blithe Spirit* (45) and *Brief Encounter* (45).
OTHER KEY FILMS: *In Which We Serve* [co-dir.] (42); David Lean's *This Happy Breed* (44)

Cowboy Films

See **Western, The**

Cox, Alex

Cox is a cheerfully idiosyncratic movie director and film theorist who has become something of a cult among buffs as much for his quirky personality as for his resolutely off-beat films. *Repo Man* (84) was an immediate critical success, and *Sid And Nancy* (86), about the doomed affair between Sex Pistol Sid Vicious and his girlfriend Nancy Spungen, played out immaculately by **Gary Oldman** and Chloe Webb, consolidated his growing reputation, while his

odd little Mexican outing, *Highway Patrolman* (91), showed a welcome burst of humanity, at a time when mainstream films were heading further and further away from an acceptance of this unhappy, but undeniably all-encompassing, state.
OTHER KEY FILMS: *Straight To Hell* (87); *Walker* (87); *Dead Beat* (94); *Floundering* (94); *Queen Of The Night* (94); *Three Businessmen* (98)

Cox, Paul

Cox's *Man Of Flowers* (83) was one of the most curious, but at the same time most exalted films of the 1980s, particularly in its preoccupation with questions of acceptance and redemption. All Cox's films seem to touch on such metaphysical aspects, even when they are at their very bleakest, as in *My First Wife* (84), in which Cox explores, in excoriating detail, the breakdown of a marriage and of family relationships. Cox is an oasis of emotional daylight in a pretty bleak world, and one can forgive him his tics and his tendency to encourage his actors to underplay their roles, for simply having the courage to try, as in *Cactus* (86), to reflect on the real and the imagined and to attempt to shuffle them into some sort of acceptable symmetry.
OTHER KEY FILMS: *Illuminations* (76); *Inside Looking Out* (77); *Kostas* (79); *Lonely Hearts* (82); *Vincent: The Life And Death Of Vincent Van Gogh* (87); *Island* (89); *The Golden Braid* (90); *A Woman's Tale* (91); *Lust And Revenge* (96); *Innocence* (00)

Crab Dolly

A camera platform equipped with a variety of hydraulic controls to allow for the maximum number of **dolly** movements in long and technically involved shots.

Crane

A moveable platform with an extensible **boom** used to carry the camera high over the set, which allows for a large number of complex lateral and horizontal movements. **Orson Welles's** famous two-minute opening sequence for *Touch Of Evil* (58) used such a crane device to magnificent effect.

Craven, Wes

A master of schlock horror and shock tactics (try saying that fast!), Craven has moved from the periphery to the commercial mainstream in tandem with society's changing tastes and widening standards of acceptance. *The Hills Have Eyes* (77), while not being his first success, was at least characteristic, in its concentration on the gruesome and the grotesque, of what was to come. Commercial heaven (in the

77

guise of the Hollywood money-men) came to Craven in recognition of the infinitely repeatable thrills of *Nightmare On Elm Street* (84), and Craven has doggedly followed (ghosted?) the same scenario and the same ghoul-strewn path ever since, most recently with the *Scream* series.

OTHER KEY FILMS: *Last House On The Left* (72); *Deadly Blessing* (81); *Swamp Thing* (82); *Deadly Friend* (86); *Shocker* (90); *The People Under The Stairs* (91); *Scream* (96); *Scream 2* (97); *Music Of The Heart* (99); *Scream 3* (00)

Crawford, Joan

Crawford spent her life being dragged through the mud – posthumously by her adopted daughter and the gossips, and during her lifetime through her predilection for such gorgeously pulpy, soap-dish material as **Michael Curtiz's** *Mildred Pierce* (45) and the later, wilder, *Flamingo Road* (49), parts that appeared to reflect her non-acting life. This could be construed as a curiously backhanded compliment to her star power, for her audience believed so strongly in the roles that she played that they found it hard to accept that they weren't seeing the real Joan Crawford on the screen. And perhaps they were right. Crawford was a 'wannabe', the redneck daughter of poor Texans, and the sum total of her life consisted in the relegation and eventual extinguishing of that reality. And she achieved this, up to a point. But her later choice of films shows her despair all too clearly, together with the sad carapace of the self-sufficient woman that she forcibly constructed around herself to disguise it.

OTHER KEY FILMS: *This Modern Age* (31); *Grand Hotel* (32); *Sadie McKee* (34); *Mannequin* (38); *The Women* (39); *Strange Cargo* (40); *Above Suspicion* (43); *Humoresque* (46); *Possessed* (47); *Daisy Kenyon* (47); *Harriet Craig* (50); *Johnny Guitar* (54);

KEY LINE:
'A woman can do anything, get anywhere, as long as she doesn't fall in love.' [Curtis Bernhardt's *Possessed*]

Credits

The list of contributors that appears either at the beginning or end of a picture (sometimes both), and which includes everyone who ever had anything to do with the making of the film right down to the trained canary. Credits can come in many different shapes or forms, including the spoken, as at the end of **Orson Welles's** *The Magnificent Ambersons* (42), or, memorably, at the beginning of Sacha Guitry's *La Poison* (51), during which the director introduces us (with an elegant speech) to the star, **Michel Simon**, the co-stars, the

musicians, the composer, singer, cameramen, script girl (he calls her the script lady), and even by means of a telephone (an amusing conceit this) to the disembodied voices of those who appear only on the soundtrack. At the end of the sequence he even introduces us to the gaffers and crew as they stand, looking rather awkward, in front of a table heaving with wine and food, no doubt patiently waiting for the off. But the most original use of credits came during **Sergio Leone's** extraordinary ten-minute opening sequence in *Once Upon A Time In The West* (69), in which the director caps the steady build-up to his initial shootout by having a credit pop up, every thirty seconds or so, from behind a hat, inside a horse trough, outside the frame, underneath a train, or, once only (for obvious reasons), from the back of baddie Jack Elam's head.

Creeper Title

A slow-moving title sequence that rolls down the screen, often during action. One of the most famous creepers (a.k.a. rollers) was **Robert Aldrich's** reverse sequence titles (they moved from the bottom of the screen upwards) in *Kiss Me Deadly* (55), which streamed out over Cloris Leachman's bare feet, as she ran, whimpering in fear, down a night-shrouded hardtop road.

Crew

Everyone involved in the technical side of making a film, from the **soundman** through to the **gaffer**.

Best Crime Films

Robert Altman's *The Long Goodbye* (73); **Claude Chabrol's** *Le Boucher* (69) and *Que La Bête Meure* [*This Man Must Die*] (69); **Joel and Ethan Coen's** *Fargo* (96); **Jules Dassin's** *Du Rififi Chez Les Hommes* (54); Michel Deville's *Eaux Profondes* (81); Carl Franklin's *One False Move* (91); **William Friedkin's** *French Connection* (71); Curtis Hanson's *LA Confidential* (97); **Alfred Hitchcock's** *Rear Window* (54); **John Huston's** *The Asphalt Jungle* (50); **Fritz Lang's** *Beyond A Reasonable Doubt* (56); **Otto Preminger's** *Anatomy Of A Murder* (59); **Raoul Walsh's** *High Sierra* (41); **Orson Welles's** *The Lady From Shanghai* (46)

Cronenberg, David

Cronenberg tried to make the horror film an art form, and failed, although **James Whale** had achieved just that, without being particularly aware of it, many years before him. *The Fly* (86), a remake

of Kurt Neumann's 1958 movie, was wildly over-praised, but with *Dead Ringers* (88) Cronenberg came closest to his aim, insofar as he moved beyond horror into the territory of the fetishist – of man as the slave of his machines – and the film works wonderfully on that level. *Crash* (97) was another good try, but there was no humanity at all at its centre, and one felt almost grateful, by the end, for the gradual disintegration of its demented protagonists. Cronenberg is the intellect made metal, and until he realises that metal cuts when sharpened, and that those cuts bleed and cause pain, he will remain the half-successful director that he is.
OTHER KEY FILMS: *Shivers* (75); *The Brood* (79); *Scanners* (81); *Videodrome* (82); *The Dead Zone* (83); *Naked Lunch* (91); *eXistenZ* (99); *Camera* [short] (00).

Crosby, Bing

Crosby was perhaps the best and most versatile popular singer of all time – he could do jazz and ballads, comic and sentimental, swing and sweetheart. His film career certainly didn't reflect this versatility, but an easygoing and likeable charm came through on the screen that was enough to comfort his audience, and to suggest to them that if a simple everyday sort of a guy like Crosby could make it, then so, perhaps, might they. Crosby made the old-fashioned seem modern, and his best part, unsurprisingly, came in a **Billy Wilder** film, *The Emperor Waltz* (48), in which modesty and simplicity (surprise, surprise) win out over royalty. But Crosby *was* royalty, of course, and he was successful also when he acknowledged this fact, as in **Charles Walters's** *High Society* (56). His screen persona was the most likeable thing about him, and his matching of it so beautifully and so seamlessly to his singing personality showed a kind of genius.
OTHER KEY FILMS: *The Big Broadcast* (32); *Mississippi* (36); *Pennies From Heaven* (36); *Road To Singapore* (40); *Holiday Inn* (42); *Going My Way* (44); *Road To Rio* (47); *White Christmas* (54); *The Country Girl* (54); *Stagecoach* (66)
KEY LINE:
'You know, if the world was run right, only women would get married.' [Victor Schertzinger's *Road To Singapore*]

Crosscutting

Two separate scenes that the audience realises, by convention, are happening at one and the same time, which the director suggests by close editing and jump cuts. Such a device is often used to imply a future meeting between two as yet un-introduced characters in a filmed love story.

Cross-Plot

An abbreviated page-long **breakdown script** which shows the director exactly what is required in terms of actors, props, studio furniture, sets, etc., during a specified shooting schedule.

Crossing The Line

Filming first from one side, then the other, of a simultaneously happening scene, in order to suggest a different perspective. Such an abrupt change of viewpoint can backfire, as in the notorious cut in **John Ford's** *Stagecoach* (39), when the stagecoach, in full process of being chased by armed Apaches, suddenly appears to be racing straight towards them, rather than away, as was implied only seconds before.

Crossover

What happens when a genre film manages to draw in an audience that would otherwise never think of attending that particular type of movie. Studio bosses dream day and night of such a happy occurrence, knowing that it can instantly double till receipts, but examples are unfortunately rare. **Charles Walters's** *High Society* (56) is a case in point, seducing even musical haters with its leisurely panache (not such an obvious contradiction in terms when one thinks about it). **Dennis Hopper's** *Easy Rider* (69) just as equally managed the crossover from independent to mainstream, earning millions for its happy producers in the process. A more recent example is Eduardo Sanchez and Daniel Myrick's ultra-low-budget *The Blair Witch Project* (99), although the king of all crossovers (and the king of all **sleepers**, too) must be **Bruce Robinson's** *Withnail & I* (87) which has leapt, by a process of almost sublime inanition, to become the cult favourite of a quite stupendously bewildering variety of people (this author modestly included).

Cruise, Tom

Possibly the most successful big box-office attraction of the past ten years, Thomas Cruise Mapother IV first made his mark in Harold Becker's *Taps* (81), at the tender age of nineteen. His big break came with Tony Scott's *Top Gun* (86), closely followed by critical success in **Martin Scorsese's** *The Color Of Money* (86) and **Barry Levinson's** *Rain Man* (88). That rare being, a major league star who can act, Cruise's best work has been in Rob Reiner's *A Few Good Men* (92) and **Sydney Pollack's** *The Firm* (93), but Hollywood loves him more for the *Mission: Impossible* series (95-00), an apparently blue chip guarantee to print money following the recent success of *Mission: Impossible 2* (00) – all this despite the series' palpable absurdities; in one scene we have Cruise worthily struggling to put on a seat belt during a hot-dogging race despite, minutes before, voluntarily dangling by his fingers from a piece of naked rock 1,000 feet above the earth without a safety harness. Cruise and his since estranged wife **Nicole Kidman** took time out from money-making to act in **Stanley Kubrick's** last film, *Eyes Wide Shut* (99), and the result, while critically hammered at the time, may still prove to be a **sleeper** in disguise. Cruise reiterated his acting credentials in his recent stand-out performance as Frank 'T J' Mackey in Paul Thomas Anderson's *Magnolia* (99).

OTHER KEY FILMS: *The Outsiders* (83); *Risky Business* (83); *Legend* (85); *Cocktail* (88); *Born On The Fourth Of July* (89); *Days Of Thunder* (90); *Far And Away* (92); *Interview With The Vampire* (94); *Jerry Maguire* (96)

Cue

When directors shout 'Action!' or 'Cut!' they are cueing the beginning or end of a scene. Cueing can also be taken to mean the prompting of an actor by someone out of the camera's eye.

Cue Card

A card or electronic device held up, off-camera, to prompt an actor or actress who has difficulty in remembering their lines. **Marlon Brando** used his shirt cuff as a cue card on more than one occasion, and was even known to read his lines from sheets pinned to another actor's back.

Cue Mark

The mark film editors make on the prints they are working on to remind themselves of sound synchronisation exigencies, such as the appearance of a particular musical theme, an essential piece of narration, or an additional sound effect or **loop**.

Cukor, George

Cukor is now celebrated as much for his homosexuality as for his perceived sensitivity in portraying women, although both facets have been exaggerated and made the expedient realities of otherwise unenlightened self-interest groups. He was quite simply a first-rate director, honed in the theatre, who had the nous and commercial intelligence to play to his strengths, and to those of his actors and actresses. He had a magical six years with *Dinner At Eight* (33), *Little Women* (33), *David Copperfield* (35), *Sylvia Scarlett* (36), *Camille* (37) and *Holiday* (38), although the run was somewhat curtailed when **David Selznick** eased him off *Gone With The Wind*. But he soon made a skilful return with *The Women* (39) and *The Philadelphia Story* (40), and later consolidated his brilliant career even more (as if that were possible) with *Adam's Rib* (49), *Pat And Mike* (52) and *A Star Is Born* (54). Always the perfect entertainer, Cukor's films had heart, and a curious, almost spontaneous integrity, and his existence is something of a miracle in the environment in which he chose to function.

OTHER KEY FILMS: *Tarnished Lady* (31); *A Bill Of Divorcement* (32); *Romeo And Juliet* (36); *Keeper Of The Flame* (43); *Gaslight* (44); *Winged Victory* (44); *A Double Life* (47); *Born Yesterday* (50); *Bhowani Junction* (56); *Let's Make Love* (60); *My Fair Lady* (64); *Travels With My Aunt* (73); *Rich And Famous* (81)

Culkin, Macaulay

Culkin is one of those anachronisms that occasionally pop up in Hollywood – a throwback to child stars like **Shirley Temple** and Jackie Coogan – and his heyday was just as brief. One fondly hopes that he had more luck than poor Jackie, and managed to pocket some of the hard-won dosh he earned, for his films are eminently forgettable. The nearest he was allowed to get to anything resembling depth came late in his career (he was all of fourteen) in Donald Petrie's *Richie Rich* (94), but that isn't saying much.

OTHER KEY FILMS: *Home Alone* (90); *Home Alone 2: Lost In New York* (92); *The Pagemaster* (94)

Cult Film

Any film that has a cult, rather than a mainstream following. Such films frequently outlast their theatrical releases, finding themselves repeated, often at art-house cinemas, ad infinitum. Jim Sharman's *The Rocky Horror Picture Show* (75) is a case in point, as is **Robert Wise's** *The Sound Of Music* (65), both of which see cult followers dressing up as characters out of the movie and re-enacting certain scenes inside the cinema in exact parallel to what is happening on the screen.

KEY LINE:

'What's a cult? It just means not enough people to make a minority.' [**Robert Altman** on cult status]

Best **Cult Films**

Robert Aldrich's *Kiss Me Deadly* (55); **Robert Altman's** *Nashville* (75); **Jean-Jacques Beineix's** *Diva* (80); **Walerian Borowczyk's** *Blanche* (71); **Philippe de Broca's** *Le Roi De Coeur* [*King Of Hearts*] (66); **Tod Browning's** *Freaks* (32); **Luis**

Buñuel and Salvador Dali's *L'Age D'Or* (30); **Luis Buñuel's** *Belle De Jour* (66); **Frank Capra's** *The Bitter Tea Of General Yen* (32); **Jean Cocteau's** *Orphée* (49); **Paul Cox's** *Man Of Flowers* (83); **Jonathan Demme's** *Caged Heat* (74); **Georges Franju's** *Les Yeux Sans Visages* [a.k.a. *Eyes Without A Face*, or *Horror Chamber Of Dr Faustus*] (60); **Jean-Luc Godard's** *A Bout De Souffle* (59) and *Vivre Sa Vie* (62); **Edmund Goulding's** *Nightmare Alley* (47); Robin Hardy's *The Wicker Man* (73); **Hal Hartley's** *Simple Men* (92); **Howard Hughes's** *The Outlaw* (41); Alejandro Jodorowsky's *Santa Sangre* (89); Edward Ludwig's *Wake Of The Red Witch* (48); **David Lynch's** *Blue Velvet* (86); **Michael Powell** and Emeric Pressburger's *I Know Where I'm Going* (45), *Black Narcissus* (47) and *Gone To Earth* (50); **Alain Resnais's** *Hiroshima Mon Amour* (58) and *Last Year At Marienbad* (61); **Bruce Robinson's** *Withnail & I* (86); **Josef von Sternberg's** *The Shanghai Gesture* (41); **Quentin Tarantino's** *Pulp Fiction* (94); **Edgar G Ulmer's** *Detour* (45); **King Vidor's** *Duel In The Sun* (47); **John Waters's** *Cry-Baby* (90)

Curtis, Jamie Lee

A fine comedienne and an outstanding screamer, particularly in **John Carpenter's** *Halloween* (78), Curtis has worked consistently since her corpse-strewn beginnings, but it is only belatedly that directors have begun to recognise her inherited talent (she is the daughter of **Tony Curtis** and **Janet Leigh**). Amy Jones's *Love Letters* (83) first revealed her potential for drama, and Charles Crichton's *A Fish Called Wanda* (88) proved how adept she was at comedy. Her career has already been a long one by current Hollywood standards (she was born in 1958), and seems set fair, given her versatility, to continue indefinitely, as has recently been manifested by her excellent turn in **John Boorman's** *The Tailor Of Panama* (01).

OTHER KEY FILMS: *The Fog* (80); *Trading Places* (83); *Blue Steel* (90); *Forever Young* (92); *True Lies* (94); *Fierce Creatures* (97); *Homegrown* (98); *Virus* (99); *Daddy And Them* (00); *Halloween 8* (01)

Curtis, Tony

Curtis has had two high points in his career, and they came within two years of each other — his reptilian Sidney Falco in **Alexander Mackendrick's** magnificent *Sweet Smell Of Success* (57), and his sublimely harassed Joe/Josephine in **Billy Wilder's** *Some Like It Hot* (59). His other

successes have always seemed variations on those themes, but the two movies revealed a genuine and surprising talent, given his inauspicious beginnings as part of **Universal's** soul-destroying star production line.

OTHER KEY FILMS: *Houdini* (53); *The Black Shield Of Falworth* (54); *Trapeze* (56); *The Vikings* (58); *Spartacus* (60); *The Great Imposter* (60); *Taras Bulba* (62); *The Boston Strangler* (68); *The Last Tycoon* (76); *Insignificance* (85); *Stargames* (98)

Curtiz, Michael

As well as directing that perennial favourite, *Casablanca* (42), Curtiz made an astonishing average of four films a year for **Warner Brothers** during his quarter of a century tenure as one of their in-house directors, no less than twelve of which starred **Errol Flynn**. Renowned for his temperamental exigencies on set, Curtiz stories abound, many relating to his often idiosyncratic use of the English language (he was Hungarian). **David Niven** named the second volume of his autobiography, *Bring On The Empty Horses*, after one of Curtiz's shouted commands on the set of *The Charge Of The Light Brigade* (36). Even a brief look at Curtiz's key films will show what an astonishing capacity the man had to reinvent himself — his directing credits include thrillers, *film noirs*, musicals, horror movies, gangster pictures and even a jazz film. To cap an extraordinary career, nearly forty-six years after directing his first silent feature he took on the **Elvis Presley** star vehicle *King Creole* (58), and made a success of it.

OTHER KEY FILMS: *20,000 Years In Sing Sing* (33); *Mystery Of The Wax Museum* (33); *Captain Blood* (35); *The Adventures Of Robin Hood* (38); *Angels With Dirty Faces* (38); *The Private Lives Of Elizabeth and Essex* (39); *The Sea Wolf* (41); *Yankee Doodle Dandy* (42); *Mildred Pierce* (45); *Young Man With A Horn* (50); *White Christmas* (54)

Cusack, John

An interesting and careful actor who has husbanded his talent well and chosen his parts with great care and attention, Cusack's star is definitely rising, and he has enough versatility to make the most of the opportunities that will no doubt keep flooding in after his success in Spike Jonze's *Being John Malkovich* (99). He was excellent, too, in **Stephen Frears's** *The Grifters* (90), and wonderfully edgy in **Woody Allen's** *Shadows And Fog* (91) and *Bullets Over Broadway* (94), and if he can only manage to keep the lid on his self-destructive urges (in 1990 he was put on probation for three years for drink driving) he should have a great career ahead of him.

OTHER KEY FILMS: *Class* (83); *Stand By Me* (86); *Broadcast News* (87); *True Colors* (91); *Bob Roberts* (92); *The Road To Wellville* (94); *City Hall* (96); *Grosse Point Blank* (97); *High Fidelity* (00)

Cushing, Peter

The **Hammer** actor par excellence, Cushing usually played the straight man to **Christopher Lee's** warped monster, and this suited his inhibited, old-fashioned style of acting (Cushing would have been entirely at home in Victorian stage melodrama). He was the ultimate Baron Frankenstein in Terence Fisher's *The Curse Of Frankenstein* (57), if only because his fall was so long, and from so erudite and informed a height. Professing himself a little fed up with the unwanted form of celebrity his horror roles brought him, Cushing nevertheless always gave of his best, and his Van Helsing, in Fisher's *Dracula* (58), was equally grave and informed by the seriousness that had become his trademark.

OTHER KEY FILMS: *The Revenge Of Frankenstein* (58); *The Hound Of The Baskervilles* (59); *The Mummy* (59); *The Brides Of Dracula* (60); *Dr Terror's House Of Horrors* (64); *The Gorgon* (64); *Torture Garden* (67); *Asylum* (72); *The Beast Must Die* (74); *Star Wars* (77)

Custard-pie Movies:

Originally a silent film convention, the throwing of custard pies has spread (if that is the word) to sound movies as well, and has even spilled over into the real world, as in the case of the notorious **Jean-Luc Godard** custard-pie stalker case (see **Cannes Film Festival**). The greatest of all filmed custard-pie fights was the one engineered (if such a thing is possible) by **Laurel and Hardy** in Clyde Bruckman's *The Battle Of The Century* (27), in which twenty-four demented combatants threw a magnificent total of 3,000 pies at each other in an ecstatic, vanilla-flavoured Armageddon.

Cut

The final command to stop filming a scene, an edited jump from one scene to another, a censored portion of a film, or the version a director chooses after the studios have returned their (often bungled) cut to him. See **Director's Cut**

Cutaway Shot

An edited jump to something slightly outside the main action of a scene. This can be a **reaction shot**, or the interposition of an inanimate object, such as a newspaper headline, which comments indirectly on the action.

Cut Back

A return back to the main theme of a movie after a **cutaway shot** to something slightly outside that theme.

Cutter

Someone who is employed in the physical act of cutting and splicing a work print in an editing room – an assistant editor, as often as not.

KEY LINE:

'Making pictures is not a one-man job. It's a collaboration of a group of people. I think a cutter does at least as much constructive work as a director, or the actors. Writing is only a part of the motion picture machine. But without the writer…' [Curt Siodmak, monster-writer – George Waggner's *The Wolf Man* (41), Robert Florey's *The Beast With Five Fingers* (47) etc. – par excellence, on the cutter and the cut]

Cutting

What the editor does in order to construct a finished and viewable film from the mass of footage shot during the course of the initial making of the film.

Cutting Negative

The parallel job of cutting a separate negative, exact in every detail to the final work print, from which a **dupe** negative may be taken.

Cutting On Action

What the editor does to disguise the cutting process during an action scene. If several differently angled and positioned shots are made of the same scene, the editor is then able to cut on action, thereby changing the emphasis of the scene without losing its continuity.

Cutting Outline

The director's initial instructions to the editor detailing the rough structure of the film he wants the editor to produce from his shot material, hopefully leading to a first **rough cut**.

Cutting Room

The room in which the film **editor** cuts and splices the completed footage of a film to create the finished work.

Cycle

A short cut used by animators allowing the use of the same drawings again and again for repetitive action, such as walking, running, waving or swimming.

Daffy Duck

Famous cartoon character created by Chuck Jones, and renowned for his evil laugh and for his appearances in **Warner Brothers' 'Looney Tunes'** series, alongside such stalwarts as **Bugs Bunny**, Tweetie Pie, Sylvester, Yosemite Sam, Road Runner, and Wile E Coyote.

Dafoe, Willem

A fine character actor with an **indie movie** face, Dafoe is yet another of the elite 1980s school of Hollywood actors (see **Tom Berenger**, **Christopher Walken** and **Kevin Bacon**) who have flirted with stardom but never quite attained it. His breakthrough came when he was allowed to play a hero (virtually for the first time) in **Oliver Stone's** *Platoon* (86), which gave him the opportunity to move on to the greatest of all heroes, Jesus Christ, in **Martin Scorsese's** *The Last Temptation Of Christ* (88). Now somewhat inured to heroic roles, Dafoe stayed on track as an investigator into the Ku Klux Klan in **Alan Parker's** *Mississippi Burning* (88), but then delighted all the fans of his darker side with an evil gem of a performance in **David Lynch's** *Wild At Heart* (90), in which he played the blinding car headlights to Laura Dern's fascinated rabbit. Rarely out of work, Dafoe has become the steady candle that burns behind many a brighter, briefer flame.
OTHER KEY FILMS: *The Loveless* (83); *Streets Of Fire* (84); *To Live And Die In LA* (85); *Off Limits* (88); *Triumph Of The Spirit* (89); *Body Of Evidence* (93); *Tom And Viv* (94); *Clear And Present Danger* (94);

The English Patient (96); *Lulu On The Bridge* (98); *American Psycho* (00); *Edges Of The Lord* (01); *Bullfighter* (01)

Daguerre, Louis

The man who, together with the lesser-known Joseph-Nicéphore Niépce (who predeceased him in 1833) may be said to have invented photography. He first presented his 'daguerreotype' photographs to the world in 1839.

Dailies

During the making of a film, each day's exposed negative is developed, then rushed back to the director, who can view the unedited results and fine-tune the next day's work accordingly. Also known as 'rushes', for obvious reasons.

Damon, Matt

Often paired in the public's imagination with his boyhood buddy **Ben Affleck** – two years his junior and also born in Cambridge MA – Damon proved in **Gus Van Sant's** *Good Will Hunting* (97) that not only could he act, he could also co-write a mean screenplay. His recent outing in **Anthony Minghella's** *The Talented Mr Ripley* (00) was most emphatically not a copy of **Alain Delon's** brilliant portrayal of Ripley in **René Clément's** *Plein Soleil* (60), and none the worse for that. Damon is obviously talented, and, more importantly, not too showy, which bodes well for the length of any future Hollywood career he may have. One to watch.

OTHER KEY FILMS: *Mystic Pizza* (88); *School Ties* (92); *Geronimo: An American Legend* (94); *Courage Under Fire* (96); *John Grisham's The Rainmaker* (97); *Saving Private Ryan* (98); *The Legend Of Bagger Vance* (00); *All The Pretty Horses* (00); *The Bourne Identity* (01)

Dassin, Jules

Dassin was always a political director, even when he swam with the sharks in the Hollywood mainstream of the 1940s, and those politics eventually got him into trouble with the HUAC (see **Hollywood Ten**), leading to his subsequent exile in Europe. His early films showed great promise, and include the superb prison drama *Brute Force* (47), the cop rite-of-passage movie *The Naked City* (48), and two of the very best **film noir** thrillers ever produced, *Thieves' Highway* (49), in which Dassin conjures up something resembling a French film in an American setting, and *Night And The City* (50), which has a doomed **Richard Widmark** running for his life through the dark streets of London and becoming progressively more demented the closer he comes to death. Dassin's hokum period only began when he arrived in Europe and met Melina Mercouri, and its apogee came with the cheery, teary, weary *Never On Sunday* (60).

OTHER KEY FILMS: *The Canterville Ghost* (44); *Rififi* (55); *He Who Must Die* (57); *Phaedra* (62); *Topkapi!* (64); *10:30 PM Summer* (66); *Circle Of Two* (80)

Davis, Bette

Star of more than ninety films, chain-smoking Ruth Davis took her new screen name from the title of Balzac's lowlife novel, *Cousin Bette*. After posing nude, aged sixteen, to model for the making of a statue of the young goddess Diana, Davis disastrously failed her first screen test, and eventually made her debut at the age of twenty-five in Hobart Henley's *Bad Sister* (31). Davis was renowned for her roles in a series of 'women's movies' during the 1930s and 1940s, in which she incarnated the tough but tender heroine who, despite girl-next-door looks, still manages to steal her man from under the noses of her more glamorous rivals. A steadfast foe of studio boss **Jack Warner**, with whom she conducted an extended court battle, Davis had the ability, above all the other actresses of her time, to make her audience want to believe in melodrama, and in the heightened words and exalted passions that are its foundation. A victim, like her near contemporary

Joan Crawford, of the vicious daughter syndrome, Davis died as she had lived – unapologetically, and on her way back from somewhere.

OTHER KEY FILMS *The Cabin In The Cotton* (32); *The Petrified Forest* (36); *Jezebel* (38); *Dark Victory* (39); *Juarez* (39); *The Private Lives Of Elizabeth And Essex* (39); *The Letter* (40); *The Great Lie* (41); *The Little Foxes* (41); *Now, Voyager* (42); *All About Eve* (50); *Whatever Happened To Baby Jane?* (62); *Hush…Hush Sweet Charlotte* (65); *The Whales Of August* (87)

KEY LINES:
'Fasten your seat belts, it's going to be a bumpy night.' [*All About Eve*]

'Oh, Jerry, don't let's ask for the moon. We have the stars!' [*Now, Voyager*]

Bette Davis in her ingénue days, only a few years after she'd posed nude for a statue of the goddess Diana

Davis, Judy

One of the most interesting and talented of all present-day screen performers, Davis has flirted with the limelight but the limelight has never quite reciprocated. She should be one of the most celebrated actresses of her generation, but in fact she is known only to dedicated movie buffs, **Woody Allen** freaks, Australians, and as an occasional character player in other people's blockbusters. She seemed set to hit the Hollywood heights following her role in **David Lean's** *A Passage To India* (84), but she contented herself with the more challenging parts offered by non-mainstream films such as Tim Burstall's excellent *Kangaroo* (86), **Gillian Armstrong's** *High Tide* (87), James Lupine's *Impromptu* (91) and Woody Allen's *Husbands And Wives* (92). Her splendidly eccentric performance in **Bob Rafelson's** seriously underrated *Blood And Wine* (97) simply adds more fuel to the Davis mystique – she's a stayer, and her reputation should definitely outlast those of her glitzier, more celebrated rivals.

OTHER KEY FILMS: *My Brilliant Career* (79); *The Winter Of Our Dreams* (81); *Heatwave* (83); *Barton Fink* (91); *Naked Lunch* (91); *Where Angels Fear To Tread* (91); *Absolute Power* (97); *Deconstructing Harry* (97); *Celebrity* (98); *A Colder Climate* (99); *Gaudi Afternoon* (00)

Dawn Process

Also known as a 'glass shot', the Dawn process was named after cameraman Norman Dawn (who invented it in 1905) and consists of a glass plate painted with whatever scene the director wants to superimpose over a live-action shot – a classic example is the Selznick building shown at the beginning of **Gone With The Wind**, in which the entire surroundings, trees, sky, magnolias, etc., are painted in. See **Soft Image**

Day, Doris

Part of the triumvirate of apparently perpetual virgins that includes **Debbie Reynolds** and **Julie Andrews**, Doris Day was actually the best actress of the bunch and a very fine singer, but she still found it impossible to shed her squeaky-clean image in any tangible (or non-tangible) way. She came closest in **Alfred Hitchcock's** *The Man Who Knew Too Much* (56) – just as Andrews did later in Hitchcock's *Torn Curtain* (66) – but her mumsie appeal was too much even for **Rock Hudson's** passion in Michael Gordon's *Pillow Talk* (59), and one is inevitably forced to assume that the 'talk' in question took place on separate pillows, in resolutely separate beds, and concerned the office picnic. Despite all this, she contrived to remain the No. 1 female star in the US and the UK pretty much continuously between 1959 and 1965.

OTHER KEY FILMS: *Romance On The High Seas* (48); *Young Man With A Horn* (50); *Tea For Two* (50); *Calamity Jane* (53); *Love Me Or Leave Me* (57); *The Pajama Game* (57); *That Touch Of Mink* (62); *Move Over, Darling* (63); *The Ballad Of Josie* (67); *Caprice* (67)

Day For Night

Day-for-night filming consists of the use of darkened filters to make a scene shot in open daylight appear as if it were shot at night. **François Truffaut's** 1973 film *La Nuit Américaine* (whose English-language title is *Day For Night*), while functioning on one level as a movie about the making of movies, also uses the day-for-night concept as a metaphor for the mimetic quality of all cinema.

Day-Lewis, Daniel

One of the best screen actors of recent years, Day-Lewis is yet another stage goodie turned movie bandit, and is renowned for his meticulous preparation for each screen role that he accepts (and they are few). He had a striking success as Johnny, the gay punk, in **Stephen Frears's** *My Beautiful Laundrette* (85), and further plaudits followed for his insufferable prig, Cecil Vyse, in **James Ivory's** *A Room With A View* (85). Hollywood suddenly took notice of him, and he appeared as a magnificently athletic Hawkeye in **Michael Mann's** *The Last Of The Mohicans* (92). His best roles to date have been as Christy Brown in Jim Sheridan's *My Left Foot* (89), and as Gerry Conlon in the same director's *In The Name Of The Father* (93). A brief glance at Day-Lewis's filmography leads one to conclude that he seems perfectly happy turning out one quality film every two years or so, with a sensible gap for hols in between.

OTHER KEY FILMS *Sunday Bloody Sunday* (71); *Gandhi* (82); *The Bounty* (84); *The Unbearable Lightness Of Being* (88); *The Age Of Innocence* (93); *The Crucible* (95); *The Boxer* (97); *Gangs Of New York* (01)

Daylight

Natural light produced by the simple fact of it being daytime, and which is measured cinematographically in terms of sunlight and skylight, sunlight being the lesser in terms of a colour temperature reading.

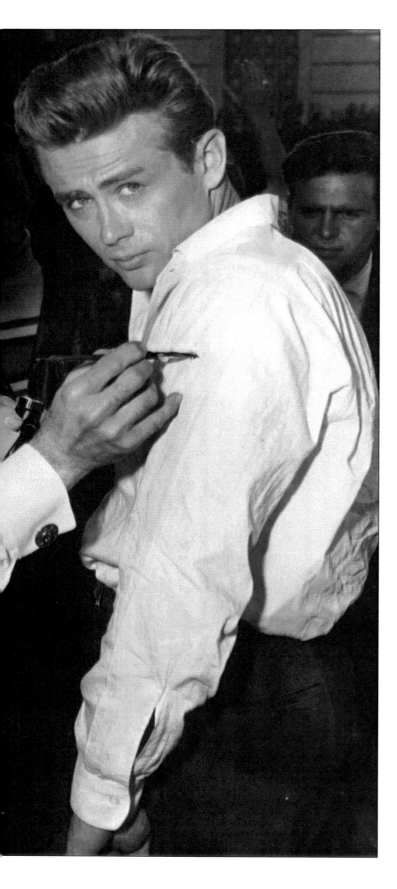

Daylight Leading Spool

Rather old-fashioned protective device used to ensure that only the outside edges of an unprocessed film are affected should a daylight changeover go wrong.

Dean, James

With his strangely tormented features and fervid **method**-style acting, Dean seemed to embody all the alienation and anger felt by teenagers brought up in the restrictive atmosphere of the Eisenhower Cold War years. The James Dean cult, however, only really began after the twenty-four-year-old manic-depressive killed himself in his Porsche on his way to a sports-car rally on 30 September 1955. It has been alleged that Dean's mangled body was covered in partially healed cigarette burns (testimony to a more than passing interest in sadomasochistic practices) and these and other posthumous acknowledgments of Dean's bisexuality mean that he has become something of a gay icon in recent years, ensuring that the titles of his earlier films now take on the appearance of a belatedly camp, Joe Orton style in-joke. The star of **Nicholas Ray's** *Rebel Without A Cause* (55), **Elia Kazan's** *East of Eden* (55) and **George Stevens's** *Giant* (56), Dean's cult status is now equalled only by that of **Rudolph Valentino** and **Marilyn Monroe**.

OTHER KEY FILMS: *Fixed Bayonets* (51); *Sailor Beware* (51); *Has Anybody Seen My Gal?* (52); *Trouble Along The Way* (53)

KEY LINES:

'Why did you run out on me? Why did you leave me alone?' [*Rebel Without A Cause*]

'It was like a strange wind that came right through the streets of Hollywood. People's rhythm changed. They began to pool into little groups like mercury rolling across a tabletop, collecting other little pieces of itself.' [Stewart Stern, who scripted **Nicholas Ray's** *Rebel Without A Cause* (55) and **Robert Altman** and George W George's *The James Dean Story* (57), on Hollywood, the day of Dean's death]

Dearden, Basil

A professional, socially conscious director who began his work at a time when British Cinema was happiest forgetting its wartime traumas in a sudsy bathful of melodramatic tosh, Dearden's subtlest film is *Frieda* (47), in which he tried to confront Britain's inevitable post-World-War-Two anti-German prejudice – *Sapphire* (59), too, was a valiant pitch (in the light of its times) for racial tolerance, and *Victim*

James Dean (as Jim) in characteristically masochistic mode, on the set of Nicholas Ray's Rebel Without A Cause *(55)*

(61) made a brave stab at reversing middle England's phobic prejudices against homosexuality. Dearden is best known among film buffs, however, for directing *The Smallest Show On Earth* (57), a gentle paean to cinema and to English eccentricity, which he followed with the amusing heist caper *The League Of Gentlemen* (60) and the less amusing *Khartoum* (66), in which **Laurence Olivier** did his notorious turn as the Mahdi, masquerading as Othello, masquerading as Richard III.

OTHER KEY FILMS: *The Captive Heart* (46); *Saraband For Dead Lovers* (48); *The Blue Lamp* (49); *The Ship That Died Of Shame* (55); *The Secret Partner* (61); *Woman Of Straw* (63); *The Man Who Haunted Himself* (70)

Debut

The first film appearance of an actor or actress only rarely heralds an overnight triumph – director's debuts, on the other hand, usually occur after a more extended rite of passage and consequently have a far greater chance of success, most notably in the case of **Orson Welles's** *Citizen Kane* (41), **Nicholas Ray's** *They Live By Night* (49) and **Charles Laughton's** *The Night Of The Hunter* (55), although Laughton's success was only retrospective. True achievement tends to come with time, and most actors and actresses would rather forget their early work in favour of the more mature and considered material of their prime. Exceptions to the rule are the glitzy and high-profile debuts of **Lauren Bacall** in **Howard Hawks's** *To Have And Have Not* (44), and of **Kathleen Turner** in **Lawrence Kasdan's** *Body Heat* (82), although both actresses have since had trouble matching the magnificent élan of their earlier achievements.

Decaë, Henri

Brilliant French cinematographer renowned for his naturalistic photography on such key French **New Wave** films as **Louis Malle's** *Ascenseur Pour L'Echafaud* (58) and *Les Amants* (58), **Claude Chabrol's** *Le Beau Serge* (58) and *Les Cousins* (58) (one hell of a run for a single year!) and **François Truffaut's** *Les Quatre Cents Coups* (59). Decaë's later films were more commercial, less exploratory, and include Anatole Litvak's pleasantly quirky *The Night Of The Generals* (67) and Franklin Schaffner's really rather turgid *The Boys From Brazil* (78).

OTHER KEY FILMS: René Clément's *Plein Soleil* (60); Serge Bourguignon's *Sundays And Cybèle* (62); Gérard Oury's *Le Corniaud* (65); Louis

Malle's *Viva Maria!* (65); **Sydney Pollack's** *Bobby Deerfield* (77); Georges Lautner's *Le Professionel* (81) and *Attention! Une Femme Peut En Cacher Une Autre* (83); Gérard Oury's *La Vengeance Du Serpent À Plumes* (84)

Deck

Hollywood slang for a studio floor.

Deep Focus

Gregg Toland, Orson Welles's cinematographic mentor on the ground-breaking *Citizen Kane* (41), was an acknowledged master of small aperture, deep focus photography, in which both near and faraway objects are simultaneously held in sharp focus, giving an awesome effect of depth and throwing everything into acute and effective contrast.

Definition

The clarity and definition of a filmic image depends on the quality of the lens used in the camera, the intensity of the light falling on the subject, and the skill of the focus puller in defining that subject, even under adverse conditions.

De Funès, Louis

Outstanding French comedian who specialised in demented, short-tempered, and accident-prone little men, De Funès worked particularly well with **Bourvil** as his calmer, more bovine partner, most notably in Gérard Oury's *Le Corniaud* (64) and *La Grande Vadrouille* (66), two films which enjoyed a spectacular success throughout the Francophone nations in the late 1960s.

OTHER KEY FILMS: *La Tentation De Barbizon* (46); *Capitaine Pantoufle* (53); *La Belle Américaine* (61); *Le Gendarme De St Tropez* (64); *Oscar* (67); *Les Aventures De Rabbi Jacob* (73); *La Zizanie* (78)

De Havilland, Olivia

Now best known for her long-standing feud with sister **Joan Fontaine** and for being the real-life object of **Errol Flynn's** attentions (she was the only one that got away), De Havilland was one of the few stars who ever bested the Hollywood studio system, winning a ground-breaking court case against **Warner's**. Squeaky-clean and saintly as Melanie in **Victor Fleming's** *Gone With The Wind* (39), she proved that she could really act in Anatole Litvak's *The Snake Pit* (48), and in **William Wyler's** *The Heiress* (49), for both of which she won well-deserved **Oscars**.

OTHER KEY FILMS: *Anthony Adverse* (36); *The Charge Of The Light Brigade* (36); *The Adventures Of*

Robin Hood (39); The Private Lives Of Elizabeth And Essex (38); Hold Back The Dawn (41); The Dark Mirror (46); My Cousin Rachel (52); Hush…Hush Sweet Charlotte (65)

De Laurentiis, Dino

Big-budget producer and husband of Italian screen star Silvana Mangano, De Laurentiis had a hand in producing both Giuseppe de Santis's Bitter Rice (49) and **Federico Fellini's** La Strada (54), before going mainline with Dinocittà, an epic-sized studio he co-founded with Carlo Ponti. He has since produced the usual array of commercial potboilers, e.g. **Michael Winner's** Death Wish (74), leavened with some seriously satisfying films such as **Ingmar Bergman's** Face To Face (75), **Don Siegel's** The Shootist (76) and John Milius's Conan The Barbarian (82), which this author obstinately persists in advocating as being particularly good of its type. De Laurentiis's greatest gift to recent cinema has been **David Lynch's** Blue Velvet (86), which reflects back to De Laurentiis's earlier, more risky productions in its quirky and lucid intelligence.

OTHER KEY FILMS: **Roberto Rossellini's** Europa '51 (52); **King Vidor's** War And Peace (56); Federico Fellini's Nights Of Cabiria (57); Richard Fleischer's Barabbas (62); **Roger Vadim's** Barbarella (68); Sergei Bondarchuk's Waterloo (70); **Sidney Lumet's** Serpico (73); **Sydney Pollack's** Three Days Of The Condor (75); Roger Donaldson's The Bounty (84)

Delerue, Georges

An extraordinarily successful film composer, and one whom a remarkable array of top directors trusted to fulfil even their most outrageous wishes, Delerue's haunting scores have graced such seminal films as **Alain Resnais's** Hiroshima Mon Amour (59), **François Truffaut's** Tirez Sur Le Pianiste [Shoot The Piano Player] (60) and Jules Et Jim (62), **Jean-Luc Godard's** Le Mépris (63), **Ken Russell's** Women In Love (69), **Bernardo Bertolucci's** The Conformist (70) and **Oliver Stone's** Platoon (86). Very few other film composers can remotely challenge his record.

OTHER KEY FILMS: François Truffaut's La Peau Douce (64); Philippe De Broca's King Of Hearts (66); **Fred Zinnemann's** A Man For All Seasons (66) and The Day Of The Jackal (74); Herbert Ross's Steel Magnolias (89); **Bruce Beresford's** Mister Johnson (90); Pierre Schoendorffer's Diên Biên Phu (92); Jean-Claude Brisseau's Céline (92)

Delli Colli, Tonino

Master cinematographer and photographer of choice for **Sergio Leone** in both The Good, The Bad, And The Ugly (66) and his masterpiece, Once Upon A Time In The West (68), Delli Colli also shot Pigsty (69), The Decameron (71) and The Canterbury Tales (72) for **Pier Paolo Pasolini**, as well as **Louis Malle's** magnificent and still underrated Lacombe Lucien (73), the single best feature film ever made about French collaboration during the Second World War.

OTHER KEY FILMS: Pier Paolo Pasolini's The Gospel According To St Matthew (64) and Salò 120 Days Of Sodom (75); Marco Ferreri's Tales Of Ordinary Madness (81); Sergio Leone's Once Upon A Time In America (84); **Federico Fellini's** Ginger And Fred (85); **Jean-Jacques Annaud's** The Name Of The Rose (86); **Roman Polanski's** Bitter Moon (92) and Death And The Maiden (94); **Roberto Benigni's** Life Is Beautiful (97)

Delon, Alain

Although sometimes known to curse his good looks ('I am an actor!' he has been heard to say, in weaker moments), Delon owes his career to them, and it is a somewhat surprising fact that he has never managed to seduce audiences across the Atlantic in the same way that he has seduced those of his native France. He was a very good screen Ripley in **René Clément's** superb thriller Plein Soleil (60) (though it is only fair to mention that **Matt Damon** was equally good, forty years later, in **Anthony Minghella's** The Talented Mr Ripley (99)), but Delon really comes into his own playing cold, marginalised characters, such as the hit-man in **Jean-Pierre Melville's** Le Samourai (67), and the corrupt art-dealer in **Joseph Losey's** Monsieur Klein (75).

OTHER KEY FILMS: Rocco And His Brothers (60); L'Eclisse (62); The Leopard (63); Borsalino (70); Un Flic (72); Red Sun (71); Le Choc (82); Swann In Love (84); Le Jour Et La Nuit (97); Les Acteurs (00)

Delpy, Julie

Delpy's is a strange and rather offbeat beauty, perfect for the cinema of thought rather than of action (and similar in essence to that of the wonderful **Dominique Sanda**), and as a result of this, and of her fine capacity for suggestion, filmmakers such as **Jean-Luc Godard**, with Détective (85), Agnieszka Holland, with Europa Europa (91), and **Krzysztof Kieslowski**, with Red (94) and White (94), have queued at her door, preferring hers to the more obvious and surface attractions of the Hollywood First Eleven.

OTHER KEY FILMS: *Bad Blood* (87); *Voyager* (91); *Killing Zoe* (94); *Before Sunrise* (95); *Tykho Moon* (97); *The Treat* (98); *L.A. Without A Map* (98); *The Passion Of Ayn Rand* (99); *Sand* (00); *Villa Des Roses* (00); *MacArthur Park* (01); *Investigating Sex* (01)

Del Rio, Dolores

A gorgeous and extremely talented Mexican actress who got fed up with being typecast as exotic plunder in films such as Thornton Freeland's *Flying Down To Rio* (33) and **Lloyd Bacon's** *Wonder Bar* (34), Del Rio threw up Hollywood in 1943 and returned to her native land where she constructed a second, and critically far more successful, career in such masterpieces as **Emilio Fernandez's** *Flor Silvestre* (43) and *Maria Candelaria* (43) (see **Gabriel Figueroa)**, only occasionally returning across the border to work for more enlightened gringo directors such as **John Ford**, in *The Fugitive* (47).

OTHER KEY FILMS: *Bird Of Paradise* (32); *In Caliente* (35); *Journey Into Fear* (42); *Bugambilia* (44); *La Otra* (46); *Historia De Una Mala Mujer* (48); *Cheyenne Autumn* (64); *The Children Of Sanchez* (78)

DeMille, Cecil B

Somewhat underrated now thanks to the false perception that all he ever did was to marshal gigantic numbers of men and women and even more gigantic sets to fulfil his megalomaniacal aims, DeMille tapped into a puritanical (call it Christian nonconformist if you like) vein in the US which likes to see and taste what it will, in private, condemn. His films mirrored, in consequence, those twin daemons of popular American culture, money and sex – money, in the enormous sets, the multifarious casts and the top-name actors he brought to the screen, and sex in his commercially astute choice of tableau-style biblical and **Western** epics and in such voluptuous and shimmering leading ladies as **Gloria Swanson**, surreally reprised in **Billy Wilder's** *Sunset Boulevard* (50); **Claudette Colbert**, in her famous naked bath in ass's milk in *The Sign Of The Cross* (32) and the carpet-rolling episode in *Cleopatra* (34); and last but not least **Hedy Lamarr**, the memory of whose naked swim in Gustav Machaty's *Ecstasy* (33) imbued each and every lubricious frame of *Samson And Delilah* (49).

OTHER KEY FILMS: *The Squaw Man* (13); *The Girl Of The Golden West* (15); *The Woman God Forgot* (17); *The Squaw Man* [remake] (18); *The Ten Commandments* (23); *The King Of Kings* (27); *Madame Satan* (30); *The Plainsman* (37); *Union Pacific* (39); *Reap The Wild Wind* (42); *The Greatest Show On Earth* (52); *The Ten Commandments* [remake] (56)

Demme, Jonathan

A former exploitation director who seemed only to benefit from his experiences directing such cult classics as *Caged Heat* (74) (a more intelligent film than the name, or the women's prison subject matter, would at first glance suggest), Demme has also made *Cousin Bobby* (91) a brilliant portrait of his fundamentalist cousin, the Rev. Robert Castle, and the riveting *Silence Of The Lambs* (91), in which he both revealed and transcended his exploitation movie background. That rare thing, a mainstream director who can still stimulate and surprise his audience, Demme was also responsible for *Swimming To Cambodia* (87), a semi-documentary in which oddball commentator Spalding Gray sounds off, in his enlightened, reactionary way, about life, films, and the absurdities inherent in being an American journalist on the razz in a country which literally massacred itself.

OTHER KEY FILMS: *Crazy Mama* (75); *Melvin And Howard* (80); *Something Wild* (86); *Married To The Mob* (88); *Philadelphia* (93); *Beloved* (98)

Dench, Judi

Renowned among the cognoscenti more for her theatre work than for her films, Dench has nevertheless made a virtue of her chameleon-like capacity for slipping in and out of character, and she has become something of a Hollywood darling recently with her performances in John Madden's *Mrs Brown* (97), in which she played Queen Victoria, and in the same director's *Shakespeare In Love* (98), in which she played Victoria's eminent (and rather more amusing) predecessor, Elizabeth I. What **Orson Welles** would have termed a queen-actress (he was a king-actor), Dench specialises in dominant women, with elements of her stage Duchess of Malfi cropping up, once again, in her M to **Pierce Brosnan's** now rather M-pecked James Bond.

OTHER KEY FILMS: *A Midsummer Night's Dream* (68); *Luther* (73); *Wetherby* (85); *A Room With A View* (86); *84 Charing Cross Road* (87); *A Handful Of Dust* (88); *Henry V* (89); *Hamlet* (96); *Tea With Mussolini* (99); *Chocolat* (00); *Thérèse Raquin* (01)

Deneuve, Catherine

Glacially beautiful star of **Roman Polanski's** *Repulsion* (65) and **Luis Buñuel's** *Tristana* (70), and never afraid of a challenge, Deneuve has become something of a French icon in recent years, retaining her elegant and sexually enticing good looks well into middle age. Erstwhile wife of photographer David Bailey, and mistress of **Roger Vadim** and **Marcello Mastroianni**, Deneuve's most famous role was that of the bored but loving housewife who took to dabbling at prostitution during the long afternoons, in Buñuel's recently reissued *Belle De Jour* (67). After a quiet period in the early 1980s, Deneuve's career took a sudden turn for the better – if one ignores Manoel de Oliveira's appalling clinker *The Convent* (95) – with well-received performances in **André Téchiné's** *Ma Saison Préferée* (92) and its follow-up, *Les Voleurs* (96).

OTHER KEY FILMS: *Les Parapluies De Cherbourg* (64); *Les Demoiselles De Rochefort* (67); *Tristana* (70); *The Last Métro* (80); *The Hunger* (83); *Indochine* (92); *L'Inconnu* (96); *Belle Maman* (99); *Le Temps Retrouvé* (99); *The Last Napoleon* (99); *Dancer In The Dark* (00)

KEY LINE:

'Sexuality is such a part of life, but sexuality in the movies – I have a hard time finding it.' [Deneuve on sex]

Denham Studios

One of the great British studios of the 1930s and 1940s, Denham was the home of many of **Alexander Korda's** landmark London Films productions, including William Cameron Menzies's *Things to Come* (36) and the magnificent *The Thief Of Bagdad* (40), directed by a sextet of directors including Ludwig Berger, **Michael Powell** and Tim Whelan, and which is quite simply the best and most inventive children's film ever made. Denham, with its thunder increasingly taken by nearby **Pinewood Studios**, was bought by Rank in 1953, becoming the company's film processing centre.

De Niro, Robert

After a stint emoting at the **Actors' Studio**, De Niro got good notices for his part in the otherwise awful **Roger Corman** flick, *Bloody Mama* (70), and this indirectly led to him being cast in John Hancock's magnificent *Bang The Drum Slowly* (73), in which his real potential showed through for the first time. **Martin Scorsese's** *Mean Streets* (73) cemented his reputation, and De Niro's filmography now reads like a guided tour through the late twentieth-century Cinematic Hall of Fame. To be fair, De Niro has made his share of turkeys, but he has also saved such otherwise shaky vehicles as **Elia Kazan's** *The Last Tycoon* (77) and Scorsese's *New York, New York* (77). His least

A studio shot of the glacially beautiful **Catherine Deneuve** *at about the time she played bored housewife Séverine Serizy in Luis Buñuel's* Belle De Jour *(67)*

mannered performances, and the ones in which he showed a real potential for humour, came in Martin Brest's *Midnight Run* (88) and John McNaughton's *Mad Dog And Glory* (92), but he is destined to be remembered, above all, for the roles of Vito Corleone in **Francis Ford Coppola's** *The Godfather Part II* (74), and of the grotesquely alienated Travis Bickle, in Scorsese's *Taxi Driver* (76).

OTHER KEY FILMS: *1900* (77); *The Deer Hunter* (78); *Raging Bull* (80); *Once Upon A Time In America* (84); *The Mission* (86); *Jacknife* (89); *Awakenings* (90); *GoodFellas* (90); *Cape Fear* (91); *Heat* (95); *Ronin* (98); *Analyze This* (99); *Flawless* (99); *Meet The Parents* (00); *15 Minutes* (01); *The Score* (01)

Density

The average density of a filmic image can be measured by a densitometer, and refers to the mass and the capacity to absorb light of the filmed subject.

De Palma, Brian

De Palma is a pretty shrewd operator – one has only to look at the steady progress of his career to realise that he's forced Hollywood to take him on his own merits rather than having Hollywood's foisted upon him. A Hitchcock devotee, De Palma's first real success came with *Sisters* (73), but this effective little movie was totally eclipsed by *Carrie* (76) three years later, which was also notable for an early appearance by **John Travolta** receiving what proved to be a particularly costly blow-job from gorgeous Nancy Allen, while driving her home in his car (no mobile phones in those days). De Palma's first dedicated blockbuster was *The Untouchables* (87), a first-class action movie, intelligently directed, and this was followed, in quality if not in chronological order, by the underrated *Carlito's Way* (93). De Palma then touched stratospheric heights with the absurd but enjoyable *Mission: Impossible* (95), which grossed a stupendous $475 million at the box office, coincidentally netting its producer and star, **Tom Cruise**, a cool $100 million in the process. In the final analysis, De Palma is an interesting and skilful director, well versed in film lore and movie history, and something of a welcome throwback to an earlier age of eclectic studio directors.

OTHER KEY FILMS: *Greetings* (68); *The Wedding Party* (69); *Hi Mom!* (70); *Phantom Of The Paradise* (74); *The Fury* (78); *Dressed To Kill* (80); *Blow Out* (81); *Scarface* (83); *Body Double* (84); *Wise Guys* (86); *Casualties Of War* (89); *Raising Cain* (92); *Snake Eyes* (98); *Mission To Mars* (00)

Depardieu, Gérard

Depardieu is a true force of nature (something reflected in his wildly fluctuating weight and girth) and for twenty years, between 1974 and 1994, he was France's most successful and hard-working screen actor. He has something of **Jean Gabin's** skill in depicting simple yet sensitive men who can rise to every occasion, but he has far more of an acting span than Gabin – which is not to say that his is a greater or more effective screen presence – for Depardieu falls more readily into the **Acteur De Composition** range rather than that of the glitzier **Monstre Sacré** which Gabin inhabited so triumphantly. Depardieu's greatest role came late, with **Jean-Paul Rappeneau's** *Cyrano De Bergerac* (90), a part that lay in waiting for him and which only someone with his acquired capacity for spouting Alexandrines could even have attempted. An international star despite (or perhaps because of?) his endearing incapacity to learn an acceptable standard of English, Depardieu regularly throws caution to the winds both in his everyday life and in his acting, and as such should be cherished over the safer, more boring stars that are spewed up so regularly and so unimaginatively from *outre-mer*.

91

Gérard Depardieu as Christopher Columbus, in Ridley Scott's 1492: Conquest Of Paradise *(92)*

OTHER KEY FILMS: *Les Valseuses* (74); *Maîtresse* (75); *Le Camion* (77); *Les Chiens* (79); *Le Dernier Métro* (80); *Mon Oncle D'Amérique* (80); *Loulou* (80); *The Return Of Martin Guerre* (82); *Danton* (83); *Jean De Florette* (86); *Sous Le Soleil De Satan* (87); *Camille Claudel* (88); *Trop Belle Pour Toi* (89); *Tous Les Matins Du Monde* (92); *Le Colonel Chabert* (94); *The Man In The Iron Mask* (98); *The Bridge* (99); *Vatel* (00); *102 Dalmatians* (00); *Le Placard* (00); *Concorrenza Sleale* (01); *Vidocq* (01)
KEY LINE:
'An artist doesn't create beauty. He simply removes what prevents us from seeing it.' [*Élisa* (95)]

Depp, Johnny

Something of an iconoclast, Depp has always tried to go his own way in movies while still retaining a wary speculator's eye on the main chance. Following TV success with '21 Jump Street' and a minor part in **Oliver Stone's** *Platoon* (86), Depp hit the big time with the title role in **Tim Burton's** *Edward Scissorhands* (90), which unfortunately eclipsed a far better film he made in the same year, **John Waters's** *Cry-Baby* (90), whose heady and imaginative mix of music and the grotesque has ensured it long-lasting cult success in such enlightened movie-going countries as France. Depp showed us he could act both in Lasse Hallström's quirky and enjoyable *What's Eating Gilbert Grape?* (93) and in Burton's *Ed Wood* (94), and he seems set to be that rare thing, an actor who is equally as popular with European art-house audiences as he is with American mainstreamers. Note for Film Buffs: 'Depp' means idiot in colloquial German.
OTHER KEY FILMS: *American Dreamers* (92); *Don Juan De Marco* (95); *Dead Man* (96); *Donnie Brasco* (97); *The Legend Of Sleepy Hollow* (99); *The Ninth Gate* (00); *Chocolat* (00); *Blow* (01); *From Hell* (01)
KEY LINE:
'I don't want to be stared at while I'm mowing my lawn. I want to wake up and wander in my yard nude, or dressed as Abe Lincoln if I feel like it.' [Depp on the price of fame]

Depth of Field

The point at which an object starts to go out of focus, depending on camera lens quality, focal length and aperture settings.

Depth of Focus

The optimal point or distance between the camera lens and the film inside the camera to ensure the sharpest focus.

Deren, Maya

A genuinely innovative avant-garde filmmaker, Deren collaborated, with her Czech cinematographer husband Alexander Hammid, on the dense, surrealistic eighteen-minute short, *Meshes In The Afternoon* (43), which still retains its power to surprise and seduce to this day. Obsessed with magic, myth and symbolic movement, Deren was moving towards a sequence of increasingly abstract structures when she fell prey to a brain haemorrhage at the tragically early age of forty-four.
OTHER KEY FILMS: *Ritual In Transfigured Time* (49); *Meditation In Violence* (53)

De Sica, Vittorio

A former romantic actor turned director (although he still acted on occasion to fund his other ventures), De Sica was that most Italian of creatures, a man who saw nothing strange in spanning three or even four different genres throughout his career, varying from the avant-garde to the blatantly commercial. A founder member of the neo-realist school with his extraordinary *Bicycle Thieves* (48), De Sica gradually returned to the sort of mainstream films in which he had begun his career, with *Stazione Termini* [*Indiscretion Of An American Wife*] (54) and *Two Women* (60). He reverted briefly and belatedly to the art cinema form with the lush and haunting *The Garden Of The Finzi-Continis* (71), which he completed just three years before his death, proving, in the process, that he had lost nothing of his consummate and golden touch behind the camera.
OTHER KEY FILMS: *Shoeshine* (46); *Miracle In Milan* (51); *Umberto D* (52); *L'Oro Di Napoli* (54); *Marriage, Italian Style* (64); *After The Fox* (66); *Una Breve Vacanza* (73); *The Journey* (74)

Detail Shot

A sudden, categorical close-up of a single object to highlight its crucial importance to a scene. One of the best examples comes in **Alfred Hitchcock's** *Young And Innocent* (37), in which a crane tracking shot swoops out over a dance floor of swirling bodies, curls down towards the dance band orchestra, then in towards the drummer, and *blam!* – the shot ends dead upon the drummer's devilishly ticking eye, allowing our heroine, Nova Pilbeam, and her tramp accomplice, Edward Rigby, to recognise him as the murderer of her boyfriend's ex-lover, despite the fact that he is wearing blackface make-up. Don't you just love those simple set-ups?

Best Detective Films

Harold Becker's *Sea Of Love* (88); **Henri-Georges Clouzot's** *L'Assassin Habite Au 21* (42) and *Quai Des Orfèvres* (47); **Howard Hawks's** *The Big Sleep* (46); Bruce Humberstone's *I Wake Up Screaming* (42); **John Huston's** *The Maltese Falcon* (41); **Fritz Lang's** *The Big Heat* (53); **Joseph H Lewis's** *So Dark The Night* (46); Claude Miller's *Mortelle Randonnée* (82); **Alan Pakula's** *Klute* (71); **Alan Parker's** *Angel Heart* (87); **Otto Preminger's** *Laura* (44); Richard Quine's *Pushover* (54); **Carol Reed's** *The Fallen Idol* (47); Dick Richards's *Farewell, My Lovely* (75); Franco Rosi's *Cadaveri Eccellenti* (75); **Ridley Scott's** *Blade Runner* (82); Bryan Singer's *The Usual Suspects* (95); W S Van Dyke's *The Thin Man* (34); **Orson Welles's** *Touch Of Evil* (58); **Billy Wilder's** *The Private Life Of Sherlock Holmes* (70); **William Wyler's** *Detective Story* (51)

Deuce

Hollywood jargon for a 2,000 watt studio lamp.

Developer

The person responsible for developing a negative film and also the chemical used in that process.

DeVito, Danny

A diminutive but important player in the Hollywood ball game, DeVito first came to the viewing public's attention playing one of **Jack Nicholson's** bewildered fellow asylum inmates in **Milos Forman's** *One Flew Over The Cuckoo's Nest* (75). He went on to star in TV's successful 'Taxi' series (78-83), and from there to directing, with *Throw Momma From The Train* (87), *The War Of The Roses* (89), *Hoffa* (92) and *Matilda* (96). Interspersed with these only occasionally successful films, DeVito has had key parts in **Barry Levinson's** *Tin Men* (87), Ivan Reitman's *Twins* (88), Barry Sonnenfeld's *Get Shorty* (95) and Curtis Hanson's *LA Confidential* (97), proving both his versatility and his astuteness at manipulating the Hollywood game to his own advantage.
OTHER KEY FILMS: *Car Wash* (76); *Terms Of Endearment* (83); *Romancing The Stone* (84); *Wise Guys* (86); *Ruthless People* (86); *Batman Returns* (92); *Junior* (94); *Mars Attacks* (96); *The Rainmaker* (97); *Man On The Moon* (99); *Drowning Mona* (00); *Heist* (01)

DFA Machine

When an exceptionally demanding director annoys the sound engineers with repeated requests above and beyond the call of duty, immemorial custom dictates that the chief sound engineer shout to his assistant something along the lines of, 'All right John, you'd better run it through the DFA!' The results obtained usually far exceed the director's expectations and the happy fellow goes home well satisfied but blissfully unaware that the letters DFA actually stand for 'Does F★★★ All!'

DGA

The powerful Directors' Guild of America, which protects the rights of film and television directors, and acts as their unofficial union.

Diagonal Action

Action that moves diagonally from one corner of the screen to another, passing, not surprisingly, through the centre. A good example would be **John Wayne's** fist in just about any of his **Westerns** one might care to name.

Diagonal Splicing

A way of avoiding the noise engendered by a straight splice through a process of diagonal splicing, thus extending and lessening the sound.

Dial

A sound editor can effectively 'dial' out extraneous noise (such as an actor or actress's inadvertent, or in the case of renowned *pétomane* **Marlon Brando**, deliberate passing of wind) in the editing room.

Dialogue

Words written by a **screenwriter** and which characters in a film later exchange. **Dialogue coaches** were formerly prevalent in Hollywood, and were no doubt surprised to find themselves amusingly parodied by **Gene Kelly** and Donald O'Connor in **Stanley Donen** and Gene Kelly's *Singin' In The Rain* (52).

Dialogue Coach

Rare fish now, dialogue coaches used to be *de rigueur* at every Hollywood studio, particularly during the 1930s, when reluctant American actors were required to mimic, or at least to attempt to mimic, English accents, in the long run of 'the sun never sets on the British Empire' films – films which included **Henry Hathaway's** *Lives Of A Bengal Lancer* (35), **Frank Capra's** *Lost Horizon* (37), and **George Stevens's** *Gunga Din* (39). It is now however, increasingly more likely that English actors will need the services of dialogue coaches to perfect their American accents. Recent examples

93

of Brits who have played Americans include **Bob Hoskins** in **Robert Zemeckis's** *Who Framed Roger Rabbit* (88), **Michael Caine** in Lasse Hallström's *The Cider House Rules* (99), and **Jude Law** in **Anthony Minghella's** *The Talented Mr Ripley* (99). Note for Film Buffs: Check out the Phoebe Dinsmore character in **Gene Kelly** and **Stanley Donen's** *Singin' In The Rain* (52) – she's the dialogue coach who receives her strident comeuppance at the hands of Jean Hagen's grotesquely vulgar Lina Lamont.

Dialogue Director
Another rare fish, the dialogue director was required to rehearse and refine an actor's delivery of his or her lines, and to go through the essential movements needed to play the scene.

Dialogue Track
A separate track that carries only the dialogue of a film, as opposed to the score or the visuals. During dubbing into a foreign language, the track can be replaced with a new, over-dubbed track, without disturbing the rest of the film's aural or visual balance.

Dialogue Writer
Very few screenplays ever reach the screen as exclusively the work of one man or one woman (despite what the screen credits may say). **Script doctors** are used extensively on most Hollywood movies, and in France *dialoguistes* may work on the finished screenplay when directors request it, toning up this scene or that with spicy and memorable dialogue, much as comedians might employ professional gagsters to jazz up their material.

Diaphragm
The fan-like structure that opens and closes over the lens of a camera to control the amount of light the film is subjected to.

Diaz, Cameron
A gorgeous and exotic-looking actress (the happy product, one supposes, of her Cuban, American Indian and Anglo-German ancestry), Diaz first made her mark opposite **Jim Carrey** in Charles Russell's *The Mask* (94), and consolidated her position as sex symbol of the 1990s and teenage heart-throb, with Jim Wilson's *Head Above Water* (97) and P J Hogan's *My Best Friend's Wedding* (97). Her recent success in Spike Jonze's *Being John Malkovich* (99) will have done nothing whatsoever to stunt her lucrative career growth.

OTHER KEY FILMS: *Feeling Minnesota* (96); *She's The One* (96); *A Life Less Ordinary* (97); *There's Something About Mary* (98); *Charlie's Angels* (00); *Gangs Of New York* (01); *The Invisible Circus* (01); *The Sweetest Thing* (01)

DiCaprio, Leonardo
Still remarkably young (he was born in 1974) for the position he has won for himself, DiCaprio is a canny operator who has made the most of his carefully chosen roles and looks set to continue the miraculous run he started with Baz Luhrmann's *Romeo And Juliet* (96), **James Cameron's** *Titanic* (97) and Randall Wallace's *The Man In The Iron Mask* (98), despite the recent blip in his rise through the stratosphere created by Danny Boyle's clinker *The Beach* (00). DiCaprio is so newsworthy, however, that even a relative failure like that is barely perceived as such by the popular press, and his largely female fans are likely to continue their worship until a similar, younger version of their hero comes mincing along. Rather surprisingly, DiCaprio *can* act, as he once showed to good advantage in his excellent turn as the brain-damaged Arnie Grape in Lasse Hallström's *What's Eating Gilbert Grape?* (93).

OTHER KEY FILMS: *Critters 3* (91); *Poison Ivy* (92); *This Boy's Life* (93); *The Basketball Diaries* (95); *A Hundred And One Nights* (95); *The Quick And The Dead* (95); *Total Eclipse* (95); *Marvin's Room* (96); *Gangs Of New York* (01)

Dickinson, Angie
There was something unbelievably sexy about Angie Dickinson, and her sex appeal proved enough to secure her numerous parts in films of which better actresses could only dream. But overt sex appeal is no small thing in the movies – in fact it's an art in itself – and Dickinson deserves considerable credit for refining it in such a luridly enticing way. Her best film was **Howard Hawks's** *Rio Bravo* (59) in which, while seeming to subsume herself within the star egos that surrounded her, she cannily contrived to remain in the memory even when the film was over and the gunplay complete. More good roles came with **Don Siegel's** *The Killers* (64) and **John Boorman's** *Point Blank* (67), in both of which she played, very effectively, women at the end of their tether and not a little out of their depth. Finally, in **Brian De Palma's** *Dressed To Kill* (80) (made when she was perilously close to 50), Angie knocked her younger rivals into a cocked hat in terms of her almost palpable sexuality.

Angie Dickinson showing 'those legs' in an early 1960s Hollywood studio shot

OTHER KEY FILMS: *China Gate* (57); *The Bramble Bush* (60); *Ocean's Eleven* (60); *The Sins Of Rachel Cade* (61); *The Chase* (66); *Cast A Giant Shadow* (66); *Big Bad Mama* (74); *Even Cowgirls Get The Blues* (94); *Sabrina* (95): *Pay It Forward* (00)

Dickinson, Thorold

A much-respected director and cinema theoretician who sadly gave up making films in mid-career, Dickinson directed both the atmospheric *Gaslight* (40), and the beautifully designed but uncomfortable to watch *Queen Of Spades* (48). Football fans (cinéphiles, no doubt, to a man) still cherish his now cult-status *The Arsenal Stadium Mystery* (40). Dickinson's true importance to cinema, however, lies in his chairmanship of the **British Film Academy** (52-3), and his presidency of the International Federation of Film Societies, in both of which roles he excelled.
OTHER KEY FILMS: *Next Of Kin* (42); *Secret People* (52); *Hill 24 Doesn't Answer* (55)

Dieterle, William

A former silent era actor who, astonishingly, played a bit role in **F W Murnau's** *Faust* (26), Dieterle made a niche for himself directing such luxury biopics as *Juarez* (39) and the excellent *Dr Ehrlich's Magic Bullet* (40), before he discovered where his real talent lay and branched out into romantic melodramas with *Love Letters* (45) and the haunting *Portrait Of Jennie* (48). His best films came earlier, however, with *The Last Flight* (31), *The Hunchback Of Notre Dame* (39), and *The Devil And Daniel Webster* (41) [a.k.a. *All That Money Can Buy*]. A committed anti-fascist, Dieterle was yet another director who fell foul of Senator Joe McCarthy's HUAC (see **Hollywood Ten**), and he never really recovered from the deeply unfair blow to his reputation that McCarthy's witch-hunters fomented on him.
OTHER KEY FILMS: *A Midsummer Night's Dream* (35); *Another Dawn* (37); *Blockade* (38); *Tennessee Johnson* (41); *Dark City* (50)

Dietrich, Marlene

Fêted in Hollywood after the release of **Josef von Sternberg's** *The Blue Angel* (30), bisexual Dietrich went on to enjoy a near fifty-year career on stage and screen. Held in high esteem for her bravely declared anti-Nazi sympathies during the Second

95

A cross-dressing **Marlene Dietrich,** *photographed, through a filter, by Richard Walling in 1934*

World War (she was affectionately nicknamed 'The Kraut' by her friend Ernest Hemingway), she starred in more than thirty films of which seven were directed by von Sternberg, her most obsessive fan, whose wife eventually divorced him after citing the cross-dressing Dietrich for having 'alienated her husband's affections'. The high point of her career came in von Sternberg's *Shanghai Express* (32) in which the director perfectly encapsulated Dietrich's beauty and the mystery of her allure – she seemed at one and the same time visually available, yet materially unattainable – while making a virtue of her voice and her highly accented English through the heightened use of slowed down, abbreviated, and brilliantly mannered dialogue. When her film roles eventually began to dry up, Dietrich skilfully recreated herself (remember the lesbian kiss in von Sternberg's *Blonde Venus* (32)?) as a *chanteuse* throughout Europe and the Americas. Note for Film Buffs: Watch out for a sensational Dietrich performance opposite a top-form **Robert Donat** in Jacques Feyder's rarely screened *Knight Without Armour* (37).

OTHER KEY FILMS: *Morocco* (30); *Dishonored* (31); *The Scarlet Empress* (34); *The Devil Is A Woman* (35); *Desire* (36); *Angel* (37); *Destry Rides Again* (39); *Stage Fright* (50); *No Highway* (51); *A Touch Of Evil* (58); *Judgment At Nuremberg* (61)

KEY LINE:
'It took more than one man to change my name to Shanghai Lily.' [*Shanghai Express*]

Differential Focusing
Relates to the **depth of field**, in that the focus of the action is kept in sharp definition, while the background remains hazy.

Diffuser
Diaphanous material used to soften the effects of a hard light source.

Digital Effects
Digitalised or scanned material that is often used as an addition to live action, as in the case of **Steven Spielberg's** *Jurassic Park* (93) in which the human beings were filmed separately from the computer- and animatronically-generated dinosaurs – the resulting action sequences were then spliced together to achieve a quasi-realistic effect. A similar result was achieved in **Ridley Scott's** *Gladiator* (00), in which digitally created tigers were seen fighting with live human beings.

Digital Projection
The next big step in film technology, digital projection is set to overtake normal celluloid film projection within a few years, producing equivalent quality pictures but obviating the wear and tear to which traditional film stock is subject. Its major advantage is that it is extremely light, can be transmitted over the Internet, via satellite or by disk, and will not require the extensive storage facilities currently needed by conventional film. To ensure that the system gets a further boost, **George Lucas** has recently announced that he is to film the remainder of his *Star Wars* series using only high-definition digital cameras.

Digital Soundtrack
A film soundtrack recorded digitally, i.e. by converting sound into a binary digital formulation, allowing a greater variation in recorded sound than that offered by a conventionally recorded soundtrack. The resultant product, however, is unquestionably more artificial, something that present-day cinema audiences no longer appear to mind. A new, split definition of sound is therefore likely in the near future, discriminating between 'real' sound and 'Hollywood' sound. Hollywood sound is deeper, more vibrant and completely safe. Real sound requires some sort of response from an auditor beyond simply the conventional chomping on a nosebag full of popcorn.

Dimension–150
A now defunct wide-screen process that required a 150-degree curved screen and projectors capable of dealing with 70mm film. The most notable Dimension–150 film was Franklin Schaffner's *Patton – Lust For Glory* (70).

DIN
The letters DIN stand for Deutsche Industrie Norm (German Industrial Standard) and refer to the emulsion speed of film and its consequent sensitivity to light. The United States uses the **ASA** rating.

Dinky Inky
Hollywood jargon for a small-sized, low-powered spot.

Diopter Lens
The lens that cinematographers use, in addition to the normal camera lens, for exaggerated close-ups.

Diorama
A tabletop mock-up of a studio set.

96

Di Palma, Carlo:

A first-rate director of photography who added his own distinctive visual voice to **Michelangelo Antonioni's** films, most notably in *Red Desert* (64) and *Blow-Up* (66), Di Palma later went on to become one of **Woody Allen's** preferred cinematographers in *Hannah And Her Sisters* (86), the sublime *Radio Days* (87), *Husbands And Wives* (92) and *Mighty Aphrodite* (95), amongst others. Somewhat surprisingly, given his artistic track record, Di Palma also shot **Brian De Palma's** [no relation] *Mission: Impossible* (96).

OTHER KEY FILMS: *Omicron* (63); *I Tre Volti* (65); *The Appointment* (69); *Tragedy Of A Ridiculous Man* (81); *Identification Of A Woman* (82); *The Secret Of My Success* (87); *Manhattan Murder Mystery* (93); *Everyone Says I Love You* (96); *Deconstructing Harry* (97)

Direct Cinema

1960s **cinéma vérité** US-style which relied on hand-held cameras, **direct sound**, and no fundamental intervention whatsoever by the director or film crew.

Direct Cut

A straight cut from one shot, or one scene, to another, without the contrived use of a dissolve or other linking device.

Directional

A catch-all term that applies to any piece of technical equipment which requires pointing, i.e. a directional microphone or directional antenna.

Direct Sound

Natural sound recorded as the action is taking place, rather than being overlaid afterwards.

Director

The person ultimately responsible for shooting an agreed script and turning it into a finished film. The director is also responsible for the guidance of actors, the control of the camera crew and for overseeing the editing and sound work leading to the **final cut** of the movie.

KEY LINE:

'If you don't work very closely with a director, you're not going to see anything you want up on the screen. There's no way. So you had better invite the gentleman to piss a little on the script. Put his mark on it. Make it *his*.' [Screenwriter Jay Presson Allen, after she had scripted *Marnie* (64) for **Alfred Hitchcock**, and *Cabaret* (72) for Bob Fosse]

Director's Cut

It is usually the studios, rather than the directors they hire, who have the final say as to the finished form (or **release print**) of a film when it hits the screens. In recent years, however, the studios have discovered that it can make sound commercial sense to re-release critically successful films in the form in which their directors, as opposed to the studios, originally intended them. **Ridley Scott's** *Blade Runner* (82) is a case in point, and a director's cut was issued ten years after the film's original release, which proved, paradoxically – and rather like John Fowles's amended version of his best-selling novel *The Magus* – considerably less enjoyable than the original.

Director of Photography:

See **Cinematographer**

Disaster Movies

A film genre that has always warmed the heart-cockles of otherwise frigidly unfeeling studio accountants, especially during the genre's heyday in the 1970s (remember John Guillermin and Irwin Allen's *The Towering Inferno* (74)?), disaster movies pit people against natural or man-made disasters and tend to come in cycles (like the weather they so often parody). **James Cameron's** blockbusting *Titanic* (97) is a recent example, but the end result, though impressive, simply cannot compare to **John Ford's** brilliant *The Hurricane* (37) in which natural forces are placed in poetic counterpart to human ones, directly following on from the great tradition of Greek Tragedy.

Discovery Shot

A subjective camera move that highlights an object or situation that was either not in view or not obvious when the scene began. A good example is the glass of milk, in **Alfred Hitchcock's** *Suspicion* (41), which Hitchcock discovers for us as **Cary Grant** carries it slowly up the stairs to a bewildered **Joan Fontaine**, and which may, or may not, contain poison – the glass certainly contains a cleverly concealed light bulb to heighten the dramatic tension of the scene even further.

Disney

The kings of cross-selling and cross-promotion, Disney are **Time Warners'** and Bertelsmann's biggest rivals in the media business. Owners of theme parks, cruise lines, stores, TV companies, music labels, publishers and film production ventures like Miramax and Buena Vista, Disney could probably sell only to their own employees and still make a profit.

Disney, Walt

Creator of **Mickey Mouse**, **Donald Duck**, **Goofy** and **Pluto**, the mercurial Disney was also responsible for such ground-breaking animated cartoons as *Snow White And The Seven Dwarfs* (37) and *Fantasia* (40). His jealously guarded trade name has since become synonymous with squeaky-clean family entertainment and a multi-billion-dollar entertainment industry legacy that includes numerous theme parks and film production companies; but what Disney really achieved, and what the company that bears his name has so singularly failed to do in the decades since his death in 1966, was to tap into popular culture while still retaining the archetypal power of the original, often literary, idea. Where the loss of Bambi's mother, in *Bambi* (42), would now be portrayed as a maudlin, mock-sentimental farce, in the original *Bambi* Disney refused to sentimentalise the lot of animals and showed the loss as simply part of the natural order of things, thus infinitely magnifying its power. More, as Hollywood still resolutely refuses to acknowledge, is not necessarily better. Disney was a true master who correctly identified the need both for enlightened sentiment in popular culture and for something to bridge the gap between the adult and the child's world, and who then went on to triumphantly fill that gap with his animated films.

OTHER KEY FILMS: *Pinocchio* (40); *Dumbo* (40); *Cinderella* (50); *Alice In Wonderland* (51); *Peter Pan* (53); *The Living Desert* (53); *Old Yeller* (57); *Sleeping Beauty* (59); *The Swiss Family Robinson* (60); *101 Dalmatians* (61); *The Incredible Journey* (63); *Mary Poppins* (64); *The Jungle Book* (67)

KEY LINE:
'Fancy being remembered around the world for the invention of a mouse!' [Disney on his deathbed]

Dissolve

An essential and subtle directing tool, dissolves can be either quick or slow, and are usually used to indicate, by a gradual melting of one scene into another, the relative passing of time. Dissolves can also point towards the beginning of a **flashback** or **dream sequence**.

Distortion

Any intended or unintended physical disturbance of a film image such that the image appears distorted or out of true. A number of factors may be the cause of this including lens malformation, incorrect positioning of the camera, or an accidental corruption of the film stock.

Distortion can be artificially created by the use of distortion optics to achieve a particular effect, such as a transformation, the mimicking of a dream, or the undermining of an audience's visual certainty.

Distributor

The distributor acts as the buffer zone between the producers of a film and its exhibitors, and they usually take a concomitant cut of the profits while steering clear of any but the most unavoidable of losses. (Cynic, Ed.)

Di Venanzo, Gianni

Before **Carlo Di Palma** (in director **Michelangelo Antonioni's** life) came Di Venanzo, a master cinematographer who contributed greatly to the almost hypnotic visual effect exerted by the last two parts of Antonioni's brilliant trilogy, *La Notte* (61) and *L'Eclisse* (62). Di Venanzo also lit and photographed **Joseph Losey's** otherwise disappointing and wantonly perverse *Eva* (62), **Federico Fellini's** masterpiece *8½* (63), and the same director's underrated *Juliet Of The Spirits* (65). A brilliant and instinctive photographer, Di Venanzo looked set fair, before his untimely death in 1966 at the age of forty-five, to become a key player in the Italian renaissance of the 1960 and early 1970s.

OTHER KEY FILMS: *Il Grido* (57); *Salvatore Giuliano* (62); *Le Mani Sulla Città* (63); *Gli Indifferenti* (64); *Il Momento Della Verità* (65); *La Decima Vittima* (65)

Dmytryk, Edward

Dmytryk, one of the original **Hollywood Ten**, fell foul of the House Un-American Activities Committee (what outrageous nomenclature − a worthy precursor to the modern-day scourge of political correctness in its grotesque ersatz logic) in 1947, and ended up, before he recanted, with a brief blacklisting. His career followed a similar pattern. He directed a trilogy of tight little thrillers in the 1940s, notable for their tough dialogue, enlightened use of location filming, and expressionistic camerawork − *Murder My Sweet* [*Farewell My Lovely*] (45), *Cornered* (45) and *Crossfire* (47). He then recanted, just as he had done before the HUAC. His remaining work varied wildly, with belated high points occurring in *The Caine Mutiny* (54), *The Young Lions* (58) and *Warlock* (59), although all these later films manifested a rather sorry looseness when compared to the tight, lowly budgeted gems that preceded them.

Director Edward Dmytryk directing a blonded-up Marlon Brando (as Christian Diestl) in The Young Lions *(58)*

Robert Donat as Ainsley Fothergill (dreaming of Dietrich?) in Jacques Feyder's Knight Without Armour *(37)*

OTHER KEY FILMS: *Hitler's Children* (43); *Tender Comrade* (44); *Till The End Of Time* (46); *The Sniper* (52); *Broken Lance* (54); *The End Of The Affair* (54); *Soldier Of Fortune* (55); *The Left Hand Of God* (55); *Mirage* (65); *Shalako* (68)

Documentary

A film that purports to be a true rendition of fact rather than fiction. John Grierson's 1929 neologism has since been used to describe everything from **Robert Flaherty's** ground-breaking work with the Eskimos, in *Nanook Of The North* (22), which relied on a scrupulous and largely objective sympathy, to **Leni Riefenstahl's** extraordinary propaganda contrivance *Olympia* (38), which relied on an unscrupulous and largely subjective apathy.

Best Documentary Films

Donald Brittain and John Kramer's *Volcano: An Inquiry Into The Life And Death Of Malcolm Lowry* (76); **Henri-Georges Clouzot's** *Le Mystère Picasso* (55); **Robert Flaherty's** *Nanook Of The North* (23) and *Man Of Aran* (34); **Georges Franju's** *Le Sang Des Bêtes* (48); Kon Ichikawa's *Tokyo Olympiad* (66); **F W Murnau** and **Robert Flaherty's** *Tabu* (31); Marcel Ophüls's *Le Chagrin Et La Pitié* [*The Sorrow And The Pity*] (69) and *Hotel Terminus* (88); **Alain Resnais** and Robert Hessens's *Guernica* (50); **Alain Resnais's** *Nuit Et Brouillard* (55); **Leni Riefenstahl's** *Olympische Spiele Parts 1 & 2* (36); **Georges Rouquier's** *Farrebique* (45); **Jean Vigo's** *A Propos De Nice* (30)

Dog

Hollywood film jargon for a downright flop. See **Worst Films**

Dolby System

Invented in 1965 by Ray Dolby, the Dolby process is used to reduce the hiss in soundtrack recordings, in parallel with a four-channel stereophonic sound system.

Dolly

A trolley device used for transporting film or television cameras around a set. Also a verb, to dolly, meaning to move a camera away from, or towards, the scene of action.

Dolly Shot

A fluid, travelling shot of a normally stationary image by means of a dolly, or trolley-tracking device. A famous example can be seen in the vast panorama of Confederate dead that the camera hovers over and slowly reveals in **Victor Fleming's** *Gone With The Wind* (39).

Donald Duck

Not related (as far as we know) to **Daffy**, wise-quacking Donald began his career in **Disney's** *The Wise Little Hen* (34)… and the rest is history.

Donat, Robert

This quintessential and beautifully spoken Englishman was in fact half-Polish, and overcame a stammer and a lifetime of chronic asthma to

become one of the most popular and best-loved stars of his generation. A consummate screen actor, Donat imbued every role (and there were, sadly, few) with his own particular brand of playful integrity. Catch him in **Alfred Hitchcock's** *The Thirty-Nine Steps* (35) or in the wonderful and little seen Jacques Feyder movie, *Knight Without Armour* (37). Donat died, aged only fifty-three, after having recorded some achingly beautiful readings from his favourite English poets for Argo records.

OTHER KEY FILMS: *The Private Life of Henry VIII* (33); *The Count Of Monte Cristo* (34); *The Ghost Goes West* (35); *The Citadel* (38); *Goodbye Mr Chips* (39); *The Young Mr Pitt* (42); *The Adventures Of Tartu* (43); *Perfect Strangers* (45); *The Winslow Boy* (48); *The Cure For Love* (49); *The Magic Box* (51); *Lease Of Life* (54); *The Inn Of The Sixth Happiness* (58)

Donen, Stanley

One of the greats of the Hollywood musical (whatever one may think of the genre in terms of its extrinsic relevance), **Gene Kelly** and Donen's *Singin' In The Rain* (52) became one of the most successful of all **crossovers**, and proved that entertainment need not presuppose stupidity on the part of an audience. *Seven Brides For Seven Brothers* (54) and *Funny Face* (57), while not threatening the status quo in any profound way, entertained pleasantly and without depth, as did his two comedy thrillers *Charade* (63) and *Arabesque* (66) – in fact Donen could be said to encapsulate virtually everything the Soviet Union thought was decadent about the West at the height of the Cold War (something which should endear him to his bewildered crossover audience far more than many of his post-*Singin'* movies). *Two For The Road* (67) was a delightful late career surprise, and showed the same sharpness of vision which characterised Donen's brilliant early work, *On The Town* (49), which he co-directed with Gene Kelly.

OTHER KEY FILMS: *Deep In My Heart* (54); *It's Always Fair Weather* (55); *The Pajama Game* (57); *Indiscreet* (58); *Staircase* (69); *Movie Movie* (78); *Blame It On Rio* (84)

Dope Sheet

A detailed memo, attached to a can of film, recording exactly which shots are contained on the reel inside.

Dors, Diana

She was intended to be the British National Serviceman's sex symbol during the early part of the 1950s, rather as **Betty Grable** had been to US draftees during the Second World War, but, apart

from a few small successes, Dors's career did not turn out as planned. Surprisingly, twenty-five years before her early death, aged fifty-two, from cancer, Dors (originally Diana Fluck, from Swindon) took off the make-up and the glitz and played against type as Ruth Ellis, the last British woman to be hanged for murder, in J Lee Thompson's *Yield To The Night* (56). Given the absurd hype surrounding her at the time, the very existence of such an unlikely piece of work in her filmography is something of a miracle – in fact it signalled her increasing desire, especially towards the end of her career, to be regarded as a serious actress.

OTHER KEY FILMS: *Holiday Camp* (47); *Oliver Twist* (48); *Value For Money* (55); *I Married A Woman* (58); *On The Double* (61); *The Sandwich Man* (66); *Berserk* (67); *There's A Girl In My Soup* (70); *Deep End* (70); *Steaming* (84)

Dot

A circular disk used to mask and diffuse the light from a spot.

Double

A labour, health, vanity or moneysaving device used, at some point or other, in most feature films, and consisting of a physically equivalent stand-in for an actor or actress, usually in non-dialogue scenes that require either stunt-work, sex-work (see **body doubles**), or location work, and in which the presence of the principal protagonist is not absolutely vital.

Double Bill

The presentation of two feature-length films in one cinema programme, usually consisting of a main feature and a **B-Movie**.

Double Broad

A double broadside normally comprises two 1,000-watt arc lamps positioned to furnish generalised, large-scale illumination on a studio set.

Double Exposure

The apparent superimposition of one image onto another to produce either a **dissolve** or a dreamlike, faded appearance. Such a **special effect** is created by the repeated exposure of the same piece of film, a process also known as multiple exposure.

Double Feature

Up to and beyond the belated but near total provision of television to the masses, most cinemas showed a programme of two big-budget feature-length films, or occasionally, in smaller cinemas, one **A-Movie** twinned with a lesser-budgeted **B-Movie**. In the case of cinema **Drive-Ins**, triple features were often the norm, no doubt to allow ample time for the three sempiternal adolescent rites of seduction, recrimination, and reparation.

Double Framing

Double framing is when each frame of a scene is printed twice, slowing down the action by fifty per cent. See **Skip Framing**

Double System

The separate but synchronous recording of image and sound – one mechanical motor drives the two or more audio and visual tracks involved, ensuring perfect synchronicity while at the same time allowing for easier editing and dubbing. Single system recording is easier, cheaper, but less malleable.

Double Take

Developed to perfection by silent film stars **Charlie Chaplin**, **Buster Keaton** and **Laurel and Hardy**, the double take consists, when done well, of a more or less normal expression of comic righteousness, followed, in the same shot, by a belatedly shocked realisation of the true nature of the thing experienced.

Douglas, Kirk

Douglas played tough men from the very beginning – he was born Issur Danielovitch of poor Russian immigrant parents, so he knew what it was like to struggle – although through some curious trick of the camera he always appeared considerably taller and broader on screen than he was in real life. Wisely, though, he leavened this toughness with a physical vulnerability and a most up-to-date capacity for angst (whether existential or otherwise is a moot point) and the films in which he succeeds best are those which reflect both sides of his Janus-like nature – the capacity not only to call down the punches on himself, but also to recover from them. Whit Sterling, in **Jacques Tourneur's** *Out Of The Past* (47), was Douglas's first really juicy role, and he already looked the complete pro he was to remain throughout his astonishing career. It was Douglas, for instance, who gave **Stanley Kubrick** the directing job on *Spartacus* (60), while cannily retaining the copyright of the film for himself (making it the only film of Kubrick's that was effectively outside the director's control). Douglas was superb at playing loners, and of all the glitzy roles he eventually filled, one remembers best his ageing, iconoclastic modern cowboy, Jack Burns, in David Miller's *Lonely Are The Brave* (62), doggedly getting into a fight in order to spring his best friend from jail and ending up bowled over by a water-closet-carrying pantechnicon on the concrete highway, his eyes cold as a bird of prey's, and with his dying horse beside him.

OTHER KEY FILMS: *I Walk Alone* (48); *A Letter To Three Wives* (49); *Young Man With A Horn* (50); *Ace In The Hole* (51); *Detective Story* (51); *The Bad And The Beautiful* (53); *Man Without A Star* (55); *Lust For Life* (56); *Gunfight At The O K Corral* (57); *Last Train From Gun Hill* (59); *Spartacus* (60); *Seven Days In May* (64); *The War Wagon* (67); *The Arrangement* (69); *Tough Guys* (86); *Diamonds* (99)

Douglas, Michael

Being **Kirk Douglas's** son was always going to be a hard act to follow, and to give him credit, Michael Douglas has made a pretty good stab at it. Power was the stock-in-trade in this family, and Douglas showed early on that he was, in symbolically Freudian terms at least, perfectly prepared to kill his own dad by persuading him (quite rightly as it turned out – for **Jack Nicholson** was born for the part) that he was too old to play the Randle Patrick McMurphy role in **Milos Forman's** *One Flew Over The Cuckoo's Nest* (75), which the thirty-year-old Michael just happened to be co-producing with **Saul Zaentz**. Never the actor his father was, Douglas has made up for this shortcoming by highlighting his charm, his butt, and his sardonic sense of humour, and his best parts, as Jack Colton, in **Robert Zemeckis's** *Romancing The Stone* (84), and as Gordon Gekko, in **Oliver Stone's** *Wall Street* (87), have used these assets to the full.

OTHER KEY FILMS: *Coma* (78); *The China Syndrome* (79); *Jewel Of The Nile* (85); *Fatal Attraction* (87); *Black Rain* (89); *The War Of The Roses* (89); *Basic Instinct* (92); *Falling Down* (93); *Disclosure* (94); *The Game* (97); *A Perfect Murder* (98); *Wonder Boys* (00); *Traffic* (00); *One Night At McCool's* (01)

KEY LINE:

'Greed – for lack of a better word – is good. Greed is right. Greed works.' [*Wall Street* – Douglas won a best actor **Oscar** for his role as Gordon Gekko]

Downey, Robert, Jr

A perennial bad boy, Downey seems like a flashback to the **Errol Flynn** years of Hollywood, where acting was simply a means to a self-indulgent end, but hardly the end in itself. Downey flits from part to part, sometimes well, sometimes indifferently, with newspaper headlines and probationary terms as half-humorous, half-tragic interstices. He was surprisingly good in Michael Hoffman's *Restoration* (95), leading one to suppose that perhaps rip-roaring Stuart England, rather than liberal bleeding-heart Hollywood, should have been his natural stamping ground.

OTHER KEY FILMS: *To Live And Die In L.A.* (85); *Less Than Zero* (87); *Chaplin* (92); *Natural Born Killers* (94); *Only You* (94); *Richard III* (95); *One Night Stand* (97); *Black And White* (99); *Wonder Boys* (00)

Downstage

The area nearest the camera on a film set.

Dowser

Device on a projector that ensures that the backlight is extinguished when a reel **changeover** occurs.

Dracula

Filmed more than 150 times to date, Bram Stoker's 1897 novel has tapped into the subconscious of more than five separate generations of filmgoers. **Bela Lugosi** played him most famously in 1931, but Max Schreck's incarnation of him as *Nosferatu* in the 1922 **F W Murnau** silent film version was far more frightening. Recent Draculas have included **Christopher Lee**, Frank Langella, and **Gary Oldman,** but most impressive of all was the demented **Klaus Kinski** in **Werner Herzog's** *Nosferatu The Vampyre* (79).

KEY LINES:

'There are far worse things facing man than death.' [Lugosi in **Tod Browning's** *Dracula* (31)]

'For one who has not lived even a single lifetime, you are a wise man, Van Helsing.' [Lugosi (you'll have to imagine the Transylvanian accent) to Edward Van Sloan]

Best Dramas

Marcel Carné's *Hôtel Du Nord* (38); **Carl Dreyer's** *Day Of Wrath* (43); Julien Duvivier's *La Fin Du Jour* (38); **Federico Fellini's** *La Strada* (54); Jacques Feyder's *La Kermesse Héroïque* (35); Mike Figgis's *Leaving Las Vegas* (95); **Georges Franju's** *Thérèse Desqueyroux* (62); **Howard Hawks's** *Only Angels Have Wings* (39); **John Huston's** *The Night Of The Iguana* (64); **Krzysztof Kieslowski's** *The Decalogue* (89); **Fritz Lang's** *M* (31); **Charles Laughton's** *The Night Of The Hunter* (55); **David Lean's** *Great Expectations* (46); **Joseph L Mankiewicz's** *All About Eve* (50); **Kenji Mizoguchi's** *Ugetsu Monogatari* (53); **Jean Renoir's** *Les Bas-Fonds* (36); **John Sayles's** *Lone Star* (95); **John Schlesinger's** *Sunday, Bloody Sunday* (71); **Josef von Sternberg's** *The Scarlet Empress* (34); **George Stevens's** *Giant* (56); **Albert Valentin's** *Marie-Martine* (42); **Luchino Visconti's** *Senso* (54); **Orson Welles's** *Chimes At Midnight* (66); **William Wellman's** *A Star Is Born* (37); **Fred Zinnemann's** *From Here To Eternity* (53)

Drapes

Curtains used either for set decoration or for dampening sound.

Dream Sequence

Sequence in a film that purports to show the unconscious or dream-life world of one of the protagonists. Most famous of all is the dream sequence in **Alfred Hitchcock's** *Spellbound* (45), which used the talents of surrealist artist and erstwhile filmmaker, Salvador Dalí, to design its imagistic sets.

DreamWorks SKG

Founded in 1994 by David Geffen, former owner of MCA records, Jeffrey Katzenberg, former head of **Disney**, and director **Steven Spielberg**, who each invested $33.3 million of their own money in the project, DreamWorks's first two films, Mimi Leder's *The Peacemaker* (97) and Spielberg's own *Amistad* (97), were undistinguished flops. The studio was, however, saved by its ensuing animation features, Eric Darnell and Tim Johnson's *Antz* (98) and Brenda Chapman, Steve Hickner and Simon Wells's *Prince Of Egypt* (98), which each took $100 million at the box office. Since then DreamWorks has cannily entered into a £150 million five-picture deal with **Aardman Studios** (the home of Nick Parks's 'Wallace and Gromit') and their first joint product has been the highly successful *Chicken Run* (00).

Dress

To 'dress' a set is to fluff it up with extra props until the exact desired effect is achieved.

Dresser

A theatrical term that has been taken over by the cinema, and which refers to the person who assists an actor or actress to dress, and who is usually subordinate to the **wardrobe** master or mistress.

Dreyer, Carl Theodor

Dreyer is one of that small band of undisputedly great directors (**Abel Gance** is another example) whose films, by some extraordinary oversight, are rarely, if ever, shown outside art theatres and university film clubs. A Dane of Swedish extraction, born illegitimately, and the product of a strictly Lutheran adoptive household following the death of his mother when he was two years old, Dreyer's art reflects the tensions inherent in such an emotionally deprived upbringing, tensions which imbue the sometimes over-fastidious visual and affective quality of his films. It seems extraordinary to us now, but most of Dreyer's films, including the magnificent *The Passion Of Joan Of Arc* (28), were commercial disasters, and he was viewed with a mixture of distaste and condescension by the mainstream Nordic film community. *Day Of Wrath* (43), *Ordet* [a.k.a. *The Word*] (55) and *Gertrud* (64) are now acknowledged as masterpieces, and it is to be hoped that enlightened festival directors and television programmers will one day give both these, and his lesser-known shorts, the belated status they deserve.

OTHER KEY FILMS: *Leaves From Satan's Book* (20); *Vampyr* (32); *Two People* (45)

Dreyfuss, Richard

He has hit the heights and plumbed the depths, and still Dreyfuss remains a difficult actor to categorise. He brings an intelligence to parts that could easily have been played unintelligently, such as that of oceanographer Matt Hooper in **Steven Spielberg's** *Jaws* (75), and he shines in light comedies, such as Herbert Ross's *The Goodbye Girl* (77), without really being a comedian. He was as excellent in Paul Mazursky's *Down And Out In Beverly Hills* (85), as he was maudlin in Stephen Herek's *Mr Holland's Opus* (95) – the jury, in the final analysis, must still be considered out.

OTHER KEY FILMS: *The Apprenticeship Of Duddy Kravitz* (74); *Close Encounters Of The Third Kind* (77); *The Big Fix* (78); *Whose Life Is It Anyway?* (81); *Stakeout* (87); *Always* (89); *Lost In Yonkers* (93); *Night Falls On Manhattan* (97); *A Fine And Private Place* (98); *The Crew* (00)

Drive-In

Quintessentially American open-air cinema with booths and sound points so that an audience may watch movies (or not, as the case may be) from the comfort of their own cars. There are still one or two drive-ins left in Texas and in a number of other southern states, but the internet, the **video** recorder, and **DVD**, together with the increasing tolerance of parents, has put paid to what, like the diner, was once seen as an inescapable part of the American way of life.

Driver, Minnie

Driver is a rare example of the true jolie-laide, and her unconventional beauty shines out and is at its best on the screen. The camera loves her, and one is constantly gripping the edge of one's seat wondering whether that love affair will continue or whether, in a sort of reverse ugly duckling scenario, all will collapse and her glass slipper turn to dust. On the basis of her recent form in **Gus Van Sant's** *Good Will Hunting* (97) and Sandra Goldbacher's *The Governess* (98), one is disposed to predict a long, rather than a short flight, for this recently feathered swan.

OTHER KEY FILMS: *Circle Of Friends* (95); *Big Night* (96); *Sleepers* (96); *The Flood* (97); *Grosse Point Blank* (97); *An Ideal Husband* (99); *Return To Me* (00); *High Heels And Low Lifes* (01)

Drop

Yet another theatrical term plundered by the cinema, a drop is a canvas backdrop painted to resemble a real location and used as background on a film set. One of the most successful of all drops is the one used in the first shot of **Michael Powell** and **Emeric Pressburger's** *Black Narcissus* (47), brilliantly conjuring up an isolated monastery in the Himalayas.

Dry Run

The movie equivalent of a theatrical dress rehearsal, a dry run is the final go-through before real shooting of a scene begins.

Duarc A double-sourced arc lamp generally used for background illumination during a studio photo shoot.

Dubbing

The post-synchronisation and provision of dialogue in the editing stage of the making of a film. British and American films, particularly in France and Spain, can be dubbed into the host language, often using specially trained actors and actresses who mimic the voices of, say, **Tom Cruise**, **Harrison Ford** or **Julia Roberts** over the entire span of their movie careers. Problems arise if, as in the case of a **John Wayne**, a **Humphrey Bogart** or a **Richard Burton**, the voices of the actors or actresses are so essential a part of their screen persona that the inferior, dubbed versions provoke only mockery. It should perhaps be mentioned that, particularly in France (see **Paris**), there is a very healthy **art house cinema** industry that disdains any dubbing at all, and contents itself, quite rightly, with **subtitles**.

Dump Tank

Enormous tanks filled with water, suspended over the set and then emptied, under rigorously controlled conditions, to simulate flooding, the coming of tsunamis, or of monsoon-style rain. **John Ford's** *The Hurricane* (37) used dump tanks to spectacular effect during the final storm sequence that destroys Thomas Mitchell's much-lamented island paradise.

Dunaway, Faye

Dunaway's is a fragile talent, best used, paradoxically, by a director – **Roman Polanski**, for instance, in *Chinatown* (74) – to whom she is temperamentally unsuited. Her face has always been her fortune, and her cold features, which bear an almost Asiatic cast despite her blonde hair and green eyes, have been well utilised by directors as disparate as **Arthur Penn**, in *Bonnie And Clyde* (67), **Sidney Lumet**, in *Network* (76), and **Sydney Pollack**, in *Three Days Of The Condor* (75). Dunaway's best acting role came in **Barbet Schroeder's** underrated *Barfly* (87), in which she bravely scraped off the paint and the glamour to reveal the soft emotional underside she normally does so much to conceal.

OTHER KEY FILMS: *The Thomas Crown Affair* (68); *The Arrangement* (69); *Little Big Man* (70); *The Towering Inferno* (74); *Eyes Of Laura Mars* (78); *Mommie Dearest* (81); *The Wicked Lady* (83); *The Handmaid's Tale* (90); *Don Juan DeMarco* (95); *In Praise Of Older Women* (97); *The Thomas Crown Affair* [remake] (99); *Messenger: The Story Of Joan Of Arc* (99); *The Yards* (00); *Stanley's Gig* (00)

Dunne, Philip

Dunne's extraordinary screenwriting career was defined by quality, wit and a literate sophistication, and his scripts for **John Ford's** *How Green Was My Valley* (41), **Joseph L Mankiewicz's** *The Ghost And Mrs Muir* (47) and **Carol Reed's** *The Agony And The Ecstasy* (65) do a great deal more than merely illustrate that fact. A committed liberal, Dunne was one of the main organisers of the anti-blacklist committee, and his career provides proof, if proof were needed, that the writers of popular movies can and do influence public perceptions and opinions. See **Hollywood Ten**

OTHER KEY FILMS: George B Seitz's *The Last Of The Mohicans* (36); **Henry King's** *Stanley And Livingstone* (39); **Henry Hathaway's** *Johnny Apollo* (40); **Elia Kazan's** *Pinky* (49); Henry Koster's *The Robe* (53)

Dupe

A copy of the valuable original negative of a film, made from a **master positive**, which is then used to provide the **release prints** when the movie is finally distributed to cinemas.

Duras, Marguerite

Duras was a literary novelist and doyenne of the 'nouveau roman' who contributed, either as a director or screenwriter, to some of the most challenging **avant-garde art house** films of the past fifty years. Her first cinematic masterpiece was her elusive but ultimately overwhelming script for **Alain Resnais's** brilliant *Hiroshima Mon Amour* (59). She followed this up with the screenplay (from her own book) for Peter Brooks's highly charged *Moderato Cantabile* (64), in which **Jeanne Moreau** suggests the obsessive quality of a Duras heroine better than any other actress either before or since. Preoccupied throughout her life with memories of her childhood in French Indochina, Duras's own directorial efforts were not always as satisfying as her collaborations, and it occasionally seemed as though the very collaborative nature of filmmaking was in some way alien to the essentially solitary state of an artist of her calibre.

OTHER KEY FILMS: René Clément's *Barrage Contre Le Pacifique* (58); **Tony Richardson's** *The Sailor From Gibraltar* (67); *India Song* [dir.] (75); *Le Camion* [dir.] (77); *Baxter – Vera Baxter* [dir.] (77); **Jean-Jacques Annaud's** *The Lover* (92)

Duvall, Robert

Duvall is a perfectionist and one of the finest of all recent screen actors. From his very first appearance as the retarded 'Boo' Radley in Robert Mulligan's *To Kill A Mockingbird* (62), it was obvious that Duvall possessed the rare quality of being able to communicate emotion through facial and bodily expression, as well as by more conventional, verbal means. His finest parts have come with Joseph Anthony's unjustly neglected *Tomorrow* (72) (based on a William Faulkner story) in which Duvall showed his extraordinary capacity for subsuming himself inside a seemingly thankless part and making it sing, and in Randa Haines's *Wrestling Ernest Hemingway* (93), in which Duvall miraculously transforms himself into the very image of an expatriate Cuban, complete with Guayabera and slicked back hair. His most memorable part came in **Francis Ford Coppola's** *Apocalypse Now* (79), in which his monstrous but all-too-credible Lt. Col. Kilgore utters his famous napalm line (see **Key Line**), a phrase which has now taken on almost mythic proportions to become one of the most memorable lines in the history of movies. Let's be brutally frank – Duvall could play just about any part, however inauspicious it might at first appear, and make it interesting.

OTHER KEY FILMS: *The Chase* (66); *True Grit* (69); *M*A*S*H* (70); *The Godfather* (72); *The Outfit* (73); *The Conversation* (74); *The Great Santini* (79); *Tender Mercies* (83); *The Natural* (84); *Belizaire The Cajun* (86); *The Lightship* (86); *Colors* (88); *Rambling Rose* (91); *The Stars Fell On Henrietta* (95); *Sling Blade* (96); *The Apostle* (97); *Deep Impact* (98); *A Civil Action* (98); *Gone In 60 Seconds* (00); *The 6th Day* (00)

KEY LINE:

'I love the smell of napalm in the morning. It smells like…victory!' [*Apocalypse Now*]

DVD

Introduced in early 1997 and formerly known as the Digital Versatile Disc or Digital Video Disc, DVD has twenty times the audio capacity of a CD Rom, is backwards compatible, and has seen its market share grow at a speed far exceeding the initial growth rates of both the CD and VHS when they too were entered into a virgin market.

Dwan, Allan

Dwan was an innovator, devising one of the earliest **dolly** devices for **D W Griffith**, and he was undoubtedly one of the first pioneers to film from the back of a moving motor vehicle. He directed more than 400 films during his fifty-year career (1911-61), a career in which he started at the bottom, at Essanay Studios, as a scenario editor, rose to the top, at **Paramount** and **Fox**, making such **Gloria Swanson** and **Douglas Fairbanks** vehicles as *The Iron Mask* (29) and *What A Widow!* (30), then sank to the bottom again after the coming of sound, with the occasional belated surge back to the surface, with *Frontier Marshal* (37), *Suez* (38), *Brewster's Millions* (45) and *The Sands Of Iwo Jima* (49). Like many of his contemporaries, he turned to **Westerns** during the 1950s, with considerable success, and the career of this remarkable man finally shuddered to a halt with an excellent **Film Noir**, *The River's Edge* (57) (featuring an unmitigatedly evil **Ray Milland**), and an underrated little sci-fi potboiler, *Most Dangerous Man Alive* (61).

OTHER KEY FILMS: *The Gold Lust* (11); *The County Chairman* (14); *The Dark Star* (19); *Robin Hood* (22); *Big Brother* (23); *Manhandled* (24); *East Side West Side* (27); *While Paris Sleeps* (32); *Heidi* (37); *Rebecca Of Sunnybrook Farm* (38); *Rise And Shine* (41); *Driftwood* (47); *I Dream Of Jeanie* (52); *The Queen Of Montana* (54); *Slightly Scarlet* (56); *Hold Back The Night* (56)

Dykstraflex

An ingenious, computer-controlled system, invented by special effects artist John Dykstra, which exactly matches camera movement to the movements of the subject being shot, e.g. the swooping and weaving battle cruisers in **George Lucas's** *Star Wars* series of films.

Dynalens

A water-cushioned camera mount used to lessen wobble while filming in a moving vehicle.

Dynamic Cutting

A staple of agitprop and propaganda films, dynamic cutting is the sudden juxtaposition of contrasting images to put across a political or philosophical point in purely visual terms. A famous example is the Odessa steps sequence in **Sergei Eisenstein's** *The Battleship Potemkin* (25), in which a pram, rattling down the steps, is juxtaposed with a woman's face, a soldier raising his rifle, then the woman's broken and bloodied glasses as we belatedly realise that she has been shot.

Ealing Comedies

Hatched and brought to chickenhood at **Ealing Studios** in west London, the famous Ealing Comedies really began, circa 1949, with Henry Cornelius's *Passport To Pimlico*, which was, in fact, the weakest and most stilted of the genre. **Alexander Mackendrick's** *Whisky Galore* (49) was better, verging on the sublime, and was swiftly followed by **Robert Hamer's** *Kind Hearts And Coronets* (49), Mackendrick's powerful satire on capitalism *The Man In The White Suit* (51), Charles Crichton's *The Titfield Thunderbolt* (52), and Mackendrick's extremely black comedy *The Ladykillers* (55), in which practically the entire cast end up dead, and with which the series gently and appositely coasted to an end.

Ealing Studios

Ealing was founded in 1931 by Basil Dean, head of Associated Talking Pictures, and was the first dedicated sound studio in Europe. Early stars were Gracie Fields and George Formby, but the studio only moved into high gear when **Michael Balcon** took over in 1937. During the Second World War Ealing was prominent in the British propaganda mission, and after the war it tried its hardest to reconcile former enemies with films such as **Basil Dearden's** *Frieda* (47), in which **David Farrar** brings home his German wife to a decidedly mixed reception from the disgruntled locals. Ealing had one final, valedictory lease of life with the **Ealing Comedies**, which lasted until the studio was taken over by BBC TV in 1956.

Eastman Color

Nearly ubiquitous **Tripac** colour system, using a single strip that requires less light than the three-negative **Technicolor** process that preceded it, and which is simpler and less idiosyncratic to develop – the results, however, never seem quite so glorious.

Eastwood, Clint

While Eastwood first made his name in **Sergio Leone's** low-budget and ground-breaking trilogy of **Spaghetti Westerns**, *A Fistful Of Dollars* (64), *For A Few Dollars More* (65) and *The Good, The Bad And The Ugly* (66), his career since then has proved that it is perfectly possible to be both commercially successful and critically discriminating at one and the same time. Using big-budget movie projects such as mentor **Don Siegel's** *Dirty Harry* (71) and James Fargo's *Every Which Way But Loose* (78) to fund his own, rather more esoteric directing projects, Eastwood has played his full part in bringing the American myth, in all its elusive subtlety, to the big screen. With films like Siegel's *The Beguiled* (71), **Michael Cimino's** *Thunderbolt and Lightfoot* (74), and his own *The Outlaw Josie Wales* (76), *Honkytonk Man* (82) and *Unforgiven* (92), Eastwood has charted the psychological course of the American male better than any other actor/director of his time. During his most commercially lucrative decade, 1974-84, Eastwood's films grossed a total of $1,400 million. **OTHER KEY FILMS:** *Where Eagles Dare* (69); *Play*

Misty For Me [also dir.] (71); *High Plains Drifter* [also dir.] (73); *Escape From Alcatraz* (79); *Tightrope* (84); *Pale Rider* [also dir.] (85); *Bird* [dir.] (88); *A Perfect World* [also dir.] (93); *The Bridges Of Madison County* [also dir.] (95); *Absolute Power* [also dir.] (97); *True Crime* [also dir.] (99); *Space Cowboys* [also dir.] (00)

KEY LINE:
'Go ahead, make my day.' [Clint Eastwood's *Sudden Impact*]

Easy Rider

Clint Eastwood in his 'The Man With No Name' mode, no doubt wondering what to say

Costing a mere $375,000 to make, and raking in a thousand times that over the years, this influential **Road Movie**, directed by **Dennis Hopper** and starring himself, **Peter Fonda** and **Jack Nicholson**, garnered **Harvard Lampoon's** worst movie award for 1970. Despite its many shortcomings, *Easy Rider* (69) did a great deal to free up the hide-bound Hollywood system in the 1970s, leading to a brief Second Golden Age of mainstream cinema.

Echo Chamber

Now largely superseded by electronic technology, echo chambers were sealed units containing both a microphone and a loudspeaker, the combined effects of which were then recorded in an effort to mimic the echo effect naturally produced inside a cave or tunnel.

Edge Numbers

Numbers etched into film stock borders to simplify copying and identification.

Edison, Thomas Alva

Edison is the man generally credited with being the inventor of motion pictures, but his assistant, W K L Dickson, was the man who actually perfected the machines that were to become Edison's **Kinetograph** and **Kinetoscope**. Edison himself considered that the moving picture was simply a novelty, which would soon pall on the paying public, but he had the foresight to take out patents on his two machines in 1892, and to buy the rights to Thomas Armat's projector in 1896, something which proved to be a wise investment when rivals began to use the same technology to make money. In 1908 Edison joined with a number of other film producers to set up The Motion Picture Patents Company, which claimed royalties to the tune of $25,000 a week on any film made using Dickson's technology, only to see the company's monopoly formally broken, in 1917, following an antitrust action.

Editing

Crucial process in which film footage is cut and assembled in an editing room until the final **release print** is ready for distribution. The process begins with the cataloguing of the **dailies** (a.k.a. rushes) into some sort of initially acceptable order. A **rough cut** follows, eventually leading to a near perfect **fine cut**. A **workprint** is then checked through by the director, following which the **sound editor** fine-tunes the **soundtrack**. A final **answer print** is then laid before the director and the studio executives who decide if there are any more belated changes that need to be made, e.g. a different ending, due to the unexpectedly critical response of a preview audience. The **final cut** is then agreed upon.

107

Editola

An editing machine that allows for an uninterrupted rather than an intermittent viewing of the piece to be edited.

Editor

The person in charge of **editing** a film, albeit under the overall creative control of the film's **director**.

Effects

Catch-all term used for any form of **special** or **sound effect** used in a film. Also known as FX in film jargon.

Effects Filter

A variable form of filter to be placed over a camera lens and capable of producing different effects such as fog, haze, mist, smoke, etc.

Effects Track

An additional soundtrack recorded independently and played behind the original soundtrack during the re-recording process, to reproduce, for example, the sound of cows lowing or the booming noise of a train passing in the far distance.

Eisenstein, Sergei

Massively influential in technical terms, and a social propagandist of heroic proportions, Eisenstein made a total of fourteen films in his brief fifty-year lifespan, most of which were either never completed or were hardly ever seen. Obsessed by design to the occasional detriment of humanity, Eisenstein struggled under the tyranny of Soviet bureaucracy as well as from the physical depredations caused by his own fervid lifestyle. His silent masterpiece, *The Battleship Potemkin* (25) (and in particular the scene on the Odessa steps) has achieved a strange sort of immortality, and his finest film, *Alexander Nevsky* (38), paradoxically (and perversely, given Hitler's abrupt about-turn on the so-called German/Soviet alliance) got the filmmaker into serious trouble with Stalin for criticising the Germans.

OTHER KEY FILMS: *Strike* (24); *October* (28); *Que Viva Mexico* (32); *Ivan The Terrible Trilogy* (43-46)

Electrician

Person in charge of the maintenance of all lighting equipment on a film set, and under the direct control of the **gaffer**.

Electronovision

An outmoded process originally designed to facilitate the transfer of video-shot films to a feature-film format.

Elevation Shot

When the camera swoops directly upwards, rather than diagonally or horizontally.

Elstree Studios

Situated near Borehamwood, on the outskirts of London, Elstree was built by Herbert Wilcox's British International Pictures in 1926, and was later acquired by **J Arthur Rank** in 1939. It was the home of **Alfred Hitchcock's** *Blackmail* (29) [the first British talkie] and was extensively used by **George Lucas** during the filming of the *Star Wars* series. Closed in the 1980s, Elstree has recently reopened, though in a smaller form, thanks to the efforts of its local council.

Emulsion

The coated part of a strip of film, consisting of a photosensitive mixture of silver salts and gelatine.

End Title

Title indicating that a film (and its often interminable credits) has finally ended. Usual forms include The End, Finis, Done, Finito, Fin, Schluss and 'That's All Folks'.

Epic

The most recent in the sun, sand, sex and sandals field is **Ridley Scott's** *Gladiator* (00), whose lavish spectacle and exotic locations perfectly encapsulate a genre that boasts such distinguished precursors as **Cecil B De Mille's** *The Ten Commandments* (56) and **Stanley Kubrick's** *Spartacus* (60). Prerequisites for any epic worth the name are the inclusion of enormous armies of either computerised or run-of-the-mill live extras (see **Soft Image**), a historical setting that allows for numerous pitched battles to take place, and heroic stars with muscular or glandular cleavages, depending on their sex — the term 'wide sweep' occurring somewhere in the publicist's blurb also helps.

***Best* Epics**

Bernardo Bertolucci's *1900* (76) and *The Last Emperor* (87); **Sergei Bondarchuk's** *War And Peace* (67); **Basil Dearden's** *Khartoum* (66); **Cecil B DeMille's** *The Ten Commandments* (56);

D W Griffith's *The Birth Of A Nation* (15) and *Intolerance* (16); **Henry Hathaway, John Ford** and George Marshall's *How The West Was Won* (62); **Howard Hawks's** *Land Of The Pharaohs* (55); **Chen Kaige's** *The Emperor And The Assassin* (99); **Akira Kurosawa's** *Kagemusha* (80); **Stanley Kubrick's** *Spartacus* (60); **Anthony Mann's** *The Fall Of The Roman Empire* (64); **David Lean's** *Lawrence Of Arabia* (62) and *Doctor Zhivago* (65); **Anthony Mann's** *El Cid* (61); **Fred Niblo's** *Ben-Hur* (25); **Laurence Olivier's** *Henry V* (44); **Ridley Scott's** *Gladiator* (00); **William Wyler's** *Ben-Hur* (59)

Episodic Film

Particularly popular in 1940s British cinema, episodic films contain two or more separate episodes, often linked by a narrator or contiguous storyline, and requiring one or more directors. The most successful of all is *Dead Of Night* (45), a truly eerie mandala-like series of ghost stories which boasts Alberto Cavalcanti, **Basil Dearden, Robert Hamer** and Charles Crichton among its directing talent.
OTHER KEY FILMS: **D W Griffith's** *Intolerance* (16); Julien Duvivier's *Tales Of Manhattan* (42); Ralph Smart, Harold French, Arthur Crabtree and Ken Annakin's *Quartet* (48) and French and Annakin's *Trio* (50); Sidney Cole's *Train Of Events* (49); **Max Ophüls's** *La Ronde* (50); **Pier Paolo Pasolini's** *The Canterbury Tales* (71); Neil Simon's *California Suite* (78); **Jim Jarmusch's** *Mystery Train* (89); **Woody Allen, Francis Ford Coppola** and **Martin Scorsese's** *New York Stories* (89)

Epstein, Julius J

Influential co-screenwriter of **Michael Curtiz's** *Casablanca* (42) and **Frank Capra's** *Arsenic and Old Lace* (44), Epstein professed himself mystified by *Casablanca*'s success, calling it 'slick shit!'. Always the consummate professional, he had, without knowing it, answered his own question. His screenwriting career spanned fifty years, and men such as he are the unsung heroes of Hollywood.
OTHER KEY FILMS: Vincent Sherman's *Mr Skeffington* (44); **Charles Walters's** *The Tender Trap* (55); **Sam Peckinpah's** *Cross of Iron* (77); Robert Ellis Miller's *Reuben, Reuben* (83)

Equity

Generic title used for both the American and the British Actors' Equity Associations, with the American version preceding the British by some sixteen years, following the creation of the parallel unions in 1913 and 1929 respectively. Both associations have engaged, on numerous occasions, in strike action, to protect and improve the interests of their members.

Erice, Victor

Downbeat and emotionally subtle Spanish director of such luminous masterpieces as *The Spirit Of The Beehive* (73), *El Sur* (83) and that punctilious and absorbing paean to artistic creation, *The Quince Tree Sun* (92), Erice has stayed resolutely clear of Hollywood and all its manifold temptations, and seems content to turn out roughly one exquisite and well-thought out film each decade. His philosophically inclined filmic meditations move slowly, but reward those with patience enough to follow them through to completion.
OTHER KEY FILMS: *Los Desafios* [part only] (68); *The Shanghai Gesture* (99)

Erotic Moments

A random, subjective, but, one hopes, enlightened selection of a few choice erotic moments from the annals of film:
Samuel Fuller's *Underworld USA* (61), when Dolores Dorn sucks on a phallic piece of ice as she is waiting in the park to meet **Cliff Robertson**. When slowed down on video (as if anyone would do such a thing) Sam Fuller's intention becomes very clear indeed.
Henri-Georges Clouzot's *Quai des Orfèvres* (47), when Suzy Delair, having returned home from a glamour photo session wearing only a fur coat and a basque, reveals herself for her husband, **Bertrand Blier**, by opening her mouth and her coat to him in unmistakable invitation (and in swooping close-up). See *The Outlaw*
Frank Capra's *Platinum Blonde* (31), when Robert Williams (whatever happened to him?) asks **Jean Harlow** to close her eyes, and she does so, turning her face up to be kissed in what has to be one of the most astonishingly erotic moments in any film, ever.
See also *Best* Films, *Best* Titles, **Heartstopping Moments, Worst Films**

Established

Once an actor, actress or location has appeared on a shot, they are deemed to be 'established', meaning that in all subsequent shots continuity of image and movement must at all costs be maintained.

Establishing Shot

A **long shot** that usually occurs early in a film's running time, and which is used to establish the locale or context of the action. Classic establishing shots include the skyline of Manhattan, London's Big Ben, Paris's La Tour Eiffel, the Pyramids and the apparently infinitely stretching lonely roads of the American Midwest (usually flanked by an equal infinity of telegraph poles).

Eustache, Jean

There are few men or women who deserve their place in cinema history on the strength of only one film, but Eustache (who died at the age of 43 in 1981) is one of them. His *La Maman Et La Putain* [*The Mother And The Whore*] (73) is so extraordinary and unique an achievement that it almost beggars belief. On seeing it on its re-release in London in 1998, this author came out of the cinema after 219 of the shortest minutes of his life, convinced, afresh (as if he ever needed convincing), that cinema, in the right hands, can be one of the greatest, noblest, and most subversively illuminating of all art forms.

OTHER KEY FILMS: *Les Mauvaises Fréquentations* (67); *Mes Petites Amoureuses* (75)

Everett, Rupert

Now something of one-track actor, Everett has recently proved how effective he is in waspish light comedy with P J Hogan's *My Best Friend's Wedding* (97) and Oliver Parker's *An Ideal Husband* (99), and one senses that such frothy fare will probably become his forte from now on. Early in his career he showed some dramatic promise with parts in Marek Kanievska's *Another Country* (84) and Mike Newell's *Dance With A Stranger* (85), films that for some obscure reason seemed to find particular favour with Continental audiences. However celebrity and his friendship with Madonna seem to have put paid to those ambitions for good, but one still dares to hope for a return to his earlier, more dramatic form.

OTHER KEY FILMS: *Duet For One* (86); *Chronicle Of A Death Foretold* (87); *The Right Hand Man* (87); *Hearts Of Fire* (87); *The Comfort Of Strangers* (91); *The Madness Of King George* (94); *Shakespeare In Love* (98); *A Midsummer Night's Dream* (99); *Inspector Gadget* (99); *The Next Best Thing* (00); *Unconditional Love* (01)

Excerpts

Short extracts taken from longer films and used as teasers, tributes, or, more commonly nowadays, for advertising purposes. Sections of film can also be excerpted and interpolated from old films into new ones, either for the purpose of reference, art, or economy, as in the reuse of filmed battle scenes, cavalry charges etc., which would be too prohibitively expensive to reshoot.

Exchange

A peculiarly American institution still in existence to this day, film exchanges were traditionally set up in different geographical regions to act as middlemen between the production companies responsible for making the movies and the distribution companies responsible for selling them.

Exciter Lamp

Used primarily in the recording and projection of optical soundtracks, an exciter lamp converts light into sound through the medium of an intensely powerful beam that is focused directly onto the soundtrack itself.

Executive Producer

A moneyman who puts together a film package – sometimes a number of them at the same time – leaving the nitty-gritty to an associate producer, who will be forced to carry the can in the event of any critical meltdown.

Exhibitor

The owner or operator of a cinema or chain of cinemas.

Existentialist Films

An alternative title for *film noir*, stemming from the appreciation certain French intellectuals, Albert Camus and Jean-Paul Sartre among them, showed for the genre during the 1940s. The existential aspect derived from the doomed condition of many of the main *noir* protagonists, and the blazing intensity with which they often chose to live their final hours.

Expanded Cinema

A mixture of live action, music, and pre-recorded film, something along the lines of a 1960s 'happening'.

Exploitation Movie

Any movie that highlights sensation and commerciality over artistic taste. Examples can occur in almost any genre, but sex, horror and violence are the exploitation movie's stock-in-trade. Post-structuralists insist on reading such films as accurate and largely uncontrived mirrors to their time and age, allowing many a stuttering and pretentious PhD thesis to coast home on the wind of schlock.

Exposure

What happens when film stock is exposed to light for a preordained amount of time in order to reveal the concealed image captured on its emulsive surface.

Exposure Meter

The gizmo used to measure the amount of light falling on a subject and to ensure that the camera filming that subject is set to the correct exposure

Exposure Sheets

Information provided by an animator to the cameraman responsible for filming a prearranged sequence of shots, and which gives details of the sequence, tenor and content of each anticipated shot.

Expressionism

Inflamed by the ideas of Freud and exacerbated by the horrors of the First World War, Expressionism took early root in German filmmaking, culminating in a remarkable series of films made during the 1920s in which exterior architecture was seen as a mirror to the interior world – twisted staircases, wildly disproportionate buildings and streets, dark shadows, and a gruesome concentration on the freakish and the macabre became, for a brief while, German cinema's stock-in-trade. Directors such as **Fritz Lang**, **F W Murnau** and **G W Pabst** are Expressionism's best-known adherents, but less well-known directors such as Paul Leni and Robert Wiene, who made the extraordinary *The Cabinet Of Dr Caligari* (19), were also devotees of expressionism's curious, and massively influential, morphology.

OTHER KEY FILMS: Paul Wegener and Carl Boese's *The Golem* (20); Fritz Lang's *Der Müde Tot* (21); F W Murnau's *Nosferatu* (21); Fritz Lang's *Dr Mabuse The Gambler* (22); Paul Leni's *Waxworks* (24)

EXT

Note on a film script indicating an exterior shot.

Extension Tube

Device used to distance the camera lens from the film inside the camera.

Extra

Someone hired, often for the day, to appear as part of a crowd, a battle, a riot, etc., during the making of a film. Few extras ever make it to the big time, Fidel Castro being an honourable example.

Extreme Close-Up

A close-up so extreme (ECU or XCU) that it only shows one detail of an actor's face or body. The phrase can also be applied to the camera's total focus on one object in order to highlight its significance. See **Close-Up**

Extreme High-Angle Shot

A crane is positioned high above the set, and the camera inside it is focused down onto an actor or scene, the better to highlight a particular action. Examples include the famous station-swooping scene in **Sergio Leone's** *Once Upon A Time In The West* (69), in which the camera lifts itself from its focus on **Claudia Cardinale** at the level of the station platform, up over the stationmaster's house, and down into the bustling main street outside, before coming to rest once again on La Cardinale's back, with the whole town spread out before her. A similar effect was achieved in the panoramic battle scenes in **Laurence Olivier's** *Henry V* (44), in which Robert Krasker's camera soared across an exquisitely choreographed Agincourt.

Extreme Long-Shot

A locating shot, taken from an extreme distance, which sets the scene for something which is about to happen, or which, in some cases, has already happened. **Raoul Walsh** used the technique in *High Sierra* (41) in order to focus on the particular corner of a mountain around which **Humphrey Bogart's** escaping vehicle was soon to slide.

Extremes

A term used in the making of animated cartoons to indicate the guiding drawings made by the senior animator denoting the beginning and end of a particular action. Assistants then draw in the missing frames.

Eye-level Angle Shot

When the camera points directly at an actor or actress's eyes to denote their particular point of view.

Eye Light

The light used to pick out and highlight the eyes and teeth of a performer. Also known as a kicker.

Eyepiece

The section of a camera the operator lays his eye to and focuses down. Some directors can regularly be seen striding around the set checking shots with a detached eyepiece, to make sure that everything is framed to their entire satisfaction.

Faction

A word first coined in literature to denote the fictional recounting of a historical fact, faction now applies to films as well, and indicates the likely use of real names and events within a fictional, notional, speculative or sensational framework. See **Film À Clef**.

Fade-in

A darkened screen gradually lightens to reveal an image, usually at the start of a film, indicating to the audience that the film has begun and that the curtain is up on the action. Fade-in can also be used for **flashback** sequences, to delineate the passage of time (rarely used in today's fast-action films), or else to imply the gradual re-emergence of one of the film's protagonists from a state of unconsciousness.

Fade-out

D W Griffith and his cameraman, 'Billy' Bitzer, stumbled, by accident, upon the convenient device of gradually darkening the screen to end a film, and the convention has been in more or less general use ever since. Tantamount to the falling of a theatre curtain, it could be argued that the closure effect appeals to our subconscious knowledge and acceptance of our own mortality, inasmuch as each film, by necessity, opens out from darkness, with the coming of light, only to return to darkness again once its story has been told – it becomes, in other words, a reflection of the passage of our lives.

Fairbanks Jr, Douglas

Son of **Douglas Fairbanks Sr** and his first wife, Anna Sully, 'Junior', as he was known by his father, made his first real mark in Paul Czinner's *Catherine The Great* (34), but only came close to matching his father's charisma when he played the swashbuckling Rupert von Hentzau in John Cromwell's *The Prisoner Of Zenda* (37). Highly decorated during the Second World War, Fairbanks was the recipient of an honorary British knighthood for his work in cementing Anglo-US relations, and died at the advanced age of 91 in 2000.

OTHER KEY FILMS: *The Dawn Patrol* (30); *The Narrow Corner* (33); *Gunga Din* (39); *The Corsican Brothers* (41); *Sinbad the Sailor* (47)

Fairbanks Sr, Douglas

Famous silent swashbuckling star who never really made the transition to sound, Fairbanks was known as the King of Hollywood, reigning jointly alongside his wife, **Mary Pickford's**, Queen. A founder of **United Artists** with Pickford, **D W Griffith** and **Charlie Chaplin**, the magically athletic Fairbanks was a charismatic master of evocative action in a long series of screen successes which included Fred Niblo's *The Mark Of Zorro* (20), **Allan Dwan's** *Robin Hood* (22) and **Raoul Walsh's** *The Thief Of Bagdad* (24).

OTHER KEY FILMS: *The Three Musketeers* (21); *Don Q Son Of Zorro* (25); *The Black Pirate* (26); *The Iron Mask* (29); *The Taming Of The Shrew* (29)

Famous Players

The precursor of **Paramount Pictures**, Famous Players was the 1912 brainchild of **Adolph Zukor**, who merged with Jesse Lassky in 1916 to create Famous Players–Lassky, one of the most important of all silent film studios, with stars of the calibre of **Douglas Fairbanks Sr** and Wallace Reid on its books. Paramount Pictures, which Famous Players – Lassky had taken over in 1917, grew so swiftly, however, that Zukor decided to fold Famous Players-Lassky back inside its subsidiary company. Zukor remained chairman emeritus of the board of Paramount until his death in 1976, at the magnificent age of 103.

Fan

See **Film Fan**

Farrar, David

There was something devil-may-care about David Farrar, epitomised by his throwing in his career in 1962 'when things got boring' and moving to Africa. This quality was best revealed in two **Michael Powell/Emeric Pressburger** films, *Black Narcissus* (47), in which he played the decadent and virile Mr Dean, who flutters the sentimental heart of **Deborah Kerr's** Sister Clodagh (particularly when singing hymns in his velvety drunken baritone) and in *Gone To Earth* (50), as Squire Reddin, where he fluttered the elemental heart of **Jennifer Jones**, particularly when she's laid over the pommel of his hunter or trying on the Stuart finery of his ancestors that he just happens to keep in an old trunk. There's a peculiar quality about *Gone To Earth*, some 'rightness', as though Powell and Farrar, **Hugh Griffith** and Cyril Cusack had managed to put their finger on a piece of Old England and encapsulate it – for it is rare for any film to give such an overwhelming, unprejudiced and honest impression of the past. Farrar was a throwback, an eighteenth-century man in a twentieth-century world, and it is for this that some of his films, particularly *The Small Back Room* (48) and *Cage Of Gold* (50), deserve reassessment.

OTHER KEY FILMS: *Went The Day Well* (42); *The Lisbon Story* (46); *Frieda* (47); *Mr. Perrin And Mr. Traill* (48); *Night Without Stars* (51); *Duel In The Jungle* (54); *The Black Shield Of Falworth* (54); *Tears For Simon* (56); *I Accuse!* (58); *Solomon And Sheba* (59)

Farrow, John:

Farrow was a weird sort of mainstream director, in that he disdained nothing in the way of work while remaining curiously literate and slightly out of place in the brash surroundings in which he found himself. His films have very little in common with each other beyond a marked emphasis on character, though never, happily, to the exclusion of action. He made one of the greatest of all **Westerns**, *Hondo* (53), and a few first-rate *film noirs*, which include *The Big Clock* (48), *The Night Has A Thousand Eyes* (48), *Where Danger Lives* (50) and *His Kind Of A Woman* (51). He was particularly good with actors, and one is left with the impression, viewing the sum total of Farrow's work, that maybe he knew something we didn't, for his films are oddly enjoyable. All in all, an extremely underrated director.

OTHER KEY FILMS: *Reno* (39); *A Bill Of Divorcement* (40); *Wake Island* (42); *Two Years Before The Mast* (46); *California* (47); *Calcutta* (47); *Alias Nick Beal* (49); *Ride Vaquero* (53); *A Bullet Is Waiting* (54)

Farrow, Mia

Once famously married to **Frank Sinatra**, and notable for her television incarnation as Alison Mackenzie in 'Peyton Place', Farrow is now best known for her scorned woman spat with ex-lover **Woody Allen**, in many of whose films she had previously (and in some cases undeservedly) starred. The child of director **John Farrow** (of **John Wayne's** *Hondo* (53) fame) and ex-Tarzan mate **Maureen O'Sullivan**, Farrow's most famous role was that of the eponymous Rosemary, in **Roman Polanski's** gripping *Rosemary's Baby* (68). A somewhat fay actress (and something of a fay woman too, one supposes) Farrow functions best as part of a group, and her most satisfying Allen outing came in the excellent *Hannah And Her Sisters* (86), in which Farrow's innate masochism and capacity for passive aggression came triumphantly to the fore.

OTHER KEY FILMS: *Secret Ceremony* (68); *John And Mary* (69); *Blind Terror* (71); *The Great Gatsby* (74); *A Midsummer Night's Sex Comedy* (82); *Zelig* (83); *Broadway Danny Rose* (84); *The Purple Rose Of Cairo* (85); *Radio Days* (87); *Crimes And Misdemeanors* (89); *Husbands And Wives* (92); *Widow's Peak* (94); *Angela Mooney* (96); *Coming Soon* (99)

Fassbinder, Rainer Werner

Very few directors have ever worked at the breakneck speed Fassbinder did during the 1970s, and one can only conjecture whether he instinctively sensed that he would die early, or whether his death at the age of thirty-six from a drug overdose was simply the result (and not the intuitive upshot) of his unbearably manic creative urges. Whatever the case, it remains indisputable that Fassbinder melded his political convictions to his cinematic artistry in a way that few directors since **Sergei Eisenstein** have achieved, and it is enlightening to note that Eisenstein, too, burnt himself out at the early age of fifty. Fassbinder's is the cinema of demoralisation, and his *Der Händler Der Vier Jahreszeiten* [*The Merchant Of Four Seasons*] (72), *The Bitter Tears Of Petra Von Kant* (72), *Chinese Roulette* (76), *The Marriage Of Maria Braun* (79) and *Veronika Voss* (82) are masterpieces of alienated urban angst. Fassbinder hated the world in which he lived but loved its people, and it is in his humanity in the face of an unwanted but very real existential torment that his genius lies.

OTHER KEY FILMS: *Katzelmacher* (69); *Warum Läuft Herr R Amok?* (70); *Beware The Holy Whore* (71); *Wildwechsel* (73); *Fontane's Effi Briest* (74); *Fox And His Friends* (75); *Fear Of Fear* (76); *Satan's Brew* (76); *Despair* (78); *Berlin Alexanderplatz* (80); *Lili Marleen* (81); *Lola* (82); *Querelle* (82)

Fast Motion
See **Accelerated Motion**

Favour
The act of giving one actor or actress the lion's share of a shot, usually by means of dedicated lighting and carefully selected camera angles. **Josef von Sternberg** was renowned for his cosseting of **Marlene Dietrich**, making sure that she had her very own lighting formula to ensure that she, and not her co-star, was the focus of every scene that she was in.

Fax
Way before it became synonymous with text sent over the telephone lines, the word fax was in general use on a film set to indicate any and all technical equipment involved in the making of the movie.

Feature
Catch-all title for a film, more than thirty-four minutes long or 3,000 feet in length, which is intended for commercial showing.

Featured Player
Another word for a supporting co-star, or important second-rank player in a film. Such parts were usually played by character actors, who became, in time, almost as well known as the major stars themselves. A good example is Jack Elam, whose wandering left eye and evil gleam gave intense pleasure to audiences in countless

Westerns and adventure films. The first ten minutes of **Sergio Leone's** *Once Upon A Time In The West* (69) give extensive prominence to Elam and to fellow featured player Woody Strode, who are both abruptly killed upon the first appearance of our real hero, **Charles Bronson**.

Feed Lines
A **cue** call from the periphery of a film set, sometimes during filming, to remind an actor of their lines.

Feed Reel
The principal reel around which a film is wound and from which it is then fed through the projector or past the camera lens onto a subsidiary **take-up** reel.

Feldman, Marty
An inspired comic loon who did most of his best work for television, Feldman was beginning to achieve considerable recognition in films prior to his premature death in 1982, aged only forty-nine, of a heart attack. With his bulging eyes and his capacity to suggest just the faintest touch of incipient dementia, he shone in a series of **Mel Brooks** and **Gene Wilder** movies including Brooks's *Young Frankenstein* (74) and *Silent Movie* (76), and Wilder's *The Adventures Of Sherlock Holmes's Smarter Brother* (75). Feldman directed himself in *The Last Remake Of Beau Geste* (77), but one will always remember him best as Igor – 'No. It's pronounced Eye-Gor!' – to Wilder's Dr Frederick Frankenstein, resolutely refusing to acknowledge the existence of his hump.

OTHER KEY FILMS: *The Bed Sitting Room* (69); *Every Home Should Have One* (70); *Yellowbeard* (83); *Slapstick (Of Another Kind)* (84)

KEY LINE:
'Comedy, like sodomy, is an unnatural act.'

Felix
The so-called European **Oscar**, given out at the European Film Awards, and intended to honour European Film (as if such a thing actually existed in a landmass which incorporates a population of perhaps 750 million people, speaking many different languages and dialects).

Fellini, Federico
Fellini is the great showman, a man at ease with himself and with the direction he has taken while remaining mildly amused that so many people have chosen to take it with him. He is the Pied Piper to

our enchanted child, and his strengths lie, not in the viewer's inevitable disenchantment and just as inevitable enforced maturity, but in the hope he holds out that we could all remain as children if only we would listen, and watch, and accept. Fellini springs his voluptuous vision upon us, confident that we will follow him, but he relies as much upon his reputation as our judgement. When watching how he uses his wife, Giulietta Masina, as the bewildered Gelsomima to **Anthony Quinn's** brutish Zampano in *La Strada* (54), it is we who become Gelsomima, with Fellini himself as the Quinn figure, forcing us onto his stage and making us twirl and caper for his amusement. In retrospect *I Vitelloni* (53) now seems to be his masterpiece, simply because it managed to encapsulate the boredom and the random but natural desire for existential recognition that underlie all his later, more self-consciously contrived films. Fellini remains a master, but a flawed one, capable of raising us briefly on his waxen wings, and making us forget that what we are seeing below us is only make-believe and papier-mâché. See **Heartstopping Moments**

OTHER KEY FILMS: *The White Sheik* (52); *The Swindlers* (55); *Nights Of Cabiria* (57); *La Dolce Vita* (it was Fellini's film that gave rise to this now common phrase) (60); *8½* (63); *Juliet Of The Spirits* (65); *Satyricon* (69); *The Clowns* (70); *Roma* (72); *Amarcord* [Fellini's filmic autobiography] (73); *Casanova* (76); *Orchestra Rehearsal* (79); *And The Ship Sails On* (83); *Ginger And Fred* (85)

Fernandel

Fernandel is the man most French people think about when they think of comedy – not **Jacques Tati**, not **Charlie Chaplin**, but Fernandel. With his elongated face, mischievous grin and strangely disingenuous eyes, Fernandel encapsulated an image of France that offered the small man a chance in the larger scheme of things if he was either cunning enough, lucky enough or stupid enough to take it. Fernandel embodied all these qualities in one man, and his humour was consequently a great deal more subtle (verging, dare one say it, on the archetypal) than at first meets the eye. His first great success came as **Marcel Pagnol's** *Angèle* (34), and his subsequent successes were legion, stretching across the Atlantic and even, astonishingly, across the English Channel. His most consistently played character was the Catholic priest, opposite Gino Cervi's intransigent communist mayor, in the Don Camillo series (once again, a reinforcement rather

than an undermining of the status quo), and his most satisfying film was Henri Verneuil's *The Cow And I* (59), in which he came perilously and effectively close to playing straight.

OTHER KEY FILMS: *Le Rosier De Madame Husson* (32); *Josette* (36); *Ignace* (37); *Le Schpountz* (39); *The Italian Straw Hat* [remake] (40); *Emile L'Africain* (49); *The Red Inn* (51); *Le Petit Monde De Don Camillo* (52); *The Sheep Has Five Legs* (54); *Ali Baba* (54); *Dynamite Jack* (61); *Heureux Qui Comme Ulysse* (70)

Fernández, Emilio

Fernández was Mexico's greatest film director (and in international terms, one of the greatest directors that ever lived) and his art was to take the innate sentimentality of the Mexican character and turn it into tragic and beautiful poetry. He was a man who lived life to the full, on occasion even to overpowering effect, as when he once shot a critic during a heated altercation, and later killed a farm labourer in a similar dispute, for which, in traditional Mexican fashion, he served only six months in jail. A veteran of the revolution, Fernández was a true Mestizo (of mixed Indian and Spanish/American blood) and his best films, *Flor Silvestre* (43), *María Candelaria* (43), *La Perla* (45) and *Río Escondido* (47) among them, put Mexico and its people back onto the map at a time when President Lázaro Cárdenas was alienating much of the rest of the industrial word by nationalising his country's oil industry. With the great cinematographer **Gabriel Figueroa** at his side, and the sublime **Pedro Armendariz** and **Dolores Del Rio** to act for him, Fernández, at his best, showed that an ancient and ill-understood country, unfairly swamped by its more recent, rather brasher neighbour, may have its **John Fords** too.

OTHER KEY FILMS: *Las Abandonadas* (44); *Bugambillia* (44); *Pepita Jiménez* (45); *Enamorada* (46); *Salón México* (48); *La Malquerida* (49); *Victimas Del Pecado* (50); *El Rapto* (53); *Una Cita De Amor* (56); *Pueblito* (62); *Un Dorado De Pancho Villa* (68); *La Choca* (73); *Zona Roja* (76)

Ferrara, Abel

A violent, visceral filmmaker who began his directing career with the serially banned *Driller Killer* (79), which he then followed with *Ms. 45* (81), a blood-curdling wish-fulfilment tale of a raped woman's revenge on her rapists, Ferrara's quest into the instinctive depths of his own Catholicism reached its fervidly (a)stigmatic height in *Bad Lieutenant* (92). This memorably began with the

115

sickeningly violent gang rape of a nun using a church crucifix, and continued with **Harvey Keitel's** misguided though ultimately redemption-seeking policeman, at first reluctantly, then righteously, and finally fetishistically, investigating her case. Ferrara is a brilliant though equally misguided filmmaker, and one suspects that Keitel's compulsively exploitative cop bears a not inconsiderable spiritual resemblance to its progenitor.

OTHER KEY FILMS: *Fear City* (84); *China Girl* (87); *King Of New York* (89); *Dangerous Game* (93); *Snake Eyes* (94); *The Blackout* (97); *New Rose Hotel* (98)

Field Camera

A hand-held camera used for shooting location scenes.

Field of View

The full extent of the physical landscape covered by the view through any particular lens.

Fields, W C

Fields was a second-generation American with an English cockney father from whom he ran away. He began his stage career as a juggler – God knows why this should be important, but it is. Suffice it to say that Fields was one of the world's greatest comic geniuses and that whatever he did, however awful and cowardly he seemed, his creations were always imbued with an overwhelming humanity. One recalls with joy his Mr Micawber, in **George Cukor's** magnificent *David Copperfield* (35), in which his playing of the role, so far from Dickens on the surface, was yet indisputably and utterly true to the Dickensian spirit – he purportedly questioned producer **David O Selznick** closely as to why there should be no juggling allowed in the part. Cuthbert J Twillie, Egbert Souse, Ambrose Wolfinger, Charles Bogle, Karl La Fong, Larson E Whipsnade, Eustace McGargle, Mahatma Kane Jeeves, Augustus Q Winterbottom, T Frothingwell Bellows, and Otis J Criblecoblis were only some of his expedient alter egos (still running away), and it was with a sort of sublime joy that one finally saw him settled, at the end of Norman Z McLeod's *It's A Gift* (34), on his well-earned Californian orange groves. Fields was the inheritor of a typically English sense of humour transcendently and serendipitously transplanted to a puritan, prohibition-minded United States, offering, God bless it, untold fresh opportunities for its exalted furtherance.

OTHER KEY FILMS: *Pool Sharks* [short] (15); *That Royle Girl* (26); *Fools For Luck* (28); *The Dentist* [short] (32); *The Barber Shop* [short] (33); *Mrs. Wiggs Of The Cabbage Patch* (34); *The Man On The Flying Trapeze* (35); *You Can't Cheat An Honest Man* (39); *My Little Chickadee* (40); *The Bank Dick* (40); *Never Give A Sucker An Even Break* (41)

KEY LINES:

'It's a funny old world – a man's lucky if he gets out of it alive.' [Charles Lamont's *You're Telling Me* (34)]

'Some weasel took the cork out of my lunch.' [George Marshall's *You Can't Cheat An Honest Man* (39)]

'Any man who hates dogs and small children can't be all bad.' [Fields on sentimentality]

'I'd rather be in Pennsylvania.' [Fields on his deathbed]

'Women are like elephants to me. I like to look at them, but I wouldn't want to own one.' [Edward Sutherland's *Mississippi* (35)]

'Don't wait up for me, my dear. I may play a little Parcheesi before coming to bed.' [William Beaudine's *The Old-Fashioned Way* (34)]

'I was in love with a beautiful blonde once. She drove me to drink. It's the one thing I'm indebted to her for.' [Edward F Cline's *Never Give A Sucker An Even Break*]

W C Fields as the harassed Harry Bissonette surreptitiously scoffing a bag of doughnuts, in Norman Z McLeod's It's a Gift (34)

Fiennes, Ralph

Fiennes's finest moment to date has come in **Steven Spielberg's** *Schindler's List* (93) in which he played concentration-camp commandant Amon Goeth with such astonishing veracity that one actually found oneself beginning to understand how the barbarities of the Nazi era could have occurred as much by moral default as by scrupulous intention. His Charles Van Doren, in **Robert Redford's** *Quiz Show* (94), was another *tour de force*, and even when he is in a film that fails, as with Jeremiah Chechik's *The Avengers* (98), Fiennes impresses with the seriousness with which he approaches even such a ludicrously underwritten role. His Almasy, in **Anthony Minghella's** *The English Patient* (96), is a prime example of Fiennes's greatest quality, his capacity for enlightened and constructive empathy even when the character he is playing is morally compromised.

OTHER KEY FILMS: *The Baby Of Macon* (93); *Strange Days* (95); *Oscar And Lucinda* (97); *Onegin* (99); *The End Of The Affair* (99)

KEY LINES:
'I veer away from trying to understand why I act. I just know I need to do it.' [Fiennes on acting]

Figueroa, Manuel

The favoured partner of director **Emilio Fernández** (with whom he made the celebrated *María Candelaria* (43) and *La Perla* (45)) and one of the ten greatest cinematographers of all time, Figueroa was the supreme master of dramatic light, preferring the deeper contrasts and heightened dramatic force of black-and-white to the softer, more dispersed tones of colour. An orphan, Figueroa was largely self-taught, only going to Hollywood when he was nearly thirty years of age to study with the great **Gregg Toland**, **Orson Welles's** mentor and the progenitor of **deep focus** photography. Although he was constantly wooed by Hollywood throughout his career, Figueroa resolutely nailed his colours to the nascent Mexican film industry (to whose renaissance he contributed not a little), only occasionally sallying across the frontier to film **John Ford's** *The Fugitive* (47) and later **Don Siegel's** *Two Mules For Sister Sara* (69). On Figueroa's own side of the legally dubious Mexican/US border, that wise old bird and old Mexico hand **John Huston** wooed Figueroa to shoot his sublime *Night Of The Iguana* (64), as well as the immaculately coloured *Under The Volcano* (84), which may rightly be seen to stand as Figueroa's epitaph.

OTHER KEY FILMS: Fernando De Fuente's *Allá En El Ranch Grande* (36); Emilio Fernández's *Flor Silvestre* (43), *Enamorada* (46), *Río Escondido* (47), *Maclovia* (48), *Pueblerina* (49) and *Salón México* (49); **Luis Buñuel's** *Los Olvidados* (50), *Él* (52), *Nazarín* (58), *The Exterminating Angel* (62) and *Simon Of The Desert* (65); Brian G Hutton's *Kelly's Heroes* (70)

KEY LINE:
'Lighting is the privilege of the cinematographer. He owns the light.' [Figueroa on the cinematographer's art]

Fill Light

Key lights create the shadows on a film set, and fill lights get rid of them again, both at the whim of the director.

Film À Clef

Not to be confused with faction, a *film à clef*, as with a roman à clef, tells the story of a real individual, but covers its trail by using false names, often in the hope of avoiding litigation. **Clint Eastwood's** *White Hunter, Black Heart* (90), for instance, actually, but not categorically, tells the story of film director **John Huston's** strange shenanigans on the set of *The African Queen* (51), and is based on Peter Viertel's book of the same name.

Film Archive

A film library in which films are conserved for scholarly or historical purposes. Unfortunately the concentration of often irreplaceable films in one place can sometimes lead to disaster, as in the case of the terrible fire of 1982 that destroyed more than 6,000 films at the Cineteca Nacional in Mexico City.

Film Base

Originally made of highly combustible cellulose nitrate, film base is the strip of material onto which emulsion is attached to produce film stock. Cellulose acetate, which is considerably more stable, has now superseded cellulose nitrate, with digital looking set to overtake the lot.

Film Club

A get together of like-minded people to form an association which allows for the viewing of esoteric, much-loved or difficult to obtain films. Most major film clubs have their own websites nowadays, and may be contacted directly or through such umbrella organisations as the BFFS (British Federation of Film Societies).

117

Film D'Art

The French production company, founded in Paris in 1908, which brought the legendary Sarah Bernhardt to the screen, Film D'Art specialised in luring stage actors into its studios. We owe our physical knowledge of the likes of Johnston Forbes-Robertson and Herbert Beerbohm Tree to its often rather stilted machinations.

Film Fan

An abbreviation for film fanatic. Hollywood has found the creation of fan clubs for its stars a convenient way to foment stability in a sometime sea of troubles. With the coming of the internet, disparate fan clubs from different countries and continents have melded and grown, and now any actor who doesn't have his or her dedicated fan-site can consider themselves something of an also-ran.

Film Festival

A showcase event held on a regular basis to foster commercial and artistic interest in (principally) new cinema. Examples might include **Cannes**, **Venice**, **Berlin**, **London** and **Sundance** Film Festivals.

Filmic

Anything to do with the technical aspect of filmmaking (and including the creative) while differentiating it from its commercial aspects.

Filmic Time

Filmic time entails a willing suspension of disbelief, so that we immediately accept, as part of the price we pay for the enjoyable convention of viewing a film, that real time no longer counts for anything, and that, by skilful editing, a man may leave his house, go down the stairs, cross the road and enter a café in the period it normally takes him to blow his nose. A good example of this occurs in *Doctor Zhivago* (65), when **David Lean** takes us from winter to spring in two or three well-chosen shots. A more laboured example occurs in the split-screen technique used by Norman Jewison in *The Thomas Crown Affair* (68), in which we follow up to five separate stories, all nominally occurring at the same time, and towards the same end.

Film Library

A source library for feature films, documentaries, *et al.*, which can have a historical, commercial or educational emphasis.

Filmmaker

The director or other principal person involved in the creative aspects of the making of a motion picture.

Film Music

The music, original or otherwise, that appears on the soundtrack of a motion picture film in order to heighten or change the atmosphere of a particular scene or emotionally charged moment, or in order to imbue the film with a particular character that the images alone might fail to suggest.

Film Noir

Generic term applied by French critics to a series of 1940s and 1950s Hollywood movies, mostly directed by European émigrés, which highlighted the dark and fatalistic side of the human condition. Using a style that incorporated elements of German **expressionism**, **pulp fiction** and the French poetic melodrama of the 1930s, the disparate pantheon of Noir directors includes **Billy Wilder**, **Fritz Lang**, **Nicholas Ray** and **Edward Dmytryk**. Some of the greatest Noir Auteurs [see **Auteur Theory**] were in fact **B-movie** directors who contrived to slip their strange films triumphantly through the Hollywood net – most notable among these was **Joseph H Lewis** whose *Gun Crazy* (49) has become massively influential in recent years, spawning an entire series of imitative, but on the whole lesser, movies. Some contemporary directors such as **Lawrence Kasdan** with *Body Heat* (81) and **Joel** and **Ethan Coen** in their debut movie *Blood Simple* (85), have made superb stabs at continuing the genre, and every few years or so there is a sudden resurgence of interest in the genre when a new film appears, such as **Dennis Hopper's** *The Hot Spot* (90), **Stephen Frears's** *The Grifters* (90), John Dahl's *The Last Seduction* (94), the Coen Brothers' *Fargo* (96), or **Oliver Stone's** *U-Turn* (97), that sees fit to acknowledge its debt to its exalted precursors.

KEY LINES:
'What do you want, Joe, my life history? Here it is in four words. Big ideas, small results.' [**Barbara Stanwyck** to Keith Andes in Fritz Lang's *Clash By Night* (52)]

'You never can depend on girls named Dolores.' [**George Raft** in Edwin L Marin's *Nocturne* (46)]

'It was the bottom of the barrel and I scraped it. But I didn't care. I had her.' [**Robert Mitchum**, about **Jane Greer**, in *Out Of The Past*]

Peggy Cummins and John Dall as the doomed film noir *lovers in Joseph H Lewis's cult favourite,* Gun Crazy *(49)*

Filmography
Akin to a writer's bibliography, a filmography lists all the films made by a particular individual during the course of his or her cinematic career.

Filmology
A catch-all phrase for the study, analysis and exposition of film.

Film Shorts
An abbreviated film form that usually relies on a single idea to fulfil its intentions. Many eminent directors, such as **David Lynch**, **Werner Herzog** and **Jean-Luc Godard**, began their careers producing low-budget short films in the hope that one of the major international Film Festivals would recognise their talent and enable them to move on to full-length features.

Film Society
Much the same as a **film club** but with a grander title, a film society gathers together those with a genuine interest in the art and history of film. Specific films are then shown, lectures given, slides slid and publications produced.

Film Stock
Unprocessed film that is intended for future use.

Film Strip
Single frame exposures from a reel of film for the purpose of education, illustration or duplication.

119

Film Theory

The in-depth analysis of the nature and psychology of the cinema, to include the placing of it within its purported sociological, philosophical, political, religious and artistic contexts by such self-styled critics and largely non-luminous intermediaries as the present author.

Filter

A coloured screen, placed over a camera lens, which affects the colour balance of a particular shot or film. Filters can also help create washed-out, sepia, haze, and vertigo effects.

Final Cut

This is the producer's cut, usually, but not always, agreed with the director, and corresponding to the **release print**. A notorious example of an unagreed final cut occurred following **Orson Welles's** filming of *The Magnificent Ambersons* (42); **RKO**, rattled by the mixed reception given to Welles's *Citizen Kane* (41), instructed **Robert Wise** to lop an hour off Welles's version of the film, and to re-shoot the ending. In later years Welles could hardly bring himself to talk about the film, and it is likely, from the fragments that still remain of the truncated material, that a masterpiece was lost on the cutting-room floor.

Finch, Peter

Finch was a subtle actor with a gentle manner and a handsome and particularly well-ageing face, and his most complex performance came in **John Schlesinger's** brilliantly sustained *Sunday Bloody Sunday* (71), as the vulnerable and civilised Dr Daniel Hirsh, who is forced, much against his will, to share his male lover with **Glenda Jackson's** equally vulnerable Alex Greville. Finch never gave a poor or ill-considered performance, and his premature death of a heart attack, aged only sixty-three, just after he had completed **Sidney Lumet's** *Network* (76), was greeted with particular sadness by all advocates of the enlightened, sensitive school of screen acting, a talent ideally characterised by Finch's portrayal of the bewildered Squire Boldwood in Schlesinger's *Far From The Madding Crowd* (67).
OTHER KEY FILMS: *The Heart Of The Matter* (53); *Father Brown* (54); *A Town Like Alice* (56); *The Nun's Story* (59); *The Trials Of Oscar Wilde* (60); *The Pumpkin Eater* (64); *England Made Me* (73); *A Bequest To The Nation* (73); *Raid On Entebbe* (77)
KEY LINE:
'I'm mad as hell and I'm not going to take it anymore.' [*Network*]

Fine Cut

One of the final stages in the editing of a film, the fine cut is a generally silent and unsynchronised last-minute version of what will eventually constitute the **release print**.

Fine-grain

A high-quality film stock in which smaller than usual particles of silver are mixed to make the emulsion, producing sharper, clearer images, particularly suitable for subsequent enlargement.

Peter Finch (as Captain Harris) on location during the shooting of Robert Aldrich's The Flight Of The Phoenix *(66)*

Finney, Albert

Finney was just the sort of talented working-class boy that post-**Free Cinema** Britain felt it needed during the 1960s to blow away the inhibited mists of an antediluvian class consciousness, and he dutifully joined the ranks of **Terence Stamp** and **Michael Caine** in an attempt to do just this. The result was a series of only vaguely subversive films and the creation of, needless to say, an entirely new and equally exclusive caste to replace the one whose apparent downfall we had so recently celebrated. If Finney were French he would be a **Monstre Sacré**, for his talent lies in his innumerable variations on himself – his consul, Geoffrey Firmin, in **John Huston's** *Under The Volcano* (84), was genuinely affecting, however, but still suffered from inevitable speculation about what a railing, drink-sodden **Richard Burton** might have made of the same role.

OTHER KEY FILMS: *Saturday Night And Sunday Morning* (60); *Tom Jones* (63); *Two For The Road* (67); *Charlie Bubbles* (67); *Gumshoe* (71); *Wolfen* (81); *Shoot The Moon* (82); *The Dresser* (83); *Miller's Crossing* (90); *The Browning Version* (94); *Washington Square* (97); *Breakfast Of Champions* (99); *Simpatico* (99); *Erin Brockovich* (00); *Traffic* (00); *Delivering Milo* (00); *Hemingway* (01); *The Hunter of Death* (01)

First Cameraman

Top of the camera-operating pecking order on a film set.

First Feature

The **A-Movie**, or main quality feature, in a double bill.

First Grip

The stagehand boss on a film set.

First Prop Man

Head of the prop crew on a film set.

First Run

The all-important first showing of a film, in carefully selected cinemas, before its general release.

Fish Eye Lens

Also known as a bug eye lens, this is the lens which gives 180° vision and which horror movie directors like to frighten us with, usually through the medium of a pretty, frightened girl, staring through a peephole in an unsatisfactorily locked door, when we all know that a drooling maniac with an ice-pick is lurking outside.

Fishing Rod (US: Fishpole)

This is the long hand-held microphone boom pole that we most often see on television being swung out over politicians, serial killers and celebrity divorcees in a (usually) vain effort to catch them out in verbal indiscretions. It is often used on film location work when a normal boom is inappropriate.

Fitzgerald, Barry

He was the stock Irishman in any number of forgettable, and some not-so-forgettable, Hollywood films, and even fellow Irishman **John Ford** did not disdain to use him as such – in fact it might be said that Fitzgerald *encapsulated* the sentimental view of Irishness that American audiences so greedily lapped up during the three decades of his screen career, and still lap up, green plastic bowler hats and all, to this day. Fitzgerald's hokum was at its most memorable in Ford's *The Long Voyage Home* (40), in which it was at least leavened with a modicum of seriousness, and again in Ford's *The Quiet Man* (52), which was so chock-full of hokum (and jolly nice hokum it was too) that Fitzgerald's performance did not, for once, stand out.

OTHER KEY FILMS: *Juno And The Paycock* (30); *Ebb Tide* (37); *Bringing Up Baby* (38); *The Dawn Patrol* (38); *The Sea Wolf* (41); *How Green Was My Valley* (41); *Going My Way* (44); *The Naked City* (48); *Union Station* (50)

Fixed Camera

A static or motionless camera that remains in the same place throughout the filming of a shot.

Fixed Focus Lens

A lens that has no focusing capacity built into its mechanism, and which is consequently useless for close-up work while paradoxically performing well in long shot, where **depth of field** is paramount.

Flag

A device used to block unwanted light sources on a film set.

Flaherty, Robert

Known by some as 'the father of the **documentary**', a title which he viewed with bemused tolerance, Flaherty was the son of a gold-miner, and from an early age he began to build up an interest in the natural world of day-to-day survival as opposed to the ever more artificial world of his native United States. His first completed film, *Nanook Of The North* (22),

121

was made almost by chance as the result of previous expeditions he had made among the Eskimo, around Hudson's Bay in Canada, and it remains one of the best films ever about survival in the face of intense natural odds. Nanook himself died of starvation just after the film was completed. It was followed by the softer, similarly heartfelt, but more self-consciously beautiful *Moana* (26), which detailed the diurnal life of a band of fishermen in the Polynesian archipelago. Flaherty's greatest achievement, however, came with *Man Of Aran* (34), which he filmed over a period of three years off the Irish coast. His final, lyrical *Louisiana Story* (48) also deserves mention, as does Flaherty's wife, Frances, who was his companion, muse, helpmeet and collaborator on many of his extraordinary and ground-breaking ventures.

OTHER KEY FILMS: *The Pottery-Maker* (25); *The Twenty-Four Dollar Island* (27); *White Shadows Of The South Seas* (28); *Tabu* (33); *Industrial Britain* (33); *Elephant Boy* (37); *The Land* (42)

Flange

An optional attachment on a film winder to ensure hitch-free rewinding in the editing room.

Flare

The equivalent of a sudden volcanic eruption on a piece of film caused by an unexpected and unwanted peripheral light source.

Flash

A sudden, short, interpolatory shot, usually comprising a single image, meant to shock, warn or intrigue the audience. **Dennis Hopper** used the technique to mixed effect in *Easy Rider* (69), particularly in the form of a flash forward to a burning motorcycle that was later shown to be that of the soon to be shotgunned Captain America (a.k.a. **Peter Fonda**).

Flashback

Near ubiquitous filmic convention to explain events that the screenwriter and director cannot get over to us in any other way. Flashback sequences can comprise dreams, as in **Alfred Hitchcock's** *Spellbound* (45), in which the final clue to a murder remains hidden inside a recurrent dream's symbolic structure; false or subjective flashbacks, as in **Akira Kurosawa's** *Rashomon* (51) in which a number of different characters, including a dead person, recount their own version of events, each progressively undermining the concept of an objective truth; and straight referrals back to the past, as in **Joseph L Mankiewicz's** *Suddenly Last Summer* (59) in which a seriously disturbed **Elizabeth Taylor** is encouraged by shrink **Montgomery Clift** to think back and unblock her own traumatic past which involved the murder and virtual cannibalisation of her homosexual cousin in front of her eyes.

Flash Cutting

A sudden sequence of quick cuts most often used to heighten tension or to instil a feeling of panic in the viewer. **Sergei Eisenstein** used the technique in the Odessa Steps sequence of his *The Battleship Potemkin* (25), and **Alfred Hitchcock** frightened millions with his meticulously constructed shower scene in *Psycho* (60), in which the editing is so brilliantly contrived that we only *think* we see **Anthony Perkins's** knife plunging again and again into the naked body of the unsuspecting **Janet Leigh**.

Flash Forward

The polar opposite of a **flashback**, the flash forward is best used to detail a character's expectations, dreads or wish-fulfilment fantasies. Tom Ewell, in **Billy Wilder's** *Seven Year Itch* (55), secretly delighted that his wife and children have left New York for the summer and that the bewitching and serially dumb **Marilyn Monroe** has moved into the apartment above him, fantasises about what may or may not occur between them in a classic case of forward-flashing comic misconception.

Flash Frame

Notorious in advertising where the only subliminally noticeable single-frame message is now banned, flash frame is normally used to unsettle and instil a sense of dread in the viewer, along the lines of 'did I or didn't I see it', and consists of an unexpected image flashed briefly onto the screen. The most amusing case of furtive flash framing came in the late 1920s, during one of **Max Fleischer's** risqué **Betty Boop** cartoons. The quite naturally unprescient cartoonist, thinking that no one would ever discover his little joke, drew Betty's vagina onto a single frame during a wind-driven upskirt sequence, leaving audiences wondering if they had fantasised Betty's nudity, or really seen it – the invention of **video**, however, rapidly uncovered his delightful and witty conceit.

Flashing

No, not the dirty brown raincoat variety of flashing, but rather the swift exposure of a film to a light source to speed up the emulsion process.

Flash Pan

A lightning fast side-to-side **pan** to effect a zappy transition between one scene and another – the effect is one of stasis, followed by sudden blurring, followed, once again, by stasis.

Flat

A theatrical term denoting a large canvas frame used as a backdrop to a static movie set.

Flat Lighting

Deadpan lighting, evenly distributed to avoid unwanted shadows and tonal infelicities on a film set.

Flat Print

A normal-sized film print, as opposed to the anamorphic (stretched or magnified) **CinemaScope** and **Panavision** variety, which were originally projected onto curved screens.

Fleischer, Max and David

The Fleischers were responsible for both the **Betty Boop** and 'Popeye The Sailorman' cartoon characters which included Bluto, Wimpy and Olive Oil (all of whom were later uncharacteristically travestied by **Robert Altman** in his live-feature *Popeye* (80)) and together they constituted the only real threat to **Walt Disney's** dominance of the animated cartoon field during the 1930s. Despite the comparative success of their first full-length cartoon, *Gulliver's Travels* (39), the brothers eventually split up and went their separate ways – as the great Jimmy Durante would no doubt have quipped, 'They were wenters.'
OTHER KEY FILMS: *Popeye The Sailor Meets Sinbad The Sailor* (36); *Hoppity Goes To Town* (41)

Fleming, Victor

Fleming's posthumous fame lies mainly in two films, *Gone With The Wind* (39), which he directed almost by default after **George Cukor** had been sacked, and *The Wizard Of Oz* (39). These came almost at the end of his career, however, and this macho man's man (he used to brothel-crawl with **Clark Gable**), had already made his mark during the 1920s and 1930s with such classics as *The Virginian* (29), *Red Dust* (32), and *Captains Courageous* (37), a grossly sentimental film which is nevertheless still able to raise the odd furtive tear in this particular correspondent (hem, hem).
OTHER KEY FILMS: *Lord Jim* (25); *The Way Of All Flesh* (27); *Bombshell* (33); *Treasure Island* (34); *Test Pilot* (38); *Dr Jekyll And Mr Hyde* (41); *Tortilla Flat* (42)

Flick

The colloquial name for a film during the 1920s to 1950s period, it is an abbreviation of the word flicker, and stems from the flickering effect given by the early (and slow) 16-frame-a-second silent features.

Flicker

'Persistence of vision' is the ability of the human eye to differentiate sufficiently between alternate images of light and darkness to allow those images to coalesce inside the brain into one continuous visual experience. Silent movies, customarily projected at 16 frames per second, did not allow for persistence of vision, and consequently the human eye detected a flicker on the screen – however, the content of the films was generally so riveting that such minor annoyances were instantly discarded.

Flies

Storage areas, up in the gods, to which stage props are conveniently stowed by pulley, only to be lowered back onto the film set when needed.

Flipover

A neat trick often used in 1930s and 1940s screwball comedies, which consists of the picture on the screen reversing itself on its axis, rather like a revolving door, thus effecting a witty transition to the next scene. A **flopover** is simply a cat flap variety of a flipover, this time from top to bottom and then vice versa. Got it?

Floating Release

A movie released to all cinemas, with no strings attached, and not contracted out to any particular circuit.

Floodlight

The usual form of lighting on most film sets, consisting of a series of powerful arc lights throwing bright beams that produce few, if any, shadows.

Floor

The location in the studio where filming is currently taking place.

Floor Manager

The person in charge of all the technical staff on a film set.

Flop

What all producers dread, a film that fails to make back even a fraction of the money that has been spent on it. A recent case is Peter Chelson's $85 million **Warren Beatty** vehicle, *Town & Country* (01), which bombed so badly that it looks set to join **Michael Cimino's** *Heaven's Gate* (80) and Elaine May's *Ishtar* (87), which also featured Beatty, as one of the most financially disastrous turkeys of all time.

Flopover

Go back to **flipover**. Do not pass Go. Do not collect £200.

Flynn, Errol

More renowned for his off-screen antics than for his on-screen acting, Flynn was actually a consummate professional. Astonishingly handsome, and with an athlete's physique to boot, Flynn's breakthrough came with **Michael Curtiz's** *Captain Blood* (35), which set the pattern for a succession of swashbuckling roles that ensured him his place in Hollywood legend. Hopelessly (and one-sidedly) infatuated with eight-time co-star **Olivia de Havilland**, Flynn took solace in drink, drugs, brawling and an increasingly crazed round of sexual shenanigans, all of which contributed to his early death at the age of fifty. He last successfully buckled his swash in William Keighley's *The Master Of Ballantrae* (53), which is better than it has any right to be given Flynn's deplorable condition at the time. One prefers to remember him as Robert Devereux, Earl of Essex, ardently proclaiming his love for both **Bette Davis** and her throne, yet still scorning the chance to use that love, at the expense of truth, to save his skin.

OTHER KEY FILMS: *The Charge Of The Light Brigade* (36); *The Adventures Of Robin Hood* (38); *The Private Lives Of Elizabeth and Essex* (38); *The Sea Hawk* (39); *Objective Burma!* (45); *The Sun Also Rises* (57)

KEY LINE:
'My dear friend, there's a little bit of Don Juan in every man. But since I *am* Don Juan, there must be more of it in me.' [Vincent Sherman's *Adventures Of Don Juan* (49)]

Focal Length

The measurement of the precise gap separating the lens from the film surface in which an image, placed at infinity, is brought into sharpest definition.

Errol Flynn cutting his usual demented swash (and his fingernails?) in a location shot for Michael Curtiz's Captain Blood *(35)*

Focus

Perfect focus requires perfect measurement, from camera lens to subject. An out-of-focus shot is either deliberate or occurs as the result of inefficient preparation on the set.

Focus Puller

Person in charge of refocusing the camera during an extended shot according to the **cinematographer's** preordained plan.

Fog

The disastrous effect unwanted light can have on film stock. Fogging can also be caused by age, poor storage, or substandard developing procedures.

Fog Filter

Neat Hollywood trick in order to produce an effect of fog on a perfectly clear day through the simple use of a **lens filter**.

Foley Artist

The sound technician in charge of recreating or enhancing noises to be heard on the soundtrack of a film by non-electronic means. A self-consciously exaggerated example occurs in **Terry Gilliam** and Terry Jones's *Monty Python And The Holy Grail* (75), in which the servants to our brave band of horseless knights mock-gallop behind them clashing coconuts together in an attempt to simulate the sound of pounding hooves.

Henry Fonda (as Tom Joad) in John Ford's The Grapes Of Wrath *(40), one of the first films to be included in the National Film Registry*

Foley State

Jack Foley, head of sound effects at **Universal** during the 1930s, was acknowledged as the greatest sound technician of his day. Foley State applies to any and every device used to create a new sound artificially, or to enhance an existing sound on a film's soundtrack.

Follow Focus

What the **focus puller** does when a lens needs constant adjustment during a **follow shot** to keep it in focus.

Follow Shot

When the camera trails after the action to give viewers the impression that they, too, are in the thick of it. Horror movies such as George Romero's *Night Of The Living Dead* (68) and Tobe Hooper's *Texas Chainsaw Massacre* (74) used jerky hand-held cameras to produce this effect, but since the arrival of the **Steadicam** (whose inventors received a special **Oscar** in 1977), things have smoothed up.

Fonda, Henry

Fonda personified integrity on the screen, and became **John Ford's** actor of choice in such American classics as *Young Mr Lincoln* (39), *The Grapes Of Wrath* (40) and the sublime *My Darling Clementine* (46). A surprisingly good straight man, Fonda also shone in **Preston Sturges's** comedy masterpiece *The Lady Eve* (41), opposite a scintillating **Barbara Stanwyck**. After exemplary wartime service in the US Navy, Fonda played a variety of tormented heroes in such movies as **Alfred Hitchcock's** *The Wrong Man* (56) and **Sidney Lumet's** electrifying courtroom drama *Twelve Angry Men* (57). In a rare outing as a bad guy, Fonda elegantly out-acted and (mostly) out-shot the opposition in **Sergio Leone's** majestic *Once Upon A Time In The West* (68).

OTHER KEY FILMS: *The Farmer Takes A Wife* (35); *Jezebel* (38); *Drums Along The Mohawk* (39); *Jesse James* (39); *The Fugitive* (47); *Fort Apache* (48); *Mister Roberts* (55); *Warlock* (59); *Fail Safe* (64); *On Golden Pond* (81)

Fonda, Jane

Excoriated by the political right for her extreme opposition to the Vietnam War, Fonda soon succeeded in living down the sex-doll image, which **Roger Vadim** had foisted on her in *Barbarella* (68). An intense, occasionally unsympathetic actress, she finally found her feet in **Alan J Pakula's** *Klute* (71), playing a hard-bitten prostitute to **Donald Sutherland's** bewildered investigator. Some politically exemplary movies followed, including **Fred Zinnemann's** *Julia* (77), **Hal Ashby's** *Coming Home* (78), and James Bridges's *The China Syndrome* (80). Her career has tailed off in recent years, and she has become more renowned for her choice of husbands (Tom Hayden and **Ted Turner**) and her fitness videos, than for her screen work.

OTHER KEY FILMS: *Cat Ballou* (65); *Barefoot In The Park* (67); *They Shoot Horses, Don't They?* (69); *California Suite* (78); *The Electric Horseman* (79); *On Golden Pond* (81); *Stanley & Iris* (90)

Fonda, Peter

Famed for his part in **Dennis Hopper's** *Easy Rider* (69), and for being the son of Henry, the brother of Jane, and the father of Bridget, Peter Fonda has been making something of a comeback in recent years with movies such as Michael Almereyda's *Nadja* (94), and Victor Nuñez's *Ulee's Gold* (97). His directorial debut, *The Hired Hand* (71), boded rather well for this Hollywood scion, but, son of a famous father that he is, Fonda has never quite seemed able to get a full grip on his undoubted talent.

OTHER KEY FILMS: *The Last Movie* (71); *Dirty Mary Crazy Larry* (74); *Race With The Devil* (75); *Wanda Nevada* [also dir.] (79); *The Cannonball Run* (81); *The Limey* (99); *South Of Heaven, West Of Hell* (00); *Wooly Boys* (01)

Fontaine, Joan

Sister and occasional public enemy of **Olivia de Havilland**, Fontaine tended towards the demure in such roles as the second Mrs de Winter, in **Alfred Hitchcock's** *Rebecca* (40), and poor Jane, in Robert Stephenson's *Jane Eyre* (44) (surely the cinema's most relentless passive/aggressive ever). In real life Fontaine was something of a derring-do, mixing pilotage, fishing and ballooning with the more decorous de Winter-like pursuits of cooking and interior design. What she had on screen, especially in her younger years, was an innocent vulnerability perfect for virile bounders such as **Cary Grant**, **Laurence Olivier** and **Orson**

Welles to threaten, thus guaranteeing the audience its fair share of thrills. Her later career marked something of a turning point, and she was allowed to stretch herself a little in more taxing, and occasionally more unsympathetic roles, such as the scheming wife in **Nicholas Ray's** *Born To Be Bad* (50).

OTHER KEY FILMS: *Gunga Din* (39); *Suspicion* (41); *The Constant Nymph* (43); *Frenchman's Creek* (44); *Ivy* (47); *The Emperor Waltz* (48); *Kiss The Blood Off My Hands* (48); *Letter From An Unknown Woman* (48); *The Bigamist* (53); *Serenade* (56); *Island In The Sun* (57); *A Certain Smile* (58); *The Witches* (66)

Footage

Either the basic length of a film, in feet, or an **extract** taken from a film and shown in a different environment or context. See **Métrage**

Footage Counter

A counter designed to adhere to a piece of equipment and which measures, in feet and frames, the exact amount of film footage exposed or viewed during a specific period.

Forced Perspective

Invented by Italian painters during the Renaissance, the technique is used on painted backdrops artificially to suggest distance through the use of a false perspective. This tricks the eye by means of height, breadth and width manipulation, for example in the case of a distant group of mountains being painted smaller than a closer-by tree.

Ford, Glenn

Ford could turn his hand to just about anything, as befitted the son of a rough, tough, railroad man, and he forged a successful career through being relaxed and at his ease in more or less any situation. His first big break came with Charles Vidor's *Gilda* (46), in which he played a down-at-heel chiseller who is taken up by a bisexual casino owner, in whose wife, **Rita Hayworth**, they have a shared interest (kinky, or what?). His best performance came in **Fritz Lang's** terrific *film noir The Big Heat* (53), and in later years Ford profitably mined the **Western** trail (where a few wrinkles more or less don't count) along with so many of his ageing male contemporaries. Out of favour now in an age that wrongly fancies it understands the subtleties better than its ancestors, Ford was always a sensitive actor in a pretty much insensitive business.

OTHER KEY FILMS: *A Stolen Life* (46); *The Undercover Man* (49); *The Secret Of Convict Lake* (51); *Affair In Trinidad* (52); *The Violent Men* (55); *The Blackboard Jungle* (55); *3:10 To Yuma* (57); *Cowboy* (58); *Santee* (73)

Ford, Harrison

A far better actor than he has any right to be, given the wonderfully obscene amount of money his most successful movies have made, Ford is equally at home as a laconic light comedian in Ivan Reitman's *Six Days And Seven Nights* (98), and as the tormented, almost *noir* protagonist of **Peter Weir's** *Witness* (85) and **Ridley Scott's** *Blade Runner* (82). It would be churlish not to give him credit for his professionalism in roles such as Han Solo in **George Lucas's** *Star Wars* series, and as Indiana Jones in **Steven Spielberg's** tetralogy of the same name, but Ford really showed what he could do with an adventurous role in Andrew Davis's superb *The Fugitive* (93) in which he played the falsely accused Dr Richard Kimble, and which, almost alone in recent years, restored one's faith in the capacity of the Hollywood mainstream to entertain without at the same time despising its audience.

OTHER KEY FILMS: *American Graffiti* (73); *The Conversation* (74); *Apocalypse Now* (79); *The Mosquito Coast* (86); *Frantic* (88); *Presumed Innocent* (90); *Regarding Henry* (91); *Random Hearts* (99); *What Lies Beneath* (00); *K-19: The Widowmaker* (01)

KEY LINE:
'It's not the age. It's the mileage.' [Steven Spielberg's *Raiders Of The Lost Ark*]

Ford, John

The former Sean Aloysius O'Feeney won six **Oscars** during his career, and deserved a number more. A true poet of the screen, he incorporated song, sound and image in a series of masterpieces that, even today, have no serious parallel in American cinema; in films like *Young Mr Lincoln* (39), *The Grapes of Wrath* (40), *My Darling Clementine* (46) and *The Searchers* (56), he became, quite literally, the emotional historian of the American soul. All his films had heart – a rare thing in the commercial world in which he operated – and a strong belief in community. Ford's people were courteous to each other (even to their enemies, when this was possible) and it was no coincidence that he chose either **John Wayne** or **Henry Fonda** to incarnate the finest of his realistically flawed heroes. Ford's conservative view of the family as the essential prop of any civilised and civilising society has received its

fair share of brickbats from the self-appointed liberal and intellectual elite of his own and more recent times, but his films obstinately retain their magic and their power to move the instincts, while the words and works of his assailants have, more often than not, simply crumbled into dust and been forgotten. See **Heartstopping Moments**

OTHER KEY FILMS: *The Informer* (35); *The Hurricane* (37); *Stagecoach* (39); *Drums Along The Mohawk* (39); *They Were Expendable* (45); *Fort Apache* (48); *She Wore A Yellow Ribbon* (49); *Rio Grande* (50); *Wagon Master* (50); *The Quiet Man* (52); *Mogambo* (53); *Mister Roberts* (55); *The Man Who Shot Liberty Valance* (62)

KEY LINE:
'It is easier to get an actor to be a cowboy than to get a cowboy to be an actor.' [Ford on acting and cowboys]

Foreground

The nearest part of the set to the camera.

Foreign Version

Following the demise of the silent movie film (which had the coincidental and not uncongenial advantage of being totally understandable to every culture under the sun), it was suddenly found necessary to redub films for foreign markets into the language of their intended audience. Certain countries, of which France is a notable example, now have a tradition of showing subtitled foreign films in their major cities while dubbed versions of the exact same film are shown in country areas – one can only assume that the film distributors take it as read that rustics and regionals are inevitably less sophisticated than their big city counterparts. Either way, dubbed films are invariably second best except when they magically revert to the language that they should have been filmed in if historical accuracy were to have been maintained. Examples that spring to mind of such 'accomplishments by default' are **Milos Forman's** *Amadeus* (84) and *Valmont* (89) (which were both even better when dubbed into German and French respectively than in their original mixed-accented English versions) and **Jean-Jacques Annaud's** *L'Amant* (92), which was infinitely better in its alternative French, rather than in its palpably absurd, internationally consumable, English variation.

Forman, Milos

A native Czechoslovakian who lost both his parents to a Nazi concentration camp, the critically acclaimed director of *A Fireman's Ball* (68) was

stranded in Paris in 1968 after the Russian takeover of his country, and eventually forsook Europe altogether and moved to Hollywood. His first big US success was *One Flew Over The Cuckoo's Nest* (75), proving, yet again, that it often takes a foreigner to best interpret a country for its own citizens. The hybrid *Amadeus* (84) followed the disappointing *Ragtime* (81) as Forman's next international success, but his excellent *Valmont* (89) was unjustly overlooked in favour of **Stephen Frears's** *Dangerous Liaisons* (88), both of which were based on the same Choderlos de Laclos epistolary novel. Forman is a fastidious director with a marked flair for atmosphere, character, and eccentricity, and his distinctly personal slant on American subjects is particularly welcome given the turgid repetitions and rank sentimentality inherent in so many home-baked productions.
OTHER KEY FILMS: *Loves Of A Blonde* [*A Blonde In Love*] (65); *Taking Off* (71); *Hair* (79); *The People Vs. Larry Flint* (96); *Man On The Moon* (99); *The Little Black Book* (99)

Format
The particular size and shape that a film is projected in, more usually known as the ratio.

Foster, Jodie
Foster was a movie brat even before the term was invented, acting in TV commercials from age three, and feature films from age ten, with Jerrold Freedman's inappropriately named *Kansas City Bomber* (72). 1976 was her *annus mirabilis*, in which she made her mark in two very different films, as Tallulah, in **Alan Parker's** *Bugsy Malone*, and as Iris Steensman, in **Martin Scorsese's** *Taxi Driver*. In her adult career (post-1983) she has sometimes verged on the worthy, almost as if she wants to be both a critical success and a mainstream darling at one and the same time, without having tumbled to the fact that the two aspirations are not necessarily compatible. But when directors have succeeded in channelling her away from her Joan-of-Arc syndrome, she has been extremely effective, most notably in **Jonathan Demme's** *The Silence Of The Lambs* (91), as the hawk-like Clarice Starling, and in Richard Donner's *Maverick* (94).
OTHER KEY FILMS: *Candleshoe* (78); *Foxes* (80); *Carny* (80); *The Hotel New Hampshire* (84); *The Accused* (88); *Little Man Tate* [also dir.] (91); *Shadows And Fog* (92); *Sommersby* (93); *Nell* (94); *Contact* (97); *Anna And The King* (99); *The Dangerous Lives Of Altar Boys* (01)

Fox
See 20th Century-Fox

Frame
There are 129,600 separate images or frames in a ninety-minute movie, at least two or more of which need to be shown in some preordained order or sequence if the appearance of motion is to be attained. Frame can also be taken to mean the extent of the view through a camera's lens.

Frame Counter
A simple measurement device attached to a camera that shows the number of frames exposed during a shot sequence.

Framing
The act of designing or composing a shot. Also the correct alignment of a film inside a film projector, taking into account the relative position of the film and of the lens aperture.

Francis, Freddie
Francis is something of a paradox – his films as a director consist almost entirely of such thoughtfully made and entertaining little thrillers as *Paranoiac* (63), *Dr Terror's House Of Horrors* (65), *Torture Garden* (68) and *The Ghoul* (75), whereas the films he has collaborated on as a cinematographer are of another ilk entirely, and include Jack Clayton's *Room At The Top* (59) and *The Innocents* (61), **Jack Cardiff's** *Sons And Lovers* (60) (Cardiff was yet another gamekeeper-cinematographer turned poacher-director), **Karel Reisz's** *Saturday Night And Sunday Morning* (60) and *The French Lieutenant's Woman* (81), **David Lynch's** *The Elephant Man* (80), and **Martin Scorsese's** *Cape Fear* (91). How to equate the two? It is almost as if it were belatedly to be discovered that Salvador Dalí had stooped to painting set designs for some rogue filmmaker's dream sequence. But then he did, didn't he? For **Alfred Hitchcock's** *Spellbound* (45).
OTHER KEY FILMS: Karel Reisz's *Night Must Fall* (64); Edward Zwick's *Glory* (89); Michael Austin's *Princess Caraboo* (94); **Bob Hoskins's** *Rainbow* (95); David Lynch's *Dune* (84) and *The Straight Story* (99)

Franju, Georges
Some reckon him one of the greatest of all French film directors; others don't reckon him at all. Franju is cult material par excellence, and from his first bravura documentary release, *Le Sang Des Bêtes* (49), in which he casts an unswerving eye on the

128

brutal business of meat slaughtering, it was obvious that Franju was not to be conveniently filed away. A co-founder of the French national film archive, La Cinémathèque Française, he alternately shocks and stimulates, as with his sensationally surreal horror classic *Les Yeux Sans Visages* [a.k.a. *Eyes Without A Face* or *Horror Chamber Of Dr Faustus*] (60), which has been a staple of university film clubs for decades. Franju's feature film masterpiece is probably *Judex* (64), in which he successfully recreates the adventurous and dreamlike silent world of Louis Feuillade, the original creator of the Judex and Fantomas characters.

OTHER KEY FILMS: *Hôtel Des Invalides* [doc.] (51); *Le Grand Méliès* [doc.] (52); *La Tête Contre Les Murs* [a.k.a. *The Keepers*] (59); *Thomas L'Imposteur* [a.k.a. *Thomas The Imposter*] (65); *L'Homme Sans Visage* [a.k.a. *Shadowman*] (74)

KEY LINE:
Franju: 'Movies should have a beginning, a middle and an end.' **Jean-Luc Godard**: 'Certainly, but not necessarily in that order.' [Franju and Godard on film]

Frankenheimer, John

A variable director, Frankenheimer has a rigorous technique which he sometimes uses to mask a lack of emotional depth in his characters. His *The Manchurian Candidate* (62), however, still stands up very well, and the recent (and finally litigation-free) re-release of *Seven Days In May* (64) confirms his reputation as a fine weaver of suspense. *French Connection II* (75) and *Black Sunday* (79) were both excellent thrillers, and one is irresistibly drawn to the conclusion, particularly in the light of his recent **Robert de Niro** vehicle *Ronin* (98), that Frankenheimer is actually a first-class 'Boy's Own' director reluctantly masquerading as a grown-up.

OTHER KEY FILMS: *The Young Stranger* (57); *Birdman Of Alcatraz* (62); *The Train* (65); *The Horsemen* (71); *The Challenge* (82); *The Holcroft Covenant* (85); *Reindeer Games* (00)

Frankenstein

Something of a genre in itself, nearly every budding director has taken a shot at Mary Shelley's *Frankenstein* (either literally or figuratively) since the birth of the cinema circa 1895. **James Whale's** 1931 *Frankenstein* is the movie most people remember, with a sad-eyed **Boris Karloff** playing the nameless monster, but Whale's follow-up, *The Bride Of Frankenstein* (35) is equally good, and benefits from an electrifying performance (forgive the pun) from the one and only **Elsa Lanchester**.

Later movie versions have varied from the comic, with Charles Barton's *Abbott And Costello Meet Frankenstein* (48) and **Mel Brooks's** *Young Frankenstein* (74), to the worthy with David Wickes's *Frankenstein* (93), to the dotty with Frank Henenlotter's *Frankenhooker* (90), to the misguided with William Beaudine's *Jesse James Meets Frankenstein's Daughter* (65) and **Kenneth Branagh's** *Mary Shelley's Frankenstein* (93), to the genuinely frightening with Jack Smight's *Frankenstein: The True Story* (73).

OTHER KEY FILMS: Erle C Kenton's *The Ghost Of Frankenstein* (42); Roy William Neill's *Frankenstein Meets The Wolf Man* (43); Terence Fisher's *Frankenstein Must Be Destroyed!* (70); Stuart Gordon's *Re-Animator* (85)

KEY LINE:
'It's alive! It's alive!' [Colin Clive's Henry Frankenstein, on first seeing Boris Karloff twitch in James Whale's *Frankenstein*]

Frears, Stephen

Something of a star on his home-grown British cinema circuit (and latterly in the US), Frears is a director of integrity who has the rare capacity to tease out an actor's performance beyond its normal range. From his debut feature *Gumshoe* (72), in which **Albert Finney's** obsession with **Raymond Chandler** and **Humphrey Bogart** leads him into more trouble than he is capable of handling, let alone explaining, through *The Hit* (84), a somewhat nihilistic and beautifully scored Costa del Sol gangster movie, to the films that have really made his name, *My Beautiful Laundrette* (85), *Prick Up Your Ears* (87) and *Dangerous Liaisons* (88), Frears has produced thoughtful and well-founded work. His best film is *The Grifters* (90), in which he effectively inhabits novelist Jim Thompson's head by unsentimentally portraying a world of small-town, penny-ante American con artists who are enmeshed in moral, amoral, and proto-Oedipal relations, far beyond their understanding.

OTHER KEY FILMS: *Bloody Kids* (80); *Sammy And Rosie Get Laid* (87); *Hero* (92); *The Snapper* (93); *Mary Reilly* (96); *The Van* (97); *The Hi-Lo Country* (98); *High Fidelity* (00); *Liam* (00)

Free Cinema

A British **documentary** movement begun by **Tony Richardson**, **Karel Reisz** and **Lindsay Anderson** in 1956, and which had as its aim the freeing up of British cinema from its long-standing class-ridden conventions. A number of documentaries were shown under the Free

Cinema aegis, including *O Dreamland* and *We Are The Lambeth Boys;* however, it was not these, but three full-length feature films, which most contributed to the eventual breaking down of the barriers during the 1960s. These were Reisz's *Saturday Night And Sunday Morning* (60), Richardson's *A Taste Of Honey* (61), and Anderson's *This Sporting Life* (63).

Freeze Frame

Not actually a frozen frame, but rather the continual repetition of a single frame to mimic a frozen effect. Its most famous use comes in the final freeze on **Jean-Pierre Léaud**, as he runs alone on the beach, in **François Truffaut's** *Les Quatre Cents Coups* [a.k.a. *The 400 Blows*] (59), an image that later came to symbolise the alienation of youth during the 1960s. Author's Note; The unobscene meaning of 'faire les quatre-cents coups' is to 'lead a wild life'.

Friction Head

The swivel at the head of a camera tripod designed to allow totally fluid camera movements.

Friedkin, William

A brilliant technician, Friedkin struck pay-dirt with two blockbusters in three years, *The French Connection* (71), with its famous (and illegal – Friedkin had not asked permission to film where and what he did) car chase, and *The Exorcist* (73), a green-vomit-stained masterpiece of inspired exploitation which spawned a host of inferior copies, and which totally changed the way Hollywood viewed word-of-mouth advertising. Friedkin seemed to lose his touch following *The Exorcist* (perhaps bemused by the film's extraordinary success), and his work since then has varied from the outrageously exploitative to the marginally pretentious.
OTHER KEY FILMS: *The Birthday Party* (68); *The Night They Raided Minsky's* (70); *The Boys In The Band* (70); *Sorcerer* (77); *To Live And Die In L.A.* (85); *Rampage* (92); *Jade* (95); *Rules of Engagement* (00)

Fröbe, Gert

Rotund German character actor even more famous in his homeland than abroad, Fröbe was renowned for his comic prowess and ability to send up himself – and the German bourgeoisie – hilariously. International audiences remember him most fondly for his Colonel Manfred von Holstein running-on-the-water scene in Ken Annakin's *Those Magnificent Men In Their Flying Machines* (65)

(in which he also demonstrated his unique ability to imitate an entire brass band through his nose) and for his sinister Mr Auric Goldfinger, in **Guy Hamilton's** *Goldfinger* (64).
OTHER KEY FILMS: *Berliner Ballade* (48); *Heroes And Sinners* (55); *The 1000 Eyes Of Dr Mabuse* (60); *The Longest Day* (62); *Die Dreigroschenoper* (63); *Tonio Kröger* (64); *A High Wind In Jamaica* (65); *Chitty Chitty Bang Bang* (68)
KEY LINE:
'This is gold, Mr Bond. All my life I've been in love with its colour, its brilliance, its divine heaviness.' [*Goldfinger*]

Front Projection

The use of cleverly placed mirrors to reflect pre-created scenes onto a screen behind the actors on a set, a process which generally produces a more convincing and less shadowy effect than **back projection** which preceded it.

Frost

Fake frost effect produced by a variety of different methods and used to coat windows, fences, cars etc., during mock-winter shooting.

Frying Pan

A circular shield that is used to lessen the effect of extraneous light sources on a film set.

F-Stop

The measured potential of a particular lens to admit light, usually in a series of staggered settings.

Fuller, Samuel

Fuller used the **B-movie** format to its full extent, writing, producing and directing his own work and retaining control over it at a time, during the 1950s and 1960s, when such a thing was virtually impossible in a mainstream context. A master of the camera and its movement, Fuller was a conservative/anarchist obsessed with criminality who refused to be bound by the conventional subject matter of Cold War America. Like **Pulp Fiction** writer Jim Thompson (whom in some ways he resembles), Fuller's view of morality and its voluble adherents is an arch one, and his characters often function more through expediency and unenlightened self-interest than through any established code. An instinctive Darwinist who believed in the rough process of natural selection, Fuller's *House Of Bamboo* (55) and *Underworld USA* (61) were devastating attacks on cupidity, human frailty and the emptiness of the revenge motive, whilst *Shock Corridor* (63) was a heady paean to the incipient insanity of those who think themselves sane, a view Fuller brought to final fruition in his magnificent but ultimately pessimistic war film, *The Big Red One* (80). Fuller is that uncomfortable thing, a man who falls between the two stools of high art and schlock commerciality, and his films are disturbing, disquieting, occasionally comically bad, and very often misunderstood. See **Erotic Moments**

OTHER KEY FILMS: *I Shot Jesse James* (49); *Fixed Bayonets* (51); *Pickup On South Street* (53); *Hell And High Water* (54); *Run Of The Arrow* (57); *Verboten!* (59); *Merrill's Marauders* (62); *The Naked Kiss* (65); *White Dog* (82); *Thieves After Dark* (84); *Street Of No Return* (89)

KEY LINE:
'When you're in the battlefield, survival is all there is. Death is the only great emotion.' [Fuller on death]

Full Figure Shot

Paradoxically refers to a waist upwards shot, rather than to the view of a complete body it initially suggests. The term can also be used in connection with inanimate objects, such as a flight of aeroplanes or a convoy of ships.

Full Shot

An 'FS' is the same as a long shot, and implies the incorporation of the entire figure of the subject being photographed onto the screen.

Fuzzy

An out-of-focus shot, either accidentally achieved or done on purpose. **Woody Allen** famously shot only **Robin Williams's** face in fuzzy to get the point across that Mel, the character Williams plays in the film *Deconstructing Harry* (97), has reached the stage where his entire life is out of focus.

Gabin, Jean

Born Jean-Alexis Moncorgé to a family of itinerant entertainers on the café circuit, Gabin, at his consummate best, outclassed even **Humphrey Bogart** as a tough guy with a tender heart. In films like **Marcel Carné's** poetic *Quai Des Brumes* (38) and **Jean Renoir's** masterpiece *La Grande Illusion* (37), Gabin played working-class men with the capacity to transcend, even if only very fleetingly, the brutalisation of their lot. Although he continued acting for more than thirty years after serving with the Free French during the Second World War, Gabin's greatest moments undoubtedly came in the 1930s, during the magnificent golden era of French cinema, which, to all intents and purposes, he encapsulated. Gabin could transmit passion, pain or disillusionment with a single glance, and his rough way with women, leavened with an innate romanticism that came as something of a pleasurable shock from a broken-nosed man who could have doubled as a middleweight boxer, endeared him to both sexes. By the time of his death, in 1976, he had become one of France's national treasures.

OTHER KEY FILMS: *Méphisto* (31); *Zouzou* (34); *La Belle Équipe* (36); *Les Bas-Fonds* (36); *Pépé Le Moko* (36); *Gueule D'Amour* (37); *La Bête Humaine* (38); *Le Jour Se Lève* (39); *The Walls Of Malapaga* (49); *La Nuit Est Mon Royaume* (51); *Le Plaisir* (52); *La Minute De Vérité* (52); *Touchez Pas Au Grisbi* (54); *Archimède Le Clochard* (58); *Les Misérables* (58); *En Cas De Malheur* (58); *Le Soleil Des Voyous* (67); *Le Clan Des Siciliens* (69); *Le Testament* (75); *L'Année Sainte* (76)

KEY LINE:
'He had the most beautiful loins I've ever seen in a man.' [**Marlene Dietrich** to a journalist, *à propos* of her one-time lover, Gabin]

A post-war Jean Gabin, photographed by Limot, still capable of showing the aura of romantic disillusion that was his trademark. See also image at Louis Jouvet

Clark Gable, aged 32, (and with his ears pinned back?), as Giovanni Severi in Victor Fleming's The White Sister *(33)*

and Tay Garnett's *China Seas* (35), Gable forged an image of the male that has lasted, more or less untainted, to the present day. He conducted passionate affairs with **Joan Crawford** and **Jean Harlow**, contracted a tender and loving marriage with the ill-fated **Carole Lombard** (whose death in a freak air accident broke his heart), and never lived to see the birth of his only son, John Clark Gable. **Frank Capra's** *It Happened One Night* (34) was Gable creating Gable, Victor Fleming's ***Gone With The Wind*** (39) was Gable out-Gabling himself, **John Ford's** *Mogambo* (53) was Gable proving that he still was Gable and that he didn't give a two-penny halfpenny damn if people knew it, and **John Huston's** *The Misfits* (60) was Gable's wise, virile and utterly en-Gabled swansong, the swansong also to an era of men who chose not to subjugate their lives to the tyranny and the oppressiveness of a neurotic and sometimes debilitating over-analysis.

OTHER KEY FILMS: *Possessed* (31); *Hell Divers* (31); *Strange Interlude* (32); *No Man Of Her Own* (33); *Manhattan Melodrama* (34); *Call Of The Wild* (35); *Mutiny On The Bounty* (35); *Wife Versus Secretary* (36); *Test Pilot* (38); *Strange Cargo* (40); *Comrade X* (40); *Somewhere I'll Find You* (42); *Lone Star* (52); *The Tall Men* (55)

KEY LINES:
'Frankly, my dear, I don't give a damn!' [***Gone With The Wind***]

'Being near him gave me twinges of a sexual urge beyond belief.' [**Joan Crawford** on the King]

'Quiet, determined – no, not determined, just quiet. I said to Hunt [Stromberg] once, "This guy's got eyes like a child and a build like a bull." ' [**John Lee Mahin**, who scripted **Victor Fleming's** *Red Dust* (32) and co-scripted Clarence Brown's *Wife Versus Secretary* (36), on Gable]

133

Gable, Clark

Despite the big ears and the alleged bad breath and all the other myriad faults that also-rans persist in seeing in him, Gable was the undisputed King of Hollywood during the 1930s, 1940s and a hefty part of the 1950s too – King not in box office necessarily, but in stature and star ranking. When people thought of Hollywood, they thought of Gable, just as when they thought of literature, they thought of Hemingway. It was something beyond the rational. And Gable played up to it wonderfully, wooing both men and women with his on-screen virility – men wanted to emulate him, women to be approved by him. He was fortunate to have begun acting at a time when licence, innuendo and sheer sex weren't frowned upon and euphemised. With films such as **Robert Z Leonard's** *Susan Lenox: Her Fall And Rise* (31), **Victor Fleming's** *Red Dust* (32)

Gaffer

Head of the electrical team on a film set; assisted by the **best boy** or best girl.

Gagmen

Joke inventors, responsible for supplying verbal gags and visual jokes for use in feature films and television comedy programmes.

Gance, Abel

Gance had been virtually ignored for thirty years before Kevin Brownlow's detailed reconstruction of his final masterpiece, *Napoléon* (27), triumphantly reappeared before an unprepared public in 1980. *Napoléon* seemed to sum up the three brief but unbelievably rich decades of the silent era, reuniting for the first and last time all the ground-breaking cinematic techniques that had been thrown up in their passing. A pioneer of the split-screen technique, in which he used three separate cameras and screens to achieve a triptych-like effect, Gance achieved early and lasting critical success with *Mater Dolorosa* (17), *La Dixième Symphonie* (18), *J'Accuse* (19) and *La Roue* (23), films in which he honed the rapid-fire editing skills he was later to use in *Napoléon*, and which were to become his trademark. The latter part of his career was distinguished by a series of superb screen biographies, *Lucrezia Borgia* (35), *The Queen And The Cardinal* (35), and *The Life And Loves Of Beethoven* (36), but it is for the wonders of *Napoléon* that he is now rightly, if somewhat belatedly, acclaimed.

OTHER KEY FILMS: *Le Nègre Blanc* (12); *La Fleur Des Ruines* (15); *Barberousse* (17); *La Fin Du Monde* (31); *Le Voleur De Femmes* (37); *Louise* (38); *Le Capitaine Fracasse* (43); *La Tour De Nesle* (55); *Cyrano Et D'Artagnan* (63)

Best Gangster Films

Jacques Becker's *Casque D'Or* (52); **Francis Ford Coppola's** *The Godfather* (72-90); **Marcel Carné's** *Le Jour Se Lève* (39); **Michael Curtiz's** *Angels With Dirty Faces* (38); **Brian De Palma's** *Scarface* (83) and *The Untouchables* (87); Julien Duvivier's *Pépé Le Moko* (36); **Howard Hawks's** *Scarface* (32); Mike Hodges's *Get Carter* (71); **John Huston's** *Key Largo* (48) and *Prizzi's Honor* (85); **Mervyn LeRoy's** *Little Caesar* (30); **Louis Malle's** *Atlantic City* (81); John Mackenzie's *The Long Good Friday* (81); Mike Newell's *Donnie Brasco* (97); **Martin Scorsese's** *Goodfellas* (89) and *Casino* (95); **Quentin Tarantino's** *Reservoir Dogs* (92); **Raoul Walsh's** *White Heat* (49)

Garbage Matte

Opaque material used to screen out unwanted objects on a shot, such as television aerials, satellite dishes and modern additions to old buildings.

Garbo, Greta:

She was the most famous screen actress of them all, although, ironically, many of the people who know her name have probably never seen a single one of her films. She was a woman whose beauty emerged from the screen as if by magic, and it is arguable that the sadness we see reflected in her face stemmed from the profoundest parts of a psyche bruised,

almost beyond endurance, by a deprived and poverty-stricken childhood. When, as **George Cukor's** *Camille* (37), Garbo takes a curiously childlike pleasure in baubles and bangles and the beautiful fripperies only rich men can provide, we are not repelled by her shallowness, but are instead forced to understand the very deprivations that can cause such a compensatory passion. In Rouben Mamoulian's *Queen Christina* (33), Garbo throws away a kingdom for an already-lost love, and in **Ernst Lubitsch's** *Ninotchka* (39) she gives up her country and her identity for the capacity to laugh. In real life she quit the screen, dramatically, at the height of her fame, arguing for the right to be herself and to live her life in all its unadorned banality, but she left behind enough of herself in the fleeting images of her brief and glittering star to remind her audience, in the decades and centuries to come, that magic contains its very own capacity for liberation.

OTHER KEY FILMS: *The Temptress* (26); *Flesh And The Devil* (27); *The Divine Woman* (28); *The Kiss* (29); *Anna Christie* (30); *Susan Lenox: Her Fall And*

Greta Garbo, photographed by C S Bull, around the time of her appearance as Grusinskaya in Edmund Goulding's Grand Hotel (32)

Rise (31); *Mata Hari* (31); *Grand Hotel* (32); *As You Desire Me* (32); *The Painted Veil* (34); *Anna Karenina* (35); *Conquest* (37); *Two-Faced Woman* (41)

KEY LINES:

'I want to be alone.' [*Grand Hotel*]

'What, when drunk, one sees in other women, one sees in Garbo sober.' [Kenneth Tynan on Garbo]

'I have been memorising this room. In future, in my mind, I shall live a great deal in this room.' [To her lover, **John Gilbert**, in *Queen Christina*]

Garcia, Andy

An intense, intelligent actor, whose Latin good looks and capacity to enshrine paradoxes on-screen have made him the choice of directors as disparate as **Brian De Palma**, in *The Untouchables* (87), **Ridley Scott**, in *Black Rain* (89), and **Francis Ford Coppola**, in *The Godfather: Part III* (90). Following these successes, Garcia seemed on the verge, for a short while at least, of taking over **Robert De Niro's** mantle, but in the final analysis his capacity for characterisation simply wasn't that extensive – proving that an actor cannot live by head alone.

OTHER KEY FILMS: *Eight Million Ways To Die* (86); *Internal Affairs* (90); *Dead Again* (91); *Jennifer 8* (92); *When A Man Loves A Woman* (94); *Things To Do In Denver When You're Dead* (95); *Night Falls On Manhattan* (97); *Desperate Measures* (98); *Just The Ticket* (99); *Lakeboat* (00); *Just Like Mona* (01)

Gardner, Ava

A stunningly beautiful share-cropper's daughter from North Carolina, Gardner flummoxed her critics by proving that she could act as well as look scenic in movies such as **Robert Siodmak's** *The Killers* (46), **Alfred Lewin's** headily romantic *Pandora And The Flying Dutchman* (51), and **John Ford's** *Mogambo* (53), in which she more than matched the formidable **Grace Kelly**. The swansong of her beauty (and incidentally one of her finest performances) came in **John Huston's** sublime *Night Of The Iguana* (64), as transplanted hotelier and devil-may-care existentialist Maxine Faulk (see **Heartstopping Moments**). Famously married (at different times, needless to say) to **Mickey Rooney**, Artie Shaw and **Frank Sinatra**, Gardner lived her life in the fast lane and resolutely refused to complain when the time finally came to pay the piper.

OTHER KEY FILMS: *Lost Angel* (43); *The Hucksters* (47); *The Bribe* (49); *My Forbidden Past* (51); *Show Boat* (51); *The Snows Of Kilimanjaro* (52); *The Barefoot Contessa* (54); *Bhowani Junction* (56);

*A classic Hollywood studio shot of **Ava Gardner** taken in 1952, when she was appearing as Cynthia, in Henry King's* The Snows Of Kilimanjaro *(52)*

The Sun Also Rises (57); *On The Beach* (59); *Seven Days In May* (64); *Mayerling* (68)

KEY LINE

'Do you really think I could be a star?' [**Joseph L Mankiewicz's** *The Barefoot Contessa*]

Garfield, John

A hard-bitten, left-leaning precursor to **Marlon Brando** and **Steve McQueen**, Garfield died at the early age of forty-one, of a heart attack following his blacklisting by the HUAC for refusing to name names (see **Hollywood Ten**). Garfield personified the loner – the man who came through the Great Depression and had been changed by it. His boxer's face fitted him perfectly for hard-boiled roles, often as working men with the courage of their convictions, but also for tragic, fatalistic roles, such as that of drifter Frank Chambers in Tay Garnett's *The Postman Always Rings Twice* (46). Capable of appearing in oddities like **Michael**

Curtiz's *The Sea Wolf* (41) and **John Huston's** *We Were Strangers* (49), and also of improving potboilers such as Delmer Daves's *Pride Of The Marines* (45), Garfield's finest moments came in mainstream movies that still somehow managed to hit home, most notably as tormented boxer Charlie Davis in **Robert Rossen's** *Body and Soul* (47), and as a self-confident lawyer, Joe Morse, who gradually allows himself to be corrupted by the underworld milieu he frequents, in Abraham Polonsky's *Force of Evil* (48).

OTHER KEY FILMS: *Juarez* (39); *East Of The River* (40); *Tortilla Flat* (42); *Fallen Sparrow* (43); *Nobody Lives Forever* (46); *Humoresque* (46); *The Breaking Point* (50); *He Ran All The Way* (51)

KEY LINE:
'Stealing a man's wife, that's nothing. But stealing a man's car, that's larceny.' [*The Postman Always Rings Twice*]

Garland, Judy

Erstwhile wife of **Vincente Minnelli** and mother of Liza, Garland received more hype, for a more variable talent, than did even **Lassie** (and Lassie could howl as well as the next person), and her messy, self-obsessed life has become so bound up with her screen career that it is almost impossible to watch **George Cukor's** melodramatic *A Star Is Born* (54) without assuming the film is about her. (It wasn't, of course. Cukor had originally shot the story as *What Price Hollywood?* in 1932, when Garland was only ten, and **William Wellman** made the original, and better, *A Star Is Born*, based loosely on the lives of **John Gilbert** and **Greta Garbo**, in 1937.) Even Garland's singing voice was overrated, although she could certainly belt out a tune loudly enough when she chose to, while utterly ignoring any particular need for characterisation beyond the strictly vocal. (Try listening first to Billie Holiday, and then go back to Garland – impossible.) Garland always seemed to be acting, and her main appeal seems to lie in this very staginess, rather as **Barbra Streisand's** (a rather similar schmaltz-merchant, come to think of it) does now. All right, she *was* genuinely winsome as Dorothy, in **Victor Fleming's** *The Wizard Of Oz* (39), but then again, can winsomeness ever *be* genuine?

OTHER KEY FILMS: *Love Finds Andy Hardy* (38); *Babes In Arms* (39); *Strike Up The Band* (40); *Girl Crazy* (43); *Meet Me In St Louis* (44); *The Clock* (45); *The Pirate* (48); *Easter Parade* (48); *Words And Music* (48)

KEY LINE:
'I was born at the age of twelve on a **Metro-Goldwyn-Mayer** lot.' [Garland on stardom]

Garmes, Lee

Garmes was one of the greatest of all the black-and-white cinematographers, pioneering the centrally concentrated use of light, while leaving the periphery of a scene in low key. He was an expert on the **dolly** as well as the static set-up, and the picture of Garmes one always remembers is of him soaring and swooping into the air, with his camera implausibly under total control, on such films as **Josef von Sternberg's** *Shanghai Express* (32) and **King Vidor's** blissfully absurd *Duel In The Sun* (46).

OTHER KEY FILMS: Josef Von Sternberg's *Morocco* (30) and *Dishonored* (31); **Howard Hawks's** *Scarface* (32); Julien Duvivier's *Lydia* (41); **Edmund Goulding's** *Nightmare Alley* (47); **William Wyler's** *Detective Story* (51)

Garson, Greer

A popular actress who specialised in five-hanky films, Garson first shone playing **Robert Donat's** wife, Katherine Ellis, in **Sam Wood's** *Goodbye Mr Chips* (39), a success which led to her role as the eponymous heroine in **William Wyler's** *Mrs Miniver* (42), alongside the man with whom she was to co-star on eight different occasions, Walter Pidgeon. Her finest moment, however, came as the self-willed Elizabeth Bennett in Robert Z Leonard's well-nigh perfect *Pride and Prejudice* (40), which boasted, among its many other felicities, a brilliant script co-written by novelist Aldous Huxley.

OTHER KEY FILMS: *Blossoms In The Dust* (41); *Random Harvest* (42); *The Youngest Profession* (43); *Madame Curie* (43); *Adventure* (46); *Desire Me* (47); *Julius Caesar* (53)

Gate

The camera or projector mechanism through which a film frame passes and which holds it steady when it is being either exposed or projected.

Gauge

The width, in millimetres, of film stock. Standard is 35, substandard is 16, and home, 8. **Epic films**, designed for grand-scale viewing, tended to use 70mm gauge during the 1950s and 1960s.

Geared Head

The fluid series of gimbals on which a camera swings, pans or tilts on its mount.

Geffen, David

See **DreamWorks SKG**

Gel
A simple strip of coloured gelatine that may be used as a camera filter.

Gemini
Meaning 'the twins', Gemini is the apposite name for the synchronous twinning of a movie camera with a video camera so that technicians may view the principal filmed image on the video monitor in real time without disturbing the camera operator.

General Release
The full release of a motion picture throughout the entire distribution area, as opposed to only a limited outlet release.

Gere, Richard
With his mincing, city boy's walk, and his all too self-conscious tics (the flicking of the hair, the cannibal kissing) Gere is an odd candidate for enduring stardom, but he has lasted longer, and at a higher level, than many of his more talented contemporaries. Does he pick his roles better? Or is it that he simply reinvents himself every five or six years, chooses an on-the-make actress to reinforce his continuing sex appeal, and takes it from there? His best role came as Jesse, the perky, existential hero of Jim McBride's *Breathless* (83), in which Gere took the Julian Kay character from **Paul Schrader's** *American Gigolo* (80) and extended him with a touch more style and a lot more energy. He was fine, too, in Taylor Hackford's brilliantly populist *An Officer And A Gentleman* (82), particularly in the early scenes with his father, played by the excellent Robert Loggia, in which Gere suggested the sort of edgy, working-class boys he might have played if fame, and the Hollywood machine, hadn't so consummately eaten him up.
OTHER KEY FILMS: *Looking For Mr Goodbar* (77); *Days Of Heaven* (78); *No Mercy* (86); *Internal Affairs* (90); *Pretty Woman* (90); *Sommersby* (92); *Mr Jones* (93); *Primal Fear* (96); *The Jackal* (97); *Runaway Bride* (99); *Autumn In New York* (00); *Dr T And The Women* (01)

German Expressionism
See **Expressionism**

Gershwin, George
The extraordinarily precocious but short-lived Gershwin (1898-1937) provided the music (his brother Ira supplied the lyrics) for well over fifty films, most, unfortunately, posthumously. The best of these, namely John Murray Anderson's *The King Of Jazz* (30), **Vincente Minnelli's** *An American In Paris* (51) and **Otto Preminger's** *Porgy And Bess* (59), conspired to push the musical off the stage and into what passes, in Hollywood Musical terms at least, for real life. Gershwin's song-writing capacity was sublime, and his rigorous technique and respect for the concert hall and for the classical repertoire allowed jazz, for almost the first time, to become something of a mainstream interest — no matter what its adherents felt about the fact.
OTHER KEY FILMS: Norman McLeod's *Lady Be Good* (41); Norman Taurog's *Girl Crazy* (43); Irving Rapper's *Rhapsody In Blue* (45); **Charles Walters's** *The Barkleys Of Broadway* (49); **Stanley Donen's** *Funny Face* (57); **Robert Wise's** *Star!* (68)

Get In Character
The ability of an actor or actress to switch off from their normal lives and enter those of the characters they are playing. Also a director's warning to the actors that the wind-up to filming a scene has begun.

> ### *Best* Ghost Films
> **Claude Autant-Lara's** *Sylvie Et Le Fantôme* (45); **Alberto Cavalcanti**, **Basil Dearden**, **Robert Hamer** and Charles Crichton's *Dead of Night* (45); **René Clair's** *The Ghost Goes West* (35); Jack Clayton's *The Innocents* (61); Basil Dearden's *The Halfway House* (43); **William Dieterle's** *Portrait Of Jenny* (49); **David Lean's** *Blithe Spirit* (45); **Anthony Minghella's** *Truly, Madly, Deeply* (91); **Peter Weir's** *Picnic At Hanging Rock* (75)

Ghost Image
An image created by double exposing or double printing a piece of film to suggest the presence of a ghost.

Ghosting
The over-dubbing of one actor or actress's voice by another, usually when singing beyond the range of that actor's capabilities is required. The most famous on-screen example of the technique comes in **Stanley Donen** and **Gene Kelly's** *Singin' In The Rain* (52), in which waspish silent star Lina Lamont, played by Jean Hagen, has her voice dubbed by the far more talented but as yet unknown, **Debbie Reynolds**. A sadder example

came in George Sidney's *Showboat* (51) when **Ava Gardner** was ghosted by Annette Warren. Gardner's exquisite rendition of 'Bill', accompanied only by a piano and string orchestra, belatedly convinces us of what a mistake, swayed by poor previews, **MGM** made.

Gibson, Mel

Mel Columcille Gerard Gibson only moved from his native New York to Australia when he was twelve (not a lot of people know that), and so it's hardly surprising that he feels so at home in both cultures. **George Miller's** cult favourite *Mad Max* (79) started him on the long return path to America, **Peter Weir's** *Gallipoli* (81) saw him briefly hesitate, but his success in Miller's *Mad Max 2* (81) [a.k.a. *The Road Warrior*] made lucrative repatriation a foregone conclusion. A more than competent stage actor, Gibson was wonderful as journalist Guy Hamilton in Weir's *The Year Of Living Dangerously* (83), and one can forgive him the blockbusting *Lethal Weapon* series (87-98) because he used his ensuing box-office clout to turn out a more than respectable *Hamlet* (90) for **Franco Zeffirelli**, followed by his own, Oscar-winning *Braveheart* (95). Obviously that rare thing, a film star with integrity, Gibson still lives in rural Australia with his wife and their seven children.
OTHER KEY FILMS: *Tim* (79); *The Bounty* (84); *Mrs Soffel* (84); *The River* (84); *Tequila Sunrise* (88); *Bird On A Wire* (90); *Forever Young* (92); *The Man Without A Face* (93); *Maverick* (94); *Ransom* (98); *Payback* (99); *The Patriot* (00); *The Million Dollar Hotel* (00); *We Were Soldiers Once…And Young* (01)

Gielgud, John

Gielgud's ninety-six-year life almost spanned the entire century, from 1904 to 2000, and he died with his mellifluous voice and unparalleled verse-speaking talents intact. Predominantly a stage actor, and a Shakespearian at that, Gielgud rarely chose to make films, but when he did he brought the same elegantly puckish grace and polish to what were often scandalously underwritten parts. Given a token **Oscar** for his beautifully modulated performance as Dudley Moore's manservant in Steve Gordon's *Arthur* (81), Gielgud really deserves his place in cinema history for having discovered and generously supported the careers of a quite extraordinary number of outstanding English actors and actresses. His own career briefly hung in the balance, in 1953, when he was fined for 'cottaging' and his misdemeanour was maliciously broadcast by the press – at his first appearance on stage after the event, his Liverpool audience gave

him a standing ovation, ensuring that justice was both done, and seen to be done.
OTHER KEY FILMS: *The Secret Agent* (36); *The Prime Minister* (41); *Julius Caesar* (53); *The Barretts Of Wimpole Street* (57); *Becket* (64); *Chimes At Midnight* (66); *The Charge Of The Light Brigade* (68); *Providence* (76); *The Shooting Party* (84); *Prospero's Books* (91); *Shine* (96); *Elizabeth* (98); *The Tichborne Claimant* (98)

Gilbert, John

Renowned as Garbo's great love (although she vehemently denied the rumour) and the only real rival to **Rudolph Valentino**, Gilbert knew how to manipulate the Hollywood system to his ends, and his brief and memorable career was as lucrative and as meteoric as it was, eventually, tragic. Dead of a heart attack at forty-one, after sound, and the audience's decreasing greed for the passion he so convincingly provided had let him down, Gilbert, at his best, encapsulated the romance and sensuality a woman might want to give herself utterly to, rather than the more cerebral, witty type of lover which came into fashion during the 1930s. Unable or unwilling to make the change, Gilbert's only real success during the sound era was as Don Antonio de la Prada, in Rouben Mamoulian's *Queen Christina* (33), but the reversal of roles with Garbo, after the heady days of Clarence Brown's *Flesh And The Devil* (26), when he was her mentor, protector and passionate friend, must have cut this proto-alcoholic to the quick. With his fortune already lost in the 1929 stock market crash, Gilbert lasted a further three years, and ended up as the model for **Frederic March's** bittersweet performance as Norman Maine in **William Wellman's** *A Star Is Born* (37).

John Gilbert (as Don Antonio de la Prada) in his final great performance opposite Greta Garbo in Rouben Mamoulian's Queen Christina *(33)*

OTHER KEY FILMS: *Heart O' The Hills* (19); *Arabian Love* (22); *Monte Cristo* (22); *He Who Gets Slapped* (24); *The Merry Widow* (25); *The Big Parade* (25); *Bardelys The Magnificent* (26); *Man Woman And Sin* (27); *Desert Nights* (29); *Downstairs* (32)

Gilbert, Lewis

Looking at Gilbert's filmography, one is struck by how extraordinarily versatile a director he is, with his work spanning a succession of genres including thrillers, with *Cast A Dark Shadow* (57), children's films, with *The Greengage Summer* (61), biopics, with *Reach For The Sky* (56) and *Carve Her Name With Pride* (58), entertainment blockbusters, with no less than three **James Bond** outings, tragicomedy, with *Alfie* (66), and adult coming-of-age comedies such as *Educating Rita* (83) and *Shirley Valentine* (88). With such a body of work, and with such a low profile outside the industry, it is an incontrovertible fact that Gilbert must be considered one of the most grotesquely underrated and intelligent of all British directors.

OTHER KEY FILMS: *Albert RN* (53); *The Sea Shall Not Have Them* (54); *The Admirable Crichton* (57); *Sink The Bismarck!* (60); *You Only Live Twice* (67); *The Spy Who Loved Me* (77); *Moonraker* (79); *Stepping Out* (90); *Haunted* (95)

Gilliam, Terry

The most precociously talented of all the Monty Python team in that he not only has a sense of humour but also the nous to use it creatively, Gilliam was behind the titles and animated interstices that did so much to raise the surreal Python humour to something approaching an art form. *Time Bandits* (81) was his first extra-Pythonian venture, and it worked surprisingly well as historical fantasy, becoming something of a favourite with the adults for whose children it was apparently intended. *Brazil* (85), too, was a critical success, but *The Adventures Of Baron Munchausen* (88), while being genuinely engaging, unaccountably fell foul of the paying public, and it was only with the over-praised *The Fisher King* (90) and the assertively curious *Twelve Monkeys* (95) that Gilliam finally succeeded in levering himself back from the corner of the classroom.

OTHER KEY FILMS: *Jabberwocky* (77); *Fear And Loathing In Las Vegas* (98)

Gimbal Mount

The ball-bearing mounting on a camera tripod which enables the camera to tilt, pan or swing in any direction.

Gish Sisters, The

Dorothy and Lillian appeared together most famously in **D W Griffith's** *The Birth Of A Nation* (15), but it was Lillian who had the more natural screen presence, and it was not long before she had become a major star, while Dorothy's career, though a worthwhile, and in any other context, a distinguished one, was forced to take second place. The sisters never fell out, however, and Lillian (ever the lady) went on to what was, at seventy-five years, one of the longest screen careers in Hollywood history. But it was Griffith who brought out the best in the demure but determined Lillian, and who understood and used her capacity for moving the audience, and it is for his *Intolerance* (16), *Hearts Of The World* (18), *Broken Blossoms* (19), and *Orphans Of The Storm* (22) that she is best known. She matured slowly, however, and in retrospect it is also for her work in Victor Sjöström's *The Scarlet Letter* (26), and especially *The Wind* (28), that she deserves to be remembered, roles which foretold the most notable of her numerous majestic but all-too-brief comebacks, as Rachel, in **Charles Laughton's** magnificent adult fairy-tale *The Night Of The Hunter* (55).

OTHER KEY FILMS: *The Madonna Of The Storm* (13); *Way Down East* (20); *Romola* (24); *Annie Laurie* (27); *His Double Life* (33); *Duel In The Sun* (47); *Portrait Of Jennie* (49); *The Unforgiven* (60); *The Comedians* (67); *A Wedding* (78); *Sweet Liberty* (86); *The Whales Of August* (87)

KEY LINE:

'Lillian had certain qualities that *seemed* ethereal, and at moments, she had great spirituality, but she was as tough as a pine knot.' [Screenwriter Horton Foote on Gish]

Glass Filter

A gelatine filter supported within two thin sheets of glass.

Glass Shot

See **Dawn Process**

Global Media Giants

Just a few companies own and control nearly all the world's media outlets, making themselves responsible for the pap we digest, the music we listen to while we digest it, and the books we read while we expel it (and quite possibly the paper we use to mop up the ensuing mess). Current kings of the block include Time **Warner**, **Disney**, Bertelsmann, **Viacom**, News Corporation, Sony, TCI, Seagram, NBC, and, to a marginally lesser extent, Thomson, Televisa, Havas, Reed Elsevier, NHK, EMI, Hachette, Canal Plus, and on and on and on. <u>Author's Note</u>: Please don't write in if I'm out of date or have any of these wrong – the whole subject simply isn't that interesting.

Gobo

No one seems to know where the name came from, but it applies to any screening device used to protect either a camera from unwanted light, or a sound recording source from unwanted sound.

Godard, Jean-Luc

Godard was a post-structuralist before the term was even invented, glorying in cinema for cinema's sake, and refusing to kow-tow (ever) to his audience's expectations. A superb critic as well as a ground-breaking director, Godard's films irritate, entertain, enlighten and obfuscate in about equal measure. *À Bout De Souffle* [*Breathless*] (60) still has the power to engender a heady sense of excitement about the very medium of cinema, and *Pierrot Le Fou* (65) takes slapstick and returns it to something resembling the innocent and anarchic art form it originally stemmed from. *Alphaville* (65) was way ahead of its time in melding **film noir** with **Science Fiction**, and *Weekend* (67) can now be seen as an almost unbearably prescient commentary on the roots of our own society's technologically advanced but morally tormented condition. In recent years Godard has busied himself with a series of documentaries about the cinema, the eight-part *Histoire(s) Du Cinéma* (89-98), and these follow a similarly instinctual and awesomely well-informed path.
OTHER KEY FILMS: *Une Femme Est Une Femme* (61); *Le Mépris* (63); *Vivre Sa Vie* (63); *Made In USA* (66); *Masculin Féminin* (66); *La Chinoise* (67); *Tout Va Bien* (72); *Passion* (82); *First Name: Carmen* (83); *Detective* (85); *Forever Mozart* (96); *Éloge De L'Amour* (99)
KEY LINES:
'Photography is truth. The cinema is truth twenty-four times per second.' [*Le Petit Soldat*]

'*Ce n'est pas une image juste, c'est juste une image.*' (This isn't a just image, it's just an image) [Godard on truth and paradox: see the quote above!]

Goddard, Paulette

Goddard never quite made it as a global star, just as she never quite made it as Scarlett O'Hara in **Victor Fleming's** *Gone With The Wind* (39) – whether because of Chaplin's interest in her (they had married secretly in 1933, though she quickly

tired of his genius) or because of an apparent coldness and dispassion that always detracted, just a little, from the strength of any performance. Outside her outings for Chaplin in *Modern Times* (36) and *The Great Dictator* (40), Goddard's best role came in **Jean Renoir's** curious *Diary Of A Chambermaid* (46), in which her coldness verged on the sadomasochistic.
OTHER KEY FILMS: *The Cat And The Canary* (39); *North West Mounted Police* (40); *Reap The Wild Wind* (42); *Unconquered* (47); *An Ideal Husband* (48); *Anna Lucasta* (49); *Gli Indifferenti* (64)
KEY LINE:
'She keeps company only with remarkable men, but she changes them often.' [Jean Renoir on Goddard's penchant for dominant and powerful men]

Gofer

See **Gopher**

Goldberg, Whoopi

A former stand-up comedienne who has made it big in the movies thanks to her auspicious debut in **Steven Spielberg's** *The Color Purple* (85), and her follow-up success, **Jerry Zucker's** *Ghost* (90), for which she received an **Oscar**. Something of an acquired taste, Goldberg has gone on to make her fortune in Emile Ardolino's pretty desperate *Sister Act* (92) and Bill Duke's even more desperate *Sister Act 2: Back In The Habit* (93). Moral: Goldberg's a funny woman verging on the arch, and Hollywood's a funny place verging on the yecch.
OTHER KEY FILMS: *Jumpin' Jack Flash* (86); *Fatal Beauty* (87); *Clara's Heart* (88); *Sarafina!* (92); *Made In America* (93); *Corrina, Corrina* (94); *Ghosts Of Mississippi* (96); *Girl, Interrupted* (99); *More Dogs Than Bones* (00); *Kingdom Come* (01); *Monkeybone* (01)

Goldblum, Jeff

Goldblum's is a charming, slightly offbeat talent, and he is capable, on the rare occasions when it is demanded of him, of leavening his humour with a nice element of tightly controlled hysteria. He was good in **Lawrence Kasdan's** *The Big Chill* (83) and again in *Silverado* (85), and he has a neat capacity to play men who do not really like themselves but cover up their insecurities with a brash self-confidence. He has recently become the face behind a thousand dinosaurs, in **Steven Spielberg's** *Jurassic Park* (93) and *The Lost World: Jurassic Park* (97), but it would be a shame if Goldblum's neat gift for comic characterisation were forever lost inside the guts of some special-effects computer.

OTHER KEY FILMS: *Nashville* (75); *St. Ives* (76); *Annie Hall* (77); *Invasion Of The Body Snatchers* (78); *The Right Stuff* (83); *Into The Night* (85); *The Fly* (87); *The Tall Guy* (89); *Mister Frost* (90); *Fathers And Sons* (92); *Independence Day* (96); *Mad Dog Time* (96); *Holy Man* (98); *Chain of Fools* (00); *Auggie Rose* (00); *Perfume* (01)

Golden Bear
See **Berlin Film Festival**

Golden Globe Awards
An award given by the Hollywood Foreign Press Association for best motion picture of the year.

Goldman, William
Goldman is the best-known screenwriter in the world thanks to his brilliant 'how to get on in the Hollywood jungle' book, *Adventures In The Screen Trade* (83), and its follow-up about the **Cannes Film Festival**, *Hype And Glory* (90). It was *Adventures* that made him, though, for every would-be screenwriter the world over bought it in the fond hope that some of its caustic and down-to-earth magic would rub off onto them. Goldman is also famous for writing the original script for George Roy Hill's *Butch Cassidy And The Sundance Kid* (69), and for being the writing brains behind **Alan Pakula's** *All The President's Men* (76). His real genius lies in his talent for script-doctoring (the highly paid prinking of other people's dud scripts), and for his sanity in continuing to write novels, like *Marathon Man* and *Magic*, which are then picked up by desperate directors who ensure that he is paid far more than the novel alone would ever have brought him for subsequently scripting them onto the screen. Goldman's is a welcome voice of sanity in a rather insane trade.
OTHER KEY FILMS: Jack Smight's *Harper* (66); George Roy Hill's *The Great Waldo Pepper* (75); Rob Reiner's *The Princess Bride* (87) and *Misery* (90); Richard Donner's *Maverick* (94); **Clint Eastwood's** *Absolute Power* (97); Simon West's *The General's Daughter* (99)

Goldwyn, Sam
The most famous independent producer of them all (and probably the most pretentious) Goldwyn came up the hard way and never allowed anyone to forget it. He liked to spend money on high-profile books and properties, stuff the set with talent, and then choose the wrong star to front the piece. On the other hand he was a great

philanthropist and something of a saint when compared to, say, a **Harry Cohn**. Now renowned more for his malapropisms than for his movies, he was nevertheless responsible for a pretty extraordinary list by anyone's standards, which included Leo McCarey's *The Kid From Spain* (32) (watch it — it will grow on you), **William Wyler's** *Dodsworth* (36), **John Ford's** *The Hurricane* (37), and **Howard Hawks's** *Ball Of Fire* (42).
OTHER KEY FILMS: William Wyler's *Wuthering Heights* (39), *The Westerner* (40), *The Little Foxes* (41) and *The Best Years Of Our Lives* (46); **Joseph L Mankiewicz's** *Guys And Dolls* (55)
KEY LINES:
'Goldwyn filled the room with wonderful panic and beat at your mind like a man in front of a slot machine, shaking it for the jackpot.' [**Ben Hecht** on Goldwyn]

'Pictures are for entertainment. Messages should be delivered by Western Union.' [Goldwyn on high-minded worthiness]

'Let me tell you, he wasn't the clown or ignoramus that the Goldwyn stories would indicate… He talked as any other sharp, intelligent man would talk and with only a slight trace of an accent.' [*Noir* writer **James M Cain** on Goldwyn]
GOLDWYNISMS:
'That's the way with these directors, they're always biting the hand that lays the golden egg.'

'A verbal contract isn't worth the paper it's written on.'

'Any man who goes to a psychiatrist should have his head examined.'

'We're overpaying him but he's worth it.'

'We have all passed a lot of water since then.'

Go-motion
A **stop-motion** animation technique in which the rods animating a particular puppet are computer-monitored, ensuring an exact duplication of the puppeteer's movements when the sequence is eventually filmed.

Gone With The Wind
The most famous movie of them all, and rightly so, director **Victor Fleming** and producer **David O Selznick's** *Gone With The Wind* (39) was the greatest **crossover** film ever made, for it contained something for just about everyone. If you wanted battles, it had battles, if you wanted romance, well then, **Clarke Gable's** passion for **Vivien Leigh**, and Vivien Leigh's passion for **Leslie Howard**, and Leslie Howard's passion for **Olivia de Havilland**, and Olivia de Havilland's passion for Leslie

141

Howard, and everyone's passion for Tara, and the Southland, and money, were enough to send the punters away happy. And Selznick, of all men, understood the fact that films are there to make people happy – they are comfort food, placebos that people turn to in times of trouble, and a vicarious way to tell oneself that all is not bad in a world in which such elegant fripperies can still be made.

KEY LINES:

'As God is my witness, they're not going to lick me. I'm going to live through this. And when it's all over, I'll never be hungry again – no, nor any of my folk. If I have to lie, steal, cheat or kill, as God is my witness, I'll never be hungry again!' [Vivien Leigh as Scarlett O'Hara]

'You come out of *Gone With The Wind* feeling that history isn't so disturbing after all. One can always make a dress out of a curtain.' [Film critic Dilys Powell]

Gong Li

One of China's finest screen actresses, and the star of choice for director **Zhang Yimou**, who has used her in *Red Sorghum* (87), *Ju-Dou* (89) and *To Live* (94), amongst other films, and also for **Chen Kaige**, for whom she played Pang Ruyi in *Temptress Moon* (97) and the Emperor Ying Zheng's concubine in *The Empress And The Assassin* (99). Li differs from her trans-Pacific counterparts in that her emotional core moves from inside out, rather than in the opposite direction as defined by the tenets of the Western acting tradition, where the idea always comes first.

OTHER KEY FILMS: *Raise The Red Lantern* (91); *The Stories of Qiu Ju* (92); *Farewell, My Concubine* (93); *Shanghai Triad* (95); *Breaking The Silence* (99)

Goodrich, Frances

With her husband, Albert Hackett, Goodrich co-scripted some of the very best and most witty Hollywood mainstream films of the 1930s and 1940s, including W S Van Dyke's *The Thin Man* (34) and *After The Thin Man* (36), **Frank Capra's** *It's A Wonderful Life* (46) (together with Capra and Jo Swerling), **Michael Curtiz's** *Father Of The Bride* (50) and **George Stevens's** *The Diary Of Anne Frank* (59). Irremediably modest, Goodrich and Hackett both steadfastly refused to play on their extraordinary, though largely unsung success.

OTHER KEY FILMS: Clarence Brown's *Ah, Wilderness!* (35); **Robert Z Leonard's** *The Firefly* (37); Stuart Gilmore's *The Virginian* (46); **Charles Walters's** *Easter Parade* (48); **Jean Negulesco's** *A Certain Smile* (58)

Goofy

Mickey Mouse's stuttering canine chum (at least one presumes he is a dog) in the famous **Walt Disney** cartoon series.

Goose

Hollywood jargon for the vehicle used for transporting film equipment from one location to another.

Gopher

Nickname for the jack-of-all-trades on a studio set whose job it is to run errands, fetch the coffee, take messages, etc., derived from the North American rodent of the same name, and presumably originating in a pun on 'go fer it'.

Go-To-Black

Instructions written into a screenplay that call for a **fade-out** to an entirely black screen.

Gould, Elliott

Gould's star has rather set of recent years, but there was a time when he was considered cool by young America (which should be enough to coax anyone from following fashion), and his crumpled self-awareness enticing. Let's forget the dross, then, and look at the gems – Gould's quirky, contemporised Philip Marlowe in **Robert Altman's** *The Long Goodbye* (73); his rather predictable but still effective casting as Jewish/American archaeologist David Kovac in **Ingmar Bergman's** *The Touch* (70); and his bewildered but ultimately triumphant bank teller, Miles Cullen, in Daryl Duke's excellent and underrated little thriller, *The Silent Partner* (78).

OTHER KEY FILMS: *The Night They Raided Minsky's* (68); *M*A*S*H* (70); *California Split* (74); *A Bridge Too Far* (77); *The Lady Vanishes* (79); *The Big Hit* (98); *Picking Up The Pieces* (00); *Puckoon* (01)

Goulding, Edmund

Goulding was a quirky director, and it is almost impossible to apply the **auteur theory** to him (not that one would necessarily wish to do so anyway), as his films are so wildly disparate. *Grand Hotel* (32) would top anyone's list of Goulding favourites, but *Dawn Patrol* (38) was a great little war movie, and *Dark Victory* (39), *The Old Maid* (39) and *The Great Lie* (41) were magnificent **Bette Davis** melodramas by anyone's standards. Like the somewhat younger **George Cukor**, Goulding was particularly good at coaxing outstanding performances from actresses with ego problems, but it is for his weird *Nightmare Alley* (47), in

which **Tyrone Power** subverts his pretty boy image to such an extent that he ends up as a live-chicken-munching fairground geek, that Goulding will be most fondly remembered by aficionados.
OTHER KEY FILMS: Henry King's *Tol'able David* [script] (21); Henry Otto's *Dante's Inferno* [script] (24); *Sally, Irene And Mary* (25); *That Certain Woman* (37); *The Constant Nymph* (43); *Claudia* (43); *Of Human Bondage* (46); *The Razor's Edge* (46); *Mister 880* (50)

Grable, Betty

Grable had a great pair of legs, ogled and slavered over by a million sex-starved GIs during the Second World War. And that's just about it. She had talent, but not in abundance. She had sex appeal, but not in abundance. And her films were largely predictable vehicles for her pedal extremities [pace Fats Waller] and her fluttering tonsils, and are, in retrospect, utterly unmemorable, save for **Jean Negulesco's** *How To Marry A Millionaire* (53), which had the virtue of finding sex humorous.
OTHER KEY FILMS: *The Kid From Spain* (32); *The Gay Divorcee* (34); *Million Dollar Legs* [clever title!] (39); *Down Argentine Way* (40); *Tin Pan Alley* (40); *Four Jills In A Jeep* (44); *The Beautiful Blonde From Bashful Bend* (49)

Grader

The person responsible for noting variations in light and colour during disparately timed shots of the same scene, allowing for eventual amendment and matching during printing.

Grading

The process a **grader** goes through to ensure that scenes are consistent visually.

Graduated Filter

A filter of variable thickness such that various parts of the same shot may be treated differently – for instance in the differentiation between sea and sky, where the colour value of one needs to be emphasised over the other. A good example would be the final shot in the first part of **Victor Fleming's** *Gone With The Wind* (39), in which **Vivien Leigh** stands, almost in shadow, highlighted against a fabulously brilliant artificial sunset to utter her immortal words, '… as God is my witness, I'll never be hungry again!'

Grahame, Gloria

There are some people who are so right for just one or two roles that the remainder of their careers

don't really matter. Grahame was one of those. Married first to director **Nicholas Ray**, and then to one of Ray's sons from a previous marriage, Grahame's screen career was as variable as her love-life. Possibly the ultimate half-tough, half-vulnerable **Film Noir** heroine, she starred in a quintet of films that are the stuff of cult legends – **Edward Dmytryk's** *Crossfire* (47), **Fritz Lang's** *The Big Heat* (53) and *Human Desire* (54), David Miller's *Sudden Fear* (52) and Nicholas Ray's sensational *In A Lonely Place* (53), where she brought out the dark and sadistic side of **Humphrey Bogart** as no other woman before or since. Her Laurel Gray was so good in that film, which glimmered with substrata from her troubled marriage with director Ray, that everything she did afterwards was inevitably somewhat anti-climactic. A tragic figure, Grahame had the rare talent of being able to suggest far more than her lines dictated on the screen, and one found oneself speculating not so much about the present, but about her character's past, of where she came from, and of what she would do next. It was a spontaneous gift, of which she was probably unaware, but which Ray, above all men, had the genius to spot. Watch any of the films below, and it's unlikely that you'll be disappointed. See under **Humphrey Bogart** for image of **Grahame**
OTHER KEY FILMS: *It's A Wonderful Life* (46); *A Woman's Secret* (49); *Roughshod* (49); *Macao* (52); *The Bad And The Beautiful* (52); *The Glass Wall* (53); *Man On A Tightrope* (53); *Naked Alibi* (54); *The Man Who Never Was* (56); *Odds Against Tomorrow* (59)
KEY LINES
Bogart 'You said you liked my face.' Grahame 'I said I liked it, I didn't say I wanted to kiss it.' [*In A Lonely Place*]
'I was born when you kissed me. I died when you left me. I lived a few weeks while you loved me.' [Grahame quoting Bogart's script back to him for real, in *In A Lonely Place*]

Grain

A grainy effect may be produced during projection by the unexpected magnification of clusters of the individual grains of silver that normally provide the dark contrast on a piece of film.

Granger, Stewart

Granger was the perfect example of a straight-down-the-line commercial actor who invariably gave excellent value and who occasionally surpassed himself (when he wasn't watching) by suggesting a deeper resonance in his roles. Second only to **Errol Flynn** in the **swashbuckling** stakes, Granger's beautiful diction, splendid physique, and long-nosed, virile profile, set female hearts a-flutter for more than twenty years, and Granger was sufficiently sure of himself even to get away with playing bounders and murderers, as in **Marc Allégret's** impassioned *Blanche Fury* (48), without queering his box-office pitch. He was a believable big-game hunter in Andrew Marton and Compton Bennett's *King Solomon's Mines* (50), a dashing, child-friendly smuggler in **Fritz Lang's** *Moonfleet* (55), and a sensitive British officer very understandably in love with the sublime **Ava Gardner** in **George Cukor's** *Bhowani Junction* (56). After all this, one ends up being rather grateful for the Grangers of this world, who never took either themselves or their art too seriously, but were, nonetheless, consummate professionals. Granger really showed what he could do when given the chance in **Richard Brooks's** little known and elegiac **Western**, *The Last Hunt* (56).

OTHER KEY FILMS: *The Man In Grey* (43); *Fanny By Gaslight* (44); *Love Story* (44); *Madonna Of The Seven Moons* (44); *Waterloo Road* (45); *Saraband For Dead Lovers* (48); *Scaramouche* (52); *The Prisoner Of Zenda* (52); *Young Bess* (53); *Green Fire* (54); *North To Alaska* (60); *The Wild Geese* (78)

KEY LINE:

'Weren't we both beautiful?' [In a touching late-night phone call to his friend, Ava Gardner, just before her death in 1990, after having seen a rerun of *Bhowani Junction* on television]

Grant, Cary

Let's clear up any misunderstandings here and now – Cary Grant was the best light comedian who ever lived, and probably the best all-round screen actor to boot. His timing was perfect, he was a master of nuance, he aged better than any other actor ever, and to blazes with his private life and his five marriages and all the other irrelevant details biographers sniff out in an effort to dilute his indissoluble star. Stick a Grant film in the video recorder or DVD machine, and you just know that you're going to be entertained and taken out of yourself for the next ninety minutes. Even better, watch him on the big screen and see how a master makes the most of every precious moment of screen time without taking anything away from his fellow actors – more than that, he gives them face, even when they don't deserve it, by playing *off* them, as well as *to* them. He was never given an **Oscar**, but he deserved at least ten, and it is to Hollywood's eternal shame that they could only come up with a

belated award that read, in pitiful fashion 'with the respect and affection of his colleagues'. Humbug! Catch his Janus-like abilities in **Josef von Sternberg's** *Blonde Venus* (32), or in **Leo McCarey's** *The Awful Truth* (37), or maybe in **Howard Hawks's** *Only Angels Have Wings* (39) or in **Alfred Hitchcock's** *Suspicion* (41), or **Joseph L Mankiewicz's** *People Will Talk* (51). Better still, see just about anything in the list below, and marvel. See **Ingrid Bergman** for further image of Grant

Cary Grant, taken around the time of his brilliant turn as Dr Noah Praetorius, in Joseph L Mankiewicz's People Will Talk *(51)*

OTHER KEY FILMS: *She Done Him Wrong* (33); *I'm No Angel* (33); *The Last Outpost* (35); *Topper* (37); *Bringing Up Baby* (38); *Holiday* (38); *Gunga Din* (39); *In Name Only* (39); *His Girl Friday* (40); *My Favourite Wife* (40); *The Philadelphia Story* (41); *The Talk Of The Town* (42); *Mr Lucky* (43); *Arsenic And Old Lace* (44); *Notorious* (46); *The Bachelor And The Bobby-Soxer* (47); *The Bishop's Wife* (47); *Mr Blandings Builds His Dream House* (48); *I Was A Male War Bride* (49); *Monkey Business* (52); *To Catch A Thief* (55); *An Affair To Remember* (57); *Indiscreet* (58); *Houseboat* (58); *North By Northwest* (59); *Charade* (63); *Father Goose* (54)

KEY LINES:

'I intended to be with you on our honeymoon, Hildy, honest I did.' [**Howard Hawks's** *His Girl Friday*]

'See, when a girl's under twenty-one, she's protected by law. When she's over sixty-five, she's protected by nature. Anywhere in between, she's fair game.' [**Blake Edwards's** *Operation Petticoat* (59)]

Grant, Hugh

It's a tricky thing to have to follow the alphabetical likes of **Cary Grant** in a book like this, especially if one happens to be a light comedian too, but it says much for Hugh Grant that he needn't blush and retire modestly, for he's an extremely talented and professional actor in his own right, and such comparisons are always monstrous anyway. Putting aside his excellent performances in Mike Newell's *Four Weddings And A Funeral* (94), Roger Michell's *Notting Hill* (99), and Sharon Maguire's *Bridget Jones's Diary* (01) in which he turned his usual good guy persona on its head, Grant was very good indeed as Frédéric Chopin in James Lapine's *Impromptu* (90), and outstanding in **Ang Lee's** *Sense And Sensibility* (95) and **Michael Apted's** much underrated thriller *Extreme Measures* (96). Grant's modest and rather shy outer skin disguises a true professional flair, and one anticipates with interest the eventual outcome of his rather classically old-fashioned (in the best sense of the word) career.

OTHER KEY FILMS: *Maurice* (87); *White Mischief* (88); *Bitter Moon* (94); *Sirens* (94); *Nine Months* (95); *Restoration* (95); *Mickey Blue Eyes* (00); *Small Time Crooks* (00); *About A Boy* (01)

Grant, Richard E

The third light comedian by the name of Grant in a row, and another real talent, blissfully shown to its full extent in **Bruce Robinson's** cult masterpiece *Withnail & I* (87). Why is the film so good? And why is Grant so good in it? Talent.

And a rigorous understanding of the camera and of what it shows and (sometimes) conceals. Grant's neologism-filled autobiography, *With Nails* (1996), is very entertaining indeed on the pretty much random way Hollywood garners its leading players from the howling pack of wannabe stars, and it is no surprise at all that Grant has floated to somewhere near the top of the character actor pond (and one confidently anticipates him remaining there). People (the present author included) will probably be collaring Grant in the street, right up until his dotage, and spluttering in his face about how much his 'Withnail' reminds us of our misspent youth. But what Grant and his director/screenwriter Bruce Robinson identified so effectively and so elusively in the character of 'Withnail' was not, of course, ourselves, but rather someone we had known and admired, sported with, despaired of, and eventually lost.

OTHER KEY FILMS: *How To Get Ahead In Advertising* (89); *Mountains Of The Moon* (90); *Henry And June* (90); *L.A. Story* (91); *The Player* (92); *Jack And Sarah* (95); *Portrait Of A Lady* (96); *Twelfth Night* (96); *Spice World* (97); *Food Of Love* (97); *The Match* (99); *The Little Vampire* (00)

Gray Scale

The normal spectrum used in the making and processing of black-and-white films, and stretching from white, through all its intermediate grey stages, to black.

Grease-glass Technique

The use of a simple glass filter, smeared with Vaseline, to produce a hazy effect over all or part of a shot.

Greasepaint

The mixture of coloured pigment and grease used by actors and actresses to disguise themselves, or to render their skin surfaces more conducive to refracted light.

Greenaway, Peter

Greenaway appeals to the French (his greatest fans) because he encapsulates and seems to give credence to the 1954 concept of the **auteur theory** promulgated for so long by its **Cahiers du Cinéma** originator, **François Truffaut**. Greenaway claims not to give a damn about his audience, but simply to make films to suit himself, and one can believe him insofar as his films abound in intellectuality (the bane of that institutional and insecure British philistine, the television film critic) but sometimes lack heart, in the grand old *nouveau roman* style. Any commercial success Greenaway enjoys comes almost by default, and we are apparently to applaud this, while brushing aside the fact that his very seriousness is his worst characteristic, and one that can occasionally verge on the pretentious. All that aside, one would rather know that Greenaway is out there beavering away at his conceits, fay as some of them are, than not have Greenaway at all. For all his showiness and the high-minded jargon with which his auxiliaries surround him, he does in fact boil down to a rigorous and professional filmmaker who resolutely refuses to be bound by either the creative ether of money, or the necessity of making it.

KEY FILMS: *The Falls* (80); *The Draughtsman's Contract* (83); *A Zed And Two Noughts* (85); *The Belly Of An Architect* (87); *Drowning By Numbers* (88); *The Cook, The Thief, His Wife, & Her Lover* (89); *Prospero's Books* (91); *The Baby Of Macon* (93); *Darwin* (93); *Pillow Book* (97); *Death Of A Composer* (99); *8¹/₂ Women* (99)

Green Print

A virgin print that has not, as yet, passed through a projector.

Greensman

The person in charge of all the greenery, real or otherwise, on a film set. Strict measurement of any quality of greenness apparent is of course achieved by the use of a greengage.

Greenstreet, Sidney

Greenstreet only started film acting when he was sixty-one years old, and although his career spanned a brief nine years, he instantly became one of the most recognisable of all 'faces' following his performance as the 'Fat Man', Kaspar Gutman, alongside **Humphrey Bogart** and **Peter Lorre** in **John Huston's** *The Maltese Falcon* (41). Greenstreet supported the pair once again in **Michael Curtiz's** *Casablanca* (42) and *Passage To Marseille* (44), though his best film is probably **Jean Negulesco's** classic *film noir* *The Mask Of Dimitrios* (44) in which he played the elusive Mr Peters. Come to think of it, he was pretty good in **Michael Curtiz's** *Flamingo Road* (49) too, playing Sheriff Titus Semple, the very incarnation of evil intent to **Joan Crawford's** not-so-innocent social climber, Lane Bellamy.

OTHER KEY FILMS: *They Died With Their Boots On* (41); *Across The Pacific* (42); *Conflict* (45); *Three Strangers* (46); *The Verdict* (46); *The Hucksters* (47); *Ruthless* (48); *The Woman In White* (48)

KEY LINES:
'As the leader of all illegal activities in Casablanca, I am an influential and respected man.' [*Casablanca*]

'I tell you right out, I'm a man who likes talking to a man who likes to talk.' [*The Maltese Falcon*]

Greer, Jane

One of the few really good female baddies (if that's not a contradiction in terms), Greer kept **Robert Mitchum** reeling in **Jacques Tourneur's** *film noir* masterpiece *Out Of The Past* (47) [a.k.a. *Build My Gallows High*] because she always behaved worse than even he expected. She played a similar trick on **Dick Powell** in Sidney Lanfield's *Station West* (48) — of course she had to die in both movies, unlike **Kathleen Turner** in **Lawrence Kasdan's** *Body Heat* (81), who, with Linda Fiorentino in John Dahl's *The Last Seduction* (94), has come closest in recent years to inheriting the Greer mantle. Greer's greatest strength in these, her two best movies, and also in one or two of the others listed below, was that she didn't mind alienating her audience, and for the exceptionally pretty woman that she was, her lack of obvious vanity in this regard was exemplary at a time when Hollywood was busy churning out sycophantic little starlets by the busload.

OTHER KEY FILMS: *Dick Tracy* (45); *The Big Steal* (49); *The Company She Keeps* (50); *The Prisoner Of Zenda* (52); *Desperate Search* (52); *The Clown* (53); *Down Among The Sheltering Palms* (53); *Man Of A Thousand Faces* (57); *The Outfit* (73); *Against All Odds* (84)

KEY LINE:
Dick Powell: 'Are you always this sweet to the men who fight over you?' Greer: 'Only the winners.' [*Station West*]

Grey Scale

See **Gray Scale**

Griffith, D W

An old-fashioned Southerner, and the son of a Civil War veteran who finally succumbed to his war wounds in 1885, Griffith allowed his gentlemanliness to leach into his films, particularly in his depictions of women, and it is this sentimentality, together with his intuitive racism, that may prevent some modern audiences from realising what an extraordinarily innovative man

Griffith really was in his tally of more than 500 shorts and feature films. *The Birth Of A Nation* (15) and *Intolerance* (16) were unique in their scope, accurately reflecting an American nation intent on temporarily damping down creativity in favour of productivity, in the aftermath of the US entry into the First World War. Griffith's way of alternating close-ups and long-shots, his fastidious editing and his enlightened use of ace cinematographer, **Billy Bitzer**, led directly to the widespread exploitation of such techniques as the **flashback**, the **matte** shot, the use of a **split screen** to show different actions happening simultaneously, and **soft focus** photography. Following the financial failure of *Intolerance*, into which Griffith had poured the major part of his personal fortune, he was forced to narrow the focus of his storytelling, and this led to the magnificent quartet of *Hearts Of The World* (18), *Broken Blossoms* (19), *True Heart Susie* (19) and *Orphans Of The Storm* (22). Co-founder of **United Artists** with **Mary Pickford, Charles Chaplin** and **Douglas Fairbanks Sr**, the studios nevertheless sidelined Griffith at the coming of sound, despite the success of the **Walter Huston**-dominated *Abraham Lincoln* (30), which proved that Griffith was perfectly capable of mastering that technique too. Griffith died in 1948, in the latest of a succession of apartment hotels that he called home, just four years after his equally neglected colleague, the by then alcoholic Bitzer.

OTHER KEY FILMS: *The Violin Maker Of Cremona* (09); *The Unseen Enemy* (12); *Judith Of Bethulia* (13); *The Mother And The Law* (14); *The Great Love* (18); *A Romance Of Happy Valley* (19); *The Fall Of Babylon* (19); *The Idol Dancer* (20); *Way Down East* (20); *Dream Street* (21); *The White Rose* (23); *Sally Of The Sawdust* (25); *The Sorrows Of Satan* (26); *The Battle Of The Sexes* (28); *The Struggle* (31)

KEY LINE:

'It is like writing history with lightning. And my only regret is that it is all so terribly true.' [President Woodrow Wilson on seeing *The Birth Of A Nation* (15)]

Griffith, Hugh

Griffith was a magnificent ruddy-faced and broad-vowelled character actor whose Welsh antecedents emerged in every word he uttered, whether as grumpy steward to **David Farrar's** Squire Reddin in **Michael Powell's** sublime *Gone To Earth* (50), or as the raunchy but possessive Squire Western in **Tony Richardson's** *Tom Jones* (63). Griffith won a well-deserved **Oscar** for his horse-loving Sheik Ilderim in **William Wyler's** *Ben-Hur* (59).

OTHER KEY FILMS: *Kind Hearts And Coronets* (49); *Laughter In Paradise* (51); *The Titfield Thunderbolt* (53); *The Beggar's Opera* (53); *Exodus* (60); *Mutiny On The Bounty* (62); *The Canterbury Tales* (72); *Luther* (73)

Griffith, Melanie

Griffith is the daughter of one of **Alfred Hitchcock's** favourite blondes, **Tippi Hedren**, and she inherits a certain nervy energy from her mother, which stood her in good stead in her outstanding debut movie, **Arthur Penn's** *Night Moves* (75). Her next major role came in **Brian De Palma's** *Body Double* (84) in which Griffith proved that she had not only grown up, but also grown out. **Jonathan Demme's** *Something Wild* (86) really established Griffith as a major star, and it suddenly seemed as if the sky were the limit, but her roles since then, with the notable exception of **Mike Nichols's** *Working Girl* (88), have, dare one say it, dumbed down, almost as if the artistic in her soul abruptly gave way to the commercial. A shame.

OTHER KEY FILMS: *The Drowning Pool* (75); *Fear City* (84); *The Milagro Beanfield War* (88); *Stormy Monday* (88); *In The Spirit* (90); *Pacific Heights* (90); *Shining Through* (91); *Nobody's Fool* (94); *Mulholland Falls* (96); *Lolita* (97); *Celebrity* (98); *Crazy In Alabama* (99); *Cecil B DeMented* (00); *Forever Lulu* (00); *Tart* (01)

Grip

The set handyman (a jack-of-all-trades really) responsible for moving machinery and props, setting up tracks for the camera dolly, scenery shifting and general maintenance.

Gross Receipts

Any returns from the making of a film that do not take into account production costs, star salaries, publicity, etc., and which include distribution returns, video sales, merchandising and any peripheral publications, musical, literary and audiovisual, which relate to the film.

Guide Track

A soundtrack recorded during the shooting of a film and which is used purely as a guide to the making of the eventual, post-synchronised article.

Guinness, Alec

Guinness died, aged eighty-seven, on 7 August 2000 – his death was a huge loss, as it was he, almost alone among the actor-knights of his generation, who embraced the 'new' with pleasure,

147

and it was he, of them all (**John Gielgud**, **Ralph Richardson**, **Laurence Olivier** and **Michael Redgrave** included), who recognised cinema early on for the great art form that it undoubtedly was. His Herbert Pocket, in **David Lean's** *Great Expectations* (46), and his Fagin, in the same director's *Oliver Twist* (48), exuded an energy that only Olivier could match, although Olivier persisted in thinking, right to the end, that cinema was a second-rate art compared to the theatre. Guinness had no such qualms, and his portrayals of Sidney Stratton in **Alexander Mackendrick's** *The Man In The White Suit* (51), and Lt. Col. Jock Sinclair in Ronald Neame's *Tunes Of Glory* (60), were masterpieces of rigorously controlled emotional acting. Most think his greatest performance came as Col. Nicholson in Lean's *The Bridge On The River Kwai* (57), but, paradoxically, his greatest moment may well have been on television, as the downbeat George Smiley in the magnificent 1979-82 BBC series based on the John le Carré spy novels.

OTHER KEY FILMS: *Kind Hearts And Coronets* (49); *The Mudlark* (50); *The Lavender Hill Mob* (51); *The Captain's Paradise* (53); *Father Brown* (54); *The Ladykillers* (55); *The Horse's Mouth* (58); *The Scapegoat* (59); *Our Man In Havana* (59); *Lawrence Of Arabia* (62); *The Fall Of The Roman Empire* (64); *Doctor Zhivago* (65); *The Quiller Memorandum* (66); *The Comedians* (67); *Cromwell* (68); *A Passage To India* (84); *Little Dorrit* (87); *A Handful Of Dust* (88); *Kafka* (92); *A Foreign Field* (93); *Mute Witness* (94)

Gyro Head

One of a multitude of camera-mount variations designed to provide judder-free camera movement during panning and tilting.

Hackman, Gene

A subtle, controlled screen actor, who can fairly claim to be one of the most successful living masters of his profession given his extensive, and often surprising, filmography, Hackman played mavericks during the 1970s and early 1980s, then graduated through heavies to warped establishment figures by way of the occasional iconoclast. His best films capture his capacity for single-minded intensity, and include **William Friedkin's** *The French Connection* (71), **Francis Ford Coppola's** *The Conversation* (74) and **Clint Eastwood's** *Unforgiven* (92), in which his performance as Sheriff 'Little Bill' Daggett spans the otherwise heady gulf between the violent and the homespun. Hackman's greatest strength lies in his ability to suggest the values the common man holds dear, together with his occasional ability to transcend them.

OTHER KEY FILMS: *Bonnie And Clyde* (67); *Prime Cut* (72); *Scarecrow* (73); *Night Moves* (75) *French Connection II* (75); *Superman* (78); *Reds* (81); *Eureka* (83); *No Way Out* (87); *Mississippi Burning* (88); *Narrow Margin* (90); *Get Shorty* (95); *Extreme Measures* (96); *Twilight* (98); *Enemy Of The State* (98); *Under Suspicion* (00); *The Replacements* (00); *The Mexican* (00); *Heartbreakers* (01); *Heist* (01)

Hair Stylists

Yul Brynner's hair stylist found himself out of a job when the star shaved his head and kept it that way following his 1951 Broadway success with *The King And I*. Other stars insist on the same stylist every time. The stylists who minister to male stars often find themselves branching out into wig artistry midway through the career of their patrons, and famous (and infamous) wig-wearers include **Humphrey Bogart**, **Fred Astaire**, **Bing Crosby** and **Burt Reynolds**. One of the most refreshing recent tendencies in films is the acceptance, by the audience, of male baldness and the resulting freedom given to follicly challenged slap-headed actors such as **Sean Connery**, **Bruce Willis**, **Nicolas Cage** and **John Malkovich** to simply be themselves, rather than some idealised notion of the perfect man. The same, unfortunately, cannot be said of female stars, who are still required to surpass themselves, and often nature too, when it comes to their hair.

Halation

This refers to the halo effect seen on some film prints which is caused by the reverse refraction of light from the film base back to the emulsion. The effect can be controlled by the use of an anti-halation coating that dampens the light and prevents flare.

Haller, Ernest

Haller shared an **Oscar** with Ray Rennahan and **Lee Garmes** for his **Technicolor** cinematography on **Victor Fleming's** *Gone With The Wind* (39), but his real forte lay in black-and-white, and he was the man behind the lighting behind **Bette**

149

Davis in **William Wyler's** *Jezebel* (38) and **Edmund Goulding's** *Dark Victory* (39). **Joan Crawford** must have been impressed with the results because she insisted on Haller filming her as **Michael Curtiz's** *Mildred Pierce* (45) when she had reached the tricky age of forty-one – needless to say Haller contrived to make her look as unblemished and as beautiful as her hard and somewhat unforgiving features would allow.

OTHER KEY FILMS: Raoul Walsh's *The Roaring Twenties* (39); Anatole Litvak's *All This And Heaven Too* (40); **Nicholas Ray's** *Rebel Without A Cause* (55); **Robert Aldrich's** *Whatever Happened To Baby Jane?* (62)

Hamer, Robert

One of the lost souls of the British film industry, Hamer died at the early age of fifty-two after a long fight with alcoholism. He was, however, responsible for four remarkable films that ensure him a place in the pantheon. *It Always Rains On Sunday* (47) was the first of a long and influential line of British underworld thrillers (that include Mike Hodges's *Get Carter* (71), John Mackenzie's recently re-released *The Long Good Friday* (80), and Guy Ritchie's *Lock, Stock And Two Smoking Barrels* (99)), while Hamer's *Kind Hearts And Coronets* (49) took dry humour to its zenith. *The Long Memory* (52) featured a brilliantly intense **John Mills**, fine location work and a magnificently extended revenge motif, and the icing on this extraordinary director's cake comes with his early 'Haunted Mirror' sequence in the genuinely creepy *Dead Of Night* (45), which knocks such modern variants as Eduardo Sanchez and Daniel Myrick's *The Blair Witch Project* (99) into the proverbial cocked hat.

OTHER KEY FILMS: *Pink String And Sealing Wax* (47); *The Spider And The Fly* (49); *School For Scoundrels* (60)

Hamilton, George

Hamilton has been the cheerful butt of suntan and cold cream jokes for years, and he has made a very good living out of it indeed. The highlights of his film career are few and far between, but then he probably wouldn't have it any other way, and he must certainly be given full credit for never allowing art to overcome his business sense. His wry, self-referential humour was best seen in Stan Dragoti's *Love At First Bite* (79), in which he played a camp Count Dracula, and all jokes aside, one can't help being left with the impression that while he is pretty much a one-horse actor, he would probably make rather a good friend.

OTHER KEY FILMS: *All The Fine Young Cannibals* (60); *Viva Maria!* (65); *L'Homme De Marrakesh* (66); *Evel Knievel* (71); *Zorro The Gay Blade* (81); *The Godfather Part III* (90); *8 Heads In A Duffel Bag* (97); *Crocodile Dundee in Los Angeles* (01)

Hamilton, Guy

Quintessential **James Bond** director that he is, with *Goldfinger* (64), *Diamonds Are Forever* (71), *Live And Let Die* (73) and *The Man With The Golden Gun* (74) under his belt, Hamilton also made the dark and rather quirky *Funeral In Berlin* (66), and the stiff-upper-lip but still fascinating *Colditz Story* (57), proving that despite his 007 credentials, acting as **Carol Reed's** assistant director during the late 1940s certainly paid off in terms of sheer technique, if in nothing else.

OTHER KEY FILMS: *The Intruder* (53); *An Inspector Calls* (54); *Manuela* (57); *The Devil's Disciple* (59); *A Touch Of Larceny* (59); *Battle Of Britain* (69); *Force 10 From Navarone* (78); *The Mirror Crack'd* (80); *Evil Under The Sun* (82); *Try This One For Size* (89)

Hamilton, Linda

Toothsome occasional star (and sometime ex-wife) of director **James Cameron**, for whom she acted in *The Terminator* (84) and *Terminator 2: Judgment Day* (91), when Hamilton leaves her muscles at home and plays straight, as in Roger Donaldson's *Dante's Peak* (97), she exudes real star quality. One wishes she would follow up her potential rather than wasting it on such weak material as George P Cosmatos's *The Shadow Conspiracy* of the same year. Actresses of Hamilton's quality and screen presence are few and far between.

OTHER KEY FILMS: *Children Of The Corn* (84); *Black Moon Rising* (86); *Silent Fall* (94); *Unglued* (99); *Skeletons In The Closet* (01)

Hammer Films

UK home of the diabolically horrible and the colourfully grotesque, Hammer Studios was founded way back in 1935 by Will Hinds [stagename: Hammer] and Enrique [John] Carreras, but it wasn't until 1957, when it first identified its niche horror market with Terence Fisher's *The Curse Of Frankenstein*, that the pounds, shillings and pence really started rolling in. Working with relatively small budgets, to a strict timetable, and using enlightened economic tactics such as the creative re-use of its sets, Hammer not so much revived as transmogrified the moribund material of the 1930s horror heyday into sometimes inelegant, but always entertaining **B-movie** fare. Staple actors

Christopher Lee and Peter Cushing carried numerous Frankenstein and Dracula films on their respectively silken- and tweed-covered shoulders, and it was only when the gothic gave way to the glossy between 1970 and 1979 that Hammer finally suceeded in bidding itself out of the auction.

OTHER KEY FILMS: Val Guest's *The Quatermass Experiment* (55); Terence Fisher's *Dracula* (58), *The Hound Of The Baskervilles* (59) and *Frankenstein Must Be Destroyed* (69); Roy Ward Baker's *Quatermass And The Pit* (67) and *Dr Jekyll And Sister Hyde* (71)

Hammerstein, Oscar II

A lawyer turned lyricist (the man must have had a way with words), Hammerstein's most fruitful partnership was with composer **Richard Rodgers**, and between them they turned out such perennial favourites as Walter Lang's *State Fair* (45) and *The King And I* (56), **Fred Zinnemann's** *Oklahoma!* (55), Joshua Logan's *South Pacific* (58) and **Robert Wise's** *The Sound Of Music* (65). It was also Hammerstein who penned the words to the immortal 'Ol' Man River' during an earlier pairing with **George Gershwin**.

OTHER KEY FILMS: James Whale's *Showboat* (36); Julien Duvivier's *The Great Waltz* (38); Norman Z McLeod's *Lady Be Good* (41)

Hammett, Dashiell

Ex-Pinkerton operative Hammett all but invented **pulp fiction**, and while he wrote relatively few original screenplays, the style of his greatest books leached through Hollywood like sulphuric acid through the face of a rogue gunsel. His pared-down and sometimes brutal prose was categorically different from that of **Raymond Chandler**, to whom many wrongly compare him; **Humphrey Bogart** was the perfect personification of his Sam Spade in **John Huston's** *The Maltese Falcon* (41), in a way that he never managed as Chandler's **Philip Marlowe** – that distinction would go to **Robert Mitchum**, in Dick Richards's sublime *Farewell My Lovely* (75). Excoriated by the House Un-American Activities Committee (see **Hollywood Ten**) for his alleged communist sympathies, the awesomely well-read Hammett gave up writing novels in favour of drink – a decision that finally killed him in 1961.

Hammid, Alexander

See **Maya Deren**

Hand-held Camera

The pre-video, hand-held **Arriflex** camera was synonymous with the French **New Wave** and with the **cinéma vérité** documentaries that flourished during the 1950s and 1960s. However, with the arrival of the **Steadicam** in the mid-1970s, cinema was freed from the 'wobble' inherent in hand-held techniques, while at the same time losing the sense of urgency that such a technique engendered. There is a fascinating essay to be written – if it has not already been done – on the effect technological advances have on artistic content.

Handlebar Mount

A camera mounted on something akin to a wheeled Zimmer frame, equipped with handlebars for smoother manoeuvring.

Hand Props

Props that actors hold or use in their hands. Obvious examples include cigarette cases, swords, handkerchiefs, handbags, fans, pistols, etc.; Leatherface's chainsaw, in Tobe Hooper's *The Texas Chainsaw Massacre* (74), could also be described as a hand prop.

151

Hanks, Tom

Now a very big name indeed thanks largely to **Robert Zemeckis's** *Forrest Gump* (94), Hanks, to look at, seems hardly cut out for stardom. Beginning his career as a comedian, most notably in **Ron Howard's** *Splash* (84), he has steadily moved towards more serious roles, such as Aids-victim Andrew Beckett in **Jonathan Demme's** *Philadelphia* (93), and as the embattled Captain Miller in **Steven Spielberg's** *Saving Private Ryan* (98), for which he netted a paltry $40 million gross (see **Money**). The voice of Sheriff Woody in **Disney's** *Toy Story* (95) and *Toy Story 2* (99), Hanks has recently tried to consolidate his 'serious' acting credentials by doing a **Robert De Niro** in reverse – this time slimming down 25lbs to play the (reasonably) emaciated Chuck Noland in Zemeckis's *Cast Away* (00). Comparable as a light dramatic actor to, say, **James Stewart**, Hanks made a surprisingly good stab at directing, acting and scripting, in *That Thing You Do!* (96), and has now turned to producing, once again alongside Steven Spielberg, with the $100 million TV wartime drama *Band Of Soldiers* (01).

OTHER KEY FILMS: *Bachelor Party* (84); *The Money Pit* (86); *Dragnet* (87); *Big* (88); *Turner And Hooch* (89); *Sleepless In Seattle* (93); *Apollo 13* (95); *The Celluloid Closet* (95); *You've Got Mail* (98); *The Green Mile* (99)

Hanna, William
See **Joseph Barbera**

Hard Light
A violent light that spares nothing and which produces extreme shadow – as opposed to a diffused, or soft light, which leaves more to the imagination but is less dramatic.

Hard-ticket Attraction
A film show for which the advanced purchase of a ticket is mandatory, on account of its likely popularity.

Hardy, Oliver
See **Laurel and Hardy**

Harlow, Jean
Killed by kidney failure at the age of twenty-six due to her Christian Scientist mother's refusal to allow treatment, Harlow was a true one-off, and her nickname 'The Blonde Bombshell' doesn't come remotely near to doing her justice. A wonderful comedienne, Harlean Carpenter, or 'Babe' as she was known to her friends, lit up any film in which she appeared. Notorious for seldom wearing underwear – something that can be deduced only too easily from a close perusal of **George Cukor's** *Dinner At Eight* (33) – she excelled as the sassy platinum blonde adept at keeping virile men's men like Clark Gable in their place (at her feet, of course) in movies like **Victor Fleming's** *Red Dust* (32), and Tay Garnett's *China Seas* (35). Catch her in **Frank Capra's** underrated *Platinum Blonde* (31), with the great Robert Williams, which also happens to contain, in the butler's 'puttering' scene, the best shaggy-dog dialogue in movie history.
OTHER KEY FILMS: *The Public Enemy* (31); *Bombshell* (33); *Hold Your Man* (33); *Libeled Lady* (36); *Wife Vs. Secretary* (36); *Personal Property* (37)
KEY LINE:
Harlow: 'I was reading a book the other day.' Marie Dressler (starting back): 'Reading a book?' Harlow: 'Yes. It's all about civilisation or something – a nutty kind of a book. Do you know that the guy said that machinery is going to take the place of every profession?' Marie Dressler: 'Oh, my dear, that's something you need never worry about.' [*Dinner At Eight*]

Jean 'Babe' Harlow, photographed by George Hurrell, with or without her elusive underwear

Harrelson, Woody

Harrelson is the sort of actor who makes the most of his resources, knowing that he cannot fall back on looks and glamour if his performance doesn't fit the bill. He works hard when he is on the screen, and he was certainly effective in the overwritten part of Mickey Knox, in **Oliver Stone's** *Natural Born Killers* (94), and again as Larry Flint, in **Milos Forman's** *The People Vs. Larry Flint* (96). The time when he seemed to be in everything has passed, however, and one looks forward to more constrained and subtle performances from him in future, now that he has made his pile and no longer needs to prove himself – perhaps along the lines of his work for Michael Winterbottom in the underrated *Welcome To Sarajevo* (97).

OTHER KEY FILMS: *L.A. Story* (91); *Indecent Proposal* (93); *The Cowboy Way* (95); *Sunchaser* (96); *Wag The Dog* (98); *The Thin Red Line* (98); *Play It To The Bone* (99); *American Saint* (00)

Harris, Ed

One of the best-kept secrets of mainstream and independent Hollywood, Harris has an impressive body of work behind him for a man who didn't get his first big break until the age of thirty-three, as astronaut John Glenn in Philip Kaufman's *The Right Stuff* (83). An unassuming man who disguises his total commitment to every part he plays behind the skilful wall of his acting, Harris, with **Robert Duvall** and **John Malkovich**, is one of that great trio of talented baldies who have had to make their way in the cutthroat world of movies through talent rather than mere surface comeliness. Even in an otherwise flawed but interesting film such as Victor Nuñez's *Flash Of Green* (85), Harris's trademark of quiet and focused concentration shines through; and he was, quite definitely, the very best thing in **Jean-Jacques Annaud's** *Enemy At The Gates* (01), playing icy master sniper, Major Erwin Konig.

OTHER KEY FILMS: *Under Fire* (83); *Places In The Heart* (84); *Walker* (87); *To Kill A Priest* (88); *Glengarry Glen Ross* (92); *The Firm* (93); *China Moon* (94); *Nixon* (95); *The Rock* (96); *Absolute Power* (97); *The Truman Show* (98); *Walking The Dead* (99); *The Prime Gig* (00); *Pollock* [also dir.] (00)

Harris, Richard

All-round hell-raiser, womaniser and self-proclaimed 'holy terror', Harris considers himself to be the last of the great survivors following the recent death of **Oliver Reed** on the set of **Ridley Scott's** *Gladiator* (00), in which Harris plays Marcus Aurelius. With nearly seventy films, two wives, and a couple of hundred sexual conquests behind him, Harris feels he has some right to crow. **Lindsay Anderson's** *This Sporting Life* (63) made him, Joshua Logan's *Camelot* (67) gave him an international following, and both Jim Sheridan's *The Field* (90) and Randa Haines's *Wrestling Ernest Hemingway* (93) have secured him a critically acclaimed dotage. What more can a man want?

OTHER KEY FILMS: *The Long And The Short And The Tall* (61); *Mutiny On The Bounty* (62); *The Red Desert* (64); *The Heroes Of Telemark* (65); *A Man Called Horse* (70); *The Molly Maguires* (70); *The Wild Geese* (78); *Cry The Beloved Country* (95); *Smilla's Feeling For Snow* (97); *To Walk With Lions* (99); *The Barber Of Siberia* (00); *The Count of Monte Cristo* (01); *My Kingdom* (01); *Harry Potter And The Philosopher's Stone* (01)

KEY LINE:
'The role of husband was never one of my strongest.' [Harris on marriage]

Harrison, Rex

Known as 'Sexy Rexy' to his friends – and to his six ex-wives? – most people remember Harrison as Professor Higgins in **George Cukor's** *My Fair Lady* (64), but in fact, he only got the part by default after **Cary Grant** refused it and insisted that Harrison be allowed to repeat his Broadway success on the big screen. His early screen work was possibly his best, and one remembers with affection his spoiled would-be novelist, Charles Condomine, in **David Lean's** *Blithe Spirit* (45). He was perfect casting, also, for Sidney Gilliat's *The Rake's Progress* (45) [a.k.a. *Notorious Gentleman*], and he injected real pathos into his role as defunct sea captain Daniel Gregg, in **Joseph L Mankiewicz's** *The Ghost And Mrs Muir* (47).

OTHER KEY FILMS: *Night Train To Munich* (40); *Major Barbara* (41); *Unfaithfully Yours* (48); *The Reluctant Debutante* (58); *Midnight Lace* (60); *Staircase* (69)

Harryhausen, Ray

Harryhausen is renowned to this day for the magical fighting skeletons that appeared in both Nathan Juran's inspired fantasy *The Seventh Voyage Of Sinbad* (58) and in Don Chaffey's *Jason And The Argonauts* (63). Harryhausen animated the skeletons through his own variation on the **stop motion** technique, Superdynamation, with which he recreated scenes that a 1950s child might well have been able to imagine, thanks to action comics, but would never have dreamed of actually seeing

153

re-enacted on the screen. Despite all the encroachments made by modern computer and **digital** technology, Harryhausen's effects still impress because they were based on a resolutely human scale, and were, as such, always believable.

OTHER KEY FILMS: Eugène Lourié's *The Beast From 20,000 Fathoms* (53); Don Chaffey's *One Million Years B.C.* (67); Desmond Davis's *Clash Of The Titans* (81)

Hartley, Hal

Hartley is the director of such medium-budget and quirkily independent movies as *Trust* (91) and the whimsically perverse *Amateur* (94) which starred Hartley's alter ego, Martin Donovan, and the luminous **Isabelle Huppert** as an ex-nun who decides to branch out into writing pornography. Both these films are far more satisfying in their scope than the blockbusters turned out by some of Hartley's more lucratively employed contemporaries. Hartley's is the cinema of intelligence, in which preconceptions are challenged, assumptions subverted, and expectations overturned – this alone is enough to ensure, thank God, that the doors to the major Hollywood studios are probably forever closed to him now. Hartley's most approachable film, *Simple Men* (92), was a touching and genuinely eccentric insight into the convolutions that families can put themselves through in their search for identity – a continuing theme in Hartley's work.

OTHER KEY FILMS: *The Unbelievable Truth* (90); *Ambition* (91); *Flirt* (95); *Henry Fool* (97); *The Book Of Life* (98); *No Such Thing* (01)

Hathaway, Henry

They don't make them like Hathaway any more, especially in the lengths of their careers – his amounted to an impressive forty-two years, all spent directing, with variable, if always entertaining results. Perhaps it was because he was so resolutely anti-intellectual that he lasted so long, for he was certainly not unintelligent, as he showed with the very strange and rather fantastical *Peter Ibbetson* (35). In that same year he had the dubious distinction of directing Adolf Hitler's favourite film, *The Lives Of A Bengal Lancer* (35), although one can hardly blame Hathaway for whatever message Hitler may have derived from it. Later successes include *Kiss Of Death* (47) – a first-class **film noir** with the serially underrated **Victor Mature** – *The Desert Fox* (51), with the ever-excellent **James Mason** as Erwin Rommel, and *True Grit* (69), for which **John Wayne** finally won the **Oscar** that had been his due for over thirty years.

OTHER KEY FILMS: *Johnny Apollo* (40); *The Shepherd Of The Hills* (41); *13 Rue Madeleine* (47); *Call Northside 777* (48); *Niagara* (53); *The Sons Of Katie Elder* (65); *Nevada Smith* (66)

KEY LINE:

'Henry Hathaway is very easy for a writer to work with. He's absolutely dreadful for actors to work with: he's probably the toughest son of a bitch in Hollywood…he's doing it deliberately, because this is the way he's discovered he can work.' [Wendell Mayes, who co-scripted Hathaway's *From Hell To Texas* (58)]

Hawkins, Jack

Hawkins ended his film career miming his words and being dubbed by other actors due to an operation for throat cancer that permanently damaged his vocal chords. This was a double tragedy for him, for Hawkins *was* his voice – a stiff upper-lip British one, to be sure, but with the capacity for sudden, surprising bursts of raw emotion. His best-known roles were as Capt. Ericson in Charles Frend's *The Cruel Sea* and as General Allenby, in **David Lean's** *Lawrence Of Arabia* (62), although he was perhaps most memorable as the Pharaoh in **Howard Hawks's** wonderfully kitsch *Land Of The Pharaohs* (55), in which Hawkins was for once allowed to show the inherent vulnerability that lay behind his otherwise ultra-dominant characters.

OTHER KEY FILMS: *The Fallen Idol* (48); *The Small Back Room* (48); *Mandy* (52); *The Cruel Sea* (53); *The Bridge On The River Kwai* (57); *Zulu* (64); *Lord Jim* (65); *Waterloo* (70); *Young Winston* (72)

Hawks, Howard

Hawks is one of the all-time greats, and proof that the Hollywood studio system of the 1930s and 1940s was every so often capable of throwing up a talent of genuine and sometimes brilliant originality. Hawks acknowledged early on that men and women are fundamentally incompatible, and then took it as his life's challenge to engender situations in which that very incompatibility would provide the main attraction. It is almost impossible to sift out just a few films from Hawks's litany of 24-carat gems and near masterpieces, but most enlightened beings would probably agree that his best comedies were the sublime *Twentieth Century* (34), together with *Bringing Up Baby* (38), *His Girl Friday* (40), *Ball Of Fire* (42), *I Was A Male War Bride* (49), *Monkey Business* (52), *Gentleman Prefer Blondes* (53) and *Rio Bravo* (59). But *Rio Bravo*, I hear you cry, is a **Western**. Not so. All Hawks's films sneered at genres, and therein lay his greatest talent – he simply didn't care what people expected of him. He was always going to make his own choice of films (which the studios would graciously fund) and follow his own star, and if this involved joking with his friends, throwing in a song or two, or having his characters debate seriously on trivial subjects, then so be it. The General Sternwood orchid-house episode in *The Big Sleep* (46) lasts a good ten minutes, and really has nothing to do with the film at all beyond providing **Humphrey Bogart** with a fine excuse to begin investigating and to fall in love with **Lauren Bacall**. But it was a great scene, and continues to give pleasure however many times one sees it. Similarly, the 'dead bee' running gag with the inimitable **Walter Brennan** in *To Have And Have Not* (44) — which on paper shouldn't even be funny — is remembered by absolutely everyone. And what the blazes was Hoagy Carmichael doing in the same movie beyond providing a few brilliant musical interludes and a lot of innocent pleasure? Yes, it may be easy to pick at Hawks, but it has proved impossible to recreate him, and on the fifteenth watching of *El Dorado* (67) — which itself only came about because Hawks had had so much fun making *Rio Bravo* that he thought, well, why not do it again? — it becomes obvious that Hawks is Hawks because his movies find time to be human. His heroes, in spite of their own better judgement, are forever dragging along unwanted sidekicks, wastrels, rummies and wild animals, so that when we emerge from the shadowy enchantment of one of Hawks's pictures, our world seems bathed in that same illogical but infinitely precious glow of optimism. See **Heartstopping Moments**

OTHER KEY FILMS: *Trent's Last Case* (29); *The Dawn Patrol* (30); *Scarface: The Shame Of A Nation* (32); *Barbary Coast* (35); *Only Angels Have Wings* (40); *Sergeant York* (41); *The Outlaw* [uncredited] (43); *Red River* (48); *The Big Sky* (52); *Land Of The Pharaohs* (55); *Hatari!* (62); *Man's Favourite Sport?* (64); *Rio Lobo* (70)

KEY LINE:
Robert Mitchum's drunken sheriff, J P Hannah: 'What are you doing here?' **John Wayne's** Cole Thornton: 'I'm looking at a tin star with a drunk pinned on it.' [Howard Hawks's *El Dorado* (67)]

Hayden, Sterling

Always something of an octagonal peg in a round hole, Hayden as a young man captained one of the last of the square-rigged schooners and subsequently never lost his passion for sailing — a passion which he would fund from his erratic acting career — occasionally disappearing for lengthy periods to complete yet another leg of his ongoing round-the-world journey. A novelist as well as an actor, Hayden's early good looks weathered over the years into something far more interesting, and they were well used by **John Huston** in *The Asphalt Jungle* (50), by **Nicholas Ray** in *Johnny Guitar* (53), and by **Stanley Kubrick** in *The Killing* (56) and *Dr Strangelove* (64). In 1951 Hayden had named names before the HUAC (see **Hollywood Ten**) in order to save his career, an act he deeply regretted and later publicly apologised for, but despite this stigma he eventually made a number of late-career comebacks, most notably as Roger Wade, the irascible writer in **Robert Altman's** *The Long Goodbye* (73).

OTHER KEY FILMS: *Arrow In The Dust* (54); *Suddenly* (54); *Terror In A Texas Town* (58); *Hard Contract* (69); *1900* (77); *King Of The Gypsies* (78)

Hays Office (Hays, Will H)

Hays is the censor who stopped Hollywood's lustful shenanigans — and the likes of the voyeuristic **Busby Berkeley** — in their tracks, in 1934, through his over-zealous implementation of the Motion Picture Association of America's production code which frowned on 'excessive and lustful kissing' and the showing of 'suggestive postures and gestures'. It was Hays also who ensured that even happily married couples were rarely seen sharing a bed, and that, if so, one partner, usually the male of the species, was to keep at least one foot firmly anchored to the floor. The production code was designed to encourage self-censorship throughout the motion picture industry, thereby avoiding the need for an unpopular, government-run censorship bureau, but its laws were increasingly flouted and its powers eroded not least by the US Supreme Court, which ruled on 26 May 1952 that states could no longer ban movies as sacrilegious. The operation of the code was finally wound up in 1968.

KEY LINE:
'Will Hays is my shepherd, I shall not want, He maketh me to lie down in clean postures.' [Gene Fowler on Will Hays]

Hayworth, Rita

Although stunning to look at and a very fine dancer and singer (as well as an often underrated actress — one of the inevitable perils, one supposes, of too much beauty), there was something fatally vulnerable about Hayworth, and the fates really did seem to conspire against her during her terrible downhill battle, towards the end of her life, with both alcohol and Alzheimer's disease. Her second husband, **Orson Welles**, captured the essence of her charms, together

with the often contradictory nature of her screen image, in the perverse Elsa Bannister in his *The Lady From Shanghai* (48); but Hayworth was also superb in **Charles Vidor's** stupendous *film noir, Gilda* (46). At her best she lit up the screen, and for some reason it is only *on* the big screen, in a darkened cinema, that she really comes to life.

OTHER KEY FILMS: *Only Angels Have Wings* (39); *You'll Never Get Rich* (41); *You Were Never Lovelier* (42); *Cover Girl* (44); *Miss Sadie Thompson* (54)
KEY LINE:
'I can never get a zipper to close. Maybe that stands for something? What do you think?' [Hayworth in *Gilda*]

Haze

A murky, misty effect that sometimes appears on film, haze can be caused by atmospheric build-up between the camera and its long-shot, exterior subject. The situation can be remedied by the use of a haze-cutting filter, which sifts and absorbs both blue and ultraviolet light.

Head, Edith

Head's name appeared on more movie credit rolls than did the copyright symbol during the 1930s, 1940s and 1950s, and she designed clothes for every great star of Hollywood's golden era. Even her occasional mistakes, as in **Bette Davis's** scene-stealing off-the-shoulder number in **Joseph L Mankiewicz's** *All About Eve* (50), turned out serendipitously perfect. Head was the mistress of the human form, and she had collected so many Academy Awards as a costumier by the end of her fifty-year career that it's a wonder she didn't set herself to designing outfits for them too.
OTHER KEY FILMS: **Howard Hawks's** *Ball Of Fire* (41); **Preston Sturges's** *Sullivan's Travels* (41); **Billy Wilder's** *Five Graves To Cairo* (43), *Double Indemnity* (44) and *Sunset Boulevard* (50); **George Stevens's** *Shane* (53); **Alfred Hitchcock's** *Rear Window* (53) (notably **Grace Kelly's** sublime frock in the dinner from Ciro's scene), *To Catch A Thief* (55), *The Birds* (63) and *Marnie* (64)

Head Shot

A close-up shot of an actor or actress's face or head.

Head-on Shot

A shot in which the camera moves directly towards the audience, who act, by default, *in loco stellae*. Director **John Woo** has perfected an action technique in films such as *Hard Target* (93), in which a bullet, rocket or arrow is shot directly, in reverse head-on, at the audience.

Head Up/Head Out

A film ready for projection, with its start leader on the outside of the reel. An unprepared reel, with its start leader on the inside, is known as tails up/tails out.

Rita Hayworth about to 'Put The Blame On Mame' and the hex on Glenn Ford's Johnny Farrell, in Charles Vidor's Gilda *(46) See also image at Orson Welles*

Heartstopping Moments

Jean Renoir's *La Grande Illusion* (37). When the soundtrack goes silent and the men in the prisoner-of-war camp suddenly become aware of a British soldier in the process of dressing up as a woman for a theatrical pageant. The muted camera tracks all the way along their faces, and in each face we are privileged to see the beyond-sexual yearning every man has for home, for female companionship, and for softness, after the vindictive harshness of their experience of war.

John Huston's *Night Of The Iguana* (64). When **Richard Burton** returns to **Ava Gardner** at the end of the film (following his polite, prescient rebuff by **Deborah Kerr**) to tell her that he will be staying after all, and the hard-nosed Gardner turns quickly away from him in an effort to hide her emotions (although not, of course, from the camera). This scene unfailingly procures sobs from all sensitive members of any audience who are viewing this magnificent film as it should be viewed, on a full-sized screen, in a proper cinema, and preferably in **Paris**.

Howard Hawks's *To Have And Have Not* (45). That little wiggle of a dance that **Lauren Bacall** does at the end of the film, to Hoagy Carmichael's music, as she walks towards **Humphrey Bogart**, and which is far more redolent of her happiness that he has accepted her than if she were to express those emotions in words. Like the *Night Of The Iguana* moment, it is pure, unadulterated, cinema.

George Marshall's *The Blue Dahlia* (46). Although not a good film in the strictest sense, there is a magic moment when **Alan Ladd** is brought up short by the luminous **Veronica Lake** when she asks him, 'Have you seen me before?' and he utters the following words (penned by **Raymond Chandler**) in a flat, resigned tone, as if he has lived with them all his life – 'Every guy's seen you before. Somewhere. The trick is to find you.'

Joseph L Mankiewicz's *The Ghost And Mrs Muir* (47). When the shadow of **Rex Harrison's** ghostly sea captain falls across **Gene Tierney's** now aged features at the exact moment of her death – superbly accompanied, of course, by **Bernard Herrmann's** swooping music. The scene appeals to the visceral instinct we all have towards the possibilities of reincarnation, and to any eventual prospects we may still entertain of finding a more than fleeting happiness.

John Ford's *My Darling Clementine* (46). When **Henry Fonda** first sees Clementine alighting from the stagecoach, and stands up, from his habitual prone position, almost in exaltation.

Alexander Korda's *Rembrandt* (36). When **Charles Laughton** silences a roomful of cynical and worldly men and their mistresses by admitting his love for his wife, Saskia, and describing her as all women to him. A moment later we realise that, during those few brief moments in which he has been extolling her, she has died. Magic.

Federico Fellini's *La Strada* (54). The scene, after a wedding, in which **Giulietta Masina** follows the children of a large, strange house up to the first floor and into the isolated bedroom of a boy with an enlarged head, and we realise, in the magical transition from adult to child's view (and without the need for any words) that this is where she really belongs, in the children's world, the place from which she was taken at the beginning of the film.

Akira Kurosawa's *The Seven Samurai* (54). The scene in which the young Samurai is told that he cannot go to fight with the older men, in the peasant village. What follows is a series of close-ups, during which Kombei tells of the years he has followed the code of Bushido, and which culminates in the grim, noble face of Kyuzo, the greatest of all the Samurai, arriving at the door.

Billy Wilder's *Sunset Boulevard* (50). The moment when one of the technicians, who would conceivably have been only an apprentice in the 1920s, recognises Norma Desmond/**Gloria Swanson** on **Cecil B DeMille's** set, where she is sitting, alone and unnoticed, in the director's chair. Slowly he spotlights her. She raises her face to the light. Gradually and magically all the extras come flocking around her, like moths to the light of a lamp. This particular scene is one of the greatest of all mute illustrations of the fundamental magic of the movies.

Jean Renoir's *Les Bas-Fonds* (36). When **Louis Jouvet** and **Jean Gabin** lie on the grass reminiscing, and an unscripted snail walks up Jouvet's arm which he incorporates, with a great actor's instincts, into the scene.

John Ford's *The Grapes Of Wrath* (40). The moment when Ma Joad (played by Jane Darwell), about to leave her condemned farm for the last time, silently tries on an old pair of earrings that she has found in a box. Ford shows us her broken, and briefly young reflection in an old mirror. The scene is silent. Words aren't necessary.

Robert Bresson's *Mouchette* (67). When a fourteen-year-old schoolgirl, clad only in a simple shift and a pair of wooden clogs, allows herself to roll slowly down the bank of a river towards her certain death. She fails the first time, gets up, and in one of the greatest and most heart-rending moments in all cinema, makes her way slowly up the bank once again, in a despair so deep that nothing can break through it, before rolling down once again, this time to her death.

Jacques Feyder's *Knight Without Armour* (37). When Russian aristocrat, **Marlene Dietrich**, in an all-but-diaphanous white nightgown, races across the empty lawns of her father's stately home, fearful that she has been abandoned to the mob by her servants and entourage. She comes to a stop by the lake, upon which a thousand angry peasants approach her from over the lee of the hill, their pitchforks and sickles held high. Hesitant at first, Dietrich slowly draws herself up and proudly faces them.

Josef von Sternberg's *Dishonored* (31). Another Dietrich moment. This time she is about to be shot as a spy. No mercy is possible. She asks for decent clothes, a lipstick, the chance to wash, and a piano. A young officer brings her these things, then breaks down at the thought of a woman suffering such a death. Dietrich comforts him before striding out to the firing squad, looking immaculate, with a cigarette dangling nonchalantly from her lips.

Ernst Lubitsch's *The Shop Around The Corner* (40). When Margaret Sullavan's Clare Novak, in love with a man (**James Stewart**) she thinks she knows only by correspondence (but who is also, unbeknown to both of them, her co-worker), searches with her gloved hand inside her post-box, only to discover that there is no letter there. The shot of her bereft face as she realises her loss is one of the most poignant moments in all cinema, and a worthy tribute to the lessons all sound directors might profitably learn, if only they had the inclination, from the art of silent filmmaking. See also **Best Titles, Erotic Moments, Worst Films**

Heavy

The thug or villain in a film, the part of a heavy is almost invariably played by a man, and one with the capacity to show malevolence, anger or the threat of evil on his features. Dedicated heavies include Jack Elam, Howard da Silva, and Mike Mazurki. Major stars who have also successfully turned heavy when required include **Robert Mitchum, Jack Nicholson,** and **Nicolas Cage** – in J Lee Thompson's *Cape Fear* (61), **Stanley Kubrick's** *The Shining* (80), and **John Woo's** *Face/Off* (97) respectively.

Hecht, Ben

Hecht is the screenwriter most people think of when they think of the wisecracking Hollywood movies of the 1930s, in which the girls are just as sassy as the boys (without feeling the need to emasculate them) and in which the screenwriter, for perhaps the very last time, occasionally succeeds in stealing the show. Hecht worked on an extraordinary succession of hit movies, often collaborating with I A L Diamond or Charles Macarthur, and as often as not received little or no billing for his pains, as in his work for **John Ford's** *The Hurricane* (37) and **Victor Fleming's** *Gone With The Wind* (39). His masterpieces are **William Wellman's** *Nothing Sacred* (37) and **Alfred Hitchcock's** *Notorious* (46), in both of which Hecht's obsession with hypocrisy, and with what constituted truth, were most apparent. He is best remembered for his play, *The Front Page*, co-written with Macarthur, that spawned two outstanding movies, Lewis Milestone's *The Front Page* (31) and **Howard Hawks's** *His Girl Friday* (40), and one pretty good one, **Billy Wilder's** *The Front Page* (74). **OTHER KEY FILMS:** Howard Hawks's *Twentieth Century* (34) and *Monkey Business* (52); **George Stevens's** *Gunga Din* (39); Alfred Hitchcock's *Spellbound* (45); **Otto Preminger's** *Where The Sidewalk Ends* (50)
KEY LINE:
'The sonofabitch stole my watch!' [*The Front Page*]

Heden Controls

After successfully developing the shutter mechanism for the Hasselblad camera during the 1960s, which is still used in production today, Swedish-born Bjorn Heden started his own engineering company to make the acknowledged Rolls-Royce of precise analogue servo-controls for use in **zoom** focus and **iris** remote control of big movie cameras. See **Hot Head**

Heflin, Van

Heflin never really made it as a big star despite a number of leading-man roles, but he was more than good in the series of varied films he did get to make. Belying his all-American boy-next-door looks, he brought a considerable emotional range to Lewis Milestone's *The Strange Love Of Martha Ivers* (46), to Curtis Bernhardt's *Possessed* (47), and, in particular, to his obsessed, dissatisfied policeman, Garwood, in **Joseph Losey's** first-class *film noir, The Prowler* (51). His most famous role was as the homesteader, Joe Starrett, in **George Stevens's** *Shane* (53).

OTHER KEY FILMS: *The Outcasts Of Poker Flat* (37); *Santa Fe Trail* (40); *Madame Bovary* (49); *Battle Cry* (55); *3:10 To Yuma* (57); *They Came To Cordura* (59)

Audrey Hepburn's Holly Golightly drinking her Breakfast At Tiffany's *(61), in the Blake Edwards movie*

Heist Movies

Heist movies are films in which the central action revolves around a robbery, and whose plots generally follow, in consecutive order, conception, perpetration, and implication. Notable examples include **John Huston's** *The Asphalt Jungle* (50), **Jules Dassin's** *Rififi* (54), **Stanley Kubrick's** *The Killing* (56), and Peter Collinson's *The Italian Job* (69). Literary-minded fans of the caper, or heist movie, might like to try the Parker books of Richard Stark, the acknowledged master of caper fiction and the originator of some of the best Hollywood heist movie clones.

Hepburn, Audrey

Hepburn may be dearly loved and esteemed by her long-standing fans, but even they cannot dispute the fact that she was never much of an actress, and that her fame lies more in her persona, her gamine charm, and the glamour she so exceptionally personified, than in any thespian talent. The only notable exception to this is her role of Sister Luke/Gabrielle Van Der Mal in **Fred Zinnemann's** *The Nun's Story* (59). Her skills were tailor-made for the sophisticated and still elitist 1950s, when the post-war boom had yet to impact on the ability of the under-classes to derive any benefit from it – instead, as a temporary placebo, they watched Hepburn, in films like **Stanley Donen's** *Funny Face* (57) and *Charade* (63), or in **Blake Edwards's** *Breakfast At Tiffany's* (61), and dreamed.

OTHER KEY FILMS: *Roman Holiday* (53); *Sabrina* (54); *Love In The Afternoon* (57); *Green Mansions* (59); *My Fair Lady* (64); *Two For The Road* (67); *Robin And Marian* (76); *Always* (89)

Hepburn, Katharine

Hepburn was the most stylised actress of her generation, and it is to her credit that she managed to ensure that the public mood accorded with her stylisations, rather than the other way around. No one ever talked or acted like Hepburn *except* Hepburn, and it was this very eccentricity and self-absorption that allowed her to extend her career beyond all reasonable limits and virtually to monopolise that singular and rarefied niche of 'Oscars for the elderly', that so warms the cockles of the Academy's ageing hearts. She acted in surprisingly few films for someone whose career spanned close to sixty-five years, and she made a conspicuous number of duds – even stranger than that was her reputation, during the 1940s, of being box-office poison, the feeling being that her upper-class accent grated on the newly democratic

159

aspirations of the returning soldiers and their girls. Hepburn swept these minor problems aside, of course, becoming democracy personified in such films as **George Cukor's** *Adam's Rib* (49) and *Pat And Mike* (52), just as she'd been elitism personified in **Howard Hawks's** *Bringing Up Baby* (38) and Cukor's earlier, and arguably best comedy of the sexes, *The Philadelphia Story* (40). Later in life, following long-term lover **Spencer Tracy's** death, she became wise and somewhat distant, reminding us, in such films as Mark Rydell's *On Golden Pond* (81) and Glenn Gordon Caron's *Love Affair* (94), what a peculiarly *American* phenomenon we had for so long been attracted to.

OTHER KEY FILMS: *A Bill Of Divorcement* (32); *Little Women* (33); *Stage Door* (37); *Holiday* (38); *Woman Of The Year* (42); *State Of The Union* (48); *The African Queen* (51); *Summertime* (55); *Suddenly Last Summer* (59); *The Lion In Winter* (68); *Rooster Cogburn* (76)

KEY LINES:
'Nature, Mr Allnutt, is what we are put into this world to rise above.' [*The African Queen*]

'I never dreamed that any mere physical experience could be so stimulating.' [*The African Queen*]

'She, Kate Hepburn, is a very bossy, humourless lady. She has a sense of wit, but no sense of humour whatsoever…and nobody is going to tell Kate Hepburn anything!' [Screenwriter Arthur Laurents on Hepburn, who starred in **David Lean's** film of Laurents's play, *Summertime* (55)]

Hero/Heroine

Traditionally these are the characters in a film with which the audience is expected, almost symbiotically, to bond. Convention dictates that the hero or heroine never do anything underhand or mean except in the most extreme of circumstances, and always for the best possible of motives. Stars, for obvious reasons, tend to allocate these parts to themselves, leaving the role of **heavy** to character actors. The classic personification of a Georgette Heyer-style hero occurs in **Victor Fleming's** *Gone With The Wind* (39), in which, although we find him instantly attractive, we initially suspect **Clark Gable** of being not quite a gentleman – the movie then goes on to show us how wrong we are. Heroines, on the other hand, as personified for example by Anna Neagle in Herbert Wilcox's *Odette* (50), are rarely required to go through this rite of passage, and we are generally convinced of their sincerity and virtue early on. A welcome exception to the rule is provided by **Katharine**

Hepburn in George Cukor's *Philadelphia Story* (40), in which our heroine is shown to have feet of clay, and to be all the more attractive and believable for it.
KEY LINE:
'If you want to make a big hero you have got to make a big villain.' [Screenwriter **Philip Yordan**, who co-scripted **Anthony Mann's** *El Cid* (61), on how to write a hero]

Herrmann, Bernard

Herrmann composed the music for **Alfred Hitchcock's** *Psycho* (60) – the famous bit when **Janet Leigh** is driving alone in her car with the rain pounding onto the windscreen so she can hardly see and then…bang!…up looms the Bates Motel and perdition. A certain sort of genius, allied with a supreme confidence in one's animal abilities, is needed to achieve such an effect. It is inconceivable that it could be bettered, just as it is inconceivable to imagine **Orson Welles's** horse rearing up over the terrified **Joan Fontaine** in Robert Stevenson's *Jane Eyre* (44) without the awesome background music, or **Robert De Niro's** Travis Bickle cruising like a shark through the mean streets of New York in **Martin Scorsese's** *Taxi Driver* (76), without Herrmann to lead us inside the tortured recesses of Bickle's mind. Herrmann's music acts as a metaphorical voice-over to the narrative, and he is the greatest master of all at framing alienation in sound, as he did so sublimely and so categorically in the case of **Robert Ryan's** disenchanted cop in **Nicholas Ray's** magnificent *On Dangerous Ground* (51).
OTHER KEY FILMS: Orson Welles's *Citizen Kane* (41) and *The Magnificent Ambersons* (42); **Joseph L Mankiewicz's** *The Ghost And Mrs Muir* (47) and *Five Fingers* (52); Alfred Hitchcock's *The Man Who Knew Too Much* (56), *North By Northwest* (59) and *Marnie* (64); J Lee Thompson's *Cape Fear* (62); **François Truffaut's** *Fahrenheit 451* (66)

Herzog, Werner

The **auteur theory** of directorial supremacy promulgated by the **Cahiers du Cinéma** boys seems tailor-made for the philosophically inclined Herzog. Indeed his single-mindedness in getting his visions onto celluloid has sometimes more resembled the compulsive tic of an incipient madman, particularly when twinned with the complementary mania of actor **Klaus Kinski**, whom Herzog, despite his better judgement and at some considerable risk to what remained of his own sanity, persisted in using as his alter ego on screen. But *Aguirre, Wrath Of God* (72) is a unique experience, and it is hard to imagine a better or more understandable vampire than Kinski's *Nosferatu* (79), a more complex *Woyzeck* (79), or a more passionate *Fitzcarraldo* (82). Herzog's best film, however, was as far removed from Kinski's creative histrionics as it is possible to be – *The Enigma Of Kaspar Hauser* (75) was a gentle, rigorously controlled and almost documentary-like insight into a truly simple man, who appeared as if from nowhere, lingered briefly to remind us that we do not possess all the answers, and then was roughly torn from the world by a man (his father perhaps) whom we neither know nor, to all intents and purposes, see. Herzog is obsessed with God, with fate and with the meaning of creation, and at the end of *Kaspar Hauser* we are left with the uncomfortable feeling that Adam and Eve's loss of the Garden of Eden may well have been occasioned by nothing more profound than a temporary fit of pique on the part of its erstwhile creator.

OTHER KEY FILMS: *Signs Of Life* (68); *Even Dwarfs Started Small* (70); *Fata Morgana* [doc.] (71); *Land Of Silence And Darkness* [doc.] (72); *Heart Of Glass* (76); *Stroszek* (77); *The Ballad Of The Little Soldier* (84); *Where The Little Ants Dream* (84); *Cobra Verde* (88); *It Isn't Easy Being God* (89); *Scream Of Stone* (91); *Lessons In Darkness* (92); *Mein Liebster Fiend – Klaus Kinski* [doc.] (99); *Invincible* (01)

Heston, Charlton

Heston is a king-actor (using **Orson Welles's** definition of a man with such innate presence that his incarnation as a mere common man would appear absurd). The two king-actors met and matched each other in Welles's magisterially expressionistic *Touch Of Evil* (58), in which the real-life Heston, through his character of Mike Vargas, arguably began to infer, in the downfall of Welles's monstrous Hank Quinlan, the fate that was to befall his own screen persona many years later. Heston bravely championed the unchampionable Welles ever after, and this courtesy – call it niceness if you will – was always a part of his charm, and was evident even when he was at his most martial, as in **William Wyler's** *Ben-Hur* (59) or **Anthony Mann's** *El Cid* (61). Heston allowed one to believe, even if ever so briefly, that history might occasionally be influenced by individual greatness. The gradual tendency of his later career towards fantasy, as in Franklin J Schaffner's *Planet Of The Apes* (68) and Richard Fleischer's *Soylent Green* (73), revealed an awkward but undoubtedly conscious acknowledgment that time and tide (and the coming of the common man) were beginning to pass him by.

OTHER KEY FILMS: *Dark City* (50); *The Naked Jungle* (54); *Secret Of The Incas* (54); *The Ten Commandments* (56); *The Big Country* (58); *The Wreck Of The Mary Deare* (59); *55 Days At Peking* (63); *Major Dundee* (65); *The Agony And The Ecstasy* (65); *The War Lord* (65); *Khartoum* (66); *Will Penny* (68); *Call Of The Wild* (72); *Gray Lady Down* (78); *Tombstone* (93); *Hamlet* (96); *Illusion Infinity* (98); *Toscano* (99); *Any Given Sunday* (99); *Town And Country* (01); *Planet Of The Apes* [remake] (01)

H I

Stands for high intensity, and refers to a powerful arc light used for studio illumination.

High-angle Shot

A shot taken from above the scene of action, looking down. Most of **Busby Berkeley's** famous choreographic set-ups start this way, but the master of the high-angle shot must surely be **Orson Welles** who, in *The Lady From Shanghai* (48), pinned his camera, as it were, to the masthead, and filmed directly down onto the prone, utterly voluptuous, and radically peroxided **Rita Hayworth**, as she sings (moans, really) to the strumming of a hidden guitar.

High Hat

Paradoxical name for a squat tripod used to snatch extremely **low-angle shots**.

High Key Lighting

Lighting designed to bring out the brashness and brightness of highly coloured set design, affording few, if any, shadows.

Highlighting

The use of a sharp beam of light to define one particular aspect of a subject's face, or one particular detail of a prop.

Highlights

The brightest, least contrasted areas of a filmed image.

High-speed Camera

A specially designed continuous-action camera, equipped with mirrors, prisms and synchronised flash, capable of photographing images at the rate of two or three thousand frames per second.

161

High-speed Cinematography

The use of special **high-speed cameras** to allow for an inordinately high frame-per-second filming rate, high-speed cinematography permits an exaggerated slow-motion effect when subsequent projection is undertaken at normal speed.

Hitchcock, Alfred

It is impossible for anyone who has seen even one of his films to deny Hitchcock his place within the cinema's pantheon of greats, for his was the most 'cinematic' mind of all, and at the same time the most isolated from 'real life' of all the great directors. Cinema made Hitchcock just as surely as the stage made **Laurence Olivier**, and he was equally in thrall to it, subsuming his unconscious mind, and ours, to its magic. He worked in England until 1939, turning out a series of bravura films including *The 39 Steps* (35), *Young And Innocent* (37) and *The Lady Vanishes* (38), and then, as if he instinctively understood how the Second World War would swing the fulcrum of power ever further westwards, he moved to America, where he began work on a new series of films. These proved unique in the annals of commercial cinema in that they successfully spanned the two worlds of the critically acclaimed and the financially viable over the immense period of thirty-six years. *Rebecca* (40), *Suspicion* (41) and *Saboteur* (42) initially harked back to his English years, but with *Spellbound* (45) he discovered his lodestone, namely the American film with an English sensibility, and this was to become his stock-in-trade during the remainder of his career. *Notorious* (46), *Strangers On A Train* (51), *Rear Window* (54), *Vertigo* (58) and *North By Northwest* (59) showed the Americans themselves as they wished to be, all the while craftily mining the very Cold War insecurities such films were ostensibly designed to obviate. *Psycho* (60), *The Birds* (63) and *Marnie* (64) were the late *chef d'oeuvres* of a master never content to rest upon his laurels, and the relative weakness of his last films can hardly, in the circumstances, afford us much cause to grumble.

OTHER KEY FILMS: *The Lodger* (26); *Blackmail* (29); *The Man Who Knew Too Much* (34); *The Secret Agent* (36); *Sabotage* (37); *Jamaica Inn* (39); *Foreign Correspondent* (40); *Shadow Of A Doubt* (43); *Lifeboat* (44); *The Paradine Case* (48); *Rope* (48); *Under Capricorn* (49); *I Confess* (53); *Dial M For Murder* (54); *To Catch A Thief* (55); *The Wrong Man* (57); *Torn Curtain* (66); *Topaz* (69); *Frenzy* (72); *Family Plot* (76)

KEY LINES:

'Actors should be treated like cattle.' [Hitchcock on the acting profession]

'Television has brought back murder into the home – where it belongs.' [Hitchcock on murder]

'There is no terror in a bang, only in the anticipation of it.' [Hitchcock on suspense]

'His whole life was motion pictures; there didn't seem to be much else in it. He just loved what he was doing, and he transmitted that feeling to you, rather than hovering over you like a giant genius.' [Screenwriter John Michael Hayes after his four-time collaboration with Hitchcock, on *Rear Window* (54), *The Trouble With Harry* (55), *To Catch A Thief* (55) and *The Man Who Knew Too Much* [co-script] (56)]

'The thing that amuses me about Hitchcock is the way he directs a film in his head before he knows what the story is.' [**Raymond Chandler**, during the co-writing of *Strangers On A Train* (51)]

HMI Lamp

A dedicated studio lamp used to achieve the effect of bright, or intermittent, sunlight.

Hoffman, Dustin

Hoffman, like his co-star **Tom Cruise** in **Barry Levinson's** *Rain Man* (88), makes a virtue of his diminutive size, using it to gather in parts that larger, more obvious men would never find it in themselves to attempt. He was an overnight sensation in **Mike Nichols's** *The Graduate* (67), and his Ratso in **John Schlesinger's** *Midnight Cowboy* (69) was an utterly cinematic creation; the character's link with everyday reality was tenuous, while its link with cinematic reality is absolute. And that is Hoffman's strength – he never forgets that he's in a movie, and his Michael Dorsey/Dorothy Michaels in **Sydney Pollack's** *Tootsie* (82) succeeds for that very reason. Hoffman can play a loser better than anyone, and even when his loser occasionally wins through, as in **Arthur Penn's** magisterial *Little Big Man* (70), or **Sam Peckinpah's** ultra-violent *Straw Dogs* (71), we are left not with the taste of champagne, but the taste of bitter aloes. In recent years Hoffman seems to have lost his way a little, and has fallen back on his reputation to the extent that he has chosen to appear in one or two no doubt lucrative pot-boilers, including **Stephen Frears's** *Hero* (92) and **Wolfgang Petersen's** *Outbreak* (95). However, in Michael Corrente's *American Buffalo* (96) he did partially redeem himself and his seriousness in the face of Hollywood madness should carry him triumphantly through to a critically acclaimed dotage.

OTHER KEY FILMS: *Papillon* (73); *Lenny* (74); *All The President's Men* (76); *Marathon Man* (76); *Agatha* (79); *Kramer Vs. Kramer* (79); *Death Of A Salesman* [TVM] (85); *Family Business* (89); *Billy Bathgate* (91); *Hook* (91); *Sleepers* (96); *Mad City* (97); *Sphere* (98); *Messenger: The Story Of Joan Of Arc* (99); *Cosm* (00)

KEY LINE:

'Mrs Robinson, you're trying to seduce me, aren't you?' [*The Graduate*]

Hold

The re-use of a single, photographed image, in cartoon animation, to suggest a **freeze-frame** effect on the screen.

Holden, William

After changing his name from William Beedle Jr (for obvious reasons), Holden first made his mark in Rouben Mamoulian's *Golden Boy* (39). Always destined for virile parts due to his peculiarly American brand of masculine good looks, Holden gradually drank himself to death — killing, in the process, the innocent bystander at one of his numerous car accidents. Holden seemed to coast along for much of the time in his movies, but when good directors did get hold of him, and when they succeeded in galvanising him out of his lethargy, he could prove excellent, as with his Joe Gillis in **Billy Wilder's** *Sunset Boulevard* (50), his Sefton in the same director's *Stalag 17* (53), and his Pike Bishop in **Sam Peckinpah's** *The Wild Bunch* (69). It was in this role that for the first and only time Holden allowed his personal despair to show through.

OTHER KEY FILMS: *Born Yesterday* (50); *Union Station* (50); *Escape From Fort Bravo* (53); *The Country Girl* (54); *Sabrina* (54); *Picnic* (55); *Love Is A Many Splendored Thing* (55); *The Bridge On The River Kwai* (57); *The Horse Soldiers* (59); *Network* (76); *Fedora* (78)

Hollywood

Now a euphemism for everything connected with commercial cinema, Hollywood was a forgotten suburb of Los Angeles when it was discovered, around 1913, by **Cecil B DeMille** and Oscar C Apfel, during a location scouting expedition for *The Squaw Man*. It was instantly deemed preferable to New York on account of the cheap labour, the almost continuous sunshine, and the privacy aspect, which, given its later nickname of Sodom-by-the-Sea, may have weighed heavily on the minds of its originators.

KEY LINE:

'…it always was a town where everybody is Cinderella and is terrified that twelve o'clock is going to strike, and eventually it does.' [Screenwriter Arthur Laurents, who numbered **Alfred Hitchcock's** *Rope* (48) amongst his numerous writing credits]

Hollywood Ten/ Hollywood Blacklist, The

The first ten unfortunate victims of Senator Joe McCarthy's anti-communist witch-hunt, which he conducted under the aegis of the House Committee on Un-American Activities during the period 1947-57, have now become known as The Hollywood Ten. Prominent members of the Hollywood film community were invited to name names before the committee or face blacklisting themselves, and the consequent loss of their ability to find jobs within the film industry. The complete list of the Hollywood Ten: Alvah Bessie, Herbert Biberman, Lester Cole, **Edward Dmytryk**, Ring Lardner Jr, John Howard Lawson, Albert Maltz, Samuel Ornitz, Adrian Scott and Dalton Trumbo.

Hope, Bob

Is Hope really funny? Or do we simply laugh at him because we are expected to do so? There is an element of the after-dinner speaker in all his performances, testing out that last tentative joke for the possibility that it might elicit one final chortle. Hope, among all screen comedians, is the most obvious product of the 'one created by the many' — he is the gagman of the nineteenth tee, a placator of the middle classes and the comforting presence that persuades us that niceness comes rewarded with riches, and that studied modesty (disguised by braggadocio) will bring with it the laurels and the reassurances of a ripe old age. That said, his is an essentially innocent and pain-free talent, best summed up in his most successful screen performance, as Wallie Campbell in Elliott Nugent's *The Cat And The Canary* (39).

OTHER KEY FILMS: *Road To Singapore* (40); *Road To Zanzibar* (41); *Caught In The Draft* (41); *Road To Morocco* (42); *Road To Utopia* (45); *Road To Rio* (47); *The Paleface* (48); *Fancy Pants* (50); *Road To Bali* (52); *The Facts Of Life* (60); *Critic's Choice* (63)

Hopkins, Anthony

It is hard to see the later, confident Hopkins in the early, ersatz **James Bond** clone he played in Etienne Perier's *When Eight Bells Toll* (71), but the nervous intensity of his acting showed through even then, as if this elusive man always had something better to do, some other place to go, and he was aching to get on with it despite the expectations of his foolish audience. We now know that his impatience was for the stardom he knew he merited (an instinctive perhaps rather than a studied haste), and that what we had allowed ourselves to miss in his youth, we would belatedly have to make up for in his prime. For Hopkins *is* the finest British screen actor of his generation, and his subtlety and dedication to his craft should serve as lessons to the short-shrifters and the ease-merchants who make up such a large proportion of the present-day generation of wannabes. Hopkins's Captain Bligh in Roger Donaldson's *The Bounty* (84) is the genuine article – a vulnerable, self-made man with homoerotic tendencies who is entirely of his time, not ours, and who is only understandable in that context. In **James Ivory's** *Howards End* (92), Hopkins was a high Victorian monolith washed up

in Edwardian England, and in the same director's *Remains Of The Day* (93) he played a man so straightened by his sense of duty that love, even the very possibility of it, remains utterly and disastrously marginalised. **Richard Attenborough's** *Shadowlands* (93) leavened the post-Edwardian despair that Hopkins controls so well, and allowed a fleeting and shocking happiness to a man nominally incapable of even comprehending it. Now that he is in such demand in Hollywood, following his bravura performances as Hannibal Lecter in **Jonathan Demme's** *Silence Of The Lambs* (91) and **Ridley Scott's** *Hannibal* (01), it is comforting to know that habit, together with an ingrained artistic integrity, will simply not allow him to give of anything but his best. <u>Note for Film Buffs</u>: Hopkins is actually just *younger* than **Dustin Hoffman**.

OTHER KEY FILMS: *The Lion In Winter* (68); *The Looking Glass War* (70); *A Doll's House* (73); *Magic* (78); *The Elephant Man* (80); *The Good Father* (86); *Blunt* (86); *84 Charing Cross Road* (87); *Desperate Hours* (90); *Legends Of The Fall* (94); *Nixon* (95); *Surviving Picasso* (96); *Amistad* (97); *The Edge* (97); *The Mask Of Zorro* (98); *Instinct* (99); *Titus* (99); *Mission: Impossible 2* (00); *Hearts in Atlantis* (01); *The Devil and Daniel Webster* (01)

KEY LINE:
'A census taker once tried to test me. I ate his liver with some fava beans and a nice Chianti.' [*The Silence Of The Lambs*]

Hopper, Dennis

Hardly the great figure he has sometimes been portrayed as, though certainly an interesting one – if only because he has survived a level of substance and alcohol abuse that has already dispatched those of his generation with somewhat lesser constitutions – Hopper's main claim to fame lies in his early link with **James Dean** in **Nicholas Ray's** *Rebel Without A Cause* (55) and **George Stevens's** *Giant* (56), and for his direction of the cult, though ultimately disappointing, *Easy Rider* (69). When not too vociferously **method**-acting, he has turned in some fine performances, particularly in **David Lynch's** *Blue Velvet* (86) and Tony Scott's *True Romance* (93). He has also directed a *film noir* thriller, *The Hot Spot* (90), which proved very good indeed. See **Overshoot** for Hopper's *The Last Movie* (71)

OTHER KEY FILMS: *True Grit* (69); *The American Friend* (77); *Apocalypse Now* (79); *Out Of The Blue* (80); *Rumble Fish* (83); *Paris Trout* (91); *Red Rock West* (93); *Waterworld* (95); *The Source* [doc.] (99); *Bad City Blues* (99); *The Spreading Ground* (00); *Luck Of The Draw* (00); *Knockaround Guys* (01)

Anthony Hopkins as repressed butler, Stevens, alongside Emma Thompson's Miss Kenton, in James Ivory's The Remains Of The Day *(93)*

Hopper, Hedda

Louella Parsons's bitter opponent in the Hollywood gossip-columnist wars of the 1930s and 1940s, Hopper was a King- and Queen-maker at a time when the Los Angeles film community was still ruled by Kings and Queens. Mistress of the celebrity scoop, Hopper dished the dirt – or withheld it, when it suited her – on just about every major Hollywood scandal of her thirty-year reign. Her son, William Hopper, later became famous as Detective Paul Drake in TV's Perry Mason series.

Best Horror Films

Roy Ward Black's *Asylum* (72); **Roger Corman's** *The Mask Of The Red Death* (64); **Wes Craven's** *A Nightmare On Elm Street* (84); **Jonathan Demme's** *Silence Of The Lambs* (91); Ruggiero Deodato's *Cannibal Holocaust* (80); **Samuel Fuller's** *Shock Corridor* (63); Robin Hardy's *The Wicker Man* (73); **Werner Herzog's** *Nosferatu The Vampyre* (79); **Alfred Hitchcock's** *Psycho* (60) and *The Birds* (63); **Stanley Kubrick's** *The Shining* (80); F W Murnau's *Nosferatu* (21); **Roman Polanski's** *Repulsion* (65) and *Rosemary's Baby* (68); **Sam Raimi's** *Evil Dead* (82); George A Romero's *The Night Of The Living Dead* (68); Kaneto Shindo's *Onibaba* (64); **Jacques Tourneur's** *Cat People* (42) and *Curse Of The Demon* [a.k.a. *Night of the Demon*] (57); **Robert Wiene's** *The Cabinet Of Dr Caligari* (19)

Horse

A racking device, used in the editing room, to prepare reels of film for error-free winding through a viewing system.

Horse Opera

Hollywood jargon for a **Western** or cowboy film.

Hoskins, Bob

A former Covent Garden porter, Hoskins is at his best playing raw, emotional men thrown into situations where they find themselves suddenly out of their depth. His gang boss, Harold, in John Mackenzie's recently re-released *The Long Good Friday* (80) is a case in point, as is his towering performance as the lovesick petty crook in **Neil Jordan's** *Mona Lisa* (86). Hoskins had a surprise success in **Robert Zemeckis's** *Who Framed Roger Rabbit* (88), which had the virtue of making him a rich man overnight, as he received a percentage

cut. Since then his roles have varied alarmingly in quality, but it is unlikely that we have heard the last of his talent.

OTHER KEY FILMS: *The Cotton Club* (84); *Brazil* (85); *The Lonely Passion Of Judith Hearne* (88); *Shattered* (91); *Nixon* (95); *Cousin Bette* (98); *Felicia's Journey* (99); *Enemy At The Gates* (01); *The Sleeping Dictionary* (01)

Hot Frame

A deliberately over-exposed frame, which appears at the beginning or end of a particular shot, and which accurately delineates that shot for later editing and sound synchronisation.

Hot Head

The A & C Hot Head was the first generation of really reliable permanent **pan-and-tilt heads** for the remote control of big movie cameras. Capable of taking even the heaviest 35mm 1,000ft magazine cameras, with all the **zoom** focus, **iris** and camera turnover controls slaved up to the camera head, it was operated remotely by the **focus puller**. See **Heden Controls**

Hot Splice

The permanent bonding together of two pieces of film by means of glue, the scraping off of a section of the emulsion, and pressure exerted by a splicing machine. See **Tape Splicing**

Hot Splicer

A machine which heats the glue used in **hot splicing**, while at the same time exerting pressure on the spliced area, thus ensuring a permanent seal.

Hot Spot

The effect too much lighting has on a particular section of the photographed set, a hot spot will later show up in the form of an over-exposed area of film during projection.

Howard, Leslie

Howard was the man who gave **Humphrey Bogart** his first big screen break by insisting that he play the part of Duke Mantee in Archie Mayo's *Petrified Forest* (36). It is perhaps hard for present-day audiences to appreciate that an actor as elusive as Howard ever had that sort of influence in Hollywood, but his was an indefinable talent, perfect for the asexual and somewhat fatalistic version of romantic idealism that flourished, very briefly, in the inter-war years. This was encapsulated best by his Holger Brandt in

165

Gregory Ratoff's *Intermezzo: A Love Story* (39), and by his brief appearance as Philip Armstrong Scott (shades of the even more fatalistic Robert Falcon Scott?) in **Michael Powell's** *The 49th Parallel* (41). Howard played passive, end-of-empire men, and he would have made a most marvellous Sir Edward Leithen if John Buchan's Leithen books had ever come to be filmed. His Ashley Wilkes in **Victor Fleming's** *Gone With The Wind* (39), so often criticised in favour of **Clark Gable's** more virile, thrusting Rhett Butler, is a pretty much perfect rendition of the lost, probably apocryphal spirit of the American South, and it is entirely fitting that Scarlett O'Hara should be idealistically attached to him, while being not so much wooed as ravished by the newly anti-heroic future incarnated by Gable. Howard died in 1943, shot down by the Nazis while travelling by air from Lisbon to London – while hesitating to call this a fitting end for such an elusive man, one is nonetheless forced to accord a measure of appropriateness to the manner of his leaving.

OTHER KEY FILMS: *Berkeley Square* (33); *The Lady Is Willing* (34); *Of Human Bondage* (34); *The Scarlet Pimpernel* (35); *Pygmalion* (38); *Pimpernel Smith* (41); *The First Of The Few* (42)

Howard, Ron

A former child star and veteran of such TV classics as *Happy Days* and *The Andy Griffith Show*, Howard found his epiphany in **George Lucas's** *American Graffiti* (73) as Steve, but he has since given up acting in favour of becoming a highly bankable director with a penchant for one-word movie titles. *Splash* (84), which was an adult breakthrough for both **Disney** and Howard himself, was followed by the slightly sickly *Cocoon* (85). Howard redeemed himself, however, with *Willow* (88), followed by the very exciting *Backdraft* (91). His best film to date has been *Apollo 13* (95), and if there were still a studio system, it would be correct to say that Howard is the perfect encapsulation of it. But there isn't. So he isn't.

OTHER KEY FILMS: *Parenthood* (89); *Far And Away* (92); *The Paper* (94); *EdTV* (99); *How The Grinch Stole Christmas* (00)

Howard, Trevor

Howard came from another generation entirely than his partial namesake, **Leslie Howard**, a generation that grew up in the shadow of England's bitter victory in the First World War. And it showed. Howard was a tougher customer altogether, a man whom one imagined *doing*

things, rather than passively contemplating the past. After being wounded in action in 1943, he was taken up by director **Carol Reed** for a small part in *The Way Ahead* (44), and it is somewhat miraculous to see him so quickly transformed into the confident Alec Harvey, in **David Lean's** *Brief Encounter* (45). He was barely thirty at the time (though he looked much older) but he had already formed the exact persona he was to inhabit in the ensuing forty-two years. Reed understood Howard better than any other director he worked with, and it is for his role as Major Calloway in Reed's *The Third Man* (49) that Howard will probably be best remembered, although his most complex and satisfying performance for Reed came later, as Peter Willems in *Outcast Of The Islands* (51). Howard's late-career films, excellent though they are, cannot stand comparison with those of his prime.

OTHER KEY FILMS: *Passionate Friends* (48); *The Golden Salamander* (49); *Odette* (50); *The Gift Horse* (52); *The Heart Of The Matter* (53); *The Roots Of Heaven* (58); *Sons And Lovers* (60); *Mutiny On The Bounty* (62); *Von Ryan's Express* (65); *The Charge Of The Light Brigade* (68); *Ryan's Daughter* (70); *Kidnapped* (71); *The Offence* (73); *Conduct Unbecoming* (75); *Sir Henry At Rawlinson End* (80); *White Mischief* (87)

KEY LINE:

'Death is at the bottom of everything, Martins. Leave death to the professionals.' [Howard to **Joseph Cotten** in *The Third Man*]

Howe, James Wong

One of Hollywood's greatest cinematographers (he first started work in **Cecil B DeMille's** cutting room in 1917), Howe undoubtedly influenced the look of **Orson Welles's** *Citizen Kane* (41) with his extraordinarily expressive camerawork on William K Howard's similarly themed *The Power And The Glory* (33). Howe's mastery of contrast and movement was also wonderfully evident in Jack Conway's *Viva Villa!* (34), but it was only later, with Robert Rossen's *Body And Soul* (47), **Alexander Mackendrick's** *The Sweet Smell Of Success* (57) and **Martin Ritt's** *Hud* (63), that his total mastery of the black-and-white medium became apparent.

OTHER KEY FILMS: W S Van Dyke's *The Thin Man* (34); John Cromwell's *The Prisoner Of Zenda* (37) and *Algiers* (38); **William Dieterle's** *Dr. Ehrlich's Magic Bullet* (40); **Sam Wood's** *Kings Row* (42); Daniel Mann's *The Rose Tattoo* (55); Joshua Logan's *Picnic* (56); Martin Ritt's *Hombre* (67)

HUAC
See **Hollywood Ten**

Hudson, Rock

Hudson gave every appearance of being heterosexual beefcake personified, a fact made all the more poignant by his forcibly unacknowledged homosexuality (except within the closed Hollywood film community) and by his death in 1985, bravely if belatedly acknowledged, from the AIDS virus. Given his physical qualifications as a heart-throb, Hudson developed into a better actor than he had any right to be given Hollywood's inevitable pigeon-holing of his talents. He predated **Randolph Scott** as a sensitive **Budd Boetticher** hero in *Seminole* (53); and **Douglas Sirk**, who had directed him in a bit part in *Has Anybody Seen My Gal?* (52), decided that there was something more than pure beefcake in this 6ft 4in hunk, and went on to prove so in the quartet of high-quality melodramas that were to make Hudson's name – *Magnificent Obsession* (54), *All That Heaven Allows* (55), *Written On The Wind* (56) and *The Tarnished Angels* (58). Other excellent Hudson roles came as Bick Benedict in **George Stevens's** *Giant* (56), and later as Antiochus 'Tony' Wilson in **John Frankenheimer's** underrated *Seconds* (66).
OTHER KEY FILMS: *Winchester '73* (50); *Bend Of The River* (52); *A Farewell To Arms* (58); *Pillow Talk* (59); *Blindfold* (66); *Tobruk* (67); *Ice Station Zebra* (68); *The Undefeated* (69)

Hughes, Howard

A true eccentric in later life, Hughes exhibited, from his very first venture into film production with Lewis Milestone's *Two Arabian Knights* (27), a compulsive need for control. The older he got, the more inspired by his actresses and his toys and his dreams did he become, culminating in the heady and machiavellian saga of *The Outlaw* (40–46) in which his obsession for both the physical and the metaphysical dimensions of **Jane Russell's** cleavage took on something of an endearingly epic quality. Hughes was the reluctant hedonist personified, and he came to represent the quintessence of an America largely unscathed by two world wars and which had come to believe that money and the convulsive spending of it were sufficient and valid compensations for vacuity. Almost despite himself, Hughes encouraged the talents of others, and it is for this, as well as for his extraordinary life, that he should be remembered.
OTHER KEY FILMS: *Hell's Angels* (30); Lewis Milestone's *The Front Page* (31); **Howard Hawks's** *Scarface* (32); **Victor Fleming's** *Bombshell* (33); **Don Siegel's** *The Big Steal* (49); John Cromwell's *The Racket* (51); **Josef von Sternberg's** *Jet Pilot* (51) and *Macao* (52); **Nicholas Ray's** *Flying Leathernecks* (51); **John Farrow's** *His Kind Of Woman* (51); **Otto Preminger's** *Angel Face* (52)

Huppert, Isabelle

An actress like Huppert would be impossible in the US, for she comfortably spans both extremes of the commercial and the *outré* in films as disparate as **Claude Chabrol's** *Violette Nozière* (78) and **Jean-Luc Godard's** *Sauve Qui Peut* (80). She first made her mark in Bertrand Blier's *Les Valseuses* (71), and it is arguable that her films as a teenager and as a young woman, up to and including Claude Goretta's *The Lacemaker* (76), were her best, in that she was so astonishingly confident and evocative an actress so early in her career. Of her later films, Maurice Pialat's *Loulou* (80), in which she played the bourgeoise to **Gérard Depardieu's** *rustre*, is perhaps the highlight, but she was characteristically excellent in **Bertrand Tavernier's** *Coup De Torchon* (81), **Paul Cox's** *Cactus* (86) and **Hal Hartley's** *Amateur* (94).
OTHER KEY FILMS: *César Et Rosalie* (72); *Glissements Progressifs Du Plaisir* (74); *Le Juge Et L'Assassin* (76); *Heaven's Gate* (80); *La Truite* (82); *La Femme De Mon Pote* (83); *Madame Bovary* (91); *Elective Affinities* (96); *La Vie Moderne* (99); *Clara* (00); *La Pianiste* (01)

Hurt, John

John Hurt is an actor whose face has corrugated and whose voice has coarsened in recent years, taking on something of the quality of a British version of France's Philippe Léotard (whom in many ways he resembles). Hurt, at his best, suggests a mixture of enlightened irony and knowing perverseness, aspects which were best used by **Stephen Frears** in *The Hit* (84) and by Michael Caton-Jones's inspired casting of him as Stephen Ward in *Scandal* (89). Richard Kwietniowski's *Love And Death On Long Island* (97) has revived what had begun to seem (outside television, at least) a somewhat moribund career, and his recent outing as Dr Iannis in John Madden's *Captain Corelli's Mandolin* (01) has brought him rightfully back to the forefront of character acting.
OTHER KEY FILMS: *A Man For All Seasons* (66); *10 Rillington Place* (71); *The Disappearance* (77); *Midnight Express* (78); *Alien* (79); *The Elephant Man* (80); *Heaven's Gate* (80); *The*

167

Osterman Weekend (83); *Champions* (84); *1984* (84); *White Mischief* (87); *The Field* (90); *Contact* (97); *The Commissioner* (98); *New Blood* (99); *Lost Souls* (00); *Tabloid* (01); *Harry Potter And The Philosopher's Stone* (01)

Hurt, William

Hurt has never fulfilled the potential so many were so keen to see in him during the 1980s, and this is because his strangely passive persona is such a dominant one, almost as though he believed that things should happen to him rather than that he must engender them himself. The majority of his best parts came early in his career, with **Ken Russell's** oddly compulsive *Altered States* (80) and **Lawrence Kasdan's** immaculate *Body Heat* (81) (which still thrills with its bravura confidence) and in which Hurt reached the apogee of his rather masochistic self-regard. He was good, certainly, as Luis Molina in **Hector Babenco's** *Kiss Of The Spider Woman* (85), and fully deserved his **Oscar**, but he was already on his way to becoming too pernickety an actor, prey to odd tics and compulsive habits, and Kasdan's *Accidental Tourist* (88) seems perilously close to self-caricature. It would be nice to be proved wrong, for Hurt is an attractive, subtle actor, but one suspects he was unsuited or in some way unprepared for stardom when it came, and that celebrity eased him, very slightly, off track.

OTHER KEY FILMS: *Eyewitness* (81); *The Big Chill* (83); *Gorky Park* (83); *Children Of A Lesser God* (86); *Broadcast News* (87); *Alice* (90); *The Doctor* (91); *Until The End Of The World* (92); *Smoke* (95); *Jane Eyre* (96); *Lost In Space* (98); *Do Not Disturb* (99); *The Contaminated Man* (00)

Huston, Anjelica

Huston has grown with the years, her face maturing, her presence strengthening, and in this respect she resembles her father, **John Huston**, and her grandfather, **Walter Huston**, who both produced their best work in mid to later life. As Lilly Dillon, in **Stephen Frears's** *The Grifters* (90), Huston, with her frantic rejection of any signs of self-weakness, beautifully complemented her earlier performance in John Huston's *The Dead* (87), in which she was all vulnerability, but distant, as if her husband, Donal McCann, had been worshipping a statue for all the years he had so misjudged her. Huston is the sort of actress writers should be writing fresh material for, not wasting their time trying to lever her into existing vehicles that may not suit her abilities.

OTHER KEY FILMS: *A Walk With Love And Death* (69); *The Postman Always Rings Twice* (81); *Prizzi's Honor* (85); *Gardens Of Stone* (87); *A Handful Of Dust* (88); *Mr North* (88); *Crimes And Misdemeanors* (89); *Enemies, A Love Story* (89); *The Witches* (90); *Manhattan Murder Mystery* (93); *The Crossing Guard* (95); *Phoenix* (98); *The Golden Bowl* (00)

Huston, John

Huston engenders mixed emotions in just about anyone brave enough to take a view on him – he has been venerated, bitched about, envied by those of lesser talent, and stabbed in the back by the very people who should have been most supportive of him. Yet even though the work, the intelligence, and the paradoxical manifestations of vainglory remain, it is still hard to decide if he is a major artist or merely a talented dilettante who found that cinema was a convenient outlet for a creative energy that could just as well have chosen any one of a dozen other paths for its fulfilment. And yet there are so many wonderful films including *The Maltese Falcon* (41), in which **Bogart** is recognisably Bogart for the first time. The war documentaries followed, a serious project to which he devoted three of the most creative years of his life – and then *The Treasure Of The Sierra Madre* (47) and *Key Largo* (48), both films dealing with men forced out of their normal rut and faced with the nightmare of moral choice. Huston's inspired *The Asphalt Jungle* (50) was the film which finally burst the glamorous balloon of the major crime heist to show the vulnerability beneath the tough outer sleeve of its protagonists. His later masterpieces, *The Misfits* (61), *Night Of The Iguana* (64) and *Fat City* (71), downgrade plot in favour of characterisation, and his people, even if they don't suffer fundamental change by the end of the film, are at least conscious of their humanity, and of the fact that, unlike Bogart's Fred C Dobbs in *The Treasure Of The Sierra Madre*, they can no longer make it on their own. Huston was a fine filmmaker, literate, adventurous and moral, who sometimes achieved, and this is no mean feat, the semblance of an enlightened understanding.
See **Heartstopping Moments**

OTHER KEY FILMS: *We Were Strangers* (49); *The Red Badge Of Courage* (51); *The African Queen* (51); *Moulin Rouge* (52); *Beat The Devil* (54); *Moby Dick* (56); *Heaven Knows, Mr Allison* (57); *Reflections In A Golden Eye* (67); *The Man Who Would Be King* (75); *Wise Blood* (79); *Under The Volcano* (84); *Prizzi's Honor* (85); *The Dead* (87)

KEY LINE:
'John Huston was a very interesting man. He could recite Shakespeare, the whole of Shakespeare, when he had a few drinks. I knew all of his wives. If I could live it all over again, I would like to live his life.' [Screenwriter Curt Siodmak, brother of director **Robert Siodmak**, on his friendship with Huston. See also **Humphrey Bogart**]

Huston, Walter

Walter Huston (the father of **John Huston**) was one of the finest screen actors of his or any other generation, and it is astonishing to realise that he only starred in his first feature film at the age of forty-six, after spending the previous twenty-five years on the stage and in vaudeville. To watch him enter into a part and then allow it to take him over, as with the elusively simple Sam Dodsworth in **William Wyler's** *Dodsworth* (36), or the wise escaped convict in **Jean Renoir's** *Swamp Water* (41), or as the compulsive but generous Howard in his son's *The Treasure Of The Sierra Madre* (48), is to see a master of instinctive, intelligent acting working at the peak of his craft. Even in such heady oddities as **Josef von Sternberg's** *The Shanghai Gesture* (41) and **Howard Hughes's** *The Outlaw* (47), Huston towers sanely over his often hysterically overacting counterparts.

OTHER KEY FILMS: *The Virginian* (29); *Abraham Lincoln* (30); *Rain* (32); *Gabriel Over The White House* (33); *Rhodes* (36); *The Light That Failed* (40); *Edge Of Darkness* (43); *Dragonwyck* (46); *Duel In The Sun* (47); *Summer Holiday* (48); *The Furies* (50)

Hype

The overblown publicity sometimes used to pre-sell the idea of a film before its release. Exaggeration and hyperbole are the stock-in-trade of the studio publicist, and audiences are inured to, while still retaining their capacity to be amused by, the sorts of spiel customarily used to foist often forgettable films onto a paying public. 'In Space, No One Can Hear You Scream'; 'The Greatest Story Ever Told'; 'The Most Exciting Adventure In A Million Years' – the words are interchangeable, but their effect, when they work, is akin to the hysterical crowd warm-up before the night's big boxing match.

Hyperfocal Distance

The point at which the first object comes into focus when a lens is focused at infinity.

Hypergonar

The anamorphic lens invented by Henri Chrétien in 1927 that was later used as part of the image distortion and subsequent rectification principle behind the **CinemaScope** process.

Hyphenates

Hollywood slang for the assumption by one person of numerous creative roles during the making of a film, necessitating the frequent use of a hyphen. One thinks, for instance of **Clint Eastwood**, the actor-producer-director of *Unforgiven* (92), or of **Jacques Tati**, actor-writer-director of *Mon Oncle* (56).

169

IAIP

Acronym for the International Association of Independent Producers, an association which aims to bring together independent filmmakers of all persuasions and all nationalities for creative and cross-collaborative purposes.

IATSE

Acronym for the International Alliance of Theatrical and Stage Employees, a US/Canadian-based union which acts for the cinema technicians, engineering crews and all support personnel involved in the production of motion pictures.

ICM

Acronym for International Creative Management, one of the foremost Hollywood agencies involved in the management, marketing and eventual syndication of individual and collective film talent. See **CAA**

IDHEC

Acronym for the Institut des Hautes Etudes Cinématographiques, an institution founded under the Pétain government in 1943, and responsible for the training of a large proportion of France's best filmmakers. In 1986 it was incorporated into a new organisation, the Institut de Formation et d'Enseignement pour les Métiers de l'Image et du Son (FEMIS).

Idiot Cards

See **Cue Card**

Idle, Eric

A founder member of the television comedy act Monty Python's Flying Circus, Idle is the blond one who talks thirteen to the dozen and starred, resplendent in a fake club blazer, in the famous 'nudge-nudge, wink-wink' sketch. He has done some movie work since the Pythons split up, most notably in Jonathan Lynn's *Nuns On The Run* (90) and Robert Young's *Splitting Heirs* (93), which he also wrote, but he is probably fated to be best remembered either singing in his reedy tenor about the glories of contraception in *Monty Python's The Meaning Of Life* (83), or otherwise hamming it up in the often surreal comic set pieces which differentiate the Pythons from the rest of the comic mob.

OTHER KEY FILMS: *And Now For Something Completely Different* (72); *Monty Python And The Holy Grail* (75); *Monty Python's Life Of Brian* (79); *Casper* (95); *The Wind In The Willows* (96); *Dudley Do-Right* (99); *102 Dalmatians* [voice over] (00)

Illumination

Any form of lighting strong enough to register on the emulsive surface of film stock.

ILM

Acronym for Industrial Light & Magic, the company set up in 1975 by **George Lucas,** ILM was responsible for creating, often from scratch, the special-effects processes used in, amongst others, the ***Star Wars*** series, *ET*, the *Indiana Jones* series, *Jurassic Park*, and a number of the ***Star Trek*** films.

Image

Image refers to the particular likeness chosen for photographic reproduction in either still or moving form. The quality of the image and its context within the work itself alters the viewer's normal perception to such an extent that the image takes on a more intense, concentrated quality than it would otherwise have. The power of this device has led to the frequent use of such images in artistic, educative and entertainment-oriented environments. Director **Josef von Sternberg**, for instance, honed **Marlene Dietrich**'s filmic image from the very beginning of their collaboration on *The Blue Angel* (30) to such an extent that she continued to use both his lighting techniques and his posing formula throughout the length of her sixty-year career.

Marlene Dietrich as Shanghai Lily – this iconic image was photographed by Don English during the filming of Josef von Sternberg's Shanghai Express *(32)*

Imax

Imax is the gargantuan wide-screen 70mm horizontal process unveiled at Expo 70 in Osaka, Japan, in 1970, following its initial development by William Shaw and P R Jones in Canada. Such a process incorporates an image projected and filmed at ten times the magnitude of a standard 35mm frame onto an immense curved screen fed by six separate soundtracks, and using a 'rolling loop' film movement. Ideal for showing natural events, catastrophes and large-scale animal life, Imax has proved an enduring hit with the thrill-seeking elements of the viewing public.

IMP

Acronym for the Independent Motion Picture Company, the precursor to **Universal**, and which **Carl Laemmle** founded in 1909 to challenge the perceived monopoly of the **Motion Picture Patents Company**. See **Thomas Alva Edison**

In-betweens

The transitional drawings, usually produced by apprentice animators, which fill in the gaps between major scenes in an animated sequence.

171

In Camera

'In camera' refers to either the full extent of a scene which is within the camera's purview, or to any process or special effect conducted within the camera itself which will ultimately affect the quality and content of the finished film.

Incident Light

The exact amount of light actually falling onto a subject, rather than the amount of light that the subject reflects back towards the camera.

Indie Movies

A long-established tradition of free-spirited and independent filmmaking, the making of Indie movies customarily takes place outside, or at the very least on the periphery, of the studio system. Benefits of this system include decreased costs, more artistic freedom, less outside interference, and the use of actors and actresses, crews and technicians, who are committed to the film rather than to its perceived effect upon their careers. Disadvantages include fewer distribution outlets, difficulties in the procurement of technical and special-effects equipment, and the reluctance of most punters even to conceive of going to a movie that does not have at least one star name on its billing.

Industrial Light & Magic

See **ILM**

Inferno

See **Soft Image**

Infinity

Not actually infinity, but simply the distance from the camera lens at which light appears parallel, thus obviating the need for any further focusing adjustment.

Infrared

Infrared is light beyond the effective range a normal camera can pick up. Infrared cameras are used to film sequences in which little or no outside illumination is present, but the quality is such that the results are rarely used in feature films — **special effects** techniques are usually brought into play instead, to suggest the use of infrared technology.

Ingénue

A female role that relies on youth and ingenuousness, rather than on skill and disingenuousness, for its effect. Notable examples might be **Marilyn** Monroe's early appearances as Miss Caswell, in **Joseph L Mankiewicz's** *All About Eve* (50) and as Angela Phinlay in **John Huston's** *The Asphalt Jungle* (50) — both roles relied on her inexperience as much as on her undoubted talent and sexual allure.

Ingram, Rex

The famous, visually innovative silent filmmaker who gave both **Rudolph Valentino** and **Ramon Novarro** their first big breaks, Ingram was the massively influential director of *The Four Horsemen Of The Apocalypse* (21), *The Prisoner Of Zenda* (22) and *Scaramouche* (23), as well as being the founder of the famous Victorine Studios in Nice. His later films came out under his own aegis, after a dispute with **MGM's Louis B Mayer**, who had refused to put Ingram in charge of *Ben-Hur* (26), which ended up being directed, very effectively, by Fred Niblo. Ingram gave up making films just after the coming of the sound era, citing, in explanation, his disgust at the venality and artistic philistinism of the Hollywood mafiosi.
OTHER KEY FILMS: *Trifling Women* (22); *Where The Pavement Ends* (23); *Mare Nostrum* (26); *The Magician* (26); *The Garden Of Allah* (27); *Baroud* (32)

Inker

The assistant animator or artist responsible for inking in the original **cell** drawings that the chief animator has already completed.

Inkies/Inky-dinky

Small, bright studio lamps, with a relatively low wattage.

In Phase

The equivalent of a horse being on the rein — in other words when all elements of the projection process are in synch, leading to the wobble-free exposure of each individual frame.

In Register

The correct positioning, or registering, of each individual frame so that they are **in phase**.

Insert

One shot, usually inserted within an existing scene, and used to illustrate a point or convey a piece of information that cannot otherwise be achieved — thus the brief shot of the brand name of a drink, a newspaper headline, or the apparently surreptitious emergence of a gun from a pocket.

Insert Stage
A dedicated studio area for the filming of **insert** shots.

INT
A screenplay notation indicating an interior, rather than an exterior, shot.

Integral Tripack
A particular form of colour film stock that incorporates three separate emulsive stages, each with a different degree of sensitivity.

Intensification
An artificial process in which the existing contrast captured on a piece of film can be deepened by the use of chemicals.

Intensity
The strength and illuminative power of a particular lighting source as measured in **candelas**.

Interchangeable Lenses
A series of lenses of varying focal lengths that can be changed as and when the camera operator sees fit.

Intercutting
See **Crosscutting**

Interlock
The exact synchronisation of any form of film reel with a soundtrack reel, ensuring that mouths, words and sounds coincide.

Intermittent Movement
The, to all intents and purposes, invisible stop-start process that goes on inside a movie camera or a projector and which ensures that each frame is momentarily stationary, in order to allow its correct exposure or projection.

International Association Of Independent Producers
See **IAIP**

International Creative Management
See **ICM**

Internegative
The original negative taken exclusively from a colour reversal film. All other negatives are known as duplicate colour negatives.

Interpositive
A particularly dense orange-coloured print used in the making of duplicate negatives.

Intertitle
The title cards used in silent films to indicate dialogue, etc.

Intervalometer
The mechanism used to set off the camera, at pre-ordained intervals, during **time-lapse photography**.

In The Can
Hollywood jargon for the completion of filming, or, alternatively, of a particular, self-contained section of a feature film or documentary.

Inverse-square Law
The ratio between diffracted light and the rapidly decreasing effect that such a light source has on a retreating object.

Invisible Cutting
Part of the art of **cutting on action**, which ensures that the audience are not overtly aware that cuts are going on, thus maintaining the continuity of a particular scene.

Invisible Splicing
The art of splicing one piece of film onto another without the join showing in any subsequent, projected action.

IPS
The inches-per-second measurement unit used in audio recording, and which has to be taken into account when recording speech (in which a slower speed may be used) and music (in which a considerably higher recording speed is necessary if true fidelity is to be achieved).

Iris
The diaphragm, or masking device, used to control the amount of light a camera lens receives. The invention of the iris has been attributed to director **D W Griffith** and his cinematographer, **Billy Bitzer**.

Iris-in/Iris-out
The use of a fan-like device that opens out from black to first reveal a scene, then closes again to black to end it – **Preston Sturges** often used the device to highlight the snappy, comedic aspects of his screwball comedies.

173

Irons, Jeremy

Irons is a master of inhibition, bringing to it all the subtlety and despair that the British class system can provide. However, this very talent seems to have limited the scope of his work, and one cannot fail to make the comparison with **Dirk Bogarde**, whom Irons somewhat resembles, but whose later range he has yet to emulate. Irons was excellent in **David Cronenberg's** *Dead Ringers* (88), although he failed to show us the full possibilities of conventional bourgeois passion in **Louis Malle's** sadly underrated *Damage* (92), leading one to question whether he isn't best suited to playing the warped outcasts of an established order, rather than the denizens of the established order itself. Born on the Isle of Wight (as was **Anthony Mingella**), Iron's islander mentality has not prevented his career from slowly moving from the distinctly artistic to the brazenly commercial – a shame, for Irons can be a consummate and edgy screen actor.

OTHER KEY FILMS: *The French Lieutenant's Woman* (81); *Moonlighting* (82); *The Mission* (86); *Reversal Of Fortune* (90); *Kafka* (91); *Waterland* (92); *Stealing Beauty* (96); *Lolita* (97); *The Man In The Iron Mask* (98); *Dungeons & Dragons* (00); *The Fourth Angel* (01); *Callas Forever* (01)

Ivory, James

For some reason the critics have always enjoyed slamming the Ivory/Ismail Merchant/**Ruth Prawer Jhabvala** triumvirate, but even a quick glance at Ivory's filmography will show that he is an unself-conscious director (along the lines of a **Henry King**) who, had he lived in the days of the great studios, would surely have turned out first-rate and highly literate commercial entertainment decade after decade. The fact that Ivory, with the help of his producer, Merchant, and their regular screenwriting partner, Jhabvala, have managed to finance and bring to fruition so many good films in the present anti-independent climate, is something of a small miracle. Ivory's best films came early, with *Shakespeare Wallah* (65), *Bombay Talkie* (70) and *Heat And Dust* (83), but of his later films, pick of the bunch is undoubtedly the masterly *Howards End* (92), closely followed by the equally well-made and impeccably acted *Remains Of The Day* (93). Ivory is that rarity among modern-day filmmakers – a man who plays to his strengths.

OTHER KEY FILMS: *The Wild Party* (75); *The Europeans* (79); *Quartet* (81); *The Bostonians* (84); *A Room With A View* (86); *Maurice* (87); *Jefferson In Paris* (95); *Surviving Picasso* (96); *A Soldier's Daughter Never Cries* (98); *The Golden Bowl* (00)

Jackson, Glenda

Now a sober and responsible UK Labour Party member of parliament, it is hard to believe that Jackson was once feted as a sex symbol. However, she certainly did exude a somewhat earthy sensuality in her first films, often quite literally, as, for example, when **Oliver Reed's** Gerald Crich ravished her Gudrun Brangwen in **Ken Russell's** *Women In Love* (69), with the mud from his father's grave still fresh on his hands. She went on to do further excellent work for Russell in *The Music Lovers* (71), but her finest and most sensitive performance came as Alex Greville in **John Schlesinger's** *Sunday Bloody Sunday* (71), one of the most literate and elegant films British cinema has ever produced. Jackson was a household name during the 1970s, taking parts, and a second **Oscar**, in Melvin Frank's *A Touch Of Class* (72) and **Michael Apted's** underrated *Triple Echo* (72), but she appeared to lose interest in acting during the 1980s, ending with a token appearance as Gudrun Brangwen's mother in Russell's *The Rainbow* (89) – D H Lawrence's precursor to *Women In Love* – and a lesser film in every way than its excellent, ground-breaking progenitor.

OTHER KEY FILMS: *The Marat-Sade* (67); *The Boy Friend* (71); *Mary Queen Of Scots* (71); *The Maids* (74); *Hedda* (75); *Stevie* (78); *The Return Of The Soldier* (81); *Turtle Diary* (85); *Doombeach* (90)

Jackson, Samuel L

Jackson had been in the business a long time before **Quentin Tarantino's** *Pulp Fiction* (94) shot the then forty-five-year-old former theatre star into the stratosphere – and to give Jackson credit, celebrity doesn't seem to have gone to his head. He was excellent in **Spike Lee's** *Jungle Fever* (91), and he can call upon a fine talent for offbeat comedy, as displayed in **Steve Buscemi's** *Trees Lounge* (96), to counteract his otherwise outstanding capacity for invoking menace. A stayer.

OTHER KEY FILMS: *Sea Of Love* (89); *Betsy's Wedding* (90); *Mo' Better Blues* (90); *GoodFellas* (90); *True Romance* (93); *Losing Isaiah* (95); *Hard Eight* (97); *Deep Blue Sea* (99); *Shaft* (00); *The Caveman's Valentine* (01)

KEY LINE:

'Oh I'm sorry. Did I break your concentration?' [Jackson to one of his victims in **Pulp Fiction**]

Jarman, Derek

A cheerfully iconoclastic product of the 1960s art scene, Jarman began his professional career set designing for **Ken Russell** on *The Devils* (71). His first feature, *Sebastiane* (75), was made on a shoestring budget and bears absolutely no resemblance whatsoever to the 1968 **Dirk Bogarde** vehicle of (roughly) the same name, apart, perhaps, from the sexual orientation of its leading men; the one proudly acknowledged; the other resolutely unacknowledged. A gay-rights activist who died from the AIDS virus in 1994, Jarman was a brave and intelligent maverick who had very little time for those who did not at least partially share the tenor of his personal and professional predilections.

His last full-length feature, *Blue* (93), was a meditation on AIDS, the colour blue, and on the dreadful paradox of an extraordinarily gifted visual artist gradually losing his sight.

OTHER KEY FILMS: *Jubilee* (78); *The Tempest* (79); *Caravaggio* (86); *The Last Of England* (87); *War Requiem* (89); *The Garden* (90); *Edward II* (91); *Wittgenstein* (93); *Glitterbug* [compilation of fragments from home movies] (94)

Jarmusch, Jim

Jarmusch looks a little like his films – individual, curious, otherworldly – and classes himself as a comedy writer rather than as the **avant-garde** director he is often taken for. Rigorously independent, he retains total control over his negatives, which include his breakthrough movie, *Stranger Than Paradise* (84), and the sublimely comic *Down By Law* (86), which introduced humorist **Roberto Benigni** to American audiences. Something of a loner himself, Jarmusch revels in the idiosyncrasies of alienation, and enjoys dropping visual and verbal quotes from his favourite directors inside the fabric of his films.

OTHER KEY FILMS: *Mystery Train* (89); *Night On Earth* (91); *Dead Man* (95); *Ghost Dog: The Way Of The Samurai* (99)

KEY LINE:

'I wanted to have always known him.' [Stephen Saban, about Jarmusch]

Jarre, Maurice

Jarre has to be considered one of the most successful of all screen composers, if only for his contribution to the films of **David Lean** – *Lawrence Of Arabia* (62), *Doctor Zhivago* (65), *Ryan's Daughter* (70) and *A Passage To India* (84) can all boast immaculate and often unnervingly intrusive Jarre scores. Noted for his inventive use of instrumentation and his subtly textured orchestrations, Jarre is equally at home composing for such cold-blooded commercial ventures as **Roger Vadim's** *Barbarella* (68) and **Clint Eastwood's** *Firefox* (82), as he is for more esoteric fare, such as **Volker Schlöndorff's** *The Tin Drum* (79) and **Peter Weir's** *The Year Of Living Dangerously* (83). He is the father of Jean-Michel Jarre, himself the ex-husband of **Charlotte Rampling** and master of city-centre laser lighting spectaculars – a true chip off the old block.

OTHER KEY FILMS: Serge Bourguignon's *Sundays And Cybèle* (62); **Georges Franju's** *Judex* (64); **John Frankenheimer's** *The Fixer* (68); **John Huston's** *The Man Who Would Be King* (75); **Peter Weir's** *Witness* (85) and *Dead Poet•¶s Society* (89);

Adrian Lyne's *Jacob's Ladder* (90); **Mike Figgis's** *Mr Jones* (93); **Michael Cimino's** *Sunchaser* (96); Hugh Hudson's *I Dreamed Of Africa* (00)

Jeanson, Henri

Jeanson, together with poet **Jacques Prévert**, was the power behind the words that gave the films in the French **Poetic Realism** tradition their peculiarly seductive style. Jeanson's greatest screenplays were for Julien Duvivier's *Pépé Le Moko* (37) and *Un Carnet De Bal* (37), and **Marcel Carné's** outstanding *Hôtel Du Nord* (38). Jeanson later went on to write a series of comedies and swashbucklers during the 1950s and 1960s, the best of which was Christian-Jaque's *Fanfan La Tulipe* (51), in which an athletic **Gérard Philipe** leaps gamely from pillar to post just nine years before his untimely death of a heart attack, aged thirty-seven.

OTHER KEY FILMS: Christian-Jaque's *Boule De Suif* (45); **René Clément's** *The Damned* (47)

Jelly

An abbreviation of the word 'gelatine', as used in the formation of film stock or in the construction of camera filters. Jelly can also refer to the screen placed in front of an arc lamp to soften its light.

Jenny

Hollywood film crew jargon for any sort of portable electric generator.

Jhabvala, Ruth Prawer

Regular scriptwriter for the producer/director team of Ismail Merchant and **James Ivory**, Jhabvala's finest script came, not unsurprisingly, from her own novel, *Heat And Dust* (83), although her scripts for *A Room With A View* (86) and *Howards End* (92) were her most successful in critical terms. *Heat and Dust* starred Greta Scacchi and **Julie Christie** as grandmother and granddaughter, both living out their lives in parallel, thanks to the almost novelistic magic of the narrative process she and Ivory chose to adopt. Jhabvala showed her keen sensitivity to nuance once again in her highly impressive script based on Kazuo Ishiguro's novel, *The Remains Of The Day* (93). The film is about Englishness, from a Japanese story, by an Indian producer, written by a Polish scriptwriter, directed by an American, with a Welshman in the lead part.

OTHER KEY FILMS: *Shakespeare Wallah* (65); *Bombay Talkie* (70); *Roseland* (77); *Hullabaloo Over Georgie And Bonnie's Pictures* (78); *The Bostonians* (84); *Jefferson In Paris* (95); *Surviving Picasso* (96); *A Soldier's Daughter Never Cries* (98); *The Golden Bowl* (00)

Johnson, Ben

An excellent character actor who left his lazy Oklahoman mark on virtually every film in which he ever acted (usually taking the nominal part of a Texan, for to this day few people in the US, let alone abroad, can readily locate Oklahoma on the map), Johnson was a **John Ford** protégé and one of the best natural horsemen the screen has ever seen. As an actor, he was possessed of a quiet, countryman's integrity that Ford used to best advantage in the last two films of his cavalry trilogy, *She Wore A Yellow Ribbon* (49) and *Rio Grande* (51). However, Johnson really came into his own when he was given the co-lead role, alongside Harry Carey Jr, in Ford's outstanding *Wagonmaster* (50). This was a film which benefited immeasurably from having no real stars among its cast list, and which is now rightly considered to be one of the finest of all the great director's **Westerns** (as well as being one of the closest to his heart). In later life Johnson became something of an iconic figure to directors such as **Sam Peckinpah** and **Peter Bogdanovich** who, along with **Lindsay Anderson**, did the most to protect Ford's posthumous reputation. Bogdanovich used Johnson to **Oscar**-winning effect as Sam The Lion, in *The Last Picture Show* (71), playing brilliantly on the instinctive sense of loss that Johnson brought to all his later roles.

OTHER KEY FILMS: *Three Godfathers* (49); *Shane* (53); *One-Eyed Jacks* (61); *Major Dundee* (65); *Will Penny* (68); *The Wild Bunch* (69); *The Undefeated* (69); *Chisum* (70); *The Getaway* (72); *Junior Bonner* (72); *The Sugarland Express* (74); *The Hunter* (80)

KEY LINE:
'Being crazy about a woman like her is always the right thing to do.' [Johnson to Timothy Bottoms in *The Last Picture Show*, about Ellen Burstyn's Lois Farrow]

Jolson, Al

Star of Alan Crosland's *The Jazz Singer* (27) – the first ever (part) talkie feature – Jolson was a master of music hall and revue, where he was renowned for his trademark 'black-face' routine. With his moribund career resuscitated due to *The Jazz Singer's* extraordinary success, he went on to star in a number of other musical films built around his powerful, cantor's voice, culminating in his very own **biopic**, Alfred E Green's *The Jolson Story* (46), for which he provided the songs, and Larry Park the histrionics. If Jolson nothing else, he certainly had energy.

OTHER KEY FILMS: *The Singing Fool* (28); *Hallelujah, I'm A Bum* (33); *Rose Of Washington Square* (39); *Swanee River* (40)
KEY LINE:
'Wait a minute! Wait a minute! You ain't heard nothin' yet!' [Jolson's catchphrase, or **shtick**, which he used in *The Jazz Singer*]

Jones, Jennifer

Jones was a true oddity. Her career was the product, not of any particular talent (although she had that too) but of a passion – the passion of **Gone With The Wind** producer **David O Selznick**. The passion, in its way, was fine (**Howard Hughes** entertained a similar one for **Jane Russell**), but in Selznick's case the passion gradually became an obsession that threatened to destroy them both – Jones attempted suicide on a number of occasions and Selznick's career limped into a neglected decline. And what came of it? Perhaps the most notorious film of the Selznick/Jones cycle is **King Vidor's** *Duel In The Sun* (46), in which Jones was inspirationally miscast – but then the film, too, was misguided, and became a success almost despite itself. One watches it today with a sort of awe that so much money and effort could have been spent on a project that so accurately mirrored, in psychological terms at least, the story-to-be of its star and of its producer. Jones's best role, in what was an exceedingly mixed career, came in **Michael Powell's** *Gone To Earth* (50), in which she played Hazel Woodus, a hunter's quarry (in this case **David Farrar's**) as if she were born for the part – which, in a way, she was.

OTHER KEY FILMS: *The Song Of Bernadette* (44); *Love Letters* (45); *Cluny Brown* (46); *Portrait Of Jenny* (49); *Madame Bovary* (49); *Carrie* (52); *Ruby Gentry* (53); *Beat The Devil* (54); *The Man In The Gray Flannel Suit* (56); *The Barretts Of Wimpole Street* (57); *A Farewell To Arms* (57)

Jones, Tommy Lee

An odd choice for stardom, Jones seems far too intelligent to have reached the heady Hollywood heights – he's quite simply a first-rate screen actor with an eye-catching (although hardly drop-dead gorgeous) face, who ploughed a lonely groove for upwards of twenty years in a succession of often very good TV movies. He appeared to have achieved a career breakthrough in **Michael Apted's** *Coal Miner's Daughter* (80), but it was only eleven years later, with his sizzling performance as Clay Shaw in **Oliver Stone's** *JFK* (91), that the Academy sat up and took notice of him. The part

177

of Deputy US Marshal Samuel Gerard, in Andrew Davis's *The Fugitive* (93) won him his best supporting actor **Oscar**, and levered him up (or down, depending on one's viewpoint) to such big-budget films as Joel Schumacher's *The Client* (94) and Barry Sonnenfeld's *Men In Black* (97). Catch him in **Tony Richardson's** *Blue Sky* (91) for a reminder of what we've lost.

OTHER KEY FILMS: *Rolling Thunder* (77); *Eyes Of Laura Mars* (78); *The River Rat* (84); *Stormy Monday* (88); *Natural Born Killers* (94); *Volcano* (97); *US Marshals* (98); *Space Cowboys* (00); *Rules Of Engagement* (00); *The Hunted* (01)

Jordan, Neil

One of the most interesting directors to work largely outside the Hollywood system, Jordan began strongly with *Angel* (82) (in which he first used actor Stephen Rae, now one of his regulars), and followed up with the challenging *The Company Of Wolves* (84), which divided the critics but worked wonderfully well on the screen. *Mona Lisa* (86) cemented his reputation, and *The Crying Game* (92) finally seduced Hollywood into making overtures, which Jordan responded to with *Interview With The Vampire* (94). Far more interesting was his 1991 film, *The Miracle*, in

which his obsession with identity, friendship and the intemperate morality of trust received full measure. His recent, underrated, *The End Of The Affair* (99), continues his preoccupation with the melancholy paradoxes inherent in moral choice.

OTHER KEY FILMS: *High Spirits* (88); *We're No Angels* (89); *Michael Collins* (96); *The Butcher Boy* (97); *In Dreams* (98)

Jouvet, Louis

Jouvet is one of the top ten screen actors who have ever lived, but his name is hardly known outside France except to the occasional wild-eyed film buff emerging from the depths of a Parisian flea-pit. Jouvet never rated film as he did theatre, but despite his devil-take-it attitude, he turned in four or five performances during the 1930s that are so majestic, so true, that any potential film actor or actress should be forced to watch them as part of their essential training. His greatest performance came as the Baron, in **Jean Renoir's** *Les Bas-Fonds* (36), a noble work, based on the writings of Maxim Gorky, but it remains a hard film to find, and potential aficionados will probably come across **Marcel Carné's** *Hôtel Du Nord* (38), Julien Duvivier's *La Fin Du Jour* (39) or **Henri-Georges**

Louis Jouvet as The Baron and Jean Gabin as Pepel in the famous snail sequence from Jean Renoir's Les Bas-Fonds *(36)*

Clouzot's *Quai Des Orfèvres* (47) with greater ease. Either way, they should endeavour to see the films in a cinema, as part of a director's season perhaps, rather than on the television.

OTHER KEY FILMS: *Topaze* (33); *La Kermesse Héroïque* (35); *Mister Flow* (35); *Mademoiselle Docteur* (36); *Un Carnet De Bal* (37); *Drôle De Drame* (37); *L'Alibi* (37); *La Marseillaise* (38); *Entrée Des Artistes* (38); *Le Drame De Shanghai* (38); *Volpone* (40); *Sérénade* (40); *Untel Père Et Fils* (40); *Un Revenant* (46); *Les Chouans* (46); *Entre Onze Heures Et Minuit* (48); *Retour À La Vie* (49); *Lady Paname* (49); *Miquette Et Sa Mère* (50); *Une Histoire D'Amour* (51)

Juicer

A juicer is the electrician in charge of the lighting arrangements on a film set.

Jump Cut

Much used in such French **avant-garde** films of the 1960s as **Jean-Luc Godard's** delightful *Une Femme Est Une Femme* (61) to suggest speed, nervous energy or a chic disregard for normal continuity, jump cuts are achieved by the removal of a portion of film from within a continuous shot. This leads to a jerky, spasmodic effect, akin to a person flashing, *Star Trek*-like, from one place to another with no intermediate staging. An alternative method to achieve the same effect consists of the camera being stopped, moved forward, and then restarted again closer to the subject.

Junge, Alfred

A great art designer, and the man who injected his trademark look of heightened romanticism into many of the best pre- and post-Second World War British films, most notably Robert Stevenson's *King Solomon's Mines* (37) and **Sam Wood's** *Goodbye Mr Chips* (39), Junge succeeded best of all in the extraordinary series of masterpieces he made with **Michael Powell** and **Emeric Pressburger**. These included *The Life And Death Of Colonel Blimp* (43), *A Canterbury Tale* (44), *I Know Where I'm Going* (45), *A Matter Of Life And Death* (46) and also the magnificent *Black Narcissus* (47), which was entirely shot at **Pinewood** and **Denham** studios, and in the

gardens of Leonard's Lee in Sussex, but which gave the impression of having been at least partly shot on location in Nepal. Junge is one of the hidden, faceless men of the cinema, without whose contribution the filmic world would be a very second-rate place indeed.

OTHER KEY FILMS: King Vidor's *The Citadel* (38); Richard Thorpe's *Ivanhoe* (52); **John Ford's** *Mogambo* (53)

Junior

A smaller 1,000 or 2,000 watt light, when compared to the more powerful **senior**.

Jurgens, Curt

Jurgens epitomised a desperate perversity on the screen, as if there were something not quite savoury beneath his smooth and handsome exterior – he was at his best in tense dramas, as men who have in some way been tricked out of what they feel to be their just deserts. He was, as such, perfectly cast in **Roger Vadim's** *And God Created Woman* (56) as **Brigitte Bardot's** frustrated older swain, Eric, and in **Nicholas Ray's** *Bitter Victory* (57) as a basically decent man warped by jealousy (shades of Macbeth), who conspires, in his madness, to bring down a better one.

OTHER KEY FILMS: *The Last Waltz* (53); *The Devil's General* (55); *The Enemy Below* (57); *The Inn Of The Sixth Happiness* (58); *Ferry To Hong Kong* (59); *Miracle Of The White Stallions* (63); *Lord Jim* (65); *Nicholas And Alexandra* (71); *The Spy Who Loved Me* (77)

Juvenile Lead

The expression 'juvenile lead' is considered pejorative now, not to say patronising, possibly on account of its unwelcome evocation of the outmoded stage practice of allowing older actors and actresses to pretend they are still aged between sixteen and twenty-five. Chirpy **Dick Powell** played the juvenile lead in a series of **Busby Berkeley** musicals until he was well into his thirties, thanks largely to a high tenor voice and a dimpled smile which he later discarded, to excellent effect, in a series of tough *film noir* movies, including **Edward Dmytryk's** *Murder My Sweet* (44) and *Cornered* (45). See **Ingénue**

179

Kael, Pauline

Notorious US film critic for the *New Yorker* magazine (68-91) who specialised in telling it as she saw it, Kael has unfortunately influenced many lesser critics who share neither her breadth of knowledge nor her mental acuity. Despite, or perhaps because of, her occasional lapses of critical taste (she 'pillified and villoried' **Orson Welles's** contribution to *Citizen Kane*, and refused even to acknowledge, let alone condone, the *auteur* theory) her reviews are always entertaining, if not quite as loftily literate as those of her eminent precursor, **James Agee**.

KEY LINE:

'The words "Kiss Kiss Bang Bang" which I saw on an Italian movie poster, are perhaps the briefest statement imaginable of the basic appeal of movies.' [Kael on where she got the name for her most famous book]

Karloff, Boris

Karloff was always the most human of monsters, a cricket-loving gentleman of the Raj who, by some extraordinary mixture of talent and serendipity, ended up in Hollywood playing ghouls, which, though terrifying, were at the same time perversely understandable. His monster, in **James Whale's** *Frankenstein* (31), was more victim than perpetrator, and the dignity inherent in Karloff's personality was beautifully brought out by **Peter Bogdanovich** in his debut film, *Targets* (68), in which the elderly horror actor offers himself in sacrifice to save the innocent victims of a demented sniper.

OTHER KEY FILMS: *The Prisoner* (23); *Man In The Saddle* (26); *The Criminal Code* (31); *The Man Who Dared* (32); *Scarface* (32); *The Mummy* (32); *The Old Dark House* (32); *The Ghoul* (33); *The Lost Patrol* (34); *The Raven* (35); *The Bride Of Frankenstein* (35); *Tower Of London* (39); *Devil's Island* (40); *The Body Snatcher* (45); *Bedlam* (46); *Corridors Of Blood* (62)

Kasdan, Lawrence

With a partial writing credit on **George Lucas's** *The Empire Strikes Back* (80) and *Return Of The Jedi* (83), and a full credit on **Steven Spielberg's** *Raiders Of The Lost Ark* (81), Kasdan could have happily sat back and watched the dollars roll in for any number of Hollywood script doctoring and screenwriting jobs. Following the success of his first feature, *Body Heat* (81), however, he chose the infinitely more frustrating director's path; successfully, in *The Big Chill* (83), worthily, in *Wyatt Earp* (94), and nobly, in *Grand Canyon* (91). His most enjoyable film is *The Accidental Tourist* (88), in which he brings to life the characters of best-selling novelist, Anne Tyler. The film was a success, despite the mannered, but for once forgivable, presence of Geena Davis.

OTHER KEY FILMS: *Silverado* (85); *I Love You To Death* (90); *French Kiss* (95); *Mumford* (99)

Katzenberg, Jeffrey

See **DreamWorks SKG**

Kaurismäki, Aki and Mika

An oddball pair of brothers who have (double-handedly?) placed Finland back on the cinematic map, Aki and Mika began as iconoclasts and have since become cosy members of the very club they started out by satirising in such films as Mika's *The Clan* (84) and Aki's *Crime And Punishment* (83), *Ariel* (89), *Match Factory Girl* (90), *I Hired A Contract Killer* (90) *and Leningrad Cowboys Go America* (90). Film buffs extraordinaire, the brothers run their own Midnight Sun film festival, and are doyens of a chain of art-house movie theatres in Helsinki.

OTHER KEY FILMS: Aki's *Calamari Union* (85); *Hamlet Gets Business* (87); *Bohemian Life* (92); *Tatjana* (94); and Mika's *Zombie And The Ghost Train* (91); *Drifting Clouds* (96); *LA Without A Map* (98); *Julia* (99); *Highway Society* (01)

Kaye, Danny

It is hard to like Kaye's screen persona, even in retrospect, because it liked itself so much. A talented ex-vaudevillian, he chose his moment well and made the brief most of it. Norman McLeod's *The Secret Life Of Walter Mitty* (47) undoubtedly struck a chord with a public fed up with the mock reality of years of war newsreels and now wanting a real bite of ersatz Never Never land, but Thurber it certainly wasn't. Charles Vidor's *Hans Christian Andersen* (52), in which Kaye played the title role, is one of the worst examples ever of Hollywood's repellent desire to foment entertainment even to the brain-dead, and is the direct precursor to dreck such as **Carol Reed's** mind-numbingly trivial *Oliver!* (68). Enough said.

OTHER KEY FILMS: *Up In Arms* (44); *Wonder Man* (45); *A Song Is Born* (48); *The Inspector General* (49); *Knock On Wood* (54); *White Christmas* (54); *The Court Jester* (56); *Merry Andrew* (58)

KEY LINE:
'The pellet with the poison's in the vessel with the pestle. The chalice from the palace has the brew that's true.' [*The Court Jester*]

Kazan, Elia

With numerous Academy Awards under his belt, Kazan should have been the toast of Hollywood; instead, he became increasingly marginalised following his agreement to name names before Senator McCarthy's House Un-American Activities Committee [see **Hollywood Ten**]. Co-founder of the New York **Actors' Studio**, Kazan directed a series of critically acclaimed and commercially successful movies in the early 1950s, amongst which *Panic in the Streets* (50), *A Streetcar Named Desire* (51), *Viva Zapata!* (52) and *On The Waterfront* (54) stand out. He helped launch many careers, most notably that of **Marlon Brando** in *Streetcar*, **James Dean** in *East Of Eden* (55) and **Warren Beatty** in *Splendor In The Grass* (61). His forte was always in social realism, allied with a poetic nostalgia for a simpler time, and his later films suffer from the lapse into sentimentality that such a preoccupation can engender.

OTHER KEY FILMS: *Pinky* (49); *Man On A Tightrope* (53); *Baby Doll* (56); *A Face In The Crowd* (57); *America, America* (63); *The Arrangement* (69); *The Visitors* (72); *The Last Tycoon* (76)

Keaton, Buster

Joseph Francis Keaton vies with **Charlie Chaplin** and **W C Fields** as the greatest of all screen comedians, and one has only to look at a still of his face to be convinced that he held within himself the secret of disguising tragedy with farce. Only really recognised as a genius towards the end of his

181

Buster Keaton as Rollo Treadway, disguising tragedy with farce in The Navigator *(24), which he co-directed with Donald Crisp*

life, in the self-directed *The Playhouse* (21), *The Navigator* (24), *Sherlock Jr* and *The General* (27), Keaton lifted comedy to sublime levels of creativity. His mistake in abandoning his own production company, and the artistic freedom it guaranteed, for a contract with **MGM**, may now be seen as a tragedy as acute, in its way, as the massacre of **Orson Welles's** *The Magnificent Ambersons* (42) or the critical disregard which attended the first screening of **Charles Laughton's** masterpiece, *The Night Of The Hunter* (55). <u>Note for Film Buffs</u>: Watch out for a brief appearance by Keaton sitting around a table playing bridge at Norma Desmond's house in **Billy Wilder's** *Sunset Boulevard* (50).
OTHER KEY FILMS: *The Scarecrow* (20); *The Haunted House* (21); *The Boat* (21); *The Paleface* (21); *The Frozen North* (22); *Our Hospitality* (23); *Seven Chances* (25); *Go West* (25); *Battling Butler* (26); *The Cameraman* (28); *Spite Marriage* (29)

Keaton, Diane

Keaton's fashion statement (or rather lack of it) in **Woody Allen's** *Annie Hall* (77) started something of a trend, and for a brief moment during the late 1970s she seemed to encapsulate everything that the modern woman thought and represented. She still retains her mannerisms, but as with all fashions, Keaton has been left to tidy up the bricks of a career founded, not so much upon talent (although she has that), as upon a fundamental misunderstanding. The difficulty was that Keaton's persona in the Allen films was simply a female extension of the director's own, and it is only when she occasionally shook off the Allen mantle, as in **Francis Ford Coppola's** *The Godfather* trilogy (72-90), in **Richard Brooks's** grotesquely disturbing *Looking For Mr Goodbar* (77), and in **Warren Beatty's** *Reds* (81), that she began to reveal something of herself. In recent years she has joined the middle-aged 'Hollywood worthies' charivari – something of a tragedy when weighed against the bitter-edged performances she gave at her best.
OTHER KEY FILMS: *Play It Again Sam* (72); *Interiors* (78); *Manhattan* (79); *Shoot The Moon* (82); *The Little Drummer Girl* (83); *Mrs Soffel* (84); *Radio Days* (87); *Manhattan Murder Mystery* (93); *The First Wives Club* (96); *The Other Sister* (99); *Town And Country* (01); *Plan B* (01)

Keaton, Michael

A stylish and stylised actor who hits and misses the mark more often than most – a tribute to his capacity for taking risks, perhaps – Keaton's screen persona may best be summed up in the words

'sinister mischievousness'. Following his success in **Tim Burton's** *Beetlejuice* (88), he acted for the same director again in the excellent *Batman* (89), and for a heady moment he teetered somewhere near the top of the Hollywood heap, before collapsing back to a more apposite level with Ron Underwood's *Speechless* (94) and **Barbet Schroeder's** astonishingly bad *Desperate Measures* (98).
OTHER KEY FILMS: *Night Shift* (82); *Pacific Heights* (90); *Batman Returns* (92); *Much Ado About Nothing* (93); *Multiplicity* (96); *Jack Frost* (98); *Road To Glory* (00)

Keitel, Harvey

Yet another ex-marine actor (see **Steve McQueen** and **Lee Marvin**), live-wire Keitel worked for **Martin Scorsese** in *Mean Streets* (73) and *Taxi Driver* (76), before making his European mark (in more ways than one) in **Ridley Scott's** *The Duellists* (77). A subtle, sympathetic actor, even when playing borderline psychotics in **Abel Ferrara's** *Bad Lieutenant* (92), Keitel was one of the main reasons for the success of **Quentin Tarantino's** debut movie *Reservoir Dogs* (92), which he both backed and acted in. At his strongest, as in the small but crucial role of Hal in Ridley Scott's *Thelma And Louise* (91), Keitel can underplay with the best of them, manifesting a quality of restraint that makes his sudden, frenetic outbursts all the more effective.
OTHER KEY FILMS: *Alice Doesn't Live Here Anymore* (75); *Bad Timing* (80); *The Last Temptation Of Christ* (88); *The Two Jakes* (90); *The Piano* (93); *Pulp Fiction* (94); *Smoke* (95); *From Dusk Till Dawn* (96); *Cop Land* (97); *Holy Smoke* (99); *U-571* (00); *Little Nicky* (00); *Nailed* (01)

Kelly, Gene

Kelly was destined, from the very beginning, to be compared to **Fred Astaire**, for no other reason than that they inhabited (for want of a better word) the same profession. Kelly, however, was muscular where Astaire was elegant, and he was modern, too, (in cinematic terms at least) where Astaire was comfortably old-fashioned. Astaire comparisons aside, one is left with Kelly as a dancer and singer of great talent, who genuinely stimulated a revival in the musical and in modern ballet at a time when both were in danger of conking out for lack of fuel. **Vincente Minnelli's** *An American In Paris* (51) may have fomented the vomit-inducingly romanticised view of the French that held sway until only relatively recently, but it also incorporated a ballet sequence, inspired by the canvases of Raoul Dufy, of astonishing ingenuity. Similarly, **Stanley Donen's** *Singin' In The Rain* [Kelly co-directed] (52), is genuinely uplifting, and is the musical of all musicals as far as the non musical-loving public is concerned. It's a pretty good record, and Kelly was a pretty nice guy.

OTHER KEY FILMS: *Cover Girl* (44); *Anchors Aweigh* (45); *The Pirate* (48); *On The Town* (49); *It's Always Fair Weather* (55); *Invitation To The Dance* (56); *Inherit The Wind* (60); *Les Demoiselles De Rochefort* (67); *That's Entertainment* trilogy [compilation] (74–94)

Kelly, Grace

Kelly was sex personified (or sex sanctified, depending on your point of view), and it was patently obvious to every man watching her on the screen that, ice-cold and frozen as she seemed, there were as yet unseen fires simmering within. Corny? Perhaps. Yet it sold films, and allowed Kelly to appeal as strongly to men as to the women she awed with

Grace Kelly as Lisa Carol Fremont (complete with portable nightdress), bonding with James Stewart's L B 'Jeff' Jeffries, in Alfred Hitchcock's Rear Window (54)

her Dior, Chanel and Balenciaga frocks and her other-worldly elegance – if a woman such as she couldn't end up marrying a prince in real life, then who could? She did find her prince, of course, and lost her career in the process, and there was something acutely touching about her later appearances, now slightly bloated, as Prince Rainier of Monaco's consort – the victim, as we belatedly found out, of strange, if rather innocent, cultish compulsions. At her best, in **Alfred Hitchcock's** *Rear Window* (54) and *To Catch A Thief* (55), and as the spoilt heiress every woman secretly yearns to be in **Charles Walters's** *High Society* (56), Kelly epitomised a quasi-insane standard of everyday glamour and made it seem something to be desired – to that extent she is one of the great daughters of the cinema, where the dream is always more important than its interpretation.

OTHER KEY FILMS: *Fourteen Hours* (51); *High Noon* (52); *Mogambo* (53); *Dial M For Murder* (54); *The Country Girl* (54); *Green Fire* (54); *The Bridges At Toko-Ri* (55); *The Swan* (56)

KEY LINES:
'Well, if there's one thing I know, it's how to wear the proper clothes.' [*Rear Window*]
'You want a leg, or a breast?' [Kelly to **Cary Grant's** John Robie in *To Catch A Thief*]

Kerr, Deborah

There was something magnificent about Deborah Kerr, as though her steel had been tempered at a familiar forge but was somehow stronger, more durable, than that of her contemporaries. She was un-neurotic and everyday, but with a luminous beauty that sometimes shone, sometimes took a back seat. Her glamour was innate, and she appeared to scorn artifice and the sins of over-emoting, and to that extent her admissions of weakness, as Sister Clodagh in **Michael Powell** and Emeric Pressburger's *Black Narcissus* (46), and as Hannah Jelkes in **John Huston's** *The Night Of The Iguana* (64), were all the more touching. Strangely, it is in the less well-known films that one appreciates her most – as Catherine Parr in George Sidney's *Young Bess* (53), or as Laura Reynolds in **Vincente Minnelli's** *Tea And Sympathy* (56) – where her innate good nature and gentleness stand out like beacons in the otherwise sargassic sea of Hollywood sharkdom.

OTHER KEY FILMS: *Major Barbara* (41); *The Life And Death Of Colonel Blimp* (43); *Perfect Strangers* (45); *I See A Dark Stranger* (46); *King Solomon's Mines* (50); *The Prisoner Of Zenda* (52); *Julius Caesar* (53); *From Here To Eternity* (53); *The End Of The*

Affair (54); *The King And I* (56); *Heaven Knows Mr Allison* (57); *An Affair To Remember* (57); *Separate Tables* (58); *The Sundowners* (60); *The Innocents* (61); *The Chalk Garden* (63); *The Assam Garden* (85)

KEY LINE:
'Years from now, when you talk about this – and you will – be kind.' [*Tea And Sympathy*, on letting the young and marginally effeminate John Kerr (no relation) make love to her]

Key Grip

The boss of the stagehand, or **grip** crew, responsible for setting up technical equipment, props, tracks and scenery on a film set.

Key Light

This is the main source of light on a movie set and the pivot around which the crucial atmosphere of the shot is constructed by the cinematographer, through the use of subsidiary lights such as **fill lights**, cross lights and **back lights**. See **High Key** and **Low Key**

Keys

Individual drawings used in the planning of animation shoots and which illustrate the main movements a character will perform during a pre-arranged sequence.

Keystone

Famous silent film production company founded in 1912 and synonymous with director **Mack Sennett**, Keystone specialised in frenetic comedy and was home to the demented **Keystone Kops**, and, briefly, to both **Charlie Chaplin** and **Fatty Arbuckle**.

Keystone Kops

A band of agile, clownishly dressed policemen, who graced, if that is the word, a sequence of **Mack Sennett** comedies brought out under the aegis of the **Keystone** Company between 1913 and 1917, Keystone Kops's stock-in-trade consisted of demented screen chases on the back of wildly gyrating fire trucks, Black Marias, omnibuses, etc. – scenes which still retain the power to amuse and amaze in roughly equal order.

Kicker

See **Eye Light**

Kidman, Nicole

Kidman is famous as much for her marriage to **Tom Cruise** and its much publicised break-up in 2001, as for her own star power, which probably galls her, but which may yet shed light on her innate talent. She impressed in the choice part of Rae Ingram in Phillip Noyce's *Dead Calm* (89), but Charles Williams's book is so strong that any one of a dozen actresses could have played the part as successfully. She was effective again in **Jane Campion's** otherwise disappointing (because loaded) *The Portrait Of A Lady* (96), but what, one asks, would **Emma Thompson** have made of the part? Such comparisons are odious, it is true, but there is something about Kidman that engenders them, as if she were to some extent a cipher, and her position as yet unresolved. Perhaps we came closest in **Stanley Kubrick's** *Eyes Wide Shut* (99), where Kidman's Alice Harford watches herself in the mirror, just as Kidman seems to in so many of her movies. One wishes she would release herself.

OTHER KEY FILMS: *Days Of Thunder* (90); *Billy Bathgate* (91); *Emerald City* (91); *Far And Away* (92); *To Die For* (95); *The Peacemaker* (97); *Birthday Girl* (00); *Moulin Rouge* (01); *The Others* (01)

Kieslowski, Krzysztof

It still seems something of a miracle that we had Kieslowski with us for so long – he was a director torn from the bowels of film, who crept up on those of us who were despairing, in the depths of the 1980s, of ever feeling enthusiasm for a modern filmmaker again. But then came *The Double Life Of Véronique* (91). Initially repelled (for at first glance the film can seem over-contrived), one returns to it despite one's early reservations, only to be won over, and then again, by the acute sensibility to nuance and to visual design exhibited by its maker. *Blue* (93), *White* (94) and *Red* (94) followed, and it became apparent that Kieslowski was almost alone among modern filmmakers in thinking along metaphysical, rather than along political or sociological lines. His death, aged fifty-four, was a dreadful blow to what used, with reason, to be called **Art-house** film; in other words, films where the intellect is first brought into play and then subsumed by the instinctive answers to the questions that have been asked under its aegis.

OTHER KEY FILMS: *Camera Buff* (79); *Talking Heads* (80); *No End* (84); *Dekalog* [*The Ten Commandments*] (88)

Kilmer, Val

Kilmer has recently gone off the boil, after a very good run at, or near, the top of the Hollywood tree. The question to be asked is, where now? Apart from his Jim Morrison in **Oliver Stone's** *The Doors* (91), his parts have been straight up the line, relying overmuch on his good looks and surly sex appeal.

Another tight *film noir*, perhaps, along the lines of one of the early **Robert Mitchum** vehicles? Not that Kilmer has the quality of a Mitchum, but he surely has the potential to age into his parts if only he can bring himself to laugh occasionally, as though he really means it, rather than merely grimacing at the discomfiture of his screen opponents.

OTHER KEY FILMS: *Top Gun* (86); *Kill Me Again* (89); *Thunderheart* (92); *True Romance* (93); *Tombstone* (93); *Batman Forever* (95); *Heat* (95); *The Ghost And The Darkness* (96); *The Saint* (97); *At First Sight* (99); *Pollock* (00); *Red Planet* (00); *The Salton Sea* (01)

Kinemacolor

Possibly the world's first dedicated colour process, Kinemacolor was introduced to audiences in 1906 and consisted of a spinning wheel placed in front of the camera lens which exposed the negative, frame by frame, to the colours of red, blue-green, then red, alternately – and it worked. Modern reprints of Kinemacolor films (e.g. the 1911 *The Durbar in Delhi*) are astonishing.

The Kong, with Fay Wray in hand, in a publicity shot for Merian C Cooper and Ernest B Schoedsack's **King Kong** *(33)*

Kinescope

Before the advent of video, television programmes were recorded on film for archival filing by the use of a Kinescope. The process, although worthwhile in a historical perspective, produced a notably poor-quality print.

Kinetograph

Acknowledged by many as the world's first motion-picture camera, the Kinetograph was constructed in 1888 by W K L Dickson for the **Edison** Company, which patented it in 1891, and used it to film story strips that were then subsequently viewed on a **Kinetoscope**.

Kinetoscope

Also patented in 1891, **Thomas Alva Edison's** Kinetoscope consisted of a wooden box with a peephole through which an individual could watch (while cranking a handle) a fifty-foot-long loop of film. The system, limited as it was to one person at a time, was soon overtaken by the collective viewing system being developed by the **Lumière Brothers**.

King, Henry

An extraordinarily versatile studio director of the old school, King spent forty-six years in the business, starting with *Who Pays?* (16) and ending with *Tender Is The Night* (62). In between, he entertained untold millions with such high-quality and intelligently thought-out star vehicles as *Tol'able David* (21), *State Fair* (33), the exquisitely photographed *Jesse James* (39), and the excellent, and still underrated, *The Sun Also Rises* (57). King loved America, and his best films are imbued with a sense of its possibilities, thus making him a rare optimist in a film world populated largely by would-be cynics.

OTHER KEY FILMS: *Lloyds Of London* (36); *Old Chicago* (38); *Alexander's Ragtime Band* (38); *The Black Swan* (43); *Captain From Castile* (48); *Twelve O' Clock High* (49); *The Gunfighter* (50); *The Snows Of Kilimanjaro* (52); *Carousel* (56); *The Bravados* (58)

King Kong

Merian C Cooper and **Ernest B Schoedsack's** *King Kong* (33) is important in the history of film because, for once, Hollywood (in the person of **David O Selznick**) allowed itself to be carried along in an experiment that, on paper, had little or no chance of succeeding. The film cost close to $700,000 to make and grossed an incredible $1,761,000 on its initial release – incredible, seeing as how the stop-motion special effects could just as easily have engendered humour, rather than awe. But the story was so strong and so resonant, above all in archetypal terms, that audiences seldom even knew why they were finding the film so satisfying. The Kong we see in the jungle and on top of the Empire State Building (an inspired touch) was in reality an eighteen-inch model designed by special-effects guru Willis O'Brien – RKO's initial plan had called for a man in a monkey suit. The film was re-released five years later, but this time with the sex removed, the gore mopped up and the monster emasculated. Modern filmmakers and scriptwriters might profitably learn from the fact that in the case of *King Kong*, the script came first and the means afterwards.

KEY LINE:
'Oh no, it wasn't the airplanes. It was Beauty killed the Beast.' [*King Kong*]

Kingsley, Ben

An elusive screen presence, who almost disappears behind the parts he plays, Kingsley first reached a large international audience with his portrayal of the title role in **Richard Attenborough's** *Gandhi* (82). More than good, as well, in John Irvin's *The Turtle Diary* (86) and **Steven Spielberg's** *Schindler's List* (93), Kingsley seems set – and is probably content – to remain on the periphery of stardom, just so long as he receives parts as challenging as his Roberto Miranda in **Roman Polanski's** *Death And The Maiden* (95), in which he was so convincing that one almost ends up rooting for him over his erstwhile victim, **Sigourney Weaver**.
OTHER KEY FILMS: *Fear Is The Key* (72); *Betrayal* (83); *Maurice* (87); *Bugsy* (91); *Sneakers* (92); *Species* (95); *Parting Shots* (98); *Rules Of Engagement* (00); *Sexy Beast* (00); *The Triumph of Love* (01)

Kinopanorama

A Russian made 360° split-screen projection system, in which the audience is entirely surrounded by the filmed image.

Kinski, Klaus

Demented German actor who spent the better part of a decade believing he was the Second Coming, Kinski was actually (when he was able to control his temper) a consummate screen actor with an extraordinary instinct for visual and emotional subtleties. Forever associated with his counterpart and sometime nemesis **Werner Herzog**, Kinski starred in four of the director's most outstanding films, *Aguirre, Wrath Of God* (72), *Nosferatu* (78), *Woyzeck* (79) and *Fitzcarraldo* (82). These two highly disparate characters alternately brought out the best and the worst in each other, and Herzog's recent TV documentary tribute to Kinski, *Mein Liebster Fiend – Klaus Kinski* (99), shows how close each came to (quite literally) driving the other mad.
OTHER KEY FILMS: *Ludwig II* (54); *For A Few Dollars More* (65); *Dr Zhivago* (65); *Circus Of Fear* (67); *Venus In Furs* (70); *Burden Of Dreams* (82); *The Little Drummer Girl* (84)

Klieg Lights

Invented by, and named after, the Kliegl brothers (J H and Anton), these powerful floodlights are used for principal and **key lighting** on closed film sets.

Kline, Kevin

Kline should really have been born around 1910, so that he could have given **Errol Flynn** a run for his money during the Golden Era of the 1930s, for he was made for **swashbuckling** – he even looks better in a moustache. Given that he was actually born in 1947, he still hasn't done too badly for himself,

Klaus Kinski as Count Dracula and Isabelle Adjani as Lucy Harker in Werner Herzog's Nosferatu, The Vampire *(78)*

186

revealing a wondrous comic touch in Charles Crichton's *A Fish Called Wanda* (88) – a gift which was already apparent in his high-octane performance as **Meryl Streep's** schizophrenic lover, Nathan Landau, in **Alan J Pakula's** *Sophie's Choice* (82). His best work to date has been as adulterer Ben Hood in **Ang Lee's** *The Ice Storm* (97).

OTHER KEY FILMS: *The Big Chill* (83); *Silverado* (85); *Cry Freedom* (87); *The January Man* (89); *Grand Canyon* (91); *Dave* (93); *French Kiss* (95); *Fierce Creatures* (97); *In & Out* (97); *Wild, Wild West* (99); *The Anniversary Party* (00)

Korda Family, The

The three Korda brothers, Alexander, a director and producer, Vincent, an art director, and Zoltán, an editor and director, were God's greatest gift to the crisis-stricken British film industry of the 1930s. Between them they made a series of what are unquestionably the most prestigious films ever produced in Great Britain. This includes Alexander Korda's own *The Private Life Of Henry VIII* (33), *The Private Life Of Don Juan* (34), *Rembrandt* (36) and *That Hamilton Woman* (41), together with an extraordinary list of productions by other directors, all notable for their outstanding quality and scrupulous design, including **René Clair's** *The Ghost Goes West* (35), Jacques Feyder's *Knight Without Armour* (36), Zoltán Korda's *The Four Feathers* (39), the multi-directed *The Thief Of Bagdad* (40) and **Carol Reed's** *The Fallen Idol* (48). Alexander also happened to be one of the nicest men in movies. See **Heartstopping Moments**

OTHER KEY FILMS: **Anthony Asquith's** *The Winslow Boy* (48); **Michael Powell's** *The Small Back Room* (49); Carol Reed's *The Third Man* (49) and *Outcast Of The Islands* (51)

Korngold, Erich Wolfgang

A classic product of the late nineteenth-century Viennese style of music (despite his 1897 'beginning of modernism' birth date), Korngold was proclaimed a child genius by Mahler, but finally settled for a high-profile career in Hollywood and the composition of such lushly romantic repertoire works as his Violin Concerto. His ecstatic scores for **Michael Curtiz's** magnificent quartet of *Captain Blood* (35), *The Adventures Of Robin Hood* (38), *The Private Lives Of Elizabeth And Essex* (39) and *The Sea Hawk* (40) contributed enormously to the atmosphere and longevity of what would otherwise have been a series of only vaguely memorable **swashbucklers**.

OTHER KEY FILMS: **William Dieterle's** *A Midsummer Night's Dream* (35); **Mervyn LeRoy's** *Anthony Adverse* (36); William Keighley's *The Prince And The Pauper* (37); Michael Curtiz's *The Sea Wolf* (41); **Sam Wood's** *King's Row* (42); **Edmund Goulding's** *The Constant Nymph* (43)

Kovacs, Laszlo

An ex-lighting cameraman, Kovacs made his real debut as a cinematographer with **Peter Bogdanovich's** *Targets* (68) and **Dennis Hopper's** *Easy Rider* (69), but his true mastery of lighting and the camera only became apparent with **Bob Rafelson's** *Five Easy Pieces* (70). Since then Kovacs has worked with the smart pack, the art pack and the brat pack, and has been responsible for the look of some of the most inventive and influential movies of the era, including stints as a co-photographer on **Steven Spielberg's** *Close Encounters Of The Third Kind* (77) and **Martin Scorsese's** entertaining documentary about The Band, *The Last Waltz* (78).

OTHER KEY FILMS: Bob Rafelson's *The King Of Marvin Gardens* (72); **Hal Ashby's** *Shampoo* (75); Graeme Clifford's *Frances* (82); Ivan Reitman's *Ghostbusters* (84); P J Hogan's *My Best Friend's Wedding* (97); Troy Miller's *Jack Frost* (98); Bunny Hunt's *Return To Me* (00); Donal Petrie's *Miss Congeniality* (00)

Krasna, Norman

One of the most independent-minded of all the mainstream studio era screenwriters, Krasna liked to adapt his own storylines for the screen, and constructed a remarkable rags-to-riches career for himself in the process. His solo credits include **Fritz Lang's** *Fury* (36) for the screen story, **Alfred Hitchcock's** *Mr And Mrs Smith* (41), and **Stanley Donen's** *Indiscreet* (58). Krasna emigrated to Europe at the height of his success, an act that, quite literally, stopped his career dead in its tracks.

OTHER KEY FILMS: Mitchell Leisen's *Hands Across The Table* (35); **Clarence Brown's** *Wife Versus Secretary* (36); Fritz Lang's *You And Me* (38); **Sam Wood's** *The Devil And Miss Jones* (41); **George Cukor's** *Let's Make Love* (60)

Kristofferson, Kris

Sexy (or so female friends tell me) and multi-talented (he also had a successful career as a singer songwriter), the Kristofferson persona shouldn't really work on the screen, but it does. He was good in Bill Norton's *Cisco Pike* (72) and better in **Sam Peckinpah's** *Pat Garrett And Billy The Kid* (73), but the undoubted high point of his film career has come recently, in **John Sayles's** utterly magnificent *Lone Star* (96), the best film about America by an American for close on a generation. Kristofferson's performance as corrupt sheriff Charlie Wade explores every false American myth going, and strikes notes that many actors spend their lifetimes trying to achieve.

OTHER KEY FILMS: *Alice Doesn't Live Here Anymore* (74); *Songwriter* (84); *Trouble In Mind* (85); *Pharaoh's Army* (95); *Blade* (98); *Payback* (99); *Planet Of The Apes* (01); *Eye See You* (01)

Kubrick, Stanley

Kubrick's recent death has robbed cinema of a true iconoclast, able to woo actors of the box-office calibre of **Tom Cruise** to take time off from other, more lucrative work, to appear in what has unfortunately turned out to be the director's last film, *Eyes Wide Shut* (99). Kubrick's greatest days came earlier, however, with such classics as *The Killing* (56), *Paths Of Glory* (57) and the one and only *Dr Strangelove: Or How I Learned To Stop Worrying And Love The Bomb* (63), a film so undeniably perfect of its type that it still improves after repeated watching. Many consider *2001: A Space Odyssey* (68) to be Kubrick's masterpiece, but his most controversial film, which has recently been re-released following the director's death, must be *A Clockwork Orange* (71), which set out to challenge existing preconceptions concerning violence and sexuality, and succeeded all too well. With an astonishing knowledge of cinema history, and a fastidious nature that involved him in frenzied and lengthy preparations for all his films, it is something of a miracle that he left us a filmography quite so rich and varied in its content.

OTHER KEY FILMS: *Fear And Desire* (53); *Killer's Kiss* (55); *Spartacus* (60); *Lolita* (62); *Barry Lyndon* (75); *The Shining* (80); *Full Metal Jacket* (87)

KEY LINE: 'What are you? Some kind of a pre-vert?' [Keenan Wynn to **Peter Sellers** in *Dr Strangelove*]

Kurosawa, Akira

The extraordinary thing about *The Seven Samurai* (54) – the film for which Kurosawa is most famous in the West – is that even an eight-year-old child can watch all three hours twenty minutes of it without twitching and without showing signs of boredom. It can't simply be the story, for at the age of eight many of the nuances will inevitably pass a

child by. So it must be the visual quality – the editing, the composition, the whole look of the film. In just the same way a child can look at the paintings of Paul Gauguin, Vincent Van Gogh, or Paul Cézanne, and be seduced by their design, without understanding the theory behind it. Kurosawa is an emotional director, in direct line to the poets, the philosophers and the painters that Japan has produced so fruitfully over a period of more than 3,000 years. His greatest films have a visual and literary universality, which explains why he was so attracted to that other master of the universal, William Shakespeare, whose *Macbeth* Kurosawa turned into *Throne Of Blood* (57), and whose *King Lear* he turned into *Ran* (85). Following a failed suicide attempt in 1970 after the failure of the studio-bound *Dodeska-den* (70), Kurosawa was invited to the Soviet Union to film *Dersu Uzala* (75), a film about the friendship, based on absolute trust, between a fur trapper and the Russian leader of a topographical expedition in nineteenth-century Siberia. The result is a masterpiece, and its success with audiences ushered in the last great creative period of this noble director – an era which encompassed not only *Ran* but also its predecessor, the visually awe-inspiring and sublimely literate *Kagemusha* (80). See **Heartstopping Moments**

OTHER KEY FILMS: *Judo Saga* (43); *Drunken Angel* (48); *Stray Dog* (49); *Rashomon* (50); *The Idiot* (51); *Ikiru* [*To Live*] (52); *The Lower Depths* (57); *The Hidden Fortress* (58); *Yojimbo* (61); *Sanjuro* (62); *Dreams* (90); *Rhapsody In August* (91)

Kusturica, Emir

Kusturica astonished everyone with his *Time Of The Gypsies* (89) – the film was at once so real and so magical, as if an entirely new voice and eye were making itself felt in the cinema. Awards poured down on Kusturica's head and he received the usual dread summons from Hollywood. It is to his great credit, therefore, that *Arizona Dream* (93), the film that emerged from the summons, is no worse. The film is part indisputably brilliant, part turgid, and it is only with his return to Yugoslavia and to his roots, that Kusturica re-emerged, not unscathed exactly, but at the very least chastened, to direct the picaresque, Palme d'Or winning *Underground* (95).

OTHER KEY FILMS: *Do You Remember Dolly Bell?* (81); *When Father Was Away On Business* (85); *Black Cat, White Cat* (98).

Lacquering

The process by which film stock is protected from scratches and abrasions.

Ladd, Alan

Shy and retiring in everyday life, Ladd was a *Boys' Own* hero in his films, appealing to a younger audience than almost any of his contemporaries. A natural athlete, his deep voice belied his five-foot six-inch frame, and when paired with the equally diminutive **Veronica Lake**, he gave an impression of stature twinned with serenity. At his best when playing loners bruised by, and wary of, women, his finest performance was undoubtedly in **George Stevens's** *Shane* (53), where, in some strange way, he managed to transcend himself and become the sort of actor he always, by implication at least, could have been.

OTHER KEY FILMS: *The Glass Key* (42); *This Gun For Hire* (42); *The Blue Dahlia* (46); *Calcutta* (47); *The Great Gatsby* (49); *Appointment With Danger* (51); *The Badlanders* (58); *The Carpetbaggers* (64)

KEY LINES:

'Call me Shane.' [*Shane*]

'I never saw another actor who moved as gracefully as Alan, who had that kind of coordination. A beautiful, deep voice. Everybody said he was a non-actor, but they were wrong. He knew what he was doing.' [Richard Maibaum, who scripted Irving Pichel's *O.S.S.* (46) and co-scripted Elliott Nugent's *The Great Gatsby* (49), on working with Ladd]

Lake, Veronica

Often twinned with **Alan Ladd** in hard-boiled thrillers (although they reputedly couldn't stand each other), the peek a boo-coiffed Lake was actually an extremely talented comedienne, as she proved in **Preston Sturges's** comic masterpiece *Sullivan's Travels* (41) and **René Clair's** delightfully idiosyncratic *I Married A Witch* (42). Her career as a top-rank star really only spanned five years, however, from 1941 to 1946, and ended with a final outing in **George Marshall's Raymond Chandler**-scripted *The Blue Dahlia* (46). All her later attempts at a comeback, even with Ladd at her side once again, fizzled out. Note for Film Buffs: Eighteen years after her last Hollywood film, Lake co-produced and starred in one of the worst and most surreally dotty horror films in movie history, B F Grinter's *Flesh Feast* (70), in which she tortures Hitler to death and ends up by shrieking anti-Nazi inanities at the audience.

OTHER KEY FILMS: *The Glass Key* (42); *This Gun For Hire* (42)

Lamour, Dorothy

Dark and exotic-looking – and therefore inevitably typecast as a dusky temptress – Lamour was excellent in **John Ford's** magnificent *The Hurricane* (37), but after hitting commercial pay dirt with **Bing Crosby** and **Bob Hope** in the *Road To...* series (1940–62), she never tried to stretch herself again, seemingly content to follow the line of least resistance and stick

189

to light romantic comedies. Nearly thirty years after first working for Ford in *The Hurricane*, she made a final brief appearance for him in *Donovan's Reef* (63). OTHER KEY FILMS: *The Jungle Princess* (36); *Tropic Holiday* (38); *Moon Over Burma* (40); *The Road To Singapore* (40); *The Road To Zanzibar* (41); *The Road To Morocco* (42); *The Road To Rio* (47); *The Road To Utopia* (46); *The Road To Hong Kong* (62)

Lancaster, Burt

Endowed by nature with a fine physique and an even finer toothy smile that, out of the blue, could light up and transform his face, Lancaster began his acting career in **Robert Siodmak's** *film noir* masterpiece *The Killers* (46), in which his brooding, panther-like presence (the result of his former career as a circus acrobat) immediately gave him entrée to the select club of Hollywood leading men. By 1948 he had formed his own production company, and he spent the rest of his life alternating (rather in the manner of **Clint Eastwood**) between art and commerce. Two great performances stand out – as J J Hunsecker, the amoral gossip columnist in **Alexander Mackendrick's** *Sweet Smell Of Success* (57), and as Lou Pasco, the self-deluding minor hood in **Louis Malle's** *Atlantic City* (80).

OTHER KEY FILMS: *Brute Force* (47); *I Walk Alone* (47); *Criss Cross* (49); *Come Back Little Sheba* (52); *From Here To Eternity* (53); *Apache* (54); *Separate Tables* (58); *Elmer Gantry* (60); *Birdman Of Alcatraz* (62); *The Leopard* (63); *The Train* (65); *The Swimmer* (68); *1900* (77); *Local Hero* (83)

KEY LINE:

Tony Curtis: 'Can I come in, J J?' Lancaster: 'No. You're dead, son. Get yourself buried.' [*Sweet Smell Of Success*]

Landscape

The natural, painted or previously filmed backdrop/surround to a filmed outdoor scene.

Lang, Charles B

Even a cursory glance at Lang's filmography will explain why he was nominated on eighteen separate occasions for Academy Awards for his cinematography. Ever the total professional, Lang was director of photography on such films as **Frank Borzage's** *A Farewell To Arms* (33), **Henry Hathaway's** *The Lives Of A Bengal Lancer* (35), **Joseph L Mankiewicz's** *The Ghost And Mrs Muir* (47), **Fritz Lang's** *The Big Heat* (53) and **Anthony Mann's** *The Man From Laramie* (55). A consummate lighting technician and one of the most respected men in the Hollywood artistic hierarchy, the, by

then, freelancing Lang was chosen by **Billy Wilder** for *Sabrina* (54) and *Some Like It Hot* (59), while **Marlon Brando**, fastidious and anxious about the look of his debut film, soon found that Lang's touch had not deserted him. The film which emerged from their collaboration, *One-Eyed Jacks*, (61) with its surging, romantic shots of the coast of California, is surely one of the most beautifully photographed **Technicolor** films of all time.

OTHER KEY FILMS: John Cromwell's *Tom Sawyer* (30); Elliott Nugent's *The Cat And The Canary* (39); Lewis Allen's *The Uninvited* (44); **Billy Wilder's** *Ace In The Hole* (51); Delbert Mann's *Separate Tables* (58); **Stanley Donen's** *Charade* (63)

Lang, Fritz

Lang cut his teeth in the **German Expressionist Movement** of the 1920s with *Die Nibelungen* (24), the ground-breaking *Metropolis* (26), and *M* (31), in which **Peter Lorre** played a tormented child-murderer. A convinced Nazi hater, Lang fled Germany for Hollywood (after an uncomfortable interview with Joseph Goebbels), where he directed **Spencer Tracy** in *Fury* (36), an anti-mob indictment that **MGM**, to Lang's unutterable horror, massacred on the cutting-room floor. Lang's continuing obsession with the psychology of human weakness made him the ideal thriller and *film noir* director, with masterpieces such as *The Big Heat* (53), *Clash By Night* (55), and *While The City Sleeps* (56) to his credit. But Lang didn't have an easy time of it in Hollywood (he was used to total control, something which the studios felt was their prerogative) and he reluctantly returned to Germany in 1956, where his last film, *The 1000 Eyes Of Dr Mabuse* (60) was made under trying circumstances. Lang was an iconoclast in a world of clones, and his fascination with the underside of life and with the pathological and morphological motivations of evil was always going to set him at odds with a studio system with a vested interest in the preservation of the status quo.

OTHER KEY FILMS: *Dr Mabuse* (21); *Western Union* (41); *Man Hunt* (41); *Hangmen Also Die* (43); *The Woman In The Window* (45); *Scarlet Street* (45); *House By The River* (50); *Rancho Notorious* (52); *The Blue Gardenia* (53); *Human Desire* (54); as actor, in **Jean-Luc Godard's** *Le Mépris* [*Contempt*] (63)

KEY LINE:

'I liked Fritz. He was a hell of a good talker. He said funny things, mostly of a dry wit and mostly detrimental about other people.' [Ring Lardner Jr, who co-scripted *Cloak And Dagger* (46), on its director, Lang]

Langdon, Harry

Now almost forgotten except by a few enlightened movie buffs, Langdon's star was brief and, towards the end, marred by sentimentality. The few fine comedies he did make seemed to succeed almost despite themselves, rather than through any consciousness by Langdon of his own potential for comic genius. Langdon, at his best, played eternity's innocent dope, and it is only in Harry Edwards's *Tramp, Tramp, Tramp* (26) and most particularly in **Frank Capra's** *The Strong Man* (26) that his talent for deadpan eccentricity really comes through.

OTHER KEY FILMS: *Long Pants* (27); *Three's A Crowd* (27); *The Chaser* (28)

Lange, Jessica

A complex and sadly underused actress, Lange's *annus mirabilis* came in 1982, when she should have won a Best Actress **Oscar** for her performance in Graeme Clifford's *Frances* (82), but had to content herself with Best Supporting Actress in **Sydney Pollack's** *Tootsie* (82) instead. Other fine performances followed, notably as doomed country singer Patsy Cline in **Bruce Beresford's** *Crimes Of The Heart* (86), and in **Tony Richardson's** marvellous last film *Blue Sky* (91), for which Lange won the Best Actress Oscar that had eluded her nine years before. Even in supporting roles, such as that of the bandit's wife in Michael Caton-Jones's *Rob Roy* (95), she always retains her integrity and refuses to take the easier path of browbeating her audience into submission.

OTHER KEY FILMS: *King Kong* (76); *The Postman Always Rings Twice* (81); *Country* (84); *Far North* (88); *Cape Fear* (91); *Night And The City* (92); *A Thousand Acres* (97); *Cousin Bette* (98); *Titus* (99); *Prozac Nation* (00)

Lanza, Mario

They tried to turn cheerful, promiscuous, golden-throated Lanza into a film star, but his eating (in the light of which his second movie, Norman Taurog's *The Toast Of New Orleans* (50), takes on an entirely new connotation), his temper and his unfortunate propensity for drink and drugs (quite a list, if you think about it) led to a fatal heart attack, aged thirty-eight. His voice was brilliant but untrained ('canned belto' some wit called it), and Lanza was never able to see live performances right through, thanks to shortcomings in his breathing technique. But on film, when he stopped acting and began to sing, he was magic, and Richard Thorpe's *The Great Caruso* (51) will have to stand as his epitaph –

although Lanza was never really 'great', and he certainly wasn't Caruso. Even so, and bearing in mind the **Technicolor** commerciality of his career, there are odd times, usually in the shower, when it is hard to get 'Call Me Fool' out of one's head and down the plughole, where it probably belongs.

OTHER KEY FILMS: *That Midnight Kiss* (49); *Because You're Mine* (52); *The Student Prince* [voiceover] (54); *Serenade* (56) [forget the film – go read the James M Cain novel instead]; *The Seven Hills Of Rome* (58); *For The First Time* (59)

Lap Dissolve

See **Dissolve**

Lassie

The brave collie-dog star of countless sentimental but well-meaning children's films between 1943 and 1978, Lassie was paradoxically played by a male dog, whose abundant fur cleverly disguised the true nature of his biological diversity from easily shockable viewers.

KEY FILMS: Fred M Wilcox's *Lassie Come Home* (43) and *Courage Of Lassie* (46); S Sylvan Simon's *Son Of Lassie* (45); Don Chaffey's *The Magic Of Lassie* (78)

Laszlo, Ernest

Laszlo received a total of eight **Oscar** nominations for cinematography throughout his career, and deserved at least eight more, with films such as **Billy Wilder's** *Stalag 17* (53), **Robert Aldrich's** *Kiss Me Deadly* (55) and **Fritz Lang's** *While The City Sleeps* (56) under his belt. He went commercial during the 1960s and 70s and the quality of his work suffered as a result, but his photography on Stanley Kramer's *Ship Of Fools* (65) won him a well-deserved Academy Award, and everyone is allowed a few duds like George Seaton's *Airport* (70) when they have such exquisite-looking black-and-whiters as Rudolph Maté's *D.O.A.* (50) to their credit.

OTHER KEY FILMS: **John Farrow's** *Two Years Before The Mast* (46); **Joseph Losey's** *M* (51); Richard Fleischer's *Bandido* (56); Stanley Kramer's *Inherit The Wind* (60)

Latensification

The slow exposure of a film negative by the faintest possible light to achieve a higher image density.

Latent Image

The embryonic image on a piece of exposed film before it has been processed into a true image.

191

Laterna Magika

A magic-lantern show originating in Eastern Europe which comprised live action performed against the backdrop of a static projected scene. Such shows were taken from village to village and were used as a means not only of entertainment, but also, on occasion, of propaganda.

Lathrop, Philip H

Lathrop is another underrated cinematographer whose name is hardly known outside film-buff circles. Well, he certainly deserves to be more highly regarded, for it is with some astonishment that one realises the consistent, frequently ground-breaking quality of his work. Look at this list: David Miller's *Lonely Are The Brave* (62), Norman Jewison's *The Cincinnati Kid* (65), **John Boorman's** *Point Blank* (67), **Sam Peckinpah's** *The Killer Elite* (75), Walter Hill's *The Driver* (78), and **Wim Wenders's** *Hammett* (82). Elegant stuff.

OTHER KEY FILMS: Blake Edwards's *Days Of Wine And Roses* (63); **Sydney Pollack's** *They Shoot Horses, Don't They?* (69); Jean-Claude Tramont's *All Night Long* (81); **Wes Craven's** *Deadly Friend* (86)

Latitude

The amount of leeway a camera operator has in his choice of lens aperture and shutter speed before the tonal quality of the image begins to suffer.

Laughton, Charles

Indisputably rotund, and with his vocal cords damaged by a First World War gassing, Laughton was, on the surface, a curious candidate for international stardom. Mercurial and insecure by nature, and deeply uneasy about his homosexuality, Laughton delighted the film world with his astonishing portrait of the king in **Alexander Korda's** *The Private Life Of Henry VIII* (33). He went on to one of the finest of all screen careers, incarnating Captain Bligh in Frank Lloyd's *Mutiny On the Bounty* (35), and Quasimodo in **William Dieterle's** *The Hunchback Of Notre Dame* (39). In 1955, he directed possibly the finest debut film ever achieved within the Hollywood system, the **James Agee**-scripted *The Night Of The Hunter*. Alas, although critically well-received and widely, if belatedly, viewed as the masterpiece it is, it was commercially unsuccessful and proved to be Laughton's only film as a director.

OTHER KEY FILMS: *If I Had A Million* (32); *Les Misérables* (35); *Rembrandt* (36); *The Beachcomber* (38); *Jamaica Inn* (39); *The Tuttles Of Tahiti* (42); *The Canterville Ghost* (44); *The Paradine Case* (48); *The Big Clock* (48); *The Bribe* (49); *Hobson's Choice* (54); *Witness For The Prosecution* (57); *Advise And Consent* (62)

KEY LINE:
'I no got wife to make happy, and I no got kids to make rich and big and strong, like me. Someday Tony die, sure. Who'll cry for Tony?' [Charles Laughton as Tony Patucci, in Garson Kanin's *They Knew What They Wanted* (40)]

Laurel and Hardy

When they were great they were very, very great, and when they were bad they were still pretty good. Paradoxically, skinny Stan Laurel was the driving force behind this sublime comic pairing, but Oliver Hardy more than held his own (on-screen as well as off) even though he received only half Laurel's salary. Leo McCarey directed many of their early shorts, but with the coming of sound they moved on to full-length features, such as **Hal**

Charles Laughton as the temperamental but tender-minded Rembrandt van Rijn in Alexander Korda's Rembrandt *(36)*

Roach and Charles Rogers's *Fra Diavolo* (33) – the mere thought of which, more than thirty years later, could still cause the author's father to giggle uncontrollably. Their relationship started to disintegrate after James W Horne's *Way Out West* (37), but they made films for a further twelve years, and together, as is only right, they still added up to considerably more than the sum of their parts.

OTHER KEY FILMS: *The Battle Of The Century* (27); *Two Tars* (28); *Night Owls* (30); *Another Fine Mess* (30); *The Music Box* (32); *Sons Of The Desert* (33); *Blockheads* (38); *A Chump At Oxford* (40)

KEY LINE

'Another fine mess you've gotten me into.' [Hardy]

Lavaliere

A concealed, or partially concealed microphone designed to be worn around a subject's neck and which does away with the need for a **boom** microphone, while still leaving the subject free to move and gesticulate in a normal (or abnormal) fashion.

Lavender

Studio jargon for a high-quality **master positive** (originally tinted lavender) from which black-and-white copies are subsequently to be made.

Law, Jude

There's not much to say about Law yet – in cinematic terms, at least, for his theatre career has been spectacular, with an Olivier award for Outstanding Newcomer and a Tony nomination for Outstanding Supporting Actor – but one suspects that there will be a great deal to say about him pretty soon, following his brilliant performance as Dickie Greenleaf, in **Anthony Minghella's** *The Talented Mr Ripley* (99). Quite apart from his perfect mastery (as an Englishman) of a particularly difficult American idiom, he managed to submerge himself inside the part to such an extent that one was left at the end of the film with the impression that one had been privileged to see a major new talent in the making. The question, as always, will be whether he is able to take advantage of the jump-start Ripley will have given his career to choose challenging, rather than merely turgidly commercial roles, such as his Russian sniper, Vasilli Zaitsev in **Jean-Jacques Annaud's** overblown *Enemy At the Gates* (01). See image at **Gwyneth Paltrow**

OTHER KEY FILMS: *Gattaca* (97); *Bent* (97); *Midnight In The Garden Of Good And Evil* (97); *Final Cut* (98); *eXistenZ* (99); *Love, Honour And Obey* (00); *A.I.: Artificial Intelligence* (01)

Lawton, Charles, Jr

Lawton is the man responsible for the camerawork on two of **Budd Boetticher's** outstanding Ranown cycle of **Westerns** featuring the great **Randolph Scott**, *Ride Lonesome* (59) and *Comanche Station* (60). These late films in the cycle have a particular look, an elegiac touch that seeks to remind us of what was lost when civilisation and its minions took over the great plains from the men and women whose spiritual home they were. It is arguable that on the basis of his work on those two films, and also on Phil Karlson's *They Rode West* (54), Delmer Daves's *Jubal* (56), *3:10 To Yuma* (57) and *Cowboy* (58) along with **John Ford's** *Two Rode Together* (61), Lawton is one of the greatest and most unsung of all cinematographers, Western-oriented or otherwise. And as if that weren't enough, Lawton also photographed **Orson Welles's** *The Lady From Shanghai* (48), which has to be one of the most gorgeously perverse-looking films ever made, with its deep contrasts, surprising angles, and massive, almost ugly close-ups.

OTHER KEY FILMS: Charles Riesner's *The Big Store* (41); **Allan Dwan's** *Brewster's Millions* (45); Curtis Bernhardt's *Miss Sadie Thompson* (53)

193

Layout

All the organisational work done before filming actually starts on sketching out and storyboarding future sequences in terms of props, lighting, camera angles, etc.

Lead

The actor or actress who takes the main role in a film, and who is known, respectively, as the leading man or the leading lady.

Leader

The safety strip at the beginning and end of a reel of film that, if it conforms to the strict guidelines laid down by the **Academy Of Motion Picture Arts And Sciences** with regard to markings, labellings and numberings, etc., is known as an Academy or **Standard Leader**.

Lean, David

Renowned (and sometimes criticised) for his later epics such as *The Bridge On The River Kwai* (57), *Doctor Zhivago* (65), *Ryan's Daughter* (70) and *A Passage To India* (84), Lean was actually a far better film-maker before he discovered wide-screen **CinemaScope**. Early classics such as *Brief Encounter* (45), *Great Expectations* (46), *Oliver Twist* (48) and *The Passionate Friends* (49), although smaller in scale, are larger in heart, and benefit from Lean's own concise editing, a talent that seemed to become looser with each successive larger-than-life blockbuster. There is no doubt that *Lawrence Of Arabia* (62) is wonderfully professional and gives much pleasure visually, but it has always seemed (dare one say it?) just a little cold at the centre.

OTHER KEY FILMS: *Blithe Spirit* (45); *Madeleine* (49); *The Sound Barrier* (52); *Hobson's Choice* (54); *Summer Madness* (55)

Léaud, Jean-Pierre

Léaud was destined for stardom the moment director **François Truffaut** chose him as his alter ego in the Antoine Doinel cycle of films, consisting of *The 400 Blows* (59), *Love At Twenty* (62), *Stolen Kisses* (68), *Bed And Board* (70) and *Love On The Run* (79). Léaud represented the quintessential French young man – with his chiselled looks and floppy hair, he could never be anything else – at the same time existentialist and conservative, hedonistic and ascetic, aesthete, philosopher and *érotomane*. **Jean-Luc Godard** saw the visual manifestations of such paradoxes in Léaud too, using him in *Masculine-Feminine* (66), *Made In USA* (66), *La Chinoise* (67) and *Weekend* (68). Léaud truly reached the heights in one great film by one great director, **Jean Eustache's** *La Maman Et La Putain* (73), which more than rustles the laurels of even **Bernardo Bertolucci's** magnificent *Last Tango In Paris* (72) in which Léaud had featured the year before. Since then, as if exhausted by his heady early fame, Léaud has fallen a little by the wayside, even though directors such as Agnès Varda, **André Téchiné** and **Aki Kaurismäki** have doggedly continued to use him.

OTHER KEY FILMS: *Le Testament D'Orphée* (60); *Pierrot Le Fou* (65); *Pigsty* (69); *Les Deux Anglaises Et Le Continent* (71); *Day For Night* (73); *Détective* (85); *I Hired A Contract Killer* (90); *J'Embrasse Pas* (91); *Personne Ne M'Aime* (94); *Irma Vep* (96); *Innocent* (98); *L'Affaire Marcorelle* (00); *Dark Circles* (01); *Le Pornographe* (01)

Leconte, Patrice

A 1969 graduate of **IDHEC**, Leconte began his professional career as a cartoonist on *Pilote* magazine, before returning to film six years later to make his directorial debut with *Les Vécés Étaient Fermés De L'Intérieur* (75) – the film flopped, but his next film, *Les Bronzés* (78), a spoof on Club Méditeranée-style holidays, was a tremendous success. Concentrating on the three themes of male bonding, deviant sexuality and incipient madness, Leconte made the tragicomic *Tandem* (87), followed by the even darker

Monsieur Hire (89). *Le Mari De La Coiffeuse* (90) was as light as a soufflé in comparison, and gave Leconte his greatest international success, and his best films since have spanned both sides of his personality – the deviant and the comedic – and include the black humour of *Tango* (93), and the brilliantly realised *Ridicule* (96), whose melding of wit, costume and politics affords a marvellously sophisticated entertainment in the grand French rococo style.

OTHER KEY FILMS: *Les Spécialistes* (84); *Contre L'Oubli* (91); *Le Batteur Du Boléro* (92); *Le Parfum D'Yvonne* (94); *Lumière Et Compagnie* (95); *Les Grands Ducs* (96); *Une Chance Sur Deux* (98); *La Fille Sur Le Pont* (99); *La Veuve De Saint-Pierre* (00); *Félix Et Lola* (00); *Rue Des Plaisirs* (01)

Lee, Ang

Lee had already established himself as a major director with *The Wedding Banquet* (93) and *Eat Drink Man Woman* (94) before the lure of Europe, and of **Emma Thompson's** immaculate screenplay, persuaded him to try his hand at an English period drama. The result was *Sense And Sensibility* (95), an unlikely subject at first glance, but one that Lee triumphantly made his own. *The Ice Storm* (97) followed, a subtle and very dark investigation into the moral fall-out from the upheavals of the 1960s in American suburbia, proving, beyond a doubt, that Lee's forte was character, atmosphere and emotional truth. Lee respects the conventions of whatever period he is filming, and it is notable that, unlike many of his New York University Institute of Film and Television counterparts, he has not, as yet, been swayed by the unholy burden of contemporary rectitude. Lee's recent *Crouching Tiger, Hidden Dragon* (00) has proved itself a most improbable triumph with the chattering classes, selling itself as a message movie to people who wouldn't be seen dead attending a swashbuckler – which is what it really is, of course.

OTHER KEY FILMS: *Ride With The Devil* (99)

Lee, Bruce

Less a film star than a phenomenon, Bruce Lee was the first great martial-arts entertainer to successfully make the crossover from China to the US. Lee's early death at the age of thirty-three from a brain oedema guaranteed his already burgeoning **cult** status, but it is only in three films, the best of which was Robert Clouse's *Enter The Dragon* (73), together with an entertaining bit part in Paul Bogart's *Marlowe* (69), that his grace and talent really showed to the full.

OTHER KEY FILMS: *The Big Boss* [a.k.a. *Fists Of Fury*] (71); *Fist Of Fury* (72)

'I owe my spirituality to Bruce Lee. In my lifetime I never met another man who was even remotely at his level of consciousness.' [Sterling Silliphant, who scripted *Marlowe* (69), in which Lee famously destroyed private eye James Garner's office with his bare hands and feet]

Lee, Christopher

Born Christopher Frank Cardini, beanpole Lee is renowned for his horror roles, in particular for his incarnation of *Dracula* in the **Hammer** Horror series. A better actor than his career might at first glance indicate, he has recently done some fine television work, notably in the BBC television adaptation of *Gormenghast* (2000), but film buffs (a law unto themselves) will always cherish his eccentric performance as the dancing, daemonic Lord Summerisle in Robin Hardy's curious *The Wicker Man* (73). In a remarkable career comeback, Lee is now playing Saruman the White in the forthcoming *Lord Of The Rings* trilogy.
KEY FILMS: *The Curse of Frankenstein* (57); *Dracula* (59); *Dr Terror's House Of Horrors* (65); *The Man With The Golden Gun* (74); *Circle of Iron* (79); *The Salamander* (81); *Howling II* (85); *Funny Man* (94); *The Legend Of Sleepy Hollow* (99)

Lee, Spike

In many ways an unprepossessing and rather vainglorious figure, Lee has real talent hidden beneath his agitprop façade. *Malcolm X* (92) is a superb meditation on commitment, but its very success shows the rest of Lee's films up in a poorer light. *She's Got To Have It* (86) and *Do The Right Thing* (89), though streetwise on the surface, seem somewhat shallow and one-track-minded by comparison.
OTHER KEY FILMS: *School Daze* (87); *Mo' Better Blues* (90); *Jungle Fever* (91); *Crooklyn* (94); *Clockers* (95); *He Got Game* (98); *Summer Of Sam* (99); *Bamboozled* (00)

Legion Of Decency

A Catholic organisation launched in 1933/4 to counter behavioural immoderation in the cinema, the Legion of Decency was largely responsible for stultifying the portrayal of emotional and sexual truth in the burgeoning US film industry. Euphemism and double entendres, those catch-alls of an inhibited society, became, under the Legion's aegis, the norm in movies, and violence, which, as far as the good Legionnaires were concerned, came a poor second place to lubricity in terms of moral danger, gradually began to replace sex as the visual opiate of the cinematic masses. Note: The frank and graphic portrayal of violence has never taken the same hold in, for instance, France, a country where a more enlightened view of sex and the delightful fallibilities of human nature has traditionally been espoused.

Lehman, Ernest

One of the most versatile and successful of all Hollywood screenwriters, Lehman's masterpiece was the adaptation of his own novella for **Alexander Mackendrick's** *Sweet Smell Of Success* (57). His own personal favourite remains his version of Rocky Graziano's autobiography in **Robert Wise's** *Somebody Up There Likes Me* (56), but many movie fans consider Lehman's script for **Alfred Hitchcock's** *North By Northwest* (59) as coming perilously close to Hollywood perfection. His final list of credits reads like a who's who of the Hollywood mainstream.
OTHER KEY FILMS: Billy Wilder's *Sabrina* (54); Walter Lang's *The King And I* (56); Robert Wise and Jerome Robbins's *West Side Story* (61); Robert Wise's *The Sound Of Music* (65); **Mike Nichols's** *Who's Afraid Of Virginia Woolf?* (66); **William Wyler's** *Funny Girl* (68); **John Frankenheimer's** *Black Sunday* (77)

Leigh, Janet

Leigh had a lot of bad years when she was forced into trivial fare by her contract with **MGM**, but suddenly, around 1958, she found herself, or rather **Orson Welles** found her, in *Touch Of Evil* (58), identifying a strange, almost innate masochism that the camera brought out, and which audiences, sadists all, lapped up. **Alfred Hitchcock**, the cinema audience's favourite ersatz sadist, sniffed fresh blood, and pounced on Leigh for the role of Marion Crane in *Psycho* (60), after which Leigh's masochism reigned supreme with put-upon roles in **John Frankenheimer's** *The Manchurian Candidate* (62) and Jack Smight's *Harper* (66), culminating in her being attacked by monster rabbits in William F Claxton's *Night Of The Lepus* (72) and menaced by a billow of angry miasma in **John Carpenter's** *The Fog* (80). And who said careers don't run in cycles?
OTHER KEY FILMS: *That Forsyte Woman* (49); *Scaramouche* (52); *The Naked Spur* (53); *The Black Shield Of Falworth* (54); *Pete Kelly's Blues* (55); *The Vikings* (58); *Wives And Lovers* (63); *Halloween H 20: Twenty Years Later* (98); *A Fate Totally Worse Than Death* (00)

Leigh, Jennifer Jason

Leigh is a true oddity in Hollywood terms – an attractive actress who decided, early on in her career, that character parts and not glamour were to be her forte. One can only utter an awestruck 'bravo!'. Fine but curious in **Paul Verhoeven's** *Flesh And Blood* (85), she was even better in Robert Harmon's *The Hitcher* (86), and really found her stride in **Barbet Schroeder's** otherwise pretty much over-the-top *Single White Female* (92) and **Robert Altman's** *Short Cuts* (93) – her incarnation of Dorothy Parker in **Alan Rudolph's** *Mrs Parker And The Vicious Circle* (94) was as eccentric as it was masterly, and remains in the memory long after the film itself has been forgotten. **Taylor Hackford's** excellent *Dolores Claiborne* (95) followed, as well as the role of **Jean Harlow**-loving Blondie O'Hara in Robert Altman's *Kansas City* (96). If Leigh can keep her nerve, and if she can avoid lesser, misdirected films such as Jocelyn Moorhouse's *A Thousand Acres* (97) and Agnieszka Holland's *Washington Square* (97), her career must surely go from strength to strength.
OTHER KEY FILMS: *The Big Picture* (89); *Miami Blues* (90); *Crooked Hearts* (91); *Rush* (92); *The Hudsucker Proxy* (94); *Georgia* (95); *eXistenZ* (99); *Skipped Parts* (00); *The King Is Alive* (00); *The Anniversary Party* (01)

Leigh, Mike

Along with fellow-iconoclast **Ken Loach**, Leigh has resolutely ignored mainstream British cinema to concentrate on such improvisational set-pieces as *Life Is Sweet* (91), *Naked* (93) and *Secrets And Lies* (96), which was the first of his films to benefit from anything like a universal release. He followed this up with the remarkable *Career Girls* (97), and his standing in France (and indeed anywhere where integrity is valued over bankability) is very high. *Secrets And Lies* won the Palme d'Or at the 1995 **Cannes Film Festival**, and is notable for the fact that, due to Leigh's insistence that his actors improvise towards a plot rather than having a plot foisted upon them, no one knew what the upshot of the film would be until it happened.
OTHER KEY FILMS: *Bleak Moments* (71); *Meantime* [TVM] (83); *Four Days In July* [TVM] (84); *High Hopes* (88); *Topsy-Turvy* (99)

Leigh, Vivien

Justly famous for landing the part of Scarlett O'Hara in **David O Selznick's** production of *Gone With The Wind* (39), Leigh's career was blighted by tuberculosis, and, to an increasing extent, by manic depression. Superb alongside husband **Laurence** Olivier in *That Hamilton Woman* (41), she also registered strongly in **Mervyn LeRoy's** *Waterloo Bridge* (40) and opposite **Marlon Brando** as Blanche DuBois in **Elia Kazan's** *A Streetcar Named Desire* (51). A tragic figure, she died at the age of fifty-four in 1967, leaving us with only the memory of her fragile beauty in the relatively small number of films she managed to make while in her prime.
OTHER KEY FILMS: *Fire Over England* (37); *Caesar And Cleopatra* (45); *Anna Karenina* (48); *The Roman Spring Of Mrs Stone* (61)
KEY LINE:
'After all, tomorrow is another day.' [*Gone With The Wind*]

Lemmon, Jack

Lemmon became something of an institution in the US, alongside the also recently deceased **Walter Matthau**, for his ability to instil hysteria with humour (and drama with hysteria). Some of his early film performances were exceptional, most notably in **John Ford** and **Mervyn LeRoy's** *Mister Roberts* (55), **Billy Wilder's** *Some Like It Hot* (59) and *The Apartment* (60), **Blake Edwards's** *Days Of Wine And Roses* (62) and Gene Saks's *The Odd Couple* (68), but a glance through Lemmon's filmography suggests that he was far more of a one-track player than is currently acknowledged. Even in such nominally dramatic roles as his Jack Godell in James Bridges's *The China Syndrome* (79) and his excellent Shelley 'the Machine' Levine in James Foley's *Glengarry Glen Ross* (92), it is the same Lemmon that tried to *Save The Tiger* in John G Avildsen's 1973 movie, or find his son in **Constantin Costa-Gavras's** *Missing* (82), who consistently reappears. It eventually comes down to a question of believability rather than talent (for Lemmon had oodles of that) – his anti-heroic characters, in the final analysis, seem contrived, as though the process from conception to finalisation were merely an intellectual equation, with no place left for instinct.
OTHER KEY FILMS: *It Should Happen To You* (54); *The Cowboy* (58); *Bell, Book And Candle* (59); *Irma La Douce* (63); *How To Murder Your Wife* (65); *The Fortune Cookie* (66); *The Out-Of-Towners* (70); *The Front Page* (74); *The Prisoner Of Second Avenue* (75); *Macaroni* (85); *JFK* (91); *Short Cuts* (93); *The Legend Of Bagger Vance* (00)

Lens

A transparent, lentil-shaped curved glass fixture for the concentration and dispersal of light rays on a camera.

Lens Adapter

An easy-change gizmo that ensures a swift swap-over of lenses during filming.

Lens Barrel

The container that houses the different elements that make up a camera lens.

Lens Cap

The protective covering for a lens when it is not in use.

Lens Coating

The transparent coating of magnesium fluoride that protects a camera lens from accidental scratching or marring.

Lens Hood

The protective cup placed around a lens to prevent unwanted light from reaching it and tarnishing the filmed image.

Lens Mount

The standard metal housing which incorporates all the essentials that go to make up a lens.

Lens Speed

The speed at which a lens can capture light and which is regulated by the relative size of the lens aperture – the lower the light, the larger the lens.

Lens Turret

A circular cartridge containing a number of different lenses which, when placed in front of a camera, facilitates and speeds up the lens-changing task of the principal cameraman.

Leonard, Robert Z

Leonard (the Z stands for Ziegler) directed one of the most underrated **Greta Garbo** vehicles, *Susan Lenox: Her Fall and Rise* (31), one of the best-ever Jane Austen adaptations, *Pride And Prejudice* (41), and one of the fruitiest quasi-*film noirs* ever conceived of in a Hollywood story department, *The Bribe* (49), and yet his name is little known outside the demented cognoscenti (this author included) who derive a vicarious pleasure from the endless perusal of screen credits. His career (he started out as an actor before turning to directing) lasted fifty years, and more than half his films are silents, now rarely seen outside the archives, but this cheerful Chicagoan whose name will be forever linked to the heyday of **MGM** was a brilliant craftsman and a thoroughgoing professional, and

even the froth on the froth of his froth has a distinctive and decidedly pleasant taste.

OTHER KEY FILMS: *The Master Key* (14); *Modern Love* (18); *Fashion Row* (23); *Bright Lights* (25); *Adam And Evil* (27); *Let Us Be Gay* (30); *Strange Interlude* (32); *The Great Ziegfeld* (36); *Maytime* (37); *When Ladies Meet* (41); *The Secret Heart* (46); *In The Good Old Summertime* (49); *The King's Thief* (55)

Leone, Sergio

One of the screen's most instinctive visual masters, Leone used the full spectrum of **CinemaScope** with controlled abandon, and will forever be remembered for the awe-inspiring crane-tracking shot in his masterpiece *Once Upon A Time In The West* (68). To the swelling lyricism of **Ennio Morricone's** music, he follows **Claudia Cardinale** as she alights from a train, then swoops over the station-house as she enters, only to pick her up again on the far side as she stares down the main street of one of the mythical West's most consummately convincing border towns. It is one of the greatest moments in all cinema – and Leone, when he was on his best form, as in *The Good, The Bad, And The Ugly* (68) and *Once Upon A Time In America* (83), *was* cinema.

OTHER KEY FILMS: *A Fistful Of Dollars* (64); *For A Few Dollars More* (66); *A Fistful Of Dynamite* [a.k.a. *Duck, You Sucker*] (72)

LeRoy, Mervyn

The diminutive LeRoy, or Le Roy, as he was sometimes known, had tried just about every job going in films (including wardrobe, acting, lab work, assistant cameraman, gag writing and comedy construction) before **Warners** discovered him as a director with *No Place To Go* (27). Just three years later he was directing **Edward G Robinson** in *Little Caesar* (31) and **Gloria Swanson** in her last major role – if one excepts **Billy Wilder's** *Sunset Boulevard* (50) – in *Tonight Or Never* (31). It wasn't long before LeRoy began fronting Warners' social dramas with the powerful and still affecting *I Am A Fugitive From A Chain Gang* (32). This success led to a sequence of high-profile films including *Gold Diggers Of 1933* (33) and *Anthony Adverse* (36), followed by a lucrative, but ultimately deadening move to **MGM**, where he worked as a producer as well as a director on a series of increasingly bland commercial vehicles, including *Waterloo Bridge* (40), *Random Harvest* (42) and *Little Women* (49). He had a minor return to form (and to Warners) in the mid-1950s, most notably with *The FBI Story* (59), which harked back to his *Little Caesar* heyday, but the spark was gone and LeRoy retired, still only in his mid-sixties, to rest on his laurels and to contemplate the Irving Thalberg Memorial Award that, in 1975, the Academy chose to award him for his lifetime's achievement.

OTHER KEY FILMS: *The Heart Of New York* (32); *Tugboat Annie* (33); *Elmer The Great* (33); *I Found Stella Parish* (35); *Blossoms In The Dust* (41); *Madame Curie* (43); *Thirty Seconds Over Tokyo* (44); *Quo Vadis* (51); *Home Before Dark* (58); *Gypsy* (62)

Level

Either the position of a camera relative to the horizontal, or the optimum setting for true fidelity in recorded sound.

Levinson, Barry

Levinson began his career as a scriptwriter, and seemed destined to remain a hack-for-hire until he surprised Hollywood, and his erstwhile employers, with the excellent *Diner* (82), a film that doesn't actually go anywhere (outside of Baltimore) but enjoys itself doing so. *Tin Men* (87) and *Avalon* (90) completed Levinson's Baltimore trilogy, and despite the commercial success of *Rain Man* (88), *Toys* (92) and *Bugsy* (91), the self-scripted trilogy remains Levinson's most heartfelt, and thus original, work.

OTHER KEY FILMS: *The Natural* (84); *Young Sherlock Holmes* (85); *Good Morning, Vietnam* (87); *Toys* (92); *Disclosure* (94); *Jimmy Hollywood* (94); *Sleepers* (96); *Wag the Dog* (97); *Sphere* (98); *Liberty Heights* (99); *An Everlasting Piece* (00); *Bandits* (01)

Lewin, Albert

Lewin was a genuine oddity in a Hollywood devoted to conformity. An intellectual in a world of boastful philistines, he worked as **Irving Thalberg's** assistant at **MGM** before moving to **Paramount**, again as a producer, in 1937. In 1942 he was finally given the chance to direct, and during the next fifteen years he produced, wrote and directed six films, all of which were quirky, and one or two downright perverse. Lewin's headiest concoction was the desperately romantic *Pandora And The Flying Dutchman* (51), which featured a brilliantly on-form **James Mason** as the Dutchman, and an **Ava Gardner** at the peak of her beauty (and immaculately photographed by **Jack Cardiff**) as the spoilt Pandora, who eventually finds an enduring love (to say the very least) with her sea-borne cavalier. Lewin's first three films had been quirky literary tales, all with a sadomasochistic bent, and all featuring the laconic talents of the doomed **George Sanders**, but his follow-up *Saadia* (54), was unfortunately a failure, marginally redeemed by his final film, *The Living Idol* (56), which returned to the strange world which Lewin had inhabited so well in *Pandora*. For a long time it was fashionable to pan Lewin for his intellectual and literary aspirations, but the Sanders films are fascinating, every one, and *Pandora* is one of those odd little miracles that occasionally thrust themselves to the surface of even the most pacific of seas.

OTHER KEY FILMS: *The Moon And Sixpence* (42); *The Picture Of Dorian Gray* (45); *The Private Affairs Of Bel Ami* (47)

Lewis, Jerry

Lewis is the Prince of hysteria, the man who could cause even a convention of Buddhist monks to tear out their non-existent hair. It is irritating even to have to talk about him, let alone think about him, but his position in the contemporary US subconscious is secure, not so much on account of his movies (which few young people have probably seen) but more on account of his demented charitable activities, which satisfy an apparently profound Western need to be seen to be doing something, rather than just to do it. Following his seven-year stint as **Dean Martin's** stooge (or was it the other way around?) from 1949 to 1956, Lewis directed himself in a series of increasingly demented, increasingly bathetic films, which include *The Bellboy* (60), *The Nutty Professor* (63) and *The Patsy* (64). Something of an institution in France, where for a long time he was preferred to the home-grown talent of **Jacques Tati**, Lewis made a sort of comeback with his appearance, as Jerry Langford, in **Martin Scorsese's** *King Of Comedy* (83).

OTHER KEY FILMS: *The Ladies' Man* (61); *The Errand Boy* (61); *The Family Jewels* (65); *Three On A Couch* (66); *The Big Mouth* (67); *One More Time* (69); *Which Way To The Front?* (70); *Arizona Dream* (93); *The Nutty Professor* (96)

Lewis, Joseph H

Lewis was that rare thing – a **B-movie** director who transcended his calling. His best films, like the sublime *Gun Crazy* (50), work on a deep psychological level. Because he wasn't a slave to highly paid, and very often vain, stars, Lewis was able to take more risks than many of his better-known contemporaries. Catch **Cornel Wilde** in *The Big Combo* (55), or **Sterling Hayden** in *Terror In A Texas Town* (58), to see both men give the sort of edgy, committed performances that simply weren't required of them in the bigger-budget movies they sometimes made.

OTHER KEY FILMS: *My Name Is Julia Ross* (46); *So Dark The Night* (47); *Undercover Man* (49); *A Lady Without Passport* (52); *Desperate Search* (53); *Cry Of The Hunted* (54); *Lawless Street* (56)

Lewton, Val

Lewton was the expressionist maestro of the **B-movie** genre, and he was largely responsible for returning horror to the mind, from where, after all, it had sprung, claws unsheathed, in the first place. His dark reign began when he joined **RKO** as a producer in 1942, and the next four years saw him responsible for **Jacques Tourneur's** *Cat People* (42), *I Walked With A Zombie* (43) and *The Leopard Man* (43), Mark Robson's *The Seventh Victim* (43), *The Ghost Ship* (43), *Youth Runs Wild* (44), *Isle Of The Dead* (45) and *Bedlam* (46), and **Robert Wise's** *The Curse Of The Cat People* (44) [co-dir. by Gunther von Fritsch], *Mademoiselle Fifi* (44) and *The Body Snatcher* (45). Not all these were the successes that Lewton devotees would have them be, but they were all inspired as much by intelligence and visual daring (often in the interests of economy), as they were by the desire to rake in the dollars and cents. *I Walked With A Zombie*, for instance, is genuinely eerie, and *The Curse Of The Cat People* is an odd little tale, more psychological fairytale than horror flick, and impossible to contemplate outside the freedom afforded by the B-movie genre. Lewton died of a heart attack, aged just forty-six, having produced only three mediocre films in his last five years of life, although it must be said that Hugo Fregonese's curious little **Western** *Apache Drums* (51) has its moments.

Library

A feature film repository, open, under certain conditions, to the general public, and which can act either as a point of reference, study or entertainment, or simply as a source for otherwise hard-to-find material.

Library Shot

Previously filmed stock footage that is then held in library conditions for later use when live, on location, or action filming is inappropriate. A classic example would be the ageless slithering crocodile that plunges into the water in all good *Tarzan* films, triggering a flustered response from a gaggle of stock-footage flamingos. Thundering herds of buffalo, impala and zebra are another firm favourite, preferably seen escaping from imminent forest fires, the hazy reflection of which will hopefully disguise the fact that the footage was actually shot by old Macumazhan himself (Allan Quatermain) forty years before, on inferior film which has subsequently deteriorated beyond any reasonable hope of redemption due to damp, mould and serial neglect.

Light Box

The illuminated desk upon which animators will customarily paint their **cells**.

Lighting

Lighting is utterly crucial to all good cinematography, and is used both to define and to highlight the atmosphere of any given film, scene or shot. Lighting is the province of the lighting cameraman (see **Cinematographer**), and a good practitioner will spend far more time setting up and defining his lighting plan than he will in actually shooting the film. Films that are particularly remarkable for their lighting effects include Clarence Brown's *Flesh And The Devil* (27) [William Daniels Ph.], **Orson Welles's** *Citizen Kane* (40) [**Gregg Toland** Ph.] and **Charles Laughton's** magical *The Night Of The Hunter* (55) [Stanley Cortez Ph.] – moonlight has never been better conjured up in a studio.

Lighting Cameraman

See **Cinematographer**

Lighting Plot

The cinematographer's personal guide to the lighting set-up that he or she plans to use in a particular scene or take.

Light Meter

See **Exposure Meter**

Lily

A sequence of coloured shots appearing at the start or finish of a roll of film which serve as a bell-wether guide to the film processor when it comes to cross-checking for colour and tonal accuracy.

Limbo

A thoroughly blacked-out set designed to highlight only the principal protagonist, or protagonists, in a shot.

Line Test

A photographed test sequence of simple animated drawings used as a quality check before the more sophisticated **cell** drawings are embarked upon.

199

Lining Up

The last-minute setting-up sequence before a cameraman can actually begin shooting and which ensures that the lighting, the camera and the subject-to-be will all be correctly positioned.

Lip Synch

The exact synchronisation of recorded sound to recorded image, particularly in the case of dialogue.

Liquid Gate

The gate through which a film passes during printing in the laboratory and which ensures that it receives a consistent coating of anti-abrasive liquid.

Live Action

Any subject or piece of film that shows real people and real action as opposed to the artificial imitation of such a thing.

Livesey, Roger

Seductively gravel-voiced star of British film throughout the 1940s and 50s, Livesey will be forever remembered for his Torquil MacNeil in **Michael Powell's** cult love story *I Know Where I'm Going* (45), opposite **Wendy Hiller's** Joan Webster. Memorable also as a tramp forced to sit, against his better judgment, for **Charles Laughton's** momentarily inspired *Rembrandt* in **Alexander Korda's** magnificent 1936 biopic, Livesey customarily played sensitive, old-school Englishmen, who yet had a glitter in their rheumy, pipe-smoke-laden eyes. His finest performance came as Dr Reeves in Powell's *A Matter Of Life And Death* (46) in which he diagnosed a cerebrally stricken **David Niven** while at the same time charming (quite innocently, of course) the gorgeous Kim Hunter. He and his gentlemanly ilk, though bitterly missed in this most ungentlemanly of ages, at least remain captured for posterity on celluloid.

OTHER KEY FILMS: *The Life And Death Of Colonel Blimp* (43); *Vice Versa* (47); *That Dangerous Age* (49); *The Master Of Ballantrae* (53); *The Intimate Stranger* (56); *The League Of Gentlemen* (60); *The Entertainer* (60); *Of Human Bondage* (64); *Hamlet* (69)

Live Sound

The simultaneous recording of sound with action, as opposed to later, in-studio **dubbing**.

Livestock Man/Girl

The person or persons responsible for the management and well-being of any animals required to appear on a film set.

Lloyd, Harold

Lloyd was the great survivor. Of all the silent stars of comedy, it was he who glided athletically through to a comfortable and secure old age, free from obvious vices and other self-destructive inroads. His two stock characters, 'Willie Work' and 'Lonesome Luke', both reflect this serene confidence in ordinariness, and even in Sam Taylor and Fred Newmeyer's *The Freshman* (25), Lloyd's eager college boy is notable for his pathetic desire to belong, at any cost, even if it means becoming a laughing stock. Lloyd's most celebrated scene, the clock-dangling trick in Taylor and Newmeyer's *Safety Last* (23), came about in an ordinary way too – his stuntman had inadvertently broken his leg and the star thought, oh well, he might as well do it himself.

OTHER KEY FILMS: *Algy On The Force* (13); *Lonesome Luke* (15); *The Big Idea* (18); *Bumping Into Broadway* (19); *His Royal Slyness* (19); *Haunted Spooks* (20); *A Sailor-Made Man* (21); *Grandma's Boy* (22); *Girl Shy* (24); *Hot Water* (24); *The Kid Brother* (27); *Speedy* (28); *Welcome Stranger* (29); *The Cat's Paw* (34); *The Milky Way* (36)

KEY LINE:

'I am just turning forty and taking my time about it.' [Lloyd aged seventy-seven]

Loach, Ken

Loach is a committed socialist whose films reflect that commitment, concentrating on the marginal and the dispossessed, and endeavouring to throw a little light on their otherwise forgotten lives. His first feature, *Poor Cow* (69), remains in the memory more than thirty years after its first showing for its scathing depiction of the commonplace brutality of an allegedly caring state apparatus – in a Loach film, it is people who care and who can make a brief difference to lives, never institutions. *Raining Stones* (93) was a magnificently human film, finding comedy in horror and yet never losing sight of the deadening, brutalising effect poverty can have on even decent people, and *Ladybird, Ladybird* (94) deserved every critical accolade it received. Loach is that rare thing – a political filmmaker who never preaches, but simply shows.

OTHER KEY FILMS: *Kes* (69); *Wednesday's Child* (71); *The Gamekeeper* (78); *Black Jack* (79); *Looks And Smiles* (82); *Fatherland* [a.k.a. *Singing The Blues In Red* (86); *Hidden Agenda* (90); *Riff Raff* (91); *Land And Freedom* (95); *Carla's Song* (96); *The Flickering Flame* (97); *My Name Is Joe* (98); *Bread And Roses* (00)

Loader Boy/Girl

The person responsible for making sure all in-use cameras are loaded with film.

Loading

The simple act of inserting film inside a camera prior to shooting.

Lobby Cards

Still in use today, lobby cards were devised by **Universal** in 1913 as a convenient form of postcard-sized advertisement for future features.

Location

Any shooting area located beyond the confines of the studio back lot. With the increasing sophistication of studios during the 1920s and 1930s, an escalating amount of film work was conducted inside the studio boundaries, avoiding the expensive and often dangerous translocation of bulky and valuable technical equipment. This situation changed in the late 1940s with the invention of lighter and more malleable equipment,

A 1933 Carole Lombard studio shot, from around the time she divorced William Powell and just before her big breakthrough as Mildred Plotka/Lily Garland in Howard Hawks's Twentieth Century *(34)*

twinned with an increasingly sophisticated audience who were simply not prepared to accept poor quality **back projection**. Location work is now the norm rather than the exception, but studio work, particularly in the **special effects** realm, still accounts for a major proportion of the schedule of most blockbusting movies.

Logo

The trademark symbol of a particular studio, a logo is intended to elicit an instant shock of recognition in the viewer. Notable examples include the **Rank** gong, the **MGM** lion, and the **Selznick** mansion.

Log Sheet

A fastidiously kept record of what has been done in terms of sound production and filming during the shooting of a feature.

Lombard, Carole

Lombard was **Clark Gable's** great love, and one of the funniest women in movies (try Gregory La Cava's *My Man Godfrey* (36) or **William Wellman's** *Nothing Sacred* (37) for an exquisite taste). She was beautiful, too, in a radiant, laconic way, as if she couldn't quite understand what all the fuss was about but, well, if men were made that way, who was she to cavil? Her life and career are made all the more poignant by the manner of her death – happily married to Gable, she briefly left his side to go on tour selling US war bonds, and her returning aircraft crashed. Gable was distraught for years, and Lombard's fans, who included President Roosevelt, bereft. Her swansong was **Ernst Lubitsch's** magnificent *To Be Or Not To Be* (42), a comedy beyond time itself, just as she is.

OTHER KEY FILMS: *The Arizona Kid* (30); *Ladies' Man* (31); *No Man Of Her Own* (32); *Twentieth Century* (34); *Hands Across The Table* (35); *Love Before Breakfast* (36); *Made For Each Other* (39); *In Name Only* (39); *Mr And Mrs Smith* (41)

KEY LINE:
'How would you like this spaghetti applied to your person?' [Carole Lombard as Amy Peters, in Garson Kanin's *They Knew What They Wanted* (40)]

London Film Festival, The

Now based at London's South Bank-located National Film Theatre and its surrounding cinemas, the annual London Film Festival was founded in 1958 to provide a forum for prestigious and worthy international and domestic films. It has now broadened its remit to

201

include separate festivals celebrating lesbian and gay filmmaking and films made for television, and also peripherally incorporates the 'Guardian Interview' series of on-stage tête-à-têtes with those involved creatively and artistically in the making of motion pictures.

Long-focus Lens

A powerful lens that is used to capture and magnify distant images because of its superior focal length.

Long Shot

The same as a full shot, or 'fs', the long shot is one which incorporates the whole of a figure or subject on the screen within a recognisable perspective, but to the detriment of individual detail. Also known as an **establishing shot**.

Looney Tunes

Together with **Merrie Melodies**, this was a long-running series of **Warner Brothers'** cartoons for which the unique **Mel Blanc** provided the voices. Stock characters include **Bugs Bunny**, **Porky Pig**, **Tweetie Pie**, **Sylvester** and **Speedy Gonzales**.

Loop

A continuous loop of film or audio-tape left running during sound editing so that the **dubbing** and **mixing** process can be effectively synchronised.

Looping

A sound technician's nightmare, looping occurs when live soundtrack has to be replaced by pre-recorded sound as in the case of a botched or misheard line, or, at the director's instigation, when the imposition or dubbing of a 'more natural' effect must be made over an existing, unwanted one, such as the howl of a jet or the barking of a distant dog.

Loren, Sophia

When the German army withdrew from Naples in 1944, Loren was barely ten years old, and the experiences she had then, of fear, hunger and uncertainty (readers of Norman Lewis's brilliant *Naples '44* will have some idea of the hell on earth the place then was) must have gone a long way towards forming the joyful, yet intrinsically serious woman we see on the screen in such films as **Vittorio De Sica's** *Two Women* (60), **Anthony Mann's** *El Cid* (61) and **Stanley Donen's** *Arabesque* (66). Always a luminous beauty, Loren has aged wonderfully well, and though she rarely appears in films now, she carries her deserved celebrity lightly and with panache.

OTHER KEY FILMS: *The Anatomy Of Love* (53); *The Miller's Beautiful Wife* (55); *Boy On A Dolphin* (57); *Houseboat* (58); *That Kind Of Woman* (59); *The Millionairess* (60); *The Condemned Of Altona* (62); *The Fall Of The Roman Empire* (64); *Lady L* (65); *The Voyage* (74); *A Special Day* (77); *Sun* (97); *Destinazione Verna* (00)

Sophia Loren as Juana in Stanley Kramer's otherwise unremarkable The Pride And The Passion *(57)*

Lorre, Peter

One of the funniest of all Spike Jones's song spoofs is his rendition of 'My Old Flame' in a Peter Lorre voice. For Lorre *was* his voice, and it's uncanny just how many people can actually imitate it very well indeed. His nervous tics, his arching eyebrows and his smarmy, too-smooth-by-half mannerisms all went to making him, along with **Walter Brennan** and **Sidney Greenstreet**, one of the most instantly recognisable character actors of them all. Think of his Joel Cairo in **John Huston's** *The Maltese Falcon* (41), or his Señor Ugarte in **Michael Curtiz's** *Casablanca* (42) – just what nationality was Ugarte meant to be? Or didn't it matter? Earlier, before his passage to Hollywood (not to Marseille), he was the cringing, murderous, doomed Franz Becker in **Fritz Lang's** *M* (31), and a superbly chilling assassin, known only as The General, for **Alfred Hitchcock**, in *Secret Agent* (36), who was so single-minded in his hatred of the enemy that even placid allies like **John Gielgud's** Edgar Brody feared him.

OTHER KEY FILMS: *Pionier In Inoplastadt* (28); *The Man Who Knew Too Much* (34); *Crime And Punishment* (35); *Think Fast, Mr Moto* (37); *Strange Cargo* (40); *All Through The Night* (42); *The Constant Nymph* (43); *Background To Danger* (43); *Passage To Marseille* (44); *The Mask Of Dimitrios* (44); *Arsenic And Old Lace* (44); *Confidential Agent* (45); *The Beast With Five Fingers* (46); *Black Angel* (46); *Beat The Devil* (54); *Tales Of Terror* (62); *The Raven* (63).

Losey, Joseph

An American director, working in England, and venerated by the French – always a contradiction in terms – Losey made films that are often perverse, sometimes hysterical, but consistently interesting. Driven out of the US by Senator McCarthy's HUAC (see **Hollywood Ten**), Losey, who had shown himself capable, with *The Prowler* (51) and *The Concrete Jungle* (60), of making commercially successful mainstream scorchers, now found himself, a bare three years later, making convoluted and pretentious trash like *Eva* (63). That, fortunately, was the low point, although the sheer unlikeability of many of his characters militated against the undoubted success of such otherwise astute social satires as *The Servant* (64) and *Accident* (68). The *Go-Between*, in 1971, was a second marvellous return to form, but even then there was no one the viewer could actually empathise with, thanks to Losey's humans-as-ants obsession.

OTHER KEY FILMS: *The Boy With The Green Hair* (49); *The Lawless* (51); *The Big Night* (52); *The Sleeping Tiger* (55); *Finger Of Guilt* [a.k.a. *The Intimate Stranger*] (57); *Chance Meeting* [a.k.a. *Blind Date*] (60); *King And Country* (66); *Mr Klein* (78)

Lot

See **Back Lot**

Best Love Films

Frank Borzage's *A Farewell To Arms* (32); **Frank Capra's** *The Bitter Tea Of General Yen* (32); **Marcel Carné's** *Quai Des Brumes* (38) and *Les Visiteurs Du Soir* (42); **Alfred Hitchcock's** *Rebecca* (40); **Krzysztof Kieslowski's** *The Double Life Of Véronique* (91); **David Lean's** *Brief Encounter* (45); **Albert Lewin's** *Pandora And The Flying Dutchman* (51); **Ernst Lubitsch's** *The Shop Around The Corner* (40); Rouben Mamoulian's *Queen Christina* (33); **Joseph L Mankiewicz's** *The Ghost And Mrs Muir* (47); **Anthony Minghella's** *The English Patient* (96); **Max Ophüls's** *Liebelei* (32); Nagisa Oshima's *Ai No Corrida* (76); **Michael Powell** and **Emeric Pressburger's** *I Know Where I'm Going* (45) and *A Matter Of Life And Death* (46); **Nicholas Ray's** *They Live By Night* (49); **Josef von Sternberg's** *The Blue Angel* (29-30), *Morocco* (30) and *Shanghai Express* (32); **François Truffaut's** *Jules Et Jim* (62); **William Wyler's** *Roman Holiday* (53)

203

Low-angle Shot

This refers to a shot taken from below, facing upwards, which is normally used either to frame an actor or subject against the sky, or to highlight size and the menacing quality inherent in it. Low-angle shots are often used to show a scene from a child's, or even an animal's, perspective – remember **Danny DeVito's** *Matilda* (96)?

Low-budget Production

A feature film made on a limited budget and usually relegated to **B-movie** or **independent** status as a result. Examples of low-budget productions which have crossed over into the mainstream are **Dennis Hopper's** *Easy Rider* (69), **Joel Coen's** *Blood Simple* (84), and Eduardo Sanchez and Daniel Myrick's *The Blair Witch Project* (99).

Low Key

Both the description of an atmosphere and the lighting style that leads to it, low key defines the moment when moral darkness and highly contrasted shadow take over from light and moral clarity. First used as a conscious aid to mood in the neo-**expressionist** films of **F W Murnau**, **Robert Wiene** and **Fritz Lang**, low-key lighting was picked up by such sublime *film noir* camera practitioners as Nick Musuraca, Sid Hickox and George E Diskant, who used it at the instigation of such directors as **Jacques Tourneur**, **Howard Hawks** and **Nicholas Ray** to reinforce the alienation and sense of betrayal felt by the characters in their stories.

Lubitsch, Ernst

A former actor, Lubitsch just occasionally took his direction of other actors to exaggerated, not to say fetishistic lengths. His best films are a delight to the eye and the ear, and are possibly the most good-natured and innocently decadent ever to have come out of Hollywood. Frequently working with screenwriter Samson Raphaelson, Lubitsch treated sex as a pleasure (something a little strange to puritan and Prohibition-minded America) whether it was in such frothy operettas as *The Merry Widow* (34), featuring **Maurice Chevalier** and Jeannette MacDonald or such sophisticated sex comedies as *Trouble In Paradise* (32), *Angel* (37) and *Ninotchka* (39), or in romance, with the delightful *The Shop Around The Corner* (40), satire (with a little sex thrown in, of course) in the sublime *To Be Or Not To Be* (42), or whimsy, with *Heaven Can Wait* (43). The 'Lubitsch touch' was a light one – Teutonic in concept and production, but rarely in the resolution. See **Heartstopping Moments**

OTHER KEY FILMS: *The Eyes Of The Mummy* (18); *The Oyster Princess* (19); *Madame Du Barry* (19); *Anna Boleyn* (20); *The Marriage Circle* (24); *The Patriot* (28); *The Love Parade* (29); *Design For Living* (33); *Bluebeard's Eighth Wife* (38); *That Uncertain Feeling* (41); *Cluny Brown* (46); *That Lady In Ermine* [completed by **Otto Preminger**] (48)

Lucas, George

Lucas began his career making promotional shorts for the films of his friend and erstwhile mentor **Francis Ford Coppola**. His first feature was an expanded version of his University of Southern California short, *THX 1138* (71), which already pointed the way to his trademark of astonishing visuals and underwritten scripts. *American Graffiti* followed in 1973, coincidentally launching the careers of a number of now veteran stars, including **Richard Dreyfuss** and **Harrison Ford**. Having earned only $20,000 from *American Graffiti* (the film, made on a tight

budget of $70,000, went on to gross $55 million), Lucas was forced to forgo the opportunity to collaborate with Coppola on *Apocalypse Now* (79), in order to work on his brainchild, *Star Wars*. Launched in 1977 but three years in the making, this proved to be a science-fiction fairy-tale which borrowed freely from just about every lucrative genre in the book, from **war movies** and **screwball comedies**, to **Westerns** and edge-of-the-seat, 'Perils of Pauline'-type cliff-hangers. Equally influential off-screen as a first-rate cutter and editor, Lucas was also the producer (through Lucasfilm) of **Akira Kurosawa's** *Kagemusha* (80), **Steven Spielberg's** *Indiana Jones* tetralogy (1981 onwards), Jim Henson's *Labyrinth* (86) and **Ron Howard's** *Willow* (88), as well as the driving force behind such technical innovations as THX sound and the Industrial Light & Magic (see **ILM**) special-effects company.

Lumet, Sidney

He started strongly, with *12 Angry Men* (57), peaked with *A Long Day's Journey Into Night* (62), *The Pawnbroker* (65) and *The Hill* (65), fought bravely on the way down with *The Anderson Tapes* (72), *The Offence* (73) and *Serpico* (73), and finally hit rock bottom with *A Stranger Among Us* (92). It's an odd career, almost as if two men were taking it in turns to direct Lumet's films. Recently, with *Guilty As Sin* (92) and *Night Falls In Manhattan* (97), he has shown a welcome, if hesitant, return to form. Lumet has been both overrated and underrated in his time, and it is probably a tribute to his intelligence that, despite a career which has lasted for upwards of fifty years, he is still impossible to pigeon-hole.

OTHER KEY FILMS: *The Fugitive Kind* (59); *A View From The Bridge* (62); *Fail Safe* (64) *The Appointment* (69); *Dog Day Afternoon* (75); *Network* (76); *The Verdict* (82); *The Morning After* (86); *Gloria* (99); *Whistle* (00); *The Beautiful Mrs Seidenmann* (00)

Lumière, The Brothers

Louis and Auguste Lumière were the first people to envisage the motion picture as something that might appeal to a mass, rather to an individual audience, as was the case with **Thomas Edison's** peep-show **Kinetoscope**, the machine upon which their subsequent invention was based. They built and patented the **Cinématographe** in 1895, a dual-purpose camera/projector capable of foxing the eye (see **Persistence Of Vision**) into believing that what it was seeing on the screen was actually moving.

Following their successful showing of *La Sortie Des Usines Lumière* [*Workers Leaving The Lumière Factory*], on 22 March 1895, they went on to present twelve short films in the cellar of the Grand Café, Boulevard des Capucines, Paris, on 28 December of the same year, which included what was probably the first-ever piece of filmed slapstick comedy, the brilliantly self-explanatory (Hollywood pitch artists please note) *L'Arroseur Arrosé* [*Watering The Gardener*]. It was at that exact moment that the cinema, as we know it, was born.

Luminaire

A composite lighting unit that already incorporates all the elements necessary for it to function, including the stand, the lamp, and the frame within which the lamp is housed.

Lupino, Ida

Descended from a long line of English stage entertainers, Lupino became one of the only women directors to work successfully within the 1950s Hollywood system. Her best film as director was *The Hitch-Hiker* (53), a convincing portrait of criminal schizophrenia, but Lupino was better known for her acting, and her waif-like, girl-of-the-people looks allowed her to shine in a variety of roles, most notably opposite **John Garfield** in **Michael Curtiz's** *The Sea Wolf* (41), in **Jean Negulesco's** intriguingly offbeat *film noir* *Road House* (48), and best of all in **Nicholas Ray's** *On Dangerous Ground* (51), where her utterly convincing blind woman (watch how she

uses the hanging plants as an orientating device) finally contrives to soften the embittered heart of **Robert Ryan's** self-hating cop.

OTHER KEY FILMS: *Her First Affaire* (33); *Peter Ibbetson* (35); *Sea Devils* (37); *The Adventures Of Sherlock Holmes* (39); *They Drive By Night* (40); *High Sierra* (41); *Devotion* (46); *Escape Me Never* (47); *Beware, My Lovely* (52); *The Big Knife* (55); *While The City Sleeps* (56); *Junior Bonner* (72)

Lynch, David

After debuting with the extraordinary, low-budget *Eraserhead* (77), Lynch joined the mainstream with *The Elephant Man* (80), a high-quality but rather empty piece of work, and *Dune* (85), which lost a fortune, and which some die-hard fans still persist in viewing as a flawed masterpiece. His next film, *Blue Velvet* (86), *was* an undisputed masterpiece, and would, in itself, be enough to ensure him a niche in the ultimate movie pantheon in the sky (if there is such a place). *Wild At Heart* (90), another fervid, surreally perverse mini-masterpiece, followed, upon which Lynch branched out into television with the cult 'Twin Peaks' series – the disastrous *Fire Walk With Me* (92), was a 'Twin Peaks' spin-off. Well, *plus ça change…* Fans live on in the hope of a renaissance. See **Worst Films**

OTHER KEY FILMS: *Weeds* (87); *The Cabinet Of Dr Ramirez* (91); *Lumière Et Compagnie* [one section] (95); *Lost Highway* (97); *The Straight Story* (99); *Mulholland Drive* (01)

M & E

The M stands for music and the E for effects (sound), and the M & E track carries just these two facets, with no dialogue, ensuring its successful use in countries that customarily dub imported films into their own language.

McConaughey, Matthew

He's had a few hesitant starts (and one entertaining brush with the law when he was caught playing a bongo drum in the street, stark naked) but Jonathan Mostow's blockbusting though historically inaccurate *U-571* (00) looks set to confirm, or at least partially to justify, McConaughey's long-mooted bankable status. It all looked as if it might happen for McConaughey after Joel Schumacher's *A Time To Kill* (96), but our boy was still in his twenties and didn't yet have the screen presence to pull off a quick double. A series of misfires followed, which included **Steven Spielberg's** *Amistad* (97), **Robert Zemeckis's** *Contact* (97) and **Ron Howard's** *EdTV* (99), but McConaughey looks to be a stayer, and, born in 1969, he still has youth on his side.

OTHER KEY FILMS: *The Texas Chainsaw Massacre 2* (86); *Dazed And Confused* (93); *Boys On The Side* (95); *Lone Star* (96); *The Wedding Planner* (01)

KEY LINE:
'If I wasn't naked, it wouldn't be funny.' [McConaughey on his brush with the law]

McCrea, Joel

An understated and modest actor who shone in both comedic and dramatic roles, McCrea graced two of the funniest films ever to come out of the Hollywood studio system – **Preston Sturges's** *Sullivan's Travels* (41) and *The Palm Beach Story* (42). Both films relied on him as the earnest straight man, baffled by the chaos surrounding his every move. Later he moved back into **Westerns**, making a fine career for himself in a series of **Jacques Tourneur** films, which included *Stars In My Crown* (50) and *Wichita* (55). His career ended on a high, with the superb **Sam Peckinpah** Western, *Ride The High Country* (62).

OTHER KEY FILMS: *The Silver Cord* (33); *Barbary Coast* (35); *These Three* (36); *Wells Fargo* (37); *Union Pacific* (39); *Foreign Correspondent* (40); *The More The Merrier* (43); *The Great Moment* (44); *Fort Massacre* (58)

KEY LINE:
'Everybody's a flop until he's a success.' [McCrea to **Claudette Colbert** in *The Palm Beach Story*]

McDormand, Frances

A favourite with independent filmmakers on account of her offbeat good looks and inspired capacity for eccentricity, McDormand has been a **Coen Brothers** regular since her first appearance in *Blood Simple* (84), and made a strong impression as pregnant police officer Marge Gunderson in *Fargo* (96), for which she received a best-actress **Oscar**. That same year she gave another knockout performance as the daddy-dominated Bunny in **John Sayles's** magnificent *Lone Star* (96), and she bids fair to continue her run as one of the finest character actresses working in American cinema.

OTHER KEY FILMS: *Raising Arizona* (87); *Mississippi Burning* (88); *Chattahoochee* (89); *Hidden Agenda* (90); *The Butcher's Wife* (91); *Crazy In Love* (92); *Passed Away* (92); *Short Cuts* (93); *Primal Fear* (96); *Paradise Road* (97); *Talk Of Angels* (98); *Wonder Boys* (00); *Almost Famous* (00); *The Man Who Wasn't There* (01)

KEY LINE:

'There's more to life than a little money, you know. Don't you know that? And here you are. And it's a beautiful day. I just don't understand it.' [McDormand's Marge Gunderson to captured killer Gaear Grimsrud (Peter Stormare) on his way to jail]

McDowell, Malcolm

McDowell had a remarkable beginning to his career, acting in a trio of arguably the most important British films to emerge from the dying fall of the 1960s – **Lindsay Anderson's** *If…* (68) and *O Lucky Man!* (73), and **Stanley Kubrick's** *A Clockwork Orange* (71). McDowell's rather repellent screen persona did not wear well, however, and he began to appear in a series of increasingly turgid commercial vehicles during the late 1970s and early 1980s, **Paul Schrader's** *Cat People* (82) notwithstanding. His recent demented lead performance in Paul McGuigan's ultra-violent thriller *Gangster No 1* (00) may go some way towards resuscitating an, of late, rather moribund screen career.

OTHER KEY FILMS: *Figures In A Landscape* (70); *Aces High* (76); *Caligula* (79); *Britannia Hospital* (82); *Gulag* (85); *Bopha!* (93); *Star Trek: Generations* (94); *The Gardener* (98); *Just Visiting* (01)

McGuffin

Alfred Hitchcock maintained that all good movies must have a McGuffin – something for the audience to latch on to but which has absolutely no real relevance to the plot. The greatest of all McGuffins came, not in a Hitchcock film, but rather in **Robert Aldrich's** *Kiss Me Deadly* (55), where private-eye Mike Hammer spends the entire film chasing after a nebulous nuclear spectre that only briefly appears as a supremely irrelevant blaze of brilliant golden light emanating from a box – the audience never do get to discover what it is, but just that everybody wants it. It gave Aldrich a damned good pretext for his movie, though.

Mackendrick, Alexander

One of Britain's greatest directors, Sandy Mackendrick proved himself that rare thing – a man who could successfully direct comedy, with *Whisky Galore!* (49) and *The Ladykillers* (55), satire, with *The Man In The White Suit* (51), romance, with *Saraband For Dead Lovers* (48), tragedy, with his American masterpiece, *Sweet Smell Of Success* (57), and even children's films, with *Sammy Going South* (63). It's as if he had to test himself, at least once, in every possible category – and it worked.

OTHER KEY FILMS: *Mandy* (52); *The Maggie* (54); *A High Wind In Jamaica* (65)

McLaglen, Victor

McLaglen was a genuine tough, with his barrel chest and cocky, big-man's walk. An ex-boxer and inveterate fighter, he was a strange choice as **Marlene Dietrich's** romantic leading man in **Josef von Sternberg's** *Dishonored* (31), but he made a more than adequate stab at the part. **John Ford** used him in a number of films, most notably as Gypo, in *The Informer* (35), for which McLaglen won a well-deserved **Oscar**. Hardly a great actor, he was rather wonderful, in a comic buffoon sort of a way, in Ford's great trilogy of **Westerns**, *Fort Apache* (48), *She Wore A Yellow Ribbon* (49), and *Rio Grande* (50), playing Sgt Festus Mulcahy, Sgt Quincannon, and Sgt-Major Quincannon, respectively. The sly, drunken characterisation, of course, was always delightfully the same.

OTHER KEY FILMS: *The Call Of The Road* (20); *Winds Of Chance* (25); *Beau Geste* (26); *Mother Machree* (28); *A Devil With Women* (30); *The Lost Patrol* (34); *Wee Willie Winkie* (37); *The Quiet Man* (52)

MacMurray, Fred

MacMurray played charming and faintly stressed pipe-smoking family men and he played *film noir* crooks. The *film noir* crooks were better. Best of all was his Walter Neff in **Billy Wilder's** *Double Indemnity* (44), entangled in **Barbara Stanwyck's** platinum blonde coils; he reprised the idea, if not the role, of the honest man drawn into deceit, in Richard Quine's *Pushover* (54), this time with a deceptively innocent-looking **Kim Novak** to tempt him. When you've seen those two, go back to Chester Erskine's *The Egg And I* (47) and weep.

OTHER KEY FILMS: *The Texas Rangers* (36); *Remember The Night* (40); *The Lady Is Willing* (42); *Above Suspicion* (43); *Murder He Says* (45); *Singapore* (47); *An Innocent Affair* (48); *Fair Wind To Java* (53); *The Caine Mutiny* (54); *Woman's World* (54); *Day Of The Badmen* (58); *Face Of A Fugitive* (59)

McQueen, Steve

Always a man's man, McQueen's weather-beaten face perfectly echoed the deprived, institutional background that made him that way. Catapulted to stardom (although not over the border into Switzerland) in **John Sturges's** *The Great Escape* (63), he was a massively successful actor despite, in many ways, running against the grain of his own times. Often playing detached, sporadically charming loners, he excelled as a high-stakes poker player in Norman Jewison's *The Cincinnati Kid* (65), and also as the hard-boiled cop in Peter Yates's *Bullitt* (68). His best performance came as *Junior Bonner* (72) for director **Sam Peckinpah**, in which McQueen looked wryly back at the traditions and culture that had formed him, while they disappeared, quite literally in a cloud of dust, beneath his eyes. He died, tragically, of an asbestos-related cancer at the age of only fifty.

OTHER KEY FILMS: *The Magnificent Seven* (60); *Love With The Proper Stranger* (63); *Soldier In The Rain* (63); *Nevada Smith* (66); *The Sand Pebbles* (66); *The Thomas Crown Affair* (68); *The Reivers* (69); *The Getaway* (72); *Junior Bonner* (72); *Papillon* (73); *The Towering Inferno* (74); *An Enemy Of The People* (77); *Tom Horn* (80); *The Hunter* (80)

KEY LINE:

'…McQueen was an impossible bastard. A third of the way through the picture, McQueen took charge. I had to rewrite his scenes and rearrange them…oh, he drove you crazy.' [Scriptwriter **W R Burnett** on the making of John Sturges's *The Great Escape* (63), which he co-scripted with novelist James Clavell]

Macrocinematography

The close-up filming of tiny objects through a variable focus macro lens, rather than through a microscope.

Madonna

Who is Madonna? A singer? A celebrity? A phenomenon? And who cares? Her film career hasn't, for certain, been particularly hot, although her debut as Susan in Susan Seidelman's *Desperately Seeking Susan* (85) was at least competent, given the context. She was perfectly acceptable, hot sex scenes and all, in Uli Edel's *Body Of Evidence* (93), and really quite good in **Alan Parker's** *Evita* (96) if you like that sort of thing, but **John Schlesinger's** *The Next Best Thing* (00), in which she partners real-life friend **Rupert Everett**, seems to represent yet another lead nail in the coffin of her screen career.

OTHER KEY FILMS: *Who's That Girl?* (87); *Dick Tracy* (90); *Shadows And Fog* (92)

Magazine

A sealed lightproof box attached to a motion-picture camera which contains both a **feed reel**, to facilitate the passing of the unexposed film stock in front of the lens, and a **take-up** reel, upon which the exposed film is automatically rewound after use.

Magirama

Abel Gance and André Debrie thought up this tri-screen projection technique in 1955, but it enjoyed only a brief run during the late 1950s, proving irritating to audiences used to more conventional screenings.

Magnetic Film

A form of magnetically coated film that allows for the instantaneous and perfect correlation of sound and image, thanks to the fact that its size exactly matches that of conventional film stock – evenly spaced perforations on both lengths of film ensure perfect post-partum synchronisation.

Magnetic Recording

The reproduction of sound by non-**digital** means, using ferromagnetic tape.

Magnetic Stripes

Iron-oxide-coated stripes running down either side of a strip of film and used for the purpose of simultaneously recording sound and image.

Steve McQueen as anti-heroic Police Lieutenant Frank Bullitt, in Peter Yates's tough 1968 thriller, Bullitt

Magnetic Tape

This is tape coated with iron oxide and used for sound recording; magnetic videotape is used for recording both sound and image simultaneously.

Magoptical Prints

Motion-picture release prints that carry both a ferromagnetic and an optical soundtrack for use in cinemas that are equipped with either one or the other system, but not both. Also useful when the requirement is for foreign-language dubbed versions.

Mahin, John Lee

Mahin was that strange example of Hollywood citizenry, the highly paid and committed studio-system screenwriter. His output was astonishing and his professionalism was complete – even Scott Fitzgerald acknowledged him as, 'among the half-dozen best picture writers in the business.' Mahin virtually created **Clark Gable's** royal persona, and even his lesser films, of which there were few, were interesting as much for the particular quality of their flaws as for their virtues. He had a hand (sometimes uncredited) in practically all **Victor Fleming's** greatest movies including *Red Dust* (32), *Treasure Island* (34), *Captains Courageous* (37), *Test Pilot* (38), **Gone With The Wind** (39), *The Wizard Of Oz* (39), *Dr Jekyll And Mr Hyde* (41) and *Tortilla Flat* (42), as well as scripting **Jack Conway's** *Boom Town* (40), **John Ford's** *Mogambo* (53) and **John Huston's** *Heaven Knows Mr Allison* (57). And that's just a fraction of his output.
OTHER KEY FILMS: **Howard Hawks's** *Scarface* (32); **W S Van Dyke's** *Naughty Marietta* (35); **Mervyn LeRoy's** *Quo Vadis* (51); John Ford's *The Horse Soldiers* (59)

Maibaum, Richard

Another great pro, but well below **John Lee Mahin** on the studio scale of greatness, Maibaum has impressive screen credits that conjure up a mixture of the commercial and the literate, with the commercial predominating. With co-script credits on a total of eleven (yes, eleven) **James Bond** films, it would be easy to forget Maibaum's earlier scripts of the quality of Elliott Nugent's *The Great Gatsby* (49) – which was far better than the **Robert Redford** version – Terence Young's *Paratrooper* (54), José Ferrer's *Cockleshell Heroes* (56) and **Nicholas Ray's** *Bigger Than Life* (56).
OTHER KEY FILMS: Terence Young's *Dr No* (63), *From Russia With Love* (64) and *Thunderball* (65); Guy Hamilton's *Goldfinger* (64), *Diamonds Are Forever* (71) and *The Man With The Golden Gun* (74); John Glen's *For Your Eyes Only* (81), *Octopussy* (83) and *A View To A Kill* (85)

Main Title

The part of the **credits** sequence which tells us, in big letters, the name of the film we are about to watch.

Make-up

One of the side-effects of both black-and-white and colour film stock is that it exaggerates existing blemishes or facial peculiarities and makes them far more noticeable than they are in real life. Make-up, or at least the sophisticated use of some of its elements, is the only answer to this. Max Factor produced the first dedicated film make-up in 1914, and stars have never looked back (although they may well have looked better) since. King of the self-make-up department was actor **Lon Chaney**, known as 'the man of a thousand faces', but despite his extreme example, few actors and actresses care to attend to their own beautification, preferring the gossip and pampering that goes with a professional job. Readers looking for a neat reverse example of the beautification principle need look no further than **Dustin Hoffman**/Jack Crabb's 121-year-old-man make-up in **Arthur Penn's** *Little Big Man* (70).

Malick, Terrence

Malick represents the obverse of the usual Hollywood coin – an erudite, literate man who chose not to make any movies for twenty years because he wasn't prepared to settle for second best. *Badlands* (73) was his first feature as producer/director/screenwriter, a canny film that took some of the elements from **Nicholas Ray's** *They Live By Night* (49) and some of the elements from **Joseph H Lewis's** *Gun Crazy* (49), and combined them into a modern parable. *Days Of Heaven* (78) was more original if marginally less satisfying, and it wasn't until the release of *The Thin Red Line* (98) that it became clear that Malick's somewhat elusive reputation was justified – it was as if (were one to believe the news reports) J D Salinger had at last brought out his long-awaited masterpiece. *The Thin Red Line* wasn't as good as all that, but it wasn't bad either. If Malick keeps up his production ratio, he'll have three more films in him before he hits eighty.

Malkovich, John

A stage actor and director who just happens to make films, Malkovich made his first mark in the movies playing a blind man, in Robert Benton's *Places In The Heart* (84). In that same year he began to construct his international reputation with Roland Joffé's *The Killing Fields* (84), but he had a set-back the following year when he botched the lead role in **Peter Yates's** *Eleni* (85). He was far better as Tom in **Paul Newman's** *The Glass Menagerie* (87), but he really found his feet as the lubricious Vicomte de Valmont in **Stephen Frears's** *Dangerous Liaisons* (88), which may still be his best film performance. Now something of a self-referential icon following the surprise success of Spike Jonze's *Being John Malkovich* (99), he is one of those rare actors who are equally at home on stage or on celluloid.
OTHER KEY FILMS: *Empire Of The Sun* (87); *The Sheltering Sky* (90); *Of Mice And Men* (92); *Shadows And Fog* (92); *In The Line Of Fire* (93); *Beyond The Clouds* (95); *Mulholland Falls* (96); *Con Air* (97); *The Man In The Iron Mask* (98); *Shadow Of The Vampire* (00); *Les Âmes Fortes* (01); *Knockaround Guys* (01)

Malle, Louis

Malle began his directing career by making one of the best thrillers ever to come out of France, *Ascenseur Pour L'Échafaud* (58) – which also benefited from a terrific Miles Davis score – which he followed up with *Les Amants* (58). With a beginning like that, it was odds on that he would fall flat on his face, and it redounds to his eternal credit that after such a garishly commercial film as *Viva Maria!* (65) he was able to come back as subtly as he did in *Le Voleur* (67), *Le Souffle Au Coeur* (71) and the magnificent *Lacombe Lucien* (73). But it is his later films, beginning with *Atlantic City* (81), and moving through *My Dinner With André* (81) and *Au Revoir Les Enfants* (87) to the delightful *Milou En Mai* (89), that have permanently secured the reputation of this elusive, deeply committed, and much lamented filmmaker.
OTHER KEY FILMS: *Le Monde Du Silence* (56); *Zazie Dans Le Métro* (60); *Pretty Baby* (78); *Damage* (92); *Vanya On 42nd Street* (94)

Maltese Cross

The apparatus, in the form of a Maltese cross, that allows **intermittent movement** to occur in a motion-picture camera or film projector.

Mankiewicz, Joseph L

One of the most erudite of all Hollywood writer/directors, this former producer and screenwriter became an actor's dream when he finally took up directing after nearly twenty years in the movie business, with such masterpieces of commercial cinema as *A Letter To Three Wives* (49), the nail-bitingly good *Five Fingers* (52) and the **Humphrey Bogart/Ava Gardner** vehicle *The Barefoot Contessa* (54). Even when he stuck his neck out with more controversial material, as in Tennessee Williams's *Suddenly Last Summer* (59), he was always interesting and sometimes, as in his earlier *All About Eve* (50) and *People Will Talk* (51), sublime. See **Heartstopping Moments**
OTHER KEY FILMS: *Dragonwyck* (46); *The Ghost And Mrs Muir* (47); *No Way Out* (50); *Julius Caesar* (53); *Guys And Dolls* (55); *The Quiet American* (58); *Cleopatra* (63); *Sleuth* (72)

Mann, Anthony

Anthony Mann made **Westerns**, thrillers and sword-fight movies, and he was, quite simply, one of the best directors ever to come out of the Hollywood system. He understood early on that making a genre film did not mean you couldn't probe the human condition, just as more pretentious directors might claim, and signally fail, to do. From his early *film noir*, *Raw Deal* (48), through his magnificent series of psychological Westerns with **James Stewart**, which included *Winchester 73* (50) and *The Naked Spur* (53), right down to the outstanding and critically underrated *El Cid* (61), Mann made magic out of material that, in other hands, might have remained simply mundane.
OTHER KEY FILMS: *T-Men* (48); *Border Incident* (49); *Side Street* (49); *The Tall Target* (51); *Bend Of The River* (52); *Thunder Bay* (53); *The Far Country* (54); *The Man From Laramie* (55); *The Tin Star* (57); *Man Of The West* (58); *The Fall Of The Roman Empire* (64); *The Heroes Of Telemark* (65)
KEY LINE:
'I avoided him because I figured, Jeez, this is a no-talent guy. You couldn't even have a conversation with him, he was so ignorant. And it turns out we made ten, eleven pictures together...he understood the camera...understood concept.' [Screenwriter **Philip Yordan** on Mann, with whom he collaborated on, among other movies, *The Man From Laramie* [co-script] (55), *El Cid* [co-script] (61) and *The Fall Of The Roman Empire* [co-script] (64)]

March, Fredric

March had what **Thelma Ritter** would have called 'class', meaning that whatever he touched was never less than impressive, and often far more. He was a character actor at a time when character actors were usually quirky, eccentric individuals with one or two standard strings to their bows and little else – but March was considerably better than that. There are moments in Rouben Mamoulian's *Dr Jekyll And Mr Hyde* (32), **William Wellman's** *A Star Is Born* (37) and John Cromwell's *Victory* (40), when we feel we are in the presence of screen greatness, and looking back to those films, one realises that March's innate modesty of performance was the only thing that stood between him and the superstar celebrity of, say, a **Spencer Tracy.**

OTHER KEY FILMS: *My Sin* (31); *Design For Living* (33); *The Barretts Of Wimpole Street* (34); *Anna Karenina* (35); *Anthony Adverse* (36); *Nothing Sacred* (37); *I Married A Witch* (42); *The Best Years Of Our Lives* (46); *Christopher Columbus* (49); *Man On A Tightrope* (53); *Executive Suite* (54); *The Desperate Hours* (55); *Inherit The Wind* (60); *Seven Days In May* (64); *Hombre* (67); *The Iceman Cometh* (73)

Mark

Chalk marks are customarily used to plan out an actor's movements before the actual filming of a scene, and also to allow for a stand-in to follow the marks while the camera operator checks his focus. An actor 'misses his mark' when he fails to pull up, or turn, or stop and stare out of the window, at the pre-arranged time and place.

Marlowe, Philip

Fictional character created by **Raymond Chandler** and the protagonist in all his novels, Marlowe was a Los Angeles private eye of a unique ilk – he had to be 'the best man in his world and a good enough man for any world'. Such a moral dimension was virtually unique in the **pulp-fiction** realm of *Black Mask* and the many other magazines that catered to this most hard-boiled of genres. **Dick Powell,** Robert Montgomery, **Humphrey Bogart, Robert Mitchum, Elliot Gould** and James Garner all made a stab at the part, but Mitchum, for whom the character of Marlowe could have been written, won hands down in Dick Richards's late but masterful *Farewell My Lovely* (75). Bogart certainly made a brave shot at him in *The Big Sleep* (46), but he wasn't Marlowe, he was Bogart.

Married Print

A composite print that comprises both the picture and the synchronised sound that accompanies it.

Martin, Dean

Martin seemed as easy-going in private life as he was on the screen, and with his good looks, fine voice and apparently innate capacity to suggest that he was drunk when perfectly sober, he made a natural transition from the stage to the movies. He was **Jerry Lewis's** straight man for nearly eleven years and sixteen movies, providing the music, the romance and the shrugs, but when he branched out on his own he made an equal success of it, much to everyone's surprise. His best dramatic screen performance came in **Edward Dmytryk's** *The Young Lions* (58), in which he got to kill reformed Nazi **Marlon Brando** in one of the most unnecessary murders in screen history, but his high point came as Dude, in **Howard Hawks's** *Rio Bravo* (59). The film is so absurdly enjoyable, and Martin so utterly perfect as **John Wayne's** wreck of a friend, that even when he picks up his guitar and duets with Ricky Nelson, we smile in happy satisfaction, knowing that in the fantasy world we are inhabiting, all is indisputably well. It was all the sadder, then, when **Frank Sinatra's** Rat Pack finally got him, ensuring that the promise he had shown at the beginning of his solo career should turn to spoof.

OTHER KEY FILMS: *The Stooge* (53); *Artists And Models* (55); *Hollywood Or Bust* (56); *Some Came Running* (59); *Ocean's Eleven* (60); *The Sons Of Katie Elder* (65); *The Silencers* (66); *Bandolero!* (68); *Five Card Stud* (68)

KEY LINE:
'He liked to swing his golf clubs, and I had heard about his drinking; but when he had something to do on the set, he was very professional.' [Screenwriter Walter Bernstein, who was working on **Marilyn Monroe's** final, unfinished project, *Something's Got To Give*, on co-star, Martin]

Martin, Steve

A former stand-up gagman (and warm-up act for The Carpenters), Martin has carved a strange niche for himself in Hollywood as the thinking man's comedian. From his first manic performance in Carl Reiner's *The Jerk* (79), through his underrated and wrongfully panned turn as the disillusioned music salesman in Herbert Ross's *Pennies From Heaven* (81), up to and beyond his quasi straight-man role in John Hughes's *Planes, Trains And Automobiles* (87), Martin has both written and acted with a full understanding of the long tradition of which he forms a part. Something of an acquired taste, when he really hits the spot, as in **Fred Schepisi's** *Roxanne* (87) [which he scripted], Martin is probably the finest screen comedian of his generation.

OTHER KEY FILMS: *Dead Men Don't Wear Plaid* (82); *All Of Me* (84); *Little Shop Of Horrors* (86); *Dirty Rotten Scoundrels* (88); *Parenthood* (89);

211

LA Story (91); *Housesitter* (92); *A Simple Twist Of Fate* (92); *Sgt. Bilko* (96); *Bowfinger* (99); *Novocaine* (01)
KEY LINE: 'I punched a totally innocent Hungarian.' [Frank Oz's *Housesitter* (92)]

Marvin, Lee

Marvin had seen darkness during his war service with the Marines, and the look and very often even the scent of death followed him throughout his career. He was a hard man in a pretty soft racket, and when he found a film to suit that hardness, as he did in **John Boorman's** *Point Blank* (67), the audience were brought just a little closer to their primitive selves, all the time wary and a little anxious that such a man may one day come their way. Marvin, of course, could ham with the best of them, and it was only rarely that a director could lever below the surface to the heart of darkness within. His most authentic films, for just that reason, were **Fritz Lang's** *The Big Heat* (53), in which he threw boiling-hot coffee in **Gloria Grahame's** face, **Michael Curtiz's** *The Comancheros* (61), **John Ford's** *The Man Who Shot Liberty Valance* (62), **Don Siegel's** *The Killers* (64) and John Boorman's elliptical *Hell In The Pacific* (68), in which Marvin was persuaded to go back over the spirit of his own war and turn it into parable.
OTHER KEY FILMS: *Eight Iron Men* (52); *Gun Fury* (53); *The Wild One* (54); *The Caine Mutiny* (54); *Bad Day At Black Rock* (55); *Violent Saturday* (55); *Attack!* (56); *Donovan's Reef* (63); *Cat Ballou* (65); *The Professionals* (66); *The Dirty Dozen* (67); *Prime Cut* (72); *The Iceman Cometh* (73); *Shout At The Devil* (76); *The Big Red One* (80); *Gorky Park* (83)

Marx Brothers, The

Chico was the eldest, followed by Harpo, Groucho, Gummo and Zeppo (something of an afterthought ten years later), but the Marx Brothers as we know them consisted of Chico, with the hat and piano, Harpo, with the hair and harp, and Groucho, with just about everything else, but mostly the moustache and the cheap cigar. Schooled by their vaudeville-performing mother, the boys finally hit Broadway in 1924, where they were snapped up by the movies. Their anarchic humour (and it was anarchy – no normal life could continue in their nihilistic presence) spawned a series of demented works in which they played havoc with bourgeois values and restored to childhood what the adult world had stolen from it. Their greatest film together is Leo McCarey's *Duck Soup* (33), and though the humour palls occasionally, and their self-obsession has a tendency to turn the audience into tourists, ogling through the bars at a cage full of chimpanzees, at his best, Groucho's insane flights of fancy incorporate all the frustrations, longings and absurdities inherent in the American male, and leave us with the ghostly impression of a vulnerable person hidden behind the carapace of levity.
OTHER KEY FILMS: *Animal Crackers* (30); *Monkey Business* (31); *Horse Feathers* (32); *A Night At The Opera* (35); *A Day At The Races* (37); *At The Circus* (39); *The Big Store* (41); *A Night In Casablanca* (46)
KEY LINES
Groucho: 'That's in every contract. That's what they call a sanity clause.' Chico: 'You can't fool me. There ain't no Sanity Clause.' [*Night At The Opera*]

'I wasn't kissing her. I was just whispering in her mouth.' [Chico to his wife, on being discovered *in flagrante delicto*]

'Either he's dead, or my watch has stopped!' [Groucho: *A Day At The Races*]

'If you can't leave in a taxi you can leave in a huff. If that's too soon, you can leave in a minute and a huff.' [Groucho: *Duck Soup*]

'Remember, you're fighting for this woman's honour…which is probably more than she ever did.' [Groucho: *Duck Soup*]

'Why, a four-year-old child could understand this report. Run out and find me a four-year-old child. I can't make head or tail of it.' [Groucho: *Duck Soup*]

Telegram – PLEASE ACCEPT MY RESIGNATION. I DON'T WANT TO BELONG TO ANY CLUB THAT WILL ACCEPT ME AS A MEMBER. [*Groucho And Me*]

'I never forget a face, but in your case I'll be glad to make an exception.' [Groucho on relationships]

Mask

A gadget with a hole in it which can be placed across the lens of a motion-picture camera to limit the size of the picture, or to produce an opening or closing effect at the beginning or end of a scene. See **Iris**

Masking

The act of using a **mask** to block out certain portions of the image or picture being taken, in order to produce a particular effect.

Mason, James

A silky-toned and suave charmer whose performances varied widely in quality, Mason was at his best in such films as **Carol Reed's**

Odd Man Out (47), **Albert Lewin's** *Pandora And The Flying Dutchman* (51) and **Joseph L Mankiewicz's** *Five Fingers* (52), where he matched, and indeed surpassed, nearly all his contemporaries. What Mason had was mystery, and virtually no other male actor of his time could equal him for haunted charm – his Rommel, in **Henry Hathaway's** *The Desert Fox* (51), was definitive, and he impressed, too, as Humbert Humbert in **Stanley Kubrick's** *Lolita* (62). In both the morning and the late afternoon of his career he played attractive villains best, but there was a time, somewhere in the late 1940s and early 1950s, when he incarnated doomed lovers in such a fated, yet detached, way that he managed to carve out a romantic niche for himself that has never quite been refilled.

OTHER KEY FILMS: *Thunder Rock* (43); *The Man In Grey* (43); *The Wicked Lady* (46); *The Prisoner Of Zenda* (52); *Face To Face* (52); *Julius Caesar* (53); *Charade* (53); *A Star Is Born* (54); *Bigger Than Life* (56); *North By Northwest* (59); *Lord Jim* (65); *Georgy Girl* (66); *The Mackintosh Man* (73); *Cross Of Iron* (77); *The Shooting Party* (84)

Master Positive

A high-quality positive print made from an original negative and destined for use in the making of **fine-grain** copies.

Master Shot

The first shot in a scene to afford the audience an overall perspective.

Mastroianni, Marcello

Renowned both for his charm and for his unabashed philandering, Mastroianni was Italy's most famous actor, and retained this status until his death in 1996. **Federico Fellini's** screen alter ego, and a favourite of such directors as **Luchino Visconti** and **Michelangelo Antonioni**, he first made his international mark standing in the Trevi fountain alongside the voluptuous Anita Ekberg's breasts in Fellini's *La Dolce Vita* (60). A subtle actor, and not afraid of showing his insecurities on screen, Mastroianni could nevertheless miss the mark, and he (correctly) ascribed such occasional lows in his career to a consummate, though always charming, idleness.

OTHER KEY FILMS: *White Nights* (57); *La Notte* (61); *Vie Privée* (62); *Marriage, Italian Style* (63); *The Tenth Victim* (65); *Leo The Last* (70); *Blow-Out* (73); *La Nuit De Varennes* (81); *Ginger And Fred* (85); *Dark Eyes* (87); *Stanno Tutti Bene* (90)

*An early **Marcello Mastroianni** studio shot, showing just why he was considered the Italian answer to Marlon Brando*

Match Cut

A sudden cut from one object to another, a match cut often takes the shape of a visual pun. An example might be the cut from the flying kestrel as it leaves the hand of one of the pilgrims in **Michael Powell** and Emeric Pressburger's *A Canterbury Tale* (44), straight to a similarly shaped Spitfire fighter plane, 550 years later. In one fell swoop, as it were, we are taken to the present-day action, whilst being shown an important point along the way.

Match Dissolve

Similar in effect, if not in process, to a **match cut**, a match dissolve sees one image fade into another image as a means of passing important visual information, very often relating to time, to the audience. An obvious example would be the sudden ageing of a human face, from child to teenager for instance, or from teenager to adult, to allow the audience, already used to the look of the character in one incarnation, to realign itself to the next.

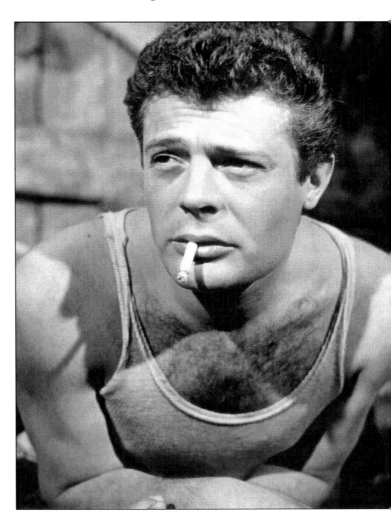

Matching

An advanced stage in the editing process during which the negative is compared to and cut to the measure of the work print.

Match Line

A form of cue marking, in animation, which indicates the moment when one object crosses another object.

Matte

A lens-blanking device that allows only part of the film to be exposed. The unexposed part can then have another image superimposed upon it, while the already exposed film is protected by a further matte device, cut to its exact dimensions.

Matte Artist

This is the person responsible for painting **matte** scenes for inclusion in partial shots. The famous Selznick mansion which appeared before the **credits** on any **David O Selznick** film is an example of a matte shot – the original mansion, far from being surrounded by gardens and graceful trees, sat in the studio back lot enclosed by building materials, which were careful blanked out and replaced, using Matte techniques.

Matte Box

See **Sunshade**

Matte Painting

A painting or partial painting of a particular background or architectural feature that is used in the composition of a **matte** shot. The famous shot of a Tibetan monastery framed against the Himalayas at the beginning of **Michael Powell** and Emeric Pressburger's *Black Narcissus* (47) is a case in point.

Matte Screen

A specially treated projection screen used during the matte process that affords equal light refraction and brightness from whatever angle it is viewed.

Matte Shot

A special-effects camera shot in which a number of different visual components go to make up the completed image.

Matthau, Walter

With his craggy features and loping, uncoordinated walk, Matthau was instantly recognisable in whatever role he played. Often teamed with **Jack Lemmon** in such comedic hits as Gene Saks's *The Odd Couple* (68), and **Billy Wilder's** *The Fortune Cookie* (66) and *The Front Page* (75), Matthau was also capable of effectively playing straight roles, such as the reluctant Sheriff Johnson in David Miller's *Lonely Are The Brave* (62), and the eponymous hero in the smooth **Don Siegel** thriller *Charley Varrick* (73), which has since become something of a cult, thanks to Matthau getting away with the heist, the dosh, *and* the acting honours.

OTHER KEY FILMS: *Charade* (63); *A Guide For The Married Man* (67); *Hello Dolly!* (69); *A New Leaf* (70); *Plaza Suite* (71); *The Sunshine Boys* (75); *Buddy Buddy* (81); *IQ* (94); *Grumpier Old Men* (95); *Out To Sea* (97); *Hanging Up* (00)

Mature, Victor

Often relegated as an also-ran in the acting stakes on account of his muscles and his glamorous good looks, Mature was actually a professional and versatile leading man who could often carry a film on his star allure alone. Excellent in *film noirs* such as Bruce Humberstone's *I Wake Up Screaming* (41) and **Henry Hathaway's** *Kiss Of Death* (47), he was the best-ever screen Doc Holliday in **John Ford's** superb *My Darling Clementine* (46), knocking later aspirants such as **Kirk Douglas** and **Val Kilmer** into a cocked hat. Thought for the Day: Never judge an actor or actress by their looks alone.

OTHER KEY FILMS: *The Shanghai Gesture* (41); *Cry Of The City* (48); *Easy Living* (49); *Samson And Delilah* (49); *Violent Saturday* (55); *The Last Frontier* (56); *After The Fox* (66); *Head* (68)

Mayer, Louis B

Marcus Loew merged his controlling interest in Metro and the Goldwyn Company with Louis B Mayer Pictures in 1924 to create **MGM**. He then instantly appointed Mayer vice-president and general manager of the new conglomerate. Always power-hungry, Mayer, the quintessential Hollywood **mogul**, soon bent MGM to his will, creating a dictatorship where his every whim was instantly gratified, and from which he could foment wholesome family values and the conservative, not to say reactionary, patriotic principles he held so dear. This said, he was a hard worker, and an even harder, sometimes whimsical taskmaster, and his enlightened choice of **Irving G Thalberg** to head MGM operations from 1924 to 1933 did somewhat lessen his otherwise deadening effect. Mayer left MGM in 1951, after having

created the longest string of feel-good pap in the history of movies – material like the *Andy Hardy* series, interspersed with such occasional gems as Robert Z Leonard's *Pride And Prejudice* (40).
KEY LINE:
'An empty taxi cab drove up and Louis B Mayer got out.' [Marshall Neilan on Mayer]

Meat Axe
A rather primitive pole device with an opaque screen hanging from it which is used to block out unwanted light from a specific area of the set.

Mechanical Effects
These are either mechanical or physical effects, produced while filming is taking place, as opposed to visual effects, which are added in later.

Medium Shot
An MS will take in a human being or group of human beings, with a little background added for good measure.

Medium-close Shot
Somewhere between a close shot and a medium shot, the MCS will span approximately two-thirds of an average human being, leaving space for a sliver of background.

Medium-long Shot
A shot which, while not expanding to a full panorama, will give a pretty good account of the middle distance, setting close action within its wider perspective.

Méliès, Georges
Méliès was the magician of early cinema, and it was through the aegis of his magic show that he first conceived of a camera to suit his fantastical requirements. By 1896 he had already made nearly eighty short films, and had fully understood the lucrative possibilities of transposing the magic to the movies, dropping his live act, and simply showing film scenes to the ever-eager punters queuing at the doors of his theatre. In 1897 he built Europe's first film studio outside Paris, at Montreuil, and it was there that he made *Cinderella* (1899), *Jeanne D'Arc* (00) and his most famous film, *Le Voyage Dans La Lune* (02). The public, however, soon tired of Méliès's tricks, and by the 1915 showing of his masterpiece, *À La Conquête Du Pole*, he was a virtual bankrupt. In desperation he sold most of his assets and reverted to the magic tricks that had pointed the way to his interim career – but by 1927 he was a totally forgotten man. Four years later, in one of the volte-face that only the French contrive so well, he was abruptly recognised for his contribution to film history by the Government, awarded the Légion d'Honneur, and settled in a rent-free apartment for the remaining seven years of his life.
OTHER KEY FILMS: *Après Le Bal* (1897); *Le Magicien* (1898); *Les Miracles Du Brahmine* (1899); *L'Homme-Orchestre* (00); *Le Temple De La Magie* (01); *Eruption Volcanique À La Martinique* (02); *Damnation Du Docteur Faust* (04); *Voyage À Travers L'Impossible* (04); *Le Palais Du Mille Et Une Nuits* (05); *Le Tunnel Sous La Manche* (07) [somewhat prescient, that one]; *Le Raid Paris-New York En Automobile* (09)

Melville, Jean-Pierre
Melville's first film was *Le Silence De La Mer* (49), in which he used his experience in the French Resistance to explore the paradox of warfare between neighbouring countries. This was quickly followed by the intriguing *Les Enfants Terribles* (50), which heralded a welcome new talent in the now rather moribund French film industry. Melville really hit his stride with the then underrated *Bob Le Flambeur* (55), presaging the superb series of gangster films which was to follow and which reached its apotheosis with *Le Samourai* (67), a masterpiece of late-period *film noir* which has influenced just about anybody who has attempted the genre ever since.
OTHER KEY FILMS: *Léon Morin – Priest* (61); *Le Doulos* (63); *L'Armée Des Ombres* (69); *Le Cercle Rouge* (70); *Un Flic* (72)

Merchandising
The art of selling memorabilia and peripherals on the back of a film success, thereby maximising investment returns.

Merchant, Ismail
See **James Ivory**, **Ruth Prawer Jhabvala**

Mercury Vapour Lamps
Powerful vacuum-filled arc lamps whose light is particularly suitable for close work.

Merrie Melodies
See **Looney Tunes**

Method Acting
An intense, largely intuitive acting technique, based on the precepts of Konstantin Stanislavsky, in which actors trawl their subconscious minds for clues to the motivations of the characters they are playing. Their

own experiences are then brought to bear in an effort to identify with the character, so that acting ceases to be acting but becomes, in a sense, 'real'. Major exponents of the 'Method' (which finds itself in direct opposition to the British theatrical tradition of screen acting) include **Marlon Brando**, **Montgomery Clift**, **Robert De Niro** and **Sean Penn**. See **Actors' Studio**

Métrage
The metrical equivalent of **footage**, in terms of film length and spool length, etc.

Metro-Goldwyn-Mayer
Founded in 1924 when Marcus Loew merged his controlling interest in Metro and the Goldwyn Company with Mayer Pictures, MGM came to represent the would-be wholesome side of the US film industry. Run by a committed conservative and an inveterate believer in family values, patriotic platitudes and the worthiness of the bourgeois ideal, MGM was dominated by **Louis B Mayer** until 1951, when his protégé, Dore Schary, finally succeeded in deposing him. In the interim, Mayer had turned the studio into the foremost comfort factory in the world, disdaining doubt and darkness and bathing his films in the artificial strip-light of his own personality. The best MGM films came during the production tenure of **Irving G Thalberg**, and include **Edmund Goulding's** *Grand Hotel* (32), **Ernst Lubitsch's** *The Merry Widow* (34), **George Cukor's** *David Copperfield* (35) and Frank Lloyd's *Mutiny On The Bounty* (35). Following Thalberg's death in 1936, Mayer bent the company increasingly towards his own reactionary world-view. A few masterpieces still slipped through the net, but they were the brainchildren of other men and women, and Mayer's real claim to fame lies in his enlightened choice of production chiefs. Alongside Irving G Thalberg, it was Dore Schary and Hunt Stromberg who made the most out of MGM's world-famous glamour factory.
OTHER KEY FILMS: Victor Fleming's *Gone With The Wind* (39) and *The Wizard Of Oz* (39); Ernst Lubitsch's *Ninotchka* (39); George Cukor's *The Philadelphia Story* (40); **John Huston's** *The Asphalt Jungle* (50); **Stanley Donen** and **Gene Kelly's** *Singin' In The Rain* (52)

Metteur-en-Scène
Old-fashioned French term for a director or filmmaker. Now often replaced by the words *réalisateur* or *réalisatrice*.

MGM
See **Metro-Goldwyn-Mayer**

Mickey Mouse
First seen in *Steamboat Willie* (28), Mickey was originally to be known as Mortimer Mouse until **Walt Disney**, who received a special **Oscar** in 1932 for creating him, thought better of it. Stupendously popular with the public and recognised around the world, his image has since become the symbol of the **Disney** empire.

Microcinematography
See **Cinemicrography**

Microphone Boom
See **Boom**

Midget
A tiny spotlight, not much stronger than a house lamp, used as a **fill light**.

Midler, Bette
A talented cabaret performer who became something of a gay icon during her tenure at Manhattan's famous Continental Baths, Midler made a strong impact in her very first starring role in Mark Rydell's veiled Janis Joplin tribute *The Rose* (79), but her subsequent film career has had as many ups and downs as has her capacity for extolling good taste. Andrew Bergman's *Isn't She Great* (00) (a title that must have seemed God's gift to any hostile reviewer) has Midler playing novelist Jacqueline Susann, of *Valley Of The Dolls* fame, a part that would appear to be tailor-made for her consistently entertaining brand of high-camp schlock.
OTHER KEY FILMS: *Divine Madness* (80); *Down And Out In Beverly Hills* (86); *Ruthless People* (86); *Outrageous Fortune* (87); *Scenes From A Mall* (91); *For The Boys* (92); *The First Wives Club* (96); *That Old Feeling* (97)
KEY LINE:
'When it's three o'clock in New York, it's still 1938 in London.' [Midler on London]

Mifune, Toshiro
The most internationally renowned of all Japanese film actors, Mifune collaborated for many years with the great **Akira Kurosawa**, most notably in *Rashomon* (50), *The Seven Samurai* (54), *I Live In Fear* (55) and *Yojimbo* (61). As comfortable in broad comedy and domestic drama as he is wielding a samurai sword, Mifune was superb as the marooned Japanese soldier opposite **Lee Marvin's** equally

The great Toshiro Mifune as Sanjuro Kuwabatake, in Akira Kurosawa's samurai swashbuckler Yojimbo (61)

marooned marine in **John Boorman's** offbeat masterpiece *Hell In The Pacific* (69), and deserves to be counted, on the strength of his Kurosawa films alone, as one of the greatest screen actors of all time. A director and producer in his own right, Mifune made a strong impression as Lord Toranaga in the 1980 television miniseries based on James Clavell's best-selling *Shogun*, in which he once again demonstrated his power for stillness and facial control.

OTHER KEY FILMS: *The Idiot* (51); *The Life Of Oharu* (52); *The Lower Depths* (57); *Throne Of Blood* (57); *The Hidden Fortress* (58); *The Bad Sleep Well* (60); *Sanjuro* (62); *Red Beard* (65); *Red Sun* (71); *Midway* (76); *Winter Kills* (79); *Inchon* (82); *Jinsei Gekijo* (83); *Taketori Monogatari* (87); *The Death Of A Tea Master* (89); *Picture Bride* (95)

Milland, Ray

In many ways a run-of-the-mill leading man, the former Reginald Truscott-Jones surpassed himself in one or two quite remarkable films, before descending into a late-career burst as an effective lead in a series of outstanding horror movies. The high point of his career came in **Billy Wilder's** *The Lost Weekend* (45), in which he played a desperate alcoholic, Don Birnam, who was incapable of staying on the wagon, and for which he won a well-deserved Best Actor **Oscar**. Another highlight

came with his performance as **Grace Kelly's** murderous husband in **Alfred Hitchcock's** *Dial M For Murder* (54). Even in the **B-movies** of which he was a staple during the late 1950s and early 1960s, Milland always gave of his best, and his capacity for playing subtly eccentric characters inside an environment of Eisenhower-era conformity marks him out as one of the more interesting and idiosyncratic of second-rankers.

OTHER KEY FILMS: *The Glass Key* (35); *French Without Tears* (39); *Beau Geste* (39); *The Major And The Minor* (42); *The Big Clock* (48); *Alias Nick Beal* (50); *Bugles In The Afternoon* (52); *A Man Alone* [also dir.] (55); *The Girl In The Red Velvet Swing* (55); *The Premature Burial* (62); *X – The Man With X-Ray Eyes* (63); *Love Story* (70); *The Thing With Two Heads* (72); *Gold* (74)

Miller, George

Action aficionados will be forever indebted to Miller for his magnificent Mad Max duet starring **Mel Gibson** – *Mad Max* (79) and *Mad Max 2* [*The Road Warrior*] (81). (The third film in the series, *Mad Max Beyond Thunderdome* (85), simply doesn't have what it takes.) Miller took action sequences that had been done a thousand times before – the car chase, the helicopter pursuing the runaway truck, the escape by night, the idyllic lull before the storm – and transformed them into something utterly different and surprisingly original. From the very first moment of the *Mad Max 2* 'war-of-the-nations' montage, we know we are in for a treat, and by the end of the film (big-screen of course), we emerge, sweating and bleary-eyed, into the street, half expecting to see Humungus howling towards us on his mighty roadster, his duelling pistol primed with the last of his precious stock of gold-tipped bullets.

OTHER KEY FILMS: *The Witches Of Eastwick* (87); *Lorenzo's Oil* (92); *Over The Hill* (92); *Babe* (95); *Babe: Pig In The City* (98)

Mills, John

Mills acted in a series of fascinating and very English films during the late 1940s and early 1950s, some of which deserve reassessment, if only for the low-key, curiously hard-boiled energy that Mills brought to his roles. Roy Ward Baker's *The October Man* (47), Anthony Kimmins's *Mr Denning Drives North* (51), and **Robert Hamer's** *The Long Memory* (52) are all fascinating for their use of location, their tiny eccentricities, tight observations of character and occasional black humour. They are the British equivalent of 1930s French **Poetic Realism** and

1940s American *film noir*, and it is possibly because they so well reflected, in all its curious drabness and downbeat reality, a psychologically ravaged, war-sick and unglamorous England, that they are less well known. There was something about Mills, some indefinable Everyman aspect that was curiously impressive. Forget the war films and the stiff-upper-lip baloney, and go check him out in Anthony Pelissier's *The Rocking Horse Winner* (49), or in J Lee Thompson's *Ice Cold In Alex* (58) or Ronald Neame's *Tunes Of Glory* (60) – not many screen actors have such range and quality, and few, if any, have been so persistently undervalued.

OTHER KEY FILMS: *The Midshipmaid* (32); *Goodbye Mr Chips* (39); *Cottage To Let* (41); *In Which We Serve* (42); *We Dive At Dawn* (43); *This Happy Breed* (44); *The Way To The Stars* (45); *Great Expectations* (46); *Scott Of The Antarctic* (48); *The History Of Mr Polly* (49); *Hobson's Choice* (54); *The Colditz Story* (55); *Town On Trial* (56); *The Chalk Garden* (63); *Oh! What A Lovely War* (69); *Ryan's Daughter* (70); *Gandhi* (82); *Hamlet* (96); *Bean* (97)

Minghella, Anthony

Minghella is a consummate professional, both as screenwriter and director, and his films hark back, in their quality and the care with which they are constructed, to the great melodramas of 1940s Hollywood. *Truly, Madly, Deeply* (91) worked on a number of levels, as comedy, drama and romance, and *The English Patient* (96) continued this eclectic trail, once again satisfying both the intellectual and the romantic in a way that has hardly been bettered in recent years. *The Talented Mr Ripley* (99) deserves to be a sleeper, despite all the **Matt Damon** and **Jude Law** hype, and despite the fact that it happens to feature an on-form **Gwyneth Paltrow**. The film should ideally be seen on the big screen, in a darkened theatre, for it is brilliant, sophisticated cinema-making at its best, and Minghella's is a rare talent.

OTHER KEY FILMS: *Mr Wonderful* (93)

Miniature

A small-scale model (see **Mock-up**) of a location, object or backdrop used when shooting the real thing would not be cost-effective. There is a danger, when the miniature is not sufficiently realistic, that the audience will find it difficult to suspend disbelief, forcing the filmmaker to waste crucial energy in recapturing their interest rather than in getting on with the story. **Alfred Hitchcock** was notoriously slapdash about his miniatures, with *The Lady Vanishes* (38) being a

case in point. The film opens with an obviously mocked-up Alpine village complete with model car jerking unrealistically through the snow. Another example might be the model car in the freight yards at the end of *Young And Innocent* (37). Both films are so good, of course, that audiences willingly overlook these relatively minor infelicities in view of the visual and verbal riches concealed elsewhere.

Minibrute

A small, powerful, 650 watt lamp used for additional outdoor lighting.

Minilite

Similar to the **minibrute**, this adjustable 650 watt lamp is mainly used for fill lighting on account of its versatility.

Minimal Cinema

An attempt, through the minimal use of technical aids and obvious photographic tricks, to instil in the viewer the sense that what they are watching is really happening. **Gillo Pontecorvo** used the technique in *The Battle Of Algiers* (65) to heighten the audience's sense of disgust at the on-screen excesses of his protagonists. The Dogme 1995 manifesto, advocating extreme simplicity and lack of technical pretence in filmmaking, adopted a similar premise.

Minimount

A camera mount specially designed to afford stability on a moving base, such as a train, car, boat, plane or helicopter.

Minnelli, Vincente

Minnelli made smooth, dark chocolaty entertainment (a bit like **Douglas Sirk**, but with music), which was always satisfying, always immaculately produced, and which occasionally, just occasionally, touched real heights of intensity. *The Clock* (45) was his first near-masterpiece, starring a still unspoiled **Judy Garland** (whom he was to marry in 1945) and the brilliant, doomed **Robert Walker**. *The Bad And The Beautiful* (52) featured a sneering **Kirk Douglas**, a sublimely winsome **Gloria Grahame**, and a pipe-chewing, typewriter-tapping **Dick Powell**, and *The Band Wagon* (53) gave much-needed late-career kudos to the inimitable Jack Buchanan, more than ably and equally elegantly abetted by the matchless **Fred Astaire**. On top of all this, Minnelli managed a really brilliant Vincent Van Gogh biopic in *Lust For*

Life (56), and possibly the most outrageously charming Maurice Chevalier vehicle ever, with *Gigi* (58). Whoever said that the Hollywood studio system couldn't produce the goods when it tried? **OTHER KEY FILMS:** *Cabin In The Sky* (43); *Meet Me In St Louis* (44); *Ziegfeld Follies* (46); *The Pirate* (48); *Madame Bovary* (49); *Father Of The Bride* (50); *An American In Paris* (51); *Brigadoon* (54); *Tea And Sympathy* (56); *Designing Woman* (57); *The Reluctant Debutante* (58); *Some Came Running* (59); *Two Weeks In Another Town* (62); *The Sandpiper* (65)

Mirror Shutter

A shutter mechanism with a mirroring facility that allows the camera operator to see exactly what is being filmed without the disadvantage of **parallax** distortion.

Robert Mitchum as the doomed Jeff Bailey, revealing all to Virginia Houston's Ann, in Jacques Tourneur's masterly Out Of The Past *(47)*

Miscasting

When the main actor in a motion picture is miscast, i.e. they are allocated a role for which they are unsuitable, either physically, mentally, or in terms of the audience's belief in them, everything else occurring in the film, no matter how realistic or apposite it may be, is instantly compromised. A recent example occurred in **Jerry Zucker's** *First Knight* (95), when **Richard Gere**, while apparently being cast amusingly against type as Lancelot, was in reality utterly miscast, something that became increasingly obvious whenever he appeared in scenes opposite **Sean Connery's** majestic King Arthur.

Mise-en-Scène

French theatrical term, appropriated by the cinema, meaning either the act of putting on a performance (with everything that involves), or the theory involved in the highlighting of each element of an individual work (the activity on set, the use of the camera, etc.) rather than simply the finished, post-**montage** whole.

Mitchum, Robert

Consummate screen presence and iconoclast (he was sentenced to sixty days on a work farm for possession of marijuana in 1948), Mitchum paved the way for many of today's quasi-tough leading men – the only difference being that Mitchum really *was* tough, yet somehow managed to retain his appeal to women, as well as to men, despite that apparent handicap. The perfect **Philip Marlowe**, he encapsulated **Raymond Chandler's** dictum that 'down these mean streets a man must go who is not himself mean, who is neither tarnished nor afraid…' Unfortunately Mitchum only got to play Marlowe when he was rising fifty-eight – his was the definitive version, however, ably abetted by Dick Richards's sublime reworking of *Farewell My Lovely* (75). Another career high was his performance as the preacher in **Charles Laughton's** unjustly neglected (until recently) *Night Of The Hunter* (55).
OTHER KEY FILMS: *The Locket* (46); *Pursued* (47); *Crossfire* (47); *Out Of The Past* (47); *Blood On The Moon* (48); *Where Danger Lives* (50); *Macao* (52); *The Lusty Men* (52); *Angel Face* (53); *Bandido* (56); *Heaven Knows Mr Allison* (57); *The Enemy Below* (58); *Thunder Road* (58); *The Sundowners* (60); *Cape Fear* (62); *El Dorado* (67); *Villa Rides* (68); *Ryan's Daughter* (70); *The Friends Of Eddie Coyle* (73); *The Yakuza* (75); *Maria's Lovers* (85); *Mr North* (88); *Cape Fear* [remake] (91); *Tombstone* (93); *Dead Man* (96)
KEY LINES:
'One of the biggest stars in the world was **Rin Tin Tin**. And that was a dog. So there can't be too much of a trick to it.' [Mitchum on stardom]

'Whatever he does he always comes back to the family.' [Dorothy Mitchum on fidelity – she was married to Mitchum for fifty-six years, until his death in 1997, aged seventy-nine]

219

Mix

The balancing and splicing together of all the disparate elements that go into making up the **soundtrack** of a film, including the **dialogue**, the musical background and all the other extraneous sounds that will eventually form an integral part of the finished product. See **Dubbing**

Mixer

The technician responsible for the correct balancing and mixing of each separate audio track and their subsequent skilful concatenation into the finished **soundtrack** that will eventually accompany the feature film on its theatrical release.

Mizoguchi, Kenji

Mizoguchi is one of the great masters of world cinema, an assertion borne out by even the few of his films that are currently available to Western audiences. The two masterpieces we know best are *The Life Of Oharu* (52) and *Ugetsu Monogatari* (53), an exquisitely photographed tale of ambition, betrayal and partial redemption, in which each fastidious set-up adds to the story, so that we find ourselves locked inside Mizoguchi's world, where character, moral force and psychological constraint vie with each other, highlighted by his elucidatory camera, until we are subsumed by the drama unfolding in front of us. Mizoguchi died, after a lengthy battle against ill-health, at the age of only fifty-eight, leaving a legacy of more than eighty films of which only a fraction have ever been seen outside his native Japan.

OTHER KEY FILMS: *Blood And Soul* (23); *A Man's Life* (28); *The Dawn Of Manchuria And Mongolia* (32); *Osen Of The Paper Cranes* (34); *The Story Of The Late Chrysanthemums* (39); *The Woman Of Osaka* (40); *The Loyal 47 Ronin* (41-2); *The Love Of Sumako The Actress* (47); *Women Of The Night* (48); *Miss Oyu* (51); *A Geisha* (53); *Chikamatsu Monogatari* (54); *Street Of Shame* (56)

Mob Scene

Movie jargon for any scene involving a large number of **extras**.

Mock-up

A full-size model of the whole, or part of the whole, of any important visual prop or element in a feature film. See *Titanic*

Model

A model, made to scale, of a set or aspect of a set that is used during filming to suggest the real thing.

Modelling Light

See **Counter Key**

Model Sheet

A sheet of precise drawings that assistant animators use to guide them in duplicating the correct dimensions of the characters they are copying from the chief animator's originals.

Moguls

A word sometimes used to describe such all-powerful studio bosses of the Hollywood Golden Era as **Harry Cohn**, **Irving G Thalberg**, **Louis B Mayer** and **Sam Goldwyn**, and referring back to the Mogul emperors who ruled India between 1526 and 1857.

Money

What Hollywood movies are all about. The best way of getting your hands on incredible amounts of dosh is to be **George Lucas**, who has just made $400 million from *Star Wars Episode 1: The Phantom Menace* (99). The next best thing is to act in and produce your very own blockbuster, as **Tom Cruise** has so effectively done with **Brian De Palma's** *Mission: Impossible* (96) and **John Woo's** *Mission: Impossible 2* (00). The first netted Cruise $75 million, and the second looks set to do the same – fifty per cent of that then goes to the Government, a further ten per cent to an agent, followed by another fifteen per cent or so to a manager, three per cent to the accountant, three per cent to lawyers, and then the rest is left to be done with as one chooses. In 1999/2000 Cruise had approximately $100 million to split, with **Tom Hanks** nudging second place in the actors' rankings with a measly $71.5 million. The only female in the top ten was **Julia Roberts**, although she will have crept up the rankings since then, with her bank account straining from a recent string of four consecutive hits, making her possibly the most commercially successful actress in Hollywood history.

Monitor

The process of checking that both the sound and picture quality of a feature film are up to scratch during shooting.

Monochrome

Deriving from the ancient Greek and meaning one colour, the term is now commonly used for black-and-white, but can just as easily indicate red, green, or brown.

220

Monogram
A **B-movie** studio specialising in **Westerns**, serials and thrillers. The young **John Wayne** was an early stalwart, and **Don Siegel** later cut his directing teeth there, after the studio had renamed itself **Allied Artists,** with *Riot In Cell Block 11* (54) and *Invasion Of The Body Snatchers* (56).

Monopack
Film stock with three separate layers of emulsion, each relating to and affected by a primary colour.

Monopole
A moveable studio light unit attached to an overhead pulley.

Monroe, Marilyn
Born Norma Jean Mortenson, Monroe became, during her brief thirty-six-year life, the ultimate Hollywood sex symbol. Following a deeply troubled childhood and a failed marriage (entered into when she was just fourteen), she first came to the public's notice as a bit player in two excellent films – **John Huston's** *The Asphalt Jungle* (50) and **Joseph L Mankiewicz's** *All About Eve* (50). Just two years and eleven movies later she was the most famous film star in the world. In 1954 she got married again, this time to baseball star Joe DiMaggio, then, a year after that, to playwright **Arthur Miller**, who wrote her final, elegiac film, Huston's *The Misfits* (61), in which Monroe played the fragile, other-worldly Roslyn Taber opposite **Clark Gable's** unregenerate Gay Langland. Following her apparent and much-debated suicide in 1962, rumour had it that Monroe had conducted unhappy affairs with two of the Kennedy brothers, Robert and Jack. True or not, her image is synonymous with sex, and, for many, she remains the ultimate screen goddess.
OTHER KEY FILMS: *Clash By Night* (52); *Gentlemen Prefer Blondes* (53); *Niagara* (53); *How To Marry A Millionaire* (53); *River Of No Return* (54); *The Seven Year Itch* (55); *Bus Stop* (56); *Some Like It Hot* (59); *Let's Make Love* (60)
KEY LINES:
'All they have to do is play eight bars of "Come To Me, My Melancholy Baby", and my spine turns to custard, I get goose-pimply all over, and I come to them.' [*Some Like It Hot*]

'What was interesting is that nobody really liked Monroe… Monroe was totally unreliable. Nobody knew what she was going to do.' [Screenwriter Walter Bernstein, co-writer on Monroe's final, unfinished project, *Something's Got*

To Give, from which she was fired two months before her death, in August 1962]

'She was a sad, sad, sad creature. She was sick. In a rightly ordered world, she would have been in a nuthouse. She was psychotic. Once you got to know her, one couldn't feel sexy about her.' [George Axelrod, who wrote the original play and co-scripted **Billy Wilder's** *The Seven Year Itch* (55), and also Joshua Logan's *Bus Stop* (56), on the Monroe myth]

Marilyn Monroe (as Cherie) checking out cowboy admirer Don Murray (Bo), in Joshua Logan's Bus Stop *(56)*

Best Monster Films

Jack Arnold's *Creature From The Black Lagoon* (54) and *Tarantula* (55); Larry Cohen's *It's Alive!* (73); **Merian C Cooper** and **Ernest Schoedsack's** *King Kong* (33); Inoshiro Honda's *Godzilla* (55); George McCowan's *Frogs* (72); John McTiernan's *Predator* (87); Kurt Neumann's *The Fly* (58); Christian Nyby's *The Thing* [a.k.a. *The Thing From Another World*] (51); **Ridley Scott's** *Alien* (79); **James Whale's** *Frankenstein* (31) and *The Bride Of Frankenstein* (35); Irvin S Yeaworth Jr's *The Blob* (58)

Monstres Sacrés

A category of actors unique to French cinema who mostly came from theatrical backgrounds and whose distinct physical or vocal presence stimulated filmmakers into constructing films around their talents, rather than levering them into already constructed scripts. They include **Jean Gabin**, **Jules Berry**, **Michel Simon**, **Arletty** and **Simone Signoret**. See **Acteurs De Composition**

Montage

The art of assembling a sequence of closely cut filmic images to suggest the passing of time, the progression of a news story, or the development of a character, in an abbreviated or concentrated form. **Orson Welles** used the technique to striking effect in his 'March of Time' sequence in *Citizen Kane* (41).

Montand, Yves

A fine cabaret singer, an elegant dancer and a more than competent actor, Montand seemed to have it all – but his background was actually one of grinding poverty and uprootal. Born Ivo Levi, in Italy's Monsummano Alto, Montand and his family fled to Marseilles when Mussolini's fascist party came to power, and Montand never forgot the sense of political injustice he derived from his truncated youth. The often penniless young man became a protégé of Edith Piaf, and later conducted a curious on/off marriage with **Simone Signoret** interspersed with numerous affairs, one of which involved the still-married **Marilyn Monroe**. Montand electrified the screen as Mario in **Henri-Georges Clouzot's** *The Wages Of Fear* (52), and later collaborated on a series of first-rate political thrillers with director **Constantin Costa-Gavras**, which included the propaganda masterpiece *Z* (69). Montand ended his life as something approaching a French national institution.

OTHER KEY FILMS: *Les Portes De La Nuit* (46); *The Wolves* (56); *Aimez-Vous Brahms?* [*Goodbye Again*] (61); *Vivre Pour Vivre* (67); *The Confession* (70); *State Of Siege* (73); *Jean De Florette* (86); *Manon Des Sources* (86)

Mood Music

Pre-recorded music available for hire and subsequent integration as part of the **soundtrack** on a feature, **documentary** or advertising film, when sufficient finance for either the commissioning of original music or the purchasing of rights to existing music is unavailable.

Moore, Demi

It is hard to understand how Moore became one of the top female box-office stars of the 1990s. It's not that she doesn't have talent – she's a perfectly acceptable screen actress, and was really quite good as Cynthia Kellogg in **Alan Rudolph's** *Mortal Thoughts* (91) – but to have the sort of clout she achieved at her height, one has to have something more than that. True, **Jerry Zucker's** *Ghost* (90) was good fun, but **Anthony Minghella's** similarly themed *Truly, Madly, Deeply* (91) was better and funnier. Rob Reiner's *A Few Good Men* (92) was an entertaining little thriller, notable for an outstanding **Jack Nicholson** performance, but what was so good about Demi Moore's Lt. Cdr. Joanne Galloway? No, the answer must be that she represented something, for a certain time, for certain women (ignoring, for a moment, the effect of her undoubted physical attributes on men) and that these characterised the greater proportion of her core audience. And somehow or other, probably with Andrew Bergman's *Striptease* (96) or with **Ridley Scott's** gruesome *G.I. Jane* (97), she contrived to lose them.

OTHER KEY FILMS: *One Crazy Summer* (86); *We're No Angels* (89); *The Butcher's Wife* (91); *Indecent Proposal* (93); *Disclosure* (94); *The Juror* (96); *Deconstructing Harry* (97); *Passion Of Mind* (00)

Moore, Roger

Suave leading man of the ironical 'I may be English but I'm certainly no gentleman' school of acting, Moore found his feet playing Maverick, Ivanhoe and the Saint for television, then landed the plum role of **James Bond**, which he incarnated, more than adequately, in seven films. Often criticised for being rather wooden, Moore is one of those rare actors who are happy sending up their own image, and his charm and unfailing modesty when teased about his apparent shortcomings have endeared him to generations of fans. Just occasionally, as in **Basil Dearden's** *The Man Who Haunted Himself* (70), Moore has proved that he is more than just a pretty face.

OTHER KEY FILMS: *Crossplot* (69); *Live And Let Die* (71); *Gold* (74); *The Man With The Golden Gun* (74); *Shout At The Devil* (76); *The Spy Who Loved Me* (77); *The Wild Geese* (78); *Moonraker* (79); *The Sea Wolves* (80); *For Your Eyes Only* (81); *Octopussy* (83); *A View To A Kill* (85); *Bed & Breakfast* (92); *The Quest* (96); *Spice World* (97); *The Enemy* (01)

Moreau, Jeanne

Moreau was the art-house director's darling during the 1960s, and rightly so, for she brought an earthy and utterly European sensuousness to all her roles, in direct opposition to the **Doris Day** and **Julie Andrews** caricatures of the US mainstream. Working for such directors as **Louis Malle** in *Ascenseur Pour L'Echafaud* (58), and **Michelangelo Antonioni** in *La Notte* (61), Moreau reminded audiences of what sex was really about – the overwhelming desire of one human being for another. Her Catherine in **François Truffaut's** *Jules Et Jim* (61) became the personification of female sexuality for countless young Frenchwomen of her time, who were themselves to prove influential in the heady Paris riots of May 1968. Addressed simply as Mademoiselle Jeanne Moreau, she recently received a well-deserved homage at the Berlin Film Festival 2000, and remains, to this day, very much the grande dame of European cinema.

Jeanne Moreau as Lidia, in a scene from Michelangelo Antonioni's La Notte *(61)*

OTHER KEY FILMS: *Touchez Pas Au Grisbi* (53); *Les Liaisons Dangereuses* (59); *Eva* (62); *Diary Of A Chambermaid* (63); *Chimes At Midnight* (66); *The Sailor From Gibraltar* (67); *The Immortal Story* (68); *Les Valseuses* (74); *Mr Klein* (77); *Plein Sud* (80); *Querelle* (82); *La Femme Nikita* (90); *Until The End Of The World* (92); *Map Of The Human Heart* (92); *Beyond The Clouds* (96); *The Prince's Manuscript* (00); *Lisa* (01); *Cet Amour Là* (01)

KEY LINE: 'Age doesn't protect you from love, but love, to some extent, protects you from age.' [Moreau on enlightened pragmatism]

Morphing

The best example of computer morphing (changing) of one pre-recorded image into another occurs in **James Cameron's** *Terminator 2: Judgment Day* (91), when the amorphous silver blob that is T-1000 morphs into the policeman he (it?) has just killed. Morphing is achieved by taking a precise correlation between the corresponding points of each image, upon which the computer calculates the most natural-seeming interim steps to bridge and then fuse the two images into one.

Morricone, Ennio

Best known as composer-in-residence to **Sergio Leone** on his **Spaghetti Westerns** series, Morricone is a master musician who has worked with directors of the stature of **Federico Fellini**, **Pier Paolo Pasolini**, **Bernardo Bertolucci**, **Gillo Pontecorvo** and **Brian De Palma**. Composer of more than 350 film scores, Morricone uses anything and everything to create his effects, most notably the human whistling in Leone's *The Good, The Bad And The Ugly* (66), and the swooping harmonica in the same director's *Once Upon A Time In The West* (68). He was also responsible for the much borrowed and infinitely haunting xylophone music in **Terrence Malick's** *Days Of Heaven* (78).

OTHER KEY FILMS: Henri Verneuil's *The Sicilian Clan* (69); Elio Petri's *Investigation Of A Citizen Above Suspicion* (70); Edouard Molinaro's *La Cage Aux Folles* (79); Roland Joffé's *The Mission* (86); **Mike Nichols's** *Wolf* (94); **Oliver Stone's** *U Turn* (97); Adrian Lyne's *Lolita* (97); **Warren Beatty's** *Bulworth* (98); Roland Joffé's *Vatel* (00); Giuseppe Tornatore's *Malèna* (00)

Mortars

Explosion-proof containers used for the safe simulation of the sound of bombs and other explosives while filming.

223

M.O.S.

Hearsay has it that the acronym marked on screenplays to indicate a silent scene (no dialogue, music or sound effects) originally stemmed from the 'mit out sound!' shouted by an unknown exiled German director whose English was, as yet, far from perfect.

Motion Control

A computer-run system that preserves the exact distance between a camera and a model (under whatever circumstances) during special-effects filming. A good example of motion control occurs during the famous pod race in **George Lucas's** *Star Wars Episode 1: The Phantom Menace* (99), in which the camera accompanies the pod wherever it goes without any lapse or possibility of human error.

Motion Picture Camera

A camera designed to record multiple consecutive images on a single motor-driven reel of light-sensitive film which, when developed, will produce an impression of movement thanks to the optical effect known as **persistence of vision**.

Motion Picture Patents Company

See **Thomas Alva Edison**

Motor

The mechanism, initially spring-driven and now electrically powered, which drives a motion picture camera.

Movietone

Early sound system that featured direct-to-film recording rather than sound recording by the expedient of a disk as in the **Warner Brothers'** system used on Alan Crosland's ground-breaking *The Jazz Singer* (27), which it superseded.

Moviola

A now somewhat outmoded editing device featuring a foot pedal that the operator tapped to engage or to stop the movement of the film being edited. Due to its poor quality of reproduction, most professional editing is now done on **Video** or digitalised **Editing Systems**.

MPAA

Acronym representing the Motion Picture Association of America, founded in 1922 (with the addition of 'Producers and Distributors' in the title, later to be dropped in favour of 'Association') to regulate the moral framework within which movies were made. It was the MPPDA which devised the censorious 'production code' so earnestly administered by the **Hays Office**, in the person of Will H Hays. The production code lasted until 1966, when it was replaced by the present ratings system.

Multibroad

A powerful set lighting unit with the added benefit of variable focusing.

Multicam

This refers to two or more cameras being used to film the same scene from a number of different perspectives, as happened in the famous final explosion in **Michelangelo Antonioni's** *Zabriskie Point* (70). Great care must be taken to ensure that none of the sight lines of the cameras overlap.

Multihead Printer

A dedicated printer that can turn out a number of copies of the same film simultaneously.

Multilayer Film

Film made with three separate layers of **emulsion**, each sensitive to one of the primary colours, together with an anti-halation backing to prevent flaring. See **Halation**

Multiplane

An animation technique that relies on a series of spaced glass slides between the camera and the animation board to give a sense of false perspective to a shot.

Multiple Exposure

The act of exposing a piece of film two or more times to achieve a doubling or tripling effect of the captured image, one on top of the other.

Multiple-image Shot

A split-frame technique that relies on the repetition of a single image again and again throughout a single frame by the use of **matte** or **digital** processes.

Multiple Roles

Perhaps the most famous example of one actor playing multiple roles occurred in **Robert Hamer's** *Kind Hearts And Coronets* (49), in which **Alec Guinness**, at his own instigation, got to play eight separate members of the same family, all of whom met their untimely ends at the hands of Dennis Price's mortally ambitious Louis Mazzini.

Multiple Runs

A special-effects technique that relies on the repetition of marginally different actions being shot, time and again, on the same piece of film.

Multiplexes

A 1970s innovation that may well have saved the tottering international film industry from going under. Out-of-town or mall-based multiplexes house numerous cinema screens inside one building, allowing an increase in viewer choice. Cafés and restaurants, bookshops and giftshops are often located nearby to increase the overall takings.

Multiscreen

A cinema projection system requiring two or more screens and a corresponding increase in projectors to present either a multi-image or an elongated picture to the viewing public.

Mural

A painting on canvas, cloth, or board, used as the backdrop to a filmed scene in order to suggest a naturalistic environment that film budgets simply do not permit the crew and cast to travel to.

Murnau, F W

Virtually nothing survives of Murnau's early work (pre-1921), but his *Nosferatu – Eine Symphonie Des Grauens* [*Nosferatu The Vampire*] (21) is a round peg in the rhomboid hole of German **expressionism**, and has been massively influential, to this day, with its use of real locations, grotesque design and atmospheric lighting. It caused filmmakers to start to think laterally, to use the whole of their available space rather than merely to view on-camera space as an extension of the theatre. Murnau completed two other masterpieces, *The Last Laugh* (24) and the exquisite, heart-breaking *Sunrise* (27) (his first Hollywood film), before his death in a car accident, aged just forty-two, on a location-scouting trip between Los Angeles and Monterey.
OTHER KEY FILMS: *Schloss Vogelöd* (21); *Der Brennende Acker* (22); *Faust* (26); *Four Devils* (28); *City Girl* (30); *Tabu* [co–dir. **Robert Flaherty**] (31)

Murphy, Eddie

Brooklyn-born Murphy, who was a successful stand-up comedian before he ever dreamed of a screen career, appeared to have the golden touch following his first star-making screen appearance in Walter Hill's *48 Hrs* (82), turning out a string of scrupulously fabricated comedy hits including Martin Brest's *Beverly Hills Cop* (84) and John Landis's *Coming To America* (88). Then his luck, and a goodly part of his audience, suddenly left him, and he found himself forced back into such increasingly moderate rehashes as Landis's *Beverly Hills Cop III* (94) and **Wes Craven's** *Vampire In Brooklyn* (95), before Tom Shadyac's *The Nutty Professor* (96) lifted him back out of the soup. Murphy's films are notable for their cheek, their energy and their visual inventiveness, but also for their uncomfortably partial plots and often dubious moral imperatives.
OTHER KEY FILMS: *Trading Places* (83); *Beverly Hill Cop II* (87); *Coming To America* (88); *Another 48 Hrs* (90); *The Distinguished Gentleman* (92); *Dr Dolittle* (98); *Bowfinger* (99); *Nutty Professor II: The Klumps* (00); *Shrek* (01) [he voiced the donkey]; *Dr Dolittle 2* (01)

Best Musical Films

Lloyd Bacon's *42nd Street* (33); Alain Corneau's *Tous Les Matins Du Monde* (91); **Clint Eastwood's** *Honkytonk Man* (82); **Milos Forman's** *Amadeus* (84); Bob Fosse's *Cabaret* (72); François Girard's *Thirty-Two Short Films About Glenn Gould* (94); Taylor Hackford's *Hail! Hail! Rock 'n' Roll* (87); **Howard Hawks's** *Gentlemen Prefer Blondes* (53); **Gene Kelly** and **Stanley Donen's** *On The Town* (49) and *Singin' In The Rain* (52); **Mervyn LeRoy's** *Gold Diggers Of 1933* (33); **Vincente Minnelli's** *The Band Wagon* (53); **G W Pabst's** *Die Dreigroschenoper* [*The Threepenny Opera*] (30); **Alan Parker's** *The Commitments* (91); **Michael Powell** and **Emeric Pressburger's** *The Red Shoes* (47); Herbert Ross's *Pennies From Heaven* (81); Mark Sandrich's *Top Hat* (35); Bert Stern's *Jazz On A Summer's Day* (59); **George Stevens's** *Swing Time* (36); **Bertrand Tavernier's** *Autour Du Minuit* [*Around Midnight*] (86); **John Waters's** *Cry-Baby* (90); **Robert Wise's** *West Side Story* (61) and *The Sound Of Music* (65)

Music Mixer

The technician responsible for balancing, synchronising and mixing the disparate elements of a film's musical soundtrack together, before the chief **sound editor** combines it with the dialogue and sound-effect tracks to create a composite.

Music Track

A separate track (from the dialogue and special-effects tracks) containing the complete musical score of a film, and which is the province of the **music mixer**. All the separate sound tracks will later be mixed together to form the whole.

Mute

A negative or positive print that does not as yet carry a sound track.

Mutoscope

A hand-cranked peep-show machine, manufactured from 1895 onwards, which rivalled Edison's **Kinetoscope** in popularity. Invented by Edison's ex-employee, W K L Dickson, the images were held on card, which was then riffled at high speed, producing the illusion of movement.

Myers, Mike

A Canadian with a British passport who became a major hit on the US *Saturday Night Live* television comedy sketch show (1989-94) with his characters Dieter and Wayne Campbell, Myers has proved himself adept at playing to his strengths, particularly in his two massively successful Austin Powers movies, Jay Roach's *Austin Powers: International Man Of Mystery* (97) and *Austin Powers: The Spy Who Shagged Me* (99). Renowned for his phobic dislike of being touched (which must play havoc with his clinches), Myers's stock has risen alongside his salary; from $1 million for Penelope Spheeris's *Wayne's World* (92), up to $7 million for *The Spy Who Shagged Me*. Recently **Universal** decided to sue the perfectionist Myers when he refused to make what he considered an inferior film (from his own screenplay) based on his famous 'Sprockets' *Saturday Night Live* sketch featuring Dieter, but he has since returned, at least vocally, as the voice of **DreamWork's** *Shrek* (01).
OTHER KEY FILMS: *Wayne's World II* (93); *So I Married An Axe Murderer* (93); *Nobody Knows Anything* (00)

Mylar

An industrial material that forms the basis of the ferromagnetic coating normally used on magnetic tape.

Narrow Gauge Film

Normal film gauge is 35mm, with 70mm used in the 1950s and 1960s for **epic**, large-scale films. Narrow gauge is anything under 35mm, commonly 16mm, but on occasion 9.5mm or even 8mm. The smaller the gauge, the lesser the quality, but the larger the economies of scale.

National Board of Review

The earliest US film censorship body, founded in 1909 allegedly to prevent the formation of a government censorship board. The board was renowned for its liberal interpretations and judgements, and was eventually emasculated (in 1921) and replaced by a number of different state and national bodies. The board continued in existence, but with its role radically changed to that of award-giver and encourager to the film industry.

National Film Preservation Act

Founded in 1988 by order of Congress, the Act chooses twenty-five American films a year (each film chosen must be more than ten years old), which are subsequently protected from colorisation, dilution, bastardisation and general ineptitude on the part of their nominal owners. These films are then placed on the National Film Registry, which acts *in loco parentis* to ensure their conservation in a manner approaching the original intentions of their makers. Up to and including the year 2000, the NFR comprised something in the region of 300 protected films.

National Film Theatre

London's centre of excellence in the showing of restored and original copies of mainstream, cult and underground films. The NFT began life as the Telekinema during the 1951 Festival of Britain before being taken over by the **BFI** in 1952. The present South Bank building, built in 1957, offers a ray of filmic sunshine in an otherwise under-filmed, under-cinemaed and under-funded capital city.

NATO

The US-based National Association of Theatre Owners represents exhibitors' interests on a state-by-state basis.

Neeson, Liam

Neeson can be a rather intense actor, but his mercurial tendencies are more than matched by his striking talent in such challenging parts as that of Oskar Schindler, in **Steven Spielberg's** outstanding *Schindler's List* (93), and his brilliant turn in John Madden's *Ethan Frome* (93). One of the masochistic school of screen actors (whose other adepts include **Marlon Brando** and **Ralph Fiennes**), Neeson was as good in Michael Caton-Jones's *Rob Roy* (95) as **Mel Gibson** was conventional in the same year's *Braveheart* (95).

OTHER KEY FILMS: *Excalibur* (81); *The Bounty* (84); *The Mission* (86); *Darkman* (90); *Under Suspicion* (91); *Nell* (94); *Before And After* (96); *Michael Collins* (96); *Les Misérables* (98); *The Hunting* (99) *Gun Shy* (00); *Gangs Of New York* (01)

Negative

A piece of processed film in which the colours are the exact opposite of what they are in real life, or, in the case of black and white, the patches of light and shade, brilliance and shadow, find themselves reversed – this situation is then rectified during positive printing.

Negative Cost

The gross cost involved in the making of a film, excluding the residual post-production costs involved in print duplication, publicity, the distribution process and eventual exhibition.

Negative Cutter

The expert involved in the cutting of a negative first to **work print** status, then to an **answer print**.

Negative Cutting

The exact matching of one print to another by means of **edge numbers**. See **Negative Cutter**

Negulesco, Jean

There is no real comparison between the early Negulesco, before *How To Marry A Millionaire* (53), say, and the later, post-**CinemaScope** Negulesco of *Three Coins In The Fountain* (54) and *Woman's World* (54) fame. In fact it is hard to believe that the director of such tight little *film noir* thrillers as *The Mask Of Dimitrios* (44) and *Road House* (48) is the same man who subsequently made *Boy On A Dolphin* (57), which is notable for nothing more than its wet-blouse publicity shot of Sophia Loren and her famous nipples. Hmm. Perhaps his self-acknowledged, impenetrable Romanian accent was to blame? Or could it have been Hollywood's fault? OTHER KEY FILMS: *The Conspirators* (44); *Three Strangers* (46); *Nobody Lives Forever* (46); *Humoresque* (46); *Deep Valley* (47); *Johnny Belinda* (48); *The Mudlark* (50); *The Rains Of Ranchipur* (55); *A Certain Smile* (58); *Jessica* (62)

Neo-realism

The style which transfigured Italian cinema during the 1940s and early 1950s, neo-realism came about partially as the result of the incredibly harsh conditions suffered by virtually all Italians in the aftermath of the Nazi pull-out of 1944. Dependent on a non-intrusive camera and on storylines that highlighted the lives of ordinary people, the cycle is often considered to have begun with **Luchino Visconti's** *Ossessione* (42), but the genuine first film of the movement was **Roberto Rossellini's** *Rome: Open City* (45), a heady mélange of documentary,

sensodrama, and direct filming on the streets, and a precursor to the Italian preference for overdubbing as later epitomised by the films of **Federico Fellini**. Prominent neo-realist films include Aldo Vergano's *Outcry* (47), **Vittorio De Sica's** *Bicycle Thieves* (48), and Giuseppe De Santis's *Bitter Rice* (49). The movement petered out in the mid-1950s when the horrors of the war had been partially forgotten, and young Italians, in thrall to an economic revival and a hero-worshipping of America, began looking to glamour, and Vespas, and girls in fluffy skirts, rather than to the lessons of the past, for their inspiration. OTHER KEY FILMS: Vittorio De Sica's *The Children Are Watching Us* (43) and *Shoeshine* (46); Roberto Rossellini's *Paisà* (46), *Germany Year Zero* (47) and *Stromboli* (49); Alberto Lattuada's *Without Pity* (48); Pietro Germi's *In Nome Della Legge* (49) and *Il Camino Della Speranza* (50)

Neutral-density Filter

An absolutely neutral filter that does not interfere with colour values but which acts instead on reducing contrast and exposure.

New Line Cinema Corporation

Founded in 1967, New Line's name became synonymous with films for teenage audiences, making its money as much from canny franchising as it did from the films themselves. Following the foundation of Fine Line Features in 1991, dedicated to intelligent mainstream movies such as **Gus Van Sant's** *My Own Private Idaho* (92) and **Robert Altman's** *The Player* (92), the company was swallowed up by **Ted Turner** in 1993.

Newman, Paul

Newman's reputation is healthier than it ought to be, notwithstanding the undoubted talent he showed in such excellent movies as **Arthur Penn's** *Left-Handed Gun* (58) and **Martin Ritt's** *Hud* (63), in which, as the amoral Hud Bannon, he gave his best-ever performance. In his many subsequent films he has often allowed his undoubted charm to get the better of him, losing the hard edge he showed in Stuart Rosenberg's *Cool Hand Luke* (67), or, even worse, endeavouring to recreate it artificially, as in George Roy Hill's utterly contrived *Slap Shot* (77). The film that most successfully combined both key elements of Newman's appeal – his coldness and his charm – was **Robert Rossen's** *The Hustler* (61), but in the forty years since then the star (and star he certainly is) may have offered much immediate gratification, but rather less long-lasting pleasure.

*Paul Newman
as Hud Bannon,
acting distinctly out
of character on the set
of Martin Ritt's
Hud (63)*

programme, finally bit the dust, but their number had been up for twenty years by then, and it is only in retrospect that one comes to realise just how influential in terms of structure, content, and bias they actually were.

Newton Rings

Coloured distortions, in the shape of a ring, which can sometimes appear on film due to unwanted light refraction between two parallel surfaces.

New Wave

The French New Wave was a reaction against what its adherents, **Claude Chabrol**, Jacques Demy, **Jean-Luc Godard**, **Louis Malle**, **Alain Resnais**, Jacques Rivette, **Eric Rohmer** and **François Truffaut**, felt was the post-Second World War 'embourgeoisification' of French film. Using theories formulated through articles in the influential *Cahiers du Cinéma* magazine, the group suggested a new order in which film would be given back to the young, with directors signing their work rather as painters like Paul Cézanne and Paul Gauguin would have done seventy years earlier. During the brief five-year life of the movement, which spanned 1958-62, there really did seem to be a new feeling abroad, of cupboards dusted out and skeletons shaken. But the iconoclasts soon found themselves 'embourgeoisified' in their turn, and the movement, as do all movements, eventually petered out, having afforded much pleasure and not a little lucrative employment to the usual phalanx of film theorists and vainglorious critics belatedly bringing up the rear.

KEY FILMS: Claude Chabrol's *Le Beau Serge* (58) and *Les Cousins* (59); François Truffaut's *Les Quatre Cents Coups* [*The 400 Blows*] (59) and *Jules Et Jim* (61); Jean-Luc Godard's *À Bout De Souffle* [*Breathless*] (60) and *Une Femme Est Une Femme* [*A Woman Is A Woman*] (61); Jacques Rivette's *Paris Nous Appartient* (60)

N G

Film director's abbreviation for 'not good', meaning that a shot should under no circumstances be used but should either be dumped, or, preferably, re-shot.

Nichols, Mike

A strangely inconsistent filmmaker, Nichols was an **Actors' Studio** protégé, and proved his theatrical worth with his effective handling of Edward Albee's *Who's Afraid Of Virginia Woolf?* (66). It is hard, in retrospect, to remember how influential his next

229

OTHER KEY FILMS: *Somebody Up There Likes Me* (56); *The Long Hot Summer* (58); *Cat On A Hot Tin Roof* (58); *Sweet Bird Of Youth* (62); *Harper* (66); *Hombre* (67); *Butch Cassidy And The Sundance Kid* (69); *Sometimes A Great Notion* (71); *The Mackintosh Man* (73); *The Sting* (73); *The Verdict* (82); *Mr And Mrs Bridge* (90); *The Hudsucker Proxy* (94); *Nobody's Fool* (94); *Twilight* (98); *Where The Money Is* (00)

KEY LINE:

'The only question I ever ask any woman is what time is her husband coming home?' [*Hud*]

Newsreel

The most famous movie newsreels belonged to Movietone, Pathé, Gaumont-British, Universal (USA) and Paramount (USA), and they predated the introduction of television by thirty years to provide some extraordinary news stories and a great deal of tacit propaganda to cinema audiences. It took until the late 1970s before the traditional newsreel, forming an integral part of the movie film, *The Graduate* (67), really was, but he certainly succeeded in capturing the Zeitgeist once again with *Carnal Knowledge* (71), in which he dissected the sexual illusions of an entire generation of American men. *Wolf* (94), once again with **Jack Nicholson**, and the more recent *Primary Colors* (98) showed a welcome return to form after a string of rather moderate precursors, which included the seriously overrated *Postcards From The Edge* (90).

OTHER KEY FILMS:
Catch-22 (70); *Silkwood* (83); *Working Girl* (88); *Regarding Henry* (91); *The Bird Cage* (96); *What Planet Are You From?* (00); *Wit* (01)

Nicholson, Jack

A perennially popular and notably promiscuous hell-raiser and rabble-rouser, Nicholson also has one of the finest bodies of work of any actor of his generation streaming along behind him. First spotted at the somewhat advanced age of thirty-two (after more than a decade in pot-boilers) in **Dennis Hopper's** *Easy Rider* (69), Nicholson surprised everybody with the depth and commitment of his performances in such outstanding films of the 1970s as **Bob Rafelson's** *Five Easy Pieces* (70), **Mike Nichols's** *Carnal Knowledge* (71), **Hal Ashby's** *The Last Detail* (73), **Roman Polanski's** *Chinatown* (74), **Michelangelo Antonioni's** *The Passenger* (75), and **Milos Forman's** *One Flew Over The Cuckoo's Nest* (75). Few actors, if any, can have achieved so much, and turned public perceptions so unequivocally around, in so short a time. His later work has varied between magnificence – his Eugene O'Neill in **Warren Beatty's** *Reds* (81) – and commercial expediency, with his Joker in **Tim Burton's** *Batman* (89). He has, however, had a most welcome recent return to form as Alex in **Bob Rafelson's** *Blood and Wine* (96), and as irascible novelist, Melvin Udall, in James L Brooks's *As Good As It Gets* (97), (at least in the first half, until the film became mawkish).

OTHER KEY FILMS: *The King Of Marvin Gardens* (72); *Goin' South* (78); *The Shining* (80); *The Postman Always Rings Twice* (81); *The Border* (83); *Terms Of Endearment* (83); *Prizzi's Honour* (85); *The Witches Of Eastwick* (87); *The Two Jakes* (90); *A Few Good Men* (92); *The Crossing Guard* (95); *Mars Attacks!* (96); *The Pledge* (01)

KEY LINES:
'Women today are better hung than men.' [*Carnal Knowledge*]

Secretary/Breathless Fan: 'How do you write women so well?' Irascible author Melvin Udall (Jack Nicholson): 'I think of a man, and take away reason and accountability.' [*As Good As It Gets* (97)]

Nickelodeon

Euphemism for a cheap cinema to which tickets used to cost a nickel (five cents). See **Odeon**

Night Effect

See **Day For Night**

9.5mm Film

A **narrow gauge film**, devised by the **Pathé** company in 1922, and much used in France and Western Europe until the introduction of 8mm film in 1932.

Nipple Count

A jokey reference to the number of exposed nipples appearing in **sexploitation** movies, with the implication that breasts equate bucks, and that there might just possibly be some correlation between sex and the cinema. Perish the thought!

Jack Nicholson as *J J Gittes (before the nose-job) in Roman Polanski's* Chinatown *(74)*

Nitrate

Before 1950, most film stock was fabricated with a highly inflammable cellulose nitrate base. Due to the unstable nature of the chemicals involved, acetate-based safety film was belatedly introduced, leading to a marked decrease in the number of archive fires, and to an increased lifespan for nitrate-based films once they had been transferred onto the new safety stock.

Niven, David

Suave leading man and notorious roisterer (with his chum and housemate, **Errol Flynn**), Niven turned in some fine performances during his more than forty-year career, notably in **Michael Powell** and **Emeric Pressburger's** *A Matter Of Life And Death* (46) and in Delbert Mann's *Separate Tables* (58). As effective in light comedy as he was in romantic derring-do, Niven was a renowned raconteur and practical joker, and wrote two best-selling autobiographical books in later life. He died in 1983 after a long, un-winnable battle against motor neurone disease.

OTHER KEY FILMS: *The Charge Of The Light Brigade* (36); *The Prisoner Of Zenda* (37); *Bluebeard's Eighth Wife* (38); *Dawn Patrol* (38); *Wuthering Heights* (39); *The Real Glory* (39); *Raffles* (40); *The Bishop's Wife* (47); *The Elusive Pimpernel* (50); *Carrington V.C.* (55); *Around The World In 80 Days* (56); *Bonjour Tristesse* (58); *The Guns Of Navarone* (61); *55 Days At Peking* (63); *The Pink Panther* (64); *The Sea Wolves* (80)

Noir

See *film noir*

Noiret, Philippe

One of France's greatest and most prolific actors, Noiret has the sort of acting range that most movie stars can only dream of. He first won international plaudits for his performance in **Louis Malle's** *Zazie Dans Le Métro* (61), and again for his role as the boring husband in **Georges Franju's** *Thérèse Desqueyroux* (62). His career now belatedly in gear, the sombre-faced Noiret began his slow rise to stardom with movies such as Marco Ferreri's *La Grande Bouffe* (73) and **Bertrand Tavernier's** *The Clockmaker* (73), which marked the start of a fruitful collaboration between the two men. Since then he has been directed by virtually every first-class French director in the business – and a good few Italian ones as well – but paradoxically, as these things so often happen, his greatest international success came with one of his lesser films, Giuseppe Tornatore's *Cinema Paradiso* (89), which, while still immensely enjoyable, can hardly bear comparison with a performance of the calibre he gave for Tavernier that same year as Commandant Dellaplane in *La Vie Et Rien D'Autre* (89).

OTHER KEY FILMS: *Alexandre Le Bienheureux* [a.k.a. *Happy Alexander*] (69); *Le Vieux Fusil* (75); *Le Juge Et L'Assassin* (75); *Coup De Foudre* (78); *La Mort En Direct* (79); *Three Brothers* (81); *Coup De Torchon* (81); *L'Étoile Du Nord* (82); *Le Cop* (84); *Round Midnight* (86); *Tango* (93); *Il Postino* (94); *Les Grands Ducs* (96); *Soleil* (97); *Le Bossu* (97); *Le Pique-Nique De Lulu Kreutz* (00); *The King Of Paris* (00)

Noise

Euphemism for unwanted sound that has been recorded inadvertently onto a film's soundtrack and requires **looping**.

Nolte, Nick

Following what studio pundits usually call an 'interesting youth', Nolte got his big break in 1976, at the ripe old age of thirty-five, in the television saga 'Rich Man, Poor Man'. A year later he was still playing beefcake opposite **Jacqueline Bisset** in **Peter Yates's** *The Deep* (77), but that all changed with **Karel Reisz's** *Dog Soldiers* [a.k.a. *Who'll Stop The Rain?*] (78), in which Nolte first suggested the true depth of his talent. He then began the roller-coaster ride he's been on ever since, both film-wise and weight-wise, and whose highlights include Paul Mazursky's *Down And Out In Beverly Hills* (86), **Martin Scorsese's** *New York Stories* (89), and **Sidney Lumet's** *Q & A* (90). Even his failures, such as **James Ivory's** *Jefferson In Paris* (95), are interesting, if only because of the intensity with which Nolte approaches every part, however unworthy some of them are of his talents.

OTHER KEY FILMS: *Cannery Row* (82); *48 Hrs* (82); *Under Fire* (83); *Farewell To The King* (89); *Cape Fear* (91); *The Prince Of Tides* (91); *Mulholland Falls* (96); *U-Turn* (97); *The Thin Red Line* (98); *The Best Of Enemies* (99); *The Golden Bowl* (00); *Investigating Sex* (01)

Non-theatrical

A film that is not intended for general commercial release, but is destined instead for a more specialised and limited audience.

Nosferatu

See *Dracula*

Notch

A mark cut into the edge of a strip of film indicating the presence of a **cue** point.

Nouvelle Vague
See **New Wave**

Novak, Kim

Novak grows on you. At first you say to yourself, oh, another big, blowzy besweatered blonde, where's the point? Then you may be fortunate enough to see her in a Richard Quine movie – *Pushover* (54) perhaps, or *Bell Book And Candle* (57), or *Strangers When We Meet* (60), or maybe even in Joshua Logan's *Picnic* (55), or in that breathtaking study of incipient paranoia, **Alfred Hitchcock's** *Vertigo* (58) – and everything suddenly falls into place. Novak shouldn't jell on screen but she does. There is a mystery about her, an allure, that a thousand other actresses can try for and fail to get. But with Novak it comes naturally, as if she is ever so slightly lost, but determined to make the best of it until someone should happen along and show her the way to the exit. This is devastatingly attractive to men, and unthreatening to women, and therein lies Novak's power and the reason why she was the US's biggest female draw in 1957.

OTHER KEY FILMS: *The Man With The Golden Arm* (55); *Jeanne Eagels* (57); *Pal Joey* (57); *Of Human Bondage* (64); *Kiss Me Stupid* (64); *Liebestraum* (91)

Novarro, Ramon

The Durango-born Novarro was the third of the great trio of Latin lover-type silent stars, along with **John Gilbert** and **Rudolph Valentino**, but now he is forgotten by all but the cognoscenti, apart from the occasional rerun of Fred Niblo's *Ben-Hur* (25) (usually consisting of just the chariot race), or George Fitzmaurice's *Mata Hari* (31), in which he co-starred with **Greta Garbo**. He made one or two lacklustre Mexican films before his final fall from grace – his last Hollywood film was **George Cukor's** aptly named *Heller In Pink Tights* (60) – when he was found battered to death on the floor of his Hollywood Hills mansion, in 1968, the victim of some venal young hustlers he had unwisely picked up earlier that day.

OTHER KEY FILMS: *The Prisoner Of Zenda* (22); *Scaramouche* (23); *The Arab* (24); *The Student Prince* (27); *The Pagan* (29); *In Gay Madrid* (30); *Laughing Boy* (34); *The Sheik Steps Out* (37); *The Big Steal* (49)

Number Board

The slate or small blackboard held up before a shot is begun so that the name of the film, the director and the cinematographer, the shot and the take number and whatever other snippets of information are deemed necessary, will be indelibly printed onto the piece of film to which they relate.

Numbering Machine

The gizmo that prints the **edge numbers** onto a strip of film.

Nykvist, Sven

Ingmar Bergman's preferred cinematographer, and the quietly presiding genius behind the look of more than a hundred films, Nykvist is a master of natural light and heightened chiaroscuro. A fine director in his own right, as with his unrelentingly downbeat *The Ox* (91), Nykvist was responsible for the gorgeous look of Charles Jarrott's underrated *The Dove* (74), as well as for the recreation of the *feel* of old New Orleans in **Louis Malle's** *Pretty Baby* (78). Although **Bob Rafelson's** *The Postman Always Rings Twice* (81) failed to match up to its 1946 Tay Garnett predecessor, no one in their right mind could deny that Nykvist conjured up depression-era America with awesome skill.

OTHER KEY FILMS: Ingmar Bergman's *The Virgin Spring* (60); Caspar Wrede's *One Day In The Life Of Ivan Denisovich* (71); **Woody Allen's** *Crimes And Misdemeanors* (89) and *Celebrity* (98); Lasse Halström's *What's Eating Gilbert Grape?* (93); Norman Jewison's *Only You* (94); **Peter Yates's** *Curtain Call* (99)

Oater

Another cinematic term used to refer to a **Western**, or cowboy film. Other expressive alternatives also include horse opera, sagebrusher, prairie dogger, oat opera, bean-scruncher and **Spaghetti western**.

Oates, Warren

Oates was suitably named, for his forte was in **oaters**, and in fact he looked as if he were bean-scrunching in just about every film in which he featured, his eyes permanently crinkled against the sun, his teeth, conceivably rotten, picked with whatever came closest to hand (in one movie, even a knife). Dead from a heart attack at fifty-three, Oates really made his mark as Lyle Gorch in **Sam Peckinpah's** *The Wild Bunch* (69), and followed this up as the aptly named GTO in his friend Monte Hellman's excellent *Two-Lane Blacktop* (71). Another great Hellman movie starring Oates was the underrated *Cockfighter* (74), which came as good as dammit to recreating the magnificent Charles Willeford novel it sprang from – something of a miracle given that the main protagonist spends virtually the whole book refusing to talk.

OTHER KEY FILMS: *Ride The High Country* (62); *Major Dundee* (65); *In The Heat Of The Night* (67); *Barquero* (70); *The Hired Hand* (71); *Badlands* (74); *Bring Me The Head Of Alfredo Garcia* (74); *Race With The Devil* (75); *92 In The Shade* (75); *The Border* (82); *Blue Thunder* (83)

Oberon, Merle

Alexander Korda, whom Oberon later married in 1939, first became obsessed by her curious, almost Asiatic beauty in 1933, when he cast her as Anne Boleyn in his *The Private Life Of Henry VIII*. Although she was a passably good actress, Oberon hardly deserved her ensuing roles in Korda's *The Private Life Of Don Juan* (34) and Harold Young's *The Scarlet Pimpernel* (35). She was much better in **William Wyler's** *Wuthering Heights* (39), but, despite her fervid private life, she never became the stuff of screen legend, as the infatuated Korda had so obviously hoped.

OTHER KEY FILMS: *I Claudius* [unfinished] (37); *Lydia* (41); *The Lodger* (44); *Berlin Express* (48); *Hotel* (67)

KEY LINE:

'I'd masturbate about her all night – with the lights off, so God couldn't see me.' [Richard Harris, on his juvenile fascination with Oberon, whom he claims he finally did get to bed]

Object Animation

An alternative term for **stop-motion** animation, object animation involves the moving of puppets, objects, etc., a single frame at a time, to give the appearance of motion when the exposed film is viewed in sequence. See **Aardman Animations**

Odeon

A famous string of distinctive British movie houses in the modern style, Odeon was initially

233

founded in 1933 by Oscar Deutsch, and then swallowed up by the omnivorous **J Arthur Rank** in 1941. The Odeon in London's Leicester Square has been, and still is, the glitzy venue for a host of star-studded film premières and is the UK's largest remaining single-screen cinema. [O.D.E.O.N. = Oscar Deutsch Entertains Our Nation although, more fittingly, *Ōideion* in Greek means place of music]

Off Camera

Anything that is out of shot, or outside the camera's capacity to 'see', either by implication or in reality.

Off Mike

Any sound that is outside the microphone's effective capacity to pick up, or is directed away from the microphone in such a way that it will either have to be dubbed in or dubbed out later on.

Off Register

Off register refers to moments when the film itself appears to shake. This can be done intentionally, as in the case of on-camera **special-effects** induced earthquakes, eruptions, explosions, detonations and eructations, or unintentionally, if the camera was vibrating unavoidably during a shot, as would undoubtedly be the case if the San Andreas fault suddenly popped **off scene**.

Off Scene

An extraneous sound that does not stem from any obvious source on the screen.

O'Hara, Maureen

O'Hara was the perfect foil for the men's men of 1940s and 1950s Hollywood, and was used to good effect by **John Ford** opposite **John Wayne** in *Rio Grande* (50) and *The Quiet Man* (52). Never a great actress, O'Hara was nonetheless an extremely professional one, and many of her roles tapped into the vein of acceptable sentimentality that audiences, deadened by the horrors of the Second World War, seemed to find necessary at the time.

OTHER KEY FILMS: *Jamaica Inn* (39); *The Hunchback Of Notre Dame* (39); *A Bill Of Divorcement* (40); *How Green Was My Valley* (41); *The Foxes Of Harrow* (47); *Our Man In Havana* (60); *McLintock!* (63)

KEY LINE:

'She looked as though butter wouldn't melt in her mouth – or anywhere else.' [Elsa Lanchester on O'Hara]

Oldman, Gary

A fine theatrical actor, Oldman uses stage technique to good effect in the handful of first-class films he has made since bursting into public awareness with **Alex Cox's** *Sid And Nancy* (85), in which he played the part of doomed punk-rocker, Sid Vicious. This was closely followed by his brilliant portrayal of Joe Orton in **Stephen Frears's** *Prick Up Your Ears* (87), which finally tipped off the US market to his precocious talent. He was astonishing as a crazed drug-dealer in Tony Scott's *True Romance* (93), and equally good in the role of a crooked policeman in Peter Medak's *Romeo Is Bleeding* (94). His best performance to date has been as Beethoven, in Bernard Rose's much underrated *Immortal Beloved* (94), but he was also a wonderfully overblown Count Dracula in **Francis Ford Coppola's** *Bram Stoker's Dracula* (92).

OTHER KEY FILMS: *Rosencrantz And Guildenstern Are Dead* (90); *JFK* (91); *Leon* [a.k.a. *The Professional*] (94); *The Scarlet Letter* (95); *Basquiat* (96); *The Fifth Element* (97); *Lost In Space* (98); *The Contender* (00); *Hannibal* (01); *Nobody's Baby* (01)

Old-timer

Jargon for the pole that supports the **gobo**, **flag** or **scrim**. In other words the supporting arm for a light-screening device.

Olivier, Laurence

Considered by many to be the greatest screen actor of them all (and by others a boring old ham), Olivier burst onto the screen (quite literally) in **William Wyler's** *Wuthering Heights* (39), followed, in the same year, by **Alfred Hitchcock's** awesomely romantic *Rebecca* – then, to complete the hat-trick, he was the definitive Darcy in **Robert Z Leonard's** *Pride and Prejudice* (40). In **Alexander Korda's** *That Hamilton Woman* (41), he starred as Horatio Nelson alongside his wife **Vivien Leigh**, and, to cap what was already a fine career, he then acted in and directed a ground-breaking *Henry V* (44) and *Hamlet* (48). His final screen triumph came playing Archie Rice in **Tony Richardson's** *The Entertainer* (60), from which moment, due to increasing ill-health, he only took occasional, largely character, roles to provide for the future of his family.

OTHER KEY FILMS: *As You Like It* (36); *Fire Over England* (37); *49th Parallel* (41); *Carrie* (52); *The Beggar's Opera* (53); *The Prince and the Showgirl* (57); *The Devil's Disciple* (59); *Spartacus* (60); *Othello* (65); *Khartoum* (66); *Oh! What A Lovely War* (69); *Sleuth* (72); *Marathon Man* (76); *The Boys From Brazil* (78); *Dracula* (79); *The Bounty* (84)

Omnidirectional Microphone

A microphone with an extremely wide field of capture.

O'Neal, Ryan

O'Neal missed his calling, which was to be a sort of Yankee **Alain Delon** figure. Instead he opted for the lovey-dovey cuddly all-American boy-wonder image, and was scuppered for good roles as soon as his age began to show. Arthur Hiller's *Love Story* (70) was schlock, and O'Neal was schlock in it, but when he played seriously, as in Walter Hill's *The Driver* (78), which was itself an oblique remake of **Jean-Pierre Melville's** *Le Samourai* (67) (featuring an equally intense Delon as loner Jeff Costello), O'Neal was simply great. *Alors pourquoi?*
OTHER KEY FILMS: *What's Up Doc?* (72); *Paper Moon* (73); *Barry Lyndon* (75); *A Bridge Too Far* (77); *Tough Guys Don't Dance* (87); *Faithful* (96); *Zero Effect* (98); *The List* (00)

One-light Print

A simple print made with the benefit of a single light setting, and only suitable for use as a workprint due to quality considerations.

One-two-threes

The in-house name for the animator's sheet on which a decision has to be made and marked as to the correct number of exposures required for each individual drawing.

Opaque

In cinematic terms, opaque refers to the relative density, or opacity, of a particular type of film.

Opaquing

When the chief animator has finished a **cell**, or individual drawing, an opaquer will fill in the remaining blank spots according to a pre-arranged colour coding.

Opening Up

Cinematographer's jargon indicating the necessity for an increase in size of the lens aperture.

Ophüls, Max

A cult director obsessed by the cyclical nature of human emotions and, as such, comparable in essence to the great **Jean Renoir**, Ophüls was falsely accused of sentimentality by some, but in fact he had recognised the fragile nature of human sexuality far better than many of the so-called 'realistically inclined' directors who surrounded him. A true poet of the cinema, his bittersweet *Letter From An Unknown Woman* (48) predated the full flowering of his talent in such films as *La Ronde* (50), *Le Plaisir* (52), *Madame de…* (53), and his masterpiece, *Lola Montés* (55).
OTHER KEY FILMS: *Die Verkaufte Braut* (32); *La Signora Di Tutti* (34); *La Tendre Ennemie* (36); *Caught* (49); *The Reckless Moment* (49)

Optical Composite

The combining of a number of separate shots onto one frame, or series of frames, by means of an **optical printer**.

Optical Printer

An essential editing tool, first conceived of during the 1920s, the optical printer allows for the duplication and subsequent combination of a number of images into one smooth whole. The system functions through a sequence of prisms and mirrors, allowing for the re-photographing and manipulation of already projected frames to create a wide variety of **special effects**.

Opticals

This is the term that refers to any and every effect achieved through the use of an optical printer.

Optical Soundtrack

More or less the obverse of a **digital soundtrack**, an optical soundtrack (until recently the world standard) records sounds through photographic means, converting them into light impulses that can then be reconverted into sound during projection.

Optical System

Any variety or arrangement of different lenses in one camera.

Option

Potential producers and directors (and occasionally stars) may take out 'options' on copyrighted literary **properties** to obtain the exclusive right to adapt the work, within a specific period of time, should they choose to do so. It is not unknown for such options to be taken out to scotch another producer's interest in a piece that the initial party has no intention whatsoever of bringing to the screen. An option will usually cost somewhere in the region of five to ten per cent of the estimated value of the completed project, and the timescale inside which the option must be picked up before it expires is generally between one and three years.

Original

The first or 'original' negative held inside the camera while filming, and the bellwether by which all subsequent prints are judged.

Original Script/Screenplay

A piece of work that is entirely original in concept and execution.

Orion Pictures Corporation

Founded by five disgruntled **United Artists** executives in 1978, Orion initially concentrated on the quality end of the commercial market with such movies as **Milos Forman's** *Amadeus* (84) and **Oliver Stone's** *Platoon* (86), before branching out into **Paul Verhoeven** *Robocop* (87) territory. Despite running into financial difficulties in the early part of the 1990s, and despite such notable successes as **Kevin Costner's** *Dances With Wolves* (90) and **Jonathan Demme's** *Silence Of The Lambs* (91), Orion soldiered on with yet another Robocop clone, this time Number Three in the series.

Orry-Kelly, John

Along with his contemporary, **Edith Head**, Orry-Kelly was one of the greatest ever **costume designers** for the cinema, being responsible for much of the **Warners** look during the 1930s and early 1940s. A master of period detail, Orry-Kelly was at home in both black-and-white and colour, and was most often associated with **Bette Davis**, although he designed costumes, at one time or another, for virtually every great star of Hollywood's Golden Era.

OTHER KEY FILMS: **Mervyn LeRoy's** *I Am A Fugitive From A Chain Gang* (32) and *Gold Diggers Of 1933* (33); **William Wyler's** *Jezebel* (38); **John Huston's** *The Maltese Falcon* (41); **Michael Curtiz's** *Casablanca* (42); Irving Rapper's *Now Voyager* (42); **Frank Capra's** *Arsenic And Old Lace* (44); Curtis Bernhardt's *A Stolen Life* (46); **Vincente Minnelli's** *An American In Paris* (51); **Billy Wilder's** *Some Like It Hot* (59)

Oscar

Nickname given to the phallic gold-plated Academy of Motion Picture Arts And Sciences statuettes handed out every year since 1929 to (no doubt) worthy recipients at a glittering ceremony now seen by billions on satellite and terrestrial TV. The story goes that **Bette Davis** named the statuette after remarking that its buttocks resembled those of her then husband, Harman Oscar Nelson. A case of posterior fame?

O'Sullivan, Maureen

O'Sullivan is now primarily remembered for being **John Farrow's** wife, **Mia Farrow's** mother and for wearing the miraculous side-split loincloth in **Jack Conway's** *Tarzan And His Mate* (34) that has fed the fantasies of millions of young cinephilic schoolboys ever since. Following her marriage in 1936 she produced seven children, giving her, one would suppose, very little time for the pursuit of her acting career. She was excellent, however, as **Greer Garson's** nicest sister, Jane, in **Robert Z Leonard's** *Pride And Prejudice* (40), a part typical of the role of sidekick, favourite sister and best friend that she honed throughout her early career.

OTHER KEY FILMS: *Strange Interlude* (32); *The Barretts Of Wimpole Street* (34); *David Copperfield* (35); *Anna Karenina* (35); *A Day At The Races* (36); *Tarzan Escapes* (36); *Tarzan Finds A Son* (39); *Tarzan's New York Adventure* (42); *The Big Clock* (48); *Where Danger Lives* (50); *The Tall T* (57)

KEY LINE:

'You Tarzan, me Jane.' [*Tarzan The Ape-Man*]

Maureen O'Sullivan (as Jane) wearing her miraculous side-slit loincloth beside ape-man lover Johnny Weissmuller, on the set of Cedric Gibbons (and Jack Conway's) Tarzan And His Mate *(34)*

O'Toole, Peter

A good-looking hell-raiser and a passable, if wildly over-stylised actor, O'Toole carved a career of sorts during the 1960s on the back of his glamorous appearance and on his capacity for shouting his dialogue, somewhat along the lines of **Laurence Olivier's** rather more controlled shouting in *Henry V* (44). O'Toole shouted his way through the part of T E Lawrence in **David Lean's** *Lawrence Of Arabia* (62) and then continued shouting as Michael James in Clive Donner's *What's New Pussycat?* (65), as King Henry II in Anthony Harvey's *The Lion In Winter* (68), and as Jack, 14th Earl of Gurney, in Peter Medak's *The Ruling Class* (72). Later, when he took to parodying himself in such films as Richard Rush's *The Stunt Man* (80), one became almost nostalgic for the time when the shouting was real, and not put on, and by the time of Richard Benjamin's delightfully silly *My Favourite Year* (82), one had begun to miss the devil-may-care O'Toole of the early days, and to regret the dilution of his often inspired vamping. Is it a case of 'they don't make them like that any more?' What does it matter? One turns to his films with a sentimental if bemused attachment, just as one turns on the critics of his stage performances with the words, 'A gentleman never shoots at a sitting target'.

OTHER KEY FILMS: *Becket* (62); *Lord Jim* (65); *The Night Of The Generals* (67); *Murphy's Law* (71); *Under Milk Wood* (71); *Caligula* (79); *The Last Emperor* (87); *High Spirits* (88); *King Ralph* (91); *Fairytale: A True Story* (97); *Phantoms* (98); *The Manor* (99); *The Final Curtain* (01)

KEY LINE:
'I'm not an actor. I'm a movie star!'
[*My Favourite Year*]

'Our Gang'

'Our Gang' ran for twenty-two years, from 1922 to 1944, during which time the regulars grew up, had families, and occasionally died. It didn't matter, for the idea was an inspired one – choose seven children and a dog, each with something memorable about them (their size, colour, hair, mannerisms, etc.), and get them into scrapes. The series was bought up for television in 1955 and renamed 'The Little Rascals', for copyright reasons, and went on to delight another couple of generations of wistful children.

Outlaw, The

Howard Hughes's *The Outlaw* (43), beautifully shot by **Greg Toland**, was originally intended as a backdrop to **Jane Russell** and her extraordinary cleavage, but she hardly appears in it except to pout at the way Billy the Kid treats her. **Walter Huston** plays it brilliantly straight, as an icy and unpredictable Doc Holliday, while Thomas Mitchell, of all people, plays Pat Garrett, with more than a dash of his Gerald O'Hara in **Victor Fleming's** *Gone With The Wind* (39). Jack Beutel, who is considerably prettier than Russell despite not having her womanly advantages, plays Billy the Kid as a bona fide New Mexican (which he wasn't), and with such a heady variation of mannerisms that some scenes, especially when taken with Huston's slow, steady delivery, become so curiously fascinating that one is forced to keep on watching despite the utter absurdity of what is actually going on. Top marks must go to Hughes for daring to use a stock-in-trade porn shot in a major Hollywood vehicle – a close-up of Russell's face turns into a close-up of her mouth quite literally going down on the recumbent Beutel, (we are deprived of the actual details, except in fade-to-black). The shot was so outré that filmmakers such as **Henri-Georges Clouzot** in *Quai Des Orfèvres* (47) [see **Erotic Moments**] have been copying it ever since, showing that high-quality dementia can sometimes excel even itself in its unplanned and unintentional originality.

Outline

The initial one-page concept for a **screenplay**, which, if the pitch goes well, will then be turned into a thirty-page treatment. If the treatment is acceptable to the studio execs, the screenwriter will hurry home clutching a largish cheque and turn that treatment into a 110-page screenplay. It will then go through an extensive doctoring process, following which, in one out of a hundred cases, it will be made into a movie (and probably one which bears little or no resemblance to the original outline).

Out Of Synch

This refers to moments when the figures on the screen and the dialogue purportedly coming from their mouths do not quite match up.

Out-takes

Aspects of shot scenes that are not used in the eventual movie, and which these days are often sold on and, in the case of lesser movies, with lesser stars, who do not have the benefit of killer attorneys and killer contracts used as TV fodder in absurd shows with names like 'Blooped Again' and 'Cock-Up Carnival'.

Overdeveloped

The opposite of underdeveloped film, in overdeveloped film the contrasts are exaggerated rather than blanched out. This results from the overuse of developing fluid and the unenlightened abuse of temperature settings.

Overexposure

This occurs when too much light is allowed to strike the undeveloped film, causing lacklustre, palely loitering prints, and, just occasionally, whiteouts.

Overhead Clusters

Clusters of lighting units situated, not surprisingly, overhead, and which afford generalised illumination on a film set.

Overhead Strips

Long strips of overhead lighting, affording large expanses of general illumination in a studio setting.

Overlap

The smooth linking of disparate scenes by means of overlapping dialogue, music or sound. Also the unused overlapping pieces of film in splicing. Can sometimes refer to extra film exposed beyond a scene's ending to allow for later dissolves, fades, or other necessary tinkering.

Overshoot

The opposite of undershooting, overshooting occurs when a director gets carried away and exposes far too much film for the budget allowed. Following his success with *Easy Rider* (69), **Dennis Hopper** bolted down to Peru with his chums (clutching a million dollars of **Universal's** money) and returned with forty hours of often incomprehensible overshots. The resulting film, *The Last Movie* [*Chinchero*] (71), when cut down to a more manageable 108 minutes (after a year of editing) won an award at Venice but remains more or less incomprehensible to the average person; Hopper, one gathers, believes it a masterpiece.

Over-the-shoulder Shot

Known as an OSS, and meant to show a character's POV (point of view), an over-the-shoulder shot generally shows the back of an ear – except in the case of Vincent Van Gogh or the unfortunate cop in **Quentin Tarantino's** *Reservoir Dogs* (92) – and part of a shoulder-blade, in the fond belief that the audience will then realise that they are meant to be that character for the length of the take.

Ozu, Yasujiro

Ozu represented the heart of Japanese cinema – he watched the world and its people with unalloyed tenderness, recording their fears, their mistakes, the complications they as often as not foisted on themselves, with a rare and paradoxically objective sensitivity. There is no escape in Ozu-land, only acceptance of one's lot, coupled with a generous, if sometimes tentative, encouragement by one generation of another. His films were little known in the West until *Tokyo Story* (53), but each is a miniature masterpiece, slow moving, sometimes discursive, always heartfelt. His usually static camera watches, records, but never judges – that is left to the viewer – and we find ourselves learning tolerance, during an Ozu film, just as we learn it from a film by **Robert Bresson**, or **Jean Renoir**. In his world, if there is to be no escape, then there must be reconciliation, accommodation, peace. It is a simple message, but can take a lifetime to understand. Ozu helps.

OTHER KEY FILMS: *The Life Of An Office Worker* (29); *I Was Born, But...* (32); *A Tokyo Woman* (33); *A Story Of Floating Weeds* (34); *The Record Of A Tenement Gentleman* (47); *Late Spring* (49); *Early Summer* (51); *The Flavour Of Green Tea Over Rice* (52); *Early Spring* (56); *Twilight In Tokyo* (57); *Equinox Flower* (58); *Late Autumn* (60); *The End Of Summer* (61); *An Autumn Afternoon* (62)

Pabst, G W

Outside film-buff circles Pabst is largely renowned for his extraordinary and wildly stylised *Pandora's Box* (29), which introduced the ill-fated but infinitely fascinating **Louise Brooks** to international audiences. The film is still powerful, with its expressionistic sets, flowing camerawork and extremities of decadent passion, but Pabst's *Die Dreigroschenoper* [*The Threepenny Opera*] (31) is the greater film, with its bizarre, nineteenth-century central character, played by the splendid Rudolf Forster, who gets closer to the heart of a Victorian pimp, both visually and through characterisation, than any number of present-day actors, tied, as they so often are, by the bonds of social and political expedience.

OTHER KEY FILMS: *Die Freudlose Gasse* (25); *Geheimnisse Einer Seele* (26); *Westfront* 1918 (30); *A Modern Hero* (34); *Le Drame De Shanghai* (38); *Das Bekenntnis Der Ina Kahr* (54)

Pacino, Al

At his best he is one of the finest screen actors working in America today, using his face, eyes and body with a confidence born, one suspects, of despair, and his best parts, as Michael Corleone in **Francis Ford Coppola's** *The Godfather* (72) and as vulnerable cop Frank Keller in Harold Becker's *Sea Of Love* (89), reflect this. His recent form has been less impressive, and Martin Brest's *Scent Of A Woman* (92) gave the impression that a lot of effort had been expended for little in the way of

insight. His performance as Ricky Roma in James Foley's *Glengarry Glen Ross* (92), on the other hand, was superb, and it was wonderful to see Pacino so confident and so enthusiastic in the self-directed *Looking For Richard* (96), in which he indulges in a fascinating thespian trawl through the making of Shakespeare's *Richard III*. He is an actor who plays to his strengths, and most of his best film roles hover within scenting distance of the US Eastern seaboard.

OTHER KEY FILMS: *The Panic In Needle Park* (71); *Scarecrow* (73); *Serpico* (73); *Dog Day Afternoon* (75); *Bobby Deerfield* (77); *Scarface* (83); *Dick Tracy* (90); *Carlito's Way* (93); *Heat* (95); *Donnie Brasco* (97); *Any Given Sunday* (99); *Chinese Coffee* (00) [also dir.]

Pakula, Alan J

A curious hybrid in Hollywood terms, Pakula started out as a producer, then turned to directing when he was more than forty. Occasionally misled by his own intelligence, Pakula directed two of the best thrillers of the 1970s – *The Parallax View* (74) and *All The President's Men* (76) – both of which were marred by an overly self-conscious use of film trickery to obtain their effects (form over substance, if you like). That said, his 1982 film of William Styron's *Sophie's Choice* worked on a number of interesting levels, and *Presumed Innocent* (90) was a more than professional stab at that most elusive of rogue elephants, an international best-seller. Pakula was killed, on 19 November 1998, when a metal pipe thrown up by another vehicle

239

smashed through the windscreen of his car. He left a sadly curtailed legacy, always fascinating, but at the same time curiously unengaging, as if its perpetrator had been conducting, not a film career, exactly, but more a lengthy experiment into the parameters of credulity.

OTHER KEY FILMS: *Klute* (71); *Comes A Horseman* (78); *Rollover* (81); *Orphans* (87); *The Pelican Brief* (93); *The Devil's Own* (97)

Palance, Jack

Palance was destined never to be offered anything but tough guy roles after his face was severely burned during the Second World War, but he successfully negotiated his way through this unwelcome rite of passage to prove himself worthy of stronger parts, thanks to the anguished depth he managed to give to roles that other, lesser actors, would simply have coasted through. Following his sinister but profound villain, Wilson, in **George Stevens's** *Shane* (53), Palance surprised everyone with his tormented performance as neurotic actor Charles Castle, in **Robert Aldrich's** *The Big Knife* (55), and his excellent turn as Jeremiah 'Jerry' Prokosch, in **Jean-Luc Godard's** *Le Mépris* [*Contempt*] (63). He made a particularly welcome comeback as amorous painter Rudi Cox in **Percy Adlon's** *Bagdad Café* (88).

OTHER KEY FILMS: *Panic In The Streets* (50); *Sudden Fear* (52); *I Died A Thousand Times* (55); *Torture Garden* (67); *The Professionals* (66); *The Horsemen* (71); *City Slickers* (91); *Salmonberries* (92); *Tombstone* (93); *Cops & Robbersons* (94); *Treasure Island* (99)

Palin, Michael

An entertaining and witty actor and one of the founder members of *Monty Python's Flying Circus*, Palin has made his post-Python reputation largely on television, but when he has acted in films he has proved himself surprisingly versatile, particularly in Malcolm Mowbray's *A Private Function* (84) and **Terry Gilliam's** *Brazil* (85).

OTHER KEY FILMS: *Monty Python And The Holy Grail* (75); *Jabberwocky* (76); *Monty Python's Life Of Brian* (79); *Time Bandits* (81); *The Missionary* (82); *Monty Python's The Meaning Of Life* (83); *A Fish Called Wanda* (88); *Fierce Creatures* (97)

Paltrow, Gwyneth

A skilful and attractive actress and something of a mistress of accent and vocal nuance, Paltrow has constructed her career with care and is now justifiably enjoying its early fruits. Douglas McGrath's *Emma* (96) ensured international interest in her, and her recent performances in John Madden's *Shakespeare In Love* (98) and **Anthony Minghella's** *The Talented Mr Ripley* (99) have cemented her reputation as a dependable and talented leading lady. Whether she has the staying power of a **Jessica Lange**, a **Michelle Pfeiffer** or a **Meryl Streep** remains to be seen.

OTHER KEY FILMS: *Hook* (91); *Flesh And Bone* (93); *Malice* (93); *Mrs Parker And The Vicious Circle* (94); *Jefferson In Paris* (95); *Seven* (95); *Great Expectations* (98); *Sliding Doors* (98); *Duets* (00); *Bounce* (00); *Possession* (01); *Shallow Hal* (01)

240

Gwyneth Paltrow's Marge Sherwood sowing discontent between Matt Damon's Tom Ripley and Jude Law's Dickie Greenleaf, in Anthony Minghella's The Talented Mr Ripley *(99)*

Pan Shot

Short for a 'panoramic shot', pan shot refers to the shot obtained when a camera moves horizontally along a pre-arranged track to cover a wider than normal filmable area, either to follow the action or to show the environment in which the action is to take place.

Pan-and-tilt Head

A support mechanism on a camera that allows it to pan horizontally and tilt vertically.

Panavision

The next big jump up from **CinemaScope**, Panavision was **MGM's** 1950s version of the wide-screen process. It encountered some initial hostility among cinema owners who did not relish having to buy an entirely new set of projectors because of the increase in size of the film stock from 35mm to 65mm (or even to 70mm in the case of Super Panavision). The system, however, eventually took off with the success of **William Wyler's** wide-screen *Ben-Hur* (59).

Panchromatic

A particularly sensitive emulsion used on black-and-white film, and which, as indicated by its name, responds to all the visible colours on the spectrum.

Panchromatic Master Positive

A print struck in black and white, but from a colour negative, which will later be used in the making of black-and-white **dupes**.

Pan Glass

A portable glass filter for viewing the approximate tonal appearance of an imminent shot, allowing the cinematographer to make last-minute changes to the set-up.

Panning Gear

Predominantly used in animation, panning gear allows the camera to move either vertically or horizontally, one frame at a time.

Paparazzi

Named after the street photographer, Paparazzo, played by Walter Santesso in **Federico Fellini's** *La Dolce Vita* (60), the paparazzi are the rogue photographers whose stock-in-trade consists of snatching candid shots of anyone on the celebrity circuit for later sale to newspapers and magazines.

Papas, Irene

An intense and unconventionally beautiful actress, Papas made her international mark playing the ill-fated widow in Michael Cacoyannis's *Zorba The Greek* (64), but her real strengths lie in Greek Tragedy – when she brings these elements to her more conventional performances, as, paradoxically, she does to the small role of Maria in J Lee Thompson's *The Guns Of Navarone* (61), she quite literally lights up the screen.

OTHER KEY FILMS: *Tribute To A Bad Man* (56); *Antigone* (60); *Electra* (62); *The Brotherhood* (68); *Anne Of The Thousand Days* (69); *A Dream Of Kings* (69); *Iphigenia* (77); *Erendira* (83); *Chronicle Of A Death Foretold* (87)

Paper Prints

Before 1912 there was no effective way to copyright a moving picture, so prints had to be taken of each frame and registered en masse with the Library of Congress. This archaic system had one coincidental benefit, namely that films registered by paper print could then be copied back, many years later, for archiving.

Parallax

The problem arising when a shot is filmed by a camera with an externally attached, rather than a through-the-lens viewfinder, necessitating a compensatory adjustment in camera position.

Parallel

A wheeled platform on which the camera and crew can be raised above the action for high-angle shooting.

Parallel Action

The cutting back and forth between two parallel and simultaneous actions to give an overview – a famous example would be the cavalry chase in **John Ford's** *Stagecoach* (39) in which we first see a shot of the stage, then a shot of the Apaches, then a shot of the cavalry, then back to the stage, and so on, all in so-called real time.

Parallelism

The exact equating of the soundtrack to the image on the screen, in terms of both sound and image/background reference. See **Counterpoint**

Paramount Pictures

Paramount Pictures is one of Hollywood's major studios and one of its oldest, with its precursor, the **Famous Players** Film Company, having been founded by **Adolph Zukor** in 1912. Paramount's featured assets have included, over the years, **Mary Pickford**, **Cecil B DeMille**, **Rudolph Valentino**, **Gary Cooper**, **Marlene Dietrich**, **Bob Hope**, **Burt Lancaster**, **Harrison Ford** and **Tom Cruise**. Despite a convoluted ownership record (they are now owned by **Viacom**) Paramount still carries its history and an important part of the Hollywood film legend with it, wherever, and to whomever, it goes.

Paris

Paris deserves an entry for being quite simply the best place on earth to watch classic and independent films as they should be seen – on the big screen. At any given moment more than 300 different films are being shown, including regular Director's Seasons. How long this glorious state of affairs will persist is a moot point, however, for the big US-output-dominated French chains such as UGC and Gaumont have recently launched unlimited access cards for a one-off flat-rate annual fee. Left Bank **art-house** cinemas such as the Action Écoles, the Quartier Latin, the Grand Action and the Action Christine, which have been Meccas for film aficionados for years, now find their futures threatened. Go to Paris while you still can, buy yourselves a 'L'Officiel des Spectacles' or a 'Pariscope' guide, and support them.

Park, Nick

See **Aardman Animations**

Parker, Alan

Something of a self-proclaimed champion of British cinema, Parker has actually made a sequence of very conventional films very well, beginning with his debut success, *Bugsy Malone* (76), a film which still has the capacity to please and to entertain. His best film is *Mississippi Burning* (88), in which he investigated the roots of racism, although a cult has formed around *Midnight Express* (78), which provided Parker with that initial, precious key to the Hollywood studio restrooms. *The Commitments* (91), about a talented Irish band doing uncannily good cover versions of Otis Redding songs, gave his career a much needed and well-deserved mid-flow boost – it's just a bit of a shame he chose *The Road To Wellville* (94) to follow it up with.
OTHER KEY FILMS: *Fame* (80); *Shoot The Moon* (81); *Pink Floyd – The Wall* (82); *Birdy* (85); *Angel Heart* (87); *Come See The Paradise* (90); *Evita* (96); *Angela's Ashes* (99)

Parsons, Louella

One of the bitchy, but indubitably influential Hollywood gossip columnists who, along with arch-rival **Hedda Hopper**, more or less dominated the celebrity-slaying and star-making fields during the 1930s, 40s and 50s, Parsons specialised in either bribing, cajoling or bulldozing her way to myriad scandalous scoops. Despised as much as feared, both she and her nemesis, Hopper, have now entered movie folklore, attaining, in posterity, the heady and empty positions that their dubious activities denied them in real life.

Pasolini, Pier Paolo

A multi-talented iconoclast, Pasolini delighted in shocking the Italian bourgeois church and laity from its customary inertia. A master of both the beautiful and the grotesque, Pasolini lived and died violently. He was a master of innovation, and in *Accatone* (61), *Theorem* (68) and *Pigsty* (69), he genuinely took the tradition of Italian neo-realist cinema a step further than it had ever intended to go. An extreme Marxist in his political views, Pasolini was, paradoxically perhaps, deeply religious, although his personal dogma was definitely not that of his baptismal Catholic Church. The victim of many censorship attempts while he was alive, Pasolini met his death at the hands of a seventeen-year-old youth who claimed that the maestro had importuned him, an act that only added to the mystique that still surrounds this bizarre and talented man.
OTHER KEY FILMS: *Mama Roma* (62); *The Gospel According To St Matthew* (64); *Oedipus Rex* (67); *The Decameron* (70); *Medea* (70); *The Canterbury Tales* (71); *The Arabian Nights* (74); *Salò – The 120 Days Of Sodom* (75); *La Ricotta* (76)

Passer, Ivan

Yet another talented European director and screenwriter who, despite one or two successes, has seemingly been humbled by the Hollywood machine. Passer had it within him to be a top-rank director, given the promise that he showed with his two early Czechoslovakian films, *A Boring Afternoon* (65) and *Intimate Lightning* (65), and with his scripts for **Milos Forman**. His talent seemed borne out by his best US film to date, the outstanding *Cutter's Way* [original title: *Cutter And Bone*] (81), which used **Jeff Bridges**, John Heard and Lisa Eichhorn in ways that they must only dream of now, lost as they are in the commercial mainstream or its peripheries. What happened? Who knows. Hollywood (whatever that may be) is not renowned for either its sensitivity or its subtlety when dealing with artists who concentrate on character and atmosphere over plot. God knows what they would have made of a genius such as **Jean Renoir** today – he, like Passer, would probably have sunk without critical trace, hoist by his inability to perfect the elusive, nay, ineffable art of the two-minute pitch.

OTHER KEY FILMS: *Law And Disorder* (74); *Crime And Passion* (76); *Silver Bears* (78); *Creator* (85); *Haunted Summer* (88); *The Wishing Tree* (99)

Passing Shot

A passing shot refers either to a stationary camera past which the object of the shot moves – think galloping horses at the beginning of **Akira Kurosawa's** *Throne Of Blood* (57) – or a stationary object past which the camera moves – think the stationary Kaspar Hauser, abandoned in the town square, in **Werner Herzog's** *The Enigma Of Kaspar Hauser* (75).

Patch Panel

A central connection board for the patching in of electrical apparatus either in the studio or on location.

Pathé, Charles

One of the earliest dedicated film exhibitors, Pathé was renting out and selling film projectors and phonographs as early as 1896, and by 1908 his business had turned into the core of an empire that would go on to dominate the industry for the next ten years. US tastes changed, however, and Pathé gradually found himself eased out of the market, and by the time of the Wall Street stock market crash of 1929 he had sold out entirely to take his well-earned retirement on the Côte d'Azur. His name did live on, however, in Pathé newsreels.

Patsy Awards

These are the animal **Oscars** for enlightened barking, neighing, mooing, howling, defecating or other forms of upstaging human actors on the screen, and which are presented annually by the American Humane Association. Picture Animal Top Star of the Year, of course, gives us the unfortunate acronym.

Peck, Gregory

Peck often gave the impression of being something of a goody-goody, a mix between a school headmaster and a lay preacher, and even when he went counter to that image, there was nevertheless something cosy in the evil he portrayed, as with Lewt, his lusty cowboy, in **King Vidor's** wildly over-the-top *Duel In The Sun* (46). Even when he kissed

a girl, one half expected Peck to step back and mildly berate her for her forwardness, but this is not to say that Peck was in any way a bad actor, for he occasionally transcended even his own saintly image and turned in excellent performances, particularly as Atticus Finch, the liberal hayseed lawyer in Robert Mulligan's *To Kill A Mockingbird* (63), and as the embattled husband and father, Sam Bowden, in J Lee Thompson's *Cape Fear* (61). Having outlasted virtually all his contemporaries, Peck's films remain as testimony to the cautiously burgeoning liberal conscience of 1940s and 50s Hollywood.

OTHER KEY FILMS: *Days Of Glory* (44); *Spellbound* (45); *The Yearling* (46); *The Paradine Case* (47); *Twelve O'Clock High* (49); *Captain Horatio Hornblower* (51); *The Snows Of Kilimanjaro* (52); *Roman Holiday* (53); *The Purple Plain* (55); *Moby Dick* (56); *On The Beach* (59); *Mirage* (65); *Arabesque* (66); *I Walk The Line* (70); *Billy Two Hats* (73); *The Omen* (76); *MacArthur* (77); *The Boys From Brazil* (78); *Old Gringo* (89); *Cape Fear* (91)

Peckinpah, Sam

Always larger than life, Peckinpah was a man's man in what was rapidly becoming (to his eyes at least) a feminised world. His heroes reflect himself – they are men who have outstayed their own times, and indulge in 'beserker' fits of suicidal bravura in a (usually) vain effort to reverse the tide. *Ride The High Country* (62), in which he paired ageing **Western** star **Randolph Scott** with **Joel McCrea**, and *The Wild Bunch* (69), in which modern life saw off **William Holden** and tamed **Robert Ryan**, are cases in point, but his most complex work (in its complete form) was *Pat Garrett And Billy The Kid* (73), in which Peckinpah appeared to suggest that nothing, despite his earlier protestations, was forever. Some of his later films slipped into self-parody, but *Junior Bonner* (72), in which Peckinpah transferred some of his real fear of change onto **Steve McQueen's** stonily bewildered face, was very fine indeed.

OTHER KEY FILMS: *Major Dundee* (65); *The Ballad Of Cable Hogue* (70); *Straw Dogs* (71); *The Getaway* (72); *Bring Me The Head Of Alfredo Garcia* (74); *The Killer Elite* (75); *Cross Of Iron* (77); *The Osterman Weekend* (83)

KEY LINE:
'I liked what I heard he was about – a guy who gave everybody a lot of shit and stood his ground…frankly, I never saw him behave badly.' [Screenwriter Walon Green, who co-scripted *The Wild Bunch* (69), on the allegedly 'mercurial' Peckinpah]

243

Penn, Arthur

Penn is the classic example of a fine director touching his peak, wobbling a little, refinding himself, and then going completely off the boil. He touched commercial heaven with *Bonnie And Clyde* (67), surpassed it with *Little Big Man* (70), which was a justifiable critical and commercial success and which remains in the memory long after the hype has been forgotten, and then, apart from two or three well-crafted thrillers, including the underrated *Night Moves* (75), made nothing of any real consequence ever again. There are too few directors of Penn's particular talent around today and it is something of a tragedy that either Hollywood, or the sum of his own particular idiosyncrasies, has let Penn down.

OTHER KEY FILMS: *The Left-Handed Gun* (58); *The Miracle Worker* (62); *Mickey One* (65); *The Chase* (66); *Alice's Restaurant* (69); *The Missouri Breaks* (76); *Target* (85); *Dead Of Winter* (87); *Inside* (97)

Penn, Sean

Only three years older than **Brad Pitt** and four years older than **Johnny Depp**, Penn seems somehow of a different generation; more of a flashback to the late 1940s **John Garfield** and the early 1950s **Marlon Brando** than the modern **Tom Cruise**-like man. A fervid, highly strung brawler, Penn is also a remarkably talented actor and director whose own *The Indian Runner* (91) was disastrously underrated on its release. Penn roused himself from a premature retirement to script and direct his friend **Jack Nicholson** in *The Crossing Guard* (95), only to find this interesting movie meeting the same fate as its predecessor. Penn is a talented and conscientious actor, and he was as outstanding as death-row victim Matthew Poncelet in **Tim Robbins's** unsentimental *Dead Man Walking* (95), as he was in **Oliver Stone's** unjustly maligned *U-Turn* (97). His recent performance as vainglorious jazz guitarist Emmet Ray in **Woody Allen's** *Sweet And Lowdown* (99) can only add to his reputation as Hollywood's most magnetically problematic son.

OTHER KEY FILMS: *Taps* (81); *The Falcon And The Snowman* (85); *At Close Range* (86); *Colors* (88); *Casualties Of War* (89); *State Of Grace* (90); *Carlito's Way* (93); *The Thin Red Line* (98); *Up At The Villa* (00); *Before Night Falls* (00); *The Weight Of Water* (00); *The Pledge* (01) [Also dir.]

KEY LINE:

'Acting is the girl who's unattractive to me. I don't enjoy it. Ever.' [Penn on acting]

Perforation

A hole punched into the edge of a strip of film, through which the sprockets of a camera, projector, or other piece of motion-picture equipment can readily engage.

Périnal, Georges

Périnal was poached from his native France by Britain's **Alexander Korda** on the strength of his extraordinary body of work for **René Clair**, and for his one-off triumph with **Jean Cocteau** on *Le Sang D'Un Poète* (31). Périnal went on to photograph Korda's *The Private Life Of Henry VIII* (33), Paul Czinner's *Catherine The Great* (34), Korda's exquisite *Rembrandt* (36), the utterly sublime multi-directed *The Thief Of Bagdad* (40), and **Michael Powell** and **Emeric Pressburger's** *The Life And Death Of Colonel Blimp* (43). A magnificent career, particularly when seen in conjunction with his early sequence of films for Clair, which included *Under The Roofs Of Paris* (30) and *Le Million* (31), after which Clair, too, was poached by Korda, for *The Ghost Goes West* (36), a film coincidentally photographed by the excellent Harold Rossen, and not Périnal, for a change.

OTHER KEY FILMS: Zoltan Korda's *The Four Feathers* (39); **Carol Reed's** *The Fallen Idol* (48); **Otto Preminger's** *Bonjour Tristesse* (58)

Perkins, Anthony

An intense, nervous and rather mannered actor, Perkins had his most famous incarnation as Norman Bates, in **Alfred Hitchcock's** *Psycho* (60), which both

Anthony Perkins as the maternally challenged Norman Bates, in Alfred Hitchcock's seminal chiller, Psycho *(60)*

244

made his reputation and at the same time destroyed him for the more conventional roles to which his talents might better have suited him. Perkins never wholly shook off the gawky, hesitant adolescent that he played in so many of his earlier films, and his best performance came, surprisingly, not in the cinema, but on television, as a superb Javert in an adaptation of Victor Hugo's *Les Misérables* (78).

OTHER KEY FILMS: *Friendly Persuasion* (56); *Fear Strikes Out* (57); *The Matchmaker* (58); *Tall Story* (60); *The Trial* (63); *The Champagne Murders* (66); *Ten Days' Wonder* (71); *Pretty Poison* (68); *Crimes Of Passion* (84)

KEY LINE:
'A boy's best friend is his mother.' [*Psycho*]

Persistence Of Vision
See **Flicker**

Petersen, Wolfgang
A German **Art-house** director who has gradually moved across to the US mainstream while nevertheless managing to keep certain key elements of his early sensitivity intact, Petersen wowed international audiences with *Das Boot* (81), his claustrophobic tale of life aboard a German submarine during the Second World War, and followed up with the effective and pleasantly offbeat thriller *Shattered* (91). His **Clint Eastwood** movie, *In The Line Of Fire* (93), further confirmed his capacity for reinvention, but *Air Force One* (97), with **Harrison Ford**, was as grotesque as it was conventional, and one fancies that Petersen, while cheerfully pocketing the loot, must secretly have hated kowtowing to the twin exigencies of both star and blockbusting potential. He looked much more comfortable directing **George Clooney** in *The Perfect Storm* (00), where his sea skills honed on (or in) *Das Boot* were once more called into play.

OTHER KEY FILMS: *Einer Von Uns Beiden* (73); *Die Konsequenz* (77); *Schwarz Und Weiss Wie Tage Und Nächte* (78); *The Neverending Story* (84); *Enemy Mine* (85); *Outbreak* (95);

Pfeiffer, Michelle
Despite her beauty (welcome distraction though it is) and despite a recent spate of rather worthy roles, Pfeiffer remains a serious contender for best mainstream actress of the 1980s and early 1990s, with her string of first-rate performances in such films as John Landis's *Into The Night* (85), **George Miller's** *The Witches Of Eastwick* (87), **Jonathan Demme's** *Married To The Mob* (88), **Stephen Frears's** *Dangerous Liaisons* (88) and Steve Kloves's

The Fabulous Baker Boys (89). This magical run continued with **Fred Schepisi's** *The Russia House* (90), Jonathan Kaplan's *Love Field* (92), **Martin Scorsese's** *The Age Of Innocence* (93) and **Mike Nichols's** *Wolf* (94) − few actresses in recent years, without the safe studio structure of the 1930s and 1940s behind them, can have managed their careers and chosen their vehicles so well.

OTHER KEY FILMS: *Scarface* (83); *Ladyhawke* (85); *Tequila Sunrise* (88); *Frankie And Johnny* (91); *Batman Returns* (92); *Up Close And Personal* (96); *A Thousand Acres* (97); *The Deep End Of The Ocean* (99); *What Lies Beneath* (00)

KEY LINE:
'You can have it all, but you can't do it all.' [Pfeiffer on life]

PG
A cinema-rating system used in both the US and Great Britain, indicating that parental guidance is required before a child is allowed to enter the cinema. PG-13 is an extra rating in the US, which advises parents, at their discretion, to be cautious in taking children under that age into the cinema because of the content of certain scenes in an otherwise innocuous, child-friendly film.

Phenakisticope
An early 'persistence of vision' (see **Flicker**) machine invented by Joseph Plateau in 1832, the phenakisticope consisted of a series of drawings glued to a circular disk that was then rotated at high speed in front of a mirror, producing an effect of continuous motion.

Philipe, Gérard
Dead from heart failure at the age of thirty-six, Philipe crammed a great deal of life into his fifteen-year screen career, becoming, in that short time, France's most popular romantic lead and one of the most successful stage actors of his generation. He managed that peculiarly French trick of mixing commercial nous with critical acuity and making a success of them both, and his capacity for plain-speaking leavened with tenderness and a melancholia that seemed in some way to foreshadow his early death, ensures him perpetual cult status with enlightened audiences. As happy in swashbuckling roles (Christian-Jaque's *Fanfan La Tulipe* (52)) as he was in romantic comedy (**René Clair's** *Les Belles De Nuit* (52)), Philipe's death in 1959 spans the exact crossover point between the old guard and the French **New Wave**.

KEY FILMS: *L'Idiot* (46); *Le Diable Au Corps* (46); *La Chartreuse De Parme* (47); *Une Si Jolie Petite Plage* (48); *Souvenirs Perdus* (49); *La Ronde* (50); *La Beauté Du Diable* (50); *Juliette Ou La Clé Des Songes* (51); *Knave Of Hearts* (54); *Le Rouge Et Le Noir* (54); *Le Joueur* (58); *Les Liaisons Dangereuses* (59)

Photoelectric Cell

An apparatus which allows light rays to be transformed into electric current, and thus eventually into sound.

Photoflood

The intentional flooding of a high-energy tungsten bulb with excess current to produce a bright, seething light, at the eventual expense of the bulb itself.

Photogenic

A term describing something or someone (or an arrangement of the two) that photographs especially well.

Photometer

An exceptionally accurate exposure meter, used to measure the intensity of light falling on a particular subject.

Photoplay

A neologism thought up in 1910, at the instigation of the Essanay film company, to accurately describe a motion picture, 'photoplay' was later superseded by the word 'movie' in the US, and 'film' in the UK. A movie-fan magazine of the same name ran from 1911 to 1980.

Pialat, Maurice

One of the foremost French directors of his generation, Pialat brings a naturalistic painter's eye to his film work, most notably in *Loulou* (80), in which yuppie **Isabelle Huppert** and butch **Gérard Depardieu** ignite chemically and sexually (if not intellectually), and *A Nos Amours* (83), a paean to adult/teenage misunderstandings. He won the Palme d'Or for *Sous Le Soleil De Satan* (87), a brooding, almost **Bressonian** exercise in misplaced spirituality, and racked up a further success with *Van Gogh* (91), in which he endeavoured to come to terms with the final few months of Vincent Van Gogh's extraordinary life, daringly using Jacques Dutronc, a French pop star, in the title role – a risk, incidentally, that paid off handsomely.

OTHER KEY FILMS: *L'Enfance Nue* (68); *La Gueule Ouverte* (74); *Passe Ton Bac D'Abord* (79); *Police* (85); *Le Garçu* (96); *Les Auto-Stoppeuses* (97)

Piccoli, Michel

Piccoli is French cinema's sophisticated Mr Sardonicus, forever taken aback by the callowness and idiocy of his fellow man, then shrugging his shoulders at his inability to do anything about it. He spans, at his best, both the **avant-garde** and the commercial mainstream in a way that few American actors can ever aspire to, and one relishes his powerful and often anarchical screen presence in such films as **Jean-Luc Godard's** *Le Mépris* [*Contempt*] (63), **Luis Buñuel's** *Belle De Jour* (67), Marco Ferreri's *La Grande Bouffe* (73), and, more recently, as the simple, almost saintly Milou, in **Louis Malle's** *Milou En Mai* (89).

OTHER KEY FILMS: *Le Doulos* (63); *Diary Of A Chambermaid* (64); *Les Demoiselles De Rochefort* (67); *The Discreet Charm Of The Bourgeoisie* (72); *Atlantic City* (80); *La Nuit De Varennes* (82); *Viva La Vie* (85); *Death In A French Garden* (85); *La Belle Noiseuse* (91); *Bête De Scène* (94); *Tykho Moon* (97); *Rien Sur Robert* (99); *Tout Va Bien, On S'En Va* (00); *Je Rentre À La Maison* (01)

Pickford, Mary

Known as 'America's Sweetheart', Pickford was, in reality, a tough cookie who knew how to cut a good deal with the studio bosses. She was still playing little girls with ringlets in her late twenties, in Marshall Neilan's *Daddy Long Legs* (19) and Paul Powell's *Pollyanna* (20), because that's what the public wanted. Together with **D W Griffith**, **Charlie Chaplin** and **Douglas Fairbanks Sr**, she formed **United Artists** in 1919. Already hugely wealthy, she married Fairbanks in 1920 and built Pickfair, their exotic mansion in Beverly Hills, in which they reigned together in state as king and queen of silent Hollywood. The coming of sound, twinned with the shearing of her golden locks, finally put paid to Pickford's screen career, but she lived on, occasionally appearing on radio, occasionally bringing out a book of memoirs, something of a belated grand dame of cinema, until her death in 1979.

OTHER KEY FILMS: *In Old Kentucky* (09); *The Little Teacher* (10); *Tess Of The Storm Country* (13); *Rebecca Of Sunnybrook Farm* (17); *A Romance Of The Redwoods* (17); *Stella Maris* (18); *Little Lord Fauntleroy* (21); *Rosita* (23); *The Gaucho* (27); *The Taming Of The Shrew* (29); *Kiki* (31)

Pickups

Extra shots completed after the shoot has been wound up to paper over continuity problems or other lacunae discovered during editing.

Picture Duplicate Negative

See **Dupe**

Picture Negative

Any negative developed in a film laboratory from previously exposed film.

Picture Print

A positive image on processed film.

Picture Release Negative

The final negative from which release prints are struck.

Pilot Pins

The sprocket pins that pop up in the gate of a camera, alternately engaging and withdrawing from the perforations at the edge of a strip of film.

Pincushion Distortion

A particular form of lens defect that leads to the distortion of square images into a pincushion shape.

Pinewood Studios

Originally opened in 1936, at staggering expense, state-of-the-art Pinewood (which has recently merged with Shepperton Studios) now possesses the world's largest purpose-built silent stage, Europe's biggest exterior tank, and a nine thousand square foot digital wide-screen television studio. All this is a far cry from the days which saw the likes of **David Lean** and **Michael Powell** making use of its premises to film *Oliver Twist* (48) and *The Red Shoes* (48) respectively. Now Pinewood, under the management of Tony and **Ridley Scott**, plays host to brainless blockbusters such as **Brian De Palma's** *Mission: Impossible* (96), Michael Caton-Jones's *The Jackal* (97), **Luc Besson's** *The Fifth Element* (97) (not quite so brainless as the others), and Simon West's *Lara Croft: Tomb Raider* (01).

Pitch

The pitch is the exact distance between two perforations on a reel of film.

Pitt, Brad

Along with **Johnny Depp**, Pitt has risen steadily to the top of his generation of actors, proving that he is as discriminating in his choice of parts as he is ambitious in his eventual intentions. He made his first international mark at the age of twenty-eight, in **Ridley Scott's** *Thelma And Louise* (91), in which he played J D (**James Dean**?), a capricious and venal drifter who nevertheless gives Geena Davis's Thelma the best sex of her life. Pitt followed this breakthrough, however, with a rather moribund turn as Paul MacClean in **Robert Redford's** *A River Runs Through It* (92), he then resurrected himself with Edward Zwick's *Legends Of The Fall* (94) (based on a brilliant Jim Harrison novella) in which he gave an almost Dean-like cast to his performance as Tristan Ludlow. Edward Fincher's recent *Fight Club* (99), together with Guy Ritchie's *Snatch* (00) and Gore Verbinski's *The Mexican* (01), has certainly done no harm to Pitt's bankability after the box-office fiasco of Martin Brest's *Meet Joe Black* (98).
OTHER KEY FILMS: *Across The Tracks* (91); *Johnny Suede* (91); *Kalifornia* (93); *True Romance* (93); *Seven* (95); *Twelve Monkeys* (95); *Sleepers* (96); *The Devil's Own* (97); *Spy Game* (01)

Platen

The glass sheet that is used to hold an animator's **cell** over a pre-drawn background while filming takes place.

Playback

The playing of pre-recorded sound or music while any action — filming, choreography, or rehearsal — that requires silent mugging on camera, is taking place. Also the swift playing back of a recently made recording to check for quality.

Pleasence, Donald

Pleasence could play sinister and he could play kind, and he made a virtue of his myopic gaze and his faculty for turning the guilty sweats on or off at will in a long sequence of films from the late 1950s to his death in 1995, amongst which Clive Donner's *The Caretaker* (64), **Roman Polanski's** *Cul-De-Sac* (66) and Delbert Mann's *Kidnapped* (71) (Pleasence's performance, and not the film) stand out. Latterly, Pleasence became something of a *rentier* in a succession of movies based on the characters from **John Carpenter's** massively successful *Halloween* (78-95), but at his best, he was one of the most subtle screen actors of his generation whose greatest skill lay in his capacity to play common men made briefly uncommon by the events surrounding them. The best example of this came in the BBC TV series based on Anthony Trollope's *Barchester Chronicles* (82), in which Pleasence brilliantly incarnated the saintly Septimus Harding.

OTHER KEY FILMS: *The Beachcomber* (54); *1984* (56); *Sons And Lovers* (60); *The Hands Of Orlac* (61); *Dr Crippen* (63); *Maniac* (64); *Eye Of The Devil* (67); *The Eagle Has Landed* (76); **Dracula** (79); *Escape From New York* (81); *Shadows And Fog* (92)

Plummer, Christopher

Plummer is the **Peter Finch** of his generation, a fine screen actor who has never quite enjoyed the superstar success that his skills and his talents should have warranted. Was it because of his looks, which were pleasant, though unconventional? Or was it because, like **Orson Welles** and **Charlton Heston**, he was a King-actor, unable to play common men with any real degree of verisimilitude? Whatever the case, in his best performances Plummer shows a rare integrity and a total commitment to the cinema, and one remembers him fondly as the young schoolteacher in **Nicholas Ray's** *Wind Across The Everglades* (58), as the squeaky-voiced Emperor Atahualpa in Irving Lerner's *The Royal Hunt Of The Sun* (69), and as the aristocratic, worldly-wise, indeed rather gentle Duke of Wellington, in Sergei Bondarchuk's *Waterloo* (70).

OTHER KEY FILMS: *The Sound Of Music* (65); *The Night Of The Generals* (67); *The Man Who Would Be King* (75); *The Disappearance* (77); *Murder By Decree* (78); *The Silent Partner* (78); *Somewhere In Time* (80); *Eyewitness* (81); *Wolf* (94); *12 Monkeys* (95); *Dolores Claiborne* (95); *Black Heart* (98); *The Dinosaur Hunter* (00); *Full Disclosure* (01)

Pluto

Mickey Mouse's dog, and the hilarious but accident-prone hero of his own series of **Walt Disney** cartoons.

Poetic Realism

Originally a uniquely French genre, but later taken up and transmogrified into an American form of poetic realism by directors such as **Nicholas Ray** in *They Live By Night* (49) and **Charles Laughton** in *Night Of The Hunter* (55), poetic realism combined a consuming interest in everyday life and ordinary people with a heightened, often poeticised dialogue that could, on occasion, seem deliriously opposed to the dramatic events unfolding on the screen. Notable films in the genre include **Jean Renoir's** *Le Crime De M. Lange* (35), *Les Bas-Fonds* (36), *La Grande Illusion* (37) and *La Règle Du Jeu* (39), Julien Duvivier's *Pépé Le Moko* (37), and **Marcel Carné's** *Quai Des Brumes* (38), the last two of which benefited from scripts by **Henri Jeanson** and **Jacques Prévert** respectively (Prévert also wrote *Le Crime De M. Lange*), the two

greatest literary exponents of the poetic realism style. There was always a strong element of despair in the original stories (an aspect later taken up by a succession of **film noir** directors in the United States), but this despair was mitigated by an existential desire to live for the moment, to take happiness, however brief it might be, and wring as much juice from it as possible before fate, or the machinations of an antagonistic state machine, could snatch it away.

OTHER KEY FILMS: Pierre Chenal's *La Rue Sans Nom* (33) and *Le Dernier Tournant* (39); Julien Duvivier's *La Bandera* (35) and *Un Carnet De Bal* (37); Jean Grémillon's *Gueule D'Amour* (37) and *Remorques* (39); Marcel Carné's *Jenny* (36), *Hôtel Du Nord* (38), *Le Jour Se Lève* (39) and *Les Visiteurs Du Soir* (45); Albert Valentin's *L'Entraîneuse* (38); Christian-Jaque's *Boule De Suif* (45)

Point-of-view Shot

The POV, as written into a screenplay, is designed to show the scene from the visual point of view of a particular actor or actress by means of the camera being positioned either in the place the character would be standing, or over the shoulder of the character, looking in the direction of the action.

Poitier, Sidney

Poitier was the first mainstream actor to appeal, on equal terms, to both black and white audiences. This remarkable crossover, which first manifested itself in

Sidney Poitier as Virgil Tibbs, in Norman Jewison's racially explosive In The Heat Of The Night *(67)*

Joseph L Mankiewicz's *No Way Out* (50) and culminated in **Stanley Kramer's** *The Defiant Ones* (58), paved the way for the gradual liberalisation of a screen that has, to this day, still not reached the stage of being totally colour-blind. Such a thing *is* possible, however, despite the carping of cynics, for it already exists in Cuba and Brazil, and should it ever be achieved in the United States and Western Europe, Poitier's name deserves to go high on the roll of honour, for he afforded the beginnings of public dignity to an enforced underclass, at a time when the night seemed at its longest.
OTHER KEY FILMS: *Cry The Beloved Country* (52); *Red Ball Express* (52); *The Blackboard Jungle* (55); *Edge Of The City* (57); *Porgy And Bess* (60); *A Raisin In The Sun* (61); *Paris Blues* (61); *In The Heat Of The Night* (67); *Sneakers* (92); *The Jackal* (97)

Polanski, Roman

Polanski steadfastly maintains that his childhood in the Cracow ghetto, the gassing of his mother at Auschwitz, the murder of his pregnant wife by drug-crazed drop-outs, and his belated flight from America to avoid a further prison term for his alleged rape of a thirteen-year-old girl at **Jack Nicholson's** house, have nothing whatsoever to do with the underlying feeling of alienation and hostility that permeates most of his films. And he may be right. He is an intelligent, self-possessed man, who has survived, apparently intact, horrors that would have crippled lesser men, and it seems patronising in the extreme not to listen to him (as Mark Cousins refused to do in a recent interview Polanski granted to the BBC). A master of many genres, following the cult success of *Repulsion* (65) Polanski made *Rosemary's Baby* (68), one of the most genuinely frightening of all horror films, and *Chinatown* (74), a masterpiece of enlightened filmmaking and the greatest of all latter-day *film noirs.* His recent *Death And The Maiden* (94) marked a fine return to form, proving that, despite his amused variability, Polanski still remains a master of the medium he respects and loves so much.
OTHER KEY FILMS: *Knife In The Water* (62); *Cul-De-Sac* (66); *Dance Of The Vampires* (67); *Macbeth* (71); *The Tenant* (76); *Tess* (79); *Frantic* (88); *Bitter Moon* (92); *The Ninth Gate* (99); *The Pianist* (01)

Polaroid Filter

An anti-reflective, anti-glare camera filter, sometimes known as a pola screen.

Polecat

A support housing for set lighting.

Polglase, Van Nest

Polglase's name is so achingly familiar from its appearance on so many Golden Age of Hollywood credit and title rolls, that it comes as something of a surprise to discover that most people have no clear idea what he did. Well, Polglase was the foremost art director and production designer of his generation, and was responsible for the overall look of the sets on such ground-breaking movies as **Merian C Cooper** and Ernest Schoedsack's *King Kong* (33), **John Ford's** *The Lost Patrol* (34) and *The Informer* (35), **William Dieterle's** *The Hunchback Of Notre Dame* (39), **Orson Welles's** *Citizen Kane* (41), and **Charles Vidor's** *Gilda* (46). Quite a record and, despite the drinking problems which caused his untimely dismissal from **RKO**, quite a man.
OTHER KEY FILMS: George Cukor's *Little Women* (33); Thornton Freeland's *Flying Down To Rio* (33); **George Stevens's** *Gunga Din* (39); **Alfred Hitchcock's** *Suspicion* (42)

***Best* Political/Satirical Films**
Lindsay Anderson's *If...* (69); Clarence Brown's *Intruder In The Dust* (49); **Frank Capra's** *Mr Smith Goes To Washington* (39); **Constantin Costa-Gavras's** *Z* (69); **Sergei Eisenstein's** *Ivan The Terrible Parts 1 & 2* (43-5); **Federico Fellini's** *La Dolce Vita* (60); **John Ford's** *The Grapes Of Wrath* (40) and *Sergeant Rutledge* (60); **Jean-Luc Godard's** *Pierrot Le Fou* (65); **Stanley Kubrick's** *A Clockwork Orange* (71); Gregory La Cava's *Gabriel Over The White House* (33); **Fritz Lang's** *While The City Sleeps* (55); **Mike Leigh's** *Secrets And Lies* (96); **Ken Loach's** *Raining Stones* (93); **Sydney Pollack's** *They Shoot Horses, Don't They?* (69); **Gillo Pontecorvo's** *The Battle Of Algiers* (66); **Leni Riefenstahl's** *Triumph Of The Will* (36); **Tony Richardson's** *The Loneliness Of The Long-Distance Runner* (62); **Volker Schlöndorff's** *The Tin Drum* (79); Lee Tamahori's *Once Were Warriors* (94); **Jean Vigo's** *Zéro De Conduite* (33); **Luchino Visconti's** *The Leopard* (63); **Peter Weir's** *The Year Of Living Dangerously* (82); **William Wellman's** *Nothing Sacred* (37)

Pollack, Sydney

Pollack likes to work regularly with his actors, initially with **Burt Lancaster** (who acted as something of a mentor before his death in 1994), and **Robert Redford**, whom he directed in, amongst others, *This Property Is Condemned* (66),

Jeremiah Johnson (73), *The Way We Were* (75) and *Out Of Africa* (85). An ambitious director who can nevertheless miss the mark badly, as in *Havana* (90), Pollack may have resuscitated **Dustin Hoffman's** career with *Tootsie* (82), but his best film is still *The Yakuza* (75), in which a suitably embittered **Robert Mitchum** literally lights up the screen as private eye, Harry Kilmer. A rather good occasional actor, Pollack appeared (very effectively) in **Stanley Kubrick's** final film, *Eyes Wide Shut* (99).

OTHER KEY FILMS: *The Scalphunters* (68); *They Shoot Horses, Don't They?* (68); *Three Days Of The Condor* (73); *Bobby Deerfield* (77); *The Electric Horseman* (79); *Absence Of Malice* (81); *The Firm* (93); *Sabrina* (95); *Random Hearts* (99)

Pontecorvo, Gillo

Pontecorvo, a leading anti-Fascist partisan in Italy during the Second World War, deserves to be remembered for more than merely his extraordinary *The Battle Of Algiers* (66), a film which still retains its capacity to shock with the audacity of its criticism of the monolithic French state. Pontecorvo was always something more than a left-wing propagandist, and his understanding of the humanity and vulnerability of even his enemies, as shown in the much underrated *Queimada!* (69), gave added power to his attacks on imperialism and on the men and women in whose vested interest many of its horrors were undertaken.

OTHER KEY FILMS: *The Long Blue Road* (57); *Kapò* (60); *The Tunnel* (79); *Ogro* (79); *I Corti Italiani* (97) [segment only]

Popeye

Max Fleischer's 'Popeye The Sailorman' cartoons of the 1930s and 1940s constituted **Paramount's** answer to the **Mickey Mouse** phenomenon, and they appeal to children today as much as ever they did (more, in many ways, than Mickey Mouse) for they offer an easy, fantasy-feeding escape from assertive authority, something which Mickey, to give both him and **Walt Disney** credit, never tried to do. With the ingestion of a single can of spinach (an unpleasant tasting thing to most children, and therefore, in some strange sense, a rite of passage), Popeye becomes miraculously all-powerful after having been humiliated by the screen's greatest perennial bully, the mighty Bluto, usually in front of the fickle Olive Oyl. And what is the ultimate key to this magic formula of Fleischer's? The *pièce de résistance*? The simple fact that nobody gets hurt as a result of this extraordinary transformation of Popeye from

weed to hero – there are no come-backs. Virtually everyone who has anything to do with animation has been copying the idea ever since.

Porky Pig
See **Looney Tunes**

Porter, Cole

One of the greatest of all composer/lyricists, Porter saw many of his Broadway successes transposed (with differing degrees of success) to film. *Anything Goes*, for instance, received a double **Bing Crosby** outing, firstly with Lewis Milestone at the helm in 1936, then with Robert Lewis twenty years later. Sophisticated and often risqué, Porter's best lyrics, like the evergreen 'I Get A Kick Out Of You', continue to delight moviegoers, and **Charles Walters's** movie version of Porter's *High Society* (56) rightly remains one of the most popular musicals of all time.

OTHER KEY FILMS: *The Gay Divorcee* (34); *You'll Never Get Rich* (41); *Night And Day* (46); *Kiss Me Kate* (53); *Silk Stockings* (57); *Can-Can* (60)

Positive
The print made from a processed negative.

Post-synchronization

The matching of a pre-recorded film to a post-recorded soundtrack, usually as the result of poor sound quality in the original recording, or following up the necessity to dub dialogue from one language to another.

Poverty Row

During the studio era (the 1930s, 1940s and early 1950s) Poverty Row was a euphemism for any commercial movie made on a shoestring budget. The expression stemmed from the geographical location of the real Poverty Row, which consisted of a bunch of run-down movie production houses situated between Gower Street and Sunset Boulevard, in downtown Los Angeles, during the 1920s.

Powell, Dick

Powell started his career in the early 1930s as a light tenor crooner in **Busby Berkeley's** sexy series of Gold Diggers musicals, and continued it into the 1940s and 50s as the often beaten-up protagonist of a convincing sequence of *film noir* thrillers. He played **Philip Marlowe** in *Murder My Sweet* (44) [a.k.a. *Farewell My Lovely*], and convincingly took on the roles of driven men in **Edward Dmytryk's** *Cornered* (45), and in André de Toth's *The Pitfall* (48).

In 1953 he directed his own tough little 'nuclear threat' **B-movie** thriller, *Split Second*.

OTHER KEY FILMS: *42nd Street* (33); *Gold Diggers Of 33* (33); *Dames* (34); *A Midsummer Night's Dream* (35); *Johnny O'Clock* (47); *Station West* (48); *The Bad And The Beautiful* (52); [and as director] *The Enemy Below* (57); *The Hunters* (58)

KEY LINE:

'I'm flattered you want me and bitter you got me.' [**Vincente Minnelli's** *The Bad And The Beautiful*]

Powell, Michael

The Michael Powell and Emeric Pressburger directing/writing team, under their trade name of The Archers, can now be seen, with the convenient hindsight of time, to have been almost single-handedly responsible for the post-war revival of quality British cinema. Cult icons to a younger generation of filmmakers in America (including **Steven Spielberg** and **Martin Scorsese**), this strange and talented duo were responsible for *The Life And Death Of Colonel Blimp* (43), the exquisitely quirky *I Know Where I'm Going* (45), and the brilliantly designed *Black Narcissus* (47). Their masterpiece was *A Matter Of Life And Death* (46), in which heaven, and the endless staircase leading to it, was paradoxically filmed in black-and-white, while the earth, with all its emotional frailty, appeared in colour. Following the dissolution of their partnership in 1956, Powell went on to direct the remarkable *Peeping Tom* (60), a film which so outraged the censors with its graphic yet sympathetic portrayal of a voyeuristically obsessed serial killer that it effectively ended this extraordinary man's career.

OTHER KEY FILMS: *49th Parallel* (41); *A Canterbury Tale* (44); *The Red Shoes* (48); *The Small Back Room* (49); *Gone To Earth* (50); *Tales Of Hoffman* (52); *The Battle Of The River Plate* (56); *Ill Met By Moonlight* (57); *Age Of Consent* (69)

Powell, William

Powell was **Dashiell Hammett's** suave Nick Charles (wrongly known as the Thin Man – that was someone else in the movie), with sexy Myrna Loy as his Nora, in the long-running series of comedy thrillers which began with W S Van Dyke II's *The Thin Man* (34), and ended, twelve pairings later (not all of them in the Thin Man series), with Edward Buzzell's *Song Of The Thin Man* (47). In-between times, Powell played in some excellent comedies, including Gregory La Cava's delightful *My Man Godfrey* (36) and **Jack Conway's** equally splendid *Libeled Lady* (36), and some first-rate little thrillers, too, including Conway's remake of Kurt

Bernhardt's 1938 pre-war French thriller *Carrefour* [renamed *Crossroads*] (42), and Chester Erskine's *Take One False Step* (49). Powell lived to the ripe old age of ninety-two despite (or perhaps because of) his famous dallyings (and occasional marriages) with such luminous ladies as **Carole Lombard** and **Jean Harlow**.

OTHER KEY FILMS: *Outcast* (22); *Romola* (24); *Beau Geste* (26); *The Great Gatsby* (26); *The Canary Murder Case* (29); *The Key* (34); *Double Wedding* (37); *I Love You Again* (40); *Love Crazy* (41); *Ziegfeld Follies* (46); *The Senator Was Indiscreet* (48); *How To Marry A Millionaire* (53); *Mr Roberts* (55)

Power, Tyrone

One of the pretty boys of the Hollywood star factory, Power showed in later, riskier films that he could really act. He played wildly against type in **Edmund Goulding's** *Nightmare Alley* (47), in which he ended up as a carnival 'geek' biting the heads off chickens, and also in **Henry King's** *The Sun Also Rises* (57), in which he took the part of Ernest Hemingway's impotent alter ego, Jake Barnes, in love with **Ava Gardner** but utterly incapable of consummating his passion (how one feels for him). He was good, too, in Rouben Mamoulian's superb *The Mark Of Zorro* (40), and also as the protagonist in King's gorgeously coloured *Jesse James* (39).

OTHER KEY FILMS: *Lloyd's Of London* (36); *In Old Chicago* (38); *The Black Swan* (42); *Captain From Castile* (47); *King Of The Khyber Rifles* (53); *Witness For The Prosecution* (57)

Praxinoscope

From the same stable as the **Zoetrope** and the **Phenakisticope** (such catchy names!), Emile Reynaud's Praxinoscope allowed the smooth viewing of consecutive images on a revolving disk, and was, of all three machines, the most realistic in giving the impression of serial motion.

Pre-credit Sequence

This is when we go straight into the action before the titles or credits have yet appeared – a good recent example would be the brilliant opening sequence of Martin Campbell's *Goldeneye* (95), in which **Pierce Brosnan's James Bond** bungee-jumps down a spectacularly deep dam complex, is betrayed by his friend Alec Trevelyan (played by Sean Bean), nevertheless succeeds in blowing up the joint, upon which…yes, the **credits** roll, and we see all those sinuous girls, phallic pistols and glaring colours that have become so comfortingly predictable over the years.

Preminger, Otto

Preminger fell between two stools – the intellectual and the expedient. The expedient finally won out, but the intellectual had quite a good run of it, with movies as idiosyncratic as his two brilliant *film noirs, Laura* (44) and *Where The Sidewalk Ends* (50). Also included in this list would be the seriously melodramatic *Angel Face* (53), a restrained **Marilyn Monroe** performance in *River Of No Return* (54), and the outstanding did-he-do-it-or-didn't-he *Anatomy Of A Murder* (59), which predated the permissive 60s in its candid discussion of sex. The film for which he is best known is *Exodus* (66), which, although excellent of its kind, pales into worthy insignificance when compared to his stylish earlier films.

OTHER KEY FILMS: *Forever Amber* (47); *Daisy Kenyon* (47); *Whirlpool* (49); *The Court-Martial Of Billy Mitchell* (55); *Bonjour Tristesse* (58); *Advise And Consent* (62); *The Human Factor* (80)

Premix

The mixing of two or more elements of the soundtrack together onto one track as a prelude to the final mixing of the soundtrack onto the finished film.

Pre-production

Any work or activity to do with a specific film that occurs before the shooting itself, pre-production includes scouting, set preparation, the completion of the shooting script, casting, etc.

Prequel

A prequel is a film that purports to show passages from the earlier lives of characters taken from an existing feature film. An obvious example might be Richard Lester's *Butch And Sundance: The Early Days* (79) which appeared a full ten years after its so-called sequel, George Roy Hill's *Butch Cassidy And The Sundance Kid* (69), when the original stars, **Paul Newman** and **Robert Redford**, were fifty-four and forty-two respectively – needless to say, younger actors had to be found to fill their parts. Parts four to six of **George Lucas's** *Star Wars* series also fall (or will fall) into the prequel category.

Prerecording

The recording of a film's soundtrack before the actual filming begins, prerecording occurs more frequently, for obvious reasons, in the making of animated cartoons, and remains a rare occurrence in feature films.

Prescoring

Something of a rarity, prescoring occurs when the composer has been asked to compose music for a scene that has not yet been filmed – possibly to act as a guide to the director in the achievement of a certain effect. Prescoring occurs far more frequently, for obvious reasons, during the construction and filming of a musical.

Presley, Elvis

One hardly thinks of Presley first and foremost as a film star, but he made a number of movies before his death at the age of forty-two, and one or two were actually quite good, notably **Don Siegel's** *Flaming Star* (60) and Phil Karlson's *Kid Galahad* (62). Die-hard fans will, of course, watch anything at all with Presley in it, and good luck to them. He is, after all, one of the greats.

OTHER KEY FILMS: *Love Me Tender* (56); *King Creole* (58); *Jailhouse Rock* (57); *Fun In Acapulco* (63); *Roustabout* (64); *Frankie And Johnny* (65)

Pressburger, Emeric

See **Powell, Michael**

Pressure Plate

The supporting plate that holds the film steady in the camera during exposure, a pressure plate can also refer to the glass or Perspex sheet used to hold an animator's **cell** drawing stable during principal photography.

Prévert, Jacques

Prévert was a poet who just happened to write for films. He mixed street intellectualism, popular ballad-making and a high-minded intensity of emotion in a way that it would be almost impossible to replicate today. His moment, curiously enough, came during the 1950s (and not during the 1930s, when he was writing most frequently), when his brand of elegant, existential despair struck a retrospective chord with a youth culture still overwhelmed by the war memories of its parents and struggling to find a philosophy that encompassed both fatalism and hope. The team of Prévert and **Marcel Carné** had turned out such films during the 1930s, in the form of *Quai Des Brumes* (38) and *Le Jour Se Lève* (39), and when the young painter in *Quai Des Brumes* tells **Jean Gabin** that he can no longer paint because when he looks at a tree he sees not only the tree, but a man hanging from it, and when he looks at the sea it is not the wind or the surf that he hears, but the cry of drowning men, young 1950s France responded to his nihilism, dressing themselves in black, reading Jean-Paul Sartre and Albert Camus, and turning to literature and music, rather than to the cult of consumerism, for their sustenance. One wishes that the same could be said of today's youth.

OTHER KEY FILMS: **Jean Renoir's** *Le Crime De M. Lange* (36); Marcel Carné's *Jenny* (36), *Drôle De Drame* (37), *Les Visiteurs Du Soir* (42), *Les Enfants Du Paradis* (45) and *Les Portes De La Nuit* (46)

Preview

The showing of a finished movie to a hand-picked audience before its release, either for purposes of advance criticism, or as a means of gauging public response to a film, thus allowing time for prinking, tweaking, or even the changing of an ending to suit, not the work in progress of course, but the perceived commercial demand.

Price, Vincent

Price was the horror supremo *par excellence* (though he began life as a straight actor), and he was possessed of a wry and endearing capacity to take himself off. With his laconic voice and indissoluble confidence, Price carried literally dozens of low-budget horror movies in the 1960s and 1970s, and one or two real stinkers as well. Something of an epicure in real life, Price gave some notable, not over-the-top performances in films such as **Otto Preminger's** *Laura* (44) and **Fritz Lang's** *While The City Sleeps* (56) before he succumbed, with an elegant disdain, no doubt, to the horror industry. His personal favourite of all his films was **Samuel Fuller's** *The Baron Of Arizona* (50) – an odd choice at first glance, but typical of Price's delightfully idiosyncratic nature.

OTHER KEY FILMS: *The Bribe* (49); *House Of Wax* (53); *The Fly* (58); *The Fall Of The House Of Usher* (60); *The Pit And The Pendulum* (61); *Masque Of The Red Death* (64); *Edward Scissorhands* (90)

Primary Colours

The basic colours in the cinematographic palette that produce all other possible colours when mixed – red-orange, blue-violet and green.

Principal Photography

Motion-picture photography dealing with the actions of the stars, as opposed to second-unit and special-effects photography, which deals in location work and tricks, respectively.

Print

The final positive copy of a film, struck from a dupe, or original negative.

Printer

A printer will replicate one piece of film onto another piece of film, either through direct contact, in the case of a contact printer, or through the medium of a lens system, in the case of an optical printer.

Printer Light

The light on a printer that can be tweaked to compensate for any differences in density caused by faulty exposure settings during filming.

Printing

The process by which a negative film is turned into a positive one, or vice versa.

Print It

The customary form a director's expression of satisfaction with a take takes.

Process Body

A mock-up of a car, train, airplane, ship's cabin, spacecraft, etc., with retractable sides, adjustable panelling or gaping holes to allow for filming and the necessary movement and positioning of the cameras. See **Process Shot**

Processing

The procedure by which negative film is processed, step by step, into positive film, processing incorporates initial exposure, chemical development and subsequent fixing and drying. The entire process is obviated in the case of **digital photography**, where everything is done by computer.

Process Shot

Any shot filmed separately from the main action, then projected against a backdrop to provide a realistic and fully focused background setting to a scene being filmed inside a **process body** (a mock-up of a car, train carriage, ship's cabin, etc.).

Producer

The person responsible for the allocation of the budget and the management of an intended feature film during the creative process; also the marketing of the finished film.

KEY LINE:

'No writer has any say about a movie! You can argue, but you can't say. *They* have the say. That's why they don't like writers. Because they wish *they* could write.' [Screenwriter Arthur Laurents, who co-scripted **Sydney Pollack's** *The Way We Were* (73), on dealing with producers]

253

Production Code
See **Hays Office**

Production Crew
See **Crew**

Production Designer
See **Art Director**

Production Manager
See **Unit Manager**

Production Track
The actual sound recorded during filming, usually consisting of the dialogue and any essential peripheral sounds whose source is visible on the screen.

Programmer
Trade slang for a **B-movie** or film which, of no interest in itself, is being used to fill up or complete the advertised programme.

Projection Booth
The room at the back of the film theatre which houses both the projectors and the projectionist, and the source of the mysterious and magical white light along which our youthful fantasies flowed.

Projectionist
The person in charge of the projection booth who is responsible for the error-free projection of the advertised film programme.

Projection Printer
See **Optical Printer**

Projection Synch
The necessary compensatory spacing between the image and its accompanying soundtrack to allow for the tiny disparity in distance between the sound head and the picture gate in a traditional sound projector.

Projector
A projector casts the image from a strip of film onto a distant screen by means of a bright light and a focused lens, and is the machine a projectionist uses to show a completed feature film to an audience. A sound projector picks up sound in addition to image, passing the sound by a series of electrical impulses to an amplifier, which converts them into sound waves that are then picked up by a series of loudspeakers and transmitted to the audience simultaneously with the images being shown on the screen.

Propaganda Films
Films designed, either overtly or covertly, to influence or to manipulate an audience into 'correcting' their taste, so that it corresponds to that of the makers or progenitors of the propaganda vehicle being shown. The most famous of all propaganda films is undoubtedly **Leni Riefenstahl's** *Triumph Of The Will* (34), which showed a godlike, mythologically bound Führer apparently walking on the water of his followers during one of the now infamous Nuremberg rallies. **Sergei Eisenstein's** *Battleship Potemkin* (25) is another case in point, with its famous Odessa steps sequence, and **Gillo Pontecorvo's** *Battle of Algiers* (66) went a long way towards changing French perceptions of the crisis in Algeria.

Property
An idea, outline, storyline, plot, novel, screenplay, script, poem, theme or pitch that someone, somewhere, might want to use as the basis for a movie.

Prop Man
The person in charge of the procurement, correct placement, and the interim maintenance of all the necessary **props** required during the shooting of a feature film.

Props
Any object, ranging from a farthing to the full-size mock-up of the *Titanic*, which is needed to add verisimilitude to the filming of a feature film. **Alfred Hitchcock** was perhaps the most fetishistic of all directors with regard to props (remember the luminous glass of milk in *Suspicion* (41)?), but objects also play a large part in the films of **André Tarkovsky** and of **Krzysztof Kieslowski** – one remembers, in particular, the transparent ball at the beginning of *The Double Life Of Véronique* (91).

Best Psychological Dramas
Bernardo Bertolucci's *Last Tango In Paris* (72); **Peter Bogdanovich's** *The Last Picture Show* (71); Youssef Chahine's *Bab El-Hadid* [*Central Station*] (58); **Milos Forman's** *One Flew Over The Cuckoo's Nest* (75); **Alfred Hitchcock's** *Spellbound* (45) and *Vertigo* (58); **John Huston's** *The Treasure Of The Sierra Madre* (47) and *Fat City* (72); **Neil Jordan's** *The Crying Game* (92); **Emir Kusturica's** *Time Of The Gypsies* (89); **Fritz Lang's** *The Woman In The Window* (44); Rouben Mamoulian's *Dr Jekyll And*

Mr Hyde (31); **Joseph L Mankiewicz's** *Suddenly Last Summer* (59); **Alexander Mackendrick's** *Sweet Smell Of Success* (57); **Bob Rafelson's** *Five Easy Pieces* (70); **Roberto Rossellini's** *Voyage To Italy* (53); Charles Vidor's *Gilda* (46); **Raoul Walsh's** *Pursued* (46); **Billy Wilder's** *Sunset Boulevard* (50) and *Ace In The Hole* [a.k.a. *The Big Carnival*] (51)

Publicist

The person in charge of publicising a movie both in advance of and during its release by means of hype, press releases, publicity junkets, and a creative manipulation of the truth.

Publicity Still

The key image (and usually the one appearing on film theatre posters) that punters must take away with them, or be attracted to, when a new movie is released – or simply an image taken from that movie, either in the form of an **action still** or a studio shot of the star, and used for subsequent publicity purposes.

Pull Back

The requirement a director makes for the camera to pull back from the action and open out the scene so that the main protagonists are put into context.

Pulp Fiction

Hard-boiled pulp fiction (the pulp referred to what happened to the paper after the disposable piece was read) first appeared in the United States during the 1920s, in such magazines as *Black Mask*, *Spicy Stories*, *Ace-High*, *Amazing*, *Astounding*, *Detective Magazine*, etc., and directly inspired the 1930s genre of **Warner** gangster movies, which began with **Mervyn LeRoy's** *Little Caesar* (31) and **William Wellman's** *Public Enemy* (31), and which culminated in the doom-laden and visually poetic 1940s and 1950s *film noir* cycle. Its principal literary progenitors and adherents were **Dashiell Hammett**, **Raymond Chandler**, John D MacDonald, Paul Cain, Jim Thompson, Donald E Westlake, Dorothy B Hughes, Mickey Spillane, Henry Kane, William S Prather, Charles Williams, Ross MacDonald and **James M Cain**, and their tight, no-nonsense style of writing, which concentrated on the ordinary man and woman caught up in the toils of fate, proved enormously influential in both verbal and visual terms to the history of American cinema, and, through that medium, to the history of European cinema also.

*Pulp fiction and film noir heroine extraordinaire **Barbara Stanwyck** as the murderous Phyllis Dietrichson in Billy Wilder's* Double Indemnity *(44). Based on a story by James M Cain and scripted by Raymond Chandler*

KEY LINE:

'When I went to college and took writing courses, they would always talk about the distinctions between the pulp writer and the slick writer and the art writer. I came to realise that was ridiculous. There are only interesting stories and dull stories, no matter where they're printed.' [Richard Matheson, prolific cult author of novels such as *I Am Legend* (1956), and scripts of the quality of Jack Arnold's *The Incredible Shrinking Man* (57) (from his own novel) and Jeannot Szwarc's *Somewhere In Time* (80), based on his novel *Bid Time Return*]

Pup

A 500-watt studio spotlight.

Purposeful Incognito

Such a thing is only possible on the European mainland, in countries where the cult of celebrity has not been overtaken by the cult of impolitic and inexpedient behaviour, and consists of stars like **Johnny Depp** giving themselves and their girlfriend of the moment an airing in a public place on the tacit understanding that anyone who sees them will have the good manners to refrain from any manifestation of the sort of inappropriate behaviour stars sometimes encounter in brasher, less sophisticated environments.

Q-Score

The Q-Score refers to a market-research-initiated popularity rating for stars, fictional characters, comic-strip cartoon heroes and TV personalities, which studios can use when considering buying the rights to films. Functioning something along the lines of a handicapping system, *Batman*, **Julia Roberts** and **Tom Cruise** might have the highest Q-scores, for example, while The Phantom, The Shadow and second-rank actors and actresses (who shall remain unnamed) would rate considerably lower on the scale.

Quaid, Dennis

Quaid always seems to have been born just a little out of his own time, as if he should have been an actor during the 1940s or 1950s rather than now. He has chosen his parts well, by and large, and has shone rather than gleamed in them, possibly on account of his marginally offbeat looks, which give him an edge over some of the purely pretty-boy actors of his generation. He was excellent in his first film, **Peter Yates's** *Breaking Away* (79), and followed that up with a brilliant performance as Gordon Cooper in Philip Kaufman's *The Right Stuff* (83). His best part to date, though, has been that of Remy McSwain, in Jim McBride's *The Big Easy* (86), where he suggested what a versatile actor he could be if someone only knew how to use him. Steve Kloves's *Flesh And Bone* (93) has come nearest to fulfilling that potential, but to date Quaid must be counted as one that got away.

OTHER KEY FILMS: *The Long Riders* (80); *All Night Long* (81); *Suspect* (87); *DOA* (88); *Come See The Paradise* (90); *Postcards From The Edge* (90); *Wyatt Earp* (94); *Dragonheart* (96); *SwitchBack* (97); *The Parent Trap* (98); *Any Given Sunday* (99); *Frequency* (00); *Traffic* (00); *Stranger Than The Wheel* (01)

Quayle, Anthony

Quayle played decent, modest men, and embodied a particular sort of Old Rugbeian Englishness which is now majestically out of fashion. Even when he played a baddie, as with his Captain Van Der Poel in J Lee Thompson's *Ice Cold In Alex* (58), he was a decent baddie (apart from those awful shorts, that is), and he seemed content to reserve his real talents for the stage, where he excelled. He was admirable, however, as Frank O'Connor in **Alfred Hitchcock's** *The Wrong Man* (57), and his Colonel Brighton in **David Lean's** *Lawrence Of Arabia* showed his screen persona at its humane, sensitive, but nevertheless rather ineffectual best.

OTHER KEY FILMS: *Hamlet* (48); *Battle Of The River Plate* (56); *The Guns Of Navarone* (61); *Operation Crossbow* (65); *Anne Of The Thousand Days* (69); *The Tamarind Seed* (74); *The Eagle Has Landed* (76); *Murder By Decree* (79)

Quick Cutting

Sequential scenes shot and edited in such a manner that they follow each other in a rapid-fire fashion on the screen.

Quickie

What oversexed people do in the backs of cars or in bus shelters – in movie terms, a 'quickie' refers to the release of a swiftly shot low-budget film to cash in on a particular market that may or may not be there in the future. Not a lot of difference from sex, then. See **Quota Quickie**

Quigley Poll

Each year exhibitors in the US are polled as to which star they think is the most popular of them all in terms of his or her box-office potential (shades of Snow White?). The results are surprisingly predictable, and generally reflect the tastes of a cross-section of the US population aged between fifteen and twenty-five – the movie-going public, in other words. Most consistent chart-toppers have been **John Wayne** and **Clint Eastwood**, with **Robert Redford** and **Tom Cruise** playing effective second stringers. **Barbra Streisand** hovered around the list

Anthony Quinn as the vainglorious Alexis Zorba, busy blowing all Alan Bates's money, in Michael Cacoyannis's Zorba The Greek (64)

for ten years, though she never became number one – that was left for **Shirley Temple** (1935 to 1938) and for **Doris Day** (four times). The last female star to be number one was **Julie Andrews** in 1967.

Quinn, Anthony

Quinn had a long wait for stardom, being called upon to play a bewildering variety of parts in his sixteen years as a character actor in the Sargasso Sea of Hollywood minor stardom. Then came an **Oscar** as **Marlon Brando's** brother in **Elia Kazan's** *Viva Zapata* (52). More disasters followed, however, among them Pietro Francisci's *Attila The Hun* (55), a strong each-way bet in the Turkey-of-all-time Olympics. Meanwhile **Federico Fellini** had directed Quinn in *La Strada* (54), and his luck began to change again. A second Oscar for his role as Gauguin, in **Vincente Minnelli's** *Lust For Life* (56), and parts in **David Lean's** *Lawrence Of Arabia* (62) and Michael Cacoyannis's *Zorba The Greek* (64) followed, and he soon became the mighty, macho Quinn we all came to know and love, still showering the world with his progeny at an advanced age, until his death, of respiratory failure, in June 2001.

OTHER KEY FILMS: *Against All Flags* (52); *The Hunchback Of Notre Dame* (57); *The Guns Of Navarone* (61); *Barabbas* (62); *A High Wind In Jamaica* (65); *Marseilles Contract* (74); *Lion Of The Desert* (81); *Last Action Hero* (93); *A Walk In The Clouds* (95); *Oriundi* (99)

Quonking

A pejorative term for any unwanted sounds picked up by the microphone during filming and which may need to be removed during the editing process. Less of a problem now with the plethora of sophisticated directional equipment available, in the early days of sound, when even the camera motors had to be masked, quonking could be a major problem.

Quota Quickies

These refer to the British **B-movies** of the 1920s and 1930s which were turned out regardless of quality in order to comply with the 1927 Cinematograph Act, which insisted that roughly a third of all films shown on British screens had to be home grown. The Act backfired, in that, rather than encouraging expertise, it promoted the second-rate.

257

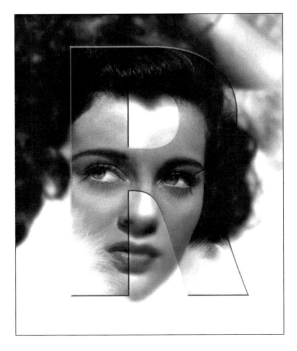

R

A Motion Picture of America Association rating, indicating that a film is deemed unsuitable for anyone under the age of seventeen unless accompanied by a parent or responsible person.

Race Movies

A series of films in all genres made specifically for black audiences during the 1920s, 30s and 40s, race movies were shown in segregated 'colored-only' cinemas. Using all-Black casts, although frequently directed and produced by Whites, such movies often markedly ran counter to the prevailing 'plantation ethos' which dogged the portrayal of Blacks in mainstream Hollywood films of the time.

Rack

Can apply to the roller system in film processing apparatus, the action of threading film, the correct alignment of the threaded film, or to the trim bin in an editing room designed for holding out-takes.

Rackover

What the cameraman does when he swings away the entire camera mechanism in order to free the lens so that he can use his viewfinder to garner a view of the scene about to be filmed without having to allow for the inevitable parallax effect produced by a side-by-side lens and viewfinder.

RADA

Acronym for the Royal Academy of Dramatic Art, Britain's foremost training ground for budding thespians. Founded in 1904, RADA has provided much in the way of crossover talent from theatre to film, but rarely, for obvious reasons, back again.

Rafelson, Bob

One of the miracles of 1970s post-*Easy Rider* US cinema, Rafelson seemed to have the future in his hands for a brief moment, but in fact it turned out to be the past – a knowledge of it and of its effects and importance on the present. *Five Easy Pieces* (70) and *The King Of Marvin Gardens* (72) can now be seen, with the vast privilege of hindsight, to be key films in the melding of two eras – the pre-1960s and the post-1960s – for it tells of the marginal people who stumbled between the slats, not really of one era or another, but out of time, just as their music, and their dreams, are out of time. Rafelson has never surpassed those two movies, not even with his recent *Blood And Wine* (97), which showed a marked return to form after nearly twenty-five years in the wilderness of commercial vacuity. Just briefly, in *Blood And Wine*, in the character played by **Judy Davis**, Rafelson achieves again that otherness which had marked him out, so early in his film career, as a potentially great auteur/filmmaker.

OTHER KEY FILMS: *Head* (68); *Stay Hungry* (76); *The Postman Always Rings Twice* (81); *Black Widow* (87); *Mountains Of The Moon* (90); *Man Trouble* (92)

Raft, George

One of the great bad guys of the cinema, Raft was actually a pretty terrible actor who managed, through a process of luck, good publicity and a deadpan face, to carve himself a particular niche (that of a gangster) and stick to it. No gangster, though, ever remotely looked or acted like Raft, and his alleged Mafia connections remain strictly that – alleged. He was OK, in a Raftian way, in **Howard Hawks's** *Scarface* (32), but when he was paired with a not-yet-iconic **Humphrey Bogart** in **Raoul Walsh's** *They Drive By Night* (40), it rapidly became apparent that Raft did not have the capacity to cast off his former mantle and don a new one. Raft is the sort of actor who is better in the memory than in the flesh.

OTHER KEY FILMS: *Night Court* (32); *Night After Night* (32); *Every Night At Eight* (35); *The Glass Key* (35); *You And Me* (38); *Background To Danger* (43); *Cairo* (53); *Black Widow* (54); *Some Like It Hot* (59)

Rail-Cam

A US idea, rail-cam tracks are laid alongside or around the intended route of a subject about to be filmed (even underwater in the case of Olympic swimming) and the remote-control camera then tracks the image at whatever pace is deemed necessary. One of the first uses of the rail-cam was by ABC at the 1988 Winter Olympics in Calgary, in order to film the speed-skaters going around the Olympic Oval. It was set up at a cost of more than $250,000, but ABC ended up by using only a mere five seconds of the ensuing successfully caught footage.

Rails

These are the ceiling-level rails in a studio set onto which movie lamps and spotlights are attached for both specific and generalised illumination.

Raimi, Sam

Cult horror director best known for his *The Evil Dead* (83-7) series and the rather more sophisticated *Darkman* (90), which starred an unlikely **Liam Neeson**, Raimi is a film buff with a finger in a lot of pies as occasional actor, screenwriter, producer and director. *The Evil Dead*, made on a spectacularly low budget, and spawner of an awful lot of junky imitations, was a witty, literate slant on the usual **Hammer**-horror clichés, and still manages to entertain, amuse and scare through its imaginative use of film trickery and the exuberance and ironical humour with which its excesses are perpetrated.

OTHER KEY FILMS: *Crimewave* (85); *Evil Dead 2* (87); *Army Of Darkness* (93); *The Quick And The Dead* (95); *A Simple Plan* (98); *For Love Of The Game* (99); *The Gift* (00)

Raimu

The great French actor who will be forever linked with, and loved for, his role as César in **Marcel Pagnol's** sublime film trilogy comprising **Alexander Korda's** *Marius* (31), **Marc Allégret's** *Fanny* (32) and Pagnol's own *César* (36), Raimu went on to delight his legion of fans in Pagnol's self-directed follow-up to the trilogy, *The Baker's Wife* (38), as Aimable, the melancholic baker who loses the will to make bread when his wife, Aurelie, leaves him for the local shepherd. In perfect Gallic fashion the deprived villagers rally together to restore both the status quo and their access to Aimable's wonderful bread. These four films between them are the best example of what French cinema can bring us that American cinema never can, namely a profoundly sophisticated insight into simplicity.

OTHER KEY FILMS: *Le Blanc Et Le Noir* (31); *Tartarin De Tarascon* (34); *Gribouille* (37); *Un Carnet De Bal* (37); *Noix De Coco* (39); *La Fille Du Puisatier* (40); *L'Arlésienne* (42); *Le Colonel Chabert* (43)

Rain Cluster

A conglomeration of sprinklers used to produce **rain effects**.

Rain Effects

Artificial rain produced through pipes, sprinklers and **rain clusters** to simulate storms, showers, downpours, monsoons and drizzle – cinema's most famous rain effect was created on the **MGM** studio lot for the scene in **Stanley Donen** and **Gene Kelly's** *Singin' In The Rain* (52) in which Kelly does just that.

Rains, Claude

A wonderful character actor and leading man whose smooth bedside manner belied the steel that he could, on occasion, summon from his heart, most notably in **Alfred Hitchcock's** *Notorious* (46), in which his Nazi sympathiser, Alexander Sebastian, married, bedded, and then tried to kill **Ingrid Bergman**, despite **Cary Grant's** rather belated objections. Rains left poor Bergman more-or-less alone in *Casablanca* (42), although not for want of carnal intent, concentrating his attentions, in a heady – but unacknowledged, one must assume – homoerotic manner, on **Humphrey Bogart's** Rick instead. He carried irony and

259

sardonic levity to extremes that only **George Sanders**, another expatriate Brit in the Hollywood maelstrom, could equal, and remained happily and fruitfully in work almost to his death, in 1967. One only wishes that Rains were still alive and available, in his prime, to play Stephen Maturin, when Patrick O'Brian's unsurpassable sea novels eventually come to be filmed.

OTHER KEY FILMS: *The Invisible Man* (33); *Anthony Adverse* (36); *The Prince And The Pauper* (37); *The Adventures Of Robin Hood* (38); *Four Daughters* (38); *The Sea Hawk* (40); *Now Voyager* (42); *Mr Skeffington* (44); *Caesar And Cleopatra* (45); *Deception* (46); *The Unsuspected* (47); *The Passionate Friends* (49); *Where Danger Lives* (50); *Lawrence Of Arabia* (62)

Rank, J Arthur

The devoutly Methodist J Arthur Rank became one of the biggest names in the British film industry during the 1940s and 1950s, expanding into most of the post-colonial markets and owning more than a thousand cinemas in the UK mainland alone, including the Gaumont and the **Odeon** chains. In his heyday, Joseph Arthur had control of both **Denham** and **Pinewood** studios, together with a considerable number of peripheral interests such as hotels, amusement arcades and Xerox copying facilities. His trademark was, and still is, known throughout the world, and consists of a bare-chested 'Bombardier' Billy Wells striking an enormous papier-mâché gong – James Blades, the much-loved percussionist who actually made the sound of the gong, delighted a generation of young children by carting around the ersatz gong and its smaller progenitor and giving lively school demonstrations during the 1950s and 1960s.

Rathbone, Basil

Rathbone was one of the screen's most effective villains – one has only to think of his appallingly cold Mr Murdstone in **George Cukor's** *David Copperfield* (35) or his heartless Sir Guy of Gisbourne in **Michael Curtiz's** *The Adventures Of Robin Hood* (38) – while at the very same time playing, in a lengthy series of films (39-46), the screen's most enduring hero, **Sherlock Holmes**. Rathbone brought two very different aspects of his personality to bear on both archetypes, focusing on acute intelligence in the case of Holmes, most notably in Sidney Lanfield's *The Hound Of The Baskervilles* (39), and sophisticated ambition in the case of such supreme villains as his Richard III in Rowland Lee's *Tower Of London* (39). With his

mellifluous voice, elegant figure and fencer's way with the sword, Rathbone was one of the great stalwarts of the Golden Age of Hollywood.

OTHER KEY FILMS: *The Great Deception* (26); *The Last Days Of Pompeii* (35); *A Tale Of Two Cities* (35); *Captain Blood* (35); *The Adventures Of Marco Polo* (38); *Dawn Patrol* (38); *The Mark Of Zorro* (40); *The Black Cat* (41); *Frenchman's Creek* (44); *The Last Hurrah* (58)

Rating System

A system by which motion pictures are rated, in terms of violence, sexual content, etc., so that children and young persons will not be subjected to scenes which they may not understand or are likely to be disturbed by. In general, rating systems tend to distinguish between pre-teenagers, young teenagers and young adults, with a generalised cut-off age occurring at around seventeen or eighteen, except in the case of certain Scandinavian countries where the cut-off age is lower. An element of discretion has recently entered into the censorship fray, in the form of the PG, or parental guidance-rating.

Ratio

See **Aspect Ratio** and **Shooting Ratio**

Raw Stock

Unexposed film footage waiting for use.

Ray, Nicholas

It was the French who first called Ray one of the greatest of all Hollywood directors, and his debut film, *They Live By Night* (48), must vie with **Charles Laughton's** *The Night Of The Hunter* (55) as one of the best-ever first features by a debut director. It was the French, too, with their long visual tradition, who best understood the concept of Ray's 'poetry of the screen', which used lighting, sound and close-ups to heighten the dramatic effect of dialogue. In *On Dangerous Ground* (51), a 'cop and blind girl' story that might have seemed simply mawkish in other hands is turned into a profound character study of an alienated man, with Ray using the exterior landscapes of town and country to mirror his character's mental state. In a number of brilliantly constructed extended scenes, **Robert Ryan's** disenchanted cop always seems on the verge of some fundamental revelation about the intricacies of his own heart. Ray's *In A Lonely Place* (50) is arguably **Humphrey Bogart's** best and most complex film, while his *Johnny Guitar* (54) raised **Joan Crawford** from the mundane to the peculiar.

Other notable films include the teen classic *Rebel Without A Cause* (55), and the underrated **Robert Mitchum** vehicle *The Lusty Men* (52). **Wim Wenders** recorded Ray's final illness in his documentary *Lightning Over Water* (80).

OTHER KEY FILMS: *Born to be Bad* (50); *On Dangerous Ground* (51); *Run For Cover* (55); *Bitter Victory* (57); *Party Girl* (58); *Wind Across The Everglades* (58); Wim Wenders's *The American Friend* (77) [as actor]

KEY LINES:

'Oh, Nick could give you cancer. Actually, I think he died of cancer. He had the most miserable life of anybody I have ever known. Nobody liked him. Nobody was close to him... It was very difficult to get anything out of him, except when he recognised it was right.' [Screenwriter **Philip Yordan**, who may or may not have scripted *Johnny Guitar* (54), on director Ray]

'I don't think he was either a compulsive liar or a Hollywood rat. I think he was a man who was *hungry* for recognition, who really didn't trust that his talent was authentic.' [Screenwriter Stewart Stern, who scripted *Rebel Without A Cause* (55), on director Ray]

Ray, Satyajit

Director Satyajit Ray getting the world back into focus around the time he made The Music Room *(63)*

Considered the doyen of all Indian filmmakers, Ray was instrumental in alerting notoriously xenophobic Western audiences to the fact that there was a film industry in India, and that it was of an extremely high quality. Ray virtually beggared himself in order to complete his first film, *Pather Panchali* (55), but the film was such a success at the **Cannes Film Festival** that both Ray's future as a director, and, just as importantly, the financial backing necessary to construct further films, was assured. He completed what is now called the Apu trilogy, with *Aparajito* (56) and *The World Of Apu* (59), before embarking on a series of films that not only changed the view the West had of India, but also the view India, or at the very least educated India, had of itself. Perhaps Ray's most exquisite film, and the one which best highlights the extraordinary paradoxes inherent in Indian society, is *The Music Room* (63), for which Ray also wrote the score. The image of the final, glorious concert held in the crumbling palace (so earnestly resented by the up-and-coming yet deeply philistine middle classes) is an enduring image of the capacity of the noumenal to transcend the present and take on the mantle of myth.

OTHER KEY FILMS: *The Goddess* (60); *Two Daughters* (61); *Charulata* (64); *The Coward And The Holy Man* (65); *Days And Nights In The Forest* (70); *Distant Thunder* (73); *The Golden Fortress* (74); *The Chess Players* (77); *The Visitor* (92)

Reaction Shot

The sudden **cutaway** to a character's face to show his or her response to the main action of a scene. A reaction shot can also occur in newsreel footage, such as the famous shot of the bystanders watching the unexpected destruction of the Challenger shuttle during its fatal take-off from the Kennedy Space Centre on 28 January 1986.

Reader

Similar to a publisher's reader, the studio reader (who is usually employed in the story department) is required to read and précis predominantly **slush-pile** outlines, scripts and treatments for the studio bosses and production executives, highlighting possible runners, and weeding out the rest. If a script has even the remotest chance of a second reading, the reader will produce an outline, in the simplest possible language, delineating the bare bones of the plot which should, ideally, be containable within a single sentence to allow for the short concentration span of the executive called upon to consider it.

Realism

A cinematic style that can only ever aspire towards what one might, with some justification, consider to be a merely ersatz, or subjective, reality, the cinema of realism relies instead on tricks to suggest reality, rather than aiming to depict reality itself.

Even such documentary footage as that of Eddy Adams's 1968 film of a Vietnamese general executing a suspected Viet Cong partisan, or the 1937 Bob Capa photographic image of a Spanish nationalist soldier throwing back his arms at the exact moment the bullet strikes him, are suspect, both morally and metaphysically, when one takes into account the alleged conditions under which the images were snatched. The camera does, of course, lie, just as every image presupposes another, mirror image. This was a fact best grasped by **expressionist** filmmakers and those dealing with a heightened, **poetic realism**, who acknowledge that the closest we are ever likely to come to reality on the screen is in the suggestion of it.

Rear Projection
See **Back Projection** and **Process Shot**

Recording Supervisor
The individual responsible, during the postproduction process, for the mixing and refining of the multiple recorded soundtracks onto one inclusive track.

Recordist
The technician responsible for the correct placement of microphones on a film set, as well as for the quality of the ensuing sound.

Redford, Robert
The big screen's original golden boy, Robert Redford has made the most of his career, acting, producing, directing, and founding the world-famous Sundance Institute for independent films and filmmakers. Despite all this, his screen persona remains more or less static, just as his looks do – one emerges from his movies impressed by their professionalism but just a little dissatisfied, as if one has been momentarily tempted by a luxurious lifestyle and then thought better of it. This is not to say that Redford is a bad actor, merely a mannered one. His directing, on the other hand, starting with *Ordinary People* (80), through *The Milagro Beanfield War* (87) and *The River Runs Through It* (93), and in particular *Quiz Show* (95), has improved with each film, and there is no earthly use denying his charm, and his obvious intelligence, and the diligence with which he has tried to follow the tenets of his own conscience.

OTHER KEY FILMS: *The Chase* (66); *Barefoot In The Park* (67); *Butch Cassidy And The Sundance Kid* (69); *Tell Them Willie Boy Is Here* (69); *Jeremiah Johnson* (72); *Three Days Of The Condor* (75); *All The President's Men* (76); *Out Of Africa* (85); *Havana* (90); *Indecent Proposal* (93); *The Horse Whisperer* [also dir.] (98); *The Legend Of Bagger Vance* [dir.] (00); *Spy Game* (01)

Redgrave, Michael
A fine screen actor and the father of an acting dynasty in **Vanessa**, Lynn and Corin, Redgrave was a Janus-like figure, uncomfortable with both his sexuality and his obvious, though frequently underused, talent. His best performances came early, in **Alfred Hitchcock's** *The Lady Vanishes* (38), the multi-directed *Dead Of Night* (45) and **Anthony Asquith's** *The Browning Version* (51), but he also brought his trademark nervous worthiness to **Tony Richardson's** *The Loneliness Of The Long Distance Runner* (62) and to Stuart Burge's film of the National Theatre's *Uncle Vanya* (63).

OTHER KEY FILMS: *Thunder Rock* (42); *The Way To The Stars* (45); *The Captive Heart* (46); *Mourning Becomes Electra* (47); *The Importance Of Being Earnest* (52); *Mr Arkadin* (55); *1984* (56); *The Quiet American* (58); *The Hill* (65); *The Go-Between* (71)

KEY LINE:
'Ah, Sir Michael Redgrave, I'll be bound!' [Sir John Gielgud, reportedly alluding to Redgrave's purported liking for homosexual bondage during their meeting in the street after hearing of Redgrave's 1959 knighthood]

Redgrave, Vanessa
On top of her form, Redgrave is one of the greatest of all screen actresses, remarkable both for her involvement with and utter commitment to any part she agrees to play. **Karel Reisz's** *Morgan: A Suitable Case For Treatment* (66) first gave an inkling of her possible range, and Michelangelo Antonioni's *Blow-Up* (66) confirmed it – whether on screen or on stage she is luminous, exuding a transcendental calm that other actresses can only marvel at. She thoroughly deserved her **Oscar** for **Fred Zinnemann's** *Julia* (77), but in recent years there has been a greater force to her now fully mature presence, that was absent before. Her small part in **James Ivory's** *Howards End* (92) was utterly sublime, and she literally carried Marleen Gorris's otherwise variable *Mrs Dalloway* (98) with the integrity and grace of her performance.

OTHER KEY FILMS: *Camelot* (67); *The Charge Of The Light Brigade* (68); *The Sea Gull* (68); *The Devils* (71); *Mary Queen Of Scots* (71); *The Seven Percent Solution* (76); *Agatha* (79); *The Bostonians* (84); *Wetherby* (85); *Prick Up Your Ears* (87); *Little Odessa* (95); *Wilde* (97); *An Interesting State* (99); *A Rumor of Angels* (00); *The Pledge* (01)

Re-dress

The remaking of a set, to include the subtle movement of props to different positions (to imply the passing of time), or to prepare the set for use in a different scene or motion picture.

Reduction Print

A reduction print, the direct opposite of a blow-up, is obtained by taking a smaller-gauge print from a larger-gauge original – a 35mm print struck from a 70mm original, for example.

Reed, Carol

Reed thought and lived in terms of cinema and of visual images, and it is curious, but somehow uplifting, to think of this illegitimate child of the great Edwardian actor, Herbert Beerbohm Tree, sloughing off the traditional English obsession with words and the workings of the intellect, to direct intuitively, in the French style, using words to fuel images, rather than vice versa. After the somewhat conventional, but still entertaining *Night Train To Munich* (40) and *The Way Ahead* (44), Reed stunned those who thought of him as unadventurous with his **expressionist** depiction of treachery, betrayal and remorse in *Odd Man Out* (47), in which **James Mason's** wounded Johnny McQueen flails through an increasingly fantastic Dublin. *Fallen Idol* (48) followed, and was an exquisite character study into the relationship between a child and **Ralph Richardson's** Baines the butler, the only person ever to show him any kindness, and who may or may not be a killer – rarely has the dark side of a child's natural ignorance of the workings of adult hearts been more sensitively shown. Reed's masterpiece is *The Third Man* (49), in which, from the very first, we are aware of Reed's total creative control over his material – from Robert Krasker's extraordinary shots of post-war Vienna to **Orson Welles's** inspired scene-stealing, to Anton Karas's haunting zither-music accompaniment, the film is an almost perfect example of cinema's capacity for intelligent, enlightened entertainment. Many critics believe that Reed faltered after *The Third Man*, but this is not strictly correct. *Outcast Of The Islands* (51) is an extraordinary film, and can bear repeated viewings, and **Trevor Howard** gives the performance of his life as Peter Willems, a man whom evil creeps up on, despite the almost saintly protection of Ralph Richardson's Captain Lingard, and in the face of Robert Morley's brilliantly hypocritical Almayer. For those four sublime films one can even forgive Reed for having agreed to direct *Oliver!* (68), which is really saying something.

OTHER KEY FILMS: *Midshipman Easy* (35); *Bank Holiday* (38); *Kipps* (41); *The Young Mr Pitt* (42); *The Man Between* (53); *A Kid For Two Farthings* (55); *Trapeze* (56); *The Key* (58); *Our Man In Havana* (59); *The Running Man* (63); *Follow Me* (72)

Reed, Oliver

A renowned piss artist and sometime heroic drunk, Reed began his screen career as a nervous, vibrant actor in a series of barely remembered **B-movies**. His uncle, **Carol Reed**, used him as Bill Sykes in the movie version of the hit musical *Oliver!* (68), where he was spotted by **Ken Russell** who, in turn, cast him as Gerald in *Women In Love* (69), which proved to be possibly Reed's most subtle screen performance. Parts in Russell's *The Devils* (71) and Richard Lester's *The Three Musketeers* (73) followed, but Reed's decline was long. He died while co-starring in what might well have been his comeback film, **Ridley Scott's** *Gladiator* (00), and he would have been amused had he known that his final scenes would have to be computer-aided with the help of **Soft Image**.

OTHER KEY FILMS: *Hannibal Brooks* (69); *The Hunting Party* (71); *Tommy* (75); *The Prince And The Pauper* (77); *Lion Of The Desert* (79); *Castaway* (86); *Prisoner Of Honour* (91); *Funny Bones* (95)

Reel

A reel is the spool on which film is wound, but it is now also used as a unit of measurement, relating to the roughly 1,000-foot, ten-minute capacity of a standard 35mm reel of film, and the approximately 400-foot, ten-minute capacity of a 16mm reel of film. Projection reels, of course, are much longer.

Reeves, Keanu

Reeves is a high-profile actor of no outstanding talent who yet possesses that rare thing – screen charisma. This is despite the po-faced look he has worn for virtually every role since *Bill And Ted's Excellent Adventure* (89). His female following is immense (and notably eclectic) and his recent role of Neo (yes, Neo) in Larry Wachowski's *The Matrix* (99) has done nothing to dent Reeves's other-worldly reputation with a set of fans who will hear no ill of their hero whatsoever.

OTHER KEY FILMS: *The Prodigal* (84); *River's Edge* (87); *Dangerous Liaisons* (88); *Parenthood* (89); *Point Break* (91); *My Own Private Idaho* (91); *Much Ado About Nothing* (93); *Speed* (94); *A Walk In The Clouds* (95); *Feeling Minnesota* (96); *Devil's Advocate* (97); *The Replacements* (00); *The Gift* (00); *Sweet November* (01); *Hardball* (01)

263

Reflector

A flat or concave panel used to reflect light in a particular direction on a film set, reflectors are also used behind spot lamps to focus their light more strongly, and also in exterior shooting, to concentrate the light of the sun onto the scene being shot.

Reflex Camera

A camera system designed to obviate the problems caused by the so-called **parallax** effect, by the use of an optical system that allows the operator to see exactly what is being filmed through the lens, without the need for parallax compensation.

Register Pins

See **Pilot Pins**

Registration

A frame is 'in register' when it is perfectly aligned in the gate of the camera. Animator's **cells** are considered to be in register in much the same way when their register holes are firmly held by register pegs before photography.

Reisz, Karel

Possibly the most influential of the 'kitchen-sink drama' school of British directors, Reisz is actually Czechoslovakian, and served in the wartime RAF following the death of both his parents in a Nazi concentration camp. His first feature was *Saturday Night And Sunday Morning* (60), which launched **Albert Finney's** screen career and which was the precursor to a seemingly endless stream of less well-made clones. *Morgan: A Suitable Case For Treatment* (66) cleverly isolated the half-manic, half-intellectual background to swinging London, and *The Gambler* (74) showed Reisz's keen eye for American nuances. *The French Lieutenant's Woman* (81) is still his most successful film to date, but *Dog Soldiers* (78) [a.k.a. *Who'll Stop The Rain?*], with Reisz's perennial leading man, **Nick Nolte**, is oddly memorable, if only for its extraordinary atmosphere.

OTHER KEY FILMS: *Night Must Fall* (64); *Isadora* (68); *Sweet Dreams* (85); *Everybody Wins* (90)

Relational Editing

A variation on traditional **montage** techniques, in relational editing the images used are designed to coalesce, by the end of the sequence, into one predominant idea or train of thought. The Russian theoretician, Vsevolod Pudovkin, designed the technique, using the terms parallelism, symbolism, juxtaposition, simultaneity and leitmotif to describe the five different modes within his conception.

Release

The general release of a feature film to selected theatres usually (but not always) follows shortly after the premiere. The year in which the release date falls is normally the year with which a film will thereafter be associated, but problems can occur, particularly in the case of European films which do not always have a formal release date for the guidance of film historians.

Release Negative

The fully authorised negative print from which all subsequent **release prints** are made.

Release Print

The final motion picture print, complete with sound, that will be distributed to film theatres for subsequent exhibition.

Relief

A particular lighting or directorial effect that ensures that a designated character or object will be the focus of the audience's attention.

Remake

The rehashing of a previously used story or script, followed by a complete refilming of the (usually successful) former movie the script or story once served, remakes are made for the delectation of present-day audiences. Examples of this unimaginative art (for the remakes are seldom better than the original movie) are **Martin Scorsese's** 1991 cover of J Lee Thompson's *Cape Fear* (62), Steve Miner's 1994 *My Father, The Hero* from Gérard Lauzier's *Mon Père, Ce Héros* (91), and George Sluizer's 1993 remake of his own far better 1988 movie, *The Vanishing*.

Rembrandt Lighting

An expression attributed to **Cecil B DeMille** and implying a highly contrasting chiaroscuro-effect lighting formula, nominally supposed to resemble that used in the paintings of Rembrandt (who will doubtless be turning in his grave at the thought).

Renaud, Madeleine

Wife of **Jean-Louis Barrault** and co-founder, with him, of the famous Renaud-Barrault stage company, Renaud was an outstanding theatrical and screen actress in her own right, although she chose to appear in only a very select number of films during her long career. She was outstanding in Julien Duvivier's *Maria Chapdelaine* (34) and in

Max Ophüls's *Le Plaisir* (52), and her name, and that of her husband, have since become synonymous with quality and excellence in the French theatre.

OTHER KEY FILMS: *Hélène* (36); *Lumière D'Été* (43); *Le Dialogue Des Carmélites* (60); *Le Diable Par Le Queue* (69); *La Mandarine* (72); *La Lumière Du Lac* (88)

Renoir, Jean

Arguably the greatest of all film directors, Renoir belonged to a long line of creative individuals which included his artist father, Pierre Auguste, his actor brother, Pierre, and his nephew, Claude Renoir, a fine cinematographer who photographed many of his uncle's films. A visual philosopher of the highest sensibility, Renoir was a down-to-earth man, obsessed by the individual and by the crucial relationship such an individual must forge between society and the natural environment. A master of extempore, Renoir extended the bounds of the cinema with such masterpieces of **poetic realism** as *Toni* (35), *La Grande Illusion* (37), and *La Règle Du Jeu* (39), exploring not only the social strata of his times, but also defining them by reference to the past and to the lessons of the importance of dignity, respect, duty and consistency already learned under its aegis. Like **John Ford**, with whom, in many ways, he can be compared, Renoir made films that exude humanity and an understanding of the disparate characteristics that differentiate people, as well as of what brings them together. His artistry, magnificent though it was, was always transcended by his search for understanding. See **Heartstopping Moments**

OTHER KEY FILMS: *La Chienne* (31); *Boudu Sauvé Des Eaux* (32); *Madame Bovary* (34); *Une Partie De Campagne* (36); *Les Bas-Fonds* (36); *Le Crime de Monsieur Lange* (36); *La Marseillaise* (38); *La Bête Humaine* (38); *Swamp Water* (41); *The Southerner* (45); *The Diary Of A Chambermaid* (46); *The Woman On The Beach* (47); *The River* (51); *Le Carosse D'Or* (52); *Eléna Et Les Hommes* (56)

KEY LINE:

'Is it possible to succeed without any act of betrayal?' [Renoir on life]

Rentals

The sum paid by the film exhibitor to the film distributor in return for the right to show the feature in question at certain agreed outlets and at certain agreed times.

Renter

The person who secures the right to exhibit a film in his or her cinema, or chain of cinemas, upon payment of a pre-arranged fee or proportion of the takings.

Republic

This was a small studio which turned out many superb films almost despite its policy of concentrating on serials and **B-movies**. John Ford's *Rio Grande* (48) and *The Quiet Man* (52) were made there, as was **Orson Welles's** eccentric *Macbeth* (48). **Nicholas Ray's** camp masterpiece *Johnny Guitar* (54) was completed just before Republic finally capitulated to the 'new behemoth' and converted itself into a television studio.

Re-recording

Re-recording can refer either to the transfer of a soundtrack from one film to another, or to the transfer of a magnetic soundtrack to tape for commercial release. It can also denote the combination of a number of different tracks (music, dialogue, extraneous sound, etc.) onto one contiguous track, in the editing room.

Re-release

Re-release refers to the reissue, often after cleaning, burnishing, or judicious recutting, of a previously successful or underrated movie, back onto the big screen. Notable examples include the re-release of **Merian C Cooper** and Ernest Schoedsack's *King Kong* (33) in 1938, and the 1999 re-release of John Mackenzie's *The Long Good Friday* (80) to cash in on the recent British success of Guy Ritchie's gangster movie *Lock, Stock And Two Smoking Barrels* (98). Massively popular films such as **Victor Fleming's** *Gone With The Wind* (39) and **Robert Wise's** *The Sound Of Music* (65) are in a near-perpetual state of re-release.

Resnais, Alain

Resnais came closer than any other film director to bringing the subtleties of the novelistic form to the screen. What he attempted in *Hiroshima Mon Amour* (59) was so original in terms of film, and yet so commonplace in terms of literature, that it deserves mention – in short, he endeavoured to remake time. By using narration, story fragmentation, and by juxtaposing documentary images with filmed narrative, Resnais used the audience's existing knowledge of literary forms to widen the scope of the purely filmic dialogue he was conducting with them. *Last Year In Marienbad* (61) was his second essay into such inherently ambiguous territory, but it is with *Muriel* (63) that he succeeded best in terms of his own cinematic ambitions. The film remains a curious and rather moving hybrid, less successful than *Hiroshima* in subverting the audience's expectations and in reaching a satisfying resolution, perhaps, but rich and dense of image, leaving the strange impression that one has inhabited, rather than merely voyeuristically viewed, the lives of its protagonists.

OTHER KEY FILMS: *Nuit Et Brouillard* [doc.] (56); *The War Is Over* (66); *Je T'Aime, Je T'Aime* (68); *Stavisky* (74); *Providence* (77); *Mon Oncle D'Amérique* (80); *Life Is A Bed Of Roses* (83); *Love Unto Death* (84); *Mélo* (86); *I Want To Go Home* (89); *Smoking/No Smoking* (93); *On Connaît La Chanson* (97)

Resolution

The quality of detail attainable by a specific lens or camera outfit.

Retake

This is the refilming of a scene or take if the previous version has been found wanting in some way. Stories abound of demented directors driving their stars to distraction by their relentless striving for perfection, but few can match the 342 retakes **Charlie Chaplin** ordered for the scene in *City Lights* (31) in which blind flower girl, Virginia Cherrill, sells Chaplin a flower in the mistaken belief that he is a rich man and not a tramp. Sometimes it is the actors who drive their directors to drink, as with renowned line-fluffer **Marilyn Monroe** – it took director **Billy Wilder** fifty-nine takes to get her to say 'Where's the bourbon?' in a convincing manner during the filming of *Some Like It Hot* (59).

Revamping

The rough equivalent of **re-dressing** a set, revamping refers more specifically to the redesigning of an existing set for reuse in another movie, or to be used unrecognisably in the same film. A notable example might be the Western town **Sergio Leone** built near Almeria, Spain, for his sequence of **Spaghetti Westerns** starring **Clint Eastwood**. This same town reappeared in the ensuing series of comic spaghettis starring Terence Hill and Bud Spencer.

Reversal Film

Film stock that does not pass through a negative stage, following exposure, but immediately becomes a positive print.

Reverse Action

Achieved by running the film backwards in a camera and then reversing it during editing, reverse action is useful in the creation of filmed stunts that require us to suspend disbelief – a dynamited chimney magically remakes itself, a diver is sucked from the water and back onto the board and so on.

Reverse Angle Shot

When a particular form of reaction shot is called for, the camera will sometimes reverse 180° on its axis to show the face of the person spoken to on screen and their response, in what is known as a 'shot/reverse shot' operation.

Reverse Scene

The mirror-like reversal of a shot scene, so that the protagonist is seen to move from left to right, as opposed to the right/left movement they conducted in reality. In such a scenario, nothing may appear on the screen that might give away the fact that the scene has been reversed – the face of a clock, signposts etc.

Rewind

A machine for the speedy and safe **rewinding** of a reel of film from one spool to another.

Rewinding

Once a reel of film has been projected, it must be rewound before a subsequent projection can occur.

Reynolds, Burt

Reynolds was hot commercial property during the late 1970s to early 80s, topping the **Quigley** Publications Poll from 1978 to 1982, thanks to such movies as Hal Needham's *Smokey And The Bandit* (77) and *The Cannonball Run* (81), which appealed to an all-teenage, all-redneck audience. Despite the usual run of duds and box-office fodder, Reynolds aspired to greater things, and he made one or two excellent films to offset the inevitable commercial dross. Such highlights included **John Boorman's** *Deliverance* (72), and the underrated *Sharkey's Machine* (81), which he also directed. He has recently made something of a comeback in Paul Thomas Anderson's excellent *Boogie Nights* (97), as, of all paradoxical things, an artistically pretentious pornographer.

OTHER KEY FILMS: *Sam Whiskey* (69); *Shamus* (73); *The Man Who Loved Cat Dancing* (73); *White Lightning* (73); *Hooper* (78); *The Man Who Loved Women* (83); *Mad Dog Time* (96); *Bean* (97); *Pups* (99); *The Crew* (00); *The Last Producer* [also dir.] (00); *The Librarians* (00); *Driven* (01); *Hotel* (01)

Reynolds, Debbie

Comparable, in effect if perhaps not in intent, to actresses such as **Julie Andrews** and **Doris Day**, Reynolds was a very talented singer and dancer with a titillating, because repressed, 1950s-style sexuality. Her best part was undoubtedly in **Stanley Donen** and **Gene Kelly's** *Singin' In The Rain* (52), in which her ebulliently virginal yet somehow still inflammatory attractions were used to good effect. Note for Film Buffs: Reynolds must be the only female dancer in the history of movies to be seen smoothing down her skirt so as *not* to show her panties in an energetic dance routine during *Singin' In The Rain*.

OTHER KEY FILMS: *The Daughter Of Rosie O'Grady* (50); *Hit The Deck* (55); *The Tender Trap* (55); *The Catered Affair* (56); *This Happy Feeling* (58); *The Rat Race* (60); *Goodbye Charlie* (64)

Richardson, Ralph

A profoundly eccentric and lovable man, Richardson was one of the foremost Shakespearian stage actors of his age, and, rather like his contemporary, **John Gielgud**, he slipped into acting for motion pictures almost by default. However, his majestic performances in **Carol Reed's** *The Fallen Idol* (48), Julien Duvivier's *Anna Karenina* (48), **William Wyler's** *The Heiress* (49), and **Sidney Lumet's** *Long Day's Journey Into Night* (62) proclaim him as one of the greatest – albeit one of the most arbitrary in his choice of parts – of all screen actors. His farewell performance as the 6th Lord Greystoke in Hugh Hudson's *Greystoke* (84), in which he recreates, in full mess kit, a famed tray slide down a set of marble steps, fatally injuring himself in the process, succeeds in bringing tears to the eyes each time one sees it, not so much on account of his performance, good as it is, but more on account of what Richardson represented as a man.

OTHER KEY FILMS: *Things To Come* (36); *The Citadel* (38); *The Four Feathers* (39); *Outcast Of The Islands* (51); *The Sound Barrier* (52); *Richard III* (55); *The Passionate Stranger* [a.k.a. *A Novel Affair*] (56); *Our Man In Havana* (60); *Woman Of Straw* (64); *The Looking-Glass War* (69); *O Lucky Man!* (73)

KEY LINE:

'The art of acting consists in keeping people from coughing.' [Richardson on acting]

Richardson, Tony

Richardson came to maturity in the rapidly changing social and industrial milieu of post-Second World War England, and he wisely made it his principal subject. With films such as *A Taste Of Honey* (61) and *The Loneliness Of The Long Distance Runner* (62), he challenged the formal authority of the unthinking middle classes, and his film version of John Osborne's seminal *Look Back In Anger* (59) was very nearly as influential as the original play. *Tom Jones* (63) was a rip-roaring and anarchically picaresque tilt at class windmills, as was his excellent *The Charge Of The Light Brigade* (68). A former husband of the actress **Vanessa Redgrave**, Richardson's work fell off in later years, but he had a marvellous and well-earned return to form with the posthumously released *Blue Sky* (94).

OTHER KEY FILMS: *The Entertainer* (60); *The Loved One* (65); *A Delicate Balance* (75); *The Border* (81)

Rickman, Alan

Neither exceptionally handsome nor exceptionably well endowed with athletic grace, what Rickman has going for him is that he can act – his most oleaginous of Mr Slopes in BBC TV's masterly *Barchester Chronicles* (82) suggested it, his Jamie in **Anthony Minghella's** *Truly, Madly, Deeply* (91) proved it, and his Colonel Brandon in **Ang Lee's** *Sense And Sensibility* (95) compounded that proof, for Rickman turned the nominally unglamorous, unthankful part of a retired, middle-aged army officer into a *tour de force* of virile acting, totally in keeping with the period in which the story was set. And that is another of Rickman's strengths – he is sufficiently confident of his skills to allow the audience time to appreciate them, rather than ramming them, in the fashion of certain celebrity actors, down people's throats.

OTHER KEY FILMS: *Die Hard* (88); *The January Man* (89); *Close My Eyes* (91); *Closet Land* (91); *Robin Hood: Prince Of Thieves* (91); *Bob Roberts* (92); *An Awfully Big Adventure* (95); *Michael Collins* (96); *The Winter Guest* [dir.] (97); *Judas Kiss* (98); *Galaxy Quest* (99); *Dark Harbour* (99); *Blow Dry* (01); *Harry Potter And The Philosopher's Stone* (01)

KEY LINE:

'Cancel the kitchen scraps for lepers and orphans. No more merciful beheadings. And call off Christmas!' [Rickman as the Sheriff of Nottingham in Kevin Reynolds's *Robin Hood: Prince Of Thieves*]

Riefenstahl, Leni

Excoriated and imprisoned for her adherence to and friendship with Adolf Hitler, no one can deny that Riefenstahl has been one of the most influential filmmakers of the past century, even if that influence can now be perceived, with the

267

benefit of hindsight, to have been largely malevolent. Professing her innocence right to the end, Riefenstahl nonetheless encapsulated the horrible and empty beauty of fascism in two masterpieces of heroic contrivance: *Triumph Of The Will* (36), which purported to be a documentary about the Nuremberg rallies but was, in fact, a Goebbels-inspired hymn to Nazi hysteria, and the two-part *Olympiad* (38), which again purported to be a documentary, this time about the 1936 Berlin Olympics, but was, in fact, a Goebbels-motivated paean to Aryan supremacy. The answer to the enigma of Riefenstahl may lie in such earlier pantheistic 'mountain' films as *The Blue Light* (32), which she both directed and acted in, and in which Germanic neo-poetic idealism finds itself allied to a curious sort of romantic folly.

OTHER KEY FILMS: *Victory Of Faith* (33); *Day Of Freedom* (35); *Berchtesgarten Über Salzburg* (35); *Tiefland* (54)

Rifle Mike

A microphone that can be aimed at one individual or particular spot.

Rifle Spot

A spotlight that produces a violent shaft of light, rather than a disseminated beam.

Riggers

The members of a movie crew responsible for erecting and maintaining scaffolding.

Rigging

The art of setting up studio lights to a pre-arranged plan before the actual shooting begins.

Rin Tin Tin

What **Lassie** was to the canine sentimentalist, Rin Tin Tin was too, only earlier. Discovered in a German slit trench during the First World War, Rin Tin Tin (whose original kennel name was probably along the lines of Rinaldo von und zu Tintenhausen) was whisked off to Hollywood, where his lack of knowledge of the English language was sure to prove no handicap (this was the silent era, remember). He mimed his way (on the **intertitles** only, of course) through a succession of smash hits, finally being allowed to bark for reel in such movies as D Ross Ledeman's *A Dog Of The Regiment* (27). Fastidious readers may find the following hard to believe, but the famous **Darryl F Zanuck** himself wrote Rin Tin Tin's dialogue, a fact which dogged him for the rest of his life. The

venerable canine finally ascended to dog heaven in 1932, aged somewhere between sixteen and eighteen, an exceptional span for a German Shepherd and doubtless due to the salutary effects of having his own valet, chauffeur, walker, veterinarian, banker and chef.

OTHER KEY FILMS: *The Man From Hell's River* (22); *Where The North Begins* (23); *Clash Of The Wolves* (25); *Rinty Of The Desert* (28); *The Million Dollar Collar* (29); *Rough Waters* (30)

KEY LINE:
'I'd better bone up on my lines, or the part will go begging. Bow Gnash may have been something of a wolf, but he liked his Bath too, and once let off the leash he didn't arf commit a few howlers.' [The alleged text of Rin Tin Tin's first serious audition]

Riser

Sometimes known by the more descriptive title of an **apple box**, a riser is used to raise an actor, a prop, or a camera, into line with, or higher than, a taller counterpart. Diminutive leading men are legion, and include within their ranks the likes of **Kirk Douglas**, **Alan Ladd** and **Dustin Hoffman**. **Lauren Bacall**, for instance, was taller than husband/co-star, **Humphrey Bogart**; **Katharine Hepburn** than lover/co-star, **Spencer Tracy**; and **Nicole Kidman** than ex-husband/co-star, **Tom Cruise**.

Riskin, Robert

New Yorker Riskin wrote the screenplays or assisted with the dialogue on a number of **Frank Capra** comedies, including *Platinum Blonde* (31), *It Happened One Night* (34) (for which he won an **Oscar**), *Mr Deeds Goes To Town* (35) and *Meet John Doe* (41). An absolute ace with the one and two liners, Riskin was also used on the Thin Man series, most notably as the scriptwriter on Richard Thorpe's *The Thin Man Goes Home* (44), which, not surprisingly, proved to be one of the funniest of the whole sequence. Another significant achievement was his script, based on James Hilton's best-selling novel, for Capra's resolutely non-comedic *Lost Horizon* (37).

OTHER KEY FILMS: **John Ford's** *The Whole Town's Talking* (35); **Henry Hathaway's** *The Real Glory* (39); **William Wellman's** *Magic Town* (47)

Ritt, Martin

A politically conscientious director whose work could, on occasion, slip into a somewhat bathetic earnestness, Ritt was at his best coaxing anti-heroic performances out of otherwise heroically inclined actors. *Hud* (63), with an electric **Paul Newman**

and an unsentimentally realist Patricia Neal, was his finest film, while *The Spy Who Came In From The Cold* (66) saw **Richard Burton** plumb the depths of existential despair. Later films, such as *The Front* (76) and *Norma Rae* (79), were thoroughly professional, but just a little worthy.
OTHER KEY FILMS: *Edge Of The City* (57); *The Long Hot Summer* (58); *The Sound And The Fury* (59); *Hombre* (67); *The Molly Maguires* (70); *Conrack* (74); *Cross Creek* (83); *Stanley & Iris* (89)
KEY LINE:
'The immediate recognition that we were dealing with a man of principle, a man with a wonderful mind, a man who was absolutely honest and direct… He fought a lot of battles for us. We were a gang of three.' [Irving Ravetch and Harriet Frank Jr on Ritt, for whom they scripted *The Long, Hot Summer* (58), *The Sound And The Fury* (59), *Hud* (63), *Hombre* (67), *Conrack* (74), *Norma Rae* (79), *Murphy's Romance* (85) and *Stanley & Iris* (89)]

Ritter, Thelma

One of the best-loved and most instantly recognisable of all character actresses, Ritter specialised in playing weary, caustic, blue-collar working women in what now seems a plethora of the best 1940s and 1950s films. Although Ritter was inevitably typecast in this way, she never cheated her audience, and there are a few real gems among her performances, particularly as **Bette Davis's** conscience in **Joseph L Mankiewicz's** *All About Eve* (50), as the murdered saleswoman in **Samuel Fuller's** *Pickup On South Street* (53), and as **Marilyn Monroe's** cynical friend in **John Huston's** *The Misfits* (60).
OTHER KEY FILMS: *A Letter To Three Wives* (49); *Perfect Strangers* (50); *Titanic* (53); *Rear Window* (54); *Pillow Talk* (59); *A Hole In The Head* (59); *Birdman Of Alcatraz* (62)
KEY LINE:
'Listen, mister. When I come in here tonight you seen an old clock running down. I'm tired. I'm through. Happens to everybody sometime. It'll happen to you too someday.' [*Pickup On South Street*]

RKO

RKO was the studio which took the original punt on **Orson Welles's** *Citizen Kane* (41), giving him unprecedented artistic control, and it was also the studio that **Howard Hughes** bought in 1948. Such a purchase was reportedly to indulge his taste for **Jane Russell** and maverick movie-making, but the shareholders then sued him for mishandling the company's affairs, securing double the value of their

initial shareholding from him in an out-of-court settlement. The original company was founded in 1904, its name graduating from the Mutual Film Corporation to Radio-Keith-Orpheum in 1921, and to RKO by 1928. Following Hughes's liquidation of the company, a tyre manufacturer acquired its assets, with the studios going to Lucille Ball and her Desilu company.
OTHER KEY FILMS: George Cukor's *A Bill Of Divorcement* (32); **Merian C Cooper** and Ernest Schoedsack's *King Kong* (33); **John Ford's** *The Lost Patrol* (34); Rouben Mamoulian's *Becky Sharp* (35); **George Stevens's** *Gunga Din* (39); **Fritz Lang's** *Clash By Night* (52)

Roach, Hal

Roach lived to be a hundred, and was finally honoured with a special **Oscar**, at the age of ninety-one, for his extraordinary contribution to film comedy. As producer to the greats, he discovered and cosseted the likes of **Laurel and Hardy**, **Harold Lloyd** and the **Our Gang** team, while at the same time aiding and abetting the early careers of directors such as Leo McCarey, George Marshall and **George Stevens**, and, hardly coincidentally, generating some of the best and most enduring of all film comedies.
OTHER KEY FILMS: Edgar Kennedy's *From Soup To Nuts* (28); Roach's own *Men Of The North* (30); Roach and Charles Rogers's *Fra Diavolo* (33); Norman McLeod's *Topper* (37); James W Horne's *Way Out West* (37); Lewis Milestone's *Of Mice And Men* (39); Gordon Douglas's *Saps At Sea* (40)

Road Movies

The United States is a country of travellers, of people who come from somewhere, stay a little, and then move on; it is natural, therefore, that a genre of film should spring up to reflect this. Road movies take place during the course of journeys, journeys that can function either as an escape from discovery or as a means of discovery. Like the best short stories, such films are about change; about the effects a stranger's passing can have on an otherwise closed community. Many of the greatest **Westerns** are road movies, as are some of the finest *films noirs*. Each generation of filmmakers rediscovers the archetype and makes it their own.
KEY FILMS: Frank Capra's *It Happened One Night* (34); **John Ford's** *The Grapes Of Wrath* (40); **Preston Sturges's** *Sullivan's Travels* (41); Tay Garnett's *The Postman Always Rings Twice* (46); **Jacques Tourneur's** *Out Of The Past* (47); **Nicholas Ray's** *They Live By Night* (49); **Joseph H Lewis's**

Gun Crazy (49); **Anthony Mann's** *Winchester '73* (50); John Ford's *The Searchers* (56); **Dennis Hopper's** *Easy Rider* (69); **Bob Rafelson's** *Five Easy Pieces* (70); **Terrence Malick's** *Badlands* (73); **Stephen Frears's** *The Hit* (85); **David Lynch's** *Wild At Heart* (90); **Ridley Scott's** *Thelma And Louise* (91); **Hal Hartley's** *Simple Men* (92); **Patrice Leconte's** *Tango* (93)

Road Show

Ultra-prestigious films, such as **Victor Fleming's** ***Gone With The Wind*** (39) or **Robert Wise's** *The Sound Of Music* (65), that, according to the studios, merit special placement at only the best-equipped theatres during their first run, are considered road show movies.

Robbins, Tim

Robbins began at the very bottom – which doesn't mean auditioning and giving away his tapes to every producer going; it means all that and then only to find that four consecutive big movies you have a major part in are flops. Yes, Robbins featured in Willard Huyck's *Howard The Duck* (86), Bill Fishman's *Tapeheads* (88), Terry Jones's *Eric The Viking* (89) and Roger Donaldson's *Cadillac Man* (90) in the space of just five years. It is to his eternal credit (and a tribute to his talent) that he survived the sort of career vicissitudes that would have floored more fragile actors. Between 1992 and 1994 Robbins played the title role of Griffin Mill in **Robert Altman's** *The Player* (92), directed and took the lead in *Bob Roberts* (92), shone as randy cop Gene Shepard in Altman's *Short Cuts* (93), redeemed *The Shawshank Redemption* from worthiness, won over waverers to **Fred Schepisi's** marginally cute *I.Q.* (94), and made sense of the **Coen Brothers'** Pythonesque *The Hudsucker Proxy* (94). All something of a miracle when one looks at his inauspicious beginnings.

OTHER KEY FILMS: *Toy Soldiers* (84); *The Sure Thing* (85); *Top Gun* (86); *Bull Durham* (88); *Dead Man Walking* [dir. only] (95); *Nothing To Lose* (97); *Arlington Road* (99); *The Cradle Will Rock* [dir.] (99); *High Fidelity* (00); *AntiTrust* (01); *Human Nature* (01)

Roberts, Julia

The girl with the biggest grin in the world, Roberts has every reason to be happy with her recent string of five consecutive hits: P J Hogan's *My Best Friend's Wedding* (97), Roger Michell's *Notting Hill* (99), Gary Marshall's *Runaway Bride* (99), **Steven Soderbergh's** *Erin Brockovich* (00) and Gore Verbinski's *The Mexican* (01). Now on $20 million a picture, with fifteen per cent of the gross thrown in

for good measure, Roberts is the thirty-something woman *par excellence*, representing female Middle America's most fervid dreams. Hardly great shakes as an actress, her stage presence, however, is electrifying, and she has that rare charisma that all major stars need if they are going to make the most of their all-too-brief time at the very top.

OTHER KEY FILMS: *Mystic Pizza* (88); *Steel Magnolias* (89); *Pretty Woman* (90); *Flatliners* (90); *Sleeping With The Enemy* (91); *Dying Young* (91); *The Pelican Brief* (93); *Mary Reilly* (96); *Michael Collins* (96); *Conspiracy Theory* (97); *Stepmom* (98); *America's Sweethearts* (01); *Ocean's Eleven* (01)

*Megastar **Julia Roberts** and her $20 million dollar grin*

Robinson, Bruce

Robinson is a fine screenwriter, an occasional actor and a subtle, sensitive director, but any notionally constructive critique of his work fetches up against the phenomenon of *Withnail & I* (86), which, to its many adherents (and this author is one), is quite simply the best British film (dare one say English?) of the past twenty years. Forget Robinson's screenplay for Roland Joffe's *The Killing Fields* (84), magnificent though it is. Forget his scripts for Joffe's *Shadow Makers* (89), and for his own *How To Get Ahead In Advertising* (89) and *Jennifer 8* (92), excellent though they are. A *Withnail & I* only comes along once in a lifetime, and that should be enough for any man. Without wishing to blow an already battered trumpet, the film is virtually faultless as both a comedy and as a record of the social mores of a recent but already bygone era, and can bear any number of repeated viewings. It thoroughly deserves its cult, and Robinson thoroughly deserves the credit for forcing through an idea that must have sounded terminally dire on paper. If there is any justice in the world, battered geriatrics will still be watching *Withnail* in thirty years time and muttering, 'Yes, that was how it was…' through their nicotine-stained beards, '… or, just maybe, how it should have been'.
OTHER KEY FILMS: **Sidney Poitier's** *Ghost Dad* [co-sc] (90); **Neil Jordan's** *In Dreams* [script] (98)
KEY LINES:
'Getinthebackofthevan!!' [A sublimely irritated police constable in *Withnail & I*]

'Baaaastards!!!' [Withnail's world-view from *Withnail & I*]

Robinson, Casey

Robinson was one of the Hollywood studio system's best literary adapters, and his scope was quite extraordinarily wide, spanning such masterpieces of commercial cinema as **Michael Curtiz's** *Captain Blood* (35), **Edmund Goulding's** *Dark Victory* (39) and *The Old Maid* (39), Anatole Litvak's *All This And Heaven Too* (40) and Irving Rapper's *Now Voyager* (42), in which Robinson penned a number of the most familiar lines in Hollywood movie history. His extraordinary capacity for empathy, and for delving deep down to the essence of a novel without losing sight of the author's intentions, mark him out as one of the unsung greats of the screenwriting profession.
OTHER KEY FILMS: **Sam Wood's** *Kings Row* (41) and *Saratoga Trunk* (46); **Henry King's** *The Snows Of Kilimanjaro* (53); **Fritz Lang's** *While The City Sleeps* (56)

Robinson, Edward G

At first glance a most unlikely candidate for major stardom, the Romanian-born Emmanuel Goldenberg constructed his career very well. He cemented his initial reputation with mean gangster roles such as that of Little Rico in **Mervyn LeRoy's** *Little Caesar* (30) and only latterly, once his reputation and name (changed to Edward G Robinson) were firmly established, moved to more challenging roles, including that of the man who invented the cure for syphilis in **William Dieterle's** *The Story Of Dr Ehrlich's Magic Bullet* (40), which, despite its subject matter, remains one of the best ever Hollywood biopics. A renowned collector of Impressionist paintings, Robinson made a fine series of *films noirs* during the 1940s, including **Billy Wilder's** *Double Indemnity* (44), and two **Fritz Lang** sizzlers, *The Woman In The Window* (44) and *Scarlet Street* (45). Possibly his finest performance, however, involved a sinister reprise of Little Rico (Johnny Rocco, this time) in **John Huston's** *Key Largo* (48), in which Robinson's face takes on an almost reptilian malevolence.
OTHER KEY FILMS: *The Man With Two Faces* (34); *Barbary Coast* (36); *Kid Galahad* (37); *Brother Orchid* (40); *The Sea Wolf* (41); *The Stranger* (46); *The Night Has A Thousand Eyes* (48); *House Of Strangers* (49); *Nightmare* (56); *Sammy Going South* (63); *Cheyenne Autumn* (64); *The Cincinnati Kid* (65); *Soylent Green* (73)
KEY LINE:
'Is this the end of Johnny Rocco?' [*Key Largo*]

Rodgers, Richard

First with lyricist Lorenz Hart, and then with **Oscar Hammerstein II**, Rodgers created a bevy of the most brilliant musical shows in cinema history, filmed versions of which include **Busby Berkeley's** *Babes In Arms* (39), A Edward Sutherland's *The Boys From Syracuse* (40), **Fred Zinnemann's** *Oklahoma!* (55), Walter Lang's *The King And I* (56), George Sidney's *Pal Joey* (57), Joshua Logan's *South Pacific* (58) and **Robert Wise's** *The Sound Of Music* (65). A filmed biopic, Norman Taurog's *Words And Music* (48), featuring Tom Drake as Rodgers and **Mickey Rooney** as Lorenz Hart (which included a smash Vera-Ellen and **Gene Kelly** dance version of 'Slaughter On Tenth Avenue') was made about Rodgers's and Hart's early lives – early, for Rodgers was only forty-six and in mid-career when the film came out.
OTHER KEY FILMS: A Edward Sutherland's *Mississippi* (35); **Mervyn LeRoy's** *Fools For Scandal* (38); Tim Whelan's *Higher And Higher* (44)

271

Roeg, Nicolas

A former clapper boy, lighting cameraman and cinematographer who belatedly moved into directing, Roeg never seems totally at ease in front of the camera (or, perhaps more accurately, beside it). His visuals are often wonderful, but his later scripts can be woeful, particularly in the case of *Eureka* (83). *Don't Look Now* (73), however, in which a Venetian serial killer becomes the final, deadly catalyst in the story of two people torn apart by the loss of their child, is a first-rate and disciplined thriller, and *Bad Timing* (80), though intellectually rather perverse, still holds together visually. Roeg's first film, *Performance* (70), which he co-directed with Donald Cammell, is now something of a cult favourite, more due to Mick Jagger's iconic presence allied to Cammell's wayward genius than to Roeg's own input. *The Man Who Fell To Earth* (76) was a genuine oddity – a brilliant idea, with striking visuals, a magnetic star presence in David Bowie, but nonetheless verging on the incoherent. If this all sounds unduly critical, it shouldn't be taken as such, for Roeg's standards and his expectations of himself are high, and his is a genuinely eclectic talent which can provoke, puzzle and satisfy in roughly equal measures.
OTHER KEY FILMS: *Walkabout* (71); *Insignificance* (85); *Castaway* (86); *Aria* [co-dir.] (87); *The Witches* (90); *Cold Heaven* (92); *Two Deaths* (95)

Rogers, Ginger

A scintillating dancer, notably alongside **Fred Astaire** in Mark Sandrich's *The Gay Divorcee* (34) and *Top Hat* (35) and **George Stevens's** *Swing Time* (36), Rogers (whose career was almost entirely run by her mother) was also a more than passable, sometimes even raunchy, comedienne, as witnessed by her earlier work in Lloyd Bacon's *42nd Street* (33) and **Mervyn LeRoy's** *Gold Diggers Of 1933* (33). Rogers had more serious aspirations, however, than hoofing and comedy, and she single-mindedly pursued them (and an **Oscar**) in **Sam Wood's** *Kitty Foyle* (40). She never really reclaimed the ground she lost when her partnership with Fred Astaire broke up in 1939 (to be briefly revived in 1949 with **Charles Waters's** *The Barkleys Of Broadway*), but her talent for mimicry was shown to good effect in **Billy Wilder's** entertaining oddity *The Major And The Minor* (42), and her capacity for melodrama in Alex Segal's *Harlow* (65). See picture at entry for **Fred Astaire**.
OTHER KEY FILMS: *Flying Down To Rio* (33); *Rafter Romance* (34); *Roberta* (35); *Vivacious Lady* (38); *The Primrose Path* (40); *Tom, Dick And Harry* (41); *Roxie Hart* (42); *Forever Female* (53)

Rogers, Roy

Rogers asked to be skinned and stuffed and placed on his beloved horse, Trigger, when he died, and one suspects that if this had been legally possible it would have been done, and the defunct cowboy and his erstwhile steed would now be waiting to greet their guests at the entrance to the Roy Rogers Museum in Victorville, California, with 'Happy Trails' gently playing in the background. Rogers made people feel good in his movies, and advocated the sort of clean-living, clean-thinking life that now seems so totally out of fashion (except with the silent majority, of course). In movies such as Joseph Kane's *King Of The Cowboys* (43) and William Witney's *Roll On Texas Moon* (47) and *Heart Of The Rockies* (51), Rogers, with his now deceased wife, Dale Evans, and his chum, Gabby Hayes, by his side, suggested security to a whole generation of children who grew up in the aftermath of the Second World War and within the toils of the lengthy, paranoid Cold War that followed. And that's quite an achievement.
OTHER KEY FILMS: *Under Western Stars* (39); *Dark Command* (40); *Sons Of The Pioneers* (42); *The Cowboy And The Señorita* (44); *My Pal Trigger* (46); *Springtime In The Sierras* (47); *North Of The Great Divide* (50)

Rogers, Will

Will Rogers was the master of the sort of ersatz homespun philosophy that had Americans queuing to see his talking pictures (he was a bit of a flop in silent movies, for obvious reasons) when they were at their most vulnerable, i.e. during the Great Depression. His great art lay in reminding people that the common man has something to say too, if he can only spit out his chaw, clear his throat and get a word in edgewise. By the time of his death, in a plane crash in 1935, the fifty-five-year-old Rogers was reportedly the most famous man in America after the President. In movies such as **John Ford's** *Doctor Bull* (33), *Judge Priest* (34) and *Steamboat Round The Bend* (35), Rogers charmed his way into American folklore, and his polo ranch above Malibu is now something of a national shrine.
OTHER KEY FILMS: *Happy Days* (29); *A Connecticut Yankee* (31); *State Fair* (33); *Mr Skitch* (33); *Doubting Thomas* (35); *In Old Kentucky* (35)
KEY LINE:
'There is only one thing that can kill the movies, and that is education.' [Rogers on film]

Rohmer, Eric

An early editor of ***Cahiers du Cinéma,*** Rohmer turned to directing in the 1960s with his series of moral tales (*Les Contes Moreaux*), which included

Claire's Knee (71), in which a lust-tormented Jean-Claude Brialy spends most of the film debating whether or not to touch his friend's daughter's patella. Rohmer's genius lies in his concentration on the mundane to highlight the larger emotional issues that face adolescents and adults. He continued this delicate process both with his comedies and proverbs (*Comédies Et Proverbes*) of the 1980s, and with his more recent seasonal tales, building a body of work notable for its delicate subtleties and complete lack of ostentation.

OTHER KEY FILMS: *La Collectioneuse* (67); *Pauline À La Plage* (83); *L'Ami De Mon Ami* (87); *Conte De Printemps* (90); *Conte D'Hiver* (92); *Conte D'Été* (96); *Conte D'Automne* (98); *L'Anglaise Et Le Duc* (00)

Role

The part an actor or actress plays in a feature film.

Roll

A quantity of film rolled around a central reel.

Roll 'em/Roll It

The director's shouted order to the camera crew to start their motors in preparation for '**Action!**', when filming proper begins.

Rolling Title

A credits sequence on a feature film that begins from the bottom and disappears through the top of the screen, i.e. the rolling titles on **Robert Aldrich's** *Kiss Me Deadly* (55).

Room Tone

This refers to the background noise in a room that is filtered out by the human ear, but is instantly picked up by a microphone. Recording engineers will make a tape of the room tone, which will be used to 'fill in' the blank spaces between dialogue in any subsequent editing.

Rooney, Mickey

Rooney epitomised what young America thought it might like to be during the late 1930s and early 1940s. A wisecracking, anti-intellectual ball of fire, he would probably have been sat on at the earliest opportunity in real life, and he actually *was* sat upon after his return from an unlikely war service. To foreign audiences, there was always something sensationally curious about Rooney, but then there seems something sensationally curious about the America he represents, an America which still mystifies onlookers to such apparently self-defeating charivaris as the Bill Clinton arraignments and the Al Gore kissathon, and in which Rooney's nine marriages and assorted bankruptcies, comebacks, sentimental outings and tough-minded statements of intent seem perfectly normal, everyday matters. That said, Rooney managed to transcend his image on one or two occasions, proving that there was indeed chicken-wire behind the papier-mâché. He was genuinely good as Puck in Max Reinhardt and **William Dieterle's** *A Midsummer Night's Dream* (35), and genuinely tough in **Don Siegel's** *Baby Face Nelson* (57). In the interim he gave America what it seemed to want, and then reminded them of the cost involved in getting it.

OTHER KEY FILMS: *A Family Affair* (37); *Boys Town* (38); *The Adventures Of Huckleberry Finn* (39); *Strike Up The Band* (40); *Babes On Broadway* (42); *National Velvet* (44); *Words And Music* (48); *The Bridges At Toko-Ri* (55); *Breakfast At Tiffany's* (61); *It's A Mad Mad Mad Mad World* (63); *The Black Stallion* (79); *Maximum Force* (92); *Lightning, The White Stallion* (96); *The First Of May* (00)

Rossellini, Roberto

Rossellini is the man who snatched **Ingrid Bergman** from her adoring fans (and her adoring husband) in the United States, impregnated her (twice), then sent her packing following his affair and subsequent (one presumes) impregnation of the Indian screenwriter, Somali Das Gupta. That's how the newspapers had it, anyway. All that aside, Rossellini just happens to be one of the main progenitors of the **neo-realist** movement in Italy, and a filmmaker, perhaps more influential than tender, more intellectual than wry, whose obsession with the necessity of 'seeing' everything, whether from the point of view of the actor or of the audience, could serve, and sometimes did, to alienate both. His greatest films were his war trilogy, *Roma Città Aperta* [*Open City*] (45), *Paisà* [*Paisan*] (46) and *Germania Anno Zero* [*Germany Year Zero*] (47), followed by *L'Amore* (48), in which his then lover **Anna Magnani** portrayed two enduring Italian archetypes, the scorned lover and the saintly peasant, and finally the extraordinary *Viaggio In Italia* (58), which succeeds despite (or perhaps because of) the fact that its two stars, Ingrid Bergman and **George Sanders**, didn't have the faintest idea what the film they were in the process of making was about.

OTHER KEY FILMS: *Stromboli* (49); *The Seven Deadly Sins* (52); *Europa '51* (52); *Joan Of Arc At The Stake* (54); *General Della Rovere* (59)

273

Rossen, Robert

A reluctant namer of names in front of the House Un-American Activities Committee (see **Hollywood Ten**), Rossen, like his contemporary, **Elia Kazan**, was a socially conscious screenwriter and filmmaker who was very nearly brought down by the enforced Cold War politicisation of 1950s Hollywood. An ex-boxer himself, he directed *Body And Soul* in 1947, with **John Garfield** playing the gradually corrupted boxing champion, Charlie Davis, an eerie pre-echo of Rossen's own slow corruption by the HUAC. *The Hustler* (61), with **Paul Newman**, brought him late acclaim, while *Lilith* (64) cemented his reputation among the French as an **auteur**, possibly on account of the presence of **Jean Seberg** among the cast.
OTHER KEY FILMS: *Johnny O'Clock* (47); *All The King's Men* (49); *Island In The Sun* (57);

Rostrum

A raised support for a camera, or for individual items of lighting equipment. Also the support used during animation shooting to ensure the correct distance between camera and subject.

Roth, Tim

Roth is one of only a handful of British actors to have made a successful long-term crossover to American cinema. Following his extraordinary performance as Mr Orange/Freddy in **Quentin Tarantino's** *Reservoir Dogs* (92) (one assumes that Tarantino had seen Roth's performance in **Stephen Frears's** *The Hit* (84), and cast him on the strength of it), he went on to feature as Pumpkin, in the same director's *Pulp Fiction* (94), and as Joshua, a hit man with family problems, in James Gray's *Little Odessa* (94). He played against type as an English aristocrat in Michael Caton-Jones's *Rob Roy* (95), before reverting once again to lucrative gangsterhood in Bill Duke's *Hoodlum* (97). All humour aside, Roth is an excellent actor who deserves to be challenged by rather more than a gun, a sword or a hypodermic needle.
OTHER KEY FILMS: *The Cook, The Thief, His Wife & Her Lover* (89); *Vincent And Theo* (90); *Rosencrantz And Guildenstern Are Dead* (90); *Bodies, Rest And Motion* (93); *Captives* (95); *Everyone Says I Love You* (96); *Gridlock'd* (97); *Vatel* (00); *Lucky Numbers* (00); *Planet Of The Apes* (01); *Inside Job* (01); *Invincible* (01)

Rotoscope

The tracing of a real object onto an animation **cell**, from which it can be improved and transposed back to the live footage that it was originally taken from.

Rough Cut

A well-advanced part of the editing process in which a film is in more or less the form in which it will eventually be exhibited, the rough cut allows the editor and director to fine-tune the film in preparation for the **fine cut**.

Roundy Round

A 180-degree change of perspective in a shot, from one speaker to another.

Rourke, Mickey

Rourke had a good run during the 1980s, trading on the success of his curiously memorable cameo as Teddy Lewis, an ex-con arsonist, in **Lawrence Kasdan's** *Body Heat* (81), to garner parts in **Michael Cimino's** *Year Of The Dragon* (85), Adrian Lyne's curious psycho-sexual hodgepodge, *9½ Weeks* (86), and **Alan Parker's** underrated *Angel Heart* (87) – and yes, Rourke doesn't dress in period, but in the context of a fantasy film like *Angel Heart*, what does it matter? His best part to date has come as Henry Chinaski (alter ego of cult author, Charles Bukowski) in **Barbet Schroeder's** *Barfly* (87), and even though his recent star has set a little, despite a number of perfectly respectable performances, there is still something about his mannered style and his existentialist, bloody-minded off-screen troublemaking that appeals. With everyone against him but the French, the guy must be doing something right.
OTHER KEY FILMS: *Heaven's Gate* (80); *Diner* (82); *Eureka* (83); *Rumble Fish* (83); *A Prayer For The Dying* (87); *White Sands* (92); *The Rain Maker* (97); *Point Blank* (97); *Shergar* (99); *Get Carter* (00); *The Pledge* (01); *Claire's Hat* (01)

Rozsa, Miklós

Rozsa wrote full-blooded music that didn't cloy, something of a cute trick in a Hollywood whose view of old Vienna involved *Sachertorte*, Sigmund Romberg (who was actually born in Hungary, just as Rozsa was) and Lily Pons trilling 'Tales of the Vienna Woods' (or something remarkably like it) to a bemused **Henry Fonda**. Hearing a Rozsa score winding itself up as a prelude to **Billy Wilder's** *Five Graves To Cairo* (43) or *Double Indemnity* (44), for instance, or maybe in **Alfred Hitchcock's** *Spellbound* (45), **Robert Siodmak's** *The Killers* (46), **John Huston's** *The Asphalt Jungle* (50) or George Sidney's *Young Bess* (53), has been known to cause grown men and women to rub their hands together in lurid anticipation of a *real* Hollywood movie, something with love and passion, drama and guts in it.

Rozsa and other composers of his ilk, including **Bernard Herrmann**, **Max Steiner**, Frederick Hollander and **Erich Wolfgang Korngold**, are more than a little responsible for the *feeling* that remains of a movie after the plot and the characters and even the context have long been forgotten.

OTHER KEY FILMS: Jacques Feyder's *Knight Without Armour* (37); **Alexander Korda's** multi-directed *The Thief Of Bagdad* (40); Billy Wilder's *The Lost Weekend* (45); **Jules Dassin's** *Brute Force* (47); **George Cukor's** *Bhowani Junction* (56); **William Wyler's** *Ben-Hur* (59)

Rudolph, Alan

Rudolph is the quirky, quasi-independent director of such fascinating after-dinner movies as *Choose Me* (84), *Trouble In Mind* (85) and the curious *Mortal Thoughts* (91), which featured the realistically slumming team of **Demi Moore** and **Bruce Willis** in their one and only non-mainstream movie. *The Moderns* (88) and *Mrs Parker And The Vicious Circle* (94) represent Rudolph in full period fig, and they are remarkably successful at conjuring up an epoch in which style was seen to equate to talent, something which is unfortunately all too true of our generation and so gives the films an added resonance. His recent *Afterglow* (97) continues the vein of character over story which Rudolph has mined so well, and it is extremely heartening to know that Rudolph is out there, like his near contemporary, **John Sayles**, quietly notching up an impressive list of recognisably consistent films.

The twenty-year-old Gail Russell, photographed by A L 'Whitey' Schaefer in 1944, showing the eyes that later conquered John Wayne

OTHER KEY FILMS: *Welcome To L.A.* (77); *Remember My Name* (79); *Roadie* (80); *Endangered Species* (82); *Songwriter* (85); *Made In Heaven* (87); *Love At Large* (90); *Equinox* (93); *Breakfast Of Champions* (99); *Trixie* (00); *Investigating Sex* (01)

Rumble Pot

Water, heated to boiling point, to which dry ice is added to create a fog or miasma effect.

Runaway Production

This refers to the filming of a feature in a foreign country to take advantage of cheaper labour costs. Spain was used for **Sergio Leone's** series of **spaghetti Westerns**, Morocco (and other places too numerous to mention) for **Orson Welles's** *Othello* (52), while Mexico has stood in for just about everywhere, including the first-class quarters (Mexico City) and the deep ocean backdrop (Baja California) during the filming of **James Cameron's** *Titanic* (97).

Runners

The rails high above a studio set from which lamps, spotlights, flats, etc., may be hung.

Running Lines

Hollywood jargon for the going over of dialogue before a scene is shot.

Running Shot

A **travelling** or **tracking** shot in which the camera, either on a **dolly**, rails or a truck, speeds to keep up with the action.

Running Speed

The speed, in frames per second, at which film stock runs past a camera gate, or through a projector.

Running Time

The official length of a movie, in hours and minutes, as measured by the time it takes to pass, from start to finish, through a projector.

Run-through

A full dress rehearsal of a scene, exactly as it is to be shot, but before the actual shooting takes place.

Rushes

See **Dailies**

Russell, Gail

The only girl whose limpid eyes could look blue in black-and-white, Russell never made it to the big time, and died tragically, aged thirty-six, after a long fight against alcoholism. A shy, unarguably beautiful woman, Russell was at her best in roles that brought out her innate masochism, and one feels almost guilty about calling her the most alluring victim in cinema history. **John Wayne**, who was rumoured to be in love with her, partnered her to good effect in two of his lesser but still underrated films, James Edward Grant's *The Angel And The Badman* (47) and Edward Ludwig's *Wake Of The Red Witch* (48), and she was also very good in John Farrow's *Calcutta* (47). **Joseph Losey**, too, recognised the power of those extraordinary, fated eyes, in his otherwise unremarkable *The Lawless* (50).

OTHER KEY FILMS: *The Uninvited* (44); *The Unseen* (45); *The Night Has A Thousand Eyes* (48); *Captain China* (49); *Seven Men From Now* (56); *The Tattered Dress* (57)

Russell, Jane

Russell is fun, and her movies, while never taking themselves too seriously, always reflect her buoyant nature and are consequently redeemed from the mediocrity that might otherwise have been their lot. Despite the mixed blessing(s) of a world-famous bust, Russell proved she could sass with the best of them, standing up to **Robert Mitchum** in **Josef von Sternberg's** *Macao* (52), to just about everybody in **Howard Hawks's** *Gentlemen Prefer Blondes* (53), and to the King himself, **Clark Gable**, in **Raoul Walsh's** *The Tall Men* (55). Mention has to be made of **Howard Hughes's** *The Outlaw* (43), the film in which Russell was first exposed to an eagerly waiting world. See entry on *The Outlaw*

OTHER KEY FILMS: *The Paleface* (48); *His Kind Of Woman* (51); *Double Dynamite* [one hell of a title, in the circumstances] (51); *The Las Vegas Story* (52); *Underwater!* (55); *Hot Blood* (56); *The Revolt Of Mamie Stover* (56); *Darker Than Amber* (70)

KEY LINE:

'I like a man who can run faster than I can.' [*Gentlemen Prefer Blondes*]

Russell, Ken

The iconoclastic director of some of the best television documentaries ever made (for the BBC *Monitor* programme), Russell had considerable success with his biographies of composers Frederick Delius, Edward Elgar and Claude Debussy and this paved the way for his extraordinary debut in feature films, *Women In Love* (69), which remains one of the best ever big-screen adaptations of D H Lawrence. Always a little prone to creative hysteria, Russell allowed his fervid love of music and his inordinate

pleasure in shocking his audience to coalesce in *The Music Lovers* (71), which took viewers on a heady ride to an inspired, rather than a base, camp. *The Devils* (71), much reviled, was brilliantly designed and as feverishly true to its origins as its author was anarchic – British cinema had never known his mainstream equal. Russell's first US film, *Altered States* (80), was a great success (despite author Paddy Chayefsky's appalled disclaimers), and Russell continues to this day, alternately missing and hitting the mark, his cherubic smile and radical intelligence intact. There is no one else quite like him.

OTHER KEY FILMS: *The Boy Friend* (71); *Savage Messiah* (72); *Mahler* (74); *Tommy* (75); *Lisztomania* (75); *Valentino* (77); *Crimes Of Passion* (84); *Gothic* (87); *The Rainbow* (89); *Whore* (91); *MindBender* (95); *The Fall Of The House Of Usher* (01)

Ryan, Meg

Ryan is an intelligent actress, somewhat along the lines of a Lee Remick, whose success seems, in some strange way, rather out of proportion to her talent. Looking through her filmography one is hard put to select an especially memorable film, and the inevitable conclusion to be drawn (and this is not meant pejoratively) is that Ryan is an actress of the moment, a condition that incorporates both her strength and her weakness. Strength, because her enjoyment of her stardom is, after all, now; weakness, in that her films, even such period dramas as Michael Hoffman's *Restoration* (95), resolutely fail to transcend the era in which they happen to be filmed. Ryan is a 1980s woman, and she carries this unfortunate condition through to any part she plays. The upside is that in the films where she plays to type, as in Rob Reiner's *When Harry Met Sally* (89) and Nora Ephron's *Sleepless In Seattle* (93), she is magnificently successful, and in thirty years time people will look back at the results with fascinated horror, rather as today they look back at bell-bottomed trousers and the beehive hairdo.

OTHER KEY FILMS: *D.O.A.* (88); *Flesh And Bone* (93); *I.Q.* (94); *When A Man Loves A Woman* (94); *French Kiss* (95); *Addicted To Love* (97); *You've Got Mail* (98); *Hanging Up* (00); *Proof Of Love* (00)

Ryan, Robert

Ryan is a movie connoisseur's actor – an adept at darker roles, he was the protagonist of choice for a number of the great *film noir* directors, who understood that Ryan had that rare thing, the ability to live a role, even if that role happened to be unsympathetic. A pronounced liberal by conviction, Ryan portrayed an anti-Semite in **Edward Dmytryk's** *Crossfire* (47), a has-been boxer in **Robert Wise's** superb *The Set-Up* (49), and a disenchanted cop on the verge of a nervous breakdown in **Nicholas Ray's** sensational *On Dangerous Ground* (51). Head and shoulders above many of the more mundane leading men of his day, Ryan improved even bad movies by his presence, and some aspects of his performances remain deep in the mind long after the movies themselves have been forgotten.

OTHER KEY FILMS: *The Woman On The Beach* (47); *Berlin Express* (48); *The Secret Fury* (50); *The Racket* (51); *Beware, My Lovely* (52); *Clash By Night* (52); *The Naked Spur* (53); *Bad Day At Black Rock* (55); *Day Of The Outlaw* (59); *Odds Against Tomorrow* (59); *Billy Budd* (62); *The Wild Bunch* (69); *The Outfit* (73)

Ryder, Winona

With her unconventional childhood (she is the daughter of LSD-exponent Timothy Leary) and her delicate good looks, Ryder might easily have drifted into feisty victim movies, along the lines of Wes Craven's *Scream* (96), but her winsomeness is cut with intelligence, and her art with cunning, as she showed from very early on, as **Dennis Quaid**/Jerry Lee Lewis's cousin Myra in Jim McBride's *Great Balls Of Fire* (89). She has chosen well since then, alternating canny commercial fare like Gillian Armstrong's *Little Women* (94), Ben Stiller's *Reality Bites* (94) and Jocelyn Moorhouse's *How To Make An American Quilt* (95), with more esoteric material, such as **Tim Burton's** *Edward Scissorhands* (90), Richard Benjamin's *Mermaids* (90) and **Jim Jarmusch's** *Night On Earth* (91). If she ignores her agent's advice and remembers to leaven her moneymaking with riskier projects, such as her Abigail Williams in Nicholas Hytner's *The Crucible* (96), she will have a career to be proud of.

OTHER KEY FILMS: *Beetlejuice* (88); *The Age Of Innocence* (93); *The House Of The Spirits* (94); *Celebrity* (98); *Autumn In New York* (00); *Lost Souls* (00); *Simone* (01)

Safety Film

Early nitrate films were easily combustible and notoriously subject to damp and decomposition, but until safety film, manufactured with less combustible cellulose and acetate bases, reached a similar production standard in the 1940s and early 1950s, filmmakers were wary of using it. Now its use is commonplace, and a great deal of nitrate-based film has already been copied onto safety film for long-term storage – but not before a lot of damage had been done, including the complete destruction of 6,506 films at Mexico City's Cineteca Nacional in March 1982. This wiped out, in one fell swoop, much of the filmic history of that country, adding further weight to urgent calls for global film preservation.

SAG

See **Screen Actors Guild**

Sagebrusher

1920s film jargon for a **Western**, cowboy, or cattleman movie, this refers to the sagebrush plant, *Artemisia Tridentata*, which can grow up to 20ft high, and which has now reached epidemic proportions in some parts of western USA.

Sample Print

An all-inclusive (composite) print that is the last step on the ladder before lab approval allows the final release prints to be struck.

Sanda, Dominique

Sanda was the intellectual film buff's pin-up during the 1970s, and something of a hit with art-house directors too, who saw in her glacial beauty a metaphorical canvas on which their visual and verbal conceits could be played out. She was the last major actress to have an air of mystery about her (excepting, perhaps, Irene Jacob and **Juliette Binoche**), and following her debut in **Robert Bresson's** *Une Femme Douce* (69), in which Bresson perfectly captured the elusive, instinctual intelligence which was her stock in trade, Sanda found herself cast as **Bernardo Bertolucci's** Anna Quadri in *The Conformist* (70), a woman destroyed by the very object of the fascination she so knowingly exerted. The third film in that great early trilogy of hers (she was aged between twenty-one and twenty-three at the time) was **Vittorio De Sica's** *The Garden Of The Finzi-Continis* (71). This proved to be a metaphor as much for the loss of Eden as it was for the lurid attractions of the snake that precipitated its fall.

OTHER KEY FILMS: *Without Apparent Motive* (71); *L'Impossible Objet* (73); *Steppenwolf* (74); *1900* (76); *Eredità Ferramonti* (76); *Caboblanco* (80); *Les Mendiants* (88); *Nobody's Children* [TV Movie] (94); *Garage Olimpo* (99); *Les Rivìeres Pourpress* (00); *The Island Of The Mapmaker's Wife* (00)

Sandbag

A sand-filled canvas counterweight used to steady set scenery and lighting.

Sanders, George

Sanders carried the world-weary, more than marginally cynical sophisticate that he played, often indifferently, in a host of sometimes indifferent films, through into his real life, when he picked up a bottle of pills, downed them, and proceeded to shuffle off his mortal coil in as elegant and flippant a manner as possible, aged sixty-five, thus fulfilling a promise he had made to himself in a typical fit of prescience nearly thirty years earlier. At his best, in **Albert Lewin's** cad-trilogy comprising *The Moon And Sixpence* (42), *The Picture Of Dorian Gray* (45) and *The Private Affairs Of Bel Ami* (47), and in **Joseph L Mankiewicz's** *All About Eve* (50), Sanders played the quintessential, albeit occasionally tender-minded bounder, the concept of which the eighteenth century had inadvertently bequeathed to the twentieth. However, just once, in **Roberto Rossellini's** magnificent *Viaggio In Italia* (53), did he stumble upon a director and a film that managed to cut beneath the glitteringly, sneeringly barbed carapace that he wore as armour, to the livid, inhibited flesh underneath. Sanders never repeated the exercise, and he went on to die, nineteen years later, just as he had chosen to live – by a process of enlightened default.

OTHER KEY FILMS: *Confessions Of A Nazi Spy* (39); *Rebecca* (40); *Foreign Correspondent* (40); *The Lodger* (44); *Hangover Square* (45); *The Ghost And Mrs Muir* (47); *Ivanhoe* (52); *While The City Sleeps* (56); *Village Of The Damned* (60)

KEY LINE:

'Dear World, I am leaving you because I am bored. I am leaving you with your worries. Good luck.' [Sanders's terminal message to the world]

Sarandon, Susan

Sarandon briefly flirted with the big time following her success in **Ridley Scott's** *Thelma And Louise* (91), but it hardly suited her, as she is a movie connoisseur's actress, renowned more for subtlety than glitz, for insight than excitement. Her best roles, but not necessarily her best performances, came early, in **Louis Malle's** *Atlantic City* (80) and in **Paul Mazursky's** *The Tempest* (82). Her best recent performance came in a somewhat flawed film, **Tim Robbins's** *Dead Man Walking* (95). Now something of a feminist icon (her roles have suffered and become a little cloying as a result), she seems a strangely European actress in an American skin.

OTHER KEY FILMS: *The Rocky Horror Picture Show* (75); *The Great Waldo Pepper* (75); *Pretty Baby* (78); *King Of The Gypsies* (79); *The Witches Of Eastwick* (87); *Bull Durham* (88); *The January Man* (89); *Light Sleeper* (92); *Lorenzo's Oil* (92); *Little Women* (94); *The Client* (94); *Dead Man Walking* (95); *Twilight* (98); *The Cradle Will Rock* (99); *Time Of Our Lives* (00); *Igby Goes Down* (01)

Saturation

The quality of intensity in a filmed colour image.

Saura, Carlos

Saura reflects the paradox of Spain as no one else does, for he understands the dual nature of a Spanish people whose temperament requires the presence of both a bullfighter and a bull, as opposed to, say, the English temperament, which of recent years seems to feel that it can get away with just the bull (and a castrated one, at that). Following a series of necessarily elliptical films produced under the totalitarian regime of Francisco Franco, including the internationally successful *La Caza* (66) and *Peppermint Frappé* (67), Saura made a trio of films soon after Franco's death in 1975. *Cría Cuervos* (76), *Elisa, Vida Mía* (77) and *Los Ojos Vendados* (78) all attempted to come to terms with the personal and familial sense of guilt left by even an unconscious participation in Franco's tyranny. Saura is now best known for his flamenco trilogy, incorporating the superb *Blood Wedding* (81), *Carmen* (83), and *El Amor Brujo* (86).

OTHER KEY FILMS: *Los Golfos* (60); *La Madriquera* (69); *El Jardín De Las Delicias* (70); *Ana Y Los Lobos* (73); *El Dorado* (88); *La Noche Oscura* (89); *Ay Carmela!* (90); *Flamenco* (97); *Tango* (98); *Goya En Burdeos* (99); *Buñuecy La Mesa De Rey Sacomón* (01)

'Save The Lights'

Director's cry to cut the lights and wind up work.

SAWA

The people responsible for promoting much of the advertising in US cinemas and abroad – SAWA stands for Screen Advertising World Association.

Sayles, John

One of the best and most literate of director/screenwriters working anywhere today (a modern **Joseph L Mankiewicz**?), Sayles surpassed even himself with his *Lone Star* (96), the finest and most perspicacious film about the American experience to have hit the screens since **Bob Rafelson's** *Five Easy Pieces* (70). A novelist, hack-for-hire, teacher and occasional actor, Sayles funds his films through these peripheral activities, creating, as a result, miracles of integrity in the sea of incipient mire that is Hollywood. *The Return*

Of The Secaucus Seven (81) alerted the alertable to Sayles's talent, while *Lianna* (83) and *Matewan* (87) triumphantly confirmed the sighting. His strange and delightful children's film, *The Secret Of Roan Inish* (94), simply added what appears to be yet another string to this extraordinarily talented man's bow, proving that if sensibility is sufficiently refined, it will become apparent in whatever it touches.

OTHER KEY FILMS: *The Brother From Another Planet* (84); *Eight Men Out* (88); *City Of Hope* (91); *Men With Guns* (97); *Limbo* (99)

Scenario

The original name for a completed screenplay, the term is now occasionally used to denote an outline or screen treatment.

Scene

A somewhat complicated term which can be used to imply anything from one uninterrupted take (if it is important enough), to an entire filmic episode taking place inside or on a particular set, and incorporating all the various shots, set-ups, variations entailed in the screenplay's numbered definition of it.

Scene Bay or Scene Dock

A repository for unwanted or temporarily unused bits of scenery at the back of a studio.

Scenery

A catch-all term to include anything that goes towards clothing, cloaking or furnishing a movie set to produce the desired effect.

Scenic Artist

The person in a film crew (usually a member of the art department) who paints the props, scenery or set.

SCG

A trade union, going under the name of the Screen Cartoonists Guild, the SCG was founded around 1935 in the US to protect the interests of its animation industry members, particularly against such giants as the **Disney** studios.

Schepisi, Fred

Schepisi is now a very successful commercial director who achieved the crossover to the US with his *The Chant Of Jimmy Blacksmith* (78), a harrowing account of tacit racism against both Aboriginals and those of mixed blood in his home country of Australia. On his arrival in North America, Schepisi made one of the most

delightful and unexpected of recent **Westerns** with *Barbarosa* (82), in which Willie Nelson and Gary Busey eat up the screen as two of the most unlikely but touching heroes in horse-opera history. His follow-up features, including the entertaining *Six Degrees Of Separation* (93), have, without exception, been intelligently made and stimulating to watch, marking Schepisi out as one of the more interesting mainstream directors working today.

OTHER KEY FILMS: *Iceman* (84); *Plenty* (85); *Roxanne* (87); *A Cry In The Dark* (88); *The Russia House* (90); *Mr Baseball* (93); *I.Q.* (94); *Fierce Creatures* (97); *Last Orders* (01)

Schlesinger, John

Schlesinger directed one of the finest and most adult of all British films, *Sunday, Bloody Sunday* (71), and arguably one of the best American films, too, in *Midnight Cowboy* (69). With such a reputation behind him, one may be forgiven for feeling a little disappointed at much of his subsequent, large-scale US work, especially when one remembers the delightful *Billy Liar* (63), and his fine evocation of Thomas Hardy's tragic world in *Far From The Madding Crowd* (67). However, he made a steady and remarkable comeback, especially after the horror of *Honky Tonk Freeway* (81), on the smaller scale that suits his fastidious and rarefied talents, with *An Englishman Abroad* (83), *A Question Of Attribution* (91) and *Cold Comfort Farm* (96), all initially made for television but proving so popular that they were given limited cinematic releases in the United States. If he had stuck to what he was good at, rather than being drawn into the commercial and moral morass, Schlesinger's reputation would not have suffered the ups and downs it has, and he would be regarded today, not merely by the few, but by the many, as one of Britain's finest living directors.

OTHER KEY FILMS: *A Kind Of Loving* (62); *Darling* (65); *The Day Of The Locust* (75); *Marathon Man* (76); *Yanks* (79); *The Falcon And The Snowman* (85); *Madame Sousatzka* (88); *Pacific Heights* (90); *The Innocent* (93); *Eye For An Eye* (96); *The Next Best Thing* (00)

Schoedsack, Ernest B

See **Merian C Cooper**

Schoonmaker, Thelma

One of the acknowledged greats of the editing world (and the wife, from 1984 until his death in 1990, of **Michael Powell**), Schoonmaker has worked almost exclusively with **Martin Scorsese**, whom she got to know when they were both freshmen at NYU. Her brilliant work on Michael Wadleigh's famous documentary about the 1969 Woodstock Festival (which she co-edited with Scorsese) followed hard on the heels of her collaboration on Scorsese's first feature, *Who's That Knocking At My Door?* (68), a film which predated her **Oscar**-winning work on *Raging Bull* (80) by a surprising twelve years. Since then she's worked on virtually all the director's films, and her work is notable for both its fluency and technical brilliance. OTHER KEY FILMS: *King Of Comedy* (83); *After Hours* (85); *The Color Of Money* (86); *The Last Temptation Of Christ* (88); *GoodFellas* (90); *Cape Fear* (91); *Age Of Innocence* (93); *Casino* (95); Alison Anders's *Cradle Of My Heart* (96); *Kundun* (97); *Bringing Out The Dead* (99); *Gangs Of New York* (01) [all directed by Martin Scorsese unless otherwise indicated]

Schrader, Paul

Schrader began his film career as a screenwriter, working with **Robert Towne** on **Sydney Pollack's** *The Yakuza* (75). He followed this with a solo credit for **Martin Scorsese's** *Taxi Driver* (76), a film which, not unsurprisingly, afforded him a relatively easy entrée into Hollywood's exclusive writer/director's list. His directional debut, *Blue Collar* (78), was an underrated little film and may just have influenced **Quentin Tarantino's** sassy dialogue for *Reservoir Dogs* (92) and *Pulp Fiction* (94). Since then he has proved himself an edgy, intellectual director, who has always stood on the periphery of the mainstream, choosing subjects that mark him out as a marginal independent. Following his commercial success with *American Gigolo* (80), and his critical success with *Cat People* (82), Schrader has alternated between scriptwriting jobs for other directors, and the making of his own tormented films, which include the excellent *Mishima: A Life In Four Chapters* (85), and the extremely overwrought *The Comfort Of Strangers* (90). A philosophy major and film theoretician, Schrader has the courage to take risks, but his self-awareness can sometimes backfire on him, as he showed in *Light Sleeper* (92), a film supposedly based (let's hope only in part) on one of Schrader's own 'lost weekends'. OTHER KEY FILMS: *Hardcore* (79); Martin Scorsese's *Raging Bull* [script] (80) and *The Last Temptation Of Christ* [script] (88); **Peter Weir's** *Mosquito Coast* [script] (86); *Light Of Day* (87); *Patty Hearst* (88); *Touch* (96); *Forever Mine* (99)

Schroeder, Barbet

Schroeder started off by producing a number of **Eric Rohmer's** early films, including *La Collectioneuse* (66) and *Ma Nuit Chez Maud* (69), before branching out into directing with the curious *More* (69), a film which has aged better than many of its psychedelic contemporaries, and can now be seen as remarkably true to the period of the mid-1960s it is depicting. A number of documentaries followed, before Schroeder, inflamed perhaps by **Bernardo Bertolucci's** *Last Tango In Paris* (73), attempted his own investigation into the subtleties of sexual role-play and power games with *Maîtresse* (76), in which **Gérard Depardieu** gets in over his head following an affair he instigates with professional dominatrix, Bulle Ogier. During the 1980s Schroeder showed his versatility by directing four very different films in succession: *Tricheurs* (84) about gambling; the Charles Bukowski/Henry Chinaski/**Mickey Rourke** curiosity *Barfly* (87); *Reversal Of Fortune* (90), which told of the Claus and Sunny von Bulow case; and *Single White Female* (92), a horror film masquerading as a psychological study. Schroeder's films entertain, stimulate and tease in roughly equal proportions, and unlike those of many of his brasher contemporaries, they grow better with time. OTHER KEY FILMS: *Kiss Of Death* (95); *Before And After* (96); *Desperate Measures* (98); *La Vierge Des Tueurs* (00)

Shtick

A regular routine (or **spiel**) originally used in stage acts, the shtick has now transposed itself to Hollywood (alt. spelling shtik). A comedian's shtick can consist of either a punchline, one particular aspect of the act that the audience have come to expect, or simply a comforting tendency. Its origin is from the German *stück*, meaning piece, and a good example might be Al Jolson's, 'Wait. Wait. You ain't heard nothing yet.'

Schüfftan Process

A trick process, invented by Eugene Shuftan (originally Schüfftan) in the 1920s, by which film is shot at forty-five degrees through a partially stripped mirror, allowing for the simultaneous use of miniature sets (reflected in the mirror) and live action (shot through the mirror), to create a reasonably effective verisimilitude.

Schwarzenegger, Arnold

Big Arnie is not everyone's cup of goulash soup, but what he does, he does very well, and with an entirely commendable lack of restraint. He first

281

showed us how prepossessing he could be on screen in **Bob Rafelson's** excellent *Stay Hungry* (76), and went on to incarnate (as no one else could possibly have done in quite the same way) **John Milius's** *Conan The Barbarian* (82), which is a far better film, along the lines of the **Alexander Korda**-produced *The Thief Of Bagdad* (40), than many otherwise enlightened critics gave it credit for being. With his moulded grin, twinkling eyes and stupendous physique, and despite his recent brush with heart disease, Arnie remains obstinately larger-than-life, and his performances in **James Cameron's** *The Terminator* (84), **Paul Verhoeven's** *Total Recall* (90) and, in particular, Cameron's follow-up in the Terminator series, *Terminator 2: Judgment Day* (91), are very nearly perfect examples of their kind – heroic, self-conscious, eager, and at the same time wryly amused both at the vagaries of the world and at a determined person's ability to manipulate them. OTHER KEY FILMS: *Pumping Iron* (77); *Commando* (85); *Predator* (87); *Red Heat* (88); *Last Action Hero* (93); *True Lies* (94); *Eraser* (96); *Batman & Robin* (97); *End Of Days* (99); *The 6th Day* (00); *Collateral Damage* (01)

KEY LINE:
John Connor: 'Jesus! You were going to kill that guy.' Big Arnie: 'Of course. I'm a Terminator.' [*Terminator 2: Judgment Day*]

Science Fiction

One of the oldest of all cinema genres (**Georges Méliès** dazzled audiences in 1898 with his *L'Homme Dans La Lune*, again in 1900 with his *Mésaventures D'Un Aéronaute*, and then in 1902 with his version of Jules Verne's *Le Voyage Dans La Lune*), in almost all cases science-fiction film is simply a transposition of other ideas and genres into space, the future, or both. Science-fiction movies have included horror films (**Ridley Scott's** *Alien* (79)), Westerns (Peter Hyams's *Outland* (81) was a virtual remake of **Fred Zinnemann's** *High Noon* (52)), fairytales (**George Lucas's** *Star Wars* series, from 1977 onwards) and even Shakespeare (Fred McLeod Wilcox's *Forbidden Planet* (56) was a reworking of *The Tempest*). Sci-fi movies tend to come in waves, usually allied to some major technical innovation in special effects, one prime mover being **Stanley Kubrick's** *2001: A Space Odyssey* (68), which preceded the moon landing by one year. However, it was undoubtedly the prodigious success of George Lucas's *Star Wars* (77) that really brought science fiction to a wider audience and made it acceptable.

Best Science-fiction Films

Jack Arnold's *The Incredible Shrinking Man* (57); **Luc Besson's** *The Fifth Element* (97); Gordon Douglas's *Them!* (54); Richard Fleischer's *Soylent Green* (73); **Jean-Luc Godard's** *Alphaville* (65); Val Guest's *The Quatermass Experiment* (55); Peter Hyams's *Outland* (81); L Q Jones's *A Boy And His Dog* (74); Philip Kaufman's *Invasion Of The Body Snatchers* (78); **Stanley Kubrick's** *2001: A Space Odyssey* (68); **Fritz Lang's** *Metropolis* (27) and *The Girl In The Moon* (29); Wolf Rilla's *Village Of The Damned* (60); Christian Nyby's *The Thing* (51); **Ken Russell's** *Altered States* (81); **Ridley Scott's** *Blade Runner* (82); **Don Siegel's** *Invasion Of The Body Snatchers* (56); **Steven Spielberg's** *Close Encounters Of The Third Kind* (77) and *E.T. The Extra Terrestrial* (82); **Paul Verhoeven's** *Robocop* (87) and *Total Recall* (90); **Robert Wise's** *The Day The Earth Stood Still* (51)

Scoop

A large floodlight that happens to share its shape with a flour scoop – thus the name.

Score

When used in the context of film, a score means a specially written musical accompaniment to a specific motion picture, designed to highlight and aggrandise emotion and to reinforce the sense of mood or place.

Scoring Stage

The sound stage upon which recording musicians sit while the film their music will eventually accompany plays in full view of the conductor – this is in order that both the conductor and the film's director may co-ordinate timings.

Scorsese, Martin

Scorsese is an enthusiast. It comes through in the way he talks (hardly stopping to draw breath) and in the way he makes his movies – passionately, with one wary eye on the past, measuring himself, a little like Ernest Hemingway in his famous letter to Maxwell Perkins, trading punches with the greats. Scorsese, to give him credit, is a more humble man than Hemingway, but he is possibly less talented too, and one can sometimes become aware, in his most prestigious films, of a process of stretching, as though he knows that he is busy composing his own epitaph and wants it to be a good one. Perhaps Scorsese's greatest gift to cinema is not so much his work as his generosity – he is a man who values others, and goes out of his way to encourage them, and he has rescued one or two reputations, **Michael Powell's** amongst them, which might otherwise have languished in the anteroom of fame. In purely filmic terms, Scorsese's real talent lies in his capacity to mould dialogue, movement and sound into one fluid, cinematic whole, and he achieves this effect most consistently with *GoodFellas* (90), which, despite its unpleasant subject matter, still succeeds in rising above its bitter roots in a marvellous series of inspired set pieces.

OTHER KEY FILMS: *Mean Streets* (73); *Alice Doesn't Live Here Anymore* (75); *Taxi Driver* (76); *New York New York* (78); *Raging Bull* (80); *King Of Comedy* (83); *After Hours* (85); *The Last Temptation Of Christ* (88); *Cape Fear* (91); *The Age Of Innocence* (93); *Casino* (95); *Kundun* (97); *Bringing Out The Dead* (99); *Gangs Of New York* (01)

Scott, Randolph

Scott was the tall-riding, slow-drawling star of the magnificent Ranown cycle of **Budd Boetticher** horse operas (the name was an elision of Scott's Christian name and producer Harry Joe Brown's surname) but Scott, who was born in 1898 and lived to be ninety years old, was a very different **Western** hero from the younger, brasher **John Wayne**, who was born nine years later. One always believed that Scott had *come* from somewhere, and that he would eventually move on once the action was over. His wonderful, deeply human films were always in passing; transitional movies, so to speak. Scott never explained himself, but let people think what they wanted, and if they came to the right decision, that was OK by him, and if they came to the wrong one – well, they took their own chances. His philosophy was that a man could make up his own mind – ride his own road – and any time he wanted he could change it. It's hard to believe that Scott was already sixty-two when he and Boetticher made their final film together, *Comanche Station* (60), and that it was to be another two years before **Sam Peckinpah** asked him to buckle on his spurs one final time, together with co-star **Joel McCrea**, for the elegiac *Ride The High Country* (62). A great man, and a great legacy – in many ways Scott *was* the myth of the West. Or how it should have been.

OTHER KEY FILMS: *Roberta* (35); *Last Of The Mohicans* (36); *Frontier Marshall* (39); *Jesse James* (39); *Western Union* (41); *Captain Kidd* (45); *Albuquerque* (47); *Santa Fe* (51); *Carson City* (52); *The Bounty*

The connoisseur's cowboy – Randolph Scott protecting the range

Hunter (54); *Lawless Street* (55); *Ten Wanted Men* (55); *Seven Men From Now* (56); *The Tall T* (57); *Decision At Sundown* (57); *Buchanan Rides Alone* (58); *Ride Lonesome* (59); *Westbound* (59)

Scott, Ridley

From his starting point in British television commercials, Scott has risen to become one of the most trusted names on the Hollywood directors' circuit. Since his wonderfully assured debut in *The Duellists* (77), through *Alien* (79), *Blade Runner* (82) and *Thelma And Louise* (91), most of his films have hit the mark both visually and verbally. When they do miss – apart from the excruciatingly embarrassing *GI Jane* (97) – they always miss worthily, and never for want of trying. His recent $100,000,000 blockbuster *Gladiator* (00) has revived yet another neglected Hollywood genre –

the 'sword, vandals and sandals' epic. Even if it is historically inaccurate – Scott has Marcus Aurelius signing letters with a wooden pen and passing them over to his secretary, whereas paper only came to Europe from China in around the year 600 – it is always entertaining.

OTHER KEY FILMS: *Legend* (85); *Someone To Watch Over Me* (87); *Black Rain* (89); *1492: Conquest Of Paradise* (92); *White Squall* (96); *Hannibal* (01)

Scott-Thomas, Kristin

She's a curiously passive actress, but her very passivity contains the emotional core that is her forte, for Scott-Thomas has a rare capacity for drama, a talent which harks back to such great screen performers as **Bette Davis** and **Barbara Stanwyck**. She can play tough, as in her magnificently horrid Brenda Last in Charles Sturridge's *A Handful Of Dust* (88), a performance so accurate that it raised hisses in certain French cinemas, and she can play tender, as in her Katherine Clifton in **Anthony Minghella's** *The English Patient* (96). Hers is a face and a technique which will age well, and one would like to see her really stretched now that she is in her prime – as Emma Bovary perhaps, or, better still, as Lawrence Durrell's Constance, a book and a character that cry out to be filmed.

OTHER KEY FILMS: *The Tenth Man* (88); *Bitter Moon* (92); *Four Weddings And A Funeral* 94); *An Unforgettable Summer* (94); *Angels & Insects* (95); *Richard III* (95); *Le Confessionale* (97); *The Horse Whisperer* (98); *Souvenir* (98); *Random Hearts* (99); *Up At The Villa* (00); *Gosford Park* (01)

Scouting

The part of the pre-production process that entails searching for suitable locations for a forthcoming film.

Scraper

The tiny scraping tool that is used by editors to thin the emulsion on two pieces of film so that the splicing glue will take a firm hold.

Scratches

Scratches on positive film are usually caused by misuse, age, or faulty projection, and show up on the screen as thin black lines. Scratches on negative film show up as white lines, and are far more serious, especially if such scratches occur on a **release negative**, from which **release prints** are made.

Scratch Print

See **Slop Print**

Screen

The expanse of material, usually painted matte white, onto which films are projected in a cinema, movie theatre or other venue. The classic-sized screen had a width-to-height ratio of approximately 4:3 (1.33:1), bringing it very close to a square shape, but following the introduction of wide-screen and **Cinerama** processes during the 1950s, the size of major screens increased considerably, leading to a variant norm of between 1.85:1 and 2.55:1, giving more of a rectangular appearance.

Screen Actors Guild

Established in 1933, the SAG is the foremost screen performers union in the USA. The Screen Extras Guild, which was established in 1945 as a separate entity, now forms part of it.

Screening Room

This refers to a room containing a screen, a projector and a few comfy chairs for the private screening of **rushes**, **workprints**, or the finished feature film before a select audience who have an interest in either the finished or the ongoing project. All major studios have their own screening rooms, ranging from the sparse to the luxurious, with a good example featuring in **Stanley Donen** and **Gene Kelly's** *Singin' In The Rain* (52), where the fact that Jean Hagen's Lily Lamont can neither sing nor, to all intents and purposes, speak, is forcibly brought home to Millard Mitchell's R F Simpson, the embattled producer of her previously silent movies, during a preview screening.

Screenplays

The creative raw material from which films are made, screenplays vary from between about 110 and 130 pages of dialogue and directions, and are subject to change right up to, and often beyond, the start of filming. Each country has their own standard format for the look of a screenplay, with the US format stipulating letter-sized paper (8.5 by 11 in) inside card covers, three-hole punched and held together with brass eyelets. Copyrights are customarily registered, for a fee, with the **Writers Guild Of America**.

Screen Test

An audition, held in front of the cameras, in order to ascertain whether an actor or actress is suitable for a part in a forthcoming feature film.

Screenwriter

The third most important category in the making of a film, after the director and the actors (although you'd sometimes not believe it), the screenwriter is responsible for writing and then rewriting the original script, until both the director and the producers feel that it warrants shooting. Screenwriters tend to fall into a number of different camps: there is the director/screenwriter, like **John Sayles**, **Billy Wilder** or **Richard Brooks**; the predominantly adaptive screenwriter, like **Ben Hecht**, **Dudley Nichols** or **Charles Bennett**; and the original screenwriter, like **William Goldman**, **Philip Yordan** or **Curt Siodmak**, an ilk that prefers to work on its own ideas but will adapt when necessary. Screenwriters often have little or nothing to do with the actual shooting of a film, the bulk of their work being done many months, and sometimes years, before shooting begins. In the days when the great studios ruled the roost, screenwriters were on salary, and were expected to tap away eclectically (and pretty much indiscriminately) to make up their hours. In modern Hollywood it is far more normal for a screenwriter to work independently, sometimes in a team with one or two others, and to be prepared to **pitch** their script (during what often amounts to a bare two-minute verbal window) at an apparently uninterested studio executive, in order to secure what may well prove to be a lucrative contract. See **Script Doctors**

KEY LINES:

'But you don't go into writing to make money anyhow. If you want to make money, sell condoms to China. One per customer and you will be rich.' [Screenwriter Curt Siodmak – **Jacques Tourneur's** *I Walked With A Zombie* [co-script] (44) and *Berlin Express* [story] (48) – on his chosen profession]

'Now the writer doesn't get any respect. You are treated like a hired hand, worse, like dirt. It is like: The toilet is clogged up. Unclog it and please get out as fast as you can and try not to track up the rug.' [Arnold Schulman, who scripted **Richard Attenborough's** *The Chorus Line* (85) and co-scripted **Francis Ford Coppola's** *Tucker: A Man And His Dream* (88), on the gradual change in studio perceptions after the early 1970s]

Screen Writers Guild

See **Writers Guild Of America**

Screwball Comedies

The Golden Age of depression-busting and war fatigue-alleviating screwball comedies came during the 1930s and 1940s, incorporating fast-talking, fast-gagging, often ludicrous plots, in which eccentric characters, notably out of synch with the status quo, get themselves into ever increasing spirals of inspired mayhem. Screwball stars included **Cary Grant**, **Jean Harlow**, **Katharine Hepburn**, **William Powell**, **Carole Lombard**, **Fredric March**, **Myrna Loy** and **Claudette Colbert**, and they were directed, as often as not, by **Ernst Lubitsch**, **Preston Sturges**, **Frank Capra** or **Howard Hawks**.

KEY FILMS: Ernst Lubitsch's *Trouble In Paradise* (32), *Ninotchka* (39), and *To Be Or Not To Be* (42); Preston Sturges's *The Lady Eve* (41), *Sullivan's Travels* (41), *The Palm Beach Story* (42) and *The Miracle Of Morgan's Creek* (44); Frank Capra's *It Happened One Night* (34), *You Can't Take It With You* (38), and *Arsenic And Old Lace* (44); Howard Hawks's *Twentieth Century* (34), *Bringing Up Baby* (38), *His Girl Friday* (40), *I Was A Male War Bride* (49) and *Monkey Business* (52); Gregory La Cava's *My Man Godfrey* (36); Leo McCarey's *The Awful Truth* (37); **William Wellman's** *Nothing Sacred* (37); **George Cukor's** *Holiday* (38); **René Clair's** *The Ghost Goes West* (36) and *I Married A Witch* (42)

Scribe

A metal editing tool used to scratch **cue marks** onto film.

Scrim

Diaphanous screen used to diffuse or soften the light from studio lamps.

Script

See **Screenplay**

Script Doctors

These are the screenwriters who are called in when a script is in crisis, to rewrite, sort out and generally save the day. Often they will be paid a daily, or bulk rate, and their names will rarely appear on the credits, unless their input on the script becomes so obvious and so influential that their agents can no longer sit idly by and see their client's work claimed by another.

KEY LINE:

'The present generation is now educated visually, not literarily as we were…looking at pictures now – and they make very good pictures – the story often falls apart.' [Screenwriter Curt Siodmak – Felix Feist's *Donovan's Brain* (53) was based on his novel – on illiteracy and the need for comprehensive editing]

285

Seberg, Jean

Dead from a drug overdose at forty, Seberg always promised more than she delivered in terms of acting ability. **Jean-Luc Godard** was the one director who really used her well, in his 1959 film *À Bout De Souffle* [*Breathless*], while **Robert Rossen** got rave reviews from the *Cahiers du Cinéma* for his direction of her in *Lilith* (64). Torn between the commercial cinema and her extreme political views (she was a supporter of the Black Panthers), her career had almost totally petered out by the time of her death in 1979.

OTHER KEY FILMS: *Bonjour Tristesse* (57); *Five Day Lover* (61); *A Fine Madness* (66); *Paint Your Wagon* (69); *Pendulum* (69)

Second Feature

The **B-movie**, or bargain basement part of a double bill.

Second Unit

A self-contained film crew whose job it is to film background locations, establishing shots, large-scale battle scenes and any other material not directly involving the principal stars.

Second-unit Director

Usually an expert in directing and marshalling large numbers of extras and prop resources in large-scale action sequences, the second-unit director is answerable to the director and producer, who are likely to insist that all film shot by the second-unit crew matches, in tone and tenor, the work in progress.

SEG

See **Screen Actors Guild**

Sellers, Peter

An inspired comic actor with a notably difficult and complex personality, Sellers learnt his trade the hard way, as part of his parents' music-hall comedy act, and then as the immortal Bluebottle in the long-running 1950s BBC radio show, *The Goons*. Sellers began his assault on the big screen in a number of **Ealing Comedies**, including **Alexander Mackendrick's** *The Ladykillers* (55), and these were followed by the **Boulting Brothers'** *I'm All Right Jack* (59) and Sidney Gilliat's *Only Two Can Play* (62). His big break came with **Stanley Kubrick's** *Dr Strangelove: Or How I Learned To Stop Worrying And Love The Bomb* (63), in which he played not only Group Capt. Lionel Mandrake (to whom **Sterling Hayden's** Gen. Jack D Ripper confides his 'precious bodily fluids' theory),

but also long-suffering President Merkin Muffley and the insane, wheelchair-bound, false-hand-possessing Dr Strangelove, whose ill-concealed devotion to the Führer is only eclipsed by his glee at the thought of repeopling a world devastated by a nuclear holocaust he has been largely instrumental in fomenting. Sellers's most lucrative creation was the bumbling Inspector Clouseau, protagonist of five and a half feature films – five and a half, because one of them, **Blake Edwards's** *The Trail Of The Pink Panther* (82), which was released three years after Sellers's death from a heart attack, consisted only of out-takes. Sellers's finest performance, and the one which brought him his only **Oscar**, came late, as Chauncey (Chance), the simple gardener turned Presidential adviser and celebrity in **Hal Ashby's** *Being There* (79).

OTHER KEY FILMS: *The Smallest Show On Earth* (57); *The Mouse That Roared* (59); *Waltz Of The Toreadors* (62); *Lolita* (62); *The Wrong Arm Of The Law* (63); *The Pink Panther* (64); *A Shot In The Dark* (64); *What's New Pussycat?* (65); *After The Fox* (66); *The Party* (68); *Hoffman* (70); *There's A Girl In My Soup* (70); *The Return Of The Pink Panther* (75); *The Pink Panther Strikes Again* (76); *Revenge Of The Pink Panther* (78)

Peter Sellers as Dr Strangelove (having a little trouble with his saluting arm) in Stanley Kubrick's Dr Strangelove: Or How I Learned To Stop Worrying And Love The Bomb (63)

Selsyn Motor

Selsyn is an abbreviation of self-synchronising motor, a mechanism designed to run two independent motion picture apparati (a camera and a sound recorder, say, or a camera and a projector) simultaneously.

Selznick, David O

One of the greatest of all Hollywood producers, Selznick is renowned both for his demented single-mindedness in bringing Margaret Mitchell's best-selling novel *Gone With The Wind* to the screen in 1939, and for inveigling England's **Alfred Hitchcock** over to Hollywood to direct *Rebecca* (40). **George Cukor's** magnificent *David Copperfield* (35) was another of his babies, as was **King Vidor's** wildly over-the-top but astonishingly successful *Duel In The Sun* (47). A renowned workaholic and worrier, Selznick produced his final film for director Charles Vidor; a remake of Hemmingway's *A Farewell To Arms* (57).

OTHER KEY FILMS: George Cukor's *A Bill Of Divorcement* (32); **Merian C Cooper** and Ernest B Schoedsack's *King Kong* (33); Clarence Brown's *Anna Karenina* (35); **Jack Conway's** *A Tale Of Two Cities* (35); **William Wellman's** *Nothing Sacred* (37); John Cromwell's *The Prisoner Of Zenda* (37); **Alfred Hitchcock's** *Spellbound* (45); **Carol Reed's** *The Third Man* (49); **Michael Powell** and **Emeric Pressburger's** *Gone To Earth* (50)

KEY LINE:

'The son-in-law also rises.' [Upon Selznick's marriage to **Louis B Mayer's** daughter]

Senior

A powerful 5,000-watt spotlight used to highlight specific performers or specific areas of a movie set.

Sennett, Mack

Sennett, together with his producer/director rival **Hal Roach**, were the two silent era kings of slapstick comedy. Sennett's contribution included **The Keystone Cops**, the Sennett Bathing Beauties, and an astonishing series of comedies starring the likes of **Charlie Chaplin**, **Harry Langdon**, Mabel Normand, and the ill-fated **'Fatty' Arbuckle**. Sennett's intense sense of fun did not outlast the silent era in terms of film productions, but his greatest comedies continue to give immense pleasure to those still fortunate enough to possess a simple heart.

KEY FILMS: *Mabel At The Wheel* (14); *The Little Teacher* (15); *Home Talent* (21); *The Lion's Roar* (28); *The Chumps* (30)

Sensitometry

The process by which the differing light responses of film emulsions are tested under laboratory conditions.

Sensurround

Universal brought out Sensurround in 1974 to accompany Mark Robson's awful *Earthquake* (74). The system was meant to thrill the audience by simulating the shaking and trembling activity of an earthquake or a battle, but it failed to catch on, and movie theatres which had invested in the fifteen or twenty huge speakers and the accompanying amplifier kit, were rather left with egg on their faces.

Best Sentimental Films

Gabriel Axel's *Babette's Feast* (87); Jean Becker's *Les Enfants Du Marais* (99); **Frank Capra's** *It's A Wonderful Life* (46); John Cromwell's *The Enchanted Cottage* (45); Julien Duvivier's *Poil De Carotte* (32) and *Sous Le Ciel De Paris* (50); **John Ford's** *Three Godfathers* (48); **Akira Kurosawa's** *Dersu Uzala* (74); **Ernst Lubitsch's** *Heaven Can Wait* (43); Robert Mulligan's *Summer of 42* (70); **Jean Renoir's** *The River* (50); **Bertrand Tavernier's** *Un Dimanche A La Campagne* (84) and *Daddy Nostalgie* [*These Foolish Things*] (90); Giuseppe Tornatore's *Cinema Paradiso* (89)

287

Sequel

A follow-up, or series of follow-ups, to a successful film which usually retains part or all of the original feature's name – thus **Francis Ford Coppola's** *The Godfather* (72), *The Godfather Part II* (74) and *The Godfather Part III* (90). The **James Bond** films are an exception to the rule, all having different names (similar only in their archness), with the producers Harry Saltzman (until 1974) and Albert 'Cubby' Broccoli relying on a heavy advertising budget, habit, and word of mouth to sell their franchise to the public.

Sequence

A succession of scenes inside a movie that link together to form an identifiable episode within the larger whole.

Serials

Serials often formed the lesser part of a double or triple bill at movie theatres, spanning the period from just before the First World War right up to the advent of mass television in the 1950s. They comprised anything up to twelve episodes, each traditionally ending in a 'cliff-hanging' situation (hence the adoption of the term 'cliff-hanger'), in which the desire to know what happened to their hero or heroine was adjudged sufficient by the producers to bring the punter back into the cinema the following week. Modern audiences, inured by television to both having their cake and eating it, no longer have the patience to wait a week for an often fake resolution. Modern television serials, therefore, while retaining the same lead characters week after week, tend to dispense with beginning, middle, and end stories, relying instead on celebrity power to hold their audience share steady – although soap-opera writers have been known to descend to old serial tricks to boost flagging audience figures, most notably in the 1985 'Who Shot JR?' storyline in *Dallas*.

Series

A series is essentially a sequence of separate films using a selection of the same stars and characters in the principal roles. Examples might be the *Tarzan* series, with **Johnny Weissmuller**, spanning 1932-48, and the British *Carry On* series of comedies, starring the likes of Kenneth Williams, Jim Dale, Sid James, Hattie Jacques, Barbara Windsor and Joan Sims, and which spanned the years 1958-78, with a somewhat belated add-on in 1992.

Serrault, Michel

An outstanding screen actor and one of France's most successful exports if one takes into account his role of Albin/Zaza in Edouard Molinaro and Georges Lautner's *La Cage Aux Folles* trilogy (78, 80 and 85), Serrault has an enormous range which spans his Raymond in **Henri-Georges Clouzot's** sensational *Les Diaboliques* (55), to the title role in Christian De Chalonge's grotesque *Dr Petiot* (90). Serrault's greatest performance came as the lawyer, Jérôme Martinaud, in Claude Miller's *Garde À Vue* (81), accused of the rape and murder of two schoolgirls by police inspectors Guy Marchand and **Lino Ventura**, and for which he won a formidably well-deserved César.

OTHER KEY FILMS: *Candide* (60); *King Of Hearts* (66); *Le Viager* (72); *Buffet Froid* (79); *Mortelle Randonée* (83); *Le Miraculé* (87); *Ennemis Intimes* (87); *Haute Époque* (94); *Nelly And Monsieur Arnaud* (95); *Rien Ne Va Plus* (97); *Le Libertin* (00); *Une Hirondelle A Fait Le Printemps* (00); *Belphégor – Le Fantôme Du Louvre* (01); *Vajont* (01)

Set

A specially constructed interior or exterior setting, designed to mimic a real or imagined locale on which the action of a feature film is played out, and which conforms to a visual, filmic, but not necessarily factual, truth.

Set Decorator

The individual in charge of carrying out the construction of film sets conceived of by the **art director**, and planned and sketched by the **set designer**.

Set Designer

Second only to the **art director** in the production crew hierarchy, the set designer is responsible for planning and laying out the art director's conceptions on paper.

Set Estimator

The individual whose task it is to cost the **art director's** concepts and the **set designer's** plans for all the sets later to be built and used as background on a motion picture shoot.

Set-up

The placement of everything from the actors, to the lighting, to the props, to the camera, before a movie scene is shot. It can also apply to the simple positioning of a camera.

Seventh Art

Italian-born theoretician and poet Ricciotto Canudo coined the expression in 1916 as a means of indicating that the art of making motion pictures was equal, in creative terms, to the art of drawing, sculpting, painting, architecture, music and prosody.

Sex

Sex has been used since the very beginnings of cinema to pull in the punter, with **Thomas Edison's** *The Kiss*, featuring May Irwin and John C Rice in carnal embrace, wowing an early clientele at Koster and Bial's Music Hall on 20 April 1896, and Eugène Pirou's *Le Coucher De La Mariée* [*The New Bride's Bed-Time*] (1896) sending all-male audiences into paroxysms of delight in the private clubs and taverns in which it was shown. Countless films purporting to show the iniquities of the white-slave trade appeared following Ole Olsen's *The White Slave* (07), in which a carrier pigeon saves our heroine from being ravaged by adepts at a riotous party, and it was not until the coming of **Will H Hays** and his production code in 1930 that the reins of censorship really tightened, forcing sex either underground or into euphemism. It re-emerged (having, of course, never been away) during the 1940s in France, the 1950s in Sweden and the 1960s in the rest of the Western world, undoing the good work of countless directors who, forced by censorship into using their imaginations, drove cinema forward into a maturity it has since lost. Now it is easier to show copulation rather than to suggest it, as was so eloquently achieved by **Paul Henreid's** kiss of **Bette Davis's** sleeping face in Irving Rapper's *Now, Voyager* (42). It seems aeons ago when a view of Virginia Valli showing her exquisitely shod foot to a patent leather-booted **William Powell** in **Howard Hawks's** *Paid To Love* (27) could inflame even the most jaded of passions.

Sexploitation Films

Films that pull in an audience by relying on their capacity to titillate a viewer rather than on any intrinsic worth.

SFX

An onomatopoeic abbreviation (one could hardly call it an acronym) for **special effects**.

Sharif, Omar

One would imagine that Sharif thoroughly enjoyed his time as a romantic lead in such European films as **David Lean's** *Doctor Zhivago* (65) and Terence Young's *Mayerling* (69), following his stunning first introduction to non-Arab audiences in Lean's *Lawrence Of Arabia* (62), but one suspects that his subsequent bridge-playing and horse-racing career have given him far more satisfaction. A former Copt who converted to Islam, Sharif would possibly concur with the view that his strengths lie in his celebrity status rather than in his acting abilities, but, that said, he was more than adequate in **James Clavell's** *The Last Valley* (70) and **John Frankenheimer's** *The Horseman* (71).

OTHER KEY FILMS: *The Night Of The Generals* (67); *Funny Girl* (68); *Mackenna's Gold* (69); *The Tamarind Seed* (74); *Funny Lady* (75); *Bloodline* (79); *Green Ice* (81); *Top Secret!* (84); *The Rainbow Thief* (90); *Heaven Before I Die* (97); *The 13th Warrior* (99); *The Patrol Officer* (01)

Sharp

A filmed image or sequence of images that is both well contrasted and clearly focused.

Shepperton Studios

See **Pinewood Studios**

Sherlock Holmes

Holmes was the creation of novelist/physician Arthur Conan Doyle (1859-1930), and most of the sixty-eight novels and stories he wrote about his hero were intended for a weekly magazine audience, forcing Doyle to keep the thrills and surprises coming, rather than to save them for the very end of the piece. This accords perfectly with the needs of the cinema and of the film screenplay, which is normally written in a three-act sequence, and the stories have proved immensely popular with movie audiences since the very inception of the medium. Holmes's first cinematic outing came only thirteen years after the famous detective's first appearance in print, in the movie short, *Sherlock Holmes Baffled* (1900). Holmes has been played by upwards of eighty actors since then, in something approaching 250 films, but his most convincing incarnation (even though Holmes found himself unwillingly modernised for wartime audiences) was by **Basil Rathbone**, with Nigel Bruce as his endearingly bumbling Dr Watson. The most successful and intelligent long-term pairing came on television, with Jeremy Brett's Holmes beautifully complemented by David Burke's intelligent (for once) Watson.

OTHER KEY FILMS: Buster Keaton's *Sherlock Jr* (24); Sidney Lanfield's *The Hound Of The Baskervilles* (39); **Billy Wilder's** *The Private Life Of Sherlock Holmes* (70); Herbert Ross's *The Seven Percent Solution* (76); **Disney's** *Basil, The Great Mouse Detective* (86); **Barry Levinson's** *Young Sherlock Holmes* (86); Fraser C Heston's *The Crucifer Of Blood* (91)

Shoot

The act of using a motion picture camera to capture a sequence of images that will eventually be contained within a feature, short or documentary.

Shooting Call

A sheet of flimsy pinned to the callboard giving notice of who will be needed, and when, on a film set.

Shooting Company

Another name for a film crew working on a specific motion picture project.

Shooting Log

The movie equivalent of a ship's log, kept by a member of the camera crew and delineating the equipment to be used and the film to be exposed during that day's shooting.

Shooting Outline

A very rough outline of what is and what is not to be shot during the making of a feature film, the shooting outline is available as a rough guide in the temporary absence of the shooting script.

Shooting Ratio

This refers to the simple ratio of the amount of film shot during the making of a feature to the amount of film used in the completed product. For example, **Fritz Lang** shot 1,960,000 feet of film during the making of *Metropolis* (26), which was reduced to 13,165 feet for the finished product – a ratio of 148.8:1. **D W Griffith's** *Broken Blossoms* (19), on the other hand, lost only 200 of its 5,200 feet of exposed film, to leave a length of 5,000 feet for the finished article – an astonishing ratio of 1.04:1.

Shooting Schedule

A working schedule that delineates when and where scenes are to be filmed and which actors and crew will be needed for them.

Shooting Script

This is the final script – the one that will end up as the shot film – complete with numbered scenes to include the dialogue, the camera set-ups and anything else deemed apposite by the director.

Shorts

See **Film Shorts**

Shot

A non-stop take, using one camera, and following a line of action that does not necessitate any new set-up, a shot can be as little as a single frame, or can last up to ten minutes (the length of a reel of film), as happened in **Alfred Hitchcock's** *Rope* (48), an experiment by the master in which the finished film consisted of eight separate ten-minute takes, incorporating only a single cut.

Showscan

An **SFX** process, invented by **Douglas Trumbull**, which gives something approaching a 3-D effect (without the need for glasses) by relying on a massive 70mm gauge of film run at two and a half times the normal speed and projected onto a curved screen.

Shrinkage

Shrinkage occurs when film dries out through contact with or proximity to excess heat, and leads to a diminution of quality and a danger of shredding or tearing.

Shutter

A camera shutter closes to protect unexposed film, and opens to expose it.

Shuttle

The mechanism that shunts the film inside a camera forward, and then holds it in place during exposure.

Siegel, Don

Siegel is a frequently underrated director whose rite of passage came as a lowly member of the **Warner Brothers' insert** department, where he even got to do a little work on *Casablanca* (42). His first feature, *The Verdict* (46), starring **Sydney Greenstreet**, was a first-class *film noir*, and Siegel went on to direct the critically acclaimed semi-documentary *Riot In Cell Block 11* (54), and the seminal *Invasion Of The Body Snatchers* (56), one of the best of all **science-fiction** films. He teased out **Elvis Presley's** finest screen performance in *Flaming Star* (60), and later directed his friend, **Clint Eastwood**, in the curious but effective *The Beguiled* (71). His best late-career thriller is *Charley Varrick* (73), with **Walter Matthau**, but he also excelled directing **John Wayne's** subtle and moving swansong movie, *The Shootist* (76).
OTHER KEY FILMS: *The Big Steal* (49); *Hell Is For Heroes* (62); *The Killers* (64); *Madigan* (68); *Dirty Harry* (71); *Telefon* (77); *Escape From Alcatraz* (79)
KEY LINE:
'If you had fought in a platoon in Vietnam, Don would have been the kind of lieutenant you'd have hoped you were lucky enough to have leading your scared ass.' [Sterling Silliphant, who scripted *The Lineup* (57) and *Telefon* (77) for Siegel]

Sight and Sound

Founded in 1932, the London-based *Sight and Sound* magazine is the longest-lasting and most prestigious of the serious cinema reviews, predating France's *Cahiers du Cinéma* by nearly twenty years.

Signoret, Simone

Similar to **Shelley Winters** in build (both began as slender blondes, then somewhat ballooned), Signoret tempered her masochism with intelligence, particularly in such early films as Jacques Becker's *Casque D'Or* (52), and **Henri-Georges Clouzot's** *Les Diaboliques* (54), in which she played Nicole Horner, the murderous mistress of Paul Meurisse's cold-blooded schoolteacher, Michel Delasalle. Following her **Oscar** success as Alice Aisgill in Jack Clayton's *Room At The Top* (58), Signoret moved on to character roles in her later films, most notably as Auschwitz-survivor Rosa in Moshe Mizrahi's *Madame Rosa* (77), for which she won a César. She enjoyed (endured?) a tempestuous thirty-four-year marriage to honorary Frenchman **Yves Montand**, with whom she co-starred in a number of films, and whose serial infidelity with the likes of **Marilyn Monroe** she seemed to take, if not in her stride, then at the very least philosophically.

OTHER KEY FILMS: *La Ronde* (50); *Thérèse Raquin* (53); *Naked Autumn* (61); *L'Armée Des Ombres* (69); *L'Aveu* (70); *Chère Inconnue* (80); *L'Étoile Du Nord* (82)

Silent Bit

A small film role (often a walk-on part) with no lines.

Silent Film

The era of silent film spanned the period from the invention of **Thomas Alva Edison's Kinetoscope** in 1889, and his **Kinetograph** in 1891, to the formal coming of sound, in the guise of Alan Crosland's *The Jazz Singer*, in 1927. During this period approximately 150,000 films were made around the world, of which probably between 20,000 and 25,000 actually survive.

Best Silent Films

Luis Buñuel and Salvador Dalí's *Un Chien Andalou* (29); **Charles Chaplin's** *The Gold Rush* (25) and *City Lights* (30); Benjamin Christensen's *Haxan* (21); **Carl Dreyer's** *The Passion Of Joan Of Arc* (28); **Sergei Eisenstein's** *Battleship Potemkin* (25); **Abel Gance's** *Napoléon* (25); **D W Griffith's** *The Birth Of A Nation* (15) and *Intolerance* (16); **Buster Keaton's** *The General* (26); **Fritz Lang's** *Metropolis* (27); **F W Murnau's** *Faust* (26) and *Sunrise* (27); **G W Pabst's** *Pandora's Box* (29); **Erich von Stroheim's** *Foolish Wives* (21) and *Greed* (23)

Silent Print

A positive print from a processed film (a.k.a. **picture print**).

Silent Speed

Silent film may be projected at a slower rate than normal (of anywhere between twelve and twenty frames per second) when it is not accompanied by a soundtrack, which requires a 24 fps projection rate.

Silhouette

If a subject is excessively backlit it will appear on the screen outlined in black, with little detail visible. **Francis Ford Coppola** used the technique to notable effect on the now-massive **Marlon Brando**, as Colonel Kurtz, in *Apocalypse Now* (79).

Simmons, Jean

Simmons was a big star during the 1950s, and one of the select few British actresses (**Elizabeth Taylor** and **Deborah Kerr** notwithstanding) to manage the tricky crossover to Hollywood, which she did accompanied by her then husband, **Stewart Granger**. She was arguably one of the most beautiful women ever to grace the big screen, and her career was a distinguished one, with notable parts, during her *annus mirabilis* of 1953, in George Sidney's *Young Bess* (53), **Otto Preminger's** *Angel Face* (53) and Henry Koster's *The Robe* (53), which were later followed by **William Wyler's** *The Big Country* (58), Stanley Kubrick's *Spartacus* (60) and husband-to-be **Richard Brooks's** *Elmer Gantry* (60). She continued her career during the 1960s and 1970s, but at a less frenetic pace, delivering a series of typically committed performances, and Simmons has recently made a small but telling comeback in Jocelyn Moorhouse's *How To Make An American Quilt* (95).

OTHER KEY FILMS: *Great Expectations* (46); *Black Narcissus* (47); *Hamlet* (48); *Desiree* (54); *Guys And Dolls* (55); *Life At The Top* (65); *The Happy Ending* (69)

Simon, Michel

One look at Simon, with his weather-beaten features, his misdirected teeth, his stand-up hair and his multitudinous chins, would be enough to persuade most sane people that the man would never stand a chance of becoming a screen actor, let alone a star. But his face and his voice were Simon's stock in trade, and in a career spanning fifty years he proved to be one of the greatest actors of this or any other era. He had a natural integrity on the screen, even in the most obnoxious of parts, such as his lascivious tramp, Boudu, in **Jean Renoir's** *Boudu Sauvé Des Eaux* (32), or his Zabel in **Marcel Carné's** *Quai Des Brumes* (38). Simon contrived to inject a grotesque, heightened reality into even such nominally sympathetic roles as his Père Jules in **Jean Vigo's** *L'Atalante* (34), and it was this consistent refusal to mar greatness with sentiment that raises him so high, and which was shown, in its ultimate perfection, in Julien Duvivier's *La Fin Du Jour* (39).

291

OTHER KEY FILMS: *La Passion De Jeanne D'Arc* (28); *La Chienne* (31); *Drôle De Drame* (37); *Vautrin* (44); *Panique* (46); *Le Poison* (51); *Le Vieil Homme Et L'Enfant* (67); *L'Ibis Rouge* (75)

Sinatra, Frank

Sinatra took the cult of celebrity to places it had never been, loafing, in purposeful *cognito* (see **purposeful incognito**), with his minders massed around him like frigates to a destroyer, through bars, hotel lobbies, casinos, airports, always the centre of attention, and always oh-so conscious of it. His career came in three stages: the bobbysoxer years (1939-45), in which his voice and his willowy form set the hearts of countless teenage girls pounding; his film-and-swing years (1953-70), from his breakthrough Maggio in **Fred Zinnemann's** *From Here To Eternity* (53) to his eponymous anti-hero in Burt Kennedy's *Dirty Dingus Magee* (70); and his comeback years (1975-93), in which he always seemed on the point of leaving us, only to hove back into view again, his flotilla and status miraculously intact, for just one final concert. He was one of the greatest popular singers of all time, a more than passable actor, and an occasionally philanthropic man.

OTHER KEY FILMS: *Anchors Aweigh* (45); *On The Town* (49); *Suddenly* (54); *Young At Heart* (55); *Guys And Dolls* (55); *The Tender Trap* (55); *The Man With The Golden Arm* (55); *High Society* (56); *Pal Joey* (57); *The Manchurian Candidate* (62); *Von Ryan's Express* (65); *The Naked Runner* (67); *Tony Rome* (67); *The Detective* (68); *Lady In Cement* (68); *The First Deadly Sin* (80)

KEY LINE:

'Everyone in the whole world who hates me is now here.' [*Guys And Dolls*]

Single-frame Exposure

The gradual, frame-by-frame exposure, used during **time lapse**, **special effects** and **stop motion** cinematography.

Single-system Recording

Single-system recording occurs when sound and image are recorded at the same time, onto the same film. A notorious disadvantage when it comes to editing (the exposed footage is subject to any extraneous sounds going at the time), the system comes into its own during pressurised documentary filmmaking and newsgathering, when the use of separate systems might often prove counter-productive.

Siodmak, Robert

Siodmak (yet another German/US transplant) may be one of the greatest of all *film noir* directors, but his best films, *Phantom Lady* (44), *The Killers* (46), *Cry Of The City* (48), *Criss Cross* (49) and *The File On Thelma Jordon* (50), transcend the genre to become a series of awesome character studies of losers, marginals and the hope-stricken, each one battling to retain a little dignity in an inimical world. He returned to Germany in 1953, and continued making films such as *Die Ratten* (55) and *L'Affaire Nina B* (62). However, once in Germany, he was no longer the outsider he had been in the United States, and this loss of role seemed to result in the demise of the edgy, chippie part of his morbid, doom-laden talent.

OTHER KEY FILMS: *Son Of Dracula* (43); *The Spiral Staircase* (45); *The Dark Mirror* (46); *The Great Sinner* (49); *Deported* (50); *The Whistle At Eaton Falls* (51); *The Crimson Pirate* (52)

Sirk, Douglas

If it hadn't been for the **auteur theory**, promulgated so serendipitously by the *Cahiers du Cinéma,* Sirk would be remembered now as merely a melodramatic precursor of the soap-opera movement, hardly worthy of more than an enlightened footnote in cinema textbooks. An expatriate Dane born in Germany, Sirk had a very real sense of not belonging to the American culture which eventually employed him, and this imbues all his finest films. These are often about people, nominally belonging, but yet pushed to the margins of their natural milieux through selfishness in *Magnificent Obsession* (54), ill-advised love affairs in *All That Heaven Allows* (56) and *Written On The Wind* (57), and unacknowledged longings and thwarted ambitions in *The Tarnished Angels* (58) and *Imitation Of Life* (59). All Sirk's Hollywood films combine a comforting, almost fetishistic love of detail and texture, with storylines that continually undermine the assumptions of a society apparently so firmly and permanently anchored in the material − to that extent he may be seen as one of the most visionary of all mainstream Hollywood directors of his era.

OTHER KEY FILMS: *La Habañera* (37); *Zu Neuen Ufern* (37); *Die Heimat Ruft* (37); *Hitler's Madman* (43); *Shockproof* (49); *Thunder On The Hill* (51); *Meet Me At The Fair* (52); *All I Desire* (53); *Sign Of The Pagan* (54); *Captain Lightfoot* (55); *There's Always Tomorrow* (56); *Interlude* (57); *A Time To Love And A Time To Die* (58)

16mm

A narrow-gauge (and consequently economical) film stock, 16mm is much used in documentary, educational and scientific work. With forty frames per foot, and single perforations for sound, double perforations for silent use, 16mm has been the low-budget and avant-garde director's obvious choice ever since its formal recognition in 1923.

Skin Flicks

Film jargon for mainstream and other movies that rely on the attractions of sex, nudity and titillation in order to pull in audiences.

Skip Framing

A developing process in which only every second or third frame is printed, giving the impression of speeded up action on the screen. See **Double Framing**

Sky Filter

A filter specifically designed to darken or heighten the contrast of the sky, usually in black-and-white films, leaving the remainder of the scene untouched.

Slapstick

The word comes from the wooden slapping stick used by nineteenth-century clowns to raise a laugh (and the exaggerated sound of a slap) whenever one of them was seen to welt the other one. In movie terms it implies a type of humour, reliant, to say the least, on physicality rather than on subtlety, for its effects. Think of **Peter Sellers** as the accident-prone Inspector Clouseau getting his hand stuck in an armoured gauntlet with a ball and chain attached to it, and the term 'slapstick' takes on its full, majestic resonance. See **Custard Pie Movies**

Slasher Movies

Films in which the principal interest lies in when and whom the cleaver/pickaxe/chainsaw/meat-hook-wielding protagonist will target next. Pointed examples might include Tobe Hooper's *The Texas Chainsaw Massacre* (74), Wes Craven's *The Hills Have Eyes* (77), **John Carpenter's** *Halloween* (78) and **Abel Ferrara's** *Driller Killer* (79). Classic devices include blades (of varying sorts) descending through walls, up bath plugs and out of graves. The title 'King of the Slashers' must go to **Jack Nicholson's** Jack Torrance, in **Stanley Kubrick's** *The Shining* (80), which, while hardly constituting a slasher movie *per se*, brilliantly invoked slasherdom in the infamous bathroom scene in which Torrance tries to claw his way through Shelley Duvall's bathroom door with an axe.

Slate

A slate, held up before the beginning of each filmed scene, on which pertinent information is chalked. When the slate is also equipped with a slapstick clapper action, capable of producing a loud bang to cue synchronisation, it is called a **clapperboard**.

Sleeper

Hollywood jargon for a film that takes a little time to build a following, rather than wowing its target audience on first showing. **Ivan Passer's** *Cutter's Way* (81) was a sleeper, as was Peter Cattaneo's *The Full Monty* (97). The most successful sleeper of all was **Dennis Hopper's** *Easy Rider* (69), which spawned numerous would-be spin-off sleepers, some of which are dozing still.

Slocombe, Douglas

An eminent British cinematographer, Slocombe began his career photographing seventeen years worth of **Ealing Studios** productions, including the multi-directed *Dead Of Night* (45), **Robert Hamer's** *It Always Rains On Sunday* (47) and *Kind Hearts And Coronets* (49), Charles Crichton's *The Lavender Hill Mob* (51) and **Alexander Mackendrick's** *The Man In The White Suit* (51). He then turned freelance, where the quality of his work has sustained him through **Joseph Losey's** *The Servant* (63), **Roman Polanski's** *Dance Of The Vampires* (67) and **Steven Spielberg's** *Indiana Jones* trilogy (81-9), garnering, in the process, a heady succession of **Academy Award** nominations. As a former journalist and Second World War newsreel cameraman, Slocombe created one of his most beautifully shot films with Alexander Mackendrick's **CinemaScope** *A High Wind In Jamaica* (65).

OTHER KEY FILMS: John Huston's *Freud* (62); Anthony Harvey's *The Lion In Winter* (68); **Ken Russell's** *The Music Lovers* (71); **Fred Zinnemann's** *Julia* (77); Irvin Kershner's *Never Say Never Again* (83)

Slop Print

A duplicate **work print** (sometimes known as a scratch print) that the editor may use as an extra tool in order that work may be done on two separate jobs in parallel.

Slow Motion

An effect of retarded motion produced by filming through a camera at a faster speed than normal, slow motion is particularly useful in nature films (to slow down the wings of a humming-bird,

293

for instance) or in sports photography. (**Leni Riefenstahl's** extraordinary slow-motion shots of the divers at the Berlin Olympiad, in *Olympische Spiele* (36), come to mind, using a total of forty-three cameramen.) Slow motion may also be used for comic effect, as when **Peter Sellers's** Inspector Clouseau makes a 'slo-mo' karate kick through the air in **Blake Edwards's** *The Return Of The Pink Panther* (75), missing Burt Kwouk but bringing down a Welsh dresser and assorted crockery, tables, chairs and flower vases, in the process, which then cascade into the flat below.

Slug

The section of **leader** used to effect a temporary repair in a **work print**.

Slush Pile

The slush pile is the ever-increasing pile of unsolicited scripts, outlines and movie treatments that are sent in to studios and agencies in the hope that they will be the next 'latest discovery'. Some studios refuse to accept unsolicited material, for fear of being sued for plagiarism if a plot in one of the unwanted scripts mirrors a plot that they later use, or are using, in a movie.

KEY LINE:
'Women know how to do makeup, and anybody can do scriptwriting.' [The ineffable **Roger Corman** on how to achieve Slush Pile status]

Smell–O–Vision

Yet another failed effort to wean viewers away from television and back into the cinemas during the desperate 1960s, Smell-O-Vision was thought up by Mike Todd Jr, and consisted of pipes, running to each cinema armchair and connected to a central console, from which smells were to emerge when triggered by a cue from the film's 'smell track'.

Smith, Maggie

Although essentially a stage actress and comedienne, Maggie Smith customarily acts everyone else off the screen when she does deign to trip the light fantastic and appear in a film. Her landmark performance came in Ronald Neame's *The Prime Of Miss Jean Brodie* (69), but she was even better in Herbert Ross's *California Suite* (78) and Jack Clayton's *The Lonely Passion Of Judith Hearne* (88). Catch her on the stage, if you can, before she retires – a rare spirit, she has remarkable sympathy for the people she plays.

OTHER KEY FILMS: *The VIPs* (63); *The Pumpkin Eater* (64); *Oh! What A Lovely War* (65); *Quartet* (81); *The Missionary* (82); *A Private Function* (85); *A Room With A View* (85); *Hook* (91); *Sister Act* (92); *Secret Garden* (93); *Richard III* (95); *The First Wives Club* (96); *Washington Square* (97); *Tea With Mussolini* (99); *The Last September* (99); *Curtain Call* (99); *Gosford Park* (01); *Harry Potter And The Philosopher's Stone* (01)

KEY LINE:
'Give me a girl at an impressionable age, and she is mine for life.' [*The Prime Of Miss Jean Brodie*]

Smith, Will

The popular star of television's *The Fresh Prince Of Bel-Air*, and an esteemed rap singer – if that's not a contradiction in terms – and light comedian, Smith starred in **Fred Schepisi's** *Six Degrees Of Separation* (93), a pointed satire on the hypocrisy inherent in much New York upper-class liberalism. He then went on to achieve star status in Michael Bay's *Bad Boys* (95), Roland Emmerich's *Independence Day* (97) and Barry Sonnenfeld's *Men In Black* (97). His recent *Wild Wild West* (99) took implausibility to new heights, but provided Smith with a nice little earner and a hit record to boot. He'll doubtless go far.

OTHER KEY FILMS: *Where The Day Takes You* (92); *Enemy Of The State* (98); *The Legend Of Bagger Vance* (00); *Ali* (01)

Smithee, Allen [a.k.a. Alan]

This is the made-up name that appears on screen credits when the director or directors of a film choose to have their real names taken off, either as the result of a dispute or because they feel that the finished product is a travesty of their original intentions. Joe Eszterhas actually wrote a movie entitled *An Alan Smithee Film – Burn Hollywood Burn* (97), which was directed by Arthur Hiller, who then, in a magnificent Hollywood moment, asked for his name to be taken off the finished product and be replaced by, yes, you've guessed it, Alan Smithee!

Smoke and Fog Effects

Artificial effects created by the use of smoke pots, chemicals, filters, etc., to reproduce an impression of fog, haze or mist on the screen.

SMPTE

The Society of Motion Picture and Television Engineers was founded in 1916 (the 'television' nomenclature, for obvious reasons, being added later), to represent and define acceptable standards and practices, on behalf of their members, throughout the film industry.

Sneak Preview

The premature showing of a motion picture to a picked or target audience (often in an out-of-the-way cinema) before its general release, in order to ascertain whether the film as it stands meets justifiable audience expectations. In severe cases of dissatisfaction, endings have subsequently been reshot and whole characters expurgated, sometimes at the expense of the artistic quality of the film. **Orson Welles's** *The Magnificent Ambersons* (42) is a case in point – after two dire previews, editor **Robert Wise** was charged by **RKO** with cutting the 130-minute film by at least a third, turning what many feel was a masterpiece into merely a good film with a sentimental new ending the quality of which, according to the extraordinary BBC 'Arena' interview Welles gave a few years before his death in 1985, broke his heart.

Snoot

A cone-shaped hood for use on studio lighting that serves to direct the beam onto a particular subject or area of the set.

Snow Effects

Mock snow created in the studio or on location (in the absence of the real thing) from either rock salt, gypsum, smashed feathers, asbestos or plastic flakes, depending on the weight, volume and consistency required.

Snuff Movie

A snuff movie is one that purports to show the actual on-screen death of an actor or actress, victim or protagonist, often as the result of sadomasochistic, cannibalistic, or various other forms of sexual and/or aggressive activity. During the late 1960s and 1970s a number of such films came out of Italy, influenced by the *Mondo* series of ghoulish semi-documentaries, showing what seemed, to the uninitiated at least, to be the genuine onscreen murder of their central characters. Ruggero Deodato's *Cannibal Holocaust* (76) was perhaps the best-made example, with Umberto Lenzi's *Eaten Alive* (79) and Sergio Martino's *Prisoner Of The Cannibal God* (81) taking distant second and third places. The films were actually cannily made mockeries, using judicious cutting (of both the film and of animal carcases) to invoke terror and disgust. They were, needless to say, massively successful, and influenced Eduardo Sanchez and Daniel Myrick's *The Blair Witch Project* (99).

Soderbergh, Steven

Soderbergh started at the top, with *sex, lies and videotape* (89), which won him the **Palme D'Or** at the **Cannes Film Festival**, and then horrified his fans with *Kafka* (91), which was actually very good indeed, followed by *King Of The Hill* (93) and *Schizopolis* (96), which were even better. Somewhat bewildered, no doubt, by his unjustified blackballing, Soderbergh fought back with the excellent *Out Of Sight* (98), starring **George Clooney** and Jennifer Lopez, a film which must have brought him to the attention of **Julia Roberts**, whom he then directed in the commercially lucrative though intellectually vapid *Erin Brockovich* (00). Now on something of a streak, thanks to the runaway success of *Traffic* (00), Soderbergh is happy proof that, even in Hollywood, talent will eventually out.

OTHER KEY FILMS: *The Underneath* (94); *Gray's Anatomy* (96); *The Limey* (99); *Ocean's 11* (01)

Soft Focus

This is what cinematographers use when the ageing stars they are filming have lost some of their previous facial definition. Gauzes, filters, or slightly out of focus lenses can all be used to obtain a soft, diffused effect, which can also bring a romantic or mysterious aura to an otherwise mundane object.

Soft Image

A type of computer software responsible for ninety per cent of the effects used in **Ridley Scott's** *Gladiator* (00), including the virtual recreation of nearly all the spectators at the Colosseum, soft image is a 2-D compositing tool which allows graphic artists to layer previously drawn pictures onto sections of live-action film. In the case of *Gladiator*, up to a hundred of these superimpositions were, at times, used on one live-action shot. See **Dawn Process**

Soft Light

A studio lighting system that diffuses rather than concentrates light, producing fewer shadows and less contrast.

Sound

The sound era formally began in 1927, with the release of Alan Crosland's *The Jazz Singer*, but sound in cinema had been present for many years before that date, often through the use of synchronised phonograph recordings alongside a nominally silent film. One of the most entertaining illustrations of the coming of sound, and its effects on the stars and players in the motion-picture industry, comes in **Stanley Donen** and **Gene Kelly's** *Singin' In The*

Rain (52), when Jean Hagen's Lina Lamont consistently forgets that she must now speak into a concealed microphone, and that it will pick up every squeak of her terminally unsuitable voice.

Sound Camera

A **blimped** (muffled) camera specifically designed to film at the same time as sounds are being recorded.

Sound Crew

The members of a feature-film production crew charged with recording the dialogue and every other peripheral sound that will eventually appear on the soundtrack of the movie.

Sound Editor

The editor or editors responsible for formulating the sound effects and dialogue tracks on a motion picture, a task that involves **looping**, **synchronising** and **mixing** the available recordings until they tally with the accompanying filmed images.

Sound Effects

This covers all sounds, other than dialogue or music, which appear on the soundtrack of a film. If the sound was not recorded analogously to the dialogue, the sound editor is responsible for adding it in later on, often through the use of pre-recorded sound tapes.

Sound Speed

Twenty-four frames per second is the standard speed at which sound film runs through a camera or a projector.

Sound Stage

A soundproof studio for the production of sound films.

Soundtrack

The strip down the side of film stock which carries the recorded sound, and which travels marginally in advance of the image to allow for subsequent synchronisation.

Soup

Jargon for the chemical bath used during film processing.

Sovcolor

The Soviet Union occupied the Agfa photographic factory in the 1940s, and it wasn't long before they adapted the Agfacolor process to their requirements, renaming it Sovcolor.

Spacek, Sissy

Spacek is one of the more interesting of the 1970s vintage of actresses, an **Actors' Studio** disciple who always wore her Strasbergian credentials lightly and with grace, from her very first appearance on screen in Michael Ritchie's pulpish *Prime Cut* (72). She made her name as Holly in **Terrence Malick's** *Badlands* (73), confirming her promise with a sensational performance in **Brian De Palma's** *Carrie* (76), returning from beyond the grave in one of the snazziest schlock finales in movie history. A very impressive sequence of films followed, including Jack Fisk's curious little love story, *Raggedy Man* (81), and **Constantin Costa-Gavras's** *Missing* (82). In recent years, however, she seems to have gone a little out of fashion as a leading lady, and this is sad, for Spacek at her best was always the thinking person's alternative to the Hollywood heavy brigade.

OTHER KEY FILMS: *Welcome To L.A.* (76); *Three Women* (76); *Heartbeat* (80); *Coal Miner's Daughter* (80); *The River* (84); *Crimes Of The Heart* (86); *The Long Walk Home* (90); *JFK* (91); *The Grass Harp* (96); *L.A. Confidential* (97); *Blast From The Past* (99); *The Straight Story* (99); *In The Bedroom* (01)

Space Opera

A space or **science-fiction** film notable for its concentration on derring-do to the exclusion of scientific fact or possibility. Good examples might be the Frederic Stephani *Flash Gordon* serials during the 1930s, and **Ed Wood's** *Plan 9 From Outer Space* (59).

Spacey, Kevin

It suddenly occurred to Hollywood that Spacey was more than just a simple character actor when his Roger 'Verbal' ('So who is Keyser Soze?') Kint stole Bryan Singer's *The Usual Suspects* (95) from under the noses of a stellar array of the usual oddball leading men, including **Gabriel Byrne**, Stephen Baldwin and Chazz Palminteri. A veteran stand-up comedian and Tony award-winner, Spacey already knew how to milk his audience, and the best supporting actor **Oscar** he took for Kint paved the way for the roles in Curtis Hanson's *L.A. Confidential* (97) and Sam Mendes's *American Beauty* (99) which have since made his name.

OTHER KEY FILMS: *Heartburn* (86); *Working Girl* (88); *Henry & June* (90); *Glengarry Glen Ross* (92); *Seven* (95); *A Time To Kill* (96); *The Negotiator* (98); *Hurlyburly* (98); *Ordinary Decent Criminal* (00); *Pay It Forward* (00); *The Shipping News* (01)

Spaghetti Westerns

A series of cowboy movies, spaghetti westerns were made during the 1960s and 1970s by Italian directors, usually in Spain, and with American actors in the lead roles. **Sergio Leone** is the acknowledged master of the genre, a genre which took the gentle loner that **Randolph Scott** played in the Ranown series of **Budd Boetticher Westerns** during the 1950s, and gave him a Japanese samurai attitude. Prominent Leone films such as *A Fistful Of Dollars* (64) and *For A Few Dollars More* (65) began the series, with **Clint Eastwood** starring, and these were followed by a whole series of spaghettis starring Terence Hill (born Mario Girotti) and Bud Spencer (born Carlo Pedersoli), which mixed broad comedy with almost continuous gunplay. The genre began satirising itself with Tonino Valerii's *My Name Is Nobody* (73), and petered out soon afterwards, but not before making its influential mark on such worthy American heirs as **Clint Eastwood's** *High Plains Drifter* (73) and **Fred Schepisi's** *Barbarosa* (82). See *Best* Western Films

Sparks

The nickname on a film set (and just about everywhere else, too) for an electrician.

Special Effects

Tricks used to temporarily convince an audience that what they are seeing on the screen is real. Special effects fall into two main categories: visual effects and mechanical effects. Visual effects require photographic manipulation before, during or after filming; mechanical effects involve live re-creations on the set of whatever phenomenon the director wishes to simulate while filming is actually going on.

Speed

The optimum speed at which film travels through a camera, projector or printer, normally measured in frames per second.

Speed!

The camera operator's call when the speed of the camera has reached a level at which filming can begin.

Speedy Gonzalez

See **Looney Tunes**

Spider

A three-pronged metal stand that is able to support a camera on a tricky surface or on angled ground – thus the sticky 'spider' analogy.

Spider Box

See **Junction Box**

Spiel

Spiel refers to a comedian's glib patter (think **Danny Kaye**, **Bob Hope**, **Eddie Cantor**), which comics use to get themselves out of tight situations when confronted by tougher, albeit less quick-thinking, adversaries. **Jack Benny** reversed the spiel brilliantly, in his famous highwayman joke. A masked man jumps out and holds Benny up with a pistol – 'Your money, or your life'. The miserly Benny puts his hand to his jaw and rubs it ruminatively. 'Come on! Come on! Your money or your life!' shouts the highwayman. Benny looks up at the bandit, surprised. 'Stop rushing me. I haven't decided yet.'

Spielberg, Steven

Director, producer, and sometime writer, Spielberg had made a number of successful shorts and television features before his TV movie, *Duel* (71/83) – the one in which a gigantic, driverless truck threatens home-bound salesman Dennis Weaver – cemented his reputation as a budding director, and gave him the opportunity to direct the well-received *Sugarland Express* (74). **Universal** then gave him *Jaws* (75), and so began the Spielberg legend; a legend based on the three all-American virtues of mechanical talent, energy and the capacity to make enormous quantities of money. It is to Spielberg's credit that he has rarely allowed his power or influence to cloud his judgement, and despite one or two fiascos (no doubt necessary, in psychological terms, to prevent vainglory), he has weaved his way skilfully between the twin pillars of popular culture and genuinely heartfelt projects with commendable restraint. *Close Encounters Of The Third Kind* (77), *Raiders Of The Lost Ark* (81), *E.T. The Extra-Terrestrial* (82) and *Jurassic Park* (93) were all brilliant forays into populist myth-making, but he has leavened these with more adult material, such as *The Color Purple* (85), *Empire Of The Sun* (87), *Amistad* (97), and *Saving Private Ryan* (98). The brightest star in Spielberg's firmament, however, is still *Schindler's List* (93), a brilliantly successful and emotionally nourishing account of the effect one person can have on a culture designed to deaden morality and replace it with a form of expedient insanity. There is hardly a false note in *Schindler*, and when Spielberg mounted the rostrum to collect his first Academy Award for Best Director, he could do so in the certain knowledge that he had justified his place in a world more notable for its moral deficiencies than for its eagerness to stand up and be counted.

OTHER KEY FILMS: *1941* (79); *Indiana Jones And The Temple Of Doom* (84); *Indiana Jones And The Last Crusade* (89); *Always* (89); *Hook* (91); *The Lost World: Jurassic Park* (97); *A. I. Artificial Intelligence* (01)

Spill Light

Unwanted or excess lighting on a film set.

Splatter Movie

Horror films which rely for their thrills on the various grotesque, wall-splattering ways in which their protagonists are killed, dismembered, maimed, tortured, discombobulated or otherwise impaired.

Splice

The act of cementing or taping together two separate pieces of film in the editing room.

Splicer

A machine designed to help the editor in the act of splicing, the splicer occurs in three main forms – the hand splicer, the machine splicer, and the heated splicer, which dries the glue virtually instantaneously.

Split Focus

Split focus is when the lens is focused at the median point between an object in the foreground and one in the distance, ensuring that both are more or less equally well defined.

Split Reel

With a detachable side, the split reel allows the editor to remove the entire spool of film without rewinding. The expression formerly referred to a silent-movie reel that contained two five-minute features.

Split Screen

A tendentious technique which involved the splitting of the main screen into two, four or more fractions, each with a separate, often synchronous activity occurring in it. The trick was unfortunately overused during the late 1960s and early 1970s, particularly in such 'trendy' films as Norman Jewison's *The Thomas Crown Affair* (68).

Spotlight

A studio lamp (with the narrow beam of a searchlight) designed to highlight a given area or individual on a set.

Sprocket Holes

The holes on one or both sides of a strip of film.

Sprockets

The toothed cog inside a camera or projector that engages with the **sprocket holes** on a strip of film, keeping the frame in precise alignment with the lens.

Spy Films

The film world has been obsessed with spies ever since the dancer and courtesan, Mata Hari, was shot dead by a French firing squad in the forests of Vincennes, on 5 October 1917, for what may (or may not) have been her spying activities on behalf of the Germans. **Greta Garbo** played her in George Fitzmaurice's *Mata Hari* (31), **Marlene Dietrich** played a variation on her (agent X27) in **Josef von Sternberg's** *Dishonored* (31), **Jeanne Moreau** played her in Jean-Louis Richard's *Mata Hari, Agent H21* (64) [co-scripted by **François Truffaut**, no less] and even Sylvia Kristel (of *Emmanuelle* fame) took a stab at her in Curtis Harrington's absurd *Mata Hari* (85). But spies and secret agents really came into their own in the film world after the Second World War, when a plethora of films purporting to tell the true story of this or that hero or heroine (or villain) appeared. Two of the best biopics, largely because the stories they told were so fascinating in themselves, were **Lewis Gilbert's** *Carve Her Name With Pride* (58), in which Virginia McKenna played Violette Szabo, and Herbert Wilcox's *Odette* (50), in which Anna Neagle played Odette Churchill. With the publication of best-selling author, John le Carré's 1963 novel, *The Spy Who Came In From The Cold*, the spy film took on a different, more self-consciously literary emphasis, as manifested by **Martin Ritt's** 1965 film of the book, starring an on-form **Richard Burton** as tormented master spy, Alec Leamas. The flip side of the coin came with the gadget-driven **James Bond** franchise, although some of Ian Fleming's original books were actually plot-driven and quite dark – read his 1953 *Casino Royale*, for instance. Recently, the spy film has taken on something of a comic, post-Graham Greene twist, with **John Boorman's** excellent *The Tailor From Panama* (01) [based on another le Carré novel], and the spoof **Mike Myers** hits, Jay Roach's *Austin Powers: International Man Of Mystery* (97) and *Austin Powers: The Spy Who Shagged Me* (99).

KEY LINES:

'I am married to an American agent.' [**Claude Rains's** astonished Nazi agent, Alexander Sebastian, to his dominating mother, eerily played by

Leopoldine Konstantine, in **Alfred Hitchcock's** *Notorious* (46)] (see lower image on front cover).

'A beautiful, mysterious woman pursued by gunmen. Sounds like a spy story.' [**Robert Donat** as John Buchan's Richard Hannay, in Alfred Hitchcock's *The Thirty-Nine Steps* (35)]

Best Spy Films

Michael Anderson's *The Quiller Memorandum* (66); **John Frankenheimer's** *The Manchurian Candidate* (62); **Guy Hamilton's** *Goldfinger* (64); **Alfred Hitchcock's** *Foreign Correspondent* (40) and *Notorious* (46); **Fritz Lang's** *Ministry Of Fear* (45); **Joseph L Mankiewicz's** *Five Fingers* (52); Ronald Neame's *The Odessa File* (74); **Michael Powell's** *The Spy In Black* (39); **Martin Ritt's** *The Spy Who Came In From The Cold* (66); **Josef von Sternberg's** *Dishonored* (31); Terence Young's *From Russia With Love* (63)

Squib

The electronically triggered explosive device used to simulate the strikes of a bullet in differing areas of the set, and which causes puffs of earth, chips of wall, and splinters of wood to erupt more or less realistically.

Stage

The part of a studio where sets are constructed and in which actual filming takes place.

Stagehand

One of numerous members of a film crew responsible for shifting props, moving scenery and a variety of other manual tasks.

Stage Left/Stage Right

A stage direction, originating in the theatre, in which an actor or actress is directed to move or exit to *their* left or right, rather than as the camera sees them.

Stallone, Sylvester

Stallone has always been an edgier actor than his great competitor in the action-movie stakes, Big **Arnie Schwarzenegger**. When this aspect of the man is allowed to come to the fore, as in Ted Kotcheff's excellent first contender in the Rambo series, *First Blood* (82), we are at once aware why Stallone managed to keep his place in the blockbuster stakes throughout the 1980s and most of the 1990s. The ensuing Rambo films, however, were turgidly run-of-the-mill, in the same way that, as the Rocky films played on, they signally

failed to improve on their progenitor, John G Avildsen's *Rocky* (76). Stallone has occasionally tried to break out from the big-action strait-jacket, most notably in Roger Spottiswoode's *Stop! Or My Mom Will Shoot* (92) and James Mangold's *Cop Land* (97), but sadly it seems that his cupidity has forever consigned him to a pumped-up, hyper-muscled, but increasingly toothless version of the Sartrean *Huis Clos* scenario.

OTHER KEY FILMS: *Farewell My Lovely* (75); *Paradise Alley* (78); *Tango & Cash* (89); *Cliffhanger* (93); *Demolition Man* (93); *Daylight* (96); *Cop Land* (97); *Get Carter* (00); *Driven* (01); *Eye See You* (01)

KEY LINE:

'Stallone has one talent – that is to have soaked up all the bullshit which has accumulated in La La Land over the years, coated it with an ersatz patina of culture and love of fine art, and created from his bootstraps a genuine, authentic Monster.' [Sterling Silliphant, who co-scripted Menahem Golan's *Over The Top* (86), which starred Stallone as a tender-hearted arm-wrestler]

Standard Leader

The strip of film at the beginning and end of a standard release print (designed to **Academy of Motion Picture Arts and Sciences** specifications) which protects the film itself, and gives the projectionist due warning either of when the projector speed is up to scratch, or that the end of the reel is approaching and it is time for a **change-over**.

Standard Stock

The standard gauge for feature films is 35mm – anything below that is considered substandard.

Stand-in

The person who doubles for a star during the lengthy preparatory stages before filming actually begins. See **Double**

Stanwyck, Barbara

Feisty leading lady who had the courage to play a number of unsympathetic characters, the former Ruby Stevens was orphaned at the age of thirteen and literally *did* start her fifty-year career in the chorus line. With a degree of maturity well beyond her twenty-five years, she shone as the missionary's wife who falls under the spell of **Nils Asther's** decadent Chinese warlord in **Frank Capra's** *The Bitter Tea Of General Yen* (32). The moment when, returning downriver to Shanghai after Yen's suicide, she turns her face up to the clouds to recall

the memory of her strange lover is undoubtedly one of cinema's greatest **Heartstopping Moments**. The perfect *film noir* scheming **vamp** in **Billy Wilder's** *Double Indemnity* (44), Stanwyck also excelled at playing fallen women, as Mae Doyle, for instance, in **Fritz Lang's** underrated *Clash By Night* (52), or as Thelma Jordon, in **Robert Siodmak's** *The File On Thelma Jordon* (49), which also featured a brilliant performance by the eccentric Wendell Corey. See also photograph at entry for *pulp fiction.*
OTHER KEY FILMS: *Ten Cents A Dance* (31); *Baby Face* (32); *Gambling Lady* (34); *The Woman In Red* (35); *Stella Dallas* (37); *Union Pacific* (39); *The Lady Eve* (41); *Meet John Doe* (41); *Ball Of Fire* (42); *Lady Of Burlesque* (43); *The Strange Love Of Martha Ivers* (46); *The Two Mrs Carrolls* (47); *Sorry Wrong Number* (48); *No Man Of Her Own* (50); *Titanic* (53); *Executive Suite* (54); *The Night Walker* (65)
KEY LINES:
'If I ever loved a man again, I'd bear anything – he could have my teeth for watch fobs.' [*Clash By Night*]

'If you waited for a man to propose to you from natural causes, you'd die of old maid-hood.' [*The Lady Eve*]

Star

A person who, on account of their talent, celebrity or physical charms, regularly takes the lead role in prestigious feature film productions, and is paid accordingly.

Starlet

A young female wannabe, whom a studio head or publicity guru hopes to turn into a bona fide star.
KEY LINE:
'There is nothing as dumb as a smart girl.' [Jay Presson Allen – she scripted *Marnie* (64) for **Alfred Hitchcock** and *The Prime Of Miss Jean Brodie* (69) for Ronald Neame – on the bumpy road to success]

Star System

This was the studio-based system by which stars were groomed and their careers rigorously monitored to ensure the optimum commercial return. When the studio system broke down with the onset of television during the 1950s, stars found themselves making their own market for the very first time. This resulted in a smaller stable of stars, but with more power. Nowadays, big-budget movies are virtually inconceivable without a major star name (or names) attached, unless the special effects are so awesome that they make up for not having one. Screenwriters regularly slant their screenplays towards the stars that they hope will climb on board the project.

Start Mark

The mark that indicates the point on a film's leader where the synchronisation of sound and image begins.

Star Trek

US television series (1966-8), *Star Trek*, with its seventy-nine episodes, spawned three further spin-offs, nine movies (and counting) and a dedicated cult following of Trekkies. For them, *Star Trek* is a passion, a way of life and sometimes even a religion; for non-Trekkies, *Star Trek* is a cause for derision and linguistic misgivings due to the most famous split infinitive in entertainment history ('to boldly go…'). *Star Trek* lore – based on a sample of nine films – has it that only the even-numbered movies pass muster.
KEY LINE:
'Live long and prosper!'

Barbara Stanwyck's foul-mouthed Sugarpuss O'Shea learning to lean on dry-as-a-stick Gary Cooper's Prof. Bertram Potts, in Howard Hawks's sublime Ball Of Fire *(41)*

Stars Wars

Star Wars is without doubt the most valuable movie franchise of all time. It is the brainchild of Californian-born **George Lucas**, who obstinately persisted with his 1977 project despite the scepticism of backers, 20th **Century-Fox**. The film eventually grossed $194,000,000, a sum that has since been dwarfed by the film's re-release in 1997, together with its two sequels, *The Empire Strikes Back* (80) and *The Return Of The Jedi* (83). Lucas has since started work on a trilogy of prequels, with number one, the underrated *Star Wars: Episode 1 – The Phantom Menace* (99) already a box-office, if not a critical, success. Episodes II and III of the prequel are due out in 2002 and 2005 respectively. See **Digital Projection**

KEY LINE:
'A long time ago, in a galaxy far, far away…' [*Star Wars* (77)]

Static Marks

Unsightly streaks on processed film resulting from static electricity discharging itself inside the camera.

Steadicam

A revolutionary harness that has changed the world of the hand-held camera from the wobbling, jerky device we were used to in the 1960s, to the smooth, infinitely adaptable tool (and shortcut to intimacy) we now benefit from in films such as **Quentin Tarantino's** *Pulp Fiction* (94). Operators can now run behind an actor, even up and down stairs, with no appreciable oscillation at all.

Steiger, Rod

Steiger is **method acting** personified, for its influence seems to leach off the screen and into real life with him, until it is sometimes hard to tell the characters from the man who plays them. His first conspicuous success was as **Marlon Brando's** crooked brother, Charley Malloy, in **Elia Kazan's** *On The Waterfront* (54), and this began the period when Steiger played heavies, deviants, venal producers and sweaty crooks, in such movies as **Robert Aldrich's** *The Big Knife* (55), Mark Robson's *The Harder They Fall* (56), **Samuel Fuller's** *Run Of The Arrow* (57) and Richard Wilson's *Al Capone* (58). Steiger has always taken himself very seriously indeed as an actor, and there are times when one feels that he tries on his parts much as a callow young woman might try on a new dress, twirling for all to see and praise her. Steiger's most memorable performance came as Bill Gillespie in Norman Jewison's *In The Heat Of*

The Night (67), but he was most convincing in a now little-seen Peter Hall film, *Three Into Two Won't Go* (69), as the unfaithful husband of (his then real-life wife) Claire Bloom, and also as the haunted Sol Nazerman in **Sidney Lumet's** *The Pawnbroker* (65). OTHER KEY FILMS: *Oklahoma!* (55); *Jubal* (56); *The Court Martial Of Billy Mitchell* (55); *The Mark* (61); *Dr Zhivago* (65); *No Way To Treat A Lady* (68); *Waterloo* (70); *A Fistful Of Dynamite* (71); *The Amityville Horror* (79); *Lion Of The Desert* (81); *Der Zauberberg* (82); *The Ballad Of The Sad Café* (91); *Mars Attacks!* (96); *Crazy In Alabama* (99); *End Of Days* (99); *Cypress Edge* (99); *The Flying Dutchman* (00); *Lightmaker* (01); *A Month Of Sundays* (01); *Poochall Junkies* (01)

Steiner, Max

Steiner was one of the great composers of Hollywood's Golden Age of the 1930s and 1940s, scoring such films (among 200-odd others) as **John Ford's** *The Informer* (35), **Victor Fleming's** *Gone With The Wind* (39), **Michael Curtiz's** *Casablanca* (42), Irving Rapper's *Now, Voyager* (42) and **John Huston's** *The Treasure Of The Sierra Madre* (48) and *Key Largo* (48). Yet another expatriate Austrian (what would Hollywood have done without them?), Steiner had actually studied under Gustav Mahler at Vienna's Imperial Academy of Music, and was so precocious a talent that he was already conducting professionally at the age of sixteen. His scores have a *fin-de-siècle* lushness and heady romanticism that ensured him a total of three **Oscars** and twenty-three further nominations. OTHER KEY FILMS: **George Cukor's** *A Bill Of Divorcement* (32) and *Little Women* (33); **William Wellman's** *A Star Is Born* (37); John Cromwell's *Since You Went Away* (44); **Howard Hawks's** *The Big Sleep* (46); John Ford's *The Searchers* (56)

Step Outline

A basic outline of the intended film, provided by the putative screenwriter to the production executive before the **screenplay** has been either commissioned or written.

Step Printing

A frame-by-frame printing technique, useful for developing film when optical effects are required.

Stereophonic Sound

Sounds recorded on more than one track and from different directions that are then played back through a number of carefully positioned channels to give a deeper, more realistic sound. See **Dolby System**

Stereoscopic Cinema
See 3-D

Sternberg, Josef von

There is no other director remotely like von Sternberg, and it is sometimes hard to conceive how he managed to get away with his delirious visual fantasies for so long in a Hollywood fundamentally devoted to Mammon and mammaries. An expatriate Austrian, brought to the US when he was not yet ten, the adult von Sternberg drifted to Hollywood and found himself work as an assistant director. Following the release of his first film, *The Salvation Hunters* (25), **Charlie Chaplin** declared him a genius, and the epithet stuck. Silent success followed, leading to a series of sound films starring his discovery and fetish object, **Marlene Dietrich**, notable for their dense, heady atmosphere, exotic lighting and mannered, almost other-worldly dialogue. The first was *The Blue Angel* (30), filmed bilingually in Germany, which introduced von Sternberg's trademark masochistic male and the song 'Falling In Love Again', that was to follow Dietrich like a lucky charm throughout her career. Von Sternberg could undoubtedly be a tyrant on set, and his artistic credo, which valued atmosphere above story, poetry above logic, allowed his actors, who were often chosen more for their looks than their acting ability, little leeway. However, his sequence of films for **Paramount**, all starring Dietrich, and which include *Morocco* (30), *Dishonored* (31), *Blonde Venus* (32), *Shanghai Express* (32), *The Scarlet Empress* (34) and *The Devil Is A Woman* (35), took cinema to realms it had never before inhabited, via visual imagery that has rarely been bettered, using sound and movement, light and darkness, in a way that no other director, before or since, has ever used them. See **Heartstopping Moments**

OTHER KEY FILMS: *Underworld* (27); *The Last Command* (28); *An American Tragedy* (31); *Crime And Punishment* (35); *The King Steps Out* (36); *I Claudius* [unfinished] (37); *The Shanghai Gesture* (41); *Jet Pilot* (50) [released 1957]; *Macao* (52); *The Saga Of Anatahan* (53)

Stevens, George

Stevens took his personal cine camera with him during his time as a major with the Army Signals Corps Unit during the Second World War, and used it to take some extraordinary colour footage, most notably of the relief of Dachau concentration camp. The experience obviously changed him, for the films he made after the war are notable for their gentle humanity and attempt to understand human motivation. *A Place In The Sun* (51) sets the audience a moral conundrum that only *Shane* (53), arguably one of the best **Westerns** ever, succeeds in answering – namely that love alone is not a sufficient foundation for happiness. When **Alan Ladd's** Shane rides off into the sunset, he is not simply abrogating responsibility, but taking it –were he to stay, he might destroy the very thing he had begun to cherish. People always count in a George Stevens film, and it is notable that even in his early comedies (and very good they are too), and in his later melodramas, he never quite allows sentiment to take over from sense, and so retains his capacity to move, rather than merely tug at the heartstrings.

OTHER KEY FILMS: *Alice Adams* (35); *Swing Time* (36); *Quality Street* (37); *A Damsel In Distress* (37); *Gunga Din* (39); *Penny Serenade* (41); *Woman Of The Year* (42); *The Talk Of The Town* (42); *The More The Merrier* (43); *I Remember Mama* (48); *Giant* (56); *The Diary Of Anne Frank* (59); *The Only Game In Town* (70)

KEY LINE:
'A great man and a marvellous drinking companion, but sometimes you never knew what the hell he was shooting. Still, it all added up.' [Screenwriter Allan Scott, who co-scripted *Swing Time* (36) and *Quality Street* (37), on director Stevens]

Stewart, James

Popular with both the public and the studios, Stewart's Princetonian drawl masked an acute intelligence and a forceful integrity. These served him well in both his film and his wartime career, where, after flying numerous bombing missions over Germany, he rose to the heady rank of Air Force brigadier general. **Frank Capra** first recognised Stewart's 'Everyman' nature in *You Can't Take It With You* (38) and *Destry Rides Again* (40), but it was only after the war that Stewart really came into his own, rather darker self, in a wonderful run of **Anthony Mann** Westerns – which includes that picaresque oddity *Winchester 73* (50) – and in the series of films he did for **Alfred Hitchcock**, most notably as driven ex-police officer, John 'Scottie' Ferguson, in *Vertigo* (58).

OTHER KEY FILMS: *The Shopworn Angel* (38); *Mr Smith Goes To Washington* (39); *The Philadelphia Story* (40); *It's A Wonderful Life* (46); *Call Northside 777* (48); *Broken Arrow* (50); *Harvey* (50); *The Naked Spur* (53); *Rear Window* (54); *The Man From Laramie* (55); *Anatomy Of A Murder* (59); *Flight Of The Phoenix* (66)

A candid, relatively unposed location shot highlighting James Stewart's movie star features – he was, it seems, as genuinely nice in real life as he appeared on screen. See also photograph at entry for Grace Kelly.

KEY LINES:

'Well I…I always feel I belong where I am.' [*The Man From Laramie*]

'I wouldn't give you two cents for all your fancy rules if behind them they didn't have a little bit of plain, ordinary kindness and a little looking out for the other feller.' [Stewart on basic human decency]

Still

A photograph shot by an outside or studio photographer before, during, or after the production of a film, and used for publicity purposes.

Stock

Virgin or 'raw' film that has not been exposed.

Stock Footage

Footage that has already been shot and archived, and which is reused in feature films or documentaries as a means of saving money or of establishing atmosphere.

Stone, Oliver

Stone dropped out of Yale and into Hollywood with similar alacrity, directing the minor cult movie *Seizure* (74), and penning the script for **Alan Parker's** *Midnight Express* (78), before taking joint writing credit on John Milius's *Conan The Barbarian* (81) and finally graduating into the super-writing league via **Brian De Palma's** *Scarface* (83). His first directing success came with *Salvador* (86), closely followed by *Platoon* (86), which was the film that finally projected him into the big time. With his emphasis on power, greed and the destructive capacity of the male when society's harness is temporarily lifted by war, great wealth or political power, Stone fits neatly into the Ernest Hemingway, Norman Mailer, Charles Bukowski line of self-abusing iconoclasts. *Wall Street* (87), *Born On The Fourth Of July* (89) and *JFK* (91) were all good in their way, but Stone excels at more out-of-the-way material, such as his underrated *U-Turn* (97), in which an increasingly disorientated **Sean Penn** backs through the door marked *film noir* and emerges somewhere close to hell.

OTHER KEY FILMS: *The Hand* (81); *Talk Radio* (88); *The Doors* (91); *Heaven & Earth* (93); *Nixon* (95); *Any Given Sunday* (99)

303

Stop

Relating to the size of the **aperture** of a camera, and how much light it lets in. See also **F-Stop** and **T-Stop**

Stop Frame

See **Freeze Frame**

Stop Motion

Used most often in **animation**, stop-motion photography allows inanimate objects to seem to be moving thanks to the time-consuming process of photographing each individual movement of the animated object (or each separate drawing of such a movement) onto a new frame, until, when the ensuing frame sequence is developed and projected, the appearance of movement is triumphantly achieved.

Stopping Down

Reducing a lens aperture so that less light can enter.

Storaro, Vittorio

One of the all-time greats of cinematography, Storaro adapts himself to each director, fleshing out their visions with the brilliance of his lighting and camerawork. Working regularly with **Bernardo Bertolucci**, for whom he created the dazzling visual tapestry of *The Conformist* (70), and the darkened, often candle-lit entrances to the soul in *Last Tango In Paris* (73), he was also responsible for the look of **Francis Ford Coppola's** masterpiece *Apocalypse Now* (79), and the strange, comic-book intensity of **Warren Beatty's** *Dick Tracy* (90), which consisted, astonishingly, of only a six-colour sequence.

OTHER KEY FILMS: **Michael Apted's** *Agatha* (79); Warren Beatty's *Reds* (81) and *Bulworth* (98); Francis Ford Coppola's *One From The Heart* (82) and *Tucker – The Man And His Dream* (88); Bernardo Bertolucci's *The Last Emperor* (87) and *The Sheltering Sky* (90); **Carlos Saura's** *Tango* (97) and *Goya En Burdeos* (99); **Alfonso Arau's** *Picking Up The Pieces* (00)

Story Analyst

Another, grander term for a studio **reader**, the story analyst has the job of ploughing through selected or **slush-pile** manuscripts and encapsulating the promising ones in brief, readable English.

Storyboard

This refers to the drawings, photographs and cut outs (and increasingly computer animation) that are used to illustrate part of or all the sequence of intended shots in a feature film, a documentary or an advertising pitch. **Alfred Hitchcock** customarily storyboarded entire movies, with each camera angle, each shot, however minor, completely delineated before shooting began. His storyboards (drawn for him by a storyboard artist, of course) for the shower scene in *Psycho* (60) and for the opening of *Marnie* (64) have virtually become expressionist works of art in themselves.

Story Conference

A get-together involving screenwriters and production staff which is used as a forum in which to discuss script developments and deadlines.

Story Editor

The person in charge of a production company's **readers** and **story analysts**, and whose responsibility it is to decide on which script outlines, screenplays and story synopses might make good movies.

Storyline

An extremely generalised outline, covering maybe three lines of text, summarising the story of a feature film.

Straight Cut

A cut from one scene to another involving no artificial or contrived transitions.

Straight Man

The straight man is the serious partner in a comedy duet who provides the straight repartee on which the comic member of the duo will frame jokes. Famous straight men include **Oliver Hardy** (to **Stan Laurel**), **Dean Martin** (to **Jerry Lewis**), and **Bud Abbot** (to **Lou Costello**).

Straight Part

A simple screen role that does not require an aptitude either for 'tragedy, comedy, history, pastoral, pastoral-comical, historical-pastoral, tragical-historical, tragical-comical-historical-pastoral, scene individable, or poem unlimited' forms of acting. [With apologies to Polonius in William Shakespeare's *Hamlet*]

Streep, Meryl

Adored by some, excoriated by others, Streep has often been compared, unfavourably, to her perceived 1980s arch-rival, **Jessica Lange**. Bitterness peaked in 1982 with Streep's **Oscar** success in **Alan J Pakula's** *Sophie's Choice*, when the critics were all for Lange's performance in Graeme Clifford's *Frances*. Streep may be a detached actress, seeming to approach a part from the outside in, but this should not detract from her often remarkable interpretations. She's a **Bette Davis**, not a **Barbara Stanwyck**, and one still remembers that first haunted look she gave **Jeremy Irons** in **Karel Reisz's** marvellously flawed *The French Lieutenant's Woman* (81). In her recent films she seems to have been searching for some role that would carry her through middle age towards a comfortable and garlanded semi-retirement, but having tried action, pseudo-feminism, worthiness and romance, she still appears to be flailing a little in her choices. This is a shame, for her serious approach to screen acting should rightly be serving as an example to younger actors still uncertain of the parameters of their profession.

OTHER KEY FILMS: *Julia* (77); *The Deer Hunter* (78); *Kramer Vs Kramer* (79); *Silkwood* (83); *Out Of Africa* (85); *She-Devil* (89); *Death Becomes Her* (92); *The Bridges Of Madison County* (95); *Dancing At Lughnasa* (98); *Music Of The Heart* (99); *Adaptation* (01)

Streisand, Barbra

In the same league as **Judy Garland** and **Al Jolson** when it comes to belting out a melody, Streisand has perhaps been over-praised, over-humoured and over-the-top in just about equal measures during her overlong screen career. Her début movie, **William Wyler's** *Funny Girl* (68), could surely only appeal to the sort of people who hang flying ducks in their living rooms and shuffle around the parquet floor on cloth pantoufles [see **Philippe Noiret** in **Patrice Leconte's** *Tango* (93)] and its follow-up, **Gene Kelly's** *Hello Dolly!* (69), did for matchmaking and **Louis Armstrong** what Elaine May's *Ishtar* (87) did for the art of comedy. Her directorial debut, *Yentl* (83), was so sublimely unconvincing that it arguably set back the cause of cross-dressing by ten years, and *The Mirror Has Two Faces* (96) took a first-class little French thriller, André Cayatte's *Le Miroir A Deux Faces* (58), and turned it into a dirge. Opinion is, of course, divided, and Barbrolaters will no doubt vociferously disagree with such a summary of their heroine's career.

OTHER KEY FILMS: *What's Up Doc?* (72); *The Way We Were* (73); *A Star Is Born* (76); *The Prince Of Tides* (91)

Stress Marks

Blemishes on a film print generally caused by mishandling or mechanical friction.
See **Static Marks**

Strike

The act of taking down a film set once it is no longer required for filming.

Striping

The application onto a reel of film of a sound 'stripe' (magnetic coating) on which to record the soundtrack.

Stroboscopic Effects

Unwanted optical effects appearing on film and caused by the time differential between the speed of movement of the action being filmed and the capacity of the camera (or the eye, of course) to pick up that speed – thus the classic example of the spokes on a car wheel seeming to revolve backwards rather than forwards.

Stroheim, Erich von

His real name was Erich Oswald Stroheim, and he was the son of a maker of straw hats, and his Hollywood incarnation, in all its demented and sometimes ill-judged glory, was largely the creation of his own fervid and obsessive imaginings. The assumed name of von Nordenwall was, however, the genuine product of the young Erich Stroheim's observation of the decadent Viennese *fin de siècle* that gave us Freud, Mahler and Schoenberg. In his greatest films as director and star, *Foolish Wives* (21), *Greed* (25), *The Wedding March* (28) and the unfinished *Queen Kelly* (28), von Stroheim perfectly inhabited that very same sensuous, disordered and fallible Habsburg Empire of the senses while remaining only too well aware of the reasons for its demise. **Jean Renoir** and **Billy Wilder** were the two great directors who understood and valued him as an actor, and in his extraordinary performances in Renoir's *La Grande Illusion* (37), and in Wilder's *Five Graves To Cairo* (43) and *Sunset Boulevard* (50), von Stroheim occasionally came close to being the man whose Golem-like image he had so fastidiously created.

OTHER KEY FILMS: as director, *Blind Husbands* (18); *The Merry Widow* (28); as an actor in *The Lost Squadron* (32); *As You Desire Me* (32); *The Great Flamarion* (45); *La Danse De Mort* (47)

KEY LINE:
'The Man You Love To Hate.' [Erich von Stroheim's publicity billing for *The Heart Of Humanity* (18)]

Erich von Stroheim (complete, no doubt, with corset and silk underwear) on the set of his truncated masterpiece, The Wedding March *(26), in which he played doomed aristocrat Prince Nikki*

Studio

Either a permanent, named location at which feature films are made, or the company that commissions, finances and sees such films through to fruition.

Studio Manager

The person responsible for the efficient running of a film studio in terms of management, staffing, maintenance, etc., but not responsible for the making of films within its aegis.

Studio System

The Studio System was the system by which stars were contracted, often for long periods of time (**Elizabeth Taylor**, for instance, signed an eighteen-year contract with **MGM**) to individual studios, which then took it upon themselves to shape and run the careers, love-lives, publicity hand-outs and beautification of their highly paid wards. Following anti-trust legislation in the late 1940s and with the coming of mass television in the mid-1950s, the system slowly collapsed, allowing the stars who remained in place after the slaughter a considerably greater say in running their own affairs.

KEY LINE:

'When you are committed to the skeleton of a beginning, a middle, and an end, the cleverness was in concealing the skeleton. This is a cliché, but you had to surprise them with what they expected.' [Screenwriter Norman Krasna on outwitting the Studio System]

Stunt Player/Stuntman

Hired to double for a star during the filming of dangerous stunts, the stunt player is required not only to resemble the star (from a suitable distance) but also to dress and coif themselves in the same way. A close look at long shots of the stars in many feature films will show up the ruse, and if one concentrates on the face rather than the stunt, fascinating discrepancies are often revealed. Hal Needham's *Hooper* (78), starring **Burt Reynolds**, and Richard Rush's *The Stunt Man* (80), starring **Peter O'Toole** and Steve Railsback, both shed interesting, if diffuse light on this somewhat dangerous occupation. Nowadays, there is even such a thing as a 'stunt bottom' – Anita Hart has doubled in this capacity during action sequences for Cindy Crawford, Pamela Anderson and Elizabeth Hurley.

Sturges, John

A top-rank action director who specialised in **Westerns** and adventure films, Sturges made his mark directing **Spencer Tracy** as one-armed war veteran John J MacReedy in *Bad Day At Black Rock* (55), before hitting the big time with *The Magnificent Seven* (60), in which he cast virtually every key male actor of the next ten years. *The Great Escape* (63) consolidated his position in the Hollywood hierarchy, and he became the director of choice of the tough-guy acting school, and, as such, he directed **Clint Eastwood** in *Joe Kidd* (72) and **John Wayne** in *McQ* (74). Sturges's final film, *The Eagle Has Landed* (76), with **Michael Caine**, is a superb example of the successful adaptation of a best-selling novel.

OTHER KEY FILMS: *The Capture* (50); *Escape From Fort Bravo* (53); *Gunfight At The OK Corral* (57); *Last Train From Gun Hill* (59); *Hour Of The Gun* (67); *Ice Station Zebra* (68)

Sturges, Preston

Scion of a rich and artistically rarefied world, and, incidentally, inventor of the kiss-proof lipstick, Sturges also made a sequence of the funniest and most inventive films ever to come out of Hollywood. He began his career as a screenwriter on such movies as A Edward Sutherland's *Diamond Jim* (35) and Mitchell Leisen's *Easy Living* (37), and this discipline stood him in good stead when he was given the opportunity to direct his own script of *The Great McGinty* (40). Already Hollywood's highest-paid writer, the floodgates then opened and in the next four years he wrote and directed *Christmas In July* (41), *The Lady Eve* (41), *Sullivan's Travels* (41), *The Palm Beach Story* (42), *The Miracle Of Morgan's Creek* (44) and *Hail The Conquering Hero* (44). These films are miracles of demented, satirical humour, and it is something of a tragedy that Sturges, exhausted perhaps by such a burst of immaculately sustained creativity, should have produced only five more films (three of which were happily up to his old standards) before his untimely death in 1959 at the predictably eccentric venue of the Algonquin Hotel in New York. It is impossible ever to forget such magnificent creations as the shotgun-toting, hound-like baying Ale and Quail Club, the Weenie King, or Rudy Vallee's J D Hackensacker III, and it is for the consistent gentleness and humanity of his humour, and his acceptance of oddity as simply a minor variation on the normal, that Sturges deserves to be honoured.

OTHER KEY FILMS: *The Great Moment* (44); *The Sin Of Harold Dibbledock* [a.k.a. *Mad Wednesday*] (47); *Unfaithfully Yours* (48); *The Beautiful Blonde From Bashful Bend* (49); *Les Carnets Du Major Thompson* (55)

Subjective Camera

This refers to those times when the camera shows only the visual point of view of a key player in a film, thereby losing its apparent objectivity. Notable (if rather flawed) examples include Robert Montgomery's **Philip Marlowe** thriller, *The Lady In The Lake* (46), and Delmer Daves's far more successful *Dark Passage* (47), in which **Humphrey Bogart's** Vincent Parry is only revealed to the audience following face-changing plastic surgery over an hour into the film's running time. (Bogart was America's highest paid star at the time, earning over $450,000 a year, so the *per capita* cost of renting his physiognomy and then not using it wasn't exactly negligible.)

Substandard Film

Any film of a smaller gauge than the standard 35mm.

Subtitles

When foreign-language films are not dubbed into the host language, the translation appears as text along the bottom of the screen in superimposed type.

Subtractive Process

A three-colour process that relies on different emulsive layers to filter out tints in order to achieve a satisfactory colour balance on the finished product.

Sundance Institute

Robert Redford inaugurated the Sundance Institute in 1980 as a means of encouraging and sponsoring young filmmakers who would otherwise have a hard time finding backing for existing projects (or finding work *per se*). The annual Sundance Film Festival is organised by the institute, highlighting and rewarding promising films from the US independent sector.

Sun Gun

A hand-held lighting unit for location shooting in conditions where the use of static lighting units would not be appropriate.

Sunlight

Daylight is light that reaches the camera's objective from any natural source, whereas sunlight comes specifically from the sun.

Sunshade

Also called the 'effects box' or 'matte box', the sunshade protects the camera from undesirable light and doubles as a holder of **mattes** and **filters** for **special effects**.

Super 8

An 8mm-gauge substandard film stock, with a fifty per cent wider gauge than standard 8mm film, which allows for the addition of sound **striping**.

Superimposition

The imposition of one piece of film, or image, over another, either through a process of double exposure, glass shots or multiple printing. The technique may be used to indicate an unconscious or dream state, or possibly the aftermath of a sapping or drugging, as in **Edward Dmytryk's** *Murder My Sweet* (45), when **Dick Powell's Philip Marlowe** gradually reawakens, following his smoking of a drugged cigarette, in a room near Jules Amthor's surgery.

Supporting Players

The important secondary actors and actresses who back up and provide necessary plot fodder for the star, and, not entirely coincidentally perhaps, much of the atmosphere of any successful movie.

Sutherland, Donald

Sutherland had been languishing in the doldrums for seven years before **Robert Altman's** *M*A*S*H* (70), in which he played the lazily anarchic Hawkeye Pearce, and Brian G Hutton's *Kelly's Heroes* (70) made him famous. He has since steered a clever course between commercial expedience and artistic integrity, and he is one of the few actors still in work to have retained, and even improved, his reputation over a forty-year career. He was impressive as John Klute, in **Alan J Pakula's** *Klute* (71), and even more so as John Baxter in **Nicolas Roeg's** *Don't Look Now* (73), and he has used his engaging quirkiness and his versatile Canadian accent to promote a steady following both in the US and in Europe, in a sequence of roles as disparate as his Calvin in **Robert Redford's** *Ordinary People* (80) (possibly the best role of his career), and Ivan in **Werner Herzog's** *Scream Of Stone* (91).

OTHER KEY FILMS: *Steelyard Blues* (72); *The Day Of The Locust* (75); *1900* (75); *The Eagle Has Landed* (76); *Casanova* (76); *Blood Relatives* (78); *The Disappearance* (78); *Invasion Of The Body Snatchers* (78); *Bear Island* (79); *Eye Of The Needle* (81); *The Winter Of Our Discontent* (83); *Crackers* (84); *The Wolf At The Door* (87); *Lock Up* (89); *A Dry White Season* (89); *Backdraft* (91); *JFK* (91); *Six Degrees Of Separation* (93); *Fallen* (98); *Instinct* (99); *Space Cowboys* (00); *The Art Of War* (00); *Final Fantasy: The Spirits Within* [voiceover] (01)

Swanson, Gloria

Swanson's rise to silent fame is inextricably linked to the star of her mentor, **Cecil B DeMille**, and to those of two other directors, **Sam Wood** and Allen Dwan. Thanks to such films as DeMille's *Male And Female* (19) and *The Affairs Of Anatol* (21), Wood's *My American Wife* (22) *And Bluebeard's Eighth Wife* (23), and Dwan's *A Society Scandal* (24) and *Wages Of Virtue* (24), Swanson was earning $17,500 a week by the time she decided to opt out of the studio system and form her own production company. Vainglory, of course, has been the bane of many lesser mortals, and it was to prove Swanson's downfall, for she arranged to star in and produce *Queen Kelly* (28), with **Erich von Stroheim** directing. The film

ruined her, to the extent that she was still paying off the debts she had incurred while making it in 1950, when **Billy Wilder** offered her the poisoned chalice of yet another comeback, this time as a grotesque parody of herself. To Swanson's credit she said yes to Norma Desmond and *Sunset Boulevard* (50), and, ironically, it is for this film that she is now best remembered, and not for the often baroque flights of fancy that were the products of her heyday.

OTHER KEY FILMS: *Don't Change Your Husband* (19); *The Great Moment* (21); *Under The Lash* (21); *The Impossible Mrs Bellew* (22); *Prodigal Daughters* (23); *Manhandled* (24); *The Coast Of Folly* (25); *The Love Of Sunya* (27); *Sadie Thompson* (28); *Indiscreet* (31); *Father Takes A Wife* (41); *Airport 1975* (74)

*The sublime **Gloria Swanson** in a publicity shot for Billy Wilder's* Sunset Boulevard *(50), in which she played the hysterically delusional Norma Desmond*

Swashbucklers

A variety of actor (and occasionally actress) who specialises in roles requiring athleticism and derring-do. A 'swash' is a violent or smashing blow, whilst 'buckler' derives from the Old French for a small round shield. The image, however, of **Douglas Fairbanks** (either father or son), **Errol Flynn** or **Stewart Granger** smashing about themselves with only a shield as a weapon, is somewhat misleading, but if one sees the shield as implying the existence of an accompanying sword, one gets nearer to the mark. Swashbuckling films are generally notable for their humour, simplicity, and general good nature, and the marked lack of any exalted ambition other than to amuse and entertain.

Best Swashbucklers

Philippe de Broca's *Cartouche* (62); Christian-Jaque's *Fanfan La Tulipe* (51); John Cromwell's *The Prisoner Of Zenda* (37); **Michael Curtiz** and William Keighley's *The Adventures Of Robin Hood* (38); Michael Curtiz's *Captain Blood* (35) and *The Sea Hawk* (40); William Keighley's *The Master Of Ballantrae* (52); **Akira Kurosawa's** *Yojimbo* (61); **Ang Lee's** *Crouching Tiger, Hidden Dragon* (00); Rouben Mamoulian's *The Mark Of Zorro* (40); Fred Niblo's *The Three Musketeers* (21); Jean-Paul Rappeneau's *Cyrano De Bergerac* (90); George Sidney's *Scaramouche* (52); Vincent Sherman's *The Adventures Of Don Juan* (49); **Robert Siodmak's** *The Crimson Pirate* (52); **Jacques Tourneur's** *The Flame And The Arrow* (50); **Raoul Walsh's** *The Thief Of Bagdad* (24)

Swish Pan

The sudden sharp panning from one scene to another or from one subject to another, creating a blurring or swish-like effect across the screen.

Sylvester

See **Tweetie Pie**

Synch/Sync

Widely acknowledged abbreviation for **synchronization**; a film is said to be in synch when both its sound and visual tracks tally.

Synchronization

Synchronization is the process by which sound and visual tracks are made to tally. When a film is out of synch, the words come out either before or after the lip movements they refer to.

Synchronizer

The sprocket-driven machine used to ensure that the visual track and its accompanying sound tracks are kept in correct alignment.

Synchronous Sound

This is sound correctly and realistically accompanying an image on the screen. Asynchronous sound is notable for its opposition to, juxtaposition with, or counterpointing of, the image on the screen

Synchronous Speed

The optimum speed (24 frames per second/90 feet a minute for 35mm film) at which camera, projector and sound recording equipment should be run if the filmed scene is to be accurately reproduced.

Synch Mark

See **Start Mark**

Synopsis

A brief (usually less than one page) résumé of the bare bones of a feature-film plot, produced before a full treatment or outline is called for, and considerably before the production of a screenplay.

Tachometer

A device that measures the exact speed, in frames per second, at which a cine camera is running.

Tail

The final blank strip of leader at the finish of a reel of film, placed there to protect the final frames and to indicate to the projectionist that the movie is over.

Tails Up/Tails Out
See **Head Up/Head Out**

Take

A take is the uninterrupted shooting of one individual scene or sequence in a film as part of the larger whole. The most famous uninterrupted take of all occurred in the opening minutes of **Orson Welles's** *Touch Of Evil* (58). This consisted of a single two-minute travelling crane shot, managed by ace cinematographer Russell Metty, and which incorporated the beginnings of a love story, a cross-border murder and the introduction of two principal characters within its awesomely complicated though deceptively simple-looking framework.

Take-up Reel

The second or subsidiary reel onto which a film is wound during projection.

Talent Agent

An agent who works on behalf of screen performers and who takes a percentage of their fees in payment.

Talent Scout

A talent scout is someone who is paid to look out for people with star quality in a non-movie environment. Mind-blowing stories abound of actors and actresses being discovered waiting at table (usually, like **Lana Turner**, at Schwab's Drugstore on Sunset Boulevard) or on the street, like the twelve-year-old **Carole Lombard**; but in reality talent scouts tend to concentrate on theatres and the stage, where they can at least count on the potential star being able to act. Movies themselves added to the mystique, with publicity departments, like that of producer **David O Selznick,** dreaming up bogus competitions, in his case to find the perfect Scarlett O'Hara from among two thousand more or less hysterical hopefuls.

Talkies

The original slang expression for 'talking pictures', in popular usage at the time of Alan Crosland's *The Jazz Singer* (27), to differentiate such movies from the nominally silent films that preceded them.

Talmadge, Norma

Sister of silent actress Constance, who was herself married to the great **Buster Keaton,** Talmadge was the biggest star in Hollywood for a short period during the 1920s, earning $250,000 a film. Not especially beautiful, and with a rather square, Victorian figure, Talmadge nevertheless struck a chord with audiences in films such as Albert Parker's *Branded Woman* (20), Clarence Brown's *Kiki*

(26) and Fred Niblo's *Camille* (27), in all of which she played tragic heroines. When her squeaky voice was finally exposed with the coming of sound, Talmadge gracefully retired from the screen to live off her extensive real estate holdings. See endpaper photograph.

OTHER KEY FILMS: *A Tale Of Two Cities* (11); *Panthea* (17); *Bluebeard's Eighth Wife* (23); *Secrets* (24); *The Dove* (28); *DuBarry, Woman Of Passion* (30)

Tank

An enormous water tank, situated on a studio lot, and used for shots involving lakes, rivers, and other expanses of water, on which it would be unprofitable and unrealistic to film in actuality.

Tape Splicing

The simple and temporary splicing together of two sections of film by the use of adhesive tape. See **Hot Splicing**

Tarantino, Quentin

It's hard to believe that Tarantino was born in only 1963, for he appears to have gone through enough career restarts to satisfy a man twice his age. A former video-store clerk with an encyclopaedic knowledge of film (in California, video stores stock *all* the great films), Tarantino wrote his breakthrough script, *True Romance* (93), for director Tony Scott, and it was a humdinger. His own debut as a director, *Reservoir Dogs* (93), quickly followed, and afforded him instant entry to that select club of brilliant first-timers which includes **Charles Laughton**, **Nicholas Ray** and **Orson Welles**. He followed up with the sensational *Pulp Fiction* (94) and then, when critics were just beginning to write him off as a burnt-out case, he completed his hat-trick with *Jackie Brown* (97). Long may he prosper.

OTHER KEY FILMS: Oliver Stone's *Natural Born Killers* (94); Robert Rodriguez's *From Dusk Till Dawn* (96)

Target

A circular screen used to protect a camera lens from unwanted light.

Tarkovsky, André

Considered by some to be the greatest Russian director since **Sergei Eisenstein**, Tarkovsky began his career working within the system, and ended it as a voluntary exile, dying of lung cancer, looking distractedly back at the culture which had made him and which he had belatedly come to feel had let him down. His films are first and foremost philosophical treatises, and this is their weakness as well as, paradoxically, being the basis for their awe-inspiring visual and poetic harmony. *Andrei Rublev* (66), his masterpiece, consists of a majestic and extended exploration into the significance of art and religion, but his first feature, *Ivan's Childhood* (62), which tells the story of a doomed boy working for the Russian partisans during the Second World War, is more accessible. His final films, *Nostalgia* (83) and *The Sacrifice* (86), were directed abroad, and reflect Tarkovsky's long-standing and well-documented obsession with the gradual dumbing down of mass culture.

OTHER KEY FILMS: *Solaris* (72); *The Mirror* (74); *Stalker* (79)

Tarzan

The burly Elmo Lincoln was, to all intents and purposes, the first screen Tarzan, in Scott Sidney's *Tarzan Of The Apes* (18), but five-time Olympic gold medal winner **Johnny Weissmuller** is the man most viewers – even now, nearly seventy years after he first appeared in the role – will forever associate with Edgar Rice Burroughs's aristocratic simian. Even **Sean Connery** has appeared in a Tarzan film, John Guillermin's *Tarzan's Greatest Adventure* (59), but only as a heavy, O'Bannion, to Gordon Scott's apeman. There have been Tarzan spoofs, and porn Tarzans; there have been Indian Tarzans, i.e. Chandrakant's *Tarzan 303*, and Chinese Tarzans – the aptly named *The Adventures Of Chinese Tarzan* (40) [director unknown]. There have been cartoon Tarzans, with Chris Buck and Kevin Lima's *Tarzan* (99), and even documentaries investigating the history and cultural impact of the apeman, including Alain d'Aix's *Investigating Tarzan* (97). **Jean-Luc Godard**, of all people, even named one of his most famous films *Tarzan Versus IBM*; all right, the film was actually *Alphaville (Une Étrange Aventure De Lemmy Caution)* (65), and the Tarzan bit was one of six alternative titles, but the trend is clear. All in all there have been more than one hundred Tarzan films and television series, and every generation seems to require their very own version of the hero. Probably the best, by public acclamation, have been W S Van Dyke's original *Tarzan The Ape Man* (32), and its follow-up, **Jack Conway** [uncredited] and Cedric Gibbons's *Tarzan And His Mate* (34), closely followed by Hugh Hudson's *Greystoke: The Legend Of Tarzan, Lord Of The Apes* (84). See also **Maureen O'Sullivan**

KEY LINE:
'Me Tarzan. You Jane.' [from *Tarzan The Ape Man* (32)]

Tati, Jacques

It is an object of faith that Tati's sense of humour was never appreciated in his native France – like most objects of faith, this is palpable nonsense. What is true is that Tati died bankrupt and unable to raise the money for his final M. Hulot film, ironically due to be called *Confusion*. Tati became increasingly self-conscious and, dare one say it, artistic, following the success of his first three features, *Jour De Fête* (49), *Monsieur Hulot's Holiday* (53) and *Mon Oncle* (58), and the French public dislikes nothing more than a message. The British and the Americans, on the other hand, adore messages (as long as they are telescoped) and they opened their hearts to Tati and Hulot, if not their wallets. *Playtime* (67) and *Traffic* (72) duly delighted the critics with their satirical edge, but alienated the French public, who preferred the less intellectual antics of **Bourvil** and **Louis de Funès**. There is no doubt that Tati was a comic genius, and an underappreciated one, but the fickle general public sees a fine line between populist comedy and enlightened social commentary, and to many, at least in his native France, Tati was perceived to have crossed it.

OTHER KEY FILMS: *Sylvie Et Le Fantôme* [act. only] (46); *Le Diable Au Corps* [act. only] (47); *Parade* (74)

Tavernier, Bertrand

A literate, deeply cultured Lyonnais – just like his father, around whom he based a sublime 1988 TV documentary, 'Lyons, Le Regard Intérieur' – Tavernier is both critic, cinéphile and director, and his best work, while remaining resolutely French in sensibility, is nonetheless imbued with his long-standing love of American cinema. His first feature, *The Watchmaker Of St Paul* (73), was an immediate success and starred **Philippe Noiret**, who performed the same mimetic function for Tavernier that **Jean-Pierre Léaud** had earlier done for **François Truffaut**. *Sunday In The Country* (84) effectively put Tavernier on a par with the greatest French directors, and both *These Foolish Things* (91), in which he drew out an absolutely luminous performance from **Jane Birkin**, and *La Vie Et Rien D'Autre* [*Life And Nothing But*] (92), in which Noiret verges on greatness, have only further confirmed Tavernier's extraordinary talent.

OTHER KEY FILMS: *Le Juge Et L'Assassin* (75); *La Mort En Direct* (80); *Une Semaine De Vacances* (80); *Coup De Torchon* (81); *Mississippi Blues* (83); *Round Midnight* (86); *La Fille De D'Artagnan* (94) *L'Appât* (95); *Ça Commence Aujourd'hui* (99)

Taviani, Paolo and Vittorio

This brilliant, film-obsessed duo have kept the reputation of Italian cinema alive through its recent period of apparent decline with their poetic meditations on myth, memory and the power of allegory. Following their Palme D'Or success at the **Cannes Film Festival** with *Padre Padrone* (77), the brothers made the magical *The Night Of San Lorenzo* (82), which continued their fascination with the Second World War and its effects upon Italian society, a fascination that first became manifest in their debut film, *San Miniato, July 44* (54). Their later films have been much bound up with the machinations of fate and the possibilities of redemption, and *Kaos* (85) remains perhaps their greatest and most poetically accomplished work.

OTHER KEY FILMS: *Un Uomo Da Bruciare* (62); *Allonsanfan* (74); *Il Prato* (79); *Good Morning, Babylon* (87); *Night Sun* (90); *Fiorile* (93); *The Elective Affinities* (96); *Tu Ridi* (98)

Taylor, Elizabeth

The last of the great studio-era screen goddesses, this 'Made In England' beauty – who has recently been made a Dame of the British Empire – left for America at the outbreak of the Second World War, aged seven. She was signed up by **MGM** three

The eighteen-year-old **Elizabeth Taylor** *played siren-like Angela Vickers to Montgomery Clift's susceptible George Eastman, in George Stevens's A Place In The Sun (51)*

years later for a mind-boggling eighteen-year contract, and the rest is, as they say, screen history. From her first appearance in Fred M Wilcox's *Lassie Comes Home* (43) it was obvious that Taylor was born to be a star, and she moved, with no apparent difficulty (thanks to MGM's star minders), from Clarence Brown's *National Velvet* (44), through **Vincente Minnelli's** *Father Of The Bride* (50) into the tentative maturity and passion of **George Stevens's** *A Place In The Sun* (51), where she realised for the first time, watching **Montgomery Clift** at work, that acting took effort. Seven marriages later, she remains an icon, an indefatigable fund-raiser for AIDS charities, and the recipient of two **Oscars**, one for Daniel Mann's *Butterfield 8* (60), a film she described as a 'heap of shit', and the other for **Mike Nichols's** *Who's Afraid Of Virginia Woolf?* (66), in which she gave the performance of a lifetime, as Martha, opposite **Richard Burton's** George.

OTHER KEY FILMS: *Little Women* (49); *Ivanhoe* (52); *Giant* (56); *Raintree County* (57); *Cat On A Hot Tin Roof* (58); *Suddenly Last Summer* (59); *Cleopatra* (63); *Reflections In A Golden Eye* (67); *Secret Ceremony* (68); *Under Milk Wood* (71); *Winter Kills* (79); *The Flintstones* (94); *The Visit* (99)

KEY LINE:
'Tell Mama. Tell Mama all.' [*A Place In The Sun*]

Taylor, Robert

Taylor (a.k.a. Spangler Arlington Brugh) was renowned for his fine profile, for his hard work, and for his wooden acting style, which relied overmuch on a serious frown and a set of flashing eyes. However, he remained a top **MGM** star for nearly thirty years, so he must have had something else to offer, but it is a little hard to decide what. He was inoffensive, like **Robert Young**, and handsome, like **Tyrone Power**, and he made an excellent corrupt lawyer in **Nicholas Ray's** *Party Girl* (58), but the magic certainly came as much from Ray as it did from Taylor (although one hesitates to begrudge him one of the few meaty parts he was ever given). Kids always loved him, though, when he buckled his swash in films like Richard Thorpe's *Ivanhoe* (52), *Knights Of The Round Table* (54) and *The Adventures Of Quentin Durward* (56), and that's no small achievement.

OTHER KEY FILMS: *Magnificent Obsession* (35); *Camille* (37); *Waterloo Bridge* (40); *Billy The Kid* (41); *Johnny Eager* (42); *The Bribe* (49); *Quo Vadis?* (51); *All The Brothers Were Valiant* (53); *The Law And Jake Wade* (58); *Miracle Of The White Stallions* (63); *The Night Walker* (64)

Téchiné, André

The subtle and elegantly intimate French director of *Barocco* (77), *Les Soeurs Brontë* (79), *Rendez-Vous* (85) and *Les Roseaux Sauvages* (94) seemed to have achieved the **crossover** he deserved with the outstanding *Ma Saison Préferée* [*My Favourite Season*] (93) and *Les Voleurs* (96), both of which starred **Catherine Deneuve** and **Daniel Auteuil**. However, it was perhaps his concentration on character, maturity, and atmosphere at the expense of plot that succeeded in alienating an English-speaking audience still made up of fifty per cent sentimentality and fifty per cent xenophobia. Apart from the handful of enlightened souls prepared to seek out Téchiné's films in the few remaining art theatres open to them, audiences now are forced to rely on rare television outings to keep up with his work. It's a sorry state of affairs when the latest **Tom Cruise** or **Julia Roberts** movie can monopolise every big screen in the country, whereas the wisdom and talent of a man like Téchiné is ghettoised. In an ideal world, shouldn't it be the other way around?

OTHER KEY FILMS: *Paulina S'En Va* (69); *Souvenirs D'En France* (75); *Hôtel Des Amériques* (81); *La Matiouette Ou L'Arrière-Pays* (83); *Le Lieu Du Crime* (86); *Les Innocents* (87); *J'Embrasse Pas* (91); *Alice Et Martin* (98); *Loin* (00)

Technical Adviser

The experts filmmakers use to advise them on the correct details of dress, manners and procedure in the making of films that have to do with the police, the army, the judiciary or any other civil or military discipline that involves codes or standards of conduct that are not normally open to public scrutiny.

Technicolor

First invented as an expensive two-colour process in 1915 by Herbert T Kalmus and Daniel F Comstock, Technicolor was improved to a three-colour process in 1932, appearing for the first time in its full glory in Rouben Mamoulian's *Becky Sharp* (35). Further improvements continued apace, culminating in **Ernest Haller**, Ray Rennahan and **Lee Garmes's** gorgeous Technicolor work on **Victor Fleming's** ***Gone With The Wind*** (39). The word Technicolor has now become a synonym for any brightly coloured object or occurrence.

Telecine

A machine used for the projection of cinema films on television.

313

Telephoto Lens

A specialist lens for taking close-up shots of faraway objects through magnification, albeit at the cost of some loss of perspective.

Temple, Shirley

The most famous child star of them all, Temple, or 'little dimples' as some bright publicist called her, first worked when she was aged only three. A precocious dancer, and imbued with an apparent self-confidence verging on the criminal, Temple became the number-one box-office attraction in the US on her seventh birthday and remained so until beyond her tenth. If anyone imagines that merchandising only began with *Star Wars*, think again. There were Shirley Temple dolls, diapers, diaries and doilies – grown men like **Cary Grant**, **Gary Cooper** and **Victor McLaglen** were forced to kowtow and hootchy-kootchy with her on screen, knowing that if they clipped the little brat around the ear (as they doubtless wanted to) they would be excoriated by all America. She had talent, and a certain fey charm, and she cheered people up, in films like Irving Cummings's *Curly Top* (35), William Seiter's *Dimples* (36), **Allan Dwan's** *Heidi* (37), and **John Ford's** *Wee Willie Winkie* (37), during the time of the Great Depression. Her career gave her up in the late 1940s, and she has spent the remainder of her life in public service, most notably as US Ambassador to Ghana and Czechoslovakia. Her autobiography was *Child Star* (88), but a better title might have been *From Dimples To Diplomat*.
OTHER KEY FILMS: *Little Miss Marker* (34); *Bright Eyes* (34); *The Littlest Rebel* (35); *Rebecca Of Sunnybrook Farm* (38); *The Little Princess* (39); *Susannah Of The Mounties* (39)

Tempo

The overall pace of a finished movie, dependent on script, timing, editing and rhythm.

Tener

An extremely powerful 10,000-watt spotlight.

Thalberg, Irving G

A sickly child, Thalberg grew into one of the best and most highly respected producers Hollywood has ever known, and the man who virtually ran **MGM** single-handed in the years from 1924 to 1933. It was during his tenure that MGM produced such commercial hits as Fred Niblo's *Ben-Hur* (26), Clarence Brown's *Flesh And The Devil* (27), **King Vidor's** *The Crowd* (28) and Tay Garnett's *China Seas* (35), and such long-term critical successes as **Tod Browning's** *Freaks* (32), **Sam Wood's** *A Night At The Opera* (35) and Sidney Franklin's *The Good Earth* (37). Thalberg had been told by his doctors when he was only a teenager that he would never reach the age of thirty – in actual fact he reached thirty-seven, and left behind him a modestly won but mightily crafted legacy, and the reputation, rare in the cutthroat world of Hollywood film production, of being a decent man.
OTHER KEY FILMS: Clarence Brown's *Anna Christie* (30); **Ernst Lubitsch's** *The Merry Widow* (34); Frank Lloyd's *Mutiny On The Bounty* (35)

Theme

The fundamental subject or leitmotif of a feature film, e.g. Ethan Edwards's search for his kidnapped niece in **John Ford's** *The Searchers* (56). Also the principal melody that recurs throughout a film as part of the soundtrack, e.g. **John Barry's** *From Russia With Love* theme from Terence Young's 1963 **James Bond** movie of the same name, or 'Lara's Theme', by **Maurice Jarre**, from **David Lean's** *Dr Zhivago* (65).

Thin Print

A positive print deficient in contrast and density.

35mm

The benchmark film gauge used on most feature films and in most movie theatres since its inception by the Lumière brothers on 28th December 1895.

Thompson, Emma

Thompson had a magnificent run between 1992 and 1995, virtually unparalleled in terms of quality and achievement since the Golden Age of the 1930s and 1940s studio system. The run began with her luminous playing of Margaret Schlegel in **James Ivory's** *Howards End* (92), continued with her unrestrained performance as Beatrice in **Kenneth Branagh's** *Much Ado About Nothing* (93), followed by her notably controlled Miss Kenton in Ivory's *Remains Of The Day* (93). She then moved on to defending the Guildford Four as Gareth Peirce in Jim Sheridan's *In The Name Of The Father* (93), transformed herself into a talented, touching Dora Carrington in Christopher Hampton's *Carrington* (95), and then, *pièce de résistance*, both wrote the screenplay and acted as Elinor Dashwood in **Ang Lee's** *Sense And Sensibility* (95). The other actresses of her generation must have heaved great sighs of relief when, in recent years, she has taken a break to start a family.

314

Emma Thompson as the luminously sensible Elinor Dashwood in Ang Lee's Sense And Sensibility *(95)*

OTHER KEY FILMS: *The Tall Guy* (89); *Henry V* (89); *Impromptu* (90); *Dead Again* (91); *Peter's Friends* (92); *Junior* (94); *The Winter Guest* (97); *Primary Colors* (98); *Judas Kiss* (98); *Maybe Baby* (00); *Wit* (01)

Thornton, Billy Bob

A character actor who found sudden fame (and an **Oscar** for the screenplay) as a result of his brilliant performance as the retarded murderer, Karl Childers, in the self-directed *Sling Blade* (96), Thornton paid his dues in a succession of second-rate films such as Adrian Lyne's *Indecent Proposal* (93) and Steven Seagal's *On Deadly Ground* (94), before hitting the big time. However, for those with the eyes to see, Thornton's talent was already on show in his magnificent script (co-written with Tom Epperson) and his excellent acting turn for Carl Franklin's still underrated edge-of-the-seat thriller, *One False Move* (92), a movie that improves with each subsequent viewing.

OTHER KEY FILMS: *For The Boys* (91); *Tombstone* (93); *The Stars Fell On Henrietta* (94); *Dead Man* (95); *Boogie Nights* (97); *U-Turn* (97); *Primary Colors* (98); *A Gun, A Car, A Blonde* (98); *All The Pretty Horses* [dir.] (00); *South Of Heaven, West Of Hell* (00); *The Man Who Wasn't There* (01); *Daddy And Them* [also dir.] (01); *Wakin' Up in Reno* (01); *Bandits* (01)

Threading

The necessary lining up of the perforations on a strip of film to the corresponding sprockets on a projector or camera before action.

3-D

This is film shot using three-dimensional cinematography techniques, and two cameras in binocular symmetry to achieve an effect, if stereoscopic glasses are worn, of quasi-realistic depth when the film is projected. The most famous 3-D film of all is André De Toth's *House Of Wax* (53), starring **Vincent Price** in his first real horror role as the hideously deformed Prof. Henry Jarrod (with **Charles Bronson**, a.k.a. Charles Buchinsky, in the role of sculptor's assistant). The paradox of the film was that the director, being blind in one eye, could not marvel at his own brilliant use of the 3-D medium.

KEY LINE:

'You never see things like this in Provincetown.' [Price]

360-degree Pan Shot

A shot in which the camera swings around the subject in a 360-degree full circle. **Krzysztof Kieslowski** used the technique in *The Double Life Of Véronique* (91), as did **Werner Herzog** in *The Enigma Of Kaspar Hauser* (75). See **Roundy Round**

Thrillers

The normal definition of a thriller is a film that has you on the edge of your seat with psychological anxiety, without actually tipping you all the way over onto the floor in abject horror. The following films all fulfil those criteria admirably. All have some twist, some diabolical plot contrivance, that won't allow the audience a let-up before the director is good and ready. Will he or won't he kill her? Will she or won't she kill him? Will the assassin actually manage to kill De Gaulle even though we all know that that is impossible? Will the killer get away with it? And if so, how? Will the fact of being locked in a lift over a long weekend spoil the perfect crime? These are all staple thriller elements, fundamental to cinema and to the success of the mega-budget entertainment industry.

KEY LINES:

Harrison Ford, as escaped murder suspect, Dr Richard Kimble: 'I didn't kill my wife.' Tommy Lee Jones, as gun-threatened Deputy US Marshal Samuel Gerard: 'I don't care.' [The Fugitive (93)]

'Two fellows meet accidentally. Each one has someone that they'd like to get rid of, and they swap murders.' [The train scene between Farley Granger's Guy Haines and Robert Walker's Bruno Anthony, from Alfred Hitchcock's Strangers On A Train (51)] Note for Film Buffs: Those immaculately written nineteen words, taken from the Patricia Highsmith novel and honed by one of the three script collaborators, Raymond Chandler, Czenzi Ormonde or Whitfield Cook, constitute an almost perfect movie pitch/concept. Chandler, given his form, must surely be odds-on favourite.

316

Best Thrillers

René Clément's *Plein Soleil* (59); Henri-Georges Clouzot's *Le Corbeau* [*The Crow*] (43) and *Les Diaboliques* (54); Andrew Davis's *The Fugitive* (93); Alfred Hitchcock's *Strangers On A Train* (51) and *North By Northwest* (59); Louis Malle's *Ascenseur Pour L'Échafaud* (57); Rob Reiner's *Misery* (92); Nicholas Ray's *On Dangerous Ground* (51); Nicolas Roeg's *Don't Look Now* (73); Martin Scorsese's *Taxi Driver* (76); John Sturges's *Bad Day At Black Rock* (55); Orson Welles's *Confidential Report* (55); Fred Zinnemann's *The Day Of The Jackal* (73)

Throw

The mean distance between the screen and the projector.

Thurman, Uma

Another oddball looker, but seriously sexy with it, Thurman has a strange, gawky grace on the screen, best seen in her early role of Cécile de Volanges, the young girl who is deflowered by John Malkovich's rapacious Vicomte de Valmont in Stephen Frears's *Dangerous Liaisons* (88). More proof that Thurman has a very particular and natural screen presence came with the role of Glory in John McNaughton's excellent *Mad Dog And Glory* (93), followed by her quirky turn as the overdosing Mia Wallace in Quentin Tarantino's brilliant *Pulp Fiction* (94). Her recent work has been curiously chosen, and she remains a connoisseur's actress, who, like vintage wine, may well improve with age.

OTHER KEY FILMS: *Adventures Of Baron Munchausen* (89); *Henry & June* (90); *Jennifer Eight* (92); *Beautiful Girls* (96); *The Truth About Cats And Dogs* (96); *Batman And Robin* (97); *Les Misérables* (98); *The Avengers* (98); *Sweet And Lowdown* (99); *Vatel* (00); *The Golden Bowl* (00); *Tape* (01); *Last Word On Paradise* (01)

Tie-in

This is the commercial exploitation, in terms of the merchandising of objects using the film's name but which have only a peripheral link to the film itself, of successful motion picture vehicles such as Tim Burton's *Batman* (89), Steven Spielberg's *Jurassic Park* (93), and James Bond franchises. Such exploitation is nothing new in the industry, its most notable early example being the multi-million dollar Shirley Temple tie-ins, which included dolls, clothes and stationery.

Tierney, Gene

The upper-crust Tierney had an other-worldly and fragile beauty about her, which the studios, to their credit, recognised, using her as the physically elusive Laura, in Otto Preminger's *Laura* (44), and as the ghost-driven Lucy, in Joseph L Mankiewicz's *The Ghost And Mrs Muir* (47). Tierney had a tragic life, giving birth to a mentally retarded child, and then succumbing to depression (following her break-up from Rita Hayworth's ex-husband, Ali Khan), a condition that necessitated a number of lengthy stays in sanatoria. At her best, as in John M Stahl's *Leave Her To Heaven* (45), or in the three first-rate *films noirs* she completed between 1949 and 1950 — Preminger's *Whirlpool* (49) and *Where The Sidewalk Ends* (50) and Jules Dassin's fatalistic *Night And The City* (50) — she transferred that other-worldliness to the screen in a way that few actresses, apart perhaps from **Kim Novak** in **Alfred Hitchcock's** *Vertigo* (58), have ever achieved quite so well.

OTHER KEY FILMS: *The Return Of Jesse James* (40); *Tobacco Road* (41); *The Shanghai Gesture* (42); *Dragonwyck* (46); *The Razor's Edge* (46); *The Mating Season* (51); *The Left Hand Of God* (55); *Advise And Consent* (62)

Gorgeous Gene Tierney, evergreen star of Otto Preminger's Laura *(44) and Joseph L Mankiewicz's* The Ghost And Mrs Muir *(47)*

Tight Shot
A shot that incorporates nearly all of a subject inside the frame, leaving little or no room for anything else.

Tilt
The up-and-down movement of the camera head, as opposed to the side-to-side movement of the camera head during a **pan** shot.

Time Lapse Photography
Time lapse photography is the photography of a slowly burgeoning object, such as a flower, where the camera's timer is set to film a single frame at a specified period (every ten minutes or every hour, say). The exposed frames will then be projected at normal speed to give an impression of accelerated motion – for instance the rapid opening of the flower's petals might take up twenty seconds of screen time, whereas the flower might have taken three hours or even three days to open in reality.

Timing
This is the art of judging one's performance, comic or otherwise, so that the rhythm of the action itself produces the desired effect on the audience. A good example might be the **double take**, where a split second of indecision can mean the difference between a laugh and a yawn.

Tinseltown
A slang name for Hollywood, deriving from its perceived shallowness and preference for glitz over substance.

Tinting
Tinting is the process by which dyes were sometimes applied, by hand, to individual frames of a black-and-white film, to produce an ersatz impression of colour. **Steven Spielberg** mimicked the technique to excellent effect in his movie *Schindler's List* (93), in which a young Jewish girl is tinted in red in an otherwise black-and-white scene, causing the audience to follow her distant progress and to remind them that they are watching human beings, and not simply an amorphous mass of potential victims.

Titanic
James Cameron's blockbusting *Titanic* (97), which cost $200 million to make and which grossed considerably more than $1 billion at the box-office, was something of a labour of love for its director. It involved twelve separate missions down to the wreck, with each mission lasting

between ten and twelve hours locked inside a submersible, with a further six hours there and back – predictably some bright spark in the publicity department then made the point that the director had actually spent more time on the ship than any of its original passengers. A seventeen-million-gallon oceanfront tank was constructed in Baja California, in which a virtually full-sized mock-up of the ship was placed to benefit from the 270° view of the sea the position afforded. Many of the sets, including the first-class salon, were constructed in Mexico City's Estudios Churubusco Azteca, no doubt to benefit from ultra low wages. (Remember the heroic view taken of the third-class passengers in the movie?) The end result was the filmic equivalent of a commercial pine forest.

Titles

Titles are essentially any written information displayed on the screen during the running of a motion picture, and range from the **credits**, listing the film's makers and participants, through the main titles, listing the name of the film, to any captions needed to provide information along the way, and culminating in the end titles, which indicate that the movie, once and for all, is over. In addition, when dealing with foreign films, subtitles may be used to show dialogue in the host language, in preference to dubbing.

Todd-AO

Todd-AO was a 65mm wide-screen process, invented by Dr Pat O'Brien in the early 1950s, and marketed by producer Mike Todd under the aegis of the Magna Corporation. Notable films to appear in Todd-AO were **Fred Zinnemann's** *Oklahoma!* (55), Michael Anderson's *Around The World In Eighty Days* (56), **Joseph L Mankiewicz's** *Cleopatra* (63) and **Robert Wise's** *The Sound Of Music* (65). Todd, the one-time husband of **Elizabeth Taylor**, was killed in a plane accident in 1958 before he was able fully to exploit the technique.

Toland, Gregg

Orson Welles's cinematographer on *Citizen Kane* (41), and the man who taught him the real potential of lighting and of **deep focus** photography, Toland was at the peak of his career when Welles was still panicking New York with his H G Wells radio spoof. Dead in 1948 at the age of forty-four, and without a single star bothering to attend his funeral, Toland realised early on that great photography was all about catching emotion on the wing. His camerawork in **William Wyler's** *Wuthering Heights* (39) and **John Ford's** *The Grapes Of Wrath* (40) and *The Long Voyage Home* (40) testifies to his genius, but his later work is curiously unemotional, as if he had somehow burnt himself out during those fervid four years from 1939 to 1942 – a period which also included Wyler's *The Westerner* (40) and **Howard Hawks's** sublime *Ball Of Fire* (41).
OTHER KEY FILMS: Leo McCarey's *The Kid From Spain* (32); Rouben Mamoulian's *We Live Again* (34); Sidney Franklin's *The Dark Angel* (35); William Wyler's *Dead End* (37); Alfred Werker's *Kidnapped* (38); Wyler's *The Best Year's Of Our Lives* (46); Henry Koster's *The Bishop's Wife* (47)

Tom and Jerry

Tom and Jerry are, of course, **MGM's** famous cat-and-mouse duo whose antics have delighted children and adults alike since their creation in 1940 by animators **Bill Hanna** and **Joe Barbera**. A travesty of a movie was made by Phil Roman in 1992, entitled, with typical Hollywood flair, *Tom And Jerry: The Movie* (92), and which bogged down the famous mouse-chaser and his vindictive rodent opponent in political correctness and bogus sentimentality.

Tonal Key

An essential tool in lighting such expressionist genres as *film noir*, tonal key refers to the predominance of either light or dark tones in a photographed image. This inevitably leads to the terms 'high key' for light tones, and 'low key' for dark tones.

Tone, Franchot

Tone had a cheerful smile that gave the impression of someone who wanted to get on with things while still not being averse to a little idling now and then. Despite the playboy image and the devil-may-care attitude and his serial marriages to a succession of increasingly lesser-known actresses (*pace* **Joan Crawford**), he produced some surprisingly good work during the 1930s and 1940s, including his Lt John Forsythe in **Henry Hathaway's** *The Lives Of A Bengal Lancer* (35), and his Roger Byam in Frank Lloyd's *Mutiny On The Bounty* (35). His best ever part came in **Billy Wilder's** *Five Graves To Cairo* (43) in the role of the brilliantly flippant John J Bramble, an English soldier marooned at a rundown hotel in the desert – a place which **Erich von Stroheim's** Erwin Rommel just happens to use as his base. Sublime.

OTHER KEY FILMS: *Gabriel Over The White House* (33); *Moulin Rouge* (34); *The World Moves On* (34); *Reckless* (36); *The Bride Wore Red* (37); *Three Comrades* (38); *Fast And Furious* (39); *Phantom Lady* (44); *Advise And Consent* (62)

Toning
The manipulation of the colour and tone qualities of a feature film either before or after exposure by artificial means.

Top Hat
A stubby, flattened camera mounting for the capture of those low-angled shots other mounts cannot reach.

Tourneur, Jacques
Tourneur is the thinking person's cult **B-movie** director, for his films grow on one over the years, showing up his A-feature commercial opposition as the also-rans they so often are. Tourneur had visual imagination, a rare attribute in the predominantly textually orientated world of the Anglo-Saxon ascendancy. A Parisian by birth, and the inheritor of a Frenchman's eye for design, harmony and contrast, Tourneur first made his mark with a sensational trio of **Val Lewton** horror features: *Cat People* (42), *I Walked With A Zombie* (43) and *The Leopard Man* (43). Just four years later he made one of the greatest and most perfect of all *film noir* thrillers, *Out Of The Past* [a.k.a. *Build My Gallows High*] (47), which paired **Robert Mitchum's** Jeff Bailey as the fly to **Jane Greer's** Kathie Moffett's (Muffet?) spider, with rapacious **Kirk Douglas's** Whit Sterling circling, and gorgeous Virginia Huston's Ann waiting hopelessly in the wings. A series of fascinating **Westerns** followed, with *Great Day In The Morning* (56) notable amongst them, but the cherry on Tourneur's cake came, surprisingly, with a British horror movie, the one and only *Night Of The Demon* [a.k.a. *Curse Of The Demon*] (57), in which an initially sceptical **Dana Andrews** combats the sinister and apparently all-powerful Niall MacGinnis. This is also the film in which we are privileged to be scared witless, first by a sensational magic-driven storm, and then by one of the most effective of all screen ghouls howling down at us from above the gushing boiler of the night express train.
OTHER KEY FILMS: *Berlin Express* (48); *The Flame And The Arrow* (50); *Circle Of Danger* (51); *Anne Of The Indies* (51); *Way Of A Gaucho* (52); *Appointment In Honduras* (53); *Wichita* (53); *Nightfall* (57)

Towne, Robert
Towne wrote the script for **Roman Polanski's** *Chinatown* (74), and that has been enough, in Hollywood terms, to ensure that he is taught on any self-respecting screenwriting course – admittedly the script *is* just about perfect of its type, despite the fact that the ending was Polanski's, and not Towne's. If one is to believe the rumours, Towne has doctored just about every major and quite a few minor scripts that have appeared since then, but, joking aside, he has never produced anything else on the majestic scale of *Chinatown*, despite other notable successes such as **Hal Ashby's** *Shampoo* (75) and *The Last Detail* (83). OTHER KEY FILMS: Buzz Kulik's *Villa Rides* (68); **Sydney Pollack's** *The Yakuza* (75); *Tequila Sunrise* [also dir.] (88); **Jack Nicholson's** *The Two Jakes* (90); **Brian De Palma's** *Mission: Impossible* (96); *Without Limits* [also dir.] (98); **John Woo's** *Mission: Impossible II* (00)

Tracking Shot
Tracking shots are those that are captured by a camera mounted on a **dolly**, train tracks, or a vehicle of some sort, allowing the camera to move in virtually any direction at the whim of the **cinematographer**. 'Tracking in' is when the camera approaches the subject, and 'tracking out' is when the camera moves away from the object being photographed.

Track Laying
The sound cutter lays the pre-recorded sound track onto the pre-filmed image during editing – thus 'track laying'.

Tracks
The railway tracks laid down for the camera to move upon during filming.

Tracy, Spencer
An actor's actor, Jesuit-educated Tracy won an unprecedented two consecutive **Oscars** for **Victor Fleming's** *Captains Courageous* (37) and Norman Taurog's *Boys Town* (38). His multi-talented persona now established, he wowed audiences once again in Fleming's *Dr Jekyll And Mr Hyde* (41), after which he began a fruitful nine movie screen partnership with **Katharine Hepburn**, beginning with **George Stevens's** *Woman Of The Year* (42). The partnership between the two stars continued off-screen as well as on, until Tracy's death in 1967 – but the actor allegedly felt unable to divorce his wife and marry Hepburn because of his Catholic principles.

OTHER KEY FILMS: *20,000 Years In Sing Sing* (33); *Northwest Passage* (40); *The Seventh Cross* (44); *Adam's Rib* (49); *Bad Day At Black Rock* (55); *The Old Man And The Sea* (58); *Inherit The Wind* (60); *Judgment At Nuremberg* (61)

KEY LINES:

'There were times my pants were so thin I could sit on a dime and tell if it was heads or tails.' [Tracy on poverty]

'I like a he to be a he and a she to be a she.' [Tracy on sex, in **George Cukor's** *Pat And Mike* (52)]

Trailer

Trailers are designed to bring the punters of another, similar film back into the cinema to view the next film on the distributor's list. In consequence film trailers usually hint at a great deal more than the actual film really has to offer in terms of sex, violence, spectacle or romance. A notable example of contrived fakery occurred in the succession of *Mondo Cane* (62) and *Mondo Cane 2* (63) trailers which showed staged footage of animal and human brutality that had been cleverly redubbed to imply a spurious reality. The term 'trailer' comes from the fact that such clips used to be situated at the end of the last reel of a film.

Training Films

These are films specifically designed to teach, instruct, enlighten, bludgeon or propagandise viewers into toeing the line of their makers, and, as such, are most often associated with the military, the industrial, the political or the social worlds. Alberto Cavalcanti's *Went The Day Well?* (42) is an impressive example of enlightened (as we see it) wartime propaganda, aimed at changing the British public's physical response to a possible German invasion.

Transfer

The process by which an original audiotape is re-recorded onto magnetic or digital film.

Transitional Effects

These are special effects designed to ease the transition from one scene to another. Common transitional tricks include the **wipe**, the **fade**, and the **dissolve**.

Translucent Screen

The see-through screen commonly used during back projection, and upon which realistic (and sometimes not so realistic) landscapes and backgrounds are recreated in order to frame the action of the actors in front.

Transparency

A transparent print on glass, celluloid or other see-through material, which only becomes visible when light is passed through it.

Travelling Matte

The travelling matte is an even more complex **matte** shot than normal, and involves a number of different pre-filmed elements being moulded together to produce a particular action effect by means of the **blue screen process**. Now, with the sophisticated use of **digital effects**, a similar outcome can be achieved with greater ease. This was demonstrated in **Ridley Scott's** *Gladiator* (00), in which a small cast of gently swaying extras was endlessly multiplied by the computer so that the crowd appeared vast enough to fill the Colosseum in ancient Rome. A similar effect was achieved in **Joseph L Mankiewicz's** *Cleopatra* (63), but the cast involved on that occasion was indeed vast, and the technical resources called on made it ruinously expensive. One of the best uses of the travelling matte occurred in Curtis Bernhardt's *A Stolen Life* (46), in which **Bette Davis** played twin sisters, both in love with **Glenn Ford**. This was so effectively shot that it is only by careful use of the pause/still button on the video recorder that the joins and shadow shortcomings can be made out.

Travelling Shot

Any shot which requires the camera to move, rather than remain stationary.

Travelogue

Short travel **documentary** films designed to pass the time as fillers in a double bill while the audience was busy buying its ice cream and popcorn. Travelogues were usually trite and uncritical in the extreme, and functioned more as wish-fulfilment fantasies than as enlightened infotainment.

Travolta, John

Living proof that there can be life after career death (followed by death again), Travolta found himself top of the tree after appearing in John Badham's *Saturday Night Fever* (77) and Randal Kleiser's *Grease* (78), only to descend into the abyss (relatively speaking, for Travolta had invested his funds carefully) for nearly sixteen years, before triumphantly re-emerging as a sassy, wise-talking minor hood in **Quentin Tarantino's** *Pulp Fiction* (94). Since then, his now slightly fleshy face has shone out in video shops all over the world from action movies such as Barry Sonnenfeld's *Get*

Shorty (95), and **John Woo's** *Broken Arrow* (96). A recent outing, however, Roger Christian's *Battlefield Earth* (00), based on Scientology founder L Ron Hubbard's erstwhile bestseller, has been welcomed by many as one of the single worst big-budget turkeys of the last hundred years of cinema. OTHER KEY FILMS: *Carrie* (76); *Urban Cowboy* (80); *Blow Out* (81); *Face/Off* (97); *Primary Colors* (98); *The Thin Red Line* (98); *The General's Daughter* (99); *Lucky Numbers* (00) *Swordfish* (01)

Treatment

Once a studio executive has shown interest in an outline or pitch idea, a fuller treatment will be required before money is paid out for the writing of a screenplay. Such a treatment will usually consist of a thirty-page retelling of the movie, from start to finish, often including short chunks of dialogue, but not including scene directives. If the treatment proves satisfactory, an initial screenplay may then be commissioned.

Triangle

A stabilising frame for a camera tripod, designed to hold the legs steady in adverse conditions.

Trick Photography

See **Special Effects**

Trim

Anything in editing concerned with cutting or shortening the **workprint**.

Trim Bin

A bin in which **out-takes** are hung for possible later use.

Trintignant, Jean-Louis

Trintignant is a board on which directors can chalk whatever emotions, or lack of emotions, they desire. He is such a consummate actor that even when he stands still, as in certain scenes during **Bernardo Bertolucci's** *The Conformist* (70), the screen still seems nervously alive. The fifteen years before his breakthrough in *The Conformist*, however, were difficult ones for Trintignant, who was in danger of being typecast as a callow romantic lead in such mediocre fare as Claude Lelouch's *Un Homme Et Une Femme* [*A Man And A Woman*] (66). Bertolucci's genius changed all that. It is arguable that Bertolucci must have seen Trintignant in **Eric Rohmer's** *My Night With Maud* (69) and noticed his latent capacity for movement even in quietude. Whatever the case,

Trintignant was suddenly in hot demand by non-commercial directors, and he made the most of his opportunities, starring in such films as Yves Boisset's *L'Attentat* (72), Serge Leroy's *Les Passagers* (76), Ettore Scola's *La Nuit De Varenne* (83), and **Krzysztof Kieslowski's** *Rouge* (94), as the manipulative Judge Joseph Kern, faced with the innocence (or lack of it) of Irène Jacob's Valentine. OTHER KEY FILMS: *And God Created Woman* (56); *Les Liaisons Dangereuses* (59); *The Sleeping Car Murders* (65); *Trans-Europ Express* (67); *Les Biches* (68); *Z* (69); *Without Apparent Motive* (71); *Flic Story* (75); *Eaux Profondes* (81); *Rendezvous* (85); *Merci, La Vie* (91); *Un Héros Très Discret* (96); *Tykho Moon* (97); *Ceux Qui M'Aiment Prendront Le Train* (98)

Tripack

Colour film with a triple emulsive coating.

Trip Gear

The mechanism by which a camera can be pre-programmed to expose a single frame or sequence of frames at a particular time, without requiring an operator. Trip gears are most often used in **time-lapse** photography and **stop-frame** animation.

Tripod

A three-pronged camera support that consists of three legs and a tripod head (fluid, gyroscopic, geared or friction) which connects directly to the camera to allow the smoothest possible horizontal and lateral movement given the circumstances in which photography is taking place.

Trombone

A trombone-shaped bracket to which light units can be connected to ensure stability.

Truffaut, François

Truffaut was a true enthusiast, a man for whom movies were life, and the filming of them the food that makes life liveable. He described much of his early childhood in his debut feature, *Les Quatre Cents Coups* [*The Four Hundred Blows*] (59), in which his alter ego compensated for an underprivileged childhood by escaping to the cinema, a habit which remained with Truffaut until his premature death of a brain tumour, aged fifty-two. André Bazin, the founder of the influential film magazine, **Cahiers du Cinéma**, first offered Truffaut a job as a film critic, and it was as such that he and his fellow cinéphiles devised what was later to become the **New Wave**. Following the success of *Les Quatre Cents Coups*, and its two brilliant follow-ups, *Tirez Sur Le Pianiste* (60) and *Jules Et Jim* (61), Truffaut became one of the most celebrated filmmakers in the world, but it is arguable that he had already given of his best. His ensuing films received mixed receptions, until he reached crisis point with the delightful *Day For Night* (73), following which he took a much-needed sabbatical, emerging wiser perhaps, but with his creative energy impaired. *Le Dernier Métro* (81) marked something of a final return to form, but Truffaut had scarcely two years left to live, and these were taken up with his new love, **Fanny Ardant**, and their infant daughter, Joséphine. Truffaut's success was, paradoxically, a triumph of intellect over the heart, and it was this fundamentally rational approach to intuition that was to hamstring his later development as an artist. OTHER KEY FILMS: *La Peau Douce* (64); *Fahrenheit 451* (66); *The Bride Wore Black* (68); *Stolen Kisses* (68); *The Wild Child* (70); *Les Deux Anglaises Et Le Continent* (71); *The Story Of Adèle H.* (75); *The Man Who Loved Women* (77); *Vivement Dimanche* (82)

Trumbull, Douglas

Trumbull is the special-effects artist who, having cut his teeth as part of the team on **Stanley Kubrick's** *2001: A Space Odyssey* (68), went on to create the dazzling and often original effects seen in such iconic **science-fiction** movies as **Steven Spielberg's** *Close Encounters Of The Third Kind* (77), **Robert Wise's** *Star Trek: The Motion Picture* (80), and **Ridley Scott's** extraordinary *Blade Runner* (82). *Blade Runner*, of all sci-fi movies, has had the greatest crossover to a mainstream audience. OTHER KEY FILMS: Robert Wise's *The Andromeda Strain* (71); *Silent Running* [also dir.] (71); *Brainstorm* [also dir.] (83)

T-Stop

A camera setting that reflects the total amount of light transmitted through a lens, taking into account any residual loss of light value due to refraction, absorption or dilution.

Turner, Kathleen

Turner had one of the spunkiest starts of any actress, appearing opposite (and under, over and around) **William Hurt** in **Lawrence Kasdan's** *Body Heat* (81), and reminding any who had been fortunate enough to see **Jacques Tourneur's** *Out Of The Past* (47) of **Jane Greer's** wonderfully wicked Kathie Moffett. But then what? The talent was there, the beauty, the husky voice, but somehow everything was dissipated in roles that

never really took her to the brink, in the way she had been taken in *Body Heat*. Yes, she was entertaining and feisty in **Robert Zemeckis's** *Romancing The Stone* (84) and Lewis Teague's *The Jewel Of The Nile* (85), but it was a contrived feistiness, giving the impression that she was simply going through the motions in readiness for her large pay-check at the end. Her beauty solidified just a little in the early 1990s, opening up character roles to her which simply did not materialise, or which she refused. Looking through her filmography for another standout such as *Body Heat*, one comes across a plethora of adequate performances but absolutely nothing that has really challenged her. She would have been fine, for instance, in the **Annette Bening** part in **Sam Mendes's** *American Beauty* (99), but Bening got that one and made it her own. Forget the fake Warshawskis, Kathleen, and convince some entrepreneurial producer to cast you in a remake of *Johnny Guitar*. OTHER KEY FILMS: *The Man With Two Brains* (83); *Crimes Of Passion* (84); *Prizzi's Honor* (85); *Peggy Sue Got Married* (86); *The Accidental Tourist* (88); *The War Of The Roses* (89); *House Of Cards* (93); *A Simple Wish* (97); *The Virgin Suicides* (99); *Beautiful* (00); *Prince Of Central Park* (00) KEY LINE: 'You're not too smart, are you? I like that in a man.' [*Body Heat*]

Turner, Lana

Turner was the epitome of the common girl plucked magically from the street (or, in her case, Schwab's Drugstore) and turned into a star. The only snag was that she had little or no talent beyond an artificial bright-eyed look of interest she could throw at any man, and a well-stacked bust which **MGM** showed off, as much as it dared, beneath a mind-boggling sequence of tightly fitting sweaters. Then Turner found her feet, and her milieu, in Tay Garnett's *The Postman Always Rings Twice* (46), as the doomed Cora Smith, a small-town girl who marries up (to the sweating, amiable owner of a diner), and then tires of the deal, and the clammy, uxorial embraces that come with it. Turner, it became clear, was the sort of girl we might today see gracing the Jerry Springer show, having stolen someone's husband or boyfriend without really wanting them, but simply as an exercise in detachment. She was great in **Vincente Minnelli's** *The Bad And The Beautiful* (52), and wonderfully schlocky in Mark Robson's *Peyton Place* (57), then real life took over from screen drama when her daughter,

Cheryl Crane, killed Turner's hoodlum lover, Johnny Stompanato, with a knife. Crane got off, and Turner wheeled out one final success, **Douglas Sirk's** *Imitation Of Life* (59). But she had little but melodrama left in her, and her looks were beginning to blowse. Turner was a natural **B-movie** actress thrown into the A-feature deep end, and it was only when her natural tackiness was coaxed into flame, as in **Mervyn LeRoy's** *Johnny Eager* (42), or in Gottfried Reinhardt's *Betrayed* (54), that she really shone.

OTHER KEY FILMS: *Rich Man Poor Girl* (38); *Ziegfeld Girl* (41); *Dr Jekyll And Mr Hyde* (41); *Honky Tonk* (41); *Green Dolphin Street* (47); *Cass Timberlane* (47); *The Merry Widow* (52); *Flame And The Flesh* (54); *The Rains Of Ranchipur* (55)

Turner, Ted

A mogul of the old style, but with thoroughly modern pretensions to political correctness, Turner built up his media empire on the back of his father's advertising business, becoming, in the process, the founder of the CNN network of twenty-four-hour cable news stations and the TNT/Cartoon Channel. A film buff (and sometime militant colorizer), Turner now works for the Time Warner conglomerate that bought him out.

Turpin, Ben

Turpin was the tiny man with the crossed eyes and the bristly moustache whose vainglorious attempts at mimicking his heroes always backfired so badly and so inevitably, in such movies as F Richard Jones's *The Shriek Of Araby* (23), Edgar Kennedy and Reggie Morris's *The Reel Virginian* (24) and Harry Edwards's *A Hollywood Hero* (26). Hardly a **Charlie Chaplin** or a **Buster Keaton**, Turpin was, nevertheless, one of the best second stringers in the business until the coming of sound curtailed his act.

OTHER KEY FILMS: *Hired And Fired* (16); *A Clever Dummy* (17); *The Battle Royal* (18); *A Small Town Idol* (21); *Love And Doughnuts* (21); *Yukon Jake* (24); *A Harem Knight* (26); *The College Hero* (27); *Saps At Sea* (40)

Turret

A forward-mounted lens attachment that facilitates the rapid changing of lenses in tight filming conditions.

Tweety Pie

Sylvester the cat's lisping quarry in the famous **Warner Brothers' Looney Tunes** cartoon series.

20th Century-Fox

Founded by William Fox in 1915, Fox went from strength to strength during the 1920s, with directors such as **John Ford**, **Raoul Walsh** and **Frank Borzage** on its books. **F W Murnau's** extraordinary *Sunrise* (27) was a Fox film, and despite the depredations of the 1929 stock-market crash, the presence of **Shirley Temple** on its books saved the day, and Fox successfully merged with Twentieth Century in 1935, acquiring the talents of **Darryl F Zanuck** in the process. This created the company that eventually went on to make the *Star Wars* films, and which now forms part of Rupert Murdoch's News Corporation media empire. It is known simply as Fox.

Two Shot

A shot with just enough leeway in its framing to incorporate the figures of two people.

Typecasting

The casting of an actor or actress again and again in the same sort of role in an effort to accede to the audience's expectations – Jack Elam played evil cowboys, Elisha Cook Jr played nervous wannabes, **Thelma Ritter** played sassy cleaners, Butterfly McQueen played sobbing maids, Rudy Vallee played friendly millionaires, Eric Blore played caustic manservants, and Edward Everett Horton played the sort of henpecked husbands with guiltily roving eyes who, when asked by St Peter why they were the only man standing in the receiving line reserved for men who dominate their wives, would reply, 'I don't know. My wife told me to stand here.'

U Certificate

The 'universal' category of film classification, in which a film is deemed suitable for everyone, regardless of age.

UFA

The Universum Film Aktien Gesellschaft produced most of the major films during the period we now think of as the Golden Age of German Cinema – the 1920s. With directors like **Michael Curtiz**, **Alexander Korda**, **Fritz Lang**, **Ernst Lubitsch**, **F W Murnau** and **G W Pabst** on its books, it could hardly fail. The tragedy is that virtually all its famous names, either voluntarily or by force, moved to the United States or England in the run-up to or immediately following the Nazi takeover in 1933, thus depriving Germany of its most precocious and uninhibited talent.

Ullmann, Liv

Lover and muse of director **Ingmar Bergman**, and a fine, intense actress in her own right, Ullmann starred in an extraordinary run of Bergman's films during the 1960s and 70s. As with her oft-times co-star **Bibi Andersson**, Bergman snatched Ullmann from the stage and cast her in a series of increasingly complex, emotionally searing parts in such films as *Persona* (66), *Hour Of The Wolf* (68), *Shame* (68) and *Face To Face* (76). Ullmann tried, in vain, to move across to the US mainstream, but soon realised that her forte lay in European art-house cinema, where she has more or less remained for the latter stages of her career.

OTHER KEY FILMS: *The Passion Of Anna* (69); *Cries And Whispers* (72); *Scenes From A Marriage* (73); *The Serpent's Egg* (77); *Autumn Sonata* (78); *Dangerous Moves* (84); *The Ox* (91); *The Long Shadow* (92); *Zorn* (94); *Faithless* [dir., with script by Ingmar Bergman] (00)

Ulmer, Edgar G

Who knows how many films Ulmer actually made? What is indisputable is that he worked on smaller budgets, and turned out better films, than many of his now forgotten, once more lauded peers. His creative use of the camera, particularly in long takes (the main object of which was to save money) and in his enlightened composition and visual design, put to shame his more financially endowed colleagues. Such films as *Isle Of Forgotten Sins* (43), *Bluebeard* (44), *Strange Illusion* (45), *Detour* (46), *Ruthless* (48) and *The Naked Dawn* (54) show a panache and a sense of style that have belatedly assured Ulmer of **auteur** status in the one country where such status still counts for something – France.

OTHER KEY FILMS: *The Black Cat* (34); *Tomorrow We Live* (42); *Club Havana* (45); *Her Sister's Secret* (46); *The Strange Woman* (47)

Umbrella

An opaque shield in the shape of an umbrella used to reflect and focus light onto specific objects, actors, or parts of actors.

Undercrank

A term stemming from the days of silent film (in which cameras were still cranked by hand), undercrank now means running a camera at below optimum speed to create an effect of drastically accelerated motion on the screen.

Underdeveloped

This occurs when a film has not been bathed sufficiently long in developing solution, leading to a blanched look, with little or no effective contrast.

Underexposed

If negative film is not exposed to light for a long enough time, or if filming is undertaken at a higher than normal speed, a washed-out effect occurs, in which both contrast and detail suffer.

Underground Film

These are feature films, documentaries and propaganda films made outside the normal studio framework, and often outside the current social, political or religious structure too. Such films are often notable for their unconventional techniques, offbeat subject matter and subversive intentions. **Crossovers** do occur from the underground to the mainstream, but these usually herald a dilution of the original message rather than an enrichment. John Cassevetes is probably the foremost example

A typically tormented shot of the cerebral Liv Ullmann, playing psychotically mute actress Elizabeth Vogler in Ingmar Bergman's Persona (66)

of an underground director adopted by the mainstream who largely managed to avoid having his work diluted; **Andy Warhol**, for all his quirky self-indulgences, is another.

Undershoot

The opposite of an **overshoot** – in other words when a director exposes too little film during the shooting of a scene so that the editor is left knowing that it is now next to impossible to make up the shortfall because the actors have been sent home, the sets destroyed and the director paid off and renamed **Allen Smithee**.

Underwater Photography

Any shooting of film under water, i.e. in a submerged tank, a submerged posture, or submerged under the sea, in a river, or beneath the surface of a lake. Special cameras are required to obviate rust, distortion and over-hydration, not to mention outfits for their operators to obviate suffocation, decompression, the bends, and a variety of other drink-related problems. See also entry on *Titanic*

Unipod

One of a number of easily transportable camera supports most often used for photographing on-the-spot news items, or as part of a **cinéma vérité** documentary set-up.

Unit

The collective noun for all the technical crew involved in the making of a motion picture.

Unit Manager

Also known as the production manager, the unit manager is responsible for ensuring that the production crew working on a particular motion picture are fed, paid, housed, transported, and, very occasionally, entertained.

United Artists

Founded by **Mary Pickford, Douglas Fairbanks, Charlie Chaplin** and **D W Griffith** in 1919, United Artists had a pretty fair sixty-two-year run until it was merged into **MGM** in 1982, following the $40 million debacle of **Michael Cimino's** *Heaven's Gate* (80). With silent successes such as Fred Niblo's *The Mark Of Zorro* (20) and **Charlie Chaplin's** *The Gold Rush* (25) under its belt, UA entered the 1930s as one of the first studios to promote films on an individual rather than on a collective studio basis. Later films completed under

the UA aegis were **Fred Zinnemann's** *High Noon* (52), **Billy Wilder's** *Some Like It Hot* (59), **John Sturges's** *The Magnificent Seven* (60) and the complete cycle of **James Bond** films.
KEY LINE:
'The lunatics have taken charge of the asylum.' [Richard Rowland, head of Metro, on first hearing of the new company]

Unit Production Manager

See **Unit Manager**

Universal

The original company was founded in 1912 by Carl Laemmle, and Universal City was built three years later on a 230-acre site in the San Fernando Valley, to include thirty-four separate sound stages, its own hospital, post office, fire station, police department, zoo, and all consequent sanitation facilities. Laemmle presided at the opening in front of more than 20,000 jubilant onlookers, and soon turned the place into something of a personal fiefdom, employing numerous family members, in-laws and acquaintances to the extent that Universal rapidly became known as 'Laemmle's faemmle', thanks to the wit of Ogden Nash. Laemmle was forced to sell the company in 1935, largely as a result of the faemmle's extravagances, only to see Deanna Durbin trill to the rescue. The old place is still going strong, but the owners have become just a little more boring, a lot less individual, and a sight more convoluted.

Universal Leader

Following on from the **Academy Leader**, the universal leader is the coded strip at the beginning and end of every reel of film that tells the projectionist when it is appropriate to begin changing reels.

Unsworth, Geoffrey

Unsworth's rite of passage as a camera operator came with **Michael Powell** and **Emeric Pressburger's** superb duo, *The Life And Death of Colonel Blimp* (43) and *A Matter Of Life And Death* (46). This then led to his promotion to officer class (i.e. Director of Photography status) on such alternately fervid and stiff-upper-lip classics as **Marc Allégret's** *Blanche Fury* (48), Roy Ward Baker's Titanic movie, *A Night*

To Remember (58), **Stanley Kubrick's** *2001: A Space Odyssey* (68), and Bob Fosse's *Cabaret* (72). Unsworth's magnificent work on **Roman Polanski's** *Tess* (79) was to prove an excellent, albeit posthumous, finale to an outstanding career.
OTHER KEY FILMS: Charles Frend's *Scott Of The Antarctic* (49); J Lee Thompson's *North West Frontier* (59); Peter Glenville's *Becket* (64); Richard Donner's *Superman* (78); Michael Crichton's *The Great Train Robbery* (79)

UPA

The United Productions of America company set up shop in 1943 following the disenchantment of some of **Walt Disney's** key animators with the great master's methods. To compensate for inevitable financial strictures, the UPA team, headed by Stephen Bosustow, Pete Burns and Bob Cannon, concentrated on characterisation rather than ostentation, and Mr Magoo and Gerald McBoing Boing were the result.

Upstage

The area furthest from the camera on a film set. Also what one actor does to another when ambition overcomes good manners.

Ustinov, Peter

Winner of a surprising two **Oscars**, for **Stanley Kubrick's** *Spartacus* (60) and **Jules Dassin's** *Topkapi* (64), Ustinov is more a force of nature than a flesh-and-blood screen actor. A raconteur, wit and general bon viveur, he directed the 1962 version of *Billy Budd* and also the curious **Richard Burton** and **Elizabeth Taylor** vehicle, *Hammersmith Is Out* (72). In later life he starred as a mannered Hercule Poirot, and indulged his passion for stand-up, or rather, given his ample size, sit-down wit, in a successful one-man show.
OTHER KEY FILMS: *One Of Our Aircraft Is Missing* (42); *The Way Ahead* (44); *Quo Vadis?* (51); *Lola Montès* (55); *We're No Angels* (55); *The Sundowners* (60); *Blackbeard's Ghost* (68); *Logan's Run* (76); *Death On The Nile* (78); *Lorenzo's Oil* (92); *Stiff Upper Lips* (98); *The Bachelor* (99)

Utility Man

On a film set, the fellow everyone gets to run the errands for them.

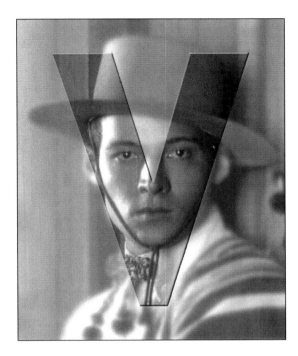

Vadim, Roger

French commercial filmmaker more notable for his marriages and liaisons with some of the most beautiful women in film history than for the quality of his work, Vadim launched first wife **Brigitte Bardot's** 'sex-kitten' career (and completely sank St Tropez in the process, turning a pleasant fishing village into a poseur's paradise) with BB and her gingham bikini in *Et Dieu Créa La Femme* [*And God Created Woman*] (56). Following a well-publicised liaison in the early 60s with **Catherine Deneuve**, who bore him a child, he then launched third wife **Jane Fonda's** brief career as a sex goddess with the titillating *Barbarella* (67). Vadim must have had something, because a troop of his ex-wives, girlfriends and lovers reappeared on the occasion of his funeral in 1999, each manifesting signs of genuine regret.

OTHER KEY FILMS: *Les Liaisons Dangereuses* (58); *Les Parisiennes* (62); *Ms Don Juan* (73)

Valentino, Rudolph

The most perfect silent-age movie icon, Valentino died at the age of thirty-one just a few weeks before **Warner Brothers** inaugurated the sound era with its **Vitaphone** system. The émigré son of a down-at-heel family of Italian aristocrats, the di Valentina d'Antonguolas, Valentino first made his mark in **Rex Ingram's** *The Four Horsemen Of The Apocalypse* (21). George Melford's *The Sheik* (21) went on to cement his fervent female following, closely followed by Fred Niblo's *Blood and Sand* (21). Two distraught

*Cult-icon **Rudolph Valentino**, complete with fetishistic accoutrements, on the set of Rex Ingram's* The Four Horsemen Of The Apocalypse *(21)*

women committed suicide on hearing of Valentino's death from peritonitis, and more than a hundred were injured in the hysteria surrounding his funeral. **OTHER KEY FILMS:** *Monsieur Beaucaire* (24); *The Eagle* (25); *Son Of The Sheik* (26)

Vamp

Theda Bara became the first screen vamp in *A Fool There Was* (15), itself the precursor to a whole raft of exotic temptress movies, in which foolish men allowed themselves to be ensnared by women with fetchingly kohl-rimmed eyes, coiled-snake breastplates and ruby-encrusted belly buttons. The genre slowly petered out in the 1920s (probably for want of accessories); however, modern-day equivalents might include **Kathleen Turner's** Matty Walker in **Lawrence Kasdan's** *Body Heat* (81) and Linda Fiorentino's Bridget Gregory in John Dahl's *The Last Seduction* (94).

Van Cleef, Lee

The 1960s **Spaghetti Western** explosion threw up a few strange characters who later made it to stardom (**Clint Eastwood** for one), but none stranger than Van Cleef, who was bald, almost indecently weird-looking, and who smoked a large corn-cob pipe for recreation. It was the eyes that did it, of course, and on such apparently insignificant features movie fortunes have been made. Van Cleef could play mean, and he could play conservative/eccentric, and never more lucratively than in **Sergio Leone's** *For A Few Dollars More* (66) and *The Good, The Bad And The Ugly* (66), which resuscitated the forty-one-year-old Van Cleef's flagging career (he always looked fifty whatever age he was) and ensured him hero status in France and Italy until his death in 1989. The one film he virtually carried on his own, Gordon Douglas's *Barquero* (70), actually wasn't half bad of its type, proving that character actors can occasionally make good after all. **OTHER KEY FILMS:** *High Noon* (52); *The Big Combo* (55); *Tribute To A Bad Man* (56); *The Young Lions* (58); *Ride Lonesome* (59); *Death Rides A Horse* (67); *El Condor* (70); *The Magnificent Seven Ride* (72); *The Rip-Off* (78); *Escape From New York* (81); *Thieves Of Fortune* (89)

Van Damme, Jean–Claude

Yes, he is the 'Muscles from Brussels' (or the 'Truffles from Brussels' as he prefers to call himself), and some of his movies may be a little over-sentimental and archetypal, but Van Damme brings a genuine and rather refreshing European sensibility to the best of his action films which give

them an edge over their blustering and often inane US rivals. In Robert Harmon's *Nowhere To Run* (93), his hero has a genuine love for children, and feet, if not of clay, at least of sand, and in Ringo Lam's *Maximum Risk* (96), Van Damme reminds us not only that Europe and America are different continents containing different cultures, but also that heady, *Boy's Own* action need not necessarily involve only the body, but can, on occasion, involve the head and the heart as well. **OTHER KEY FILMS:** *Missing In Action* (84); *Double Impact* (91); *Universal Soldier* (92); *Hard Target* (92); *Timecop* (94); *Sudden Death* (95); *Double Team* (97); *Legionnaire* (98); *Universal Soldier: The Return* (99); *The Replicant* (01); *The Order* (01); *The Monk* (01)

Vanel, Charles

Vanel will be forever remembered by film buffs and edge-of-the-seat anxiety aficionados for his role as the tough/tender buddy of **Yves Montand** in **Henri-Georges Clouzot's** *The Wages Of Fear* (52). Montand single-mindedly humiliates Vanel/Jo (who has set himself up as a man of means in the pestilential Central American oilfield community that none of them can afford to leave) before running over his legs with his truck in a mud-filled bog. The fact that Vanel can convince us of his utter change of heart and character is a testimony to his long and distinguished career in French cinema (let's face it, the best in the world), where he played parts ranging from the evil Javert in Raymond Bernard's *Les Misérables* (34), to the tinder-dry Inspector Fichet in Clouzot's *Les Diaboliques* (55). Extraordinarily, Vanel made his first film, *Jim Crow*, in 1912, and his last, Francesco Rosi's *Three Brothers*, in 1980 — a magnificent career of sixty-eight years. **OTHER KEY FILMS:** *Waterloo* (28); *L'Arlésienne* (31); *Michel Strogoff* (36); *Le Diable Souffle* (47); *Si Versailles M'Était Conté* (54); *To Catch A Thief* (55); *Le Piège* (58); *La Vérité* (60); *Ballade Pour Un Chien* (69); *Illustrious Corpses* (76); *Ne Pleure Pas* (78); *La Puce Et Le Privé* (79)

Van Sant, Gus

An off-beat filmmaker whose best work, *Mala Noche* (85), *Drugstore Cowboy* (89) and *My Own Private Idaho* (91), shows a particularly distinctive view of the United States underscored as much by drug abuse, bisexuality and incipient mania, as it is by friendship, the trust of strangers and the importance of country, and the free passage within it, to the heart. His people are searchers, movers and feelers, and Van Sant's films only fall down when they become static and overly intellectual.

328

OTHER KEY FILMS: *Even Cowgirls Get The Blues* (94); *To Die For* (95); *Good Will Hunting* (97); *Psycho* (98); *Don't Worry, He Won't Get Far On Foot* (00); *Finding Forrester* (00)

Variable-area Soundtrack

The standard optical soundtrack that shows modulations in the form of oscillating dark lines, when compared to **variable-density**.

Variable-density Soundtrack

A further variation on the optical soundtrack, the variable-density soundtrack shows modulations in the form of horizontal barred lines of varying colours and densities, from grey to black, and was used almost exclusively by **MGM** from the 1930s to the 1950s.

Variable-focus Lens

See **Zoom Lens**

Variable Shutter

A camera with two separate shutter mechanisms which revolve simultaneously, allowing the operator greater control over such variables as exposure and depth of field.

Variable-speed Motor

Used exclusively in silent filmmaking due to the non-variable motor requirements of sound filming, the 'wild' or variable-speed motor consists of a camera motor capable of a variety of different speeds, and is adjustable during filming.

Variety

The film world's very own weekly industry magazine, trade journal and generalised rumour repository, *Variety* lists the deals made, the films and TV programmes shot, and the box-office takings of all extant projects, including everything and anything at all pertaining to the filmic jungle and its denizens, including marriages, divorces, fallings out and eventual demises.

Vault

A foolproof, fireproof, and damp-proof storage room for the conservation of delicate nitrate- and non-nitrate based films, usually to be found in National Film Archive libraries or the better-funded universities.

Veidt, Conrad

Veidt became a British citizen in 1939 following Nazi threats against his Jewish wife, and he died three years later of a heart attack, aged just fifty. His German career had been a long and distinguished one, including the role of Cesare in **Robert Wiene's** *The Cabinet Of Dr Caligari* (19), and he and his extraordinary English pronunciation were soon in great demand in France, Britain and the US. This led to parts in Walter Forde's *Rome Express* (32), **Alexander Korda's** magical and multi-directed (by **Michael Powell** among others) *The Thief Of Bagdad* (40), in which Veidt played the evil Jaffar, and **Michael Curtiz's** evergreen *Casablanca* (42), as the sinister Major Heinrich Strasser. Veidt had a sudden posthumous burst of celebrity when his atrociously accented 1930s version of the song 'There's A Lighthouse Across The Bay' became a cult hit on disc jockey Terry Wogan's popular 1980s BBC radio programme.

OTHER KEY FILMS: *Nocturno Der Liebe* (18); *Around The World In 80 Days* (19); *Lady Hamilton* (21); *King Richard III* (22); *Lord Byron* (22); *William Tell* (23); *The Hands Of Orlac* (25); *Rasputin* (32); *King Of The Damned* (36); *The Spy In Black* (39); *A Woman's Face* (41); *All Through The Night* (42); *Above Suspicion* (43)

Velocilator

A larger version of a **dolly**, or movable camera mount, incorporating operator's seats for both the cameraman and the focus-puller and capable of raising the camera up to six feet above the ground.

Venice Film Festival

Founded in 1932 at the instigation of Benito Mussolini to raise Italy's international standing and to afford his government a much needed publicity coup, the Venice Film Festival was the first of the international film festivals to offer prizes for outstanding achievement in the cinema. Its main prize is the Golden Lion (the symbol of Venice), and there is, in addition, the Special Jury Prize, whose recipient is decided on by the votes of a caucus of international critics, and also the President of the Senate's Special Award, which usually goes to a film that, despite its particular excellence, is otherwise likely to pass unnoticed.

Ventura, Lino

Lino Ventura and pock-marked Eddie Constantine were France's tough men during the 1950s, 60s and early 70s — they played cops, thieves, crooks, thugs, hit men, bandits, private eyes, gunsels and murderers. Ex-boxer Ventura was the more talented actor of the two, and when he was paired with first-rate directors, as in **Louis Malle's** *Ascenseur*

Pour L'Echafaud (58) or Henri Verneuil's *The Sicilian Clan* (69), he turned in performances of tremendous power. Francesco Rosi was also quick to recognise Ventura's star presence, using him to excellent effect in his *Illustrious Corpses* (76) as the dogged police inspector uncovering a sinister and far-reaching right-wing conspiracy. The French counted on Ventura, for nearly thirty years, to turn out tough, unsentimental and utterly professional films, and he rarely, if ever, disappointed them.

OTHER KEY FILMS: *Touchez Pas Au Grisbi* (54); *Le Gorille Vous Salue Bien* (58); *Taxi For Tobruk* (61); *Les Barbouzes* (64); *L'Armée Des Ombres* (69); *The Valachi Papers* (72); *The Slap* (74); *The Medusa Touch* (78); *Garde A Vue* (81)

Verhoeven, Paul

Dr Paul Verhoeven PhD (physics) has, it seems, always been fascinated by voyeuristic sex, even in his earlier Dutch films such as *Turkish Delight* (73), *The Fourth Man* (79) and *Spetters* (80). However, after arriving in the US on a tide of dollars, either he or his producers had the bright idea of replacing the sex with violence (a taste much more to Hollywood's liking), leading to two mega-hits, *Robocop* (87) and *Total Recall* (90). *Basic Instinct* (92) marked a partial return to Verhoeven's original roots (if that is the right word), combining sex, violence *and* voyeurism to produce a third major commercial winner. No doubt inflamed by his success, Verhoeven tried to repeat the trick with *Showgirls* (95), which proved so awful that it has now become a camp cult classic, somewhat along the lines of **Ed Wood's** *Glen Or Glenda?* (53). In an effort to redress the balance in his favour, Verhoeven made *Starship Troopers* (97), which was seen by some as an attack on US militarism, and by others as a fundamental Nazi game plan. The talented Verhoeven, it seems, will always conjure up such paradoxes. It is, of course, possible that the man just may be the iconoclast he sells himself as, and he is certainly capable, when he wants to be, of an almost visceral panache.

OTHER KEY FILMS: *Business Is Business* (71); *Flesh & Blood* (85); *The Hollow Man* (00)

Viacom

One of the giants of the media industry, alongside **Disney**, Time **Warner**, Bertelsmann and News Corporation, Viacom are the blockbuster people, and own something in the region of thirteen US television stations, not to mention theme parks, publishers and **Paramount** pictures.

Video

A medium-quality visual and audio recording system in which magnetic tape is used for the eventual playback of previously filmed material, the video was devised during the 1950s, but the system only really came into its own during the late 70s and early 80s (in a domestic rather than an industry context). This provided an outlet not only for major films, but also for the second-rate and offbeat features that may not have benefited from a wide initial distribution. Now set to be superseded by **DVD**.

Video Assist

A parallel recording technique using a video camera attached to the main motion-picture camera, the video assist was pioneered in the UK in the early 1980s. It allows the camera operator and his assistant to view through a monitor exactly what is being filmed at the very moment it is being filmed, this serving as a basis for the informed production of rushed **dailies**.

Video Colour Analyser

A system that allows an operator or editor to tinker with the colour and density of a recorded moving image before the final print is struck.

Video Editing System

The transference of film frames to videotape as an aid to film editing, allowing for the electronic manipulation and sorting of images on a video screen before the actual cutting process takes place.

Vidor, King

Vidor first made his mark with *The Big Parade* (25), one of the greatest and most successful of all mainstream silent films, which represented the peak of matinee idol **John Gilbert's** screen career. He followed this up with the considerably less lucrative, but equally penetrating *The Crowd* (28), a film about the vicissitudes of poverty and the power of love to transcend it. Vidor cared about people, and his films, which include *Stella Dallas* (37) (in which **Barbara Stanwyck's** Stella Dallas sacrifices her own happiness for that of her daughter), *The Citadel* (38), *Duel In The Sun* (47) and *Ruby Gentry* (52) are notable for their strong female roles.

OTHER KEY FILMS: *Peg O' My Heart* (22); *The Champ* (31); *Cynara* (32); *Northwest Passage* (40); *Comrade X* (40); *The Fountainhead* (49); *Man Without A Star* (55); *War And Peace* (56); *Solomon And Sheba* (59)

KEY LINE:

'Marriage isn't a word... it's a sentence!' [*The Crowd*]

Viewer

A rapid-action viewing machine, either hand-cranked or machine-operated, which allows for the swiftest possible movement from one part of a film to another, and which is particularly useful in the search for specific scenes.

Viewfinder

A small device attached to the camera, the viewfinder allows for the balanced composition of any shot about to be filmed, by virtue of recreating the shot exactly as seen by the camera lens. It incorporates within its mechanism a compensation for any parallax errors by the use of reflex technology.

Vignette

Either a small, exquisite, or especially noticeable scene set within the larger context of a feature film, or alternatively one particular aspect of a filmic performance that stands out from the whole. Glorious examples include the 'puttering' scene from **Frank Capra's** *Platinum Blonde* (31), the 'snail' scene from **Jean Renoir's** *Les Bas-Fonds* (36), and the 'blind linesman' scene from **The Coen Brothers'** *O Brother, Where Art Thou?* (00)

Vigo, Jean

Vigo's is a tragic story. Stricken with tuberculosis following the mysterious death of his anarchist father in the infamous Fresnes prison in 1917 (when Vigo was just twelve years old), Vigo produced only one forty-five-minute and one full-length feature, a documentary, and a short, before succumbing to septicaemia at the age of twenty-nine. But his films have genius in them, and illustrate a sensibility so refined and so profoundly original in the context of the environment in which he was living (or in any context for that matter) that the French Government now belatedly awards an annual prize in Vigo's name for films that manifest a similar independence of spirit. Vigo's masterpiece is *L'Atalante* (34), in which **Michel Simon** plays a free-thinking, foul-mouthed bargee, who at first challenges the swiftly consummated marriage of his beloved boss, and then becomes instrumental in its reinstatement. The film shows scenes as curious and as moving as they are universal, including the famous shot of Simon's tattooed belly button apparently smoking a cigarette. The earlier *Zéro De Conduite* (33) was Vigo at his most anarchic and most influenced by his father, and the famous pillow fight (immaculately shot by Boris Kaufman) was later used as the basis for numerous theoretical arguments on existentiality, and on the power of the young to challenge authority, before their inevitable corruption by its influence. Regardless of fashion, mores, and the trivial vicissitudes of social expediency, Vigo's unique voice lives on.

OTHER KEY FILMS: *A Propos De Nice* (30); *Taris, Champion De Natation* (31)

Visconti, Luchino

Visconti was an aristocrat and a Marxist, two things that, in Milanese society during the time of Mussolini, were hardly as incompatible as they might seem elsewhere, and at other times. His first film was the magnificent *Ossessione* (42), adapted, without permission, from James M Cain's novel *The Postman Always Rings Twice*, and by far the best film ever made on a subject that filmmakers as disparate as Tay Garnett (46) and **Bob Rafelson** (81) have since attempted. Visconti's most famous film is undoubtedly *Death In Venice* (71), in which **Dirk Bogarde** gives a performance of such magnificent intensity that the entire film lurches headily around him like a frenzied, barely controllable merry-go-round. Visconti's most satisfying film, however, is his last, *L'Innocente* (76), an extended paean to aestheticism and the decline of the haute-bourgeoisie in nineteenth-century Italy.

OTHER KEY FILMS: *La Terra Trema* (48); *White Nights* (57); *Rocco And His Brothers* (60); *The Leopard* (63); *The Damned* (69); *Ludwig II* (72); *Conversation Piece* (75)

VistaVision

A 35mm horizontal wide-screen process, VistaVision was introduced by **Paramount** into its most prestigious cinemas in the form of **Michael Curtiz's** *White Christmas* (54), to take the sting out of 20th Century-Fox's successful introduction of **CinemaScope**, with Henry Koster's *The Robe* in 1953. It was designed to produce very high-quality wide-screen images without the need for **anamorphic** lenses.

Visual Effects

Any effect that results from the alteration or dilution of a 'naturally' filmed image or series of images, into something akin to fantasy, surrealism, or merely, as often as not, a doctored version suggestive of reality. See **Blue Screen Process, CGI, Back Projection, Digital Effects, Process Shot, Matte,** etc.

Vitagraph

Vitagraph was an enormously successful silent-movie studio, founded in 1896, which boasted **Rudolph Valentino**, **Norma Talmadge**, Maurice Costello, Florence Turner, Lillian Walker and Earle Williams amongst its stars.

Vitaphone

A disc-based recording system synchronised to the movie reel, the Vitaphone technique was used in Alan Crosland's *The Jazz Singer* (27), the film that inaugurated the era of sound in the movies.

Voiceover

Voiceover is any narration or commentary spoken off-screen but which appears on the soundtrack of a film or documentary. A notable example would be Dick Richards's *Farewell My Lovely* (75), which includes a **Robert Mitchum/Philip Marlowe** voiceover throughout its entire length, sometimes even when the actor himself is silently on screen. The ultimate voiceover, however, must surely be that of **William Holden's** Joe Gillis, in **Billy Wilder's** *Sunset Boulevard* (50), who dispassionately narrates his own death, followed by the events that led up to it.

Voice Test

An audition specifically designed to test the qualities of an actor or actress's voice for use either directly on screen, or in a voiceover or dubbing capacity.

Voight, Jon

Voight had it all and then somehow lost it. He is a superb screen actor, as he proved beyond question in **John Schlesinger's** *Midnight Cowboy* (69), **John Boorman's** *Deliverance* (72), and Andrei Konchalovsky's *Runaway Train* (85), but one now searches with increasing desperation for his appearance in parts that might afford him a filmography worthy of his talents. Instead he has featured in such mundane films as **Brian De Palma's** *Mission: Impossible* (96) and Luis Llosa's *Anaconda* (97), although it remains patently obvious that Voight should be playing the sort of parts a great actor like **Robert Duvall** still contrives to find for himself. Note for Film Buffs: Angelina Jolie, of Simon West's *Lara Croft: Tomb Raider* (01) fame, is Jon Voight's daughter.

OTHER KEY FILMS: *Conrack* (74); *Coming Home* (78); *Heat* (95); *Rosewood* (97); *The General* (98); *Enemy Of The State* (98); *A Dog Of Flanders* (99); *Pearl Harbor* (01); *Lara Croft: Tomb Raider* (01)

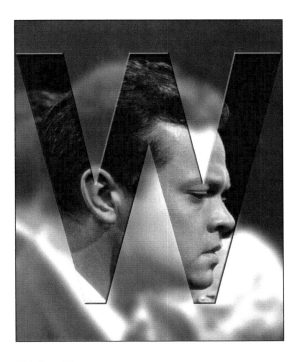

Waits, Tom

This eccentric-looking and quirkily individual musician and singer occasionally deigns to appear in movies that appeal to his intelligence and sense of humour, and his filmography has become surprisingly impressive as a result. On screen he is as odd and seductive as his songs, and his most notable performances have all occurred in the independent-minded films of such directors as **Jim Jarmusch**, with *Down By Law* (86) and *Mystery Train* (89), **Hector Babenco**, with *Ironweed* (87), **Robert Altman**, with *Short Cuts* (93), and **Francis Ford Coppola**, with *Bram Stoker's* **Dracula** (92), in which Waits got to play the ever-charming, fly-and-spider-crunching R M Renfield. Waits is that rare thing, a genuinely innovative human being who always pushes the boundaries just that little bit further than his more conventional contemporaries.

OTHER KEY FILMS: *Paradise Alley* (78); *The Outsiders* (83); *Rumble Fish* (83); *The Cotton Club* (84); *The Fisher King* (91); *At Play In The Fields Of The Lord* (91); *Mystery Men* (99); *In The Boom Boom Room* (00); *Cadillac Tramps* (00)

Wajda, Andrzej

An eminent and brave filmmaker, Wadja became, during the 1950s, quite literally the voice of Poland. His masterwork is his trilogy – *Generation* (54), *Kanal* (57) and *Ashes And Diamonds* (58) – two of which starred the ill-fated Zbigniew Cybulski, who was known as the James Dean of Poland and who died in a railway accident in 1967 at the tragically early age of thirty-nine. Wajda later went on to map the original sources and progress of the Solidarity movement in *Man Of Iron* (81), but his main strength has always been in his instinctive understanding of how the past affects the present, a concept to which he has brought an often inspired visual slant, most notably in the scenes of the partisans' doomed escape through the claustrophobic Warsaw sewers in *Kanal*.

OTHER KEY FILMS: *Lotna* (59); *Ashes* (65); *Everything For Sale* (68); *Landscape After Battle* (70); *Man Of Marble* (77); *Without Anaesthetic* (79); *Danton* (82); *The Possessed* (87); *Nastazjai* (94); *Pan Tadeusz* (99)

Walbrook, Anton

A marvellously romantic actor whose star shone briefly in a series of quality films during the 1940s and early 1950s, Walbrook had a marked advantage in his voice, an elegantly Austrian instrument that turned spoken English into something verging on the sublime. Scion of a family that had provided clowns for the Austro-Hungarian Empire's circuses for generations, Walbrook made his mature mark in Brian Hurst's *Dangerous Moonlight* (41) and in **Michael Powell's** brilliant and perspicacious *The Life And Death Of Colonel Blimp* (43), in which he played a sympathetic German, a rare role in wartime Britain. Walbrook's masterpiece, and the part for which he, above all men, was most perfectly suited, came as the master of ceremonies in **Max Ophüls's** *La Ronde* (50). His career wound slowly down after that, and by the time of his death in 1967, he was something of a forgotten man.

OTHER KEY FILMS: *Viktor Und Viktoria* (33); *Maskerade* (34); *Allotria* (36); *Michael Strogoff* (37); *Victoria The Great* (37); *Gaslight* (40); *49th Parallel* (41); *The Red Shoes* (48); *The Queen Of Spades* (49); *Oh Rosalinda* (55); *I Accuse!* (58)

Walken, Christopher

An offbeat and intense character actor whose very frigidity on screen constitutes his main advantage over lesser performers, Walken first came to prominence in **Michael Cimino's** *The Deer Hunter* (78), in which he played an action-addicted Vietnam veteran utterly unable to lay off the kick he got out of risking his life, again and again, at Russian roulette. He made a surprisingly effective all-singing, all-dancing pimp in Herbert Ross's sadly underrated *Pennies From Heaven* (81), and his recent parts, though scarcer than one would wish, have all been effective, in particular in Tony Scott's *True Romance* (93) and John Badham's otherwise rather dotty *Nick Of Time* (95). Walken is about the best baddie in the business, and his cold smile must be hell-on-earth if it's the final thing one sees before oblivion.

OTHER KEY FILMS: *The Anderson Tapes* (71); *Annie Hall* (77); *Roseland* (77); *The Dogs Of War* (80); *Heaven's Gate* (80); *Brainstorm* (83); *The Dead Zone* (83); *Biloxi Blues* (88); *The Milagro Beanfield War* (88); *King Of New York* (90); *Things To Do In Denver When You're Dead* (95); *Last Man Standing* (96); *The Opportunists* (00); *Scotland, P.A.* (01); *Joe Dirt* (01); *America's Sweethearts* (01); *Inside Job* (01)

Walker, Robert

A sadly self-destructive actor, Walker had the chance to shine (which he did) in one utterly memorable performance, that of psychotic rich-boy Bruno Anthony in **Alfred Hitchcock's** *Strangers On A Train* (51). Why is Walker so convincing in the part? It would be trite to ascribe his skill to his having lived on the psychological edge for most of his adult life – suffice it to say that in *Strangers*, and to a lesser extent in **Vincente Minnelli's** *The Clock* (45), as the vulnerable young soldier who falls in love with, and marries, a non-singing **Judy Garland** during a forty-eight hour furlough, Walker hinted at a depth of characterisation and a capacity for simplicity that must surely afford him a finer posthumous reputation than his tragically curtailed filmography would at first glance suggest.

OTHER KEY FILMS: *Bataan* (43); *Madame Curie* (43); *Thirty Seconds Over Tokyo* (44); *Since You Went Away* (44); *The Sea Of Grass* (46); *Till The Clouds Roll By* (46); *One Touch Of Venus* (48); *Vengeance Valley* (51); *My Son John* (52)

KEY LINE:
'Some people are better off dead. Like your wife and my father, for instance.' [Walker, making his proposition to Farley Granger, in *Strangers On A Train*]

Walk-on Part

A part in a film that requires an actor to walk on, keep quiet, and walk off again. Many stars have begun their careers in this way, and some have ended them in a similar fashion.

Walk-through

A physical, as opposed to a verbal rehearsal, in which protagonists rehearse only the movements, without the dialogue, of the scene in which they will soon be appearing, so that cameramen, lighting technicians and sound crew can set up their equipment in advance, and in the most effective manner possible.

Wallach, Eli

Wallach was a smiling baddie who never seemed quite as bad as he made out. He first impressed audiences as the seducer in **Elia Kazan's** hard-to-watch *Baby Doll* (56), and later went on to more lucrative, if less skilled parts, as the Mexican bandit leader in **John Sturges's** *The Magnificent Seven* (60) (where his onscreen bandit chums apparently stuck to and protected him in real life, too, during shooting), and 'the ugly' in **Sergio Leone's** *The Good, The Bad And The Ugly* (67), although that part might just as well have been taken by the seriously weird-looking **Lee Van Cleef**. When he was offered a really juicy part, as in **John Huston's** *The Misfits* (61), Wallach quite surpassed his baddie status and became again the original and talented actor he so obviously was.

OTHER KEY FILMS: *Lord Jim* (65); *Mackenna's Gold* (69); *The Deep* (77); *Movie Movie* (78); *Circle Of Iron* (79); *The Hunter* (81); *The Two Jakes* (90); *The Godfather Part 3* (90)

Wallis, Hal B

The poor-boy-made-good producer of a quite extraordinary number of high-quality Hollywood mainstream films, ranging from **Mervyn LeRoy's** *Little Caesar* (31) to **John Wayne's** *True Grit* follow-up, Stuart Millar's *Rooster Cogburn* (75),

Wallis could be said not only to have spanned, but to have more than partially created the great years of Hollywood cinema through which he lived. A modest man in comparison with some of his more bull-like contemporaries, Wallis had an astonishing filmography of more than 400 films, remarkably few of them clinkers, which attests both to his taste and to his fundamental humanity in a pit otherwise chock-full with ersatz vipers.

OTHER KEY FILMS: Mervyn LeRoy's *I Am A Fugitive From A Chain Gang* (32); **Michael Curtiz's** *Captain Blood* (35); **William Wyler's** *Jezebel* (38); Michael Curtiz's *The Adventures Of Robin Hood* (38); **Raoul Walsh's** *High Sierra* (41); Irving Rapper's *Now Voyager* (42); Michael Curtiz's **Casablanca** (43); **John Sturges's** *Last Train From Gun Hill* (59); Peter Glenville's *Becket* (64); **Henry Hathaway's** *True Grit* (69)

Walsh, Raoul

Real-life cowboy and wearer of an eye-patch after an unfortunate collision with a flying rabbit, Walsh was one of the unsung paladins of Hollywood, producing splendid action films with often complex anti-heroes. After silent successes such as *What Price Glory?* (26), he made **Humphrey Bogart's** name with *High Sierra* (41), and provided **Errol Flynn** with one of his better roles, as Custer, in *They Died With Their Boots On* (41). Director of more than a hundred films, Walsh was a true professional with a hint of genius, as was shown in *White Heat* (49), in which **James Cagney** gets to immolate himself in a triumphant *Götterdämmerung* on top of a petrol refinery.

OTHER KEY FILMS: *Sadie Thompson* (28); *In Old Arizona* (29); *The Big Trail* (30); *The Roaring Twenties* (39); *They Drive By Night* (40); *Background To Danger* (43); *Objective Burma!* (44); *Pursued* (47); *The Naked And The Dead* (58)

Walters, Charles

A former choreographer turned **MGM** director, Walters was responsible for only one truly influential film in his career, *High Society* (56), and it is for this that he gets his entry. With it he achieved that rare thing in a film, a true **crossover**, in that he managed to persuade people who would never ordinarily have gone anywhere near a Hollywood musical, much less a **Bing Crosby** one, to give the thing a try. It's still fun, and it still plays to full houses when shown commercially.

OTHER KEY FILMS: *Easter Parade* (48); *The Tender Trap* (55); *Please Don't Eat The Daisies* (60); *The Unsinkable Molly Brown* (64)

Wardrobe
See **Costumer**

War Films
When cinema started, circa 1895 [see **The Brothers Lumière**], war was one of the last things on people's minds. Twenty years later it was on everybody's mind, and cinema had found one of its great motifs. There have arguably been more great war films made than films in any other genre except the **Western**, and the list below represents some of the finest ones. War, by its very nature, can comprise horror, comedy, love, friendship, hate, and the solace of brief happiness − all the great themes, therefore. As with novels, so with movies: **Sergei Eisenstein's** *Alexander Nevsky* (38) is cinema's *War And Peace*; **Jean Renoir's** *La Grande Illusion* (37) is cinema's *Servitude Et Grandeur Militaires*; Lewis Milestone's *All Quiet On The Western Front* (30) is at least comparable, in its cumulative effect, to the 1929 novel by Erich Maria Remarque that it was drawn from. **Francis Ford Coppola's** *Apocalypse Now* (79) created a metaphor for the Vietnam conflict that is arguably stronger, and potentially more long-lasting, than true-life images from the war itself, while **Anthony Minghella's** *The English Patient* (96) took war as the universal context for an exploration of love, friendship, and the mechanics of betrayal.

KEY LINES:
'You'll have to forgive me, comrade.' [**Lew Ayres** as Paul Baumer, in *All Quiet On The Western Front* (30), asking the Frenchman he has just killed for understanding]

'He wished that he, too, had a wound. A red badge of courage.' [From the narration accompanying **John Huston's** *The Red Badge Of Courage* (51)]

> ### *Best* **War Films**
> Claude Autant-Lara's *La Traversée De Paris* (56); Sergei Bondarchuk's *Waterloo* (70); **Robert Bresson's** *Un Condamné A Mort S'Est Échappé* (56); Christian de Chalonge's *Docteur Petiot* (89); Grigori Chukrai's *Ballad Of A Soldier* (59); **Michael Cimino's** *The Deer Hunter* (79); James Clavell's *The Last Valley* (70); **René Clément's** *Jeux Interdits* (51); **Francis Ford Coppola's** *Apocalypse Now* (79); **Sergei Eisenstein's** *Alexander Nevsky* (38); **John Huston's** *The Red Badge Of Courage* (51); **Stanley Kubrick's** *Paths Of Glory* (58); **David Lean's** *The Bridge On The River Kwai* (57); **Joseph Losey's** *Monsieur Klein* (76); **Louis Malle's** *Lacombe Lucien* (74);

Jiri Menzel's *Closely Observed Trains* (66); **Jean-Pierre Melville's** *L'Armée Des Ombres* (69); **Lewis Milestone's** *All Quiet On The Western Front* (30); **Sam Peckinpah's** *Cross Of Iron* (77); **Michael Powell** and **Emeric Pressburger's** *The Life And Death Of Colonel Blimp* (43); **Nicholas Ray's** *Bitter Victory* (57); **Jean Renoir's** *La Grande Illusion* (37); **Roberto Rossellini's** *Paisà* (46); **Steven Spielberg's** *Schindler's List* (93); **Bertrand Tavernier's** *La Vie Et Rien D'Autre* (89); **Billy Wilder's** *Five Graves To Cairo* (43) and *Stalag 17* (53)

Warhol, Andy

Warhol is seen by some as an avant-garde cultural icon and by others as a tiresome parvenu, and his film work falls somewhere in between the two camps, while nonetheless managing to draw interminably pretentious twaddle from people one might otherwise assume should know better. Suffice it to say that Warhol took himself seriously, and that some of the work produced by his film 'factory' was highly prescient in its undermining of standard moral parameters (although it might conceivably be seen as splendidly irrelevant to those living outside such sophisticated cultural environments as New York). Paul Morrisey's *Flesh* (68) and *Andy Warhol's Dracula* (74) are the most celebrated of Warhol's post-gunshot creations, and will no doubt continue to delight and bore, for generations to come, the denizens of museum retrospective showings.

OTHER KEY FILMS: *Sleep* (63); *Harlot* (64); *Bitch* (65); *The Velvet Underground And Nico* (67); *The Chelsea Girls* (66); *L'Amour* (73)

Warner Brothers

Founded by Jack L Warner in 1923, with his brothers Sam, Harry and Albert along for the ride, Warner Brothers is the studio many people subconsciously think of when they think of Hollywood. Jack Warner was a genius when it came to delegating and choosing his production executives, and it is to him that we owe the extraordinary string of films produced by **Darryl Zanuck** and **Hal Wallis** between 1929 and 1944, and also those by Jack Warner himself until the sale of his studio to Seven Arts in 1967. The impressive list includes **Raoul Walsh's** *The Roaring Twenties* (39), **John Huston's** *The Maltese Falcon* (41), **Michael Curtiz's** *Casablanca* (43), **Elia Kazan's** *A Streetcar Named Desire* (51), **George Stevens's** *Giant* (56), and **John Ford's** *The Searchers* (56). Warner Brothers is now owned by Time Warner.

Washing

The action of rinsing off chemicals from an already fixed and developed film.

Washington, Denzel

Washington first attracted real notice as Pfc. Peterson in Norman Jewison's *A Soldier's Story* (84), and the prestigious part of Steve Biko in **Richard Attenborough's** *Cry Freedom* (87) soon followed. His best break, however, came in Edward Zwick's *Glory* (89), and he has hardly looked back since. He was excellent as penniless private investigator Easy Rawlins in Carl Franklin's *Devil In A Blue Dress* (95), and looks set for a long, lucrative, if possibly somewhat over-earnest career. Perhaps it's about time he played a 'good' baddie.

OTHER KEY FILMS: *For Queen And Country* (88); *Ricochet* (91); *Malcolm X* (92); *Much Ado About Nothing* (93); *The Pelican Brief* (93); *Philadelphia* (93); *Crimson Tide* (95); *The Hurricane* (99); *Remember The Titans* (00); *Training Day* (01); *John Q* (01)

Waters, John

Blissfully irreverent cult filmmaker who has flirted with the mainstream without ever actually choosing to go to bed with it, Waters first came to the attention of the moralists with his *Mondo Trasho* (69), in which gargantuan transvestite Divine (an ex-school chum of Waters's) first erupted onto the big screen. History was made during Waters's follow-up, *Pink Flamingos* (72), when Divine scoffed a dog turd. However, Waters's best film by far, *Cry-Baby* (90), proved, paradoxically, to be a box-office failure, despite the presence of a teardrop-tattooed **Johnny Depp** at the head of the cast list. The continentals loved it, though, and the film did much to bolster Depp's subsequent career as the thinking Frenchwoman's favourite American.

OTHER KEY FILMS: *Female Trouble* (72); *Desperate Living* (77); *Polyester* (81); *Hairspray* (88); *Serial Mom* (94); *Pecker* (98); *Cecil B DeMented* (00)

KEY LINES:
'Hysterectomy pants, I call them.' [*Cry-Baby*]

Wave Machine

The wave machine is designed to churn up studio water tanks in order, Neptune-like, to produce waves on command. Possibly the greatest and most inventive use of this technology came in **John Ford's** *The Hurricane* (37), which still contains the best storm sequence ever shot. See **Wind Machine**

Waxing

The act of lubricating the edges of a strip of film to prevent unwanted hitches.

Waxman, Frank

One of the best of the romantic school of Hollywood film music composers, Waxman was responsible for a multitude of distinguished scores, including that for **Alfred Hitchcock's** *Rebecca* (40), Peter Godfrey's *The Two Mrs Carrolls* (47), Anatole Litvak's *Sorry Wrong Number* (48), **Billy Wilder's** *Sunset Boulevard* (50) and **George Stevens's** *A Place In The Sun* (51). As with his distinguished colleagues, **Max Steiner**, Friedrich Hollander, **Bernard Herrmann**, and **Erich Wolfgang Korngold**, Waxman was a classically trained musician who felt out of touch with modernism and preferred the well-staffed orchestras and well-stocked pocket books of Hollywood to the short rations on offer on the concert circuit.

Wayne, John

Arguably the best-loved and most enduring of all Hollywood stars, Marion Michael Morrison remains the focus of an ongoing cult that shows no sign of abating. Embodying the manly virtues of moral consistency and an invariable decency towards women, six-foot four-inch 'Duke' Wayne starred in more than 140 feature films during his fifty-year career. The chosen star for **John Ford** in his sublime cavalry trilogy, *Fort Apache* (48), *She Wore A Yellow Ribbon* (49) and *Rio Grande* (50), Wayne was often reviled for his consistently held right-wing views, most notably by those who had failed either to see or to appreciate the profound humanism of his greatest films. Dignified to the last, he made his farewell to the screen in **Don Siegel's** *The Shootist* (76), playing John Bernard Books, a gunfighter mortally ill with cancer (just as Wayne was at the time) and a man who was gently but resolutely concerned with the process of 'making' his soul (and thus, coincidentally, cleansing the town of bad men) before dying.

OTHER KEY FILMS: *The Oregon Trail* (36); *Stagecoach* (39); *The Long Voyage Home* (39); *They Were Expendable* (45); *Red River* (48); *Wake Of The Red Witch* (48); *Three Godfathers* (49); *The Quiet Man* (52); *Hondo* (53); *The Searchers* (56); *Rio Bravo* (59); *The Man Who Shot Liberty Valance* (62); *El Dorado* (67); *True Grit* (69)

KEY LINES:

'A long time ago I made me a rule – I let people do what they want to do.' [*Hondo*]

'That'll be the day!' [*The Searchers*]

John Wayne as The Ringo Kid in Stagecoach *(39), John Ford's majestic paean to ethical humanism*

'Don't apologise. It's a sign of weakness.' [*She Wore A Yellow Ribbon*]

'I won't be wronged, and I won't be insulted, and I won't be laid a hand on. I don't do these things to other people, and I require the same from them.' [*The Shootist*]

'John Wayne never blows a line. He'll come in letter perfect. The other actors will blow lines, but he will stand there patiently, wait for them to get their lines, then say his in his own way.' [Wendell Mayes, who scripted **Otto Preminger's** *In Harm's Way* (65), which featured Wayne as Captain Rockwell Torrey]

Weave

What happens when a film miscarries in a projector, causing the image on the screen to duck and dive.

Weaver, Sigourney

Refreshingly independent in a film world formed largely of wannabe clones, Weaver has constructed her career with care and has acted in remarkably few turkeys. She shot to fame, quite literally, as Ripley (shades of Patricia Highsmith?) in **Ridley Scott's** *Alien* (79), and then consolidated her reputation for quality acting opposite **Mel Gibson** in **Peter Weir's** excellent *The Year Of Living Dangerously* (82). She would have been sensational in **Lawrence Kasdan's** *Body Heat* (81), which she turned down because of the sex scenes involved, while paradoxically agreeing to appear in Bob Swaim's much inferior *Half Moon Street* (86), in which she cheerfully shed her clothes and cavorted in front of a mirror (and her audience) in stockings, suspender belt and precious little else. Since then she's been far more cautious (and just a little worthy).

OTHER KEY FILMS: *Gorillas In The Mist* (88); *Working Girl* (88); *Dave* (93); *Death And The Maiden* (95): *Galaxy Quest* (99); *Company Man* (00); *Heartbreakers* (01)

Webb, Clifton

A fondly remembered character actor who nevertheless had enough box-office clout to carry many films on his own, Webb Parmallee Hollenbeck specialised in over-bred, over-mannered know-it-alls with hearts of gold, as personified by his perennial Mr Belvedere in Walter Lang's *Sitting Pretty* (48). Webb's best part, because it allowed full play to his innate waspishness, came as Waldo Lydecker in **Otto Preminger's** magnificent, ground-breaking *Laura* (44).

OTHER KEY FILMS: *The Dark Corner* (46); *The Razor's Edge* (46); *For Heaven's Sake* (50); *Titanic* (53); *Three Coins In A Fountain* (54); *The Man Who Never Was* (56)

KEY LINES:

'How I detest the dawn! The grass always looks like it's been left out all night.' [**Henry Hathaway's** *The Dark Corner*]

'It's lavish, but I call it home.' [Waldo Lydecker, in *Laura*]

Best Weepies

Marcel Carné's *Les Portes De La Nuit* (46); John Cromwell's *The Enchanted Cottage* (45); **Edmund Goulding's** *Dark Victory* (39); Jean Grémillon's *Remorques* (39-40); **David Lean's** *Brief Encounter* (45); **Ang Lee's** *Sense And Sensibility* (95); Mervyn LeRoy's *Waterloo Bridge* (40); **Joseph L Mankiewicz's** *A Letter To Three Wives* (49); **Max Ophüls's** *Letter From An Unknown Woman* (48); Irving Rapper's *Now, Voyager* (42); **Douglas Sirk's** *Magnificent Obsession* (53) and *All That Heaven Allows* (55); **Sam Wood's** *King's Row* (42)

Weir, Peter

One of the best of Australia's 1970s 'New Wave' directors and something of a poet of emotional and physical claustrophobia, Weir is adept at maintaining the basic integrity of his films while still securing success at the box office. *Picnic At Hanging Rock* (75) mystified an entire generation (and still persists in doing so – what really happened to those three girls, for God's sake?) whilst *Gallipoli* (81), following the grand old filmic tradition of historical inaccuracy, was, emotionally speaking at least, right on the nail, which can be the only conceivable justification, apart from propaganda, for tinkering with historical truth. Weir's best film to date is *The Year Of Living Dangerously* (83) in which he successfully conjured up an entire lost decade that may be close to us in time but is far away in comprehension. Fans of *Witness* (85) and of *Dead Poets Society* (89), however, may wish to dispute that choice.

OTHER KEY FILMS: *The Cars That Ate Paris* (74); *The Last Wave* (77); *The Plumber* (80); *The Mosquito Coast* (86); *Green Card* (90); *Fearless* (93); *The Truman Show* (98)

Weissmuller, Johnny

Undeniably the greatest-ever screen **Tarzan**, Weissmuller was not in fact the first – that privilege fell to burly Elmo Lincoln, complete with impala loincloth and a shoulderful of coiled lianas, in Scott Sidney's *Tarzan Of The Apes* (18). Weissmuller, however, brought an Olympic swimmer's physique to the part, and his initial success in W S Van Dyke's *Tarzan, The Ape Man* (32) led to a further eleven spin-offs, culminating in Robert Florey's *Tarzan And The Mermaids* (48), in which good living and good loving had obviously taken their toll on our hero's once noble frame. During Weissmuller's brief but tempestuous marriage to Mexican firecracker Lupe Velez, the body make-up department were kept in a permanent state of mild hysteria by the marks Lupe's passionate temper and equally passionate carnality inflicted on the naked frame of their ape man. Fed up to the back teeth with Lupe's habit of flinging her skirt over her head in public places to reveal her invariable lack of underwear, Weissmuller divorced Velez in 1938 — sadly, she was to commit suicide six years and countless exhausted lovers later, by overdosing on Seconal tablets. See photograph at entry for **Maureen O'Sullivan**.

OTHER KEY FILMS: *Tarzan And His Mate* (34); *Tarzan Escapes* (36); *Tarzan Finds A Son* (39); *Tarzan's Secret Treasure* (41); *Tarzan's New York Adventure* (42); *Tarzan Triumphs* (41); *Tarzan's Desert Mystery* (43); *Tarzan And The Amazons* (45); *Tarzan And The Leopard Woman* (46); *Tarzan And The Huntress* (47)

Welch, Raquel

Almost incapable of acting in the normal sense of the word, the half-Bolivian, half-English Welch founded and maintained her career on the triple assets of her face and figure, which, quite reasonably, given the laws of biology, have provided her with an extremely good living ever since. The famous image of her (in a leopard-skin loincloth and little else) which first skewered an entire generation of spotty adolescents by the groin came in Don Chaffey's *One Million Years B.C.* (66), a film which may well mark the high-water point of Welch's screen career. Welch has always been remarkably astute at marketing her sexuality and disguising her lack of real acting talent, and it would be absurd, in the context of her era, to have expected any more of her than that.

OTHER KEY FILMS: *Fantastic Voyage* [in which she utters nary a word] (66); *Fathom* (67); *Bedazzled* (67); *Bandolero!* (68); *100 Rifles* (69); *Myra Breckenridge* (70); *The Magic Christian* (70); *The Last Of Sheila* (73); *The Three Musketeers* (74); *The Final Insult* (94)

KEY LINES:
'Being a sex symbol is rather like being a convict.' [Welch on the price of fame]
   'Tumak!' [*One Million Years B.C.*]

Welles, Orson

Welles was the closest Hollywood ever came to having a wayward genius in its commercially inhibited midst, and they made the worst of it. Whatever **Pauline Kael** or other carpers may have to say about *Citizen Kane* (41), the fact remains that Welles largely conceived and directed it, and absolutely certainly acted in it, and all this at the tender age of twenty-five, when most would-be geniuses are still busy chasing girls. Welles chased girls too, of course, and caught a good few of them, including **Rita Hayworth**, whom he married, then divorced, after showing her to the public in all her complexity in *The Lady From Shanghai* (48). Six years before, his heart had been torn out, along with a good deal of his film, when **RKO** let editor **Robert Wise** loose on what might have proved to be Welles's greatest masterpiece, *The Magnificent Ambersons* (42). His later films may have fallen off in budget terms as a result of the *Ambersons* failure, but they never fell off in imagination and creative design, and *Touch Of Evil* (58) was masterly in all those departments, including Welles's acting. His Hank Quinlan, a grotesque yet strangely sympathetic human whale, out of place and out of mind in an imaginary borderland of the soul, lingers on in the memory as hardly any conventional film hero ever does. All through his life, Welles was obsessed with Shakespeare and with a merry, older England, where inhibitions do not stifle enterprise and where creativity isn't forced to feed off the fluff from its own navel, and his final mighty bow to that tradition came with *Chimes At Midnight* (66), in which noble Falstaff is brought low by the iron hand of a soulless institution. Such was Welles's tragedy too, for he was *our* Falstaff figure, and his presence lingers in the ether, and will continue to linger, long after his tormentors, and their counterfeit memorials, have crumbled into dust.

OTHER KEY FILMS: *Journey Into Fear* (43) [co-dir]; *The Stranger* (46); *Macbeth* (48); *Othello* (52); *Mr Arkadin/Confidential Report* (55); *The Trial* (62); *The Immortal Story* (68); *F For Fake* (75)

KEY LINES:
'In Italy for thirty years under the Borgias they had warfare, terror, murder, bloodshed — and they

Orson Welles's bewildered Michael O'Hara facing up to Rita Hayworth's provocatively wayward Elsa Bannister, in his The Lady From Shanghai *(48)*

produced Michelangelo, Leonardo da Vinci and the Renaissance. In Switzerland they had brotherly love, five hundred years of democracy and peace and what did they produce? The cuckoo clock.' [*The Third Man*]

'I hate television. I hate it as much as peanuts. But I can't stop eating peanuts.' [Welles on nuts]

'The biggest electric train set any boy ever had…' [Welles on the **RKO** studios]

'He was some kind of a man. What does it matter what you say about people?' [**Marlene Dietrich** gives Hank Quinlan (and Welles?) his epitaph, in *Touch Of Evil*]

'With Welles, everything began with the writing. And he was very good at it. He was a terrific guy…his wealth of information and background about story lines was inexhaustible. He was inventive. Fearless.' [Writer/Director **Richard Brooks** on Welles, with whom he worked on the Mercury Theatre radio series]

Wellman, William

One of the tough boys of the early US film industry, Wellman was a bona fide First World War aviation hero who simply could not shake off the

habit of abrupt wartime command, even behind the camera. His tendency of treating his actors like recalcitrant fighter-bombers from the Lafayette Squadron got him into a fist-fight with **Spencer Tracy** and into a face-off with big **John Wayne**. Despite, or perhaps because of, these eccentricities, he managed to make a number of very fine motion pictures, including *Wings* (29), *The Public Enemy* (31), *Call Of The Wild* (35) [see **Loretta Young**], *Nothing Sacred* (37) and the magnificent *A Star Is Born* (37), a film which showed a quite uncharacteristic understanding of women on Wellman's part.

OTHER KEY FILMS: *Frisco Jenny* (33); *Small Town Girl* (36); *Beau Geste* (39); *The Light That Failed* (39); *Roxie Hart* (42); *The Ox-Bow Incident* (43); *Lady Of Burlesque* (43); *Yellow Sky* (48); *Battleground* (49); *Across The Wide Missouri* (51); *The High And The Mighty* (54)

Wenders, Wim

Wenders is the classic example of a post-war German (he was born in 1945) who grew up in a country imbued, for the first time ever, with a totally alien yet heady sense of cultural freedom entirely emanating from the US. American films, books and music entered his native culture as if by osmosis, and his gentle and often sensitive films reflect this, in particular *The American Friend* (77), *Hammett* (82) and *Paris, Texas* (84), for which he won the Palme d'Or at the **Cannes Film Festival**. His work turned increasingly fey during the late 1980s and early 90s, with *Wings Of Desire* (87) and *Until The End Of The World* (92), almost as if Wenders the filmmaker was seeing life from the very height of the angels he was depicting. But he came triumphantly down to earth again with his inspired documentary, *The Buena Vista Social Club* (99), in which he resuscitated the careers of a group of sensational Cuban 'son' musicians who had last enjoyed real success way back in the good old pre-Castro days.

OTHER KEY FILMS: *The Goalkeeper's Fear Of The Penalty* (71); *Alice In The Cities* (74); *Wrong Move* (75); *Kings Of The Road* (76); *Lightning Over Water* (80); *Tokyo-Ga* (85); *Faraway, So Close* (93); *Beyond The Clouds* [co-dir. with **Michelangelo Antonioni**]; *The End Of Violence* (97); *The Million Dollar Hotel* (99); *In America* (01)

West, Mae

The mother of all **vamps** (with apologies to **Theda Bara**), West began by shocking Broadway with her play, *Sex*, then moved on to shock Hollywood in turn, almost single-handedly bringing down the wrath of the **Hays Office** onto a mewling Tinseltown with her fruity double entendres. Her screen career began at the age of forty, when her figure already resembled (even when corseted) the lifebelt that the US Navy triumphantly named after it. But none of this mattered because West had that rare thing, innate sex-appeal, and she certainly knew how to use it, and could rattle the knees of screen swains such as **Cary Grant** with her straight from the shoulder invitations to 'come up sometime, and see me' in Lowell Sherman's *She Done Him Wrong* (33). By 1935 she was the best-paid woman in Hollywood, but the high point of her camp, if not of her sex, appeal, came five years later, when she starred opposite **W C Fields** in Edward Cline's *My Little Chickadee* (40). See photograph at **X-rated**

OTHER KEY FILMS: *Night After Night* (32); *I'm No Angel* (33); *Belle Of The Nineties* (34); *Goin' To Town* (35); *Klondike Annie* (36); *Go West Young Man* (36); *Every Day's A Holiday* (38); *The Heat's On* (43); *Myra Breckenridge* (70); *Sextette* (78)

KEY LINES:

'I always say, keep a diary and some day it'll keep you.'

'Beulah, peel me a grape.'

'It's not the men in my life that counts, it's the life in my men.'

'Is that a gun in your pocket, or are you just glad to see me?'

'I used to be Snow White… but I drifted.'

'You can say what you like about long dresses, but they cover a multitude of shins.'

Western, The

The Western is the song of the United States, a symbolic journey into just about every psychological and spiritual state imaginable, becoming, in the process, whatever the writer or the director chooses to make of it. It is for this reason that the Western will never die, despite numerous sombre warnings of its impending doom from the customary cluster of harbingers that hang around any genre open to disapproval. The Western can be about love, violence, brotherhood, poetry, or mental exploration, but it can just as easily be about heroes and heroines, bad guys and good guys, sanctity and perfidy. At its best, as in **John Ford's** *My Darling Clementine* (46) or **Anthony Mann's** *Winchester '73* (50), the Western takes on something of the characteristics of a country of the soul, where the landscape is of as much importance as the motives of the small, lonely characters within its often grotesque embrace. Sometimes, as in Ford's *The Searchers* (56), the landscape becomes the soul, and a simple shot of a man riding away, framed through a doorway, with a woman standing to one side, back-on, watching, can transcend its own context, becoming a universal image of alienation and possible reconciliation in starkly silent, utterly visual terms – the essence, in other words, of the cinema. See also **Spaghetti Westerns**

KEY LINES:

'Don't forget the Western is not only the history of this country, it is what the Saga of the Nibelungen is for the European.' [**Fritz Lang** on the Western]

Henry Fonda: 'Mac, you ever been in love?' Mac: 'No. I've been a bartender all my life.' [*My Darling Clementine*]

'Badges? We ain't got no badges. We don't need no badges. I don't have to show you any stinking badges!' [Alfonso Bedoya to **Humphrey Bogart** in *The Treasure Of The Sierra Madre*]

'Lady, the things I don't know you could herd like cows.' [Harry Carey, John Ford's 'bright star of the early Western sky', in Garson Kanin's *They Knew What They Wanted* (40) – the film may not be a Western in the strictest sense, but Carey's sentiments exemplify the spirit of the Western, of which he was an icon]

'I think all the stories about the West are probably full of shit. Cowboys were probably uneducated and very dull.' [Screenwriter **Julius J Epstein**, who co-scripted **Michael Curtiz's** *Casablanca* (42) and **Frank Capra's** *Arsenic And Old Lace* (44), on his detestation of Westerns – he didn't like Science Fiction either]

'The Western hero is the last hero…he's a man who is accountable only to himself and God.' [Screenwriter **Philip Yordan**, who co-scripted **Nicholas Ray's** *Johnny Guitar* (54) and **Anthony Mann's** *The Man From Laramie* (55), on Westerns]

Best Western Films

Budd Boetticher's *Seven Men From Now* (56), *The Tall T* (57), *Decision At Sundown* (57), *Buchanan Rides Alone* (58), *Comanche Station* (60) and *Ride Lonesome* (59); **Clint Eastwood's** *The Outlaw Josey Wales* (76) and *Unforgiven* (92); **John Farrow's** *Hondo* (53); **John Ford's** *Stagecoach* (39), *My Darling Clementine* (46); *Fort Apache* (48), *She Wore A Yellow Ribbon* (49), *Rio Grande* (50), *Wagon Master* (50) and *The Man Who Shot Liberty Valance* (63); **Henry Hathaway's** *True Grit* (69); **Howard Hawks's** *Red River* (48) and *Rio Bravo* (59); **Fritz Lang's** *Rancho Notorious* (52); **Sergio Leone's** *Once Upon A Time In The West* (69); **Anthony Mann's** *Winchester '73* (50), *The Naked Spur* (53), *The Man From Laramie* (55) and *Man Of The West* (58); **George Marshall's** *Destry Rides Again* (39); **David Miller's** *Lonely Are The Brave* (62); **Sam Peckinpah's** *Ride The High Country* (61); **Arthur Penn's** *Little Big Man* (69); **Nicholas Ray's** *Johnny Guitar* (54) and *Run For Cover* (55); **George Stevens's** *Shane* (53); **John Sturges's** *The Magnificent Seven* (60); **Raoul Walsh's** *Pursued* (47); **Robert Wise's** *Blood On The Moon* (48); **Fred Zinnemann's** *High Noon* (52)

WGA

See **Writers Guild Of America**

Whale, James

One of the great progenitors of the horror genre, Whale has recently been celebrated in a Hollywood biopic, Bill Condon's *Gods And Monsters* (98), being played on screen by no less a figure than Ian McKellen. With *Frankenstein* (31) [whose images would later run through and imbue **Victor Erice's** haunting *The Spirit Of The Beehive* (73)], *The Old Dark House* (32), *The Invisible Man* (33) and his camp masterpiece, *The Bride Of Frankenstein* (35), Whale covered just about every conceivable variation, from outright comedy to naked fear, that later generations of horror filmmakers would so eagerly claim as their own. An ex-First World War prisoner-of-war, Whale knew both the darkness of the trenches, the humiliation of apparent defeat, and the joy of eventual victory, all of which are reflected in his films. This strange man eventually gave up films to paint full time, before dying, in rather odd circumstances, in his own swimming pool.
OTHER KEY FILMS: *Journey's End* (30); *By Candlelight* (33); *Show Boat* (36); *Sinners In Paradise* (37); *The Man In The Iron Mask* (39); *Green Hell* (40); *They Dare Not Love* (41)

White Telephone Movies

These are the sort of movies where the characters live in penthouses, never have to think about money, have flunkeys to do all their dirty work, and chat to their friends on white, as opposed to any other coloured, telephones – white being taken by 1930s Hollywood filmmakers to represent, by some convoluted process of filmic logic, extreme luxury. **Edmund Goulding's** marvellous *Grand Hotel* (32) is a classic white telephone movie, as is **Howard Hawks's** *Twentieth Century* (34) and W S Van Dyke's *The Thin Man* (34).

Wide-angle Lens

A wider than normal lens of at least sixty-degrees perspective, most often used to film panoramas or other forms of **establishing shot**.

Wide-screen Process

A loose term for post-1953 non-Academy ratio films (that were, however, not in **CinemaScope**), the wide-screen process uses a wider than normal aspect ratio of at least 4:3, and a film gauge usually in the region of 65 or 70mm, to present moving pictures that are of an epic, or almost epic scale, e.g. **Ridley Scott's** *Gladiator* (00). Usual ratio is between 1:1.66 and 1:1.75, and the world standard in multiplexes is 1:1.85. Wide-screen TV is different again.

Widmark, Richard

It's hard to pin Widmark down, because he was never really a leading man in the conventional sense of the term, although he was very certainly a star. Perhaps it was the mean streak that did it, constantly bubbling just below the surface and ready to erupt in grotesque violence at the slightest opportunity, as in **Henry Hathaway's** *Kiss Of Death* (47), in which Widmark, shrieking with maniacal glee, sends a wheelchair-bound old lady to her death down a vertical flight of steps. But then the man could play gentle characters too, with that faraway look in his eyes and his sudden, boyish grin. Perhaps he was simply a one-off – a blond man in a predominantly dark world, who turned the tables on blondness, unlike his contemporary **Alan Ladd**, to become one of the very best screen villains going. Whatever the case, it is impossible to forget his panting, petrified hood in **Jules Dassin's** *Night And The City* (50), as he runs for his life, impervious even to the achingly beautiful, well-intentioned **Gene Tierney**, in his headlong descent into hell.

OTHER KEY FILMS: *Road House* (48); *Panic In The Streets* (50); *No Way Out* (50); *Pickup On South Street* (53); *Broken Lance* (54); *The Trap* (58); *Warlock* (59); *The Alamo* (60); *Two Rode Together* (61); *Cheyenne Autumn* (64); *Madigan* (68); *Death Of A Gunfighter* (69); *To The Devil A Daughter* (76); *Against All Odds* (83)

Wiene, Robert

One of the most influential of the German **expressionist** directors, Wiene made the extraordinary *The Cabinet Of Dr Caligari* (19), a film which marked that style's high point, but also, unfortunately, the director's, for he never made anything remotely as impressive again. Critics now take the view that Wiene himself was less than totally responsible for the look of the film, something which perhaps owed more to his assistants, Hermann Warm, Walter Röhrig and Walter Reimann, than was previously thought – a view which somewhat spikes the guns of the French **auteur** theory as advocated by **François Truffaut** and others of his ilk.

OTHER KEY FILMS: *Der Mann Im Spiegel* (16); *Salome* (22); *The Hands Of Orlac* (25); *Der Rosenkavalier* (26); *Unfug Der Liebe* (28)

Wigwag

The flashing red warning light outside a studio door which warns that filming is under way.

Wilde, Cornel

Best seen as a top-of-the-tree **B-movie** actor, Wilde had a lot going for him in terms of looks and physique, and, remarkably for one of his beefcake calling, he also proved that he could, on occasion, act too. Similar in many ways to his near-contemporary **Dana Andrews**, his never-quite-conventional looks and obvious intelligence no doubt precluded him from rising any higher in the Hollywood firmament than he did. His best mainstream films were the tight little **Jean** Negulesco *film noir* *Road House* (48), in which he was teamed with **Richard Widmark** and **Ida Lupino** in a scintillatingly murderous, hard-talking emotional triangle, and also **Joseph H Lewis's** sensational *The Big Combo* (54), in which Wilde's eardrums were subjected to a particularly painful form of torture by a cold-blooded Richard Conte. Of the number of independent movies Wilde eventually directed under the aegis of his very own production company, it is *The Naked Prey* (66), in which he finds himself stripped and allowed to run for his life from the bush tribe his clients have so unwisely and so lethally angered, that stands out.

OTHER KEY FILMS: *High Sierra* (41); *A Song To Remember* (46); *Leave Her To Heaven* (46); *Forever Amber* (47); *The Scarlet Coat* (55); *Hot Blood* (56); *Beach Red* (68) [also dir.]

Wilder, Billy

If he's not the best comic director and scriptwriter the cinema ever produced, then Wilder comes pretty darned close. With his colleague, **Charles Brackett**, he co-wrote the words for **Ernst Lubitsch's** *Ninotchka* (39) and for **Howard Hawks's** *Ball Of Fire* (42), and his first directing success soon followed with the quirky and wonderful *Five Graves To Cairo* (43). With *Double Indemnity* (44), one of the greatest of all *film noirs,* under his belt, he then made the ultimate film about alcoholism, *The Lost Weekend* (45), quickly followed by the best ever film about film, *Sunset Boulevard* (50), and the best ever film about the newspaper business, *Ace In The Hole* (51). And as if that wasn't enough, he then went on to make the best ever prisoner-of-war film, *Stalag 17* (53), and the best ever itinerant-musicians-dressing-up-as-women-and-being-pursued-by-demented-Mafiosi-while-still-taking-time-out-to-seduce-Marilyn-Monroe-and-Joe-E-Brown film. Yes. You've guessed it. He made *Some Like It Hot* (59) too. A master. No, *the* master. See **Heartstopping Moments**

OTHER KEY FILMS: *The Major And The Minor* (42); *The Emperor Waltz* (48); *Sabrina* (54); *The Seven Year Itch* (55); *Love In The Afternoon* (57); *Witness For The Prosecution* (58); *The Apartment* (60); *One Two Three* (61); *The Fortune Cookie* (66); *The Private Life Of Sherlock Holmes* [try and catch it – desperately underrated] (70)

KEY LINES:

Ninotchka: 'Why should you carry other people's bags?' Porter: 'Well, that's my business, Madame.' Ninotchka: 'That's no business. That's social injustice.' Porter: 'That depends on the tip.' [*Ninotchka*]

343

Wilder, Gene

A dotty and multi-talented comedian, Wilder will be forever cherished by film aficionados for his demented turn as Leo Bloom in **Mel Brooks's** *The Producers* (68), which quite coincidentally happens to be one of the funniest films ever made and the source for 'Springtime For Hitler' and other popular melodies now on Broadway. Wilder's 'Fat! Fat! Fat!' scene with Zero Mostel took neurosis to its illogical limits, and in doing so, became a classic, and nothing Wilder ever did later can really come close, although he was predictably splendid in Brooks's *Blazing Saddles* (74) and in Arthur Hiller's immaculately timed *Silver Streak* (76). Apropos of nothing whatsoever (and simply as a matter of passing interest), Wilder may be said to have the most unconventional hair (one assumes, still) of any major Hollywood figure, always excepting that of Jack Nance in **David Lynch's** *Eraserhead* (76).

OTHER KEY FILMS: *Bonnie And Clyde* (67); *Willy Wonka And The Chocolate Factory* (71); *Young Frankenstein* (74); *The Adventure Of Sherlock Holmes's Smarter Brother* (75); *Stir Crazy* (80); *The Woman In Red* (84); *See No Evil, Hear No Evil* (89); *Funny About Love* (90); *Another You* (91)

Wild Sound

Sound filmed outside the normal shooting schedule and which is added to the soundtrack at a later date to provide extra atmosphere.

Wild Track

Sound that does not have to be synchronised to the images in a film but which can be allowed to run randomly behind them – the noise of cicadas, a running stream, a distant storm, dogs barking in a yard, etc.

Williams, John

Composer of such majestic and stirring scores as those for **Steven Spielberg's** *Jaws* (75), *Close Encounters Of The Third Kind* (77), *Raiders Of The Lost Ark* (81) and *E.T.* (82), not to mention **George Lucas's** entire *Star Wars* series (77 onwards), Williams seems to have been the composer of choice for just about any famous blockbuster one may care to mention during the 1970s and 1980s, and it is to his credit that his music does not seem to have turned either stale or predictable in the process. Some of his best work, however, has been on much smaller films, most notably **Robert Altman's** *The Long Goodbye* (73) and **Lawrence Kasdan's** *The Big Chill* (83).

OTHER KEY FILMS: **Don Siegel's** *The Killers* (64); **Alfred Hitchcock's** *Family Plot* (76); Richard Donner's *Superman* (78); Mark Rydell's *The River* (84); **George Miller's** *The Witches Of Eastwick* (87); Steven Spielberg's *Jurassic Park* (93); **Oliver Stone's** *Nixon* (95); **Alan Parker's** *Angela's Ashes* (99); Roland Emmerich's *The Patriot* (00); Steven Spielberg's *A.I. – Artificial Intelligence* (01)

Williams, Robin

Occasionally irritating but undoubtedly talented, Williams took a long time to get off the mark in movies, and he was all of thirty-five when **Barry Levinson's** *Good Morning Vietnam* (88) notified the general public that he was here to stay. **Peter Weir's** *Dead Poets Society* (89) made him something of a cult in continental Europe, and his recent form, both in a series of children's movies which includes Joe Johnston's *Jumanji* (95), and also in more adult fare, such as **Gus Van Sant's** excellent *Good Will Hunting* (97), indicates that the talent of this comedian should maintain him both in fine style and in close proximity to the top of the Hollywood heap.

OTHER KEY FILMS: *Popeye* (80); *The World According To Garp* (82); *The Adventures Of Baron Munchausen* (89); *The Fisher King* (91); *Hook* (91); *Mrs Doubtfire* (93); *Father's Day* (95); *Patch Adams* (98); *Jakob The Liar* (99); *Bicentennial Man* (99); *One Hour Photo* (01)

Williams, Tennessee

A brilliant playwright and the source for many a fervid, sometimes fetid, but always literate Hollywood film, Williams was the star of his own life, and virtually all the films made from his plays and scripts stem from this fact, as is shown in their treatment of adults as the unconscious progeny of their own sexual and emotional natures. For many viewers during the 1950s and 60s, Williams and his work represented the acme of what could or could not be acknowledged in terms of adult emotional truths – the high points of his career were consequently legion, and include **Elia Kazan's** *A Streetcar Named Desire* (51), **Richard Brooks's** *Cat On A Hot Tin Roof* (58), **Joseph L Mankiewicz's** *Suddenly Last Summer* (59), and, best of all, **John Huston's** *The Night Of The Iguana* (64).

OTHER KEY FILMS: Irving Rapper's *The Glass Menagerie* (50); Elia Kazan's *Baby Doll* (56); José Quintero's *The Roman Spring Of Mrs Stone* (61); Richard Brooks's *Sweet Bird Of Youth* (62)

Willis, Bruce

One of the most intelligent and humorously self-deprecating of the latter-day big box-office macho men, Willis made his name in the television series *Moonlighting*, which gave him enough clout to land the star part in John McTiernan's *Die Hard* series (88–95 and beyond?). Three successive turkeys, Norman Jewison's *In Country* (89), **Brian De Palma's** *The Bonfire Of The Vanities* (90) and Michael Lehmann's *Hudson Hawk* (91), forced him to review his strategy, and he now seems to have plumped for the **Clint Eastwood** road of a big actioner, followed by a more thoughtful character performance, as in **Alan Rudolph's** *Mortal Thoughts* (91), **Robert Altman's** *The Player* (92) and **Quentin Tarantino's** *Pulp Fiction* (94), to leaven the commercial sourdough. Willis has had a recent surprise hit with M Night Shyamalan's brilliant ghost story, *The Sixth Sense* (99), and of all the blockbuster stars, he may still be the one to watch.

OTHER KEY FILMS: *Blind Date* (87); *Billy Bathgate* (91); *The Last Boy Scout* (91); *Death Becomes Her* (92); *The Story Of Us* (00); *The Kid* (00); *Unbreakable* (00); *The Whole Nine Yards* (00); *Bandits* (01)

KEY LINE:
'I said to Bruce Willis, "Anyway, whoever you are, you're standing in my space – so f★★★ off!" '
[**Richard Harris**, on his first encounter with the star]

Willis, Gordon

Woody Allen's favourite **cinematographer**, Willis was the master behind the look of some of Allen's best loved films, including *Annie Hall* (77), *Manhattan* (79), *Stardust Memories* (80), *Zelig* (83) and *The Purple Rose Of Cairo* (85). He can also, when his director requires it, indulge in the sort of screen trickery seen in **Alan J Pakula's** *The Parallax View* (74) and *All The President's Men* (76), for which one easily forgives him, bearing in mind the conventional yet magnificent work he did on **Francis Ford Coppola's** *The Godfather Parts I, II and III* (74–90).

OTHER KEY FILMS: Alan J Pakula's *Klute* (71); **Herbert Ross's** *Pennies From Heaven* (81); Alan J Pakula's *The Devil's Own* (97)

Winding

The delicate process of transferring, often at high speed, one full reel of film to another empty reel.

Wind Machine

An enormous mechanical fan designed to blow up a storm in artificial studio conditions when the filming of wild and inclement weather is on the agenda. See **Wave Machine**

Winger, Debra

A sadly underused actress who was, perhaps, simply not winsome enough for mass popular taste, Winger first made her mark in **Taylor Hackford's** *An Officer And A Gentleman* (82) as the spunky (in more senses than one) working-class heroine whom **Richard Gere** gets to carry off in his willowy arms at the end of the movie (to well-earned cheers from the audience). Her best performance (*c'est la vie*) came in her biggest flop, **Bernardo Bertolucci's** disastrously underrated *The Sheltering Sky* (90), although her understated playing of Joy Gresham in **Richard Attenborough's** *Shadowlands* (93) was equally outstanding. She deserves better both from her public and the studios.

OTHER KEY FILMS: *Urban Cowboy* (80); *Terms Of Endearment* (83); *Legal Eagles* (86); *Black Widow* (87); *Betrayed* (88); *Forget Paris* (95); *Big Bad Love* (01)

Winner, Michael

Master of the violent screen moment and resident gourmet for *The Sunday Times*, Winner had the misfortune (or the luck) to fall foul of the liberal elite with his *Death Wish* series (74–85) starring **Charles Bronson**, and he has never been allowed to forget it. A more professional and a better director than he is given credit for, Winner has shown canny judgement in deciding what the public wants, and then giving it to them. Outspoken and unregenerate, one nevertheless retains a soft spot for him despite his often outrageous foibles.

OTHER KEY FILMS: *West 11* (63); *The System* (64); *The Jokers* (67); *I'll Never Forget What's 'is Name* (67); *The Games* (70); *Lawman* (71); *Chato's Land* (72); *The Nightcomers* (72); *The Mechanic* (72); *The Stone Killer* (73); *Appointment With Death* (88); *Bullseye* (90); *Parting Shots* (98)

Winslet, Kate

Flavour-of-the-year following her turn as Rose DeWitt Bukater (God help us!) in **James Cameron's** *Titanic* (97), Winslet is a far better actress than her co-star **Leonardo DiCaprio** is an actor, and her career, if she plays it right, should be considerably longer (if commensurately less lucrative). She was outstanding in her first big feature, Peter Jackson's *Heavenly Creatures* (94), and she followed this up, very effectively indeed, with a notable performance in **Ang Lee's** brilliant Jane Austen outing, *Sense And Sensibility* (95), a film which almost single-handedly restored one's faith in the cinema's ability to produce emotionally satisfying, high-quality, mainstream entertainment. Michael Winterbottom's downbeat *Jude* (96) was another career highlight, and one only hopes that this still very young actress (she was born in 1975) can keep her nerve and talent intact over the long term.

OTHER KEY FILMS: *Hamlet* (96); *Hideous Kinky* (98); *Holy Smoke* (99); *Quills* (00); *Thérèse Raquin* (01); *Enigma* (01)

Winters, Shelley

A screen victim who nevertheless managed to turn the tables on her tormentors to become a confident, skilful actress, Winters has expanded over the years from the slip of a girl who appeared so effectively as one of **Ronald Colman's** murderees in **George Cukor's** *A Double Life* (47), to the star she is today. With each successive film she seemed to gain in confidence and poise, even though the combined star power of **Elizabeth Taylor** and **Montgomery Clift** nearly blew her off the screen in **George Stevens's** *A Place In The Sun* (51). But she got her own back as yet another murder victim in **Charles Laughton's** utterly splendiferous *The Night Of The Hunter* (55), where her death scene is among the most poignant in cinema history. Her filmography is extensive and startling in its diversity, and Winters is the classic example of the bridesmaid who occasionally, and rightly, manages to outshine the bride.

OTHER KEY FILMS: *The Great Gatsby* (49); *Winchester '73* (50); *Executive Suite* (54); *The Big Knife* (55); *I Died A Thousand Times* (55); *Odds Against Tomorrow* (59); *Lolita* (62); *Alfie* (66); *Harper* (66); *Bloody Mama* (70); *The Tenant* (76); *King Of The Gypsies* (79); *Stepping Out* (91)

Wipe

The 'wipe' is the moment, often in a 1930s or 40s screwball comedy, when the scene we are watching on the screen is gradually replaced by a new scene, sliding or rolling or juddering across it. Such wipes come in many shapes, forms and sizes and have fallen into disfavour in recent years, just as any 'obvious' artifice has fallen into disfavour. What directors don't seem to appreciate is that 1930s audiences were every bit as sophisticated as we are, and were just as aware that what they were watching was a movie approximation to real life, and not an accurate reflection of it.

Wisdom, Norman

A pratfalling English comedian, Wisdom is still thought of with considerable affection even though he has appeared in no more than one or two films in the past thirty years. However, it would be absurd in his case to single out one particular film for particular praise – he is either loved or hated, and those who love him look beyond the sheer ordinariness of much of his work to the exalted comic timing and genuine inventiveness he occasionally showed.

KEY FILMS: *Trouble In Store* (53); *Man Of The Moment* (55); *Just My Luck* (57); *On The Beat* (62); *The Early Bird* (65); *The Sandwich Man* (66); *The Night They Raided Minsky's* (68)

Wise, Robert

Despite being the man whom **RKO** chose to massacre **Orson Welles's** *The Magnificent Ambersons* (42) [he'd already been editor on *Citizen Kane* (41)], Wise partially redeemed himself with a string of excellent *film noirs*, not to mention a further duet of screen musicals that included, yes, *The Sound Of Music* (65) and *Star!* (68). Wise's best movie is undoubtedly *The Set-Up* (49), with **Robert Ryan** on the top of his form as an ageing boxer playing out his final fight in tense real time, though Wise's earlier *Born To Kill* (47) was another corker for the *film noir* connoisseur. The undervalued *Tribute To A Bad Man* (56), a movie in which **James Cagney** managed the difficult task of moving from an unsympathetic to a sympathetic character without making the audience throw up in horror, fulfilled a similar function for **Western** aficionados. Come to think of it, *Blood On The Moon* (48), with **Robert Mitchum** as its tormented post-Freudian protagonist, made a pretty good stab at being a double genre Western *film noir*, and his two best **science-fiction** movies, *The Day The Earth Stood Still* (51) and *The Andromeda Strain* (71), were more than passable, stacking the odds even more in favour of Wise's post-Wellesian redemption.

OTHER KEY FILMS: *The Body Snatcher* (45); *Mystery In Mexico* (48); *Executive Suite* (54); *Run Silent Run Deep* (58); *Odds Against Tomorrow* (59); *West Side Story* (61) [co-dir.]; *The Sand Pebbles* (66);

Woo, John

Cantonese director of innovative, balletic action films, in which the editing, camera angles and cutting all play their part, Woo has continued his successful run with *Mission: Impossible 2* (00), in which **Tom Cruise** reprised the role of actor and producer that brought him a $75-million payout for *Mission: Impossible* (95). Woo's cut of the take was considerable too, based on his recent string of hits that includes *The Killer* (89), *Hard Target* (93), *Broken Arrow* (96) and *Face/Off* (96). An awesome technician, Woo woos his actors, allowing them to perform the sort of macho stunts that appeal to those who like their action both well done and bloody at the same time.

OTHER KEY FILMS: *The Sunset Warrior* (83); *Run Tiger Run* (85); *A Better Tomorrow* (86); *Bullet In The Head* (90); *Once A Thief* (91); *Hard-Boiled* (92); *Wind Talkers* (01)

KEY LINE:

'Woo's action is like a dance, and he has that mythic quality in his pictures…' [Tom Cruise on Woo]

Wood, Ed

Considered by some to be the world's worst film director, Wood was the happy, albeit posthumous, beneficiary of a biopic to that effect in **Tim Burton's** *Ed Wood* (94), starring **Johnny Depp** as its eponymous hero. But Wood actually wasn't that bad if one takes into account his mania for cross-dressing (particularly in fluffy tops) and his rock-bottom budgets. Among his numerous masterpieces of retrospective camp, special acclaim must go to *Glen Or Glenda?* (53) for its lessons in the use of voiceover, and to *Plan 9 From Outer Space* (59) for just about everything, and particularly the ghoul.

OTHER KEY FILMS: *Bride Of The Monster* (53); *Jail Bait* (54); *Night Of The Ghouls* (60); *Necromancy* (72)

Wood, Natalie

She died tragically in a boat accident in 1981, aged forty-three, and one would like to be able to rate her career more highly as a result, but the fact remains that if it wasn't for her early death, Natalie Wood would probably be acting alongside Farrah Fawcett and Victoria Principal in nothing but run-of-the-mill TV movies by now. What's interesting about her is that she was very much a Hollywood product from the beginning, making her first film at the tender age of five, and she remained one, sadly, until the end. Her best performances were in **Nicholas Ray's** *Rebel Without A Cause* (55) and **Robert Wise** and Jerome Robbins's *West Side Story* (61).

OTHER KEY FILMS: *The Ghost And Mrs Muir* (47); *The Star* (53); *The Searchers* (56); *Gypsy* (62); *Sex And The Single Girl* (64); *Bob & Carol & Ted & Alice* (69)

Wood, Sam

Wood is the sort of director whose filmography looks considerably more impressive than the extent of his actual talent would suggest. He was put in charge of two of the greatest **Marx Brothers** films, *A Night At The Opera* (35) and *A Day At The Races* (37), but, according to Groucho, the films were successes despite, and not because of, Wood. He directed the sublime **Robert Donat** in *Goodbye Mr Chips* (39), but the film was always Donat's, never Wood's, and the same can be said of *For Whom The Bell Tolls* (43), which relies on the star chemistry of **Gary Cooper** and **Ingrid Bergman** to attract attention away from its stolid mechanics. All carping aside, Wood's best films came near the end of his career, with *The Devil And Miss Jones* (41) and *Ivy* (47).

OTHER KEY FILMS: *Madame X* (37); *Raffles* (39); *Kitty Foyle* (40); *Kings Row* (42); *Guest Wife* (45); *Command Decision* (49); *Ambush* (50)

Woods, James

One of the best character actors working in Hollywood today, Woods has brought energy, commitment and unconventional looks to films as diverse as Harold Becker's *The Onion Field* (79), **David Cronenberg's** *Videodrome* (83), Taylor Hackford's *Against All Odds* (84) and **Sergio Leone's** *Once Upon A Time In America* (84). However, the high point of his career must surely be his brilliantly nuanced and utterly unsentimental performance in the title role of Tim Metcalfe's *Killer: A Journal Of Murder* (96), in which he knocked the opposition [and **Sean Penn** in **Tim Robbins's** commercially more successful *Dead Man Walking* (95)] into a cocked hat, with his portrait of an entirely unregenerate killer.

OTHER KEY FILMS: *Eyewitness* (81); *Split Image* (82); *Cat's Eye* (85); *Salvador* (86); *The Getaway* (94); *Casino* (95); *Nixon* (95); *Contact* (97); *Any Given Sunday* (99); *Race To Space* (00); *John Q* (01)

Woodward, Joanne

Paul Newman's wife since 1958 (they must be approaching something of a Hollywood record), Woodward has appeared in many movies that more often miss the mark than not. This is not to take away from her good performances (when she's not being worthy, that is) but merely to put her career in a just perspective. Career highlights include Nunnally Johnson's *The Three Faces Of Eve* (57) and **Sidney Lumet's** *The Fugitive Kind* (59), and she was excellent, too, in **James Ivory's** downbeat *Mr And Mrs Bridge* (90). It's a curious thing, though, but her reputation, which is excellent, has always seemed to outstrip the reality.

OTHER KEY FILMS: *Count Three And Pray* (55); *A Kiss Before Dying* (56); *The Long Hot Summer* (58); *Paris Blues* (61); *Rachel, Rachel* (68); *The Effect Of Gamma Rays On Man-In-The-Moon Marigolds* (72); *Summer Wishes, Winter Dreams* (73); *The Glass Menagerie* (87); *Philadelphia* (93)

Working Title

This is the tentative title used during the writing of the screenplay or by the director and crew during the making of the film, before the true title of the released version of a film is decided upon. Remember Paul Weitz's *American Pie* (99)? – its working title was *East Great Falls High*, and Peter Hewitt's *Bill And Ted's Bogus Journey* (91) was for a long time known as *Bill And Ted Go To Hell*. Phil Alden Robinson's *Field Of Dreams* (89) was originally *Shoeless Joe* while Peter Cattaneo's *The Full Monty* (97) was otherwise known as *Eggs, Beans and Chippendales* – catchy or what? And how about Garry Marshall's *Pretty Woman* (90) [a.k.a. *$3,000*] and Billy Wilder's *Some Like It Hot* (59) [a.k.a. *Not Tonight, Josephine*]?

Workprint

The editor's working print used during the **rough cut**, **fine cut** and pre-**release print** stages of a film's editing.

Worst Films

There have been innumerable bad movies made over the past century of cinema and innumerable bad movie awards to celebrate them, and the subject must always, by its very nature, be an entirely subjective one. However, some films are so bad that they simply transcend fashion, naturally falling into a category of their very own. Here are just a few from the past ten years, in date order, that were foisted upon us by directors who really should have known better:

The Coen Brothers's *Barton Fink* (91), in which a trio of otherwise excellent actors, John Turturro, John Goodman and **Judy Davis**, battle against the incoherence of a script which purports to examine the condition of writer's block and only succeeds in making one wish that it occurred more frequently. 'We all want it to have that Barton Fink feeling. I mean, I guess we all have that Barton Fink feeling, but since you're Barton Fink, I'm assuming you have it in spades.' [Studio boss Lipnick to Barton Fink]

David Lynch's *Twin Peaks: Fire Walk With Me* (92), in which pretension overcomes discretion and inanition replaces elucidation until…well, it just doesn't make any sense at all, even to those who consider the same director's *Blue Velvet* (86) to be one of the very best and most original films of the past fifty years.

Manoel de Oliviera's appalling turkey *The Convent* (95), in which **Catherine Deneuve** and **John Malkovich** walk from room to room looking uncomfortable. As well they might. Was Shakespeare really Spanish? And do we care? And is Luis Miguel Cintra really Mephistopheles? These abuses must be put an end to…

Claude Lelouch's *Les Misérables* (95), in which an apparently disintegrating **Jean-Paul Belmondo** cavorts geriatrically around France, machine-gunning all and sundry in a demented attempt to mimic Victor Hugo's invariably unarmed Jean Valjean. And fails.

Michael Cacoyannis's *The Cherry Orchard* (98), in which the acting is more wooden than the eponymous orchard, and the staccato, ill-edited direction obliterates all trace of Chekhov's intended comic portrayal of the Russian ruling class in witless decline. The decelerating dénouement is relieved only by a convincingly purple-nosed Michael Gough as decaying butler Feers who, abandoned in the locked-up country house after its forced sale, is entrusted with the film's last line: 'My long life is coming to an end, and there has been no point to it.' A suitable valediction indeed.

Roger Christian's *Battlefield Earth* (00), in which an ever more porky **John Travolta** dresses up in dreadlocks and a metal tiara, with what appear to be two feeding tubes stuck up his nose, in a vain effort to frighten the rest of the world into embracing Scientology.

Jeremiah Chechik's *The Avengers* (98) must be the supreme example of Hollywood's capacity to take a much-loved television series, misunderstand what constitutes its cult, and reformat it for an unsophisticated, and largely uninterested contemporary audience. Sex appeal, badinage, spoof spying - how good they must have sounded to the Warner Bros accountants after the runaway success of Jay Roach's *Austin Powers: International Man Of Mystery* (97). The difference between the two movies, lies, of course, in the fact that one of them was made with heart, incorporating a genuine affection for the chosen genre, and the other with venality, incorporating a genuine respect for the anticipated bottom line.

It becomes obvious, right from the start of Steven Soderbergh's *Erin Brockovich* (00), that **Julia Roberts** is now so much in love with her onscreen image (sassy, mock vulnerable, manipulative) that it would be sheer madness to actually expect her to act. Instead she presents us with the caricature of ordinary working woman and former Miss Pacific Coast 1981, Erin (née Patee) Brockovich, filtered through the Hollywood commercial gauze that has become Roberts's reality. Star egos are notoriously large and notoriously fragile, and one can hardly blame Soderbergh, and to a lesser extent, **Albert Finney**, for succumbing to the hype and dumbing down. The film was a huge commercial success, managing, in the process, to turn a genuinely uplifting story into something about as believable as a 'little-green-men-on-Mars story' – sadly, approximately eighty per cent the US population actually do believe that there are little green men on Mars, so **Roberts** has the final laugh.

Jean-Jacques Annaud's *Enemy At The Gates* (01) takes a brilliant premise, the true-life battle of wits between two master snipers during the siege of Stalingrad, and turns it into expensive hokum. Actors **Jude Law** (Sergeant Vassili Zaitsev), **Joseph Fiennes** (Commissar Danilov) and **Ed Harris** (brilliant, as usual, as Major Erwin Konig), really seem to take the movie seriously, but Annaud, inured, by now, to the curious rules which apply only to potential international blockbusters, snatches the structure from beneath them and contrives to turn Armageddon into Armani, until even the immaculately applied facial dirt seems a contrivance. Go watch Andrzej Wajda's **Kanal** (56), or read Guy Sajer's *The Forgotten Soldier* instead.

See also **Best Titles, Erotic Moments, Heartstopping Moments**

Writers Guild Of America

Formerly known as The Screen Writers Guild, this influential Los Angeles and New York-based association represents both film and television writers by protecting copyrights, recommending work practices, and advising on legal and contractual disputes.

Wyler, William

An obsessive perfectionist while on set, Wyler spanned the wholesome, culturally aspiring middle ground of the movie spectrum, and produced an extraordinary number of high-quality hits. His films were always literate if rarely deep, and *Dodsworth* (36), which benefited from a superb **Walter Huston** performance in the title part, was his high-water mark artistically. The rest of his films, however, are both visually satisfying and downright enjoyable, and include *Dead End* (37), *Jezebel* (38), *Wuthering Heights* (39), *Mrs Miniver* (42) and *The Heiress* (49). Highest profile of all was his 1959 epic version of *Ben-Hur*, though it is arguable that the lesser-known *Detective Story* (51), which Wyler imbued with a semi-documentary feel, is the more challenging film. In later years Wyler began to take a few risks, most notably with *The Collector* (65), a film based on the John Fowles novel of the same name,and which was considerably underrated at the time of its release.

OTHER KEY FILMS: *These Three* (36); *The Letter* (40); *The Westerner* (40); *The Little Foxes* (41); *The Best Years Of Our Lives* (46); *Carrie* (52); *Roman Holiday* (53); *The Desperate Hours* (55); *The Children's Hour* (62); *Funny Girl* (68)

X-rated

A film censorship rating once used in the US for pornographic films or films with a heavy and explicit sex content (now superseded by the NC-17 – No Children under seventeen), and in the UK (from 1951 to the mid-1980s) for films with an exclusively adult content. After the X-rating had been current for some time in the US, it was belatedly discovered that the X had not been copyrighted and that anyone could assign an X (or even an XX or, Heaven help us, an XXX) to their flick in the hope of conning gullible viewers into believing that anyone watching the thing was, at the very least, risking excommunication.

XLS

Abbreviation for '**extreme long shot**'.

Xi'an Film Studios

Ground-breaking Chinese film studio whose heyday was in the 1980s, Xi'an's motto was 'to make a profit with one hand and to take awards with another'. It was also the location for Tian Zhuangzhuang's *The Horse Thief* (86) and **Zhang Yimou's** visually splendid, Golden Bear award-winning *Red Sorghum* (87).

Xie Jin

A veteran Chinese director who was silenced by Mao Zedong's Red Guards during the Cultural Revolution but who has since returned to directing, Jin is notable for the sympathetic portrayal of women in his films, particularly in his catchily titled *Woman Basketball Player No 5* (57), and *The Red Detachment Of Women* (60).

OTHER KEY FILMS: *Two Stage Sisters* (64); *Youth* (77); *The Herdsman* (82); *Qiu Jin* (84); *Hibiscus Town* (84); *Wreaths At The Foot Of The Mountain* (85); *The Last Aristocrats* (89); *An Old Man And His Dog* (93); *Behind The Wall Of Shame* (96); *The Opium War* (97)

The X-rated **Mae West** *waiting for someone to come up sometime and see her, in the original 1928 Broadway production of her play,* Diamond Lil

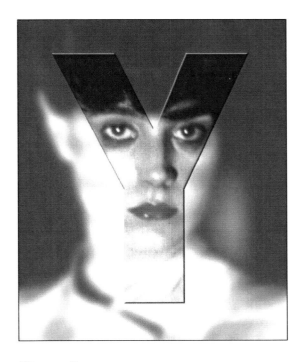

Yanne, Jean

A very French actor and director, committed both artistically and emotionally to his country of origin, Yanne is best known to international audiences for his complex portrayals of a murderer in **Claude Chabrol's** *Le Boucher* (70) and in *Que La Bête Meure* (69), the latter being based on the brilliant Cecil Day Lewis [writing as Nicholas Blake] novel *The Beast Must Die*. Yanne had a deserved success with his first feature film as actor/writer/director, *Tout Le Monde Il Est Beau – Tout Le Monde Il Est Gentil* (72), and has split his career ever since between subtle, carefully chosen appearances in other people's films, and a commitment to his own work. His particular strength as an actor lies in his ability to make the grotesque, in some strange way, sympathetic.

OTHER KEY FILMS: *Weekend* (67); *Nous Ne Vieillirons Pas Ensemble* (72); *La Raison D'Etat* (78); *Asphalte* (81); *Choucroute* (85); *Le Paltoquet* (86); *Madame Bovary* (91); *Victory* (95); *Désiré* (96); *Mo'* (96); *The Raft Of The Medusa* (98); *Belle Maman* (99); *Le Pacte Des Loups* (01)

Yates, Peter

Yates is a curious director who veers alarmingly from commercial dross, with *Krull* (83), to emotional truth and critical success, with *Breaking Away* (79) and *The Dresser* (83). At his best, and when he doesn't espouse short-term visual tricks and trendy filmic short cuts, he has shown himself capable, in films like *The Friends Of Eddie Coyle* (73), of digging far deeper into character and atmosphere than would be expected of the man responsible for **Steve McQueen's** famous car chase in that otherwise routine thriller, *Bullitt* (68).

OTHER KEY FILMS: *Summer Holiday* (63); *Robbery* (67); *Murphy's War* (71); *The Hot Rock* (72); *The Deep* (77); *Eyewitness* (81); *Eleni* (85); *The Suspect* (87); *Year Of The Comet* (92); *Roommates* (95); *The Run Of The Country* (95); *Curtain Call* (99)

Yordan, Philip

Yordan is one of the near greats – a screenwriter who combines commercial nous with a critical and intellectual intensity that is only deepened by his uncanny way with vernacular and the red pencil, the so-called 'Yordan touch'. The 'near', however, came from his habit of hiring 'surrogates' (often consisting of blacklisted artists) to write some of his scripts, a practice which inevitably throws some doubt on one or two of his contributions to cinematic history, but none at all on his talent for incisive editing. Despite this proviso, Yordan's credits or co-credits read like a roll-call of intense and satisfying Hollywood movie-making, and include Max Nosseck's *Dillinger* (45), **William Wyler's** *Detective Story* (51), Byron Haskin's *Naked Jungle* (54), **Nicholas Ray's** *Johnny Guitar* (54), **Joseph H Lewis's** *The Big Combo* (55) and Mark Robson's *The Harder They Fall* (56). Whether Yordan wrote the finished scripts or not, his mark is all over these movies, and his uncanny way with dialogue puts him in the august company of such masters as **Ben Hecht** and Charles MacArthur.

OTHER KEY FILMS: Frank Tuttle's *Suspense* (46); **Anthony Mann's** *The Man From Laramie* (55); Nicholas Ray's *King Of Kings* (61); Anthony Mann's *El Cid* (61); Irving Lerner's *The Royal Hunt Of The Sun* (69)

York, Michael

A rather dated actor, York appears to straddle, sometimes awkwardly, the gulf between the 1960s and the present day. He was a wartime baby, the product of time-warp 1950s England, and he has always seemed a little ill at ease playing trendy 'liberated' men, fitting far better into period films such as Etienne Périer's *Zeppelin* (71) and Richard Lester's *The Three Musketeers* (73). His best moments have always come when either he or his director has had the courage to overcome the inhibited part of York's nature and reveal the seething vulnerability beneath, as Bob Fosse briefly succeeded in doing in *Cabaret* (72).

OTHER KEY FILMS: *The Taming Of The Shrew* (67); *Logan's Run* (76); *The Island Of Dr Moreau* (77); *Wide Sargasso Sea* (91); *Gospa* (95); *Dark Planet* (96); *Austin Powers: International Man Of Mystery* (97); *Wrongfully Accused* (98); *Austin Powers: The Spy Who Shagged Me* (99); *Borstal Boy* (00)

York, Susannah

There were a couple of years during the 1960s when York seemed to be in just about every big British film going, but her career tailed off just as suddenly during the late 1970s and one is now left feeling slightly mystified by her ephemeral and strangely dated charm. She first made her adult mark in **John Huston's** curiosity *Freud: The Secret Passion* (62), and then shot to stardom with the role of Sophie Western in **Tony Richardson's** flavour-of-the-month *Tom Jones* (63). Her best performance, however, came in the little-known **Robert Altman** film, *Images* (72), which was based around her own writings for children but which remained impenetrable to the audience it was meant to enlighten.

OTHER KEY FILMS: *The Greengage Summer* (61); *Kaleidoscope* (66); *Sebastian* (68); *The Killing Of Sister George* (68); *They Shoot Horses, Don't They?* (69); *Jane Eyre* (71); *Gold* (74); *The Shout* (78); *Loophole* (80); *Alicja* (82); *Melancholia* (89); *Loop* (97)

Young, Freddie

A doyen of British cinematography, Young photographed nearly all the large-scale **David Lean** movies, including *Lawrence Of Arabia* (62), *Dr Zhivago* (65) and *Ryan's Daughter* (70). However, his best work (a contentious issue, this) came in black-and-white, and included **Sam Wood's** magnificent *Goodbye Mr Chips* (39), **Michael Powell's** *49th Parallel* (41) and Young's masterpiece, **Richard Brooks's** *Lord Jim* (65). The plot and treatment of *Lord Jim* may have been unfaithful to Joseph Conrad's original, but the film's lighting and photographic atmosphere, thanks to Young's brilliancy, were surely all that the creator of *Heart Of Darkness* could have desired.

OTHER KEY FILMS: **Carol Reed's** *The Young Mr Pitt* (42); **Anthony Asquith's** *The Winslow Boy* (48); **John Ford's** *Mogambo* (53); Franklin J Schaffner's *Nicholas And Alexandra* (71)

Young, Loretta

It's quite hard to understand the appeal of actresses such as Loretta Young today, but she did make over a hundred films and was surprisingly successful at keeping herself in the public eye. She seemed to make her good movies almost by default, as though she stumbled into them rather than appeared in them through any conscious critical effort. Take *Platinum Blonde* (31) for instance – it was **Frank Capra's** baby, **Jean Harlow** was its star, and Robert Williams was at his subtly anarchic best as the penniless reporter. Oh, and then there was Loretta Young. That seems to be the story of her life. Having said that, she was a professional, hard-working actress, and she was more than good in **Orson Welles's** *The Stranger* (46). <u>Note for Film Buffs</u>: Young's 'adopted' daughter later claimed that she was actually the fruit of a torrid love affair between **Clark Gable** and Young during the filming of **William Wellman's** *Call Of The Wild* (35).

OTHER KEY FILMS: *Laugh, Clown, Laugh* (28); *Four Men And A Prayer* (38); *China* (43); *The Farmer's Daughter* (47); *The Bishop's Wife* (47); *Rachel And The Stranger* (48)

Young, Robert

The most un-neurotic of actors, Young wafted through upwards of eighty films with consistent good humour and professionalism, his audience appeal lasting right through until his late sixties, when he enjoyed a successful run on television in *Father Knows Best* and *Marcus Welby M.D.* In the movies he specialised in playing good friends and unthreatening swains, and his best performances came in **Frank Borzage's** *Three Comrades* (38), **King Vidor's** *H. M. Pulham, Esq.* (41) and **John Cromwell's** wildly romantic *The Enchanted Cottage* (45).

Scintillating but wayward Sean Young as Rachael the 'replicant', in Ridley Scott's influential Blade Runner (82)

OTHER KEY FILMS: *The Kid From Spain* (32); *The Secret Agent* (36); *Northwest Passage* (40); *The Canterville Ghost* (44); *Crossfire* (47); *Secret Of The Incas* (54)

Young, Sean

An absolutely gorgeous actress who failed, largely on account of her temperament, to benefit from the opportunities she carved out for herself, Young was chosen by director **Ridley Scott** to play Rachael in *Blade Runner* (82), and her career, given her beauty and obvious talent, should have been plain sailing from there on in. But it was not to be. She shone briefly in Roger Donaldson's *No Way Out* (87), but since then her film choices have been eccentric, to say the least, and her only hope seems to lie in a **Tallulah Bankhead**-like renaissance on the back of her cult-fame as a 'was she or wasn't she' android.

OTHER KEY FILMS: *Stripes* (81); *Dune* (85); *Wall Street* (87); *A Kiss Before Dying* (91); *Ace Ventura Pet Detective* (94); *Even Cowgirls Get The Blues* (94); *The Proprietor* (96); *Men* (97); *Out Of Control* (98); *Sugar & Spice* (01); *Mockingbird Don't Sing* (01); *Night Class* (01); *Control* (01)

354

Zaentz, Saul

Eminent producer who has almost single-handedly managed to corner the market in literary adaptations, Zaentz first made his mark co-producing **Milos Forman's** *One Flew Over The Cuckoo's Nest* (75) along with **Michael Douglas**. His follow-ups, apart from the occasional blip like **Peter Weir's** unjustly maligned *The Mosquito Coast* (86), have been equally high-minded while still retaining their capacity to pull in the dollars. In some ways, therefore, he's the model of the perfect producer, allowing directors like **Anthony Minghella** more or less free rein for their talents in such movies as *The English Patient* (96).

OTHER KEY FILMS: Ralph Bakshi's *The Lord Of The Rings* (78); Milos Forman's *Amadeus* (84); Philip Kaufman's *The Unbearable Lightness Of Being* (88); **Hector Babenco's** *At Play In The Fields Of The Lord* (91); Peter Jackson's *Lord Of The Rings: The Fellowship Of The Ring* (01)

Zane, Billy

Impressively smooth-looking and smooth-talking actor who seems at home in both light comedy and drama, Zane was particularly effective as unwanted passenger Hughie Warriner, in Philip Noyce's excellent thriller, *Dead Calm* (88), based on a smashing Charles Williams story. Zane's recent high-profile appearance as Cal Hockley in **James Cameron's** *Titanic* (97) will have done nothing to injure his still burgeoning career.

OTHER KEY FILMS: *Critters* (86); *Orlando* (93); *Tombstone* (93); *Only You* (94); *The Phantom* (96); *This World, Then The Fireworks* (97); *Morgan's Ferry* (99); *The Believer* (01); *Claim* (01); *Landspeed* (01)

Zanuck, Darryl F

A tough-minded and old-fashioned movie mogul who fulfilled his lifelong ambition by taking over 20th Century-Fox in 1962, following the financial losses incurred by **Joseph L Mankiewicz's** mega-budget *Cleopatra* (63). (Zanuck had founded the original 20th Century Pictures in 1933, and been production manager at Fox itself until 1956, before turning independent.) He then found that the movie industry had moved beyond him while his back was turned. Zanuck's greatest days were in the 1930s and early 1940s, when his word at Fox counted for everything, and during which he saw to fruition **Mervyn LeRoy's** *Little Caesar* (31), **John Ford's** *The Grapes Of Wrath* (40) and Rouben Mamoulian's *Blood And Sand* (41). His later career encompassed a number of other classics, largely through his association with Mankiewicz and **Elia Kazan**, including Mankiewicz's *All About Eve* (50) and *People Will Talk* (51), and Kazan's *Pinky* (49) and *Viva Zapata!* (52). Zanuck is also remembered for smoking the largest cigars in the business.

OTHER KEY FILMS: Henry King's *Jesse James* (39); John Ford's *How Green Was My Valley* (41); John Cromwell's *Anna And The King Of Siam* (46); Robert Rossen's *Island In The Sun* (57); the multi-directed *The Longest Day* (62)

KEY LINES:

'For God's sake, don't say yes until I finish talking!' [Zanuck on one-upmanship]

'At MGM every picture was talked either to death or to life…whenever a picture got made, it was a miracle. At Fox there was only a script and Darryl Zanuck. He okayed it or he threw it out.' [Screenwriter Walter Reisch on the Zanuck touch]

Zavattini, Cesare

One of the greatest of all screenwriters and the founding father of Italian post-war neo-realism, Zavattini wrote the scripts for such disparate masterpieces as **Vittorio De Sica's** seminal *Bicycle Thieves* (48) and the same director's hauntingly beautiful *The Garden Of The Finzi-Continis* [uncredited] (71). A noted theoretician and an influential and iconic presence in Italian cinema, Zavattini never contemplated a formal move over to the US, as so many of his contemporaries had done, but seemed content to work from his intellectually rewarding and esteemed European base.

OTHER KEY FILMS: Vittorio De Sica's *Miracle In Milan* (51); **René Clément's** *The Walls Of Malapaga* (56); **Federico Fellini, Luchino Visconti** and Vittorio De Sica's *Boccaccio '70* (62)

Zeffirelli, Franco

Zeffirelli's films are permeated with the happy fallout from their creator's early background as a set and costume designer for a number of Italian opera companies, and it is to this background as well that Zeffirelli owes his success at adapting Shakespeare to the cinematic medium. *The Taming Of The Shrew* (67) marked his first tentative stab at the Bard, followed by the lush *Romeo And Juliet* (68), which had the virtue of casting adolescents of a suitable age in the lead parts almost for the first time. A number of excellent opera adaptations followed, before the inspired casting of **Mel Gibson** as *Hamlet* (90) in a very effective if truncated version of the play.

OTHER KEY FILMS: *Brother Sun, Sister Moon* (73); *Endless Love* (81); *La Traviata* (82); *Otello* (86); *Sparrow* (93); *Jane Eyre* (96); *Tea With Mussolini* (99); *Callas Forever* (01)

Zemeckis, Robert

Something of a Hollywood one-off, Zemeckis has cleverly used a mixture of special effects and dramatic action in a series of blockbusters that have put him into roughly the same commercial league as his erstwhile mentor, **Steven Spielberg**. *Romancing The Stone* (84) was his first mega-hit,

followed by the *Back To The Future* series (85-90) and the outstanding *Who Framed Roger Rabbit?* (88), which mixed live action and animation to superb effect. *Forrest Gump* (94) was a phenomenon of its time, and was a far more intelligent film than its critics ever implied, and his recent back-to-back hits, *What Lies Beneath* (00) and *Cast Away* (00), have only increased his commercial credibility.

OTHER KEY FILMS: *Used Cars* (80); *Death Becomes Her* (92); *Contact* (97)

Zetterling, Mai

A successful actress who later became one of the first female directors to make their mark on the cinema, Zetterling began her career as a teenage star in Sweden, before moving to Britain to act in a series of often rather poor melodramas. Her first directorial effort was *The War Game* (63), a documentary short that won her a prize at the **Venice Film Festival**, and her subsequent films, which include *Loving Couples* (64) and *Night Games* (66), were always heartfelt, if sometimes a little dour.

OTHER KEY FILMS: **Basil Dearden's** *Frieda* (47); **Sidney Gilliat's** *Only Two Can Play* (62); *Vincent The Dutchman* (72); *Visions Of Eight* [co-dir.] (73); *Love* (81); *Scrubbers* (83); *Amorosa* (86); **Ken Loach's** *Hidden Agenda* (90) [all directed by Zetterling unless otherwise indicated]

Zhang Yimou

A fine director and cinematographer, Zhang has been consistently harassed by the Chinese authorities for his perceived criticism of the state apparatus. His first feature, *Red Sorghum* (87), showed intense visual and intellectual promise, something borne out by his succeeding features, *Ju-Dou* (90), the brilliant *Raise The Red Lantern* (91), and *To Live* (94). The latter includes one of the most magnificent crane shots in the history of cinema, in which two men, alone on a plain, are suddenly engulfed by an entire army of thunderously running soldiers.

OTHER KEY FILMS: *The Story Of Qiu Ju* (92); *Shanghai Triad* (95); *Keep Cool* (97); *The Road Home* (99); *Not Less One* (99)

Zinnemann, Fred

A thoroughly professional middlebrow director, Zinnemann was a technical perfectionist whose films always satisfied, although it is certain that he hoped and believed they would do much more. Both *The Search* (48) and *The Men* (50) were worthy social and commercial vehicles, which, seen with hindsight and within the constraints of their time, now seem rather brave, while *High Noon* (52) achieved a truly remarkable resonance, although to read the movie as a veiled comment on Cold-War America is palpably absurd. *From Here To Eternity* (53) genuinely opened the can of worms that was America's prurient on-screen attitude to sex, whilst *The Sundowners* (60) was first-rate family entertainment. Zinnemann's most accomplished and **Oscar**-garlanded film was *A Man For All Seasons* (66), although, paradoxically, it is in *The Day Of The Jackal* (73), a film he made towards the end of his career, that his sheer technical ability reaches its apogee. The film is a model of how to construct a taut, almost nihilistic thriller from a naturally extended bestseller source without losing any of the original fictional nuances.

OTHER KEY FILMS: *Eyes In The Night* (42); *Act Of Violence* (49); *Oklahoma!* (55); *The Nun's Story* (59); *Behold A Pale Horse* (64); *Julia* (77); *Five Days One Summer* (83)

Zoetrope

Invented by William George Horner in 1834 and functioning on roughly similar lines to the later 'What The Butler Saw' machines, the Zoetrope consisted of a wooden box with a spyhole, inside which a sequence of drawings were seen to revolve at speeds to give an impression of sequential action.

Zoetrope Studios

Francis Ford Coppola founded American Zoetrope in 1969 with the help of **Warner Brothers**, but the film company was forced into bankruptcy twenty-one years later after a series of box-office failures, and eventually re-emerged as Zoetrope Studios.

Zone Focusing

A rather generalised form of focusing that relies on a standard lens and does not concentrate on any particular area within the cameraman's field of vision.

Zoom

The zooming movement to or from the subject of a shot – not by the camera itself, but by the use of the camera's lens. **Alfred Hitchcock** used zoom to dizzying effect in *Vertigo* (58), in which James Stewart's height-fearing cop, John 'Scottie' Fergusson, has his inner turmoil cruelly mimicked by the camera, which zooms backwards, bringing more foreground into the picture, thus giving a gut-wrenching vertiginous depth to the shot.

Zoom Lens

A lens that mimics the movement of a camera to or from the subject of a shot by a process of extended focus.

Zoom Shot

The real or artificial process by which a cameraman approaches his subject (zooms in) or retreats from his subject (zooms out), achieved by the use of either a **zoom lens**, a camera shuttle or **dolly**, on tracks.

*A classic **zoom shot** from Alfred Hitchcock's* Vertigo *(58), in which Hitchcock exaggerates the foreground and increases the focal length by the use of a telephoto lens*

Zsigmond, Vilmos

A hard-working and extremely professional mainstream cinematographer, Zsigmond is a master of light filters, and his name appears on some of the finest and most visually satisfying movies of the past thirty years. His masterpiece, purely in terms of cinematic atmosphere, is **Robert Altman's** *McCabe And Mrs Miller* (71), but his sure touch with the camera and with lighting worked to equal effect in **Michael Cimino's** *The Deer Hunter* (78) and in **George Miller's** *The Witches Of Eastwick* (87).

OTHER KEY FILMS: **John Boorman's** *Deliverance* (72); Robert Altman's *The Long Goodbye* (73); Michael Cimino's **Heaven's Gate** (80); **Brian De Palma's** *Blow Out* (81); **Sean Penn's** *The Crossing Guard* (95); Stephen Hopkins's *The Ghost And The Darkness* (96); Jonas McCord's *The Body* (01)

Zucker, David and Jerry

Co-producers and directors, with **Jim Abrahams**, of *The Kentucky Fried Movie* (77), *Airplane!* (80) and *The Naked Gun* series (88-94), the team were, for a while, the comic heroes of Hollywood, but their place seems to have been usurped, of recent years, by the **Farrelly** brothers, of *Dumb & Dumber* (94) fame. What is it about brothers? The **Coens** are pretty funny too.

OTHER KEY FILMS: *Top Secret!* (84); *Ruthless People* (86); *Ghost* (90); *First Knight* (95); *Phone Booth* (01); *Unconditional Love* (01); *Rat Race* (01)

Zukor, Adolf

Founder of the **star system** and arguably the man who, with his **Famous Players** studio, put the very concept of the motion picture onto the map as a commercial reality, Zukor was renowned for his extraordinary tenaciousness in the face of adversity. It is to this that we owe the continued existence of **Paramount** studios, which was Zukor's baby ever since its takeover in 1917 and its first formal inception, in 1927, as the holding company for the Famous Players-Lasky corporation. Zukor died in 1976 at the age of 103, still chairman emeritus of the company he had founded, fought for, and apparently lost.

357

*Silent stars, Constance and **Norma Talmadge**, in 1920s Malibu*

MARIO READING

The Music-Makers

Jonathan Audley, approaching fifty, has been given the all-clear after his cancer treatment and can now get on with the rest of his life. The trouble is, he has never moved on from the day almost thirty years ago when he betrayed Frances, the only woman he ever truly loved.

Theirs was a childhood of innocence, of shared carefree summer holidays at the big house, and of running away from Clara and Lisa, their tedious younger sisters. As the years passed, the two developed a passionate relationship, defying their parents' wishes and living life to the full, tasting rebellion and planning their forbidden future together. Yet jealousy was never far away and it was only a matter of time before Clara destroyed the delicate status quo.

Once shattered, could the fragments of their former love ever be pieced together to form some kind of friendship? As he travelled back to the house for Helen's funeral, Jonathan was about to find out.

'a very good first novel… I am sure it will do well'
– *Rosamunde Pilcher*

ISBN 0-7551-0142-1
£9.99

HOUSE OF STRATUS

Internet:	**www.houseofstratus.com** including author interviews, reviews, features.
Email:	**sales@houseofstratus.com** **info@houseofstratus.com** (please quote author, title and credit card details.)
Tel:	**Order Line** **0800 169 1780 (UK)** **800 724 1100 (USA)** **International** **+44 (0) 1845 527700 (UK)** **+01 845 463 1100 (USA)**
Fax:	**+44 (0) 1845 527711 (UK)** **+01 845 463 0018 (USA)** (please quote author, title and credit card details.)
Send to:	**House of Stratus Sales Department** **House of Stratus Inc.** **Thirsk Industrial Park** **2 Neptune Road** **York Road, Thirsk** **Poughkeepsie** **North Yorkshire, YO7 3BX** **NY 12601** **UK** **USA**